Venezuela

Krzysztof Dydyński

Charlotte Beech

Contents

Caracas p53

The Northwest p137

The Central North p96

The Northeast p228

The Andes p179

Los Llanos p212

Guayana p277

Destination: Venezuela

Venezuela is a land of incredible variety, from snow-capped Andean peaks to Caribbean coastline; from the legendary wilderness of the Amazon to the wildlife-rich savannas where flat-topped mountains called tepuis rise vertically from the plains, each summit a moonscape of unique endemic flora that inspires visions of a lost world. From the top of one of these tepuis the unforgettable Angel Falls (Salto Ángel) plummets 979m – the world's highest waterfall and Venezuela's most famous attraction.

For outdoor adventurers there are jungle treks and high-altitude ice-climbs, while eco-tourists can seek out caimans, capybaras and anacondas. For water-lovers there is wind-surfing, snorkeling or diving off white-sand shores – or simply downing a Polar beer as the sun sets into the Caribbean and the drummers start up in a beachside bar.

The country's culture is as diverse as its geography, where the Stone Age lifestyle of the indigenous Yanomami co-exists with Caracas' striking modern architecture, mile-wide motorways, and super-slick shopping malls. The US influence is superficially pervasive, but the currents of Latin, African and Caribbean culture run deep, especially in the Venezuelans' passion for salsa, the frenzy of Carnaval and the colorful festivals of the Dancing Devils.

The casino-like economy may boom and bust, but oil-rich or prodigiously poor, Venezuela's sheer sensuality excites and seduces – the vitality of a youthful population that lives for today and dances all night; the enjoyment of everything from showbiz and baseball to fashion, flirtation and fast cars; plus the gorgeous good looks of people for whom attractiveness is an obsession and the beauty pageant is a national sport.

Festival de Los Diablos Danzantes (Festival of the Dancing Devils), San Francisco de Yare (p106)

KRZYSZTOF DYDYŃSKI

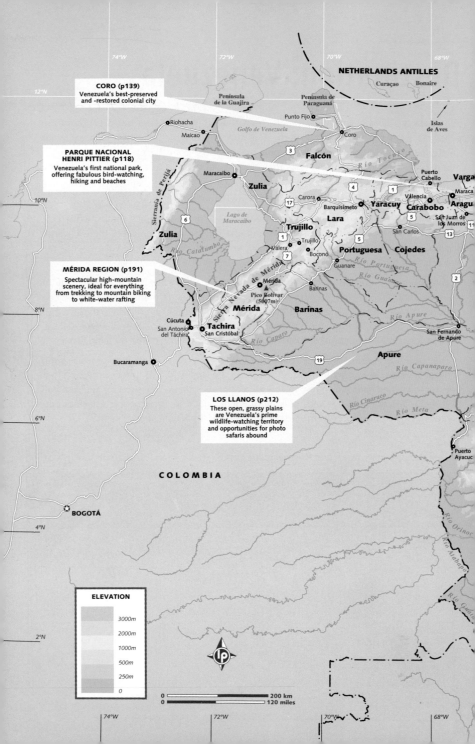

NETHERLANDS ANTILLES

Curaçao   Bonaire

CORO (p139)
Venezuela's best-preserved and -restored colonial city

Islas de Aves

Península de la Guajira

Península de Paraguaná

Punto Fijo

Riohacha

Maicao

Golfo de Venezuela

Coro

Puerto Cabello

Varga

Falcón

Río Tocuyo

PARQUE NACIONAL HENRI PITTIER (p118)
Venezuela's first national park, offering fabulous bird-watching, hiking and beaches

Maracaibo

Zulia

Carora

Barquisimeto

Yaracuy

Valencia

Carabobo

Maraca

Aragu

San Juan de los Morros

Zulia

Lago de Maracaibo

Lara

San Carlos

Trujillo

Trujillo

Valera

Cojedes

Río Catatumbo

MÉRIDA REGION (p191)
Spectacular high-mountain scenery, ideal for everything from trekking to mountain biking to white-water rafting

Boconó

Portuguesa

Guanare

Río Portuguesa

Río Guai

Mérida

Pico Bolívar (5007m)

Barinas

Río Apure

Cúcuta

San Antonio del Táchira

Táchira

San Cristóbal

Mérida

Barinas

San Fernando de Apure

Bucaramanga

Río Caparo

Apure

Río Capanaparo

LOS LLANOS (p212)
These open, grassy plains are Venezuela's prime wildlife-watching territory and opportunities for photo safaris abound

Río Cinaruco

Río Meta

Puerto Ayacuc

COLOMBIA

Río Orinoc

Río Atapapc

★ **BOGOTÁ**

ELEVATION

3000m
2000m
1000m
500m
250m
0

0   200 km
0   120 miles

74°W   72°W   70°W   68°W

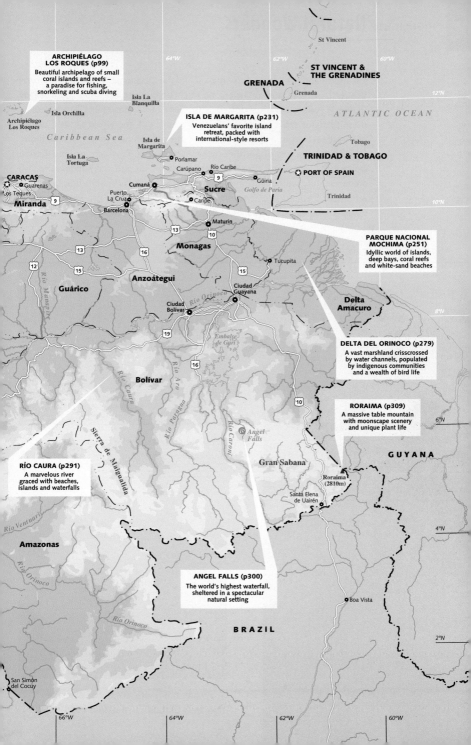

ARCHIPIÉLAGO LOS ROQUES (p99)
Beautiful archipelago of small coral islands and reefs – a paradise for fishing, snorkeling and scuba diving

ISLA DE MARGARITA (p231)
Venezuelans' favorite island retreat, packed with international-style resorts

PARQUE NACIONAL MOCHIMA (p251)
Idyllic world of islands, deep bays, coral reefs and white-sand beaches

DELTA DEL ORINOCO (p279)
A vast marshland crisscrossed by water channels, populated by indigenous communities and a wealth of bird life

RORAIMA (p309)
A massive table mountain with moonscape scenery and unique plant life

RÍO CAURA (p291)
A marvelous river graced with beaches, islands and waterfalls

ANGEL FALLS (p300)
The world's highest waterfall, sheltered in a spectacular natural setting

Encompassing the Andes, the Amazon and the Caribbean, Venezuela's natural beauty is diverse and unique. One such unique region is the **Gran Sabana** (p305), a rolling savanna dotted with giant table mountains. From one of these plateaus spills **Angel Falls** (Salto Ángel; p300), the world's tallest waterfall, best seen from a viewpoint at its base or from an exciting scenic flight. Or climb to the top of another mesa, **Roraima** (p309), which inspired Conan Doyle's *The Lost World*. The **Delta del Orinoco** (p279) and the **Amazonas** (p314) are fascinating wild environments, while the **Andes** (p179) offer dramatic high mountain scenery. The hypnotic **Los Llanos** (p212) is a vast grassy plain full of wildlife, whereas the **Médanos de Coro** (p143) shelters unusual sandy dunes.

Guayana's spectacular Angel Falls
(Salto Ángel; p300)

KRZYSZTOF DYDYŃSKI

KRZYSZTOF DYDYŃSKI

Horse-riding through the desert-like landscape of the Médanos de Coro (p143)

KRZYSZTOF DYDYŃSKI

Guayana's unique tepuis tower over the highlands of the Gran Sabana (p305)

It's hard to resist the call of Venezuela's 2800km-long Caribbean coastline with its vast array of offshore islands and isolated bays. You can escape from it all to the unspoiled coral islands of **Archipiélago Los Roques** (p99), or spend days hopping among the islands of **Parque Nacional Mochima** (p251) or **Parque Nacional Morrocoy** (p152). If it's international-style comfort you're after, try the tourist haven of **Isla de Margarita** (p231). Venezuela also has plenty of beautiful mainland beaches – some offer great people-watching, while others are secluded places to escape the crowds; try those around **San Juan de las Galdonas** (p269) and **Puerto Colombia** (p120).

Sunset at Juangriego, Isla de Margarita (p241)

A fisherman from Playa Manzanillo, Isla de Margarita (p243)

The popular beaches of Parque Nacional Henri Pittier, near Puerto Colombia (p120)

Venezuela's outdoor activities range from mild relaxation to extreme excitement. The diverse topography makes Venezuela a paradise for hiking, trekking and bird-watching in over 40 national parks scattered across the country. Visit the Amazon basin near **Puerto Ayacucho** (p316) or tackle paragliding, mountaineering, white-water rafting and mountain biking amid the rugged high-mountain scenery around **Mérida** (p182). Marvel at the unique lightning phenomenon of **Catatumbo** (p177), or take a wildlife safari in **Los Llanos** (p224). Challenge the exhilarating heights of **Roraima** (p309) in Guayana, or trek to the top of **Píco Bolívar** (p194). Venezuela's coastline and offshore islands offer fantastic scuba diving and snorkeling, plus world-class windsurfing and kitesurfing at **Adícora** (p148) and **El Yaque** (p243).

Spectacular bird-watching at the hatos in Los Llanos (p224)

Hikers taking a break en route to the summit of Roraima, Guayana (p309)

Rafting through the amazing Parque Nacional Canaima, Guayana (p302)

Getting Started

Venezuela has all the usual facilities and services – hotels, restaurants and transport – that you can get at home, but cheaper. It's a destination for any budget, from backpacker to business class. The main things to check before your departure are the vaccination requirements (p343), and the latest exchange rates and currency situation (p329). And remember that your visit will be infinitely richer if you take the time to learn some Spanish.

WHEN TO GO

The tourist season in Venezuela runs year-round, but consider the climate and Venezuelan holidays before finalizing your travel plans.

Venezuela has one dry season (roughly November/December to April/May) and one wet season (the rest of the year). The dry season is certainly more pleasant for traveling, and particularly for hiking or other outdoor activities, though sightseeing in cities or towns won't be greatly disturbed by rain. Some sights, such as waterfalls, are actually more impressive in the wet season. The Angel Falls, for example, is absolutely spectacular after heavy rains in the wet months, but it may be not much more than a thin ribbon of water in the dry season. Furthermore, the falls can be inaccessible by boat in dry months, cutting off a great attraction from your itinerary.

See the Directory (p321) for more details on climate, festivals and events.

Venezuelans are mad about traveling over the Christmas season (running up till mid-January), Carnaval (several days prior to Ash Wednesday) and Holy Week (the week before Easter Sunday). During these three peak times, air and bus transportation are busy and hotels fill up quickly, so you'll have to book ahead. On the other hand, these periods are colorful and lively, with a host of festivities. Schools also break for annual vacations in August, but this doesn't significantly affect public transportation or accommodations.

COSTS & MONEY

Venezuela is a reasonably cheap country for visitors, though prices are volatile (see the boxed text, p10). Budget travelers prepared for basic conditions and willing to put up with some discomfort on the road

---

DON'T LEAVE HOME WITHOUT...

- Required and recommended vaccinations (p343).
- Comprehensive insurance policy (p328).
- Photocopies of your essential documents (p326).
- Snorkeling equipment – if snorkeling is on your agenda.
- Electrical adapter (p321).
- Torch – useful for most off-the-beaten-track excursions.
- Good insect repellent – essential for a Roraima trek and in many other areas.
- Travel alarm clock – for those early-morning buses.
- Small Spanish-English dictionary and/or Lonely Planet phrasebook.
- Flip-flops or thong sandals – to protect feet against fungal infections in hotel bathrooms.

can get by on $20 to $25 per day. This would cover accommodations in budget hotels, food in low- to middle-range restaurants, and travel by bus, and should still leave a small amount for some drinks, movies and taxis. You shouldn't have to spend more than $5 to $10 a night (on average) for a budget hotel, and the cost will be lower if you travel with someone else, especially if you're sharing a bed (see Accommodations, p322). For budget dining, the set lunch or dinner will cost $2 to $4 each. This budget wouldn't cover rental cars, tours or internal flights.

Travelers who want more comfort, including mid-range hotels and restaurants, will find that $35 to $50 per day should easily cover their expenses, and even allow an occasional flight. Mid-range travelers can expect to spend between $10 and $25 per day on accommodations anywhere, less if traveling in a party or as a couple. A fine à-la-carte dinner will cost $5 to $10 for an average main course.

Bus is the main means of transportation, and it's reasonably priced, about $1.50 to $2 per hour of a journey. City buses cost next to nothing. Taxis aren't expensive either, particularly when you're in a group and can split the cost.

Churches and cathedrals don't have an admission charge. Most museums don't have an admission charge either, and those that do usually keep the fee low. Cultural events (cinema, theater, music etc) are all fairly inexpensive. On the other hand, a drinking session in a nightclub can deplete your funds quickly – especially if you drink at the same rate as Venezuelans.

What can really eat into your budget are organized tours. They cost roughly between $25 and $100 per day and are rarely just day trips. Some of the country's major attractions can only be reached by taking a tour (Angel Falls, Delta del Orinoco and Los Llanos, among others).

TRAVEL LITERATURE

Venezuela's unique table mountains have captivated writers for over a century. One of the most unusual accounts is by Sir Arthur Conan Doyle who, inspired by fabulous stories of explorers of Roraima, gave play to his imagination in the rollicking 1912 tale *The Lost World*, in which dinosaurs roam the top of the plateau.

Plenty of travelers were in turn inspired by Conan Doyle's story, including actor and author Brian Blessed, who tells how he fulfilled his childhood dream of visiting the 'Lost World' in his beautifully entertaining *Quest for the Lost World*.

Churún Merú, the Tallest Angel, by Ruth Robertson, is a report of the expedition to Auyantepui, during which the height of Angel Falls was measured for the first time, confirming its status as the world's highest waterfall.

Mad White Giant, by Benedict Allen, is an exciting account of the author's trip from the Delta del Orinoco to the mouth of the Amazon River,

PRICE WARNING

Due to the instability of the Venezuelan economy and a high inflation rate, prices of goods and services are extremely volatile and rise frequently. Prices in this book are given in US dollars, but they may not exactly reflect the local prices and should be regarded as guidelines only. An additional complication is the black market (see p330), which existed when this book was researched and may still be operating when you visit. The prices in this book were calculated on the official rate, but travelers changing dollars on the black market are likely to be much better off.

TOP TENS
BEACHES & ISLANDS

Pack your sunblock and floppy sun-hat – Venezuela's Caribbean coast is brimming with fine beaches, incredible marine life and exotic islands.

- **Puerto Colombia** (p120) Chilled out jumping-off point for isolated bays accessible only by boat.
- **Archipiélago Los Roques** (p99) Holiday brochure of idyllic islands and abundant marine life.
- **Isla de Margarita** (p231) Venezuela's top island destination, encircled by white beaches.
- **Parque Nacional Mochima** (p251) Storybook islands, coral reefs and sparkling seas.
- **Playa Pui Puy** (p266) Long, sweeping bay with good surf for body-boarders.
- **Playa Medina** (p266) Secluded, palm-fringed cove famous for its beauty.
- **El Playón Area** (p120) Popular mainland beach near Puerto Colombia.
- **San Juan de Las Galdonas** (p267) Remote seaside fishing village with pristine beaches.
- **Puerto Cabello Area** (p134) The coastline east of this port has several tranquil islands to explore.
- **Parque Nacional Morrocoy** (p152) Spectacular world of islands and beaches on the west coast.

HIDDEN JEWELS

Most travelers know about Venezuela's greatest natural wonders such as Angel Falls and Delta del Orinoco, but there are plenty of lesser-known natural marvels which are just as fascinating.

- **Médanos de Coro** (p143) Striking mini-Sahara Desert near Coro.
- **Cerro Autana** (p318) Gigantic tree trunk–shaped tepui in Amazonas.
- **Brazo Casiquiare** (p318) Unusual water channel linking the Orinoco and Río Negro.
- **Sierra de San Luis** (p150) Attractive, lush mountains near Coro.
- **Península de Paria** (p271) Marvelous peninsula graced with coves and beaches.
- **Catatumbo** (p178) Place famous for unique lightning without thunder.
- **Salto Aponguao** (p307) Gran Sabana's most spectacular waterfall.
- **Reserva Biológica de Montecano** (p148) Beautiful forest in the arid Peninsula de Paraguaná.
- **Quebrada de Jaspe** (p311) Small waterfall rolling over amazing red jasper rock.
- **Salto Pará** (p291) Lovely waterfall on the Río Caura.

OUTDOOR ADVENTURES

From relaxed beach walks to extreme canyoning, the opportunities are almost unlimited – outdoor adventures are exciting, affordable and well organized.

- **Hiking in Parque Nacional El Ávila** (p93) Beautiful mountainous environment near Caracas.
- **Trekking to the top of Roraima** (p310) Spectacular trek to the famous 'Lost World.'
- **Piranha fishing in Los Llanos** (p225) A popular part of wildlife safaris.
- **Whitewater-rafting around Mérida** (p196) Wet, wild and terrifying – Venezuela's best rafting.
- **Kitesurfing in Adícora** (p149) Ideal conditions attract world-class kitesurfers.
- **Scuba diving at Los Roques** (p100) Clear water, colorful fish and spectacular coral.
- **Windsurfing at El Yaque** (p243) Internationally acclaimed site with good facilities.
- **Paragliding around Mérida** (p186) Take to the sky in a tandem glider – all thrills, no skills.
- **Mountain biking around Mérida** (p187) Rent a bike for the day, or take a challenging tour.
- **Caiman hunting in Delta del Orinoco** (p282) Capture a caiman – on film of course; a highlight of your delta tour.

and his experience with the jungle and its indigenous tribes along the way.

Redmond O'Hanlon's *In Trouble Again* is a hilarious story of his four-month expedition in a dugout canoe through the upper Orinoco and the Amazon to the homelands of the Yanomami.

In *The Hacienda: My Venezuelan Years*, English-born author Lisa St Aubin De Teran writes with a healthy dose of dry humor of her extraordinary experience running a rural hacienda in the Venezuelan Andes.

The famous German geographer and botanist Alexander von Humboldt explored and studied various regions of Venezuela and describes it in his three-volume *Personal Narrative of Travels to the Equinoctial Regions of America, 1799–1801*. Volume No 2 covers the Venezuelan section of his journey. It may sound like a dry, scientific study, but it's fascinating reading, full of amazing details.

INTERNET RESOURCES

Lonely Planet (www.lonelyplanet.com) Summaries on Venezuela travel; the Thorn Tree bulletin board; travel news and links to useful travel resources.

Think Venezuela (www.think-venezuela.net) General information on Venezuela, including politics, geography, economy, culture, education and national parks.

University of Texas (www.lanic.utexas.edu/la/venezuela) Comprehensive directory of Venezuelan websites provided by the Latin American Network Information Center of the University of Texas.

Venezuelan Embassy in the USA (www.embavenez-us.org) Government information, including updates on visa regulations, plus plenty of links to everything from Venezuelan cuisine to beauty queens.

Venezuela's Ecoturism (www.internet.ve/wildlife) Site focusing on ecotourism and adventure trips, but with plenty of links to general information.

Your Venezuela (www.venezuelatuya.com) Multi-language travel website richly illustrated with photos.

Itineraries
CLASSIC ROUTES

BEACH BUM ROUTE

Three to Four Weeks

Venezuela's Caribbean coastline will wow you with its wealth of beautiful beaches, islands and other natural attractions. The exquisite coral archipelago of **Los Roques** (p99) is many people's first or last destination, easily accessible from **Caracas** (p154). West of Caracas, nestled in the eastern mountains, is the pretty German town of **Colonia Tovar** (p116). From here, it's a spectacular ride down to the lowlands. A little further west you can take one of two scenic roads up and over the coastal mountains, through the wildlife-rich cloud forests of **Parque Nacional Henri Pittier** (p118). One road emerges at the coastal village of **Puerto Colombia** (p120), surrounded by secluded beaches reached only by boat. The other road goes to **Ocumare de la Costa** (p120) and the picturesque bay of **Playa Cata** (p121).

Taking the long haul back past Caracas, **Puerto La Cruz** (p246) is the jumping-off point to explore the stunning beaches and islands of **Parque Nacional Mochima** (p251). You can hop on a ferry to Isla de Margarita here, or continue first to the historic city of **Cumaná** (p256). You may also want to take a detour southeast to the impressive cave, **Cueva del Guácharo** (p275), or east to **Río Caribe** (p265) and the remote, undeveloped beaches nearby, including idyllic **Playa Medina** (p268). You can then take a boat from Chacopata or Cumaná to the soft, white shores of tourist mecca **Isla de Margarita** (p231).

It's possible to cover this 1450km route in three weeks at a squeeze, but if you're after rest and relaxation don't try to fit in too much. Pick and choose your destinations carefully so you can spend more time chilling out on a beach rather than sitting on a bus.

AROUND GUAYANA

Four to Six Weeks

Guayana is famed for its natural beauty and is one of the most traveled regions in the country. Most of its attractions, though, are well off the beaten track and inaccessible by road, and the usual way of visiting them is by tour.

Guayana's major travelers' base is the old colonial port of **Ciudad Bolívar** (p284), easily accessible from Caracas by daily flights or a comfortable nine-hour bus ride. Stay a few days in town to stroll about the charming streets and museums, before taking a tour to **Canaima** (p302) and the famous **Angel Falls** (Salto Ángel; p300). Back in Ciudad Bolívar, your next adventures might be the vast, enchanting highlands of **Gran Sabana** (p305) and the massive table mountain of **Roraima** (p309). Tours to both places can be bought in Ciudad Bolívar, or you can go by bus along a spectacular road to **Santa Elena de Uairén** (p311) and buy both tours more cheaply from here.

Ciudad Bolívar is also a springboard for the **Río Caura** (p291), a lovely river 200km to the southwest, which again is only accessible on a tour. Guayana's other big attraction is the **Delta del Orinoco** (p279), and this trip can also be organized from Ciudad Bolívar, or you can go to **Tucupita** (p281) and shop around for a tour.

Some travelers go by bus to **Puerto Ayacucho** (p316) to explore the upper Orinoco and Amazon basins – another virgin corner of the country, another off-the-beaten-track adventure and another tour.

Visiting all the listed attractions will take four to six weeks, and a large slice of your budget. Many travelers cross Guayana on their way to Brazil and just visit the main sights en route (Gran Sabana and Roraima, plus the spectacular Angel Falls). Put aside two weeks for these three sights.

WESTERN LOOP

Three to Six Weeks

This loop covers a mixed bag of natural and cultural attractions. Starting from **Caracas** (p54), you can make the first stop in **Las Trincheras** (p131), near Valencia, and warm up in the world's second-hottest springs. To cool yourself down, take an hour's bus ride to **Parque Nacional Morrocoy** (p152), where you can bathe in the beautiful turquoise waters of the Caribbean.

Next port of call, **Coro** (p139), shelters some of Venezuela's best colonial architecture and is a base for the arid **Península de Paraguaná** (p144) and the lush **Sierra de San Luis** (p150), two lovely and completely different environments. Continuing west, you reach the hot, modern city of **Maracaibo** (p167), from where you can take a side trip to **Laguna de Sinamaica** (p177), where Venezuela's name was born 500 years ago.

A night bus from Maracaibo will whisk you straight to **Mérida** (p162), where you'll probably hang your hat for a week or more, taking advantage of the wide selection of adventure tours, from rafting and paragliding to mountain biking and wildlife safaris.

From Mérida, take a bus on one of Venezuela's most spectacular and dramatic mountain roads to **Valera** (p196). Take a short detour to the old town of **Trujillo** (p198) or head northwest to **Barquisimeto** (p157), from where it's worth exploring surrounding towns noted for their fine crafts. You can then return directly to Caracas, or stop at the various regional attractions along the way.

You can do this 1975km loop comfortably by bus in three to four weeks, but you should allow an extra week or two for outdoor activities in the scenic Mérida region – it's the highlight of a fantastic circuit.

TAILORED TRIPS

VENEZUELA IN A CAPSULE   Three to Four Weeks

'I have a three-week holiday – how can I see the best Venezuela has to offer?' This frequently asked question usually comes from travelers with limited time and a mid-range budget; it's easy to do if you invest in local flights and organized tours, arranged in advance by Internet or phone.

Stay a day or two in **Caracas** (p54) to see the museums, then fly to **Los Roques** (p99), a lovely, coral Caribbean archipelago, for two or three days.

Mérida (p182) is the next stop, by air or a full-night bus ride from Caracas. This adventure sports region offers every kind of activity – rafting, paragliding, trekking and mountain biking – so allow a few days for some action. Also consider a four-day wildlife-safari tour to **Los Llanos** (p196), organized from Mérida.

Next stop is **Ciudad Bolívar** (p284), where your priority is a three-day tour to the famous **Angel Falls** (p300). Back in town, take a four-day tour to the **Gran Sabana** (p305), an amazing rolling savanna dotted with table mountains and waterfalls. If you have an extra week to spare, consider a fantastic trip to the top of **Roraima** (p309).

It's then time to relax on some of Venezuela's fabulous beaches, like the lively and trendy **Playa El Agua** (p242) on Isla de Margarita. Allow a few days before flying back to Caracas for some last-minute shopping and the flight home.

VENEZUELA ON FOOT

Venezuela has walking for everybody, whether it's a leisurely beach stroll or a trek to a snowcapped peak.

When you arrive in Caracas, you'll find fantastic hiking territory with over 200km of well-signposted trails in **Parque Nacional El Ávila** (p93), just north of the city. More hiking awaits you in **Parque Nacional Henri Pittier** (p118), just two hours west of Caracas by bus, where there are two-day treks from Turmero to Chuao, or shorter hikes. Further west along the

coast, you can hike to the top of the unusual **Cerro Santa Ana** (p147), in the middle of the arid Península de Paraguaná, north of Coro.

The widest choice of hiking opportunities is around **Mérida** (p182), where you can easily spend a month tramping local mountain paths. A hike from Mérida to **Los Nevados** (p194) is one of the most popular trips, but if you need something more challenging, the trek to the tops of **Píco Bolívar** (p193) and **Pico Humboldt** (p193), the country's highest peaks, is the way to go.

The ultimate adventure is a trek up **Roraima** (p309) in Guayana; you need at least five days to complete the trip, plus a couple more days to get to this remote corner of the country.

The Authors

KRZYSZTOF DYDYŃSKI
Coordinating Author,
Northwest, Andes, Los Llanos & Guayana

A native Pole from Warsaw, Krzysztof lived in Colombia for four years and traveled extensively in Latin America, from Mexico to Argentina. On one such trip he discovered Venezuela, which enchanted him with its people and its landscapes, and what began as an extension of his Colombian adventure turned into an entirely new fascination. He now lives in Australia, but like a migratory bird has returned to Venezuela almost every year for more than a decade to explore new, less-traveled paths and delve deeper into the country's heart. Krzysztof has authored Lonely Planet's three previous editions of *Venezuela*.

My Favorite Trip

Roraima (p309) was my first big Venezuelan adventure, in 1993, and it remains a compelling fantasy. I obviously didn't expect dinosaurs but, partly inspired by Conan Doyle's *The Lost World*, I had hoped to find something unique atop this mysterious table mountain. My wife, Angela, and I went without any guides and completely unprepared – but full of youthful energy. It was an exhausting climb, but the top fulfilled our wildest fantasies: before us lay a unique world of bizarre landforms and strange plants. I returned to Roraima's summit exactly 10 years later, this time on a guided tour. I was worried that the magic of the previous trip might not be repeated, but the 'lost world' was still there, waiting to be found again, and like nothing else on earth.

CHARLOTTE BEECH
Caracas, Central North & Northeast

Charlotte's love affair with Latin America began in Venezuela, her first port of call on a marathon trip that took her halfway round the continent. Initially arriving as a stiff and reserved Brit, she was quite literally swept off her feet by the warmth and generosity of the people she met, not to mention their single-minded determination to teach her salsa. She is now addicted. Charlotte has also worked on Lonely Planet guidebooks *Peru* and *South America on a Shoestring*, as well as contributed to numerous guides as an editor. When not on the road, she lives in London with her South American partner.

My Favorite Trip

It comes as no surprise when travelers cite Parque Nacional Canaima as the highlight of their trip to Venezuela – with good reason (see the boxed text, p44). In all my subsequent travels through the country, I've never felt such exhilaration as on my very first trip, when I swam in the river immediately below the incredible Angel Falls (don't try it in the wet season!). I'll never forget that feeling of awe, floating on my back and looking up at the highest waterfall in the world looming over me. If, like me, you go in the low season, you'll see few other people, but expect plenty of puff pushing your dugout when it gets stuck in the riverbed!

CONTRIBUTING AUTHORS

Dr David Goldberg MD wrote the Health chapter (p342). David completed his training in internal medicine and infectious diseases at Columbia-Presbyterian Medical Center in New York City, where he has also served as voluntary faculty. At present, he is an infectious diseases specialist in Scarsdale, New York state, and the editor-in-chief of the website MDTravelHealth.com.

Tobias Mendelovici wrote the Environment chapter (p40). He was born in Caracas and became an avid traveler while still a teenager. He has traveled extensively in Latin America and Australia and has put his passion for nature into practice over the last decade through a number of environment-related projects in Israel, Australia and Venezuela. For the last four years Tobias has been at the forefront of ecotourism development in Venezuela. During his thesis work at the University of Sydney he came across a copy of Lonely Planet's *Venezuela* and had a strong feeling that one day he would find himself writing for Lonely Planet. Five years later his hunch has become a reality.

Snapshot

Outside South America, Venezuela is best known for its beauty queens, its oil resources and its history of political instability. Inside the country, these are issues of public interest and general conversation, but often in unexpected ways. The beauty of Venezuelan women is a source of national pride, and they have won all the major international beauty contests, including four Miss Universe pageants and five Miss Worlds. The surprise is how seriously this is taken, and how it's supported by an enormous industry that includes cosmetics, plastic surgery and fashion. Much less discussed are feminist issues and the place of women in society. The cult of the beauty contest could be a metaphor for Venezuelan values, where appearance is paramount and charm counts for more than achievement – just so long as you keep smiling and laughing.

Oil wealth has bankrolled most of the country's economic development, and when oil prices boomed in the 1970s, Venezuela became the wealthiest country in Latin America. For decades Venezuelans lived within a petrol bubble, in which wealth, comfort and stability seemed assured. When oil prices fell, the country borrowed, and when the national debt became unsupportable, crisis was inevitable. Oil still accounts for a third of GDP, half of the government revenue, and three-quarters of export earnings, but even with the recent revival of world oil prices, around 75% of families live below the poverty line. To talk about oil is to talk about the economy, but it's more like a lottery prize than a management outcome or a return on investment.

As for politics, it was scarcely an issue as long as the oil money rolled in. But President Hugo Chávez, in his trademark red beret, has brought political theater to the national stage. His unconventional style and populist rhetoric have divided opinion, and demonstrations for or against him are a sporting event in which everyone takes sides. Chávez has proclaimed a continuing 'Bolivarian Revolution,' which frequently invokes the name of national hero Simón Bolívar, but rarely delivers anything of substance on serious issues like poverty, inequality, environmental damage, drug abuse and lawlessness on the Colombian border. Meanwhile, there is more enthusiasm for the traditional national interests – drinking, dancing and music, sport (especially baseball), and of course the TV soap operas which frequently present the latest political scandals and crises thinly disguised as fictional drama.

The common denominator that unites the nation is an overwhelming passion for life, love and sheer enjoyment. When the tropical sun sets and evening breezes cool hot bodies, Venezuelans strut their stuff in swanky nightclubs, frenetic discos and laid-back beach bars. From downtown Caracas to upcountry Mérida, from *gaita* bars in Maracaibo to salsa clubs on Isla de Margarita, the country rocks to Latino, Afro and Caribbean rhythms that resonate with the energy of a people living for the moment. Above all, the youth and vitality of Venezuela is exciting, enjoyable and infectious – it's an irresistible attraction and the hottest highlight of all.

FAST FACTS

Population (2004): 25.5 million

Population growth rate: 2.2%

Adult literacy: 92%

Area: 916,445 sq km

Inflation (2003): 27.1%

GDP growth rate (2003): -7.1%

Unemployment (2003): 15.4%

Number of Miss Worlds won by Venezuelans: 5

Number of Venezuelan baseball players in the US major leagues: 36

History

PRE-COLUMBIAN TIMES

The first inhabitants of the Americas came from Siberia across the Bering Strait, spread over the North American continent, then moved down to Central and South America in several waves of migration. In Venezuela, the oldest archaeological evidence of human habitation has been dated to around the 14th millennium. The oldest samples come from the northwest of the country.

The Explorers of South America, by Edward J Goodman, brings to life some of the adventurers who opened the continent to Europeans, from Columbus to Humboldt. Captivating reading.

Various nomadic groups evolved from that time, using rough stone for tools and weapons. Agriculture was established by the 1st millennium, leading to the country's first permanent settlements. From this stage on, separate groups began to develop into distinct cultures belonging to three main linguistic families: Carib, Arawak and Chibcha. By the time of the Spanish conquest at the end of the 15th century, some 300,000 to 400,000 indigenous people inhabited the region that is now Venezuela.

The warlike Carib tribes occupied the central and eastern coast, living off fishing and shifting agriculture. Various Arawak groups were scattered over the western plains and north up to the coast. They lived off hunting and food-gathering, and occasionally practiced farming.

The Timote-Cuica tribes, of the Chibcha linguistic family, were the most advanced of Venezuela's pre-Hispanic societies. They lived in the Andes and developed advanced agricultural techniques, including irrigation and terracing. They were also skilled craftspeople, as we can judge by the artifacts they left behind – examples of their fine pottery are shown in museums across the country – though no important architectural works have survived.

SPANISH CONQUEST

Christopher Columbus was the first European to set foot on Venezuelan soil, anchoring at the eastern tip of the Península de Paria, opposite Trinidad, on his third voyage to the New World in 1498. He thought he had discovered another island, but continuing along the coast, he found the voluminous mouth of the Río Orinoco – sufficient proof that the place was much more than an island. Astonished with his discovery, he wrote in his diary, 'Never have I read or heard of so much sweet water within a salt ocean,' and named the gulf El Mar Dulce (Sweet Sea). Today it is called the Golfo de Paria.

DID YOU KNOW?

Venezuela is the only South American mainland country where Columbus landed.

A year later another explorer, Alonso de Ojeda, accompanied by the Italian Amerigo Vespucci, sailed up to the Península de la Guajira, at the western end of present-day Venezuela. On entering Lago de Maracaibo, the Spaniards saw the local indigenous people living in *palafitos* (thatched huts on stilts above the water). Perhaps as a sarcastic sailor joke, they called the land 'Venezuela' (literally 'Little Venice'), as these rustic reed dwellings didn't exactly match the opulent palaces of the Italian city they knew. The name of Venezuela appeared for the first time on a map in 1500 and has remained to this day. You can go to the place where the

TIMELINE	14,000 BC	AD 1498
	The earliest record of human occupation in Venezuela	Christopher Columbus lands in northeastern Venezuela, the first European to see the South American continent

first Spanish sailors saw the *palafitos* and see similar huts (p177), and ponder upon how Venezuela's name was born.

Alonso de Ojeda sailed further west along the coast and briefly explored parts of what is now Colombia. He saw local aborigines wearing gold adornments and was astonished by their wealth. Their stories about fabulous treasures inland gave birth to the myth of El Dorado, a mysterious land abundant in gold. Attracted by these supposed riches, the shores of Venezuela and Colombia became the target of Spanish expeditions, an obsession with El Dorado driving them into the interior. Their search resulted in the rapid colonization of the land, though El Dorado was never found.

The Spanish established their first settlement on Venezuelan soil around 1500, at Nueva Cádiz, on the small island of Cubagua, just south of Isla de Margarita. Pearl harvesting provided a livelihood for the settlers, and the town developed into a busy port until an earthquake and tidal wave destroyed it in 1541. The earliest Venezuelan town still in existence, Cumaná (p256), on the northeast coast, dates from 1521 and is an enjoyable place to visit, even though earthquakes ruined much of the early Spanish colonial architecture.

Officially, most of Venezuela was ruled by Spain from Santo Domingo (present-day capital of the Dominican Republic) until 1717, when it fell under the administration of the newly created viceroyalty of Nueva Granada, with its capital in Bogotá. In practice, however, the region was allowed a large degree of autonomy. Spaniards gave it low priority, considering it an unimportant and sparsely populated backwater and focusing instead on gold- and silver-rich Colombia, Peru and Bolivia. In many ways, Venezuela remained a backwater until the oil boom of the 1920s.

The colony's population of indigenous communities and Spanish invaders diversified with the arrival of black slaves, brought from Africa to serve as the workforce. Most of them were set to work on plantations on the Caribbean coast. By the 18th century, Africans surpassed the indigenous population in number.

The demographic picture became even more complex when the three racial groups began to mix, producing various fusions, including mestizos (people of European-Indian ancestry), mulattos (of European-African ancestry) and *zambos* (of African-Indian ancestry). Yet, throughout the colonial period, power was almost exclusively in the hands of the Spaniards.

INDEPENDENCE WARS

Apart from a few brief rebellions against colonial rule, Spanish Venezuela had a relatively uneventful history for its first 300 years. All this changed at the beginning of the 19th century, when Venezuela gave Latin America its greatest ever hero, Simón Bolívar (see the boxed text, p22). El Libertador, as he is commonly known, together with his most able lieutenant, Antonio José de Sucre, was largely responsible for ending colonial rule all the way to the borders of Argentina.

The revolutionary flame was lit in 1806 by Francisco de Miranda, Venezuela's first leader of the independence movement, but his efforts

John Hemming's *The Search for El Dorado* is a fascinating insight into the Spanish conquest of Venezuela and Colombia. It reads like a thriller, yet is admirably factual.

Gabriel García Márquez' historical novel *The General in his Labyrinth* recounts the tragic final months of Simón Bolívar's life. It's a powerful and beautifully written work from one of Latin America's most celebrated literary figures.

1527

The town of Coro is made the first capital of colonial Venezuela

1577

Caracas, founded in 1567 by Captain Diego de Losada, becomes the capital of Venezuela to set up an independent administration in Caracas ended when fellow conspirators handed him over to the Spanish. He was shipped to Spain and died in jail, and Bolívar then assumed leadership of the revolution. After unsuccessful initial attempts to defeat the Spaniards at home, he withdrew to Colombia, then to Jamaica, until the opportune moment came in 1817.

The Napoleonic Wars had just ended, and Bolívar's agent in London was able to raise money and arms, and recruit 5000 British veterans of the Peninsular War. With this force and an army of horsemen from Los Llanos, Bolívar marched over the Andes and defeated the Spanish

THE EXTRAORDINARY EL LIBERTADOR

'There have been three great fools in history: Jesus, Don Quixote and I' – this is how Simón Bolívar summed up his life shortly before he died. The man who brought independence from Spanish rule to the entire northwest of South America – today's Venezuela, Colombia, Panama, Ecuador, Peru and Bolivia – died abandoned, rejected and poor.

Simón Bolívar was born in Caracas on July 24, 1783 into a wealthy Creole family, which had come to Venezuela from Spain 200 years earlier. Simón was just three years old when his father died, and six years later his mother died too. The boy was brought up by his uncle and was given an open-minded tutor and mentor, Simón Rodríguez.

At the age of 16, Bolívar was sent to Spain and France to continue his education. The works of Voltaire and Rousseau introduced him to new, progressive ideas of liberalism, yet he didn't think about a political career at that stage. He married Spaniard María Teresa and the young couple sailed to Caracas to start a new life at the old family hacienda in San Mateo. Unfortunately, María Teresa died of yellow fever just eight months later. Bolívar never married again, though he had many lovers. The most devoted of these was Manuela Sáenz, whom he met in Quito in 1822 and who stayed with him almost until his final days.

The death of María Teresa marked a drastic shift in Bolívar's destiny. He returned to France, where he met with the leaders of the French Revolution, then traveled to the USA to take a close look at the new order after the American Revolutionary War. By the time he returned to Caracas in 1807, he was full of revolutionary theories and experiences taken from these two successful examples. It didn't take him long to join clandestine pro-independence circles.

Bolívar's military career began under Francisco de Miranda, but after Miranda was captured by the Spaniards in 1812, Bolívar took command. Over the following decade, he hardly had a moment's rest, as battle followed battle with astonishing frequency. He personally commanded the independence forces in 35 victorious battles, including the key Battle of Carabobo, which brought freedom to Venezuela.

Bolívar's long-awaited dream of a unified republic comprising Colombia, Venezuela and Ecuador became reality, but Gran Colombia soon began to disintegrate. As separatist tendencies escalated, Bolívar assumed dictatorship in 1828, yet this step brought more harm than good and his popularity waned. A short time later, he miraculously escaped an assassination attempt in Bogotá. Disillusioned and in bad health, he resigned from the presidency in early 1830 and decided to leave for Europe.

When he reached Santa Marta, Colombia, to board a ship bound for France, he was already very ill and depressed. He died at a local hacienda on December 17, 1830, at the age of just 47. A priest, a doctor and a few officers were by his bed, but none of his close friends. One of the last bitter remarks written in Bolívar's diary reads, 'America is ungovernable. Those who serve the revolution plough the sea.'

1725	1783
Venezuela's first university, the Universidad Real y Pontificia de Caracas, is founded	National hero Simón Bolívar is born in Caracas on July 24

at the Battle of Boyacá, bringing independence to Colombia in August 1819. Four months later in Angostura (present-day Ciudad Bolívar), the Angostura Congress proclaimed Gran Colombia, a new state unifying Colombia, Venezuela and Ecuador (though the last two were still under Spanish rule). The memories of the event are still alive in Ciudad Bolívar (p284), and you can see the great mansion where the first congress debated. Venezuela's liberation came on June 24, 1821 at Carabobo, where Bolívar's troops defeated the Spanish royalist army.

Though the least important of Gran Colombia's three provinces, Venezuela bore the brunt of the fighting. Venezuelan patriots fought not only on their own territory, but also in the armies that Bolívar led into Colombia and down the Pacific coast. By the end of 1824, Bolívar and Sucre had liberated Ecuador, Peru and Bolivia. It's estimated that a quarter of the Venezuelan population died in the independence wars.

Gran Colombia began to collapse right from the moment of its birth, as the central regime was incapable of governing such an immense country with its great racial and regional differences. Bolívar, the president of the vast republic, was busily fighting for the independence of Peru, while real power was left in the hands of a federalist vice-president. The new state existed for only a decade before splitting into three separate countries. Bolívar's dream of a unified republic fell apart even before he died in 1830.

Following Venezuela's separation from Gran Colombia, the Venezuelan Congress approved a new constitution and – incredibly – banned Bolívar from his homeland. It took the Venezuelan nation 12 years to acknowledge its debt to the man to whom it owed its freedom. In 1842, Bolívar's remains were brought from Santa Marta, Colombia, where he died, to Caracas and entombed in the cathedral. In 1876 they were solemnly transferred to the Panteón Nacional (p66) in Caracas, where they now rest in a bronze sarcophagus.

Today venerated by Venezuelans almost as a god, El Libertador was a man of exceptional gifts. An idealist and visionary with a poetic mind, his goal was not only to topple Spanish rule but also to create a unified America. This was an impossible ideal, yet the military conquest of five million square kilometers remains a phenomenal accomplishment for an inspired amateur without any formal training in war strategy. The campaign over the Andean Cordillera in the rainy season was described 100 years later as 'the most magnificent episode in the history of war.'

AFTER INDEPENDENCE

Venezuela's post-independence period was marked by serious governmental problems that continued for more than a century. These were times of despotism and anarchy, with the country being ruled by a series of military dictators known as caudillos. The governments were almost entirely in the hands of Creoles, or persons of European descent. They paid little attention to Indians and blacks, and not much more to mestizos or mulattos, who continued to be exploited under conditions similar to, or worse than, those prevailing under Spanish rule. Although slavery was officially abolished in 1854, in many regions it continued

DID YOU KNOW?

The arc of seven white stars on the Venezuelan flag represents the seven original provinces of Venezuela in 1811, when the country's independence was first declared.

A moving film directed by Diego Rísquez, *Manuela Sáenz: La Libertadora del Libertador* (2000) jumps between an old woman in a plague-ridden Peruvian town and her former life as the feisty mistress of Simón Bolívar.

1811	1812
Congress declares the independence of Venezuela (but it takes another 10 years to achieve it)	A catastrophic earthquake ruins many towns in central and western Venezuela, all the way from Caracas to Mérida

well into the 20th century. It wasn't until 1947 that the first democratic government was elected.

The first of the caudillos, General José Antonio Páez, controlled the country for 18 years (1830–48). It was a tough rule, but it established a certain political stability and put the weak economy on its feet. The period that followed was an almost uninterrupted chain of civil wars that was only stopped by another long-lived dictator, General Antonio Guzmán Blanco (1870–88). He launched a broad program of reform, including a new constitution, and assured some temporary stability, but his despotic rule triggered wide, popular opposition, and when he stepped down the country plunged again into civil war.

Written with an insider's knowledge by the prominent Venezuelan novelist, historian and politician Arturo Uslar Pietri, *Half a Millennium of Venezuela* provides a comprehensive record of the country's events, from the Spanish conquest to modern times.

In the 1840s, Venezuela raised the question of its eastern border with British Guiana (present-day Guyana), claiming as much as two-thirds of Guiana, up to the Río Essequibo. The issue was a subject of lengthy diplomatic negotiations and was eventually settled in 1899 by an arbitration tribunal, which gave rights over the questioned territory to Great Britain. Despite the ruling, Venezuela maintains its claim to this day. All maps produced in Venezuela have this chunk of Guyana within Venezuela's boundaries, labeled 'Zona en Reclamación.'

Another conflict that led to serious international tension was Venezuela's failure to meet payments to Great Britain, Italy and Germany on loans accumulated during the government of yet another caudillo, General Cipriano Castro (1899–1908). In response, the three European countries sent their navies to blockade Venezuelan seaports in 1902.

20TH-CENTURY DICTATORSHIPS

The first half of the 20th century was dominated by five successive military rulers from the Andean state of Táchira. The longest lasting and most tyrannical was General Juan Vicente Gómez, who seized power in 1908 and didn't relinquish it until his death in 1935. Gómez phased out the parliament, squelched the opposition and monopolized power. The discovery of oil helped Gómez's regime to stabilize the country. By the late 1920s Venezuela was a major oil exporter, which not only contributed

---

VENEZUELA'S BLACK GOLD

Oil is Venezuela's principal natural resource and the heart of its economy. Discovered here in 1914, it soon turned Venezuela from a poor debtor nation into one of South America's richest countries. Until 1970, Venezuela was the world's largest oil exporter, and though it was overtaken by Middle Eastern countries, its oil production has expanded year after year.

As cofounder of the Organisation of the Petroleum Exporting Countries (OPEC), Venezuela was influential in the fourfold rise in oil prices introduced in 1973–74, which quadrupled the country's revenue. On this strength, Venezuela borrowed heavily from foreign banks to import almost everything other than oil. Predictably, oil has overshadowed other sectors of the economy.

Today Venezuela is the world's fourth-largest oil producer, and the state oil company PDVSA is one of the world's biggest oil corporations. Oil provides 80% of Venezuela's export revenues, yet this dependence on oil leaves Venezuela vulnerable to fluctuations in the global economy. The main oil deposits are beneath and around Lago de Maracaibo, but other important reserves have been discovered and exploited in Los Llanos and the Delta del Orinoco.

1819	1821
The Angostura Congress proclaims the unified republic of Gran Colombia, comprising Venezuela, Colombia and Ecuador	Bolívar's victory in the Battle of Carabobo seals the independence of Venezuela

to economic recovery but also enabled the government to pay off the country's entire foreign debt.

Little of the oil-related wealth filtered down to people on the street. The vast majority continued to live in poverty with little or no education or health facilities, and not even reasonable housing. As agriculture was virtually abandoned, food had to be imported and prices rose rapidly. When Gómez died in 1935, the people of Caracas went on a rampage, burning down the houses of his relatives and supporters and even threatening to set fire to the oil installations on Lago de Maracaibo.

Tensions rose dangerously during the following dictatorships, exploding in 1945 when Rómulo Betancourt, leader of the left-wing Acción Democrática (AD) party, took control of the government. A new constitution was adopted in 1947, and noted novelist Rómulo Gallegos became president in Venezuela's first democratic election. On the wave of political freedom, the conservative Partido Social Cristiano (Copei) was founded by Rafael Caldera to counterbalance the leftist AD. But the pace of reform was too fast, given the strength of the old military forces greedy for power. The inevitable coup took place only eight months after Gallegos' election, with Colonel Marcos Pérez Jiménez emerging as leader. Once in control, he crushed the opposition and plowed oil money into public works and into modernizing Caracas. The spectacular buildings mushrooming in the capital were, however, poor substitutes for a better standard of living, and opposition rapidly grew.

For a comprehensive directory of Venezuelan websites on just about everything, check out www.lanic.utexas.edu/la /venezuela, put together by the Latin American Network Information Center of the University of Texas.

DEMOCRACY AT LAST

Pérez Jiménez was overthrown in 1958 by a coalition of civilians and navy and air-force officers. The country returned to democratic rule and Rómulo Betancourt was elected president. He enjoyed popular support and actually completed the constitutional five-year term of office – the first democratically elected Venezuelan president to do so. Since then, all changes of president have been by constitutional means, although the last decade has seen a few hiccups.

During the term of President Rafael Caldera (1969–74), the steady stream of oil money flowed into the country's coffers keeping the economy buoyant. President Carlos Andrés Pérez (1974–79) benefited from the oil bonanza – not only did production of oil rise but, more importantly, the price quadrupled following the Arab-Israeli war in 1973. In 1975 Pérez nationalized the iron-ore and oil industries and went on a spending spree; imported luxury goods crammed shops, and the nation got the impression that El Dorado had finally materialized. Not for long, though.

For a concise and to-the-point introduction to the country's historic, economic, societal and contemporary issues, read *In Focus: Venezuela – A Guide to the People, Politics and Culture,* by James Ferguson.

BACK TO INSTABILITY

In the late 1970s, the growing international recession and oil glut began to shake Venezuela's economy. Oil revenues declined, pushing up unemployment and inflation, and once more forcing the country into foreign debt. The 1988 drop in world oil prices cut the country's revenue in half, casting doubt on Venezuela's ability to pay off its debt. Austerity measures introduced in 1989 by Pérez (elected for the second time) triggered a wave of protests, culminating in the loss of more than 300 lives in three

1830	1849
Simón Bolívar dies in Santa Marta, Colombia	Rich lodes of gold are found in Guayana, generating one of the world's greatest gold rushes in modern history

days of bloody riots known as 'El Caracazo.' Further austerity measures sparked protests that often escalated into riots. Strikes and street demonstrations continued to be part of everyday life.

To make matters worse, there were two attempted coups d'état in 1992. The first, in February, was led by paratrooper Colonel Hugo Chávez. Shooting throughout Caracas claimed more than 20 lives, but the government retained control. Chávez was sentenced to long-term imprisonment. The second attempt, in November, was led by junior air-force officers. The air battle over Caracas, with war planes flying between skyscrapers, gave the coup a cinematic, if not apocalyptic, dimension. The Palacio de Miraflores, the presidential palace, was bombed and partially destroyed. The army was called to defend the president, and this time more than 100 people died.

Things became even more complicated in 1993 when Pérez was charged with embezzlement and misuse of public funds. He was automatically suspended from office, then judged, sentenced and placed under house arrest.

Amid the Pérez corruption scandals, Rafael Caldera was elected president for a second, non-consecutive term, but it was plagued by serious financial problems right from the start. The domino-like failure of a dozen banks in 1994 cost the government US$10 billion to pay off depositors, and several more banks failed in 1995. In all, the disaster cost the state some 20% of its GDP – one of the largest national financial collapses in recent history.

In 1995 Caldera was forced to devalue the currency by more than 70%, and a year later the government introduced more drastic rescue measures, including a 500% increase in petrol prices. By the end of his term in 1998, two-thirds of Venezuela's 23 million inhabitants were living below the poverty line. Drug-trafficking and crime had increased and Colombian guerrillas had dramatically expanded their operations into Venezuela's frontier areas.

TURN TO THE LEFT

The 1998 election put Hugo Chávez (see the boxed text, p27), the leader of the failed 1992 coup, into the presidency. After being pardoned by President Caldera in 1994, Chávez had embarked on an aggressive populist campaign, with nationalist Bolivarian rhetoric targeting the poor – roughly 70% of Venezuelans. As a platform for his campaign, he founded the Movimiento Bolivariano Revolucionario party, which in 1997 was transformed into the Movimiento Quinta República (MVR). He showed little enthusiasm for privatization and a free-market economy, vowing instead to produce the Bolivarian Revolution, a great if unspecified 'peaceful and democratic social revolution.'

Shortly after taking office, Chávez held a referendum in which a constituent assembly was approved to rewrite the existing constitution. The new document was approved in another referendum and came into force in December 1999. The new constitution gave the chief executive sweeping powers and introduced extensive changes – so extensive, in fact, that general elections had to be held again. In July 2000, still enjoying widespread popular support, Chávez easily won the new elections.

The gripping film *Amaneció de Golpe* (1999), directed by Carlos Azpúrua, portrays Venezuelan political unrest in the early 1990s. It tells how military man Hugo Chávez led an unsuccessful coup against then president Carlos Andrés Pérez.

DID YOU KNOW?

The 1999 constitution changed the country's name from República de Venezuela to República Bolivariana de Venezuela, requiring replacement of everything bearing the name, from coins and banknotes to passports and the coat of arms.

1908–35	1914
Venezuela experiences a period of tyrannical dictatorial rule under General Juan Vicente Gómez	The first oil well is sunk in Lago de Maracaibo, precipitating the oil boom and completely changing Venezuela

Since then, however, Chávez's 'peaceful social revolution' has been anything but peaceful. The introduction of a package of new decree laws in 2001 was met with angry protests, followed by a massive strike in April 2002 in Caracas, in which half a million people took to the streets. The protest turned violent, claiming 24 lives and injuring 114. Most of the fatalities were demonstrators allegedly shot dead by pro-government armed civilian groups.

The strike culminated in a coup d'état orchestrated by military leaders sponsored by business lobby. Chávez was taken under military custody and a prominent businessman, Pedro Carmona, was hastily placed as interim president. The next day, though, Chávez's supporters fought back in another round of violent protest and he miraculously regained power. The events only intensified the conflict and left people poised for violence. Meanwhile, the economy continued to slump.

While tensions rose, the opposition called a general strike in December 2002, in another attempt to oust the president. The nationwide strike paralyzed the country, including its vital oil industry and a good part of the private sector. After 63 days the opposition finally called off the strike which had cost the country 7.6% of its GDP and further devastated its oil-based economy. Chávez again survived and claimed the victory, yet

> To keep track of the country's current political and economic affairs, the best English-language news websites are www.venezuelanalysis.com and www.americas.org/venezuela

WHO IS HUGO CHÁVEZ?

A former paratrooper and leader of a failed 1992 coup, the current president of Venezuela is not exactly your average politician. Once he took office in 1998, he swiftly embarked on changing the constitution, which he achieved within a year. The new document extends presidential terms from five to six years with consecutive one-time re-elections, which means Chávez can potentially stay in office until 2012. Critics haven't missed the opportunity to comment that the era of the caudillos is back.

Comparing himself to the hero of the 19th-century independence wars, Simón Bolívar, Chávez apparently has another great friend and mentor, Fidel Castro, and is a frequent guest in Havana. His opponents accuse him of dragging the country down the Cuban path, while hundreds of Cuban doctors and teachers arrive in Venezuela, presumably to help provide educational and medical services in the provinces.

Born in 1954 in a small provincial town in Los Llanos, Chávez seems to inherit much of the tough and resistant nature of hardy *llanero* cowboys, the inhabitants of the plains. His language is not politically correct and he doesn't mince his words when clashing with opponents. His lengthy chats during his weekly television appearances are a new soap-opera entertainment, and were described by some as 'mesmerizing.' Not exactly a classic Latin dictator, he has bitterly divided the nation.

On the international front, Chávez caused a lot of talk in 2000, when he became the first foreign head of state since the Gulf War of 1991 to visit Baghdad and meet Saddam Hussein. He allegedly turns a blind eye to the presence of Colombian guerrillas in Venezuela and is carefully watched by Uncle Sam, who sees him as a destabilizing force in the region.

A strong opponent of globalization, Chávez has been credited with the revitalization of the Organisation of Petroleum Exporting Countries (OPEC) and the campaign to keep oil prices high by carefully controlling supply. He also tries to portray OPEC as a consumer-friendly advocacy organization and blames high fuel prices on the heavy taxes charged by Western governments.

1947	1998
Venezuela holds its first ever democratic election, in which popular novelist Rómulo Gallegos becomes president	Hugo Chávez is elected president in a landslide victory

he was increasingly isolated. According to the polls, his popular support dropped to a record low of about 30% by mid-2003.

AN UNCERTAIN FUTURE

Though divided and dispirited by the failure of the strike, the opposition closed ranks and came up with a new weapon against Chávez – his own new constitution, which included legislation allowing a mid-term vote on the president's leadership. According to the document, a minimum of 20% of the electorate (or 2.4 million votes) was required to call the referendum.

The so-called 'Reafirmazo' took place in November 2003 and the opposition immediately claimed the victory, saying they collected over 3.5 million signatures. Chávez swiftly fought back, accusing the signature collection process of 'megafraude,' even though observer teams from the Organization of American States (OAS) and the Carter Center considered it clean. The official verification and count of the signatures faces legal and bureaucratic roadblocks and will take months to complete, while the government and the opposition collect ammunition for the next battle. The Bolivarian Revolution goes on, while the country's economic crisis worsens.

Shot by two Irish documentary filmmakers, Kim Bartley and Donnacha O'Briain, who were inside the presidential palace during the coup d'état of April 2002, *The Revolution Will Not Be Televised* contains compelling firsthand footage of the events.

1999	2002–03
Violent mudslides devastate the central Caribbean coast, claiming up to 50,000 lives	A 63-day general strike in December and January paralyzes the country

The Culture

THE NATIONAL PSYCHE

Despite all its problems, Venezuela remains a proud and patriotic country. Its victorious role in the War of Independence is a source of tremendous national pride and Venezuelans celebrate their independence champion Simón Bolívar as one of the continent's greatest heroes: you won't find a town without a Plaza Bolívar or a school without his portrait on the wall.

Almost as strong as Venezuelan's pride in their history, however, is their pride in the beauty of their women, who have repeatedly won all the major international beauty contests. Supported by an enormous beauty industry that includes cosmetics, plastic surgery and fashion, girls are trained from a very young age to become queens. Glamor is not just a duty in urban Venezuela – it's a religion. Perhaps unsurprisingly, this is also an unabashedly macho country and men celebrate women's efforts to the full.

However, when the men aren't discussing women or politics, chances are they will be talking about baseball – all the rage among the country's ardent sport aficionados. And the national sport seems to go hand-in-hand with the national drinks of rum and beer.

On the whole, Venezuelans are a supremely courteous and hospitable people, full of life and warmth. They are open, willing to talk and not shy about striking up conversations with strangers. Wherever you are, you're unlikely to be alone or feel isolated, especially if you can speak a little Spanish. You'll meet many friendly people promising you the earth, though don't expect all promises and appointments to be honored. Venezuelans believe in the concept of life *aquí y ahora* (here and now), and give little import to the future. This is a party nation, renowned for the energy and joie de vivre of its inhabitants. Everybody who's anybody is out to have a ball, wherever you go, foot-tapping, hip-wriggling rhythms will follow you and there's always a *rumba* (party) brewing somewhere. The sparkle and good humor of Venezuelans' social interplay is also echoed by their wit and penchant for wordplay. Coastal Venezuelans are famed for their jokes, double meanings and innuendos, which pepper conversations about even the most mundane of things.

But it isn't all salsa and innuendos in the land of petrol and politics. Profound social scars have deepened during the oil crisis of the last few decades, and the revolutionary rhetoric of President Chávez has whipped up the long-simmering resentment of the lower classes (who make up the vast majority of the population) toward their oil-rich compatriots. On the other hand, the middle- and upper-class psyche still feeds upon the lingering confidence of the good old days of the petrol bubble, when a comfortable – even lavish – lifestyle was taken for granted and anything seemed possible.

LIFESTYLE

Visitors from the USA and Europe will find Venezuela superficially more familiar than any other Andean country. Although the country hosts a palette of ethnic blends, and traditional culture is very much alive in the countryside, the urban population went through an intensive course of 'Yankification' when oil money hit the nation from the 1960s to the 1980s. Local shops glittered with the latest in styles and gadgets, US cars

DID YOU KNOW?

Venezuelan women have won more international beauty competitions than any other country, including five Miss Worlds, four Miss Universes and countless other titles.

DID YOU KNOW?

Remember the story that Caracas has the highest female–male ratio in the world? Well the ratio is only 10:9, and that difference is in the over 50-year-olds. Sorry boys!

AND THE WINNER IS... MISS VENEZUELA!

Over the last 50 years, Venezuela has won more international beauty contests than anywhere else in the world. As such, it is a country afflicted with beauty-pageant fever, and has a thriving industry dedicated to finding the nation's next winner. The television station that broadcasts the Miss Venezuela pageant pays all the costs of grooming and dressing the women selected, and their full-time training (yes, training) costs many tens of thousands of dollars each.

Here are five more facts about the beauty industry in Venezuela that may surprise you:

- Beauty Queen or President – Winner of Miss World in 1981, Irene Saez, was subsequently elected mayor of Chacao in Caracas and governor of Isla Margarita. She even ran in the presidential elections of 1999 (losing to Hugo Chávez).
- Surfeit Salons – Caracas lists over 900 beauty salons in the *Yellow Pages:* that works out as one beauty salon to every two restaurants or cafés!
- Big Spenders – A market research study has found that the average Venezuelan spends one-fifth of their income on personal grooming and beauty products.
- Body Perfect – The plastic surgery industry in Caracas is the most profitable industry on the continent pro rata.
- Double Cup – Venezuelans have twice won the annual Miss Universe and Miss World competitions simultaneously – an achievement unmatched by any other nation.

---

were imported in the thousands, and middle-class Venezuelans jetted off for shopping sprees in Miami – and these habits have stuck, even through the last belt-tightening years.

However, scratch beneath the glossy international veneer and you'll find that local habits, manners and attitudes are often quite different from those at home. For one thing, everyday life is remarkably open and public. The climate, and restricted space of the majority of Venezuelan homes, invites the outdoor life. Consequently, much of family life takes place outside the home: in front of the house, in the street, in a bar or at the market. Don't be surprised to see people dancing to the tune of the car stereo in the streets or drinking a leisurely beer together on the sidewalk curb. The setting doesn't matter so long as the company's good.

And Venezuelans don't hold back in public places either. Personal affairs are discussed loudly and without embarrassment, irrespective of who may be listening. Office employees happily gossip about private love affairs and personal problems, completely oblivious to the glares of their waiting customers. Personal space is similarly disregarded in much of Venezuela; people waiting to use public phones will squash themselves up against the person calling, and streets and parks are filled with couples kissing passionately, blind to everyone passing around them. The exception to this rule is for gays and lesbians. Sexuality is highly stereotyped in Venezuela's macho male culture, and in this environment homosexuality tends to be swept under the carpet, except for a small community of more open gays in Caracas.

Noise is also a constant companion in Venezuela. Locals go undisturbed by blaring music, vehicles as noisy as tanks, and horns that are used constantly, even in traffic jams. Street vendors screech at potential customers, and people converse at a volume that to outsiders can suggest a heated argument.

However, while Venezuelans are open and laid-back in their public habits, security is high priority in the home. An estimated 75% of families live below the poverty line, and a similar percentage of the population

Alejandro Saderman's film *Cien Años de Perdón* (1999) is a humorous look at Venezuela's recent monetary meltdown and middle-class crisis. Financial ruin drives four previously law-abiding friends into robbing a bank, during which they discover high-level corruption.

live tightly packed together in urban towns and cities. As such, it's all too common for haphazardly built *barrios* (shantytowns) to sit directly alongside opulent hillside mansions. In the resulting scramble for security, city apartment blocks have come to resemble enormous birdcages with their abundance of iron-barred windows and security fences.

A peek inside the family home further emphasizes the chasm between rich and poor. While a family from the slums of Caracas might scrape together the wherewithal for food on the table and a small television, the average middle-class family has a maid, cable TV and two cars. The rich of Venezuela lead a truly extravagant lifestyle, with holiday homes, several cars and a number of servants at their disposal.

Regional differences in lifestyle are also dramatic. The consumer-led coastal society is a world apart from the slower, traditional life in the Andes, the isolated fisherfolk of the Delta del Orinoco or remote areas of the Amazon, where tribes of seminomadic hunter-gatherers struggle to maintain their lifestyle in the face of disputed land rights, pushy oil companies, miners and cattle ranches.

One common factor of Venezuelan life is the central importance of family, and especially the mother figure. Children almost always live with their families until they are married and care for their aging parents. It's therefore a particularly sad fact that political upheavals are driving increasing numbers of the young and educated away from their families to set up their lives abroad.

Discrimination

Given that the vast majority of Venezuelans are of mixed race, it's not surprising that they profess to be a nation that doesn't judge a person by their skin color. However, under the surface there remains a subtle prejudice against the darker-skinned descendants of African slaves. The pervading ideal of beauty, embedded by North American propaganda, values light skin, blond hair and light-colored eyes – a rather sad state of affairs given that only 20% of the population are classified as 'white.' Having said that, you're more likely to be barred from clubs for wearing out-of-fashion clothes than for your skin color.

The more openly expressed social distinction in Venezuela is by wealth and power. Success and money can gain almost anyone respect, especially among the upper classes. Highbrow *caraqueños* (persons born or residing

Sicario (José Ramón Novoa, 1995) is the harrowing story of a child assassin who lives and works in the violent *barrios* (shantytowns). It's a dramatic and thought-provoking film – but definitely not a feel-good movie!

While many books have been written on the Yanomami culture, *Into the Heart* (Kenneth Good and David Chanoff, 1991) is one of the most engaging. It describes Good's life and marriage in the Amazonian tribe.

VENEZUELAN TIME & SPACE

Like many Latin Americans, Venezuelans have their own notion of time. And time-related terminology here is not necessarily predictable. For example, *mañana* (literally 'tomorrow') can mean anytime in the indefinite future. Similarly, the word *ahora* (literally 'now' or 'in a moment'), often used in charming, diminutive forms such as *ahorita* or *ahoritica*, also has a flexible meaning. If you're waiting for a bus and ask bystanders when it should arrive, take it easy when they reply *ahorita viene* (it's coming) because this can just as easily mean in a few hours as in a minute's time.

Venezuelans invited to lunch also regard it as normal to arrive a few hours late. So be prepared: take a newspaper! Many offices have a similarly flexible grasp of working hours. Don't expect to arrange anything if you arrive less than half an hour before its statutory lunch break or official closing time.

Some Venezuelans, particularly rural dwellers, also have a different notion of space. If they say that something you're looking for is *allí mismito* (just around here) or *cerquitica* (very close), it may still be an hour's walk to get there.

DOS & DON'TS

■ Never show any disrespect for Bolívar – he is a saint to Venezuelans. Even sitting with your feet up on a bench in Plaza Bolívar, crossing the plaza wearing shorts, or carrying bulky parcels (or even a backpack) across the square may provoke piqued strangers to hassle you.

■ Litter is a fact of life, and trash is thrown thoughtlessly. Don't draw attention to this as it will offend people. Try rather to lead by example.

■ If you ask for information or directions, don't bank on a correct answer. Polite *campesinos* (country folk) may often tell you anything just to appear helpful. Ask several people to be sure and avoid questions that can be answered by just 'yes' or 'no'; instead of 'Is this the way to...?' ask 'Which is the way to...?'

---

in Caracas) frequently ridicule the lower social classes as *monos* (monkeys), and deride the 'unsophisticated' ways of the *campesinos* (country folk). Recent political turmoil has further polarized this rich-poor mentality, and there is often deep resentment of the richer classes from the poorer sectors of society.

POPULATION

Venezuela's population density, at about 26 people per square kilometer, is low, but varies dramatically. Over one-fifth of its population live in Caracas alone, while Los Llanos and Guayana are very sparsely populated indeed. In total, more than 75% of Venezuelans live in towns and cities, causing serious problems with overcrowding and unemployment.

DID YOU KNOW?

Almost half of the total population of Venezuela is age 19 or younger.

Venezuela is a country of mixed races. About 70% of the population is a blend of European, Indian and African ancestry, or any two of the three. The rest are whites (about 20%), blacks (8%) and Indians (2%).

Of that 2%, there are about 24 highly diverse indigenous groups, comprising some 532,750 people, scattered throughout the country. The main Indian communities include the Guajiro, north of Maracaibo; the Piaroa, Guajibo, Yekuana and Yanomami, in the Amazon; the Warao, in the Delta del Orinoco; and the Pemón, in southeastern Guayana.

Venezuela's rate of population growth stands at 2.2%, one of the highest in Latin America. It has also been the destination for significant post–World War II immigration from Europe (estimated at about one million), mostly from Spain, Italy and Portugal, but it nearly stopped in the 1960s. From the 1950s on, there has been a stream of immigrants from other South American countries, particularly Colombia. Venezuela also has some Middle Eastern communities, notably from Lebanon.

SPORTS

Never mind soccer. It may be the sport of choice across Latin America, but in Venezuela, *béisbol* (baseball) rules. The professional baseball league is composed of eight teams (based in Caracas, La Guaira, Maracaibo, Valencia, Barquisimeto, Maracay, Puerto La Cruz and Cabimas), which often feature US players during their winter season (October to February). Similarly, many Venezuelans have gone on to fame and fortune in US Major League Baseball. The biggest clash in the season is always between the two top teams: Leones del Caracas and Navegantes del Magallanes (Valencia).

The next most popular sport is *baloncesto* (basketball), followed by *fútbol* (soccer), which has a professional league that plays from August till May. In the past the national side has been prone to embarrassing defeats against fellow Latin American sides, though recent successes are slowly raising soccer in the popularity stakes.

Horse races have been run in Los Llanos for centuries, but they are now run on international-style racetracks, betting included. A more blood-thirsty spectator sport is cockfighting, and *galleras* (cockfight rings) can be found in most cities.

The Spanish *corrida* (bullfight) also found fertile soil in Venezuela, and most cities have their own *plaza de toros* (bullring). The bullfighting season peaks during Carnaval, when top-ranking matadors are invited from Spain and Latin America. Also thrilling – but bloodless – is the *coleo* or *toros coleados,* a rodeo popular in Los Llanos, in which four riders compete to bring down a bull after grabbing it by the tail from a galloping horse.

Less risky to participate in is *bolas criollas,* the Venezuelan variety of lawn bowling, each team aiming wooden balls at the smaller *mingo.* Similarly, street games of chess and dominoes have plenty of addicts throughout the country, and visitors are welcome to join in.

MEDIA

Freedom of the press has become a more sensitive subject in Venezuela during recent times. President Chávez' hands-on relationship with the media has had a mixed reception, invoking some mutterings of dictatorship and muzzling of free expression.

Two government and four private TV stations operate out of Caracas and reach most of the country. In October 2003 the government seized broadcasting equipment from the private news channel, Globovision, after it strongly criticized Chávez' administration. (The government asserted that they had been broadcasting on illegal channels.) In contrast, the president has won the hearts of many through his use of the government-run media. He will frequently talk informally to the nation via television appearances that can last for hours, and he hosts a regular radio program called *Hola, Presidente* in which he speaks directly to the people about current issues, encouraging a feeling of inclusion and openness in his government.

'The president talks informally to the nation via television appearances that can last for hours, and hosts a regular radio program called *Hola, Presidente'*

RELIGION

About 95% of Venezuelans are Roman Catholics. Many Indian groups adopted Catholicism and only a few isolated tribes still practice their ancient beliefs. Various Protestant churches in Venezuela have also gained importance, and there are small populations of Jews and Muslims.

A few curious religious cults have also spread throughout the country, including that of María Lionza (see the boxed text, p161). And the country's most important holy figure is José Gregorio Hernández (see the boxed text, p67). You'll see his well-attired statuettes in homes, shops and churches. Look for the black felt hat and smart suit.

ARTS
Music

Music plays a central part in Venezuelan life. Wherever you go – through markets, on buses and in restaurants – you'll be surrounded by everything from the energetic rhythms of salsa to African drumbeats.

The Spanish, and with them the Africans, introduced new rhythms and instruments, which gradually merged with pre-Hispanic indigenous music, producing what is now Venezuela's diverse folk music. The country's most popular folk rhythm is the *joropo*, also called *música llanera*, which developed in Los Llanos (see p218). The *joropo* is usually sung and accompanied by the harp, *cuatro* (a small, four-stringed guitar) and maracas. The *joropo* song 'Alma Llanera' has become an unofficial national anthem.

Joropo apart, regional beats are plentiful. In the eastern part of the country you'll hear, depending on where you are, the *estribillo*, *polo margariteño*, *malagueñas*, *fulías* and *jotas*. In the west, the *gaita* is typical of the Maracaibo region, while the *bambuco* is a popular Andean rhythm. The central coast echoes with African drumbeats, a mark of the sizable black population.

European classical music emerged in Venezuela only in the 19th century. The first composers of note include José Angel Lamas (1775–1814) and Cayetano Carreño Rodríguez (1774–1836), both of whom wrote religious music. However, the most prominent figure in Venezuela's classical music was Teresa Carreño (1853–1917), a pianist and composer. Born in Caracas, she was just seven years old when she composed her first work, a polka that was performed by a military band in Caracas. At the age of nine, she held her first concert in New York.

Of foreign rhythms that have taken hold in Venezuela, salsa and merengue from the Caribbean basin and *vallenato* from Colombia have been best absorbed. The king of Venezuelan salsa is Oscar D'León (1943–), also one of the world's top salsa stars. During his 40-year-long musical career, he has entered the books of Latin American music history and recorded a staggering 60 albums.

And, of course, Western pop – everything from rock to rap – is hugely influential among the urban youth (who account for the majority of the population). Caracas is an exciting center of Latin pop and the *rock en español* movement, which harnesses the rhythm and energy of Latin beats like salsa, merengue, mambo and calypso, and combines it with international trends. For many people Caracas is an international melting pot of Latin music second only to Miami.

RECOMMENDED LISTENING

- *Inolvidable* (José Luis Rodriguez, 1997) The silky voice of 'El Puma' crooning impossibly romantic Latin ballads is enough to make icebergs melt.

- *Al Pueblo lo que es de César* (Ali Primera, 1968) Prolific folk singer of the '60s; an icon to Venezuelan revolutionaries.

- *The New Sound Of The Venezuelan Gozadera* (Amigos Invisibles, 1998) For irreverent Venezuelan funk music, you won't get much better than these guys.

- *Songs of Venezuela* (Soledad Bravo, 1995) Venezuelan institution Soledad Bravo has recorded more than 30 albums and taken her heartfelt voice all around the world.

- *Donde Esta el Futuro* (Desorden Publico, 1999) Features many remixed early hits for this ever-energetic ska band.

- *Carreño – Piano Works* (2000) The wonderful classical works of pianist and composer Teresa Carreño, performed by Alexandra Oehler.

- *Venezuela y su Folklore: A Taste of Venezuela* (Grupo Barlovento, 1998) Broad range of traditional folk music from *joropo* to *bambuco*.

- *El Diablo Suelto: Guitar Music of Venezuela* (Sony International, 2003) A masterclass in the harp, guitar and *cuatro* (small four-stringed guitar).

Dance

Given the importance of music in Venezuela, it's not surprising that dance also plays a vital role. Indeed it's all too common to hear mothers threatening their sons to learn 'or you'll never find a girlfriend!' Dancing here is more than a pastime – it's an essential social skill.

Dances were also an integral part of ritual in Venezuela's early civilizations. These early forms merged with colonial and immigrant influences creating diverse and colorful folk dances. Such traditions are at their more energetic among black communities on Venezuela's central coast, where everybody rushes to dance when homegrown drummers spontaneously take to their instruments in the streets. The most dramatic time to see African-influenced dancing in Venezuela is during the festival of the Dancing Devils in May/June (p328).

You can often see amateur folk-dance ensembles in action during annual feasts. Folk dance has sown seeds for the creation of professional groups that now promote their musical folklore to the public and abroad, such as Danzas Venezuela, founded by internationally famous folk dancer Yolanda Moreno.

Among the neoclassical dance groups, the best known is the Ballet Nuevo Mundo de Caracas, led by Venezuela's most famous ballerina, Zhandra Rodríguez. The Ballet Teresa Carreño and the Ballet Contemporáneo de Caracas (www.caracasballet.com) also perform in the neoclassical style. Contemporary dance is probably best represented by the groups Coreoarte, the Danza Hoy, the Dramo, and Acción Colectiva, whose productions can all be seen regularly in Caracas theaters (see p88) and in touring shows around the country.

Elia Schneider's *Huelepega* (1999), literally 'glue-sniffer,' pulls no punches in its portrayal of the lives of Caracas street children. The film uses genuine street children, lending authenticity to the nonstop, sometimes schizophrenic action.

Cinema

Venezuelan cinema hasn't reached the heights of other Latin American nations such as Mexico or Argentina, and local film production is generally sparse. But while Venezuelans will tell you that their film industry is still in diapers, it doesn't stop them producing hard-hitting social critiques and carefully crafted historical dramatizations.

Venezuela's first short film was shot in 1909, just 13 years after the first films by the Lumière brothers took place in Paris. The country's first international hit was *La Balandra Isabel Llegó Esta Tarde* (The Ship Isabel Arrived this Afternoon; 1950), by Carlos Hugo Christensen, a prize-winner at the 1951 Cannes film festival.

It wasn't until the 1970s that local cinematography began to develop at a faster pace, producing several thought-provoking films. Román Chalbaud, who began his career during this period, is Venezuela's best known film director. His film *El Pez que Fuma* (The Fish That Smokes; 1977) received international critical acclaim. His most well-known works include *La Quema de Judas* (The Burning of Judas; 1974), *La Oveja Negra* (The Black Sheep; 1987) and *Pandemónium* (Pandemonium; 1997).

Recent trends in Venezuelan filmmaking have leant heavily towards contemporary social commentary on the one hand and historical narratives on the other. Film buffs interested in recent highlights of Venezuelan cinematography should track down some of the following films: *Jericó* (Jerico; Luis Alberto Lamata, 1991), the historical account of a 16th-century Dominican monk in the Amazon; a son's look at his pioneering father in *El Misterio de Los Ojos Escarlata* (The Mystery of the Scarlet Eyes; Alfredo Anzola, 1993); the story of the scientist Humboldt in *Aire Libre* (Out in the Open; Luis Armando Roche, 1995); and *Amaneció de Golpe* (A Coup at Daybreak; Carlos Azpúrua, 1999), the story of how

President Hugo Chávez burst onto the political scene. More recent films include the recommended *Oro Diablo* (Devil Gold; Elia Schneider, 2000), a bold and heartrending story set amid the poor youth of Venezuela; and *Manuela Saenz* (Manuela Saenz; Diego Risquez, 2000), the War of Independence through the eyes of Bolívar's mistress.

However, in general Venezuelan film distributors tend to come down in favor of foreign movies, which are more likely to realize a profit (hence tracking down copies of Venezuelan films can be easier in the USA than in Venezuela!).

In contrast to cinema, TV production is a booming industry. This is especially true of soap operas (see the boxed text below).

Literature

A rich world of pre-Hispanic Indian tales, legends and stories preserved and passed from generation to generation provided invaluable information on the pre-Columbian culture for the first Spanish chroniclers. For a taste of the first chronicles narrating the early history of Venezuela, try to hunt down *Brevísima Relación de la Destrucción de las Indias Occidentales*, by Fray Bartolomé de las Casas, or *Elegías de Varones Ilustres de Indias* (1589) by Juan de Castellanos. More analytical and comprehensive is one of the later chronicles, *Historia de la Conquista y Población de la Provincia de Venezuela* (1723) by José de Oviedo y Baños.

The dawn of the 19th century saw the birth and crystallization of revolutionary trends. The first 30 years of that century were more or less dominated by political literature. Among the pivotal historical works was the autobiography of Francisco de Miranda (1750–1816). Simón Bolívar (1783–1830) himself also left an extensive literary heritage, including letters, proclamations, dissertations and also literary achievements such as *Delirio sobre El Chimborazo* (My Delirium on Chimborazo) – an expression of ideals for a nation fighting for independence. Bolívar was influenced by his close friend Andrés Bello (1781–1865), the first important Venezuelan poet, as well as noted philologist, historian and jurist.

With independence achieved, political writing gave way to other literary forms. In the 1920s, Andrés Eloy Blanco (1896–1955) appeared on the scene to become one of the best poets Venezuela has ever produced. *Angelitos Negros* (Little Black Angels) is the most popular of his numerous poems.

At the same time, several notable novelists emerged, among whom Rómulo Gallegos (1884–1969) was the most outstanding; he remains the country's internationally best-known writer. *Doña Bárbara*, his most

DID YOU KNOW?

Internationally renowned novelist Rómulo Gallegos (1884–1969) was also Venezuela's first democratically elected president.

TELENOVELAS

While flicking between channels on your hotel TV, take a minute to enjoy the intense melodrama of a good ol' Venezuelan *telenovela*. These ubiquitous soap operas with their impossibly beautiful stars, hammy acting and theatrical drum rolls transfix the nation on a nightly basis. Their habitual formula is a racy mix of romance, seduction, glamor and a healthy dose of blood-and-thunder.

And it works. More than 50% of Venezuelans are obsessive fans, and producers do everything they can to meet demand. It's a thriving multimillion dollar industry, and Venezuelan soaps have been distributed all over the world (breaking rating records in foreign countries more than once). Over the last two decades Venezuela has even come to rival the two traditional *telenovela* powers, Mexico and Brazil.

Unlike ongoing European or American soaps, each *telenovela* runs for just a few months, climaxing in dramatic endings that have the power to bring the country to a standstill.

popular novel, was first published in Spain in 1929 and has since then been translated into a dozen languages. Miguel Otero Silva (1908–85) was another remarkable novelist of the period. He's best remembered for *Casas Muertas* (Dead Houses), a bestseller published in 1957.

Arturo Uslar Pietri (1906–2001) stands out as a novelist, historian, literary critic, journalist and even a politician, having been a minister and a presidential candidate. He was not only the most versatile writer in modern Venezuela, but also the most inexhaustible: since his first novel, *Lanzas Coloradas* (The Red Lances), in the 1930s, he wrote tirelessly right up until his death in 2001.

Other veteran Venezuelan writers include Denzil Romero (novels), Salvador Garmendia (short forms), Aquiles Nazoa (humor, poetry) and Francisco Herrera Luque (historical novels). The books of Herrera Luque (1928–91) are particularly interesting as they give a profound and beautifully readable insight into Venezuela's history. His novels include *Los Viajadores de la India* (The Travelers from India), about the Spanish conquest.

The 1960s saw the start of many fresh, experimental trends in contemporary Venezuelan literature. Many writers took up magical realism, while others became more and more introspective. The increasing freedom of speech and the example of the Cuban Revolution also encouraged writers to explore the vast divides within their own oil-rich society. A groundbreaking experimental novel from the middle of the century is *El Falso Cuaderno de Narciso Espejo* by Guillermo Meneses (1911–78); a slightly later seminal work by Adriano Gonzalez Leon (1931–) is the powerful magical-realism novel *Pais Portatil* (Portable Country), which contrasts rural Venezuela with a monstrous vision of Caracas.

Ednodio Quintero is another contemporary writer to look out for. His work *La Danza del Jaguar* (The Dance of the Jaguar; 1991) is one of several translated into other languages. Other contemporary writers worth tracking down include Carlos Noguera, Luis Brito García, Eduardo Liendo and Orlando Chirinos.

Theater

Caracas has developed a strong theater tradition since it founded Venezuela's first venue, Teatro del Conde, in 1784. Several more theaters opened at the end of the 19th century in Caracas, Maracaibo, Valencia, Barquisimeto and Barcelona, all presenting a steady diet of European fare. The national theater was born only a few decades ago, with its major center in Caracas. Today, there are several dozen theatrical groups, most in Caracas. Rajatabla, tied to the Ateneo de Caracas, is Venezuela's best-known theater on the international scene. Other Caracas-based groups of note include La Compañía Nacional de Teatro and the Teatro Profesional de Venezuela. It's also worth watching out for the Teatro Negro de Barlovento, formed by the black community of the central coast and taking inspiration from African roots.

Visual Arts

Venezuela has one of the strongest contemporary art movements in Latin America. The streets and public buildings of Caracas are filled with modern art and the city houses some truly remarkable galleries.

But the history of Venezuelan art goes back before even the Spaniards. Surviving pre-Colombian works include a scattering of cave paintings in Bolívar and Amazonas states and enigmatic rock-carvings, which have been found at about 200 locations throughout the country. Some

For a biography of Venezuela's most famous poet, Andrés Eloy Blanco, plus many of his most beloved poems, visit www.los-poetas.com/b /blanco.htm (in Spanish).

of the best collections of petroglyphs can be seen on Piedra Pintado, a 50m-high cliff near Puerto Ayacucho (p319), and Piedra Pintada near Valencia (p130).

Shuffling forward in time, the painting and sculpture of the colonial period had an almost exclusively religious character. Although mostly executed by local artists, the style was influenced by the Spanish art of the day. But when independence loomed, painting departed from strictly religious themes and began to immortalize historical events. The first artist to do so was Juan Lovera (1778–1841), whose most famous paintings can be seen in the Capilla de Santa Rosa de Lima, in Caracas (p64).

When General Guzmán Blanco took power in the late 19th century, Venezuelan painting blossomed. The most outstanding painter in this period – and Venezuelan history as a whole – is Martín Tovar y Tovar (1827–1902), particularly remembered for his monumental works in Caracas' Capitolio Nacional (p65). Another important 19th-century artist, Arturo Michelena (1863–98), received international recognition despite his short life. He spent much of his life in Paris, then the world's art capital. Another Venezuelan living in France, Emilio Boggio (1857–1920) acquired an international reputation for impressionist works influenced by Van Gogh.

For more information and biographies of Venezuelan writers, performers and artists, visit the culture page of the website of the Venezuelan Embassy in the US www.embavenez-us.org

The epic historical tradition of Tovar y Tovar was continued by Tito Salas (1888–1974), who dedicated himself to commemorating Bolívar's life and achievements in huge murals (see p65 and p66).

Many claim that modern Venezuelan painting began with the unique expressionist Armando Reverón (1889–1954) and the transitional painter Carlos Otero (1886–1977). Francisco Narváez (1905–82) is commonly acclaimed as one of Venezuela's most groundbreaking modern sculptors. The art museum in Porlamar, on his native Isla de Margarita (p234), has the largest collection of his diverse and experimental works.

Recent Venezuelan art has been characterized by a proliferation of different schools, trends and techniques. One of the most remarkable exemplars of this movement was the painter Héctor Poleo (1918–89), who expressed himself in a variety of styles, switching easily from realism to surrealism, with some metaphysical exploration in between. Equally captivating is the expressionist painting of Jacobo Borges (1931–91), who by deforming human figures turns them into caricatures.

There's a lot of activity among the current generation. Watch out, for example, for works of Carlos Zerpa (painting), the quirky ideas of José Antonio Hernández Díez (photo, video, installations) and the emblematic paintings, collages and sculptures of Miguel von Dangel. And you'll see plenty more in the contemporary art museum of Caracas (see p67).

Culture Shock: Venezuela (Kitt Baguley, 1999) is a light-hearted and irreverent commentary on almost every sector of Venezuelan society, from fast-paced urban life to the wilds of the Andes.

However, Jesús Soto (1923–) is Venezuela's number one internationally renowned contemporary artist. He's a leading representative of kinetic art (art, particularly sculpture, that contains moving parts). His large distinctive works adorn numerous public buildings and plazas in Venezuela and beyond (including Paris, Toronto and New York). The largest collection of his work is in the museum dedicated to him in Ciudad Bolívar (p288).

Architecture

There isn't a lot left to see of pre-Hispanic dwellings in Venezuela as many were made from perishable materials such as adobe, wood and vegetable fibers. However, the homes of remote indigenous communities in the Amazon still give a glimpse of the design of early Indian structures.

The arrival of the Spanish brought the introduction of solid building materials such as brick and tile to Venezuelan architecture. The newly founded towns were direct reflections of the Spanish style, laid out on a square grid with the main plaza, cathedral and government house forming the center. But colonial architecture in Venezuela never reached the grandeur that marked neighbors like Colombia, Ecuador and Peru. Churches were mostly small and houses were usually undecorated one-story constructions. Only in the last half-century of the colonial era did a wealthier merchant class emerge that built grand residences that reflected their stature. A handful of notable examples survive in Coro (see p139).

Independence initially had little impact on Venezuelan architecture, but in the 1870s a dramatic overhaul of the capital city was launched by Guzmán Blanco. He commissioned many monumental public buildings in a hodgepodge of styles, from neo-Gothic to neoclassical, largely depending on the whim of the architect in charge.

A real rush toward modernity came with oil money and culminated in the 1970s. This period was characterized by indiscriminate demolition of the historic urban fabric and its replacement by modern architecture. Many dilapidated colonial buildings fell prey to greedy urban planners. Accordingly, Venezuela's colonial legacy can be disappointing when compared to that of other Andean countries. On the other hand, Venezuela has some truly remarkable modern architecture. Carlos Raúl Villanueva, who began work in the 1930s, is considered the most outstanding Venezuelan architect. The campus of Universidad Central de Venezuela in Caracas (p71) is regarded as one of his best and most coherent designs and has been included on Unesco's Cultural Heritage list.

Environment Tobias Mendelovici

THE LAND

Occupying 916,445 sq km in the northernmost reaches of South America, Venezuela is 18 times larger than Costa Rica and just over twice the size of California. Part of the charm of visiting Venezuela is its remarkable diversity of landscapes. The traveler can encounter all four primary South American landscapes – the steamy Amazon, the snowy peaks of the Andes, the hot and flat savannas and the beaches and islands of the Caribbean – all in a single country.

The country has two mountain ranges. The lower Cordillera de la Costa reaches an altitude of 2725m at Pico Naiguatá, the tallest peak of the Ávila Mountains, which separates the valley of Caracas from the Caribbean. This mostly green and warm-to-temperate region is the most developed and populated of the country. The other, taller mountain range is the northernmost section of the great Andes mountain range. The tallest Andean point in Venezuela rises to 5000m at the Sierra Nevada de Mérida. These slopes give birth to rivers that roll down the treeless hills of the *páramos* (open highlands above about 3300m) to the downstream temperate forests before finally reaching Los Llanos and the lowlands around Lago de Maracaibo.

Lago de Maracaibo is the largest lake in South America and is linked to the Caribbean Sea. The region around the lake is the traditional oil-producing region of the country. While the Maracaibo basin still produces 50% of the country's oil, its significance is being displaced by drilling in other areas.

The Río Orinoco watershed embraces the sparsely populated low-lying region of Los Llanos ('the plains'), which are characterized by prairies with a variety of savanna and forests. The Llanos makes up nearly a third of the country. The Río Orinoco itself runs for 2150km down to the delta's wetlands and is South America's third largest river.

South of the Orinoco lies another sparsely populated area, the Guayana region. This area, which makes up nearly half the country, includes the Río Caura watershed, the largely impenetrable Amazon rain forest, and the famous plateaus of the Guayana highlands where hundreds of tabletop mountains called tepuis tower over the forest. The Guayana highlands are considered one of the geologically oldest places on earth. The area also holds the world's highest waterfall – the famous Angel Falls (Salto Ángel) – which plummets nearly a kilometer from one of the tepuis found here.

Finally, let's not forget the country's 2813km-long stretch of Caribbean coast, featuring a 900,000 sq km Caribbean marine zone with numerous islands and cays. The largest and most popular of these is Isla Margarita, followed closely by the less-developed Archipiélago Los Roques.

WILDLIFE

Venezuela offers great opportunities for wildlife watching. The huge diversity of ecosystems, each with its own flora and fauna, results in a relative abundance of wildlife, much of which cannot be seen outside of its native zone. Indeed Venezuela is the 10th most biologically diverse country on the planet. A tip: your chances of spotting the country's rarest and most impressive specimens will improve dramatically if you hire specialized guides who know where and when to look for wildlife.

DID YOU KNOW?

The Río Orinoco's watershed is one of the largest and most complex fresh-water ecosystems on earth. It's home to more than 1000 fish species – more than Europe and North America combined.

Emilio Perez and Adrian Warren's *Map to Mount Roraima* is more than a map: it's actually a brochure with great illustrations and information about this tepui's geology, climate, history, flora and fauna.

As with anywhere, geography has influenced the evolution of plant and animal species. One of the best places on earth to see this is in the Guayana region, where dramatic contrasts in geology and altitude have produced a huge range of habitats for a diverse selection of plants and animals. The finest example is the 'lost worlds' atop the tepuis, where flora and fauna is isolated from the forest below and from the other tepuis, and therefore has developed independently from its surroundings. Some of the tabletop habitats have been isolated for millions of years and many of the species found on the tops of tepui exist only on their particular summit. For example, half of the plant species found on Roraima do not exist anywhere else in the world.

Leslie Pantin's beautifully illustrated *Genio y Figura de la Fauna Venezolana* describes Venezuela's fauna and includes folktales in Spanish.

Animals

Again, diversity is the key word when it comes to describing Venezuela's fauna. There are 341 species of reptiles, 284 species of amphibians, 1791 species of fishes, 351 species of mammals and many butterflies and other invertebrates. More than 1360 species of birds – approximately 20% of the world's known species – reside in the country, and 46 of these species are endemic. The country's geographical setting on a main migratory route makes it a bird-watcher's heaven.

The evergreen forests of the Cordillera de la Costa are a good place to look for sloths, monkeys and marsupials, and are a definite must for bird-watchers, who will delight in such rare species as Venezuela's endemic parakeets, screamers (*Anhimidae* family), trogons, rare thrushes and many species of toucan and toucanet. Parque Nacional El Ávila (p93), north of Caracas, provides an excellent starting point to search for hummingbirds, parakeets and fruit-eaters, among the more than 300 species identified there. West of Caracas, Parque Nacional Henri Pittier (p118) is another birder's paradise with some 582 bird species. Further west, in the Cuare fauna refuge, you can spot one of the country's largest flamingo colonies. If you visit the Cueva del Guácharo (p275), 12km east from Caripe, you can't miss the unique *guácharo* (oilbird). This blind bird is about half a meter long, has reddish-brown feathers and curved beak and lives in the caves. The Andes are home to the endangered South American bear or spectacled bear, plus many birds including curassows, quetzals, owls, hawks and a small population of the recently reintroduced Andean condor.

DID YOU KNOW?

The Anaconda is the largest snake on earth. Its average length is 3m to 4m, but specimens as long as 11m have been found.

Along the Caribbean coastline and on the islands you will spot many waterbirds including the colorful scarlet ibis. At some of the islands you may also see endangered parrots, such as the *cotorra cabeciamarilla* (yellow-shouldered parrot) – look for its green feathers and yellow face. Although this bird has become nearly extinct in the Caribbean, Isla Margarita (p231) is home to one of the largest remaining populations. Dolphins are abundant along Venezuela's coastline, and around Archipiélago Los Roques (p99) you will be surprised by the health and vitality of the reefs and the abundant marine life that rivals any of the better-known diving destinations in the Caribbean. Endangered green sea turtles nest on the archipelago and in the Parque Nacional Península de Paria (p271) on the eastern mainland coast.

The seasonally flooded plains of Los Llanos (p196) are among Venezuela's best places to spot wildlife. You stand a good chance of seeing capybara (locally known as *chiguire*), spectacled caiman, monkeys, giant anteaters, armadillo, anaconda, piranhas, ocelot and even the elusive jaguar. Birds flock here by the millions: it's one of the planet's most important bird-breeding reserves, with well over 350 species including

The Birds of Venezuela 2003, by Stephen L Hilty, is a must for bird-watchers. Similarly, William H Phelps' and Rodolphe Meyer de Schauensee's A Guide to the Birds of Venezuela was the first of its kind and remains a classic.

waterfowl species such as ibis, herons, jacanas and egrets. Seed-eating birds, macaws, raptors and the strange *hoatzin* – a prehistoric-looking bird with punky yellow feathers on its head – all make their home here. South of Lago de Maracaibo, within the Parque Nacional Ciénagas del Catatumbo, you can find howler monkeys, spectacled caiman, endemic river dolphins, and many birds including ospreys, kingfishers, herons, masked ducks and ibises. Manatees and otters are also found here, but are notoriously hard to spot. In the Delta del Orinoco (p279) you can expect some of the species found in the Llanos.

The Guayana region contains many rare, unique and endangered species, including the endemic birds of the tepuis (such as the amazing cock of the rock with its brilliant orange crest), jaguar, puma, otters, harpy eagles and the tapir (the biggest mammal in the country). It's also home to the native, endangered Orinoco crocodile, which grows up to 8m long and is the largest crocodile in the Americas.

Plants

Otto Huber's Ecological Guide to the Gran Sabana provides excellent information on the environmental features of Parque Nacional Canaima, including lists of animals and plants.

Venezuela boasts 650 types of vegetation and thousands of plant species in several major habitats. Tropical lowland rain forests still cover a very large part of the country. Cloud forests are confined to the mountain slopes between 1000m and 2800m above sea level, and are a primary feature of Parque Nacional Henri Pittier (p118) and the Sierra Nevada de Mérida (p196). Dry forests are found mainly on the larger Caribbean islands and in the hills between Coro and Barquisimeto. The coasts and islands feature mangrove forests. Grasslands and savannas are mainly on the plains and in Parque Nacional Canaima (see the boxed text, p44). Finally, you can see the Mérida *páramos*, highland meadows that are found just above the cloud forests.

The national flower, the Flor de Mayo *(Cattleya mossiae)*, is just one of the more than 25,000 species of orchid found in Venezuela's forests; its sensuous pink flower blossoms in May. Another Venezuelan specialty is the *frailejón (Espeletia)*, a typical plant of the *páramos*; it has pale green leaves coated in white velvety fur, which are arranged in a rosette pattern around a thick trunk. The *frailejón* can grow to more than 3m tall and its yellow flowers bloom from September to December.

If you drive along the Caracas–Valencia highway between December and April, you are likely to see the splendid yellow blossoming of Venezuela's national tree, the *araguaney* (trumpet tree). Endemic to Roraima is the little carnivorous *Drosera roraima*, which is found in the humid areas atop of the tepui and has intense red leaves with sticky tentacles that catch insects. When visiting the Gran Sabana, look along the main road for the *morichales* (palm groves), which are groups of *moriches* (oily palms) that grow along waterways or in flood-prone areas. These are very common in the eastern plains of the Llanos as well. The adult plant features a 15m-tall trunk dotted with fan-shaped leaves that are used by indigenous people for construction. The palm's reddish fruit serves as a local food source.

NATIONAL PARKS

Think Venezuela (www.think-venezuela .net) provides a good overview of the country's national parks – just click on the national parks link.

Some 46% of the country is protected under national law as ABRAEs (Areas Under Special Administration). About 16% of this protected territory includes 43 national parks and 21 natural monuments; the remaining 30% is designated under a variety of categories, including wildlife refuges, forests and biosphere reserves.

Venezuela's national parks offer a diverse landscape of evergreen and snowy mountains, sandy beaches, tropical islands, coral reefs, high

Protected Area	Features & Activities	Best Time to Visit	Page
Parque Nacional Henri Pittier	steep, forested mountains rolling into Caribbean beaches, hiking & interpretation trails at Estacion Biológica Rancho Grande; bird-watching (500 species, 22 endemic), monkeys, sloths, snakes	late June for drumming at the Fiesta de San Juan	121
Parque Nacional Guatopo	rain forest & mountains embrace a freshwater reservoir, camping, walking trails, visitors center at La Macanilla, Hacienda La Elvira; 50 species of bats, 8 species of marsupials, howler & capuchin, monkeys, armadillo, jaguar, harpy eagles	year-round	107
Parque Nacional Canaima	arguably 'the jewel in the crown' with Angel Falls, hiking the tepuis & Roraima, jaguars, anteaters, cock of the rock, harpy eagle, tapir	year-round	boxed text 44
Parque Nacional Mochima	hills with dry tropical forest penetrating deep-water beaches on the east coast, rain forest inland, diving, snorkeling, rafting, camping; dolphins, abundant marine life, marine birds, iguanas	year-round	251
Parque Nacional Archipiélago Los Roques	mangrove coastline embraced by the Caribbean's turquoise waters, secluded cays with white-sand beaches & coral reefs, extraordinary diving & snorkeling, fishing, sailing, windsurfing & kitesurfing, marine biological station; green turtle nesting area, abundant marine life & birds (over 90 species)	year-round	99
Parque Nacional Morrocoy	palm-fringed cays with sandy beaches protected by mangroves & coral reefs on the western coast, diving, snorkeling, camping, Golfete de Cuarefauna refuge; abundant marine life & birds, alligators, large scarlet ibis colonies	September	152
Parque Nacional Sierra Nevada	snowy mountains of the Andes descend into temperate & tropical forest, hiking & biking, Venezuela's tallest mountain Pico Bolivar (5001m); spectacled bear & Andean condor (both endangered), deer, ocelot, frailejón endemic plant	year-round	193

plateaus and rainforests, so it's no surprise that most of the country's domestic and international tourism occurs within them. While some parks, especially those in coastal and marine zones, are easily accessible and tend to be overcrowded by locals during holiday periods and weekends, others remain unvisited despite their location and year-long season. A few of the parks offer tourism facilities, but they're generally not very extensive.

PARQUE NACIONAL CANAIMA

Parque Nacional Canaima comprises 30,000 sq km in the remote southeastern corner of the country. In 1994 Unesco declared it a World Natural Heritage Site because of its outstanding natural features that include cloud forest, savanna, rivers, huge waterfalls, *moriche* palm groves, shrublands and swamp forests – and, most notably, the extraordinary geologic formations called tepuis. The tepuis are the remains of mighty sandstone plateaus. These tabletop habitats have been isolated for millions of years, allowing the development of unique flora and fauna that attracts research scientists from around the world. The highest of the tepuis is the legendary Roraima (2810m), which is located in the eastern sector of the park. The park is also home to the world's highest waterfall – the famous Angel Falls (Salto Ángel) – which descends nearly a kilometer from Auyantepui in the western sector of the national park. See p302 for tours to Angel Falls.

For some parks, such as Morrocoy, you'll need to get a permit and pay a small fee for camping. Always ask about safety when going camping. Few parks charge admission fees; the most expensive fees are for Los Roques ($5) and Canaima ($3).

Parques Nacionales de Venezuela, edited by Oscar Todtman, is a review of Venezuela's 43 national parks. It showcases some wonderful photography, but lacks the more practical information a traveler needs to get around.

Inparques (Instituto Nacional de Parques Nacionales; www.inparques.gov.ve in Spanish), an autonomous institute attached to the Ministry of Environment, was created to manage the national parks and natural monuments. Unfortunately the park authorities lack the funding, equipment, personnel and the enforcement capacity to fully manage this huge territory. Some parks do require permits for camping or hiking, but there is usually an Inparque office in most main towns, or posts at the national parks themselves, which can provide information. Other types of protected lands are managed by other organizations designated by the Ministry of Environment.

While the Venezuelan populace looks to the park system to protect the nation's biodiversity and provide a recreation amenity, many parks are inhabited by local indigenous and peasant communities that have lived in the parks since before they were designated as such by the government. This creates a conflict between each park's conservation needs and the local population's use of a natural resource. The greatest hope in combining conservation with economic sustainability for locals lies in a planned and responsible development of ecotourism within the protected areas.

ENVIRONMENTAL ISSUES

The most visible and perhaps the most emblematic of all Venezuelan environmental issues is waste management – the country has no recycling policy, dumping of garbage in cities and natural areas is a common practice by locals, and untreated sewage is sometimes dumped in the sea and other water bodies. Fortunately, the Ministry of Environment has begun to make major investments in water-treatment plants for many areas. There continues to be a general lack of clear environmental policy and the provision of environmental education is poor.

Another major environmental issue is the hunting and illegal trade of fauna and flora that takes place in many parts of the country, including protected areas. You may see 'traders' along the roadside selling monkeys, parrots and other endangered species, many of which are taken out of the country to become pets in the so-called 'developed' world. Also affecting wildlife is the destruction of habitats, particularly the clear-cutting of forests for agriculture and the illegal mining, both of which are seriously threatening the still-pristine lands south of the Orinoco.

ECOTOURISM OPPORTUNITIES

Venezuela's incredible variety of natural attractions and biodiversity makes it an understandably attractive destination for nature lovers. Most of the country's important features fall inside one of Venezuela's protected areas. Many of the country's 43 indigenous groups live on or near protected areas as well.

There are more than 800 posadas or lodges in natural areas that provide accommodation for nature tourists, ranging from the most rustic camps to very comfortable lodges. A growing number of tour operators include ecotourism tours and accommodation in their packages, but do be aware that not all tours marketed as 'eco' are committed to high standards of ecological conservation or to local community participation. Tour guides seldom belong to the local communities, but porters, cooks and drivers usually do. Also know that while some guides speak English and even a second foreign language, others do not, so make sure you shop around.

Perhaps the country's most successful conservation stories are in the Llanos, where some *hatos* (cattle ranches) have preserved their fauna and built a tourism infrastructure to make it accessible to visitors. These wildlife ecotourism reserves combine accommodation and tours, and some even have research facilities. Tours in the *hatos* usually include trucks specially outfitted for photo safaris.

In addition to these, there are many other ways travelers can experience Venezuela's ecotourism. The following are some examples of what the country can offer the ecotourist:

Hato Piñero (p226; ☎ 58-212-991-8935; www.hatopinero.com; s/d May-Nov $130/190, Dec-Apr $150/230) In the upper Llanos, this ranch is home to more than 300 bird species and contains a herbarium featuring a diversity of floral species of the plains. Prices include meals.

Hato El Cedral (p225; ☎ 58-212-781-8995, 58-212-793-6082; www.hatocedral.com; s/d May-Nov $140/240, Dec-Apr $165/290) Located in the lower Llanos, this ranch is outstanding for the opportunity to see a vast number of wildlife, including some 350 bird species and a population of 30,000 capybaras. Prices include meals.

Hato El Frio (p225; ☎ 58-414-743-5329; www.elfrioeb.com; s $115-145, d $170-230) Located in the lower Llanos, 150km west of San Fernando de Apure, this wildlife refuge was established in 1974. It has its own biological station where you can see anacondas and endemic crocodiles raised in captivity. Prices include meals.

Hato Río de Agua (☎ 0294-332-215, 0294-332-0527; merle@telcel.net.ve) Located on the Península de Paria, this place combines buffalo ranching, conservation and ecotourism (see p269).

Los Guardianes de la Biodiversidad (☎ 0274-252-6341, 0414-745-3154; auratours@cantv.net) This Mérida-based NGO runs boat tours in the Parque Nacional Ciénagas de Catatumbo through Aura Marcucci Expeditions, and sponsors education campaigns for schools.

Fundación Bioandina (maria@bolivar.funmrd.gov.ve) Has reintroduced the condor to the Venezuelan Andes. Contact the organization direct to learn more about the program.

Provita (http://www.wpti.org/ven.htm) Runs the Bioinsula Program (☎ 580-295-416-2541; Urbanización Augusto Malavé Villalba, Av 9, Casa No 15 Boca de Río, Península de Manacao, Isla Margarita), which targets the endangered *cotorra cabeciamarilla* (yellow-shouldered parrot). Small groups can participate in monitoring during April, July and October.

Sociedad Conservacionista Audubón de Venezuela (☎ 0414-336-0464; www.birdlife.net/worldwide /national/venezuela/) Based in Caracas (see Tour Companies p75), this is one of the country's oldest environmental NGOs; it runs bird-watching tours and volunteer monitoring programs.

Ecochallenge (www.ecochallenge.ws in Spanish) This private business monitors sharks and offers scuba-diving safaris.

Campamento Nuevo Mundo (☎ 0414-825-3122, 0281-416-1599) Preserves a patch of rain forest in the south of Miranda state, and has a rustic ecolodge that provides a communal experience.

Programa Andes Tropicales (☎ 0274-263-6884, 0274-263-8633; www.andestropicales.org) Rural tourism experience in the upper Andes; stay with local farming families in traditional rural lodges called *mucuposadas*.

Fundación Mario Abreu (☎ 00-58-289-995-1415; www.lastrefuge.co.uk) Located in Santa Elena, near the Brazilian border, this foundation provides ecotourism training courses for indigenous people, and designs ecological brochures and maps. The organization can refer travelers to the few indigenous-run tourism operations in the country.

The website
www.planeta.com has a
useful directory and inter-
active forum promoting
'practical ecotourism' in
Latin America.

In some locations, the development of road systems has triggered environmental problems.

A final major ecological concern is pollution from oil refineries and drilling: Lago de Maracaibo has witnessed many oil spills, and much of the petroleum infrastructure is old and in need of repair.

This said, there is a sector of the population – including community organizations, cooperatives, NGOs (nongovernmental organisations), universities and governmental agencies – that is working to reduce environmental degradation. Following is a list of major organizations working for the Venezuelan environment:

Conservation International (www.conservation.org) Works on conservation issues in several Latin American countries, including Venezuela.

Fundación Polar (www.fpolar.org.ve/index.html) Leading NGO working in biodiversity, sustainable agriculture and water-management issues.

Ministerio del Ambiente (www.marnr.gov.ve/ in Spanish) Leading government organization at national level in charge of environmental legislation, planning and zoning of protected areas.

Ocean Futures Society (www.oceanfutures.org) Works on environmental issues related to coastal areas.

Food & Drink

Venezuelans love to eat, and eat well. From home-cooked corn turnovers to authentic Spanish paella or downright indulgent desserts, there's plenty for your taste buds to discover. The national cuisine is characterized by a rich fusion of indigenous and European roots. Caracas itself is an internationally renowned culinary melting pot, while the regions of Venezuela have their own peculiarities and specialties. The *costeños'* (coastal peoples) plates overflow with fish and exquisite seafood, while the Amazonian peoples have plenty of imaginative uses for the humble yucca (edible root). Wheat and trout dishes rule in the Andes, and those bursting for a barbecued platter will adore the obscenely juicy steaks of Los Llanos.

DID YOU KNOW?

Venezuelans are so keen on meat that in some areas they classify capybara (an aquatic rodent) as 'fish' so they can eat it through Lent and Easter.

STAPLES & SPECIALTIES

The Venezuelans have a saying, *lo que no mata engorda* (what doesn't kill you makes you fat), and it's true that many of their tasty common dishes appear decidedly on the fattening side, from steaks as thick as bricks to deep-fried cheese.

Many staples rely on the use of corn, especially *arepas* and *empanadas*, which are as common as hotdogs and hamburgers in the US. The *arepa* is a hamburger-sized corn pancake that is split and stuffed so full of juicy fillings that it takes a special talent to avoid getting it all over your face. *Areperas* (*arepa* restaurants) offer a hundred and one fillings to choose from, but a favorite is the tasty *reina pepiada* (chicken, mayo and avocado). They're a surprisingly heavy-going, filling snack so don't be surprised if your jaw aches and you feel full by your third bite.

Deep-fried *empanadas* (corn turnovers) filled with meat, chicken or cheeses are also a common snack. And the sweet and greasy *cachapa* pancake is another corn-based favorite, usually with slabs of cheese and ham slapped on top. At Christmas, families lovingly prepare *hallacas* (corn dough with chopped meat and vegetables), steamed in banana leaves.

But let's not get fixated on corn alone. Other Venezuelan cuisine, collectively referred to as *comida criolla,* uses plenty of rice, yam, plantain, beans and carefully prepared meat, chicken or dozens of fresh seafood varieties. The *salsas* (sauces) make generous use of *ají dulce* (small sweet peppers) and *cilantro* (coriander leaves used as a garnish). There's also a vast array of tropical fruits, including papaya the size of US footballs and

For a list of typical Venezuelan recipes to get cooking at home, see www.venezuelatuya.com /cocina/ (in Spanish)

WE DARE YOU!

If you can track them down, these unusual Venezuelan dishes should give you plenty to chew on.

- *Hormigas culonas* – deep-fried Amazonian ants with big, juicy rear ends (hence the ungraceful name meaning literally 'big-bottomed'). Sometimes coated in chocolate!

- *Katara* – along the same theme, the Yekwana Indians' chili sauce is made with the heads of leaf-cutter ants and is reputedly an aphrodisiac.

- *Paticas de grillo* – don't be scared off by the name (cricket legs); this tasty dish from Lara is actually finely shredded beef.

- *Chivo en coco* – though it sounds odd, goat in a coconut sauce is a favorite dish in Coro.

- *Consomé de chipi chipi* – coastal clam broth; another rumored aphrodisiac.

more types of banana than you can shake a monkey at. And of course, if you're ripe for rump steak, you've come to the right place. Venezuela is famous for its cheap and abundant grill-houses, serving steaks supplied in truckloads from the ranches of Los Llanos.

Spanish, Italian, Chinese and Middle Eastern restaurants are all well represented too, thanks to sizable immigrant populations, and since Venezuela is one of the most Yankified countries on the continent, expect a dense array of gringo fast-food joints.

DRINKS

Strong, espresso coffee is excellent in Venezuela. Ask for *café negro* if you want it black; for *café marrón* if you want milk; or for *café con leche* if you like it very milky. When it has more milk than coffee, it's given the tongue-in-cheek title of *tetero* (baby's bottle). For an extra kick, *café bautizado* (literally 'baptized') contains a shot of rum.

Given the mind-boggling variety of fruit in the country, you'll also be spoilt for choice of juices (see the Menu Decoder p50), which come as *batidos* (pure or watered down) or as *merengadas* (milk shakes). Also good for the sweet-toothed are the local drinks *chicha*, a thick milky liquid made with rice and sugar, and *papelón con limón*, sugar-cane juice mixed with lemon – very sweet!

The number one alcoholic drink is of course beer, sold at icy temperatures for only $0.50 a bottle (about 0.22L) in the cheapest bars and eateries. If you ever wonder why Venezuelans don't like larger bottles, the answer is simple: the beer could get warm before you finish it. Particularly popular is the local brand Polar beer (look for the cute polar bear logo).

Among Venezuelan spirits, rum heads the list and the smooth, dark Ron Añejo Aniversario Pampero is one of the best. Another specialty is the throat-stripping *miche*, an anise-flavored spirit made from sugarcane, similar to the Colombian *aguardiente*, and so-called in some areas. The local production of wine is small, except for some good Altagracia wines (p166).

However, it's imported whisky that wins the prize as the chic drink of choice, and upper-crust restaurants stock enough to rival any Scotch bar. Indeed Venezuelans manage to get through about five million cases per year!

Colorful *cocteles* (cocktails) also abound: from the hugely popular *guarapita*, a fruity combination of sugarcane spirit and fresh juices that is all-too-easy to gulp down, to Andean *calentados*, hot toddies to warm the cockles of your heart on cold mountain nights.

WHERE (& WHEN) TO EAT & DRINK

For a filling *desayuno* (breakfast), do what many locals do and grab something in the local *panadería* (bakery). Venezuelans take their *almuerzo* (lunch) more seriously, however. In fact, it's taken for granted that a 'lunch hour' is more likely two lunch hours, and will tend to be a drawn-out social affair. For a good-value lunch, look at the *menú del día* or *menu ejecutivo*, a set meal consisting of soup and a main course. It costs just $2 to $5, cheaper than most à-la-carte dishes.

For a quick bite, grab some spit-roasted chicken or a stuffed *arepa*, or markets always offer fresh local fare. Street vending is also common, though hygiene can be iffy. Particularly popular are *churro* machines, which churn out long, thin pastry sticks sprinkled with sugar.

To linger over a more sedate evening meal, visit one of the many traditional Spanish tascas (Spanish-style bar-restaurants) found throughout

DID YOU KNOW?

Whole bottles of spirits are commonly poured over coffins (and the coffin-bearers) at Venezuelan funerals.

DID YOU KNOW?

The per capita consumption of Black Label Scotch whisky in Venezuela is the highest in the world.

the country. Here you can choose to chow down on tapas with the local barflies or sit down for a filling meal of succulent seafood or meats with the family. In cities, upmarket restaurants come to life from 7pm to 8pm. However, in small towns, everything may be shut by 9pm.

VEGETARIANS & VEGANS

A popular fridge magnet in Venezuela reads *Soy vegetariano, vivo en vainitas* (I'm vegetarian, I live on green beans). Sure enough, vegetarianism isn't a concept well grasped in a country where rump steak is king.

That said, it's relatively easy to get by in Venezuela if you don't mind a little monotony. The country has plenty of cheeses, eaten with ubiquitous staples such as *arepas* and *cachapas*. *Perico* is another filling made with scrambled eggs, tomato and onion. A popular appetizer is *tostónes* (hard plantain cakes), which generally come with vegan-friendly sauces. You can also enjoy a wide selection of beans, salads and fruit juices. When ordering salads, it's not enough to ask if it has any *carne* (meat) because chicken and fish are in a separate linguistic class and aren't necessarily considered meat – see the following Useful Phrases section for ordering.

In tourist haunts, there are always vegetarian pizzas, pasta and omelets available, and there are even a few dedicated vegetarian restaurants in larger cities such as Caracas. Self-catering is the safest option for vegans; markets have a great selection of fruit and vegetables.

HABITS & CUSTOMS

At all levels of society, food preparation is done with care and eating is to be savored, not hurried. Food is a central means of showing hospitality, so expect huge portions and constant refills if you're invited to somebody's house. Festivals, especially Christmas, call for displays of generosity by filling stomachs that are already fit to burst.

If somebody invites you out to eat, you can expect them to pay. Of course, the flipside is that when you invite somebody out, the bill falls to you. Before tucking in, it's polite to wish your fellow diners *buen provecho* (bon appetit), and when drinking, to say *salud* (good health).

EAT YOUR WORDS

Want to know what ordering a cup of *leche de burra* (donkey's milk) or a *teta* (breast) will really bring to your table? Discover the secrets of the local cuisine by getting to know the language. For pronunciation guidelines see p351.

Restaurants and cafés automatically add 10% service charge to the bill. Upscale restaurants, particularly in Caracas, are also notorious for not including the 16% IVA tax on the menu, so brace yourself to pay 25% more (or 35%, if you include a 10% tip).

The annually updated, bilingual *Caracas Gastronomic Guide*, published by Miro Popic, covers more than 600 restaurants in the capital and is a great help in discovering the local food scene. See www.miropopic.com for the latest recommendations.

TYPES OF RESTAURANTS

arepera – serves *arepas* (stuffed corn pancakes) and other typical dishes
charcutería – pork butcher selling hams, sausages, salamis etc
fuentes de soda – budget café serving snacks and drinks
frutería – fruit shop or place that serves fruit salads and juices
heladería – serves ice-cream and sometimes fast food
lunchería – cheap restaurant serving staple food and snacks
panadería – bakery selling cakes, coffee, pastries and bread
parrillada – Argentine-style restaurant serving mixed grills
pollo en brasas – cheap restaurant/takeaway serving grilled chicken and fries
refresquería – sells soft drinks and snacks
restaurante turístico – designed to showcase regional cuisine to visitors
tasca – Spanish-style bar-restaurant, serving tapas, paella and other Spanish dishes

Useful Phrases

I'm a vegetarian.
soy ve-khe-ta *rya*-no/a

Soy vegetariano/a. (m/f)

Do you have any vegetarian dishes?
tye-nen al-*goon* pla-to ve-khe-ta-*rya*-no?

¿Tienen algún plato vegetariano?

I don't eat meat, chicken or fish.
no *ko*-mo *kar*-ne nee *po*-yo nee pes-*ka*-do

No como carne, ni pollo ni pescado.

I'm allergic to peanuts/wheat/eggs.
soy a-*ler*-khee-ko/a al ma-*nee/tree*-go/*we*-vo

Soy alérgico/a al maní/trigo/huevo.

Is this water purified?
es-ta *a*-gwa es poo-ree-fee-*ka*-da?

¿Ésta agua es purificada?

Do you have a menu (in English)?
tye-nen oo-na *kar*-ta (en een-*gles*)?

¿Tienen una carta (en Inglés)?

I'd like the set meal.
kee-*sye*-ra el men-*oo*

Quisiera el menú.

Does that come with salad/fries?
ve-e-ne kon *pa*-pas *free*-tas?

¿Viene con ensalada/papas fritas?

What do you recommend?
ke me re-ko-*myen*-da?

¿Qué me recomienda?

Not too spicy please.
seen *tan*-to pee-*kan*-te, por fa-*vor*

Sin tanto picante, por favor.

I didn't order this.
no pe-*dee es*-to

No pedí esto.

The bill, please.
la *kwen*-ta, por fa-*vor*

La cuenta, por favor.

Thanks, that was delicious.
gra-syas, es-*ta*-ba sa-*bro*-so

Gracias, estaba sabroso.

Menu Decoder

FOOD

aceite (a-*say*-te) – oil

aguacate (a-gwa-*ka*-te) – avocado

ají (a-kh*ee*) – chili pepper

ajo (*a*-kho) – garlic

aliño (a-*lee*-nyo) – combination of spices

arepa (a-*re*-pa) – small, grilled maize pancake stuffed with cheese, beef, sausage, shrimp, eggs, salad etc; Andean *arepa de trigo* is made from wheat

atún (a-*toon*) – tuna

✗ **batata** (ba-*ta*-ta) – sweet potato

berenjena (be-ren-*khe*-na) – eggplant

cachapa (ka-*cha*-pa) – round, juicy corn pancake, served with cheese and/or ham

cachito (ka-*chee*-to) – croissant filled with chopped ham and served hot

calabaza (ka-la-*ba*-za) – squash

camarón (ka-ma-*ron*) – small shrimp

✗ **cambur** (*kam*-boor) – banana

cangrejo (kan-*gre*-kho) – crab

canilla (kan-*ee*-ya) – small baguette

carabina (ka-ra-*bee*-na) – Mérida version of *hallaca*

caraota (ka-ra-*o*-ta) – black bean

carne de res (*kar*-ne de res) – beef

casabe (ka-*sa*-be) – huge, flat bread made from *yuca amarga* (bitter yucca, grated, pressed and dried); a staple in Indian communities

cebolla (se-*bo*-ya) – onion

chayote (cha-*yo*-te) – choko; green pear-shaped fruit

chicharrones (chee-cha-*ro*-nes) – pork cracklings

chivo (*chee*-vo) – goat ✖

chorizo (cho-*ree*-zo) – seasoned sausage

chuleta – (chu-*le*-ta) – chop, rib steak

cochino (ko-*chee*-no) – pork

coco (*ko*-ko) – coconut

cordero (kor-*de*-ro) – lamb

durazno (door-*az*-no) – apricot

empanada (em-pa-*na*-da) – crescent-shaped, deep-fried cornmeal turnover stuffed with beef (*carne de res*), chicken (*pollo*) or cheese (*queso*)

fresa (*fre*-za) – strawberry

frijoles (*free*-kho-les) – red beans

guanábana (gwa-*na*-ba-na) – soursop ✖

guasacaca (gwas-a-*ka*-ka) – piquant sauce made of peppers, onions and seasoning

guayaba (gwa-*ya*-ba) – guava ✖

hallaca (a-*ya*-ka) – maize dough with chopped pork, beef or chicken with vegetables and olives, wrapped in banana leaves and steamed; popular during Christmas

hervido (er-*vee*-do) – hearty soup made of beef or chicken with root vegetables

huevo frito/revuelto (*we*-vo *free*-to/re-*vwel*-to) – fried/scrambled egg

jamón (kha-*mon*) – ham

langosta (lan-*gos*-ta) – lobster

lau lau (lau-lau) – catfish ✖

lechón (le-*chon*) – baked pig stuffed with its own meat, rice and dried peas

lechosa (le-*cho*-sa) – papaya ✖

lechuga (le-*choo*-ga) – lettuce

limón (lee-*mon*) – lemon

mamón (ma-*mon*) – small, green fruit with reddish flesh ✖

mandarina (man-da-*ree*-na) – mandarin

manzana (man-*za*-na) – apple

mariscos (ma-*rees*-koz) – shellfish, seafood

mejillones (me-khe-*yon*-es) – mussels

melocotón (me-lo-ko-*ton*) – peach ✖

melón (me-*lon*) – honeydew, rock melon

milanesa (mee-la-*ne*-sa) – thin steak

mondongo (mon-*don*-go) – seasoned tripe cooked in bouillon with maize, potatoes and vegetables

mora (*mor*-a) – blackberry

muchacho (moo-*cha*-cho) – hearty roasted beef dish

naranja (na-*ran*-kha) – orange

nata (*na*-ta) – thick, sweet cream

natilla (na-*tee*-ya) – sour-milk butter

ñame (*nya*-me) – a type of yam ✖

pabellón (pa-be-*yon*) – national dish of shredded beef, rice, black beans, cheese and fried plantain ✖

papa (*pa*-pa) – potato

papelón (pa-be-*lon*) – crude brown sugar; flavoring for drinks

parchita (par-*chee*-ta) – passion fruit ✖

parrilla (parrillada) (pa-*ree*-ya) – mixed grill, including steak, pork, chicken and sausages

pasapalos (pa-sa-*pa*-los) – hors d'oeuvres, small snacks, finger food

patilla (pa-*tee*-ya) – watermelon ✖

pernil (per-*neel*) – leg of pork

perro caliente (*pe*-ro ka-*lyen*-te) – hot dog

piña (*pee*-nya) – pineapple

plátano (*pla*-ta-no) – plantain ✖

pollo (*po*-yo) – chicken

quesillo (ke-*see*-yo) – caramel custard

raspao (ras-*pa*-o) – sweet, flavored ice shavings

salchicha (sal-*chee*-cha) – sausage

sancocho (san-*ko*-cho) – vegetable stew with fish, meat or chicken
tapas (*ta*-pas*)* – typical Spanish hors d'oeuvres, including *empanadas*, tortillas, *jamón serrano*, *camarones* (shrimp), and grilled sausage
tequeño (te-ke-*nyo*) – cheese strips wrapped in pastry and deep fried
teta (*te*-ta) – iced fruit juice in plastic wrap, consumed by sucking
tocineta (to-see-*ne*-ta) – bacon
tomate (to-*ma*-te) – tomato
tortilla (tor-*tee*-ya) – omelet
tostón (tos-*ton*) – fried unripe plantain
trucha (*troo*-cha) – trout
yuca (*yoo*-ka) – yucca (edible root)
zanahoria (za-na-*o*-ree-a) – carrot

DRINKS
agua (*a*-gwa) – water
aguardiente (a-gwar-*dyen*-te) – sugarcane spirit flavored with anise
café (ka-*fe*) – coffee
calentado (ka-len-*ta*-do) – hot Andean drink with anise-flavored spirit, milk, herbs and brown sugar
cerveza (ser-*ve*-sa) – beer
chicha (*chee*-cha) – usually nonalcoholic drink made from corn or rice
cocuy (ko-*kooy*) – sugarcane liqueur
guayoyo (gwa-*yo*-yo) – weak black coffee
jugo (*khoo*-go) – juice
leche (*le*-che) – milk
leche de burra (*le*-che de *boo*-ra) – Andean beverage made of *miche*, egg and (cow's) milk
miche (*mee*-che) – anise-flavored sugarcane-based spirit; *aguardiente*
refresco (re-*fres*-ko) – soft drink
ron (*ron*) – rum
té (*te*) – tea
vino blanco/tinto/espumoso (*vee*-no *blan*-ko/*teen*-to/es-poo-*mo*-so) – white/red/sparkling wine

Food Glossary

pan	pan	bread
mantequilla	man-te-*kee*-ya	butter
torta	*tor*-ta	cake
queso	*ke*-so	cheese
maíz	ma-*eez*	corn/maize
postre	*pos*-tre	dessert
bebida	be-*bee*-da	drink
pescado	pes-*ka*-do	fish
comida	ko-*mee*-da	food
papas fritas	*pa*-pas *free*-tas	fries
fruta	*froo*-tas	fruit
hielo	ee-*e*-lo	ice
helado	e-*la*-do	ice-cream
carne	*kar*-ne	meat
pastel	pas-*tel*	pastry
pimienta	pee-*myen*-ta	pepper
arroz	a-*roz*	rice
ensalada	en-sa-*la*-da	salad
sal	sal	salt
sopa	*so*-pa	soup
azúcar	a-*zoo*-kar	sugar
legumbres	le-*goom*-bres	vegetables
trigo	*tree*-go	wheat

Caracas

CONTENTS

Its spectacular setting in a valley amid rolling hills, striking modern architecture, and a spider's web of motorways makes Caracas unique among South American capitals. Fast-paced, progressive and cosmopolitan, it is a cocktail of all things Latin American, with a dash of the Caribbean and an aftertaste of Miami. In a race toward modernity, this love-it-or-hate-it city has almost 440 years of history buried beneath its glass-and-concrete monuments to oil-fueled affluence.

The center of Venezuela's political and economic life, Caracas is also the cultural capital, boasting a vibrant arts scene. Its acclaimed Museo de Artes Contemporáneo is perhaps the best on the continent, and you'll see numerous sculptures, mosaics and murals gracing the streets. The bright lights of Caracas' stylish nightlife also provide myriad opportunities for clubbers, bar-hoppers and live salsa aficionados to mingle with the city's famously die-hard party crowd, and there is an abundance of upmarket restaurants in gastronomic hubs like Las Mercedes, where every international gourmet can indulge.

Of course, while Caracas enjoys every modern convenience, it also suffers visibly from third-world problems. Vast expanses of haphazardly built shantytowns creep up the surrounding hillsides, a constant reminder of the city's contrast between wealth and poverty, and political divisions and strikes have rocked the capital particularly hard over recent years.

Caracas' northern edge abuts the steep, wooded slopes of Parque Nacional El Ávila, where miles of walking trails wind through scented forests. At an altitude of about 900m, the city enjoys an agreeable, sunny climate often described as 'eternal summer.'

HIGHLIGHTS

- Hike or catch the **teleférico** (cable car) to the summit of El Ávila (p94)
- Explore the bars and clubs of **Las Mercedes & La Castellana** (p85)
- Souvenir shop in the winding streets of **El Hatillo** (p73)
- Enjoy international art at the acclaimed **Museo de Arte Contemporáneo** (p67)
- Stroll around the green haven of **Parque del Este** (p71)
- Discover lost treasure at the small but perfect **Museo de Arte Colonial** (p67)
- Join the cuisine scene of **Las Mercedes** (p83), **Altamira** (p84) and **La Candelaria** (p82)
- Visit the tomb of national treasure, Simón Bolívar, in the **Panteón Nacional** (p66)

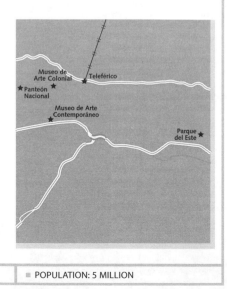

- TELEPHONE CODE: 0212

- POPULATION: 5 MILLION

O11-58-

HISTORY

Caracas had a precarious beginning in 1560 when Francisco Fajardo of Isla de Margarita discovered the verdant valley – then inhabited by Toromaima Indians. He founded a settlement named San Francisco, but was soon driven out by natives. A year later the town was resurrected, but years of bitter struggle against Indian attacks followed.

In 1567, a decisive conquest of the valley was ordered and 136 men led by Diego de Losada overcame a brave Indian resistance before re-establishing the settlement once and for all on July 25. The new township was named Santiago de León de Caracas, 'Caracas' being the name of a decidedly less troublesome Indian group that inhabited the coastal cordillera.

In 1577, the governor chose the young town to be the third and final capital of Venezuela (after Coro and El Tocuyo). But from the beginning, the new capital was besieged by vicious pirate raids, plagues and natural disasters, including a devastating earthquake in 1641.

In 1728, a Basque trading company called the Real Compañía Guipuzcoana was based in La Guaira and given a monopoly over trade with Spain. Its later corruption aroused widespread anger among the colonists. In 1749, 800 men marched on Caracas to protest against the company's oppressive tactics, a riot that many believe sowed the seeds of the independence movement. The company was eventually dissolved in 1785.

On March 28, 1750, Caracas became the birthplace of Francisco de Miranda, and on July 24, 1783, that of Simón Bolívar. The former was to pave the way to independence; the latter was to realize that aim. On April 19, 1810, a group of councilors and notable *caraqueños* (inhabitants of Caracas) denounced the Spanish governor and formed a Supreme Junta to replace the government. The political struggle raged until July 5, 1811, when congress declared the country's independence.

On Maundy Thursday of 1812, an earthquake wrecked the town, killing some 10,000 people. The conservative clergy swiftly declared that it was a punishment from heaven for the rebellion, but the independence movement was not to be stopped. It eventually reached its aim nine years later, sealed by Bolívar's victory at the battle of Carabobo on June 24, 1821. Despite this, Spain stubbornly refused to recognize Venezuela's sovereignty until 1845.

Caracas grew at a modest pace until the 1870s, when an extensive modernization program was launched by General Guzmán Blanco, known as 'El Modernizador.' His rule saw a swathe of new monumental buildings totally transform the character of the city center.

Then came the oil boom, and things began to change at breakneck speed. Oil money was pumped into modernization, transforming the bucolic colonial town into a vast concrete sprawl. Colonial buildings were demolished and their place taken by modern commercial centers and steel-and-glass towers.

Spurred on by the illusory dream of wealth, thousands of rural dwellers rushed into Caracas, but the majority never saw their share of the city's prosperity, leading a hand-to-mouth existence in *ranchos* (ramshackle huts) that covered the hills around the central districts. Over the last 50 years, the city's population has shot up from around 400,000 to over five million.

ORIENTATION

Nestled in a long and narrow valley, the city spreads at least 20km from east to west. To the north looms the steep, verdant wall of Parque Nacional El Ávila, refreshingly free of human dwellings. To the south, by contrast, the city is devouring the hillsides, with modern *urbanizaciones* (suburbs) and derelict *barrios* (shantytowns) invading every reasonably flat piece of land.

The valley itself is a dense urban fabric, with forests of skyscrapers sticking out of a mass of low-rise buildings like needles through patchwork. The area from El Silencio to Chacao is the central downtown area, packed with commercial centers, offices and hotels. The metro's main line (No 1) goes right along this axis, making many of Caracas' attractions readily accessible.

The historic quarter (called the 'Center' in this chapter) is at the west end of the greater downtown area and is recognizable on the map by the colonial chessboard layout of the streets. About 1.5km to the east is Parque Central, noted for its museums and theaters. Another 2km east is Sabana Grande, centered on a busy pedestrian mall

CARACAS

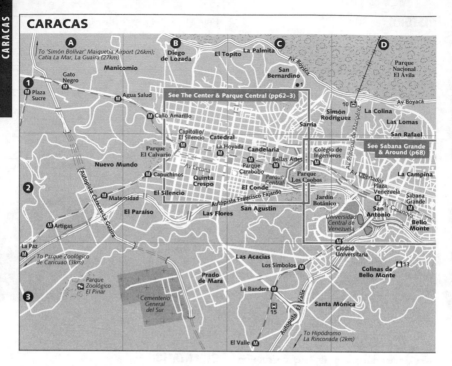

CARACAS

brimming with shops and stalls. Continuing east, you come to Chacao, a commercial district good for upmarket shopping, and then to the trendy Altamira, which boasts scores of upmarket restaurants and nightspots. El Rosal and Las Mercedes, south of Chacao, also cater to gourmets and night trippers.

A curiosity of Caracas is the center's street address system. It's not the streets that bear names here, but the *esquinas* (street corners); therefore, addresses are given 'corner to corner.' So if an address is 'Piñango a Conde,' the place is between these two street corners. If a place is situated on a corner, just the corner will be named (eg Esq Conde). However, note that a few major thoroughfares, such as Av México and Av Universidad, generally supercede this rule.

Authorities have given numbers and cardinal-point designations to the streets (Este, Oeste, Norte and Sur), but locals continue to stick with the *esquinas*. Outside the colonial center, the conventional system is used, though street numbers are still rare.

The Venezuelan system of designating floors resembles that of the UK. The ground floor is the *piso bajo* or *planta baja*, the 1st floor is the *primer piso*, then comes the *segundo piso* (2nd floor) etc. In elevators, abbreviations used include PB (ground floor), M (mezzanine), S (basement level) and PH (penthouse).

Maps

Most bookshops will sell folded Caracas city maps with a map of Venezuela on the reverse. If you can't get any of these, look for the Caracas city maps in the back of the local phone directory. It's also worth remembering that most metro stations have city maps posted near the ticket booth and the train platform.

To find specialist maps for the rest of Venezuela, visit the **Instituto Geográfico de Venezuela Simón Bolívar** (IGVSB; Map pp62-3; ☎ 546-1203; mapaven@igvsb.gov.ve; 2nd fl, Edificio Camejo, Av Este 6, Center; ☉ 8:30am-noon & 2-4:30pm Mon-Thu, 8:30am-noon Fri).

INFORMATION
Airline Offices
For airline details see p335.

CARACAS

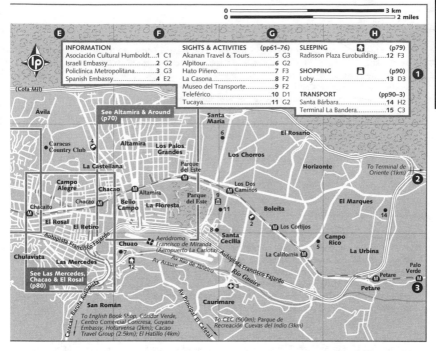

INFORMATION
Asociación Cultural Humboldt...1 C1
Israeli Embassy.........................2 G2
Policlínica Metropolitana..........3 G3
Spanish Embassy.....................4 E2

SIGHTS & ACTIVITIES (pp61–76)
Akanan Travel & Tours.............5 G3
Alpitour................................6 G2
Hato Piñero...........................7 F3
La Casona..............................8 F2
Museo del Transporte............9 F2
Teleférico............................10 D1
Tucaya...............................11 G2

SLEEPING (p79)
Radisson Plaza Eurobuilding.....12 F3

SHOPPING (p90)
Loby.....................................13 D3

TRANSPORT (pp90–3)
Santa Bárbara.......................14 H2
Terminal La Bandera..............15 C3

Bookstores

American Book Shop (Map p70; ☎ 285-8779; Nivel Jardín, Centro Comercial Centro Plaza, Los Palos Grandes) Fair selection of Lonely Planet guidebooks and secondhand books in English.

El Libro Italiano (Map p68; ☎ 763-1964; Av Francisco Solano, Sabana Grande) For books in Italian.

English Book Shop (Map pp56-7; ☎ 979-1308; Centro Comercial Concresa, Prados del Este) Phone in advance as it has extremely irregular opening hours; 2km south of town.

Librería La France (Map p68; ☎ 952-0890; Centro Comercial Chacaíto, Plaza Brión/Chacaíto) The best selection of books in French.

Librería Alemana Oscar Todtmann (Map p68; ☎ 762-5244; Centro Comercial El Bosque, Av Libertador, Chacaíto) Extensive choice of German-language publications.

Librería Rizzoli (Map p70; ☎ 286-2442; Centro Comercial Centro Plaza, 1a Transversal btwn 1a Av & Av Andrés Bello, Los Palos Grandes) More books in Italian.

Read Books (Map p80; ☎ 991-9509; Av Orinoco, Las Mercedes) Has texts, guidebooks and magazines in English, French and Spanish. Recommended.

Tecni-Ciencia Libros (CCCT) Centro Ciudad Comercial Tamanaco (Map p80; ☎ 959-5547; fl C-2, Chuao);

Centro Sambil (Map p70; ☎ 264-1765; Nivel Acuario, Av Libertador, Chacao) One of Venezuela's best bookshops has half a dozen branches around the city. Both large branches listed here have heaps of publications, including well-stocked travel sections that feature plenty of Lonely Planet titles, and some local tourist maps.

Books are not cheap in Venezuela. If you want to save some bolívares, first check the secondhand bookshops and markets. The cheapest place to buy Spanish-language books is the street **book market** (Map pp62-3; Plaza España a Romualda). These bookstalls have a haphazard range of new and secondhand books, including some rare old editions that are virtually unobtainable elsewhere.

There are also a dozen or so bookstalls in the grounds of the **Universidad Central de Venezuela** (Map p68) that sell new books, CDs and DVDs at excellent prices.

Cultural Centers

Alianza Francesa (Map p68; ☎ 763-1581; www.afcaracas.org in Spanish/French; 1st fl, Edificio Centro Solano, Av Francisco Solano, Chacaíto; ☺ 8am-1pm & 3-8pm Mon-Fri, 8:30am-12:30pm Sat) Has publications in French.

CARACAS

CARACAS IN...

Two Days

On your first morning take a trip round the historical heart of the city (see the Walking Tour boxed text p72), stopping for an espresso in **Café del Sacro** en route and finishing at Bolívar's tomb at the **Panteón Nacional**. Once you've worked up an appetite, treat yourself to lunch at a traditional tasca in **La Candelaria**. In the afternoon, take your pick of the museums in Bellas Artes and don't miss the **Museo de Arte Contemporáneo**. Alternatively, it's worth the trip north to the **Museo de Arte Colonial**. Finish off your day with a meal and perhaps a nightcap in the glitzy restaurants and bars of **Las Mercedes**.

On your second day, escape the urban jungle and take a trip up El Ávila mountain on the newly reconstructed **teleférico** (cable car). Once you're back on terra firma, catch a bus out to the charming colonial suburb of **El Hatillo** for some serious souvenir shopping after a meal in one of its numerous excellent restaurants. Finally, when you've deposited any bulky buys back in your hotel, those who have still got a spring in their step can treat themselves to a meal in upmarket **Altamira** followed by a night out in the chic clubs and bars of **Centro Comercial San Ignacio**.

Four Days

If you're sticking around for longer, follow the two-day itinerary, but leave El Hatillo and Altamira until your third day, and take advantage of spending the entire second day in the mountains, roaming further along the tranquil woodland paths of **Parque Nacional El Ávila** from the **teleférico** (cable car). Then on your fourth day, wind down by taking a walk through the sprawling **Parque del Este**, perhaps ending at the **Museo del Transporte**, or pay a visit to the animals in **Parque Zoológico de Caricuao**.

British Council (Map p68; ☎ 952-9965; www.british council.org.ve; 3rd fl, Torre Credicard, Av Principal El Bosque, Chacaíto; ☺ 8am-9pm Mon-Thu, 8am-8pm Fri, 9am-1pm Sat) Has the widest selection of English-language resources and offers Internet connection for $1.25 per hr.

Centro Venezolano Americano (CVA; Map p80; ☎ 993-7911; www.cva.org.ve; Av Principal de Las Mercedes) Has many English-language publications and offers Spanish courses.

Emergency

All the services listed below operate 24 hours. Don't expect the attendants to speak English. If your Spanish is not up to scratch, try to get a local to call on your behalf.

Emergency Center (Ambulance, Fire, Police; ☎ 171)
Fire (☎ 166)
Police (☎ 169)
Traffic Police (☎ 167)

Immigration

DIEX (Dirección de Identificación y Extranjería; Map pp62-3; ☎ 482-0977, 483-2070; www.onidex.gov.ve in Spanish; Av Baralt, Plaza Miranda, El Silencio; ☺ 7:30am-4:30pm Mon-Fri) Visas and tourist cards can be extended here for up to three months ($40). Passport, two photos and a letter explaining the purpose of the extension are required, plus the form you'll be given to fill in. Processing takes three working days.

Internet Access

Caracas is chockablock with places offering Internet services, and new ones are popping up all the time.

British Council (see Cultural Centers opposite)
CANTV Net (see Telephone & Fax p60)
CompuMall (Map p80; ☎ 993-0111; 1st fl, Edificio CompuMall, Av Orinoco, Las Mercedes; per hr $1.25; ☺ 9am-9pm Mon-Sat, 11am-8pm Sun)
Cyber Café M@dness (Map p70; ☎ 267-1866; Centro Sambil, Av Libertador, Chacao; per hr $1.50; ☺ 9am-9pm Mon-Sat, 10am-8pm Sun)
Cyber Office 2020 (Map p68; ☎ 762-9407; Edificio San Germán, Calle Pascual Navarro at Av Francisco Solano, Sabana Grande; per hr $1; 8am-11pm)
Digitel Cyberdepot (Map p70; ☎ 959-7296; Centro Sambil, Av Libertador, Chacao; per hr $1.20; ☺ 9am-9pm)
Digital Planet (Map p70; ☎ 261-0509; Yamin Family Center, 2nd fl, Av San Juan Bosco, Altamira; per hr $1.25; ☺ 9am-midnight Mon-Sat, 10am-midnight Sun)
Galileus (Map p80; ☎ 953-8372; Centro Lido, Av Francisco de Miranda, El Rosal; per hr $2.50; ☺ 9am-10pm Mon-Sat)

Infocentro (Map pp62-3; www.infocentro.gov.ve in Spanish) Biblioteca Metropolitana Simón Rodríguez (☎ 862-1521; Calle Norte 4, Esq El Conde; ☺ 9am-4pm Tue-Sat); Galería de Arte Nacional (☎ 578-1818; Plaza de Los Museos, Los Caobos; ☺ 9am-5pm Tue-Fri, 10am-5pm Sat & Sun); Palacio de las Academias (Av Universidad) These centers are the product of a government initiative to give Internet access to all. They are generally found in libraries and public buildings, and allow anybody 30 minutes' free access. Connections can be slow.

Internet Para Todos (Map p80; ☎ 992-4155; Centro Comercial Paseo Las Mercedes, Nivel Mercado, No 143, Las Mercedes; per hr $1.90; ☺ 10am-6pm Mon-Sat)

Link (Map p80; ☎ 993-9941; Calle New York, Las Mercedes; per hr $1; ☺ 9am-10pm Sun-Thu, 9am-midnight Fri & Sat)

M@dness Internet (Map pp62-3; ☎ 503-5000; Hotel Hilton Caracas, Av Sur 25 at Av Mexico, Parque Central; per hr $2; ☺ 9am-9pm) Opposite the Complejo Cultural Teresa Carreño.

Post.net (Map p68; ☎ 952-2005; Av Los Jabillos 7, Sabana Grande; per hr $0.65; ☺ 8am-7:30pm Mon-Sat, 8am-5pm Sun)

Laundry

Many hotels offer laundry facilities, though it is cheaper to use *lavanderías* (launderettes). There are a few self-service laundries; most provide serviced washes. Bring your dirty clothes in the morning and pick them up clean and dry in the afternoon. Most *lavanderías* work from about 7am until 6pm Monday to Friday with a break for lunch, and from 7am to 1pm Saturday. A 5kg load will cost $1 to $3. Recommended *lavanderías*:

Lavandería Autolanka (Map pp62-3; ☎ 576-4203; Centro Comercial Doral Centro, Av Urdaneta, La Candelaria)

Lavandería Chapultepex (Map p68; Calle Bolivia, Sabana Grande) Self-service.

Lavandería El Metro (Map p68; Calle Los Manguitos, Sabana Grande)

Lavandería El Rey (Map p68; ☎ 763-2643; Calle Pascual Navarro 6, Sabana Grande)

New York City Lavandería (Map p70; ☎ 265-7737; Av Ávila, Altamira Sur)

Libraries

Asociación Cultural Humboldt (Map pp56-7; ☎ 552-6445; Av Jorge Washington a Av Juan Germán Roscio, San Bernardino) Library featuring German-language books, papers and periodicals.

Biblioteca Metropolitana Simón Rodríguez (Map pp62-3; ☎ 862-1521; Calle Norte 4, Esq El Conde; ☺ 9am-4pm Tue-Sat) Free Internet service.

Biblioteca Nacional (Map pp62-3; ☎ 505-9121, 564-3043; www.bnv.bib.ve in Spanish; Av Norte 1, El Panteon; ☺ 9am-4pm Mon-Sat) Next to the Panteón Nacional, this is the best-stocked library in Caracas; it also houses the principal archives of national documents, books, newspapers and audiovisual records.

Medical Services

Most minor health problems can be solved in a *farmacia* (pharmacy), of which Caracas has a wide array, and there's always one in every suburb that takes its turn to stay open all night. They are listed in the local press, but you can easily recognize them by a lit board or neon sign reading 'Turno.' Some central *farmacias* include **Farmatodo** (Map p68; ☎ 763-4631; Edificio El Celeste, Blvd de Sabana Grande) and **FarmAhorro** (Map p70; ☎ 263-5275; Av Luis Roche, Altamira).

If you get really sick, Caracas has a number of public hospitals, private clinics, specialist medical centers and dentist offices. If you're insured, use private clinics rather than government-owned institutions; though they are more expensive, they are better equipped. Most private clinics offer inpatient and outpatient services, and have specialist doctors, some of whom speak English.

Most private clinics also offer vaccinations, but you can get them at no cost in public health centers called *unidades sanitarias*, which are in most suburbs. They can inoculate you against yellow fever and administer a series of jabs against rabies if you've been bitten by a suspect animal.

Following are reputable medical facilities:

Centro Médico de Caracas (Map pp62-3; ☎ 552-2222, 555-9111; Plaza El Estanque, Av Eraso, San Bernardino)

Clínica El Ávila (Map p70; ☎ 276-1003, emergency ☎ 276-1090; Av San Juan Bosco at 6a Transversal, Altamira)

Clínica Instituto Médico La Floresta (Map p70; ☎ 285-2111, 285-3222; Av Principal de la Floresta at Calle Santa Ana)

Policlínica Metropolitana (Map pp56-7; ☎ 908-0100, 908-0140; Calle A at Av Principal de Caurimare)

For dental work try **Centro de Emergencias Odontologicas** (Map p70; ☎ 693-4946; CCCT, Torre C, 5th fl, Chauo).

Money

Cash advances on Visa and MasterCard can be easily obtained at most Caracas banks. Many banks also have ATMs on the Cirrus and Plus networks, but foreign plastic was being denied by most at the time of writing. It is also safer to withdraw money within the bank (see the boxed text p330). Convenient central branches:

Banco de Venezuela Center (Map pp62-3; Av Universidad); Chacao (Map p80; Av Francisco de Miranda); La Candelaria (Map pp62-3; Av Urdaneta); La Castellana (Map p70; Av San Juan Bosco); Sabana Grande (Map p68; Blvd Sabana Grande)

Banco Mercantil Center (Map pp62-3; Av Universidad); Sabana Grande (Map p68; Av Las Acacias)

Banesco Altamira (Map p70; 6a Transversal); Altamira (Map p70; Av Sur Altamira); Center (Map pp62-3; Av Fuerzas Armadas); Center (Map pp62-3; Av Universidad); Chacao (Map p80; Av Francisco de Miranda); La Candelaria (Map pp62-3; Av Urdaneta); Las Mercedes (Map p80; Calle Monterrey); Sabana Grande (Map p68; Blvd de Sabana Grande); Sabana Grande (Map p68; Av Las Mercedes); San Bernardino (Map pp62-3; Av Panteón)

BBVA (Map p70; Av San Juan Bosco, La Castellana)

Corp Banca Bello Campo (Map p70; Calle Coromoto); El Rosal (Map p80; Av Francisco de Miranda); La Castellana (Map p70; Plaza La Castellana); La Castellana (Map p70; Av San Felipe); San Bernardino (Map pp62-3; Av Panteón)

Few banks exchange US cash dollars unless you have an account with them. The usual places to change foreign cash are *casas de cambio* (money-exchange offices), such as **Italcambio** (☎ 562-9555; www.italviajes.com in Spanish; ✆ 8:30am-5pm Mon-Fri, 9am-1pm Sat) Altamira (Map p70; Av Ávila); Chacao (Map p70; Centro Sambil, Av Libertador); La Candelaria (Map pp62-3; Av Urdaneta); Las Mercedes (Map p80; Calle California); Maiquetía airport (Map pp56-7; International terminal); Sabana Grande (Map p68; Av Casanova).

Amex (☎ 800-100-4730) offers local refund assistance for traveler's checks. If you need money sent to you quickly, Western Union is represented by **Grupo Zoom** (☎ 800-767-9666), which has about 25 offices scattered around the city.

Post

Ipostel Main Office (Map pp62-3; ☎ 0800-4767-835; www.ipostel.gov.ve; Av Urdaneta, Esq Carmelitas, Center; ✆ 7am-7:45pm Mon-Fri, 8am-5pm Sat, 8am-noon Sun) This is close to Plaza Bolívar and offers a poste-restante service. Address letters as follows: recipient's last name capitalized and underlined, their first name, Lista de Correos, Ipostel, Carmelitas, Caracas 1010. Ipostel branches which open Monday to Friday include Altamira (Map p70; Av Francisco de Miranda); La Candelaria (Map pp62-3;

Plaza La Candelaria); Sabana Grande (Map p68; Centro Comercial Arta, Plaza Chacaíto).

There are a number of international and local courier companies:

DHL (☎ 800-225-5345)

FedEx (☎ 205-3333)

UPS (☎ 204-1353)

Telephone & Fax

Public phones are everywhere, though those that work are all too often besieged by people. Many public phones have access to an international network, so you can call abroad using a phonecard (widely available in kiosks, pharmacies and shops) or by making a collect (reverse-charge) call. For more on phonecard varieties, see the Directory p332.

CANTV has many telecommunication offices called 'Centros de Comunicaciones CANTV,' which offer international and domestic calls; calls are charged by the minute, without the three-minute minimum charge. Some outlets also provide Internet facilities.

There are dozens of CANTV outlets in Caracas, including **Chacao** (Map p70; ☎ 263-0881; Centro Sambil, Av Libertador; ✆ 9am-9pm Mon-Sat, 10am-6pm Sun; Internet per hr $1); **Las Mercedes** (Map p80; ☎ 959-5099; CCCT, fl C-1, No 47-F; ✆ 9am-9pm Mon-Sat, 10am-6pm Sun; Internet per hr $1); and a couple in the center at **Esq El Conde** (Map pp62-3), **El Chorro at Dr Díaz** (Map pp62-3) and **Parque Central** (Map pp62-3).

Many hotels will place your call through CANTV but will add a hefty charge on top of this service. All the CANTV offices listed above also provide fax service.

Tourist Information

Inatur (www.inatur.gov.ve); Domestic terminal (Map pp56-7; ☎ 355-1191; Maiquetía airport; ✆ 7am-8pm); International terminal (Map pp56-7; ☎ 355-1060; Maiquetía airport; ✆ 8am-midnight); Parque Central (Map pp62-3; ☎ 0800-462-8871, 576-5138; 35th fl, Mirador de la Torre Oeste; ✆ 8:30am-12:30pm & 2-5pm Mon-Fri) When you enter the Mirador de la Torre Oeste, take the elevator from Nivel Lecuna to get to the information office – elevators from other levels don't go to this floor.

Information desk (☎ 503-5000; Hotel Hilton Caracas, Av Sur 25 at Av Mexico, Parque Central; ✆ 7am-10pm) This service in Hotel Hilton's main lobby is officially for hotel guests only, but the friendly and knowledgeable English-speaking staff are likely to attend to you if they are not too busy.

Inparques (Instituto Nacional de Parques Nacionales; Map p70; ☎ 285-4859; www.inparques.gov.ve in Spanish; Av Rómulo Gallegos; ☹ 8am-noon & 1:30-4pm Mon-Fri) This office doesn't provide maps or brochures about the parks, but it has a specialized library.

Travel Agencies

IVI Idiomas Vivos (Map p80; ☎ 993-6082, 993-8738; www.ividiomas.com; Ground fl, Residencia La Hacienda, Av Principal de Las Mercedes; ☹ 8am-6pm Mon-Fri) Offers attractive airfares to Europe and elsewhere for foreign students, teachers and people under 26 years of age. It issues ISIC and ITIC cards for full-time students or teachers. IVI has agreements with various businesses around the country that give cardholders discounts (about 10% to 30%) on their goods or services (hotels, restaurants, shops, medical services etc).

DANGERS & ANNOYANCES

Volatile political demonstrations, especially in the center of Caracas, have made sightseeing an unpredictable affair in recent years. Keep an eye on the news and take local advice about the current political climate and possibility of demonstrations.

Petty crime in general, and armed robbery in particular, are also on the rise. Since the late 1980s, Caracas has become increasingly unsafe due to the city's rapidly growing population, the majority of which lives in *ranchos* far below the poverty level. Poor *barrios* are where the majority of violent crimes are reported, but more affluent districts are not immune, so be on your guard. Flashing jewelry, watches or cameras will multiply your chances of being mugged.

Don't venture into *barrios* at any time of the day, let alone at night. The historic center is relatively safe for daytime strolls, but stay aware and don't take valuables as armed robberies do occasionally occur. The area becomes dangerous after dark. Sabana Grande is heading the same way, though it's reasonably secure until 8pm or 9pm, when crowds rapidly dwindle. Altamira, La Castellana, Los Palos Grandes and Las Mercedes are much safer at night.

Caracas' traffic is heavy, fast and wild, so be careful! Drivers don't obey traffic rules, and they may run red lights or crawl against the flow up a one-way street if they feel like it. Air pollution is also a by-product.

Nonsmokers may have a hard time. Venezuela is a smoking nation, and it's permitted nearly everywhere: in restaurants, offices, and at the bus and airport terminals. The metro is technically no-smoking territory, however.

SIGHTS

The Center & Around   Map pp62–3

The historic sector, where the city was born, still retains glimpses of its colonial identity. In a rush toward modernization, many colonial houses were replaced with a flood of new buildings, ranging from nondescript concrete edifices to futuristic tinted-glass towers, although a few colonial treasures have since been restored by oil money. Architectural ragbag that it is, it's a lively and colorful area, and boasts some important Bolívarian sights. See the Walking Tour boxed text (p72) for a suggested route.

PLAZA BOLÍVAR

This leafy square is the nucleus of the old town and is always busy with huddled groups of *caraqueños* chewing the fat, and children feeding freshly popped corn to black *ardillas* (squirrels) in the trees, avoiding the swirling flock of pigeons. In the center is the inevitable monument to Bolívar – the equestrian statue was cast in Europe, shipped in pieces, and eventually unveiled in 1874 after the ship carrying it foundered on the Archipiélago de Los Roques.

The plaza is a favorite playground for political visionaries and religious messiahs, who deliver their passionate speeches to a casual audience. In recent years the plaza has been a focus for supporters of President Chavez, and stalls have sold videos, paintings and photos of him alongside saints and musical legends.

CATEDRAL

Set on the eastern side of Plaza Bolívar, this **cathedral** (☎ 862-4963; ☹ 7:30am-11am Mon-Fri, 8:30am-11am Sat, 9am-11am & 5-6pm Sun) started its life as a mere mud-walled chapel. A church later replaced it, but this was flattened by the 1641 earthquake. Built from 1665 to 1713, the new cathedral was packed with dazzling gilded alters and elaborate side chapels. The wide five-nave interior, supported on 32 columns, was largely remodeled in the late 19th century. The **Bolívar family chapel** is in the middle of the right-hand aisle and

THE CENTER & PARQUE CENTRAL

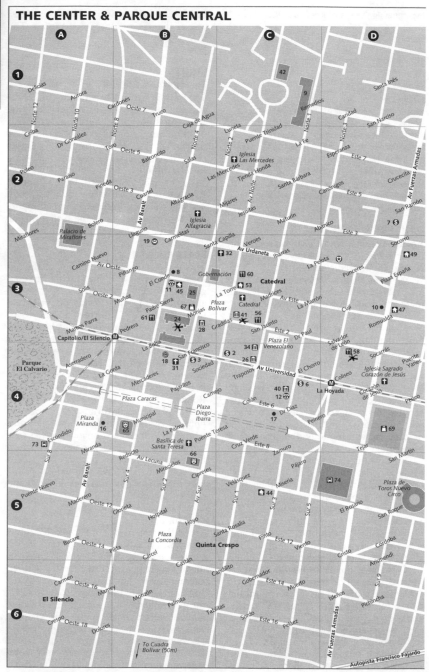

A • B • C • D

1

Delicias
Aurora
Oeste 7
Truco
Caja de Agua
Luneta
42
9
Santa Inés
Remedios
Norte 1
Caridad
Santa Narciso

Ceiba
Norte 12
Norte 10
Cardones
Oeste 8
Norte 4
Norte 2
Puente Trinidad
La Fe
Norte 3
Esperanza
Este 7
Av Fuerzas Armadas

Dr González
Toro
Oeste 5
Balconcito
Salas
Iglesia
Las Mercedes
Tienda Honda
Santa Bárbara
Canónigos
Este 5
San Ramón

2

Poleo
Paraíso
Pineda
Oeste 3
Cuartel
Altagracia
Las Mercedes
Av Norte
Mijares
Jesuitas
Santa Bárbara
Maturín
Este 3
Abanico
Crucecita
7 ⓢ

Miraflores
Palacio de
Miraflores
Bolero
Uraguno
Iglesia
Altagracia
Carmelitas
Santa Capilla
Veroes
Av Urbaneta
Ibarras
Socorro
49

Camino Nuevo
Av Oeste
Piñango
El Conde ● 8
Gobernación
60
53
Catedral
La Pelota ⊕
Punceres
Plaza España

3

Solis
Oeste 2
Muñoz
11 45 25
La Torre
Catedral
Madices
Av Este
La Marrón
Cují
10 ●
47

Padre Sierra
67
Plaza
Bolívar
Catedral
41 56
Monjas
Gradillas
San Jacinto
Este 2
Dr Paul
Romualda

Marcos Parra
Pedrera
61 24
28
Salvador
de León
58
Socarrás

Capitolio/El Silencio Ⓜ
La Bolsa
Plaza El
Venezolano
Puente
Yanes
Iglesia Sagrado
Corazón de Jesús

4

Parque
El Calvario
Aserradero
La Gorda
San Francisco
18 31 ⓢ 3
Sociedad
ⓢ 2
34 26
Av Universidad
El Chorro
Coliseo
Corazón
de Jesús
Peñco

Mercaderes
Pajaritos
Camejo
Traposos
40 12
Ⓜ 6
La Hoyada

Plaza Caracas
Colón
Este 6
Dr Díaz
● 17

Plaza
Miranda
16
Municipal
65
Plaza
Diego
Ibarra
La Palma
Peñero
69

73
Escondido
Miranda
Reducto
Basílica de
Santa Teresa
Puente Teresa
Cruz Verde
Zamuro
Tejar
San Martín

5

Av Lecuna
Miracielos
66
Cipreses
Velásquez
Pájaro
Misería
44
El Rosario
Plaza de
Toros Nuevo
Circo

Puente Nuevo
Madero
Oeste 12
Glorieta
Sur 4
Sur 2
Av Sur
Sur 1
Sur 3
Sur 5
74
San Roque

Bucare
Oeste 14
Pilita
Cárcel
Hospital
Hoyo
Santa Rosalía
Pinto
Este 12
Viento
Cristo
Córdoba
Ansmendi

Plaza
La Concordia
Quinta Crespo
Castán
Candilito
Gobernador
Este 14
Muerto
Iseños
Sur 9
Pichincha

6

Carmen
Oeste 16
Mamey
Monzón
Palmita
Tablitas
Sordo
Este 16
Peláez

El Silencio

Crespo
Oeste 18
Dolores

To Cuadra
Bolívar (50m)

Av Fuerzas Armadas
Autopista Francisco Fajardo

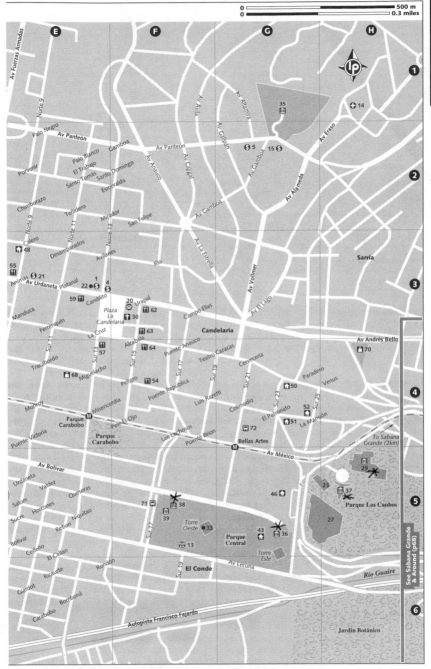

can be easily recognized by a modern sculpture of El Libertador mourning his parents and Spanish bride. Also take a look at the fine colonial altarpiece at the back of the chapel.

MUSEO SACRO DE CARACAS

Accommodated in a meticulously restored colonial building next to the cathedral, this **museum** (☎ 861-5814; Plaza Bolívar; adult/student $0.30/0.25; 🕙 10am-4:30pm Tue-Sun) displays a modest but carefully selected collection of religious art. Duck down through the low doorway into the dark, old ecclesiastical prison, where remains of early church leaders still lie in sealed niches. Museo Sacro also hosts a cultural program featuring theater, poetry, musical recitals and concerts, plus a pleasant café (see Café del Sacro p82).

CONCEJO MUNICIPAL

Occupying half of Plaza Bolívar's southern side, the **city hall** (☎ 409-8236; admission free; 🕙 9am-noon & 2-4:30pm Tue-Fri, 10am-4:30pm Sat & Sun) was erected by the Caracas bishops from 1641 to 1696 to house the Colegio Seminario de Santa Rosa de Lima. In 1725, the Real y Pontificia Universidad de Caracas, the province's first university, was established here. Bolívar renamed it the Universidad Central de Venezuela, the moniker it continues to keep to this day, though it has moved to a vast campus outside the historic center. Today the building is the seat of the Municipal Council, but part of it is open to the public.

Museo Santana, on the ground floor, has a unique 'doll's-house version' of the city's development, filled with elaborate miniature models of turn-of-the-19th-century Caracas. All the models were created by local artist, Raúl Santana. There are also grand historic paintings, banners, and some fascinating ceiling murals; look for the one depicting Bolívar in the heavens.

On the 1st floor is a collection of 80 paintings by Emilio Boggio (1857–1920), a Venezuelan artist who lived in Paris. It's normally closed, but the attendants by the main entrance might show you around.

The western side of the building houses the **Capilla de Santa Rosa de Lima**, where congress declared Venezuela's independence in 1811 (though it was another 10 years before this became a reality). The chapel has been restored with the decoration and furniture of the time.

While strolling around the courtyard, look for the reproduction of the very first Caracas map, drawn in 1578. It shows the old town when it stretched just two blocks from the plaza in each direction.

CASA AMARILLA

The 17th-century balconied mansion called the 'Yellow House,' on the western side of Plaza Bolívar, was originally an infamous royal prison. Wholly revamped and painted lemon yellow (hence its name) after independence, the building was converted into a presidential residence. Today it's the seat of the Ministry of Foreign Affairs and can't be visited, but have a good look through the archway and note the well-preserved colonial appearance of its exterior.

IGLESIA SANTA CAPILLA

The neo-Gothic **church** (☎ 860-8894; ⊙ 7am-6pm; Av Urdaneta, Esq Sta Capilla), one block north of Plaza Bolívar, is modeled on the Sainte Chapelle of Paris and looks a bit like a wedding cake. It was ordered by Guzmán Blanco in 1883 and built on the site of the first mass celebrated after the foundation of the town.

Illuminated by the warm light passing through colorful stained-glass windows, the marble and white-washed interior boasts an elaborate stone altar and an unusual open-work vault. One of the treasured possessions of the church is the sizable painting *Multiplication of the Bread,* by Arturo Michelena, hanging in the right-hand aisle.

CAPITOLIO NACIONAL

As part of his mad dash toward modernization in the 1870s, Guzmán Blanco commissioned an ambitious, new neoclassical seat of congress, the **National Capitol** (☎ 564-7589; admission free; ⊙ 9am-noon & 2-5pm Tue-Sun), to occupy the entire block just southwest of Plaza Bolívar. The two-building complex was to be erected on the site of a convent, whose occupants were promptly expelled by the dictator and their convent razed.

Personnel on the gate of the Capitolio Nacional will give you a visitor sticker and instruct you where to go. In the central part of the northern building is the famous **Salón Elíptico**, an oval hall topped by an extraordinary domed ceiling. Covering this dome is an all-encompassing mural, which almost seems to move as you walk beneath it. The painting, depicting the battle of Carabobo, was done in 1888 by the

most notable Venezuelan artist of the day, Martín Tovar y Tovar. The southern wall of the hall is crammed with portraits of the distinguished leaders of the independence wars. In front of this wall is Bolívar's bust on top of a marble pedestal; the 1811 Act of Independence is kept in the chest inside the pedestal. It's put on public view on July 5, Independence Day.

Tovar y Tovar also left more military works of art in two adjoining halls: the **Salón Amarillo** has on its ceiling a depiction of the battle of Junín, while the **Salón Rojo** has been embellished with a scene from the battle of Boyacá.

IGLESIA DE SAN FRANCISCO

Just south of the Capitolio Nacional, the **Church of San Francisco** (☎ 482-2442; Av Universidad; ⊙ 6am-7am, noon-1pm & 5-7pm Mon-Sat, 7am-6pm Sun) was built in the 1570s, but was remodeled on several occasions during the 17th and 18th centuries. Guzmán Blanco, unable to resist his passion for modernizing, placed a new neoclassical facade on the church to match the just-completed capitol building. Fortunately, the interior of the church didn't undergo such an extensive alteration, so its colonial character and much of its old decoration have been preserved. Have a look at the richly gilded baroque altarpieces distributed along both sidewalls, and stop at the statue of San Onofre, in the right-hand aisle. He is the most venerated saint in the church due to his miraculous powers of bringing health, happiness and a good job.

It was in this church in 1813 that Bolívar was proclaimed 'El Libertador,' and also here that his much-celebrated funeral was held in 1842, after his remains had been brought from Santa Marta in Colombia, 12 years after his death.

CASA NATAL DE BOLÍVAR

Bolívar's funeral took place just two blocks from the house where, on July 24, 1783, he was born. The interior of **Bolívar's birthplace** (☎ 541-2563; San Jacinto a Traposos; admission free; ⊙ 9am-4:30pm Tue-Sun) has been enthusiastically reconstructed though it lacks its original fittings. The ceilings and walls are splashed with a score of huge paintings by Tito Salas depicting Bolívar's heroic battles and scenes from his life.

CARACAS

MUSEO BOLIVARIANO

If you've not yet had your fill of Bolíviarian memorabilia, this is the place for you. Just a few paces north of Casa Natal de Bolívar, this **museum** (☎ 545-9828; San Jacinto a Traposos; admission free; ⊙ 9am-4:30pm Tue-Fri, 10am-4:30pm Sat & Sun) has more successfully preserved its colonial style and displays a variety of independence memorabilia, from muskets to medals and shaving sets to swords. It also has some fascinating documents and letters written by the man himself, and numerous portraits. More on the macabre side are the coffin in which the remains of Bolívar were brought from Santa Marta, and the *arca cineraria* (funeral ark) that transferred his ashes from the cathedral to the Panteón Nacional.

MUSEO FUNDACIÓN JOHN BOULTON

This small **museum** (☎ 564-4366; www.fundaboulton.es.mn; 11th fl, Torre El Chorro, Esq El Chorro; admission free; ⊙ 8:30am-11:30am & 1:30-4:30pm Mon-Fri) features a collection of historic and artistic objects accumulated over generations by the family of British merchant John Boulton (1805–75). Among the exhibits are paintings by Arturo Michelena, Bolívar memorabilia and a vast collection of ceramics from all over the world. The foundation was gearing up to move to the national library in 2004.

CUADRA BOLÍVAR

Located in the far southern section of the historic center, this is the **Bolívar family's summer house** (☎ 415-8617; Bárcenas a Piedras; admission free; ⊙ 9am-noon & 2-4pm Tue-Fri, 10am-1pm & 2-4:30pm Sat & Sun), where Simón spent much of his youth. Restored to its original appearance and stuffed with period furniture, the house is today a museum dedicated to El Libertador. It's a curious sight to see the one-story colonial block sitting isolated amid the ugly urban sprawl that encloses it.

PANTEÓN NACIONAL

The entire central nave of the imposing **National Pantheon** (☎ 862-1518; Av Norte; admission free; ⊙ 9am-noon & 2-5pm Tue-Fri, 10am-noon & 2-4:30pm Sat & Sun) is dedicated to national hero Simón Bolívar, underlining the almost saint-like reverence with which he is held in Venezuela. His bronze sarcophagus is placed in the chancel instead of the high altar, and the path to reach his tomb is lined with red carpet and covered by a ceiling filled with paintings of Bolívar's life, all done by Tito Salas in the 1930s.

No less than 140 white-stone tombs of other eminent Venezuelans are crammed into the aisles, though there are only three women (War of Independence heroine Luisa Cáceres de Arismendi, pianist Teresa Carreño and writer Teresa de la Parra) buried here.

One tomb is empty and open, awaiting the remains of Francisco de Miranda, who died in a Spanish jail in 1816 and was buried in a mass grave. There are two more empty tombs, but they are sealed. One is dedicated to Antonio José de Sucre, who was assassinated in Colombia and whose remains are in the Quito Cathedral; he is considered by Ecuadorians as the liberator of their country. The other tomb commemorates Andrés Bello, a Caracas-born poet, writer and friend of Bolívar's who later went to live (and die) in Chile.

There is also a huge crystal chandelier, made on the centennial of Bolívar's birth, that consists of an incredible 4000 pieces and 230 lights. It was undergoing restoration in late 2003, but should be back on display when you read this.

The pantheon is at the opposite, northern edge of the old town, five blocks due north of Plaza Bolívar. There was once a church on the site, but it was destroyed in the 1812 earthquake. After being reconstructed, it continued as a place of worship until 1874, when Guzmán Blanco decided that it would make a suitable resting place for revered Venezuelans.

There is a ceremonial changing of the guard held several times a day during the opening hours.

IGLESIA DE LA CANDELARIA

This **church** (Plaza La Candelaria), seven blocks east of Plaza Bolívar, stands amid an area tingling with Spanish flavor, thanks to Iberian migrants who settled here and opened up tascas (Spanish-style bar-restaurants). The church itself has richly gilded monumental retables that cover the chancel's walls. The central retable dates from about 1760, while the lateral ones are modern replicas.

But the holiest place in the church for Venezuelans is doubtless the tomb of José Gregorio Hernández (see the boxed text

SAINT IN A SUIT

Ask Venezuelans to name their most important saint and most will answer 'José Gregorio Hernández.' Indeed, the surprisingly well-to-do image of this treasured saint is omnipresent in private homes, shrines and religious stalls. Look for the guy with a black felt hat, well-tailored suit and Charlie Chaplin moustache. It's hardly the usual get-up of saints – but don't worry, it's him. In reality, Hernández doesn't appear on the Vatican's list of saints, though he was elevated to venerable status in 1985. But this doesn't deter his faithful followers.

Born into a humble Andean family in 1864, Hernández studied medical sciences in Caracas and Paris before embarking on a brilliant career as university professor and doctor to the president. He was a passionately religious person, and distinguished himself by treating the poor without charge. He tried to dedicate himself to a monastic life on various occasions, but always returned to plough his energy into caring for the poor.

Hernández died in a car accident in 1919, and a cult soon emerged around him and spread throughout the country and beyond. Countless miracles are attributed to him, including numerous healings. Hernández was even adopted as one of the principal deities of the mysterious María Lionza cult (see p161).

above), in the first chapel off the right-hand aisle. Though not canonized, José Gregorio is considered the most important saint by many Venezuelans, more so than many official saints whose images adorn the altars of this and other churches.

MUSEO DE ARTE COLONIAL
The **Museum of Colonial Art** (☎ 551-4256; www .quintadeanauco.org.ve; Av Panteón, San Bernardino; admission & 45-min tour adult/student $2.50/1.25; ◷ 9am-11:30am & 2-4:30pm Tue-Fri, 10am-5pm Sat & Sun) is housed in an elegant country mansion known as **Quinta de Anauco**, laid out around a charming patio and enclosed by lush, shady gardens. A ball was staged here in honor of Simón Bolívar's very last night in Caracas: he was never to return alive.

When built in 1797, the mansion was well outside the historic town; today it's just a green oasis in the inner suburb of San Bernardino, a 10-minute walk northeast of La Candelaria. You'll be rewarded with a guided tour around meticulously restored interiors filled with carefully selected works of art, furniture and household paraphernalia. Tours depart roughly every half-hour. Regular chamber-music concerts are held in the adjacent former stables, usually on weekends (see the website for the latest programs and prices).

Parque Central & Around   Map pp62–3
Parque Central is not, as you might expect, a green area, but rather a concrete complex of five high-rise residential slabs of somewhat apocalyptic appearance, crowned by two 53-story octagonal towers, the tallest in the country. You may not be impressed by the architecture, but don't retreat yet as there's plenty of sights around, especially for culture vultures.

The Parque Central area is Caracas' art and culture hub, boasting half a dozen museums, the major performing arts center, two art cinemas and arguably the best theater in town. Additionally, you can go to the top of one of the towers for an impressive 360-degree bird's-eye view of the city. The park is 1.5km southeast of Plaza Bolívar, next to the Bellas Artes metro station.

MIRADOR DE LA TORRE OESTE
This open-air **viewpoint** (admission free; ◷ 8am-11am & 2-4pm Tue-Fri) sits high on the 52nd floor of the Torre Oeste (which also houses Inatur, p60) and provides some fabulous views of the city. It's run as a courtesy of the tower's security department, which lets visitors ascend.

You first need to go to the department's office, CSB División y Departamento de Seguridad, on the tower's basement level (Nivel Sótano Uno). Upon exiting the elevator, you'll see the office right in front of you. The staff will ask to see your passport before somebody accompanies you up to the lookout.

MUSEO DE ARTE CONTEMPORÁNEO
Occupying the eastern end of the Parque Central complex, the **Museum of Contemporary Art** (☎ 573-8289; maccsi@cantv.net; admission free;

CARACAS

SABANA GRANDE & AROUND

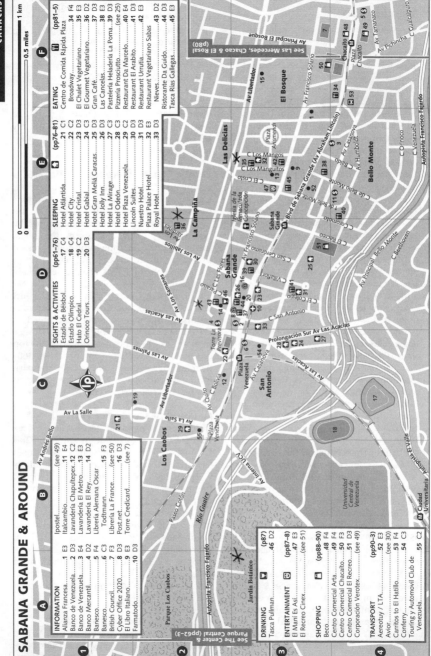

See The Center &
Parque Central (pp62–3)

See Las Mercedes, Chacao & El Rosal
(p80)

0   0.5 miles
0   1 km

🕑 10am-5:45pm Tue-Sun) is by far the best in the country, if not the continent. In 16 halls on five levels, you'll find many big, bold and shocking works by many prominent Venezuelan artists, including Jesús Soto, famous for his kinetic pieces.

There are also some remarkable paintings by international giants such as Picasso, Chagall, Matisse, Monet, Leger and Miró, and – the pride of the museum – a collection of a hundred or so engravings by Picasso, created by the artist from 1931 to 1934. Part of the exhibition space is given to changing displays that showcase both locally and internationally renowned artists. There's also a pleasant little café outside in a sculpture garden.

MUSEO DE LOS NIÑOS
The brightly colored **Children's Museum** (☎ 575-0295; Parque Central; adult/child $5.60/5; 🕑 9am-4pm Tue-Fri, 10am-5pm Sat & Sun) is an excellent science museum with lots of colorful, hands-on exhibits combining learning with fun – in fact, adults can have as much (or perhaps more) fun than the kids. There's a small planetarium too. Avoid weekends, when families besiege the museum. The museum is at the opposite end of the complex from Museo de Arte Contemporáneo.

MUSEO DEL TECLADO
This highly eclectic little **Museum of Historic Keyboards** (☎ 572-9024; museodelteclado@cantv.net; Edificio Tacagua, Parque Central; admission free; 🕑 9am-4pm Tue-Sun) holds concerts and recitals Saturday at 4pm and Sunday at 11am.

COMPLEJO CULTURAL TERESA CARREÑO
Rising like a gigantic concrete bunker across the street from Parque Central (and linked to it by a footbridge), the Complejo Cultural Teresa Carreño is a modern performing arts center. Opened in 1983, it has an enormous main auditorium, theatre and side hall that regularly host concerts, ballets, plays and recitals by local and visiting performers. It has also become a popular point for political rallies and public addresses from the president.

Hour-long guided **tours** (☎ 574-9122; $0.35; 🕑 10am-5pm Tue-Sat) around the complex are conducted several times a day. Call a day or two in advance if you need an English-speaking guide. At the back of the building is a small museum dedicated to Teresa

Carreño (1853–1917), the best pianist Venezuela has ever produced (see Music p33).

ATENEO DE CARACAS
Next to the Complejo Cultural, this **cultural center** (☎ 573-4400; Bellas Artes) comes complete with a concert hall, theater, cinema, art gallery, bookshop and café. The centre is home to the Rajatabla, the country's best-known theater company.

MUSEO DE CIENCIAS NATURALES
The **Natural Sciences Museum** (☎ 577-5103; www.museo-de-ciencias.org.ve; adult/child under 16 $1.50/0.30; 🕑 9am-5pm Tue-Fri, 10:30am-6pm Sat & Sun), behind the Ateneo, tracks the history of evolution, displaying minerals, fossils, stuffed animals and artifacts of pre-Hispanic communities from Venezuela and beyond.

GALERÍA DE ARTE NACIONAL & MUSEO DE BELLAS ARTES
The **National Art Gallery** (☎ 578-1818; Plaza de Los Museos, Parque Los Caobos; admission free; 🕑 9am-5pm Tue-Fri, 10am-5pm Sat & Sun) has a vast collection of artwork embracing five centuries of Venezuela's artistic expression. It alternates this diverse collection in temporary exhibitions showcasing everything from pre-Hispanic art to some truly mind-boggling modern kinetic pieces. The graceful building radiates from a neoclassical-style courtyard with a pond and weeping willow, and was designed in 1935 by renowned Venezuelan architect, Carlos Raúl Villanueva. The gallery also houses Caracas' leading art cinema.

Adjoining the gallery, the **Museo de Bellas Artes** (Museum of Fine Arts; ☎ 578-1816; museodebellasartes@cantv.net; Parque Los Caobos; admission free; 🕑 9am-5pm Tue-Fri, 10am-5pm Sat & Sun) is in a more functional modern six-story building also designed by Villanueva. The museum features mostly temporary exhibitions, and has an excellent little shop selling contemporary art and crafts.

The sculptural garden outside is recommended, and you can ponder the purpose of the various revolving sculptures from the comfort of the garden café, while sipping on your coffee and hobnobbing with local art students.

Sabana Grande & Around   Map p68
Sabana Grande, 2km east of Parque Central, is an energetic district packed with hotels,

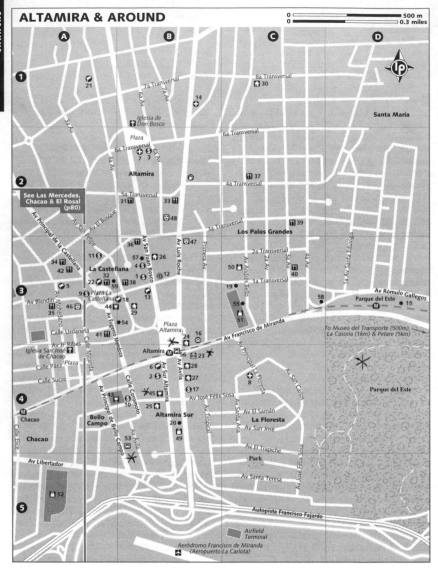

ALTAMIRA & AROUND

restaurants and shops. Locals come en masse to stroll along its vibrant, teeming mall, the **Blvd de Sabana Grande**, which stretches between Plaza Venezuela and Plaza Chacaíto. Its wide western end has room for several open-air cafés – a great place to sit over an espresso and watch the world go by.

✈ JARDÍN BOTÁNICO

From Sabana Grande, it's a 10-minute walk west across hectic roads to reach the **Botanical Gardens** (☎ 605-3989; www.ucv.ve/fibv.htm in Spanish; Av Interna UCV; adults/child under 14 $0.60/ 0.30; ⏰ 8:30am-4:30pm), but once you're inside it's a blissful escape from the madness outside, and the deeper you delve into the intertwining trees, draped vines and lush plants, the traffic noise fades away and birdsong takes over. The gardens are extensive, with plants from all over the world represented. The sole entrance to the gardens is from Av Interna UCV.

UNIVERSIDAD CENTRAL DE VENEZUELA (UCV)

With its 70,000 students, the UCV is Caracas' (and Venezuela's) largest university and is a hub of cultural activity, not to mention a hotbed of frequent student protests.

The vast campus was designed and built all in one go in the early 1950s by Carlos Raúl Villanueva, and it's dotted with abstract sculptures and murals throughout its grounds.

There's an excellent concert hall, **Aula Magna** (see Classical Music & Ballet p88) capable of seating 2700, and thought to have the best acoustics in the country. Curiously, a US sculptor, Alexander Calder, contributed to this by hanging a set of *platillos volantes* (flying saucers) from the ceiling.

The campus can be reached from Sabana Grande or by metro (Ciudad Universitaria).

Altamira & Eastern Suburbs

East of Sabana Grande lie some of Caracas' most fashionable suburbs, especially in Altamira and its immediate environs. As you proceed further east, you gradually descend the social ladder, reaching a low point at Petare. Eastward from here are vast expanses of appalling *barrios*.

PARQUE DEL ESTE

At weekends, as you ascend from Parque del Este metro station, you'll be greeted by bubbles, ice-cream and a crowd of colorful toy stalls clustered outside the gates to **Parque del Este** (Map p70; Av Francisco de Miranda; adult/student/child under 12 $0.15/0.10/0.05; ⏰ 5am-5pm Tue-Sun). There's just as much activity inside the extensive grounds, from children playing hide-and-seek among the rock gardens, to soccer games, religious groups, martial arts classes and, of course, a profusion of lycra clad bodies jogging with cellular phone in one hand and stop-clock in the other. The park is the largest in Caracas, and a great place to explore on a leisurely stroll. You can visit the snake house, aviary and cactus garden, and at weekends enjoy a show in the **Planetario Humboldt** (adult/child under 12 $1.25/0.65; hourly 1pm-4pm Sat & Sun, closed Sep).

MUSEO DEL TRANSPORTE

If planes, trains and automobiles flick your ignition switch, you'll want to visit the **Museum of Transportation** (Map pp56-7; ☎ 234-2234; admission $0.65; ⏰ 8am-2pm Wed, 9am-4:30pm Sun, closed Sep), just east of the Parque del Este and reached directly from the park by a pedestrian bridge (if it's closed, go through the nearby parking-lot gate). The museum

WALKING TOUR

The Bolívar Trail

The national hero Simón Bolívar (see the boxed text, p22) is an inescapable presence in downtown Caracas, where he was born, raised and eventually entombed, and reminders of his life can be found at every corner. To take a tour of the principal sites, start at the Capitolio/El Silencio metro station (see the map opposite). Take the exit for El Capitolio and you'll find yourself emerging a block east of the station into a busy street market. Battle your way right, and across Av Universidad before following it west until you come to **Iglesia San Francisco** (1; p65), where Bolívar was declared El Libertador (The Liberator). It was here also that his funeral took place.

From the setting for the great man's funeral, it's just a short stroll two blocks east and up a street on your left to reach his birthplace, the mansion **Casa Natal de Bolívar** (2; p65), now a museum. In addition, another museum dedicated to Bolívar is a few steps north. This good little **Museo Bolivariano** (3; p66) charts the independence movement with stacks of Bolivarian accoutrements.

From here it's just a block north and then west to the city's symbolic heart, **Plaza Bolívar** (4; p61), presided over by Bolívar's statue and still a focal point for modern-day social revolutionaries. While you're here, take a quick peek at **Museo Sacro de Caracas** (5; p66) and, if it's open, don't miss the **Catedral** (6; p61), just north of the museum, where Bolívar was once buried, and his family and wife still lie. Retrace your steps southwest around the plaza to the **Concejo Municipal** (7; p64).

Take a quick and worthwhile detour to the crisp, white **Capitolio Nacional** (8; p65), just southwest of the plaza. You'll see a small gatepost to your right; ask here to enter and view the Salón Elíptico, the oval seat of congress, smothered in glorious battle scenes of Bolívar et al.

After retracing your steps to the plaza, stroll up its left-hand side past the **Casa Amarilla** (9; p65) and take the street heading north to **Iglesia Santa Capilla** (10; p65). From here, head one block east, then left up a northbound pedestrian boulevard dotted with telephone stands and white-haired old men playing chess.

At the top of the boulevard, you'll pass under a low bridge where local artists sometimes peddle their work and look up toward the **Panteón Nacional** (11; p66), sitting grandly at the top of several flights of steps. This is where El Libertador's extravagant tomb lies in pride of place, flanked by other great Venezuelans.

This tour covers a distance of about 2km and should take 2½ to 3½ hours including time to stop and explore the museums. It visits all the vital sights, but of course, if you still have the legs for it, there are many other sites related to the life of Bolívar throughout Caracas!

---

features everything from old steam locomotives to tractors and cable-car capsules. The highlights are extensive collections of old horse-drawn carriages and vintage cars linked with former rulers. If you arrive by road, look for the American AT-60 'Texan' airplane precariously perched on a circular building.

LA CASONA

A short walk south of the museum is **La Casona** (Map pp56-7; ☎ 286-8030, 286-8070), the home of Venezuela's presidents. Established at the beginning of the 18th century as a cacao hacienda, it was later decreed the presidential residence, and in 1966 Raúl Leoni became its first resident. Part of the sprawling hacienda used to be open to the public, but visits have been suspended for several years due to political upheavals – call ahead for an update.

LA ESTANCIA

Just steps from Altamira metro station is this renovated 200-year-old coffee **hacienda** (Map p70; ☎ 208-0422; estancia@reacciun.ve; Av Francisco de Miranda; admission free; ☿ 9am-4:30pm Tue-Sat, 10am-4pm Sun) that now houses changing displays on the development of Caracas. It is surrounded by beautiful gardens.

PETARE

Today, **Petare** (Map pp56-7) is just an outer suburb of Caracas easily accessible by metro,

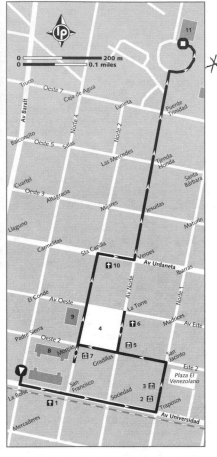

but it was once an independent colonial town founded in 1621 and developed side by side with Caracas. Although it has been swallowed by the metropolis, Petare preserves some of its historic character around the restored Plaza Sucre. The eastern side of the square is occupied by the large mid-18th-century **Iglesia del Dulce Nombre de Jesús**, and two blocks south of the plaza is a small art museum set in a colonial house.

Don't take valuables with you to Petare and do not go alone: the suburb is close to dangerous slum areas.

Southern Suburbs   Map pp56–7

The southern part of Caracas, set on rolling hills, is the most heterogeneous. Here are some of Caracas' wealthiest suburbs and also numerous pockets of ramshackle *barrios*, sometimes neighboring each other.

PARQUE ZOOLÓGICO DE CARICUAO

Caracas' main **zoo** (☎ 431-2045; Av Principal de Caricuao, Caricuao; admission $1; ☽ 9am-4pm Tue-Sun) is situated in the beautifully kept grounds of an old coffee plantation. It has a good selection of native birds, reptiles and mammals, plus some imported big cats and elephants. Most animals enjoy a fair degree of freedom in their enclosures, and some birds, including peacocks, ibis, flamingos and macaws, are almost free. Monkeys also mingle with the visitors, so keep an eye on your lunch if you don't want it disappearing up the nearest tree.

The zoo is located in the far southwestern suburb of Caricuao, 10km southwest of the center but easily accessible by metro. Get off at Zoológico metro station, from where it's a seven-minute walk to the zoo's entrance.

EL HATILLO

Now a trendy getaway for *caraqueños*, the characterful 16th-century town of El Hatillo lived its own life for centuries until it was eventually absorbed by the burgeoning city. Its narrow central streets and pretty plaza still retain many of their colonial buildings, now painted in sugary, bright colors and filled with fancy restaurants (see p85 for recommendations), art galleries and craft shops.

Located 15km southeast of the city center, this little village overflows with people at the weekend. There's always a wonderful atmosphere in the afternoon and early evening, when children can still be found skipping in the square, fairy lights illuminate the streets and musical *grillos* (crickets) shrill from all around.

The biggest and best craft shop is the **Hannsi** (see p89), half a block north of the plaza, but you'll find countless other boutiques tucked away in the narrow streets. Also take a look at the **parish church** on Plaza Bolívar, which has a particularly well-preserved exterior, though its interior was radically (and rather controversially) modernized.

Unfortunately, there are no hotels in El Hatillo.

Getting There & Away

Frequent carritos (small buses; $0.30, 45 minutes) run to El Hatillo from Av Humboldt, just off Blvd de Sabana Grande near the Chacaíto metro station (Map p68). Alternatively, metro bus No 202 leaves from Altamira metro station (Map p70) on weekdays only.

ACTIVITIES

Caracas has good options for outdoor activities. The best place for **hiking** near Caracas is Parque Nacional El Ávila (p93). If you're looking for organized hiking trips, contact one of the *centros excursionistas* (see Excursion Centers p75).

Parque de Recreación Cuevas del Indio (Map pp56-7; ☎ 273-2882; Av Principal de la Guairita; ⏰ 8:30am-5pm Tue-Sun) is a favorite rock-climbing spot; local climbers flock here at the weekend. It's 9km southeast of the city on the southern continuation of Av Principal el Cafetal.

There are few public tennis courts in the city, but some private clubs hire out their courts to nonmembers. Contact the **Federación Venezolana de Tenis** (☎ 979-6523) for details.

Public golf courses are nonexistent in Caracas, but some private golf clubs are willing to offer their facilities to the general public – for a fee, of course. You can obtain information from **Federación Venezolana de Golf** (☎ 731-4507).

COURSES
Language

Caracas has many language institutions, though they concentrate on teaching English to Spanish speakers. However, most can also arrange Spanish classes and individual tuition. Try the following:

Centro de Idiomas Berlitz (Map p80; ☎ 993-6851; www.berlitz.com; Centro Comercial Paseo Las Mercedes, Las Mercedes)

Centro Venezolano Americano (CVA; see Cultural Centers p58)

Centro Venezolano de Español (CEVES; Map p68; ☎ 793-9265, 793-2434; www.ceves.org.ve; 19th fl, Torre Phelps, Plaza Venezuela)

TOURS

Caracas tour companies can send you almost anywhere in Venezuela, but the trips won't be cheap. It's cheaper to reach the region on your own and contact a local operator. But remember that some tours organized from Caracas may be unavailable in the region, and Caracas companies may conveniently link various regional tours into one chain to reduce transfer time.

Tour Companies

There are over 500 travel agencies in Caracas. Some of them (the so-called *mayoristas*, or wholesalers) simply sell tours organized by other companies. Many agencies use some of the services of selected regional operators, adding their own guides and transfers, and sometimes altering routes and upgrading lodging facilities. Some Caracas operators, though, organize the entire trip themselves, using their own camps and means of transportation. Some companies can prepare tailor-made trips, which will cost considerably more than standard tours. Prices vary significantly depending on the number of people in the tour.

The following listed companies focus on responsible tourism and have English-speaking guides (some also have guides that speak German and/or French):

Akanan Travel & Tours (Map pp56-7; ☎ 234-2103, 234-2323; www.akanan.com; Edificio Claret, Mezzanina, Av Sanz at Calle La Laguna, El Marques) This company specializes in quality (though not cheap) adventure trips, including treks to the top of Auyantepui (eight days) and Roraima (eight days), as well as bicycle trips from La Paragua to Canaima (six days).

Alpitour (Map pp56-7; ☎ 283-1433, 283-1966; www.alpi-group.com; 1st fl, Torre Centro, No 11, Centro Parque Boyacá, Av Sucre, Los Dos Caminos) One of the more expensive operators, this company specializes in fishing trips, but also offers a range of mainstream packages and some adventurous tours in the Amazonas.

Aventura Trotamundos (Map pp62-3; ☎ 576-6160; www.trotamundos.com; 4th fl, Torre Sur, No 423, Hotel Hilton Caracas, Parque Central) This is one of Caracas' well-established wholesalers, with wide if not budget offerings of mainstream and mild adventure tours to most regions.

Cacao Travel Group (Map pp56-7; ☎ 977-1234; www.cacaotravel.com; Quinta Orquidea, Calle Andrómeda, Urbanización El Peñón, Vía Baruta) This agency, 2.5km south of Las Mercedes, has expertize in Río Caura tours (five days in total, $315 to $374 depending on accommodation type), where it has its own lodge. It also has a lodge in the Amazonas, serving as a base for boat trips in the region.

Cóndor Verde (Map pp56-7; ☎ 975-4306, 975-3660; www.condorverde.com; Av Río Caura, Torre Humboldt, Mezzanina 03, Prados del Este) This German-run agency, 2km south of Las Mercedes, offers one of the widest ranges of tours, from beach holidays on Isla de Margarita to adventurous boat trips in the Amazonas, plus special-interest packages such as fishing, diving and golf. Tours include Delta del Orinoco (three days), Gran Sabana (four days), Roraima (seven days) and Río Caura (five days). It also has a special no-frills offer for budget travelers.

Orinoco Tours (Map p68; ☎ 761-8431; www.orinoco tours.com; 7th fl, Edificio Galerías Bolívar, No 75-A, Blvd de Sabana Grande) This German-run agency offers various levels of adventure tours. Programs include Gran Sabana, Roraima and Los Llanos.

Sociedad Conservacionista Audubón de Venezuela (SCAV; ☎ 992-3268; ◔ 9am-1pm Mon-Fri) For more information on responsible traveling, contact this leading environmental society. It can provide information on ecological issues and recommend tour companies; it also organizes bird-watching tours itself.

Tucaya (Map pp56-7; ☎ 234-9401; www.tucaya.com; Quinta Santa Marta, 1a Av Urbanización Campo Claro, Los Dos Caminos) This small, French-run agency caters principally to French-speaking clientele, but it also organizes English-speaking tours. The tours feature some major tourist destinations, including Gran Sabana (four days), Roraima (nine days), Los Llanos (four days) and Delta del Orinoco (three days).

ANGEL FALLS TOUR OPERATORS

Angel Falls (Salto Angel) is one of Venezuela's top tourist attractions, so many Caracas tour companies (including most listed earlier) have it in their program. You can also find a couple of agencies in the domestic terminal at Maiquetía airport. See Ciudad Bolívar (p288) for more tour options. **Hoturvensa** (☎ 976-0530; www.hoturvensa.com.ve in Spanish; Av Río Caura, Torre Humboldt, Nivel Mezzanina 1 & 2, Prados del Este) is two kilometres south of Las Mercedes. It is an offspring of Avensa airlines and owns the Canaima camp. A three-day trip to Canaima costs $485 to $510, which includes room and board at the Canaima camp plus several excursions, including an all-day tour to Angel Falls. The Caracas–Canaima flight costs extra, as do any flights over the falls (about $80). This is one of the more expensive offers on the market. You can buy these packages at Avensa offices and in most travel agencies.

LOS ROQUES TOUR OPERATORS

Archipiélago Los Roques is serviced from Maiquetía airport by a number of small airlines – see p102 for more information. They all offer a flight-only option, and some airlines also offer tours. The following

airlines are based at the airport (usually departing from the auxiliary terminal):

AeroEjecutivos (☎ 991-7942, 991-7942; www.aero ejecutivos.com.ve)

Avior (☎ 355-2767; www.avior.com.ve)

Chapi Air/Transavén (☎ 355-2786, 355-1179)

Línea Turística Aereotuy (LTA; ☎ 355-2060; www.tuy.com/aereotuy.htm) Caracas (Map p68; ☎ 761-8043; 5th fl, Edificio Gran Sabana, Blvd de Sabana Grande) LTA is the largest Los Roques tour operator.

Sol de América (☎ 355-1797)

LOS LLANOS REPRESENTATIVES

If you plan on taking tours to the *hatos* (ranches) in Los Llanos (p224), note that some may require you to book and pay beforehand through a Caracas agent:

Hato El Cedral (Map p68; ☎ 781-8995; www .hatocedral.com; 5th fl, Edificio Pancho, No 33, Av La Salle, Los Caobos)

Hato La Fe (☎ 991-4321; piedrasvivascs@telcel.net.ve)

Hato Piñero (Map pp56-7; ☎ 991-1135, 992-4413; www.hatopinero.com; 6th fl, Biotur Hato Piñero, Edificio General de Seguros, No 6-B, Av La Estancia, Chuao)

Excursion Centers

An alternative to tour companies, *centros excursionistas* (excursion centers) are associations of outdoor-minded people who organize independent excursions in their spare time. These are essentially one- or two-day weekend trips around Caracas and the central states, but longer journeys to other regions are often scheduled for long weekends and holiday periods. The focus is usually on nature and walking, though cultural sights are often part of the program. Each trip is prepared by a member of the group, who then serves as a guide. The *excursionistas* use public transportation and take their own food and camping gear if necessary. Foreign travelers are welcome, and you can usually find a companion for conversation in English, German etc.

Centro Excursionista Caracas (CEC; Map pp56-7; Polideportivo Santa Sofía) This center is about 8km southeast of the center off Av Principal El Cafetal. Founded in 1929, it is the oldest and best-known club of its kind. Its members include people of all ages, and it has regular weekend trips. Club meetings are on Saturday (if there is no excursion that day) between 2:30pm and 5pm in the Polideportivo. It's best to call a member beforehand to ask about forthcoming trips and to check the meeting's details; contact Andrea Würz (☎ 0212-235-3053; English & German) and Fritz Werner (☎ 0212-945-0946; German only).

Centro Excursionista Universitario (CEU; www
.ucv.ve/ceu.htm in Spanish) Another club which bands
together mostly university students keen to take on faster,
more adventurous trips. Contact persons include Roberto
González (☎ 762-0424), José Daniel Santana (☎ 371-
1871, 0414-253-2384; English) and Mirna Carolina Ríos
(☎ 661-5644, 0412-738-7473; Spanish). The club meets
on Tuesday between 6pm and 8pm in the Edificio de
Deportes ground floor, alongside the Judo Club, at the
Universidad Central de Venezuela.

Guides

The **Asociación Venezolana de Instructores y Guías
de Montaña** (☎ 0414-311-2149; www.zonam.com/avigm
in Spanish) is an association consisting of
over 30 experienced guides. It can provide
mountain-guide services (mountaineering,
rock climbing, trekking etc) and find guides
for other activities such as caving, kayaking,
paragliding or bird-watching.

Henry González (☎ 283-3260, 0414-286-2970;
henryg@unete.com.ve) is a photographer who can
organize and guide expeditions to several
tepuis (flat-topped sandstone mountains
with vertical flanks), including the top of
Auyantepui in Canaima National Park
(see the boxed text p44). These are 12- to
15-day strenuous treks from the base of the
tepui to the point from which Angel Falls
spills down.

FESTIVALS & EVENTS

Christmas, Carnaval and Easter are celebrated with fervor in Caracas. During these
times all offices close, as do most shops,
and intercity bus transportation is frantic.
Flights are usually fully booked.

The biggest religious feast in Caracas is
the **Semana Santa** (Holy Week, culminating
in Easter) celebration in Chacao, which begins with the Bajada de Palmeras (literally,
'taking down of the palms') on the Friday
before Palm Sunday, and goes on for over a
week, culminating with solemn processions
on Maundy Thursday and Good Friday. It
concludes with the Quema de Judas (Burning of Judas) on Easter Sunday.

Traditional suburbs often celebrate holy
days with more vigor than central districts.
El Hatillo boasts local feasts on several occasions during the year (May 3, July 16 and
September 4), as does Petare (January 30
and 31 and the last Sunday of September).

More characteristic of Caracas are cultural events, of which the **Festival Interna-**

cional de Teatro (www.fitcaracas.com in Spanish) is
the city's highlight. Initiated in 1976, it has
been held in March/April of every even-
numbered year and attracts national and
international groups to Caracas' theatres.

El Hatillo is home to the still very young
and small **Festival de Música El Hatillo**, which
covers everything from jazz to ethnic to
classical to contemporary music and takes
place sometime between September and
November.

A similarly wide range of musical genres
characterizes the **Festival El Piano de Bach a
Chick Corea**, which is held in Caracas' Complejo Cultural Teresa Carreño in June/July.
Another event, the **Temporada de Danza**, runs
for several weeks in July and August, bringing together some of the leading national
dance groups, plus international guests.

The week around July 25 also witnesses an
increase in concerts, exhibitions and theater
performances, organized to celebrate the
anniversary of Caracas' foundation on July
25, 1567.

Also see the boxed text on the festival
of **Diablos Danzantes** (p106) in Francisco de
Yare, a day trip from Caracas.

SLEEPING

Accommodations in Caracas are much
more expensive than elsewhere in the country. A double room costing $10 elsewhere
won't be available for less than $15 here;
the price breakdowns following reflect that
reality. All hotels listed in this chapter have
rooms with private bathrooms and either
fan or air-conditioning (as indicated), and
almost all have TV sets.

On the whole, Caracas' budget accommodations are poor, lacking charm and
located in unimpressive, sometimes unsafe
areas. Most budget haunts double as love
hotels (rent by the hour) and some as
brothels; business is particularly brisk on
Friday and Saturday. Allow time for possible hotel hunting at these times.

A reminder of wealthier decades, Caracas
also has plentiful four- and five-star hotels
charging hefty rates. Some top-end hotels
offer temptingly low rates on weekends;
ask in advance. Upmarket hotels have
noiseless central air-conditioning, instead
of the rattling, dripping boxes used in
budget and mid-range hotels. In high-rise
hotels, try asking for a room on one of

the upper floors, for better views and less noise. Always have a peek at the room before booking in.

Taxes are included in the following prices.

The Center   Map pp62–3

The cheapest accommodations in the center are found south of Av Bolívar. However, this entire area is unattractive and is unsafe at night; even during the daytime you should be on your guard. Furthermore, most of the budget hotels are scruffy shelters, mostly renting rooms by the hour.

BUDGET

Hotel Center Park (☎ 542-4110; Av Lecuna; s with fan $4.40, d with fan $7.50-10, with air-con $10; 🞐) One of the few acceptable places in the area. It's cheap and reasonably clean (a few cigarette marks on sheets is the worst of it) and packs a lot of rooms into a very small space.

Hotel New Jersey (☎ 571-4624; Esq Paradero; d $15-21, tr $22.50; P 🞐) This nine-story option is a decent choice, though you enter the hotel through the entrance to a car park and will most likely be led to your room by a bellboy in a boiler suit. Ask for one of the better rooms on the top floors. Rooms have hot showers.

Hotel Hollywood (☎ 514-9946; Av Fuerzas Armadas, Esq Romualda; d $14-19; 🞐) One of the cheapest options in the area, Hotel Hollywood sits opposite the Av Fuerzas Armadas book market. It has a smart polished-stone entrance, and the spacious rooms, though shade dark and characterless, have cable TV and hot water.

Hotel Inter (☎ 564-0251; Esq Calero; s/tr $14/22, d $15.50-17.50; 🞐) This is a quieter hotel, with a more old-fashioned feel. It's reasonably well kept, popular with business people, and run by a couple of charming old Italians.

Hotel Ribot (☎ 571-3433; Av Andrés Eloy Blanco, Esq La Mansión; s/d/tr $11.50/13/15.50) This is the cheapest place in the area closer to Bellas Artes' museums, and has a striking Egyptian-temple theme with plenty of gold paint and hieroglyphics liberally scattered around the entrance. However, the rooms themselves are particularly dark and basic. You may want to bring your own pillowcase.

Hotel Metropol (☎ 562-8666; Plaza España a Socorro; d $11.50-14, tr $18; 🞐) You may also consider this claustrophobic, old hotel with rattling air-con; it's OK for a night's kip.

MID-RANGE

Hotel Renovación (☎ 571-0133; renov@telcel.net.ve; Esq El Patronato; s $15.50, d $19-22; P 🞐) This modern orange-brick building is the best lower middle-range option in the area. The staff are extremely helpful and everything is kept spick-and-span. Rooms have cable TV, new tiles and low beds, and the maids take as much pride cleaning as though it were their own home. Ask for a room on one of the highest floors.

Plaza Catedral Hotel (☎ 564-2111; plazacatedral@cantv.net; Plaza Bolívar; s/d $17.50/19; 🞐) This hotel has an unbeatable position on the corner of the plaza: ask for one of the four rooms with a plaza view (room 106 even has a mini balcony). It's not for light sleepers, though, as the cathedral's bells ring every 15 minutes and daytime vendors haggle noisily below. A bonus is the hotel's top-floor restaurant (see Restaurant Les Grisons p82).

Hotel El Conde (☎ 860-1171; hotel_elconde@hotmail.com; Esq El Conde; s/d/tr $29/32/35; P 🞐) One of very few mid-range options in the center, the three-star Hotel El Conde is just one block west of Plaza Bolívar. The grand polished entrance up a wide staircase is a reminder of more salubrious times, though corridors and rooms are plainer. Good solid value in an excellent position.

TOP END

Hilton Caracas Residencias Anauco (☎ 573-4111; anaucosuits@cantv.nct; Parque Central; s/d/tr plus breakfast $62/73/89; P 🞐) This is the Hilton's four-star neighbor within the concrete-dominated Parque Central complex. Faded suites in a uniformly neutral color range from spacious studios to three bedrooms with kitchen included, especially good for larger parties. Many come with a concrete balcony-cum-yard.

Hotel Hilton Caracas (☎ 503-5000; www.hiltoncaracas.com.ve; Av Sur 25 at Av México, Parque Central; d/ste $163/210; P 🞐 🖳 🖾) Opposite Complejo Cultural Teresa Carreño, this aging five-star hotel faces Parque Central and is one of the most-established upmarket hotels in town. Its trump cards are a convenient location for museum hopping, lofty views of the concrete jungle from the top floors, a helpful tourist information desk, tennis courts, swimming pool and a gym. The hotel has old and new sections, the former being a touch dated and claustrophobic – so specify if you want a room in the new wing.

Sabana Grande & Around   Map p68

This area is a popular place to stay among budget travelers. There are about 30 cheap hotels in the western end of the district, all within a few minutes' walk of the Plaza Venezuela metro station. Note that most of these hotels cater primarily to passionate local couples looking to have sex. It can be a rough area after dark – try to stay in a group if you're going out. There is also a good choice of hotels in the mid-range bracket, though Altamira is generally a safer neighborhood.

BUDGET

Nuestro Hotel (☎ 761-5431; bhotelccs@yahoo.com; Calle El Colegio, Sabana Grande; s/d/tr/q $10.50/12.50/15.50/19) This is a long-established choice that calls itself 'the only one for budget travelers in Caracas.' True to form, the friendly Portuguese owners are well versed in travelers' needs, though English is not spoken. Located on a relatively quiet side street, the rooms are plain and functional with fans and a private bathroom, and the hotel has a miniature balcony-terrace drenched with plants. Bookings placed over the Internet are not reliable.

Hotel Odeón (☎ 793-1345; Av Las Acacias, Sabana Grande; d $12.50-15.50; P ⊠) This Colombian-run hotel has eight floors of starkly simple rooms and there is a tasty cheap café below. Good value.

Hotel La Mirage (☎ 793-2733; Prolongación Sur Av Las Acacias, Sabana Grande; d $12.50-14, tr/ste $15.50/22; P ⊠) There are over a dozen budget hotels further south on Prolongación Sur Av Las Acacias, including this good but undistinguished nine-floor block, that are popular with Venezuelan families. The boxy rooms come with bright tartan bedspreads and a cramped bathroom.

Hotel Cristal (☎ 761-9131; Blvd de Sabana Grande, Sabana Grande; d $16.50; ⊠) If you need somewhere more central, try this perfectly located spot just off the main boulevard. It's not the classiest place around, but it has lots of spacious, serviceable rooms. Ask for a room with a balcony overlooking the mall.

Hotel Jolly Inn (☎ 762-3665; fax 761-4887; Av Francisco Solano, Sabana Grande; d $15.5-19, tr $22; ⊠) The Jolly Inn has very eager-to-please – slightly manic – staff, and light, carpeted rooms with stacks of storage space. But note that rooms facing the street cop plenty of noise.

MID-RANGE

Hotel Plaza Venezuela (☎ 781-7811; fax 781-9542; Av La Salle, Los Caobos; d $25-28, ste $31; P ⊠) Just above the traffic hubbub on Plaza Venezuela, this is a space-efficient hotel with a tiny lift, nice but compact rooms (with cable TV) and a small restaurant. It's well decorated, light-filled and plays piped music in its compact corridors. Consider paying the additional $6 for a large suite. English is spoken.

Hotel City (☎ 793-5785; fax 782-6354; Av Bolivia, Sabana Grande; s/d/ste $28/30/31; P ⊠) Hotel City is perched on a slight rise next to a busy junction and a mere hop, skip and a jump to the metro. Despite having nine floors, the narrow, somewhat lonesome-looking building is positively dwarfed by the skyscrapers looming around it. Inside it has a smart entrance and restaurant, but dated '70s decor in the rooms. Small windows minimize street noise.

Hotel Atlántida (☎ 793-3211; hotelatlanti@cantv .net; Av La Salle, Los Caobos; d $19-25, tr/ste $31/44; P ⊠) A few minutes' walk uphill on the same street as the Hotel City, the friendly, secure Atlántida has a cool, spacious feel and its spotless corridors are dotted with modern art. Rooms are slightly faded but still good value, with bonus points for safety deposit boxes and hairdryers. There's a restaurant below. Ask at reception for cable TV.

Plaza Palace Hotel (☎ 762-4821; plaza_palace _hotel@hotmail.com; Calle Los Mangos, El Bosque; d/ste $36/40; P ⊠) Plaza Palace is a very smart, cool, businesslike hotel on a quiet street close to Blvd de Sabana Grande. The well-tended rooms have plenty of mod cons including cable TV and a hairdryer, and some also boast a mini-terrace. There's also a good restaurant. English is spoken.

Royal Hotel (☎ 762-5494; fax 762-6459; Calle San Antonio, Sabana Grande; s/tr $22.50/27.50, d $24-25; P ⊠) This less salubrious hotel is in a busy area close to the boulevard. It's fine for a few nights, though the bland rooms do not fulfil the promise of the hotel's smart entrance.

Hotel Gabial (☎ 793-1156; fax 781-1453; Prolongación Sur Av Las Acacias, Sabana Grande; d $33-39, ste $46; P ✶) This very efficient, tightly-run operation has seven floors of fresh, modern rooms. Suites have a Jacuzzi. Its large, modern restaurant and bar is dark but warmly lit, and often hosts live music.

TOP END

Hotel Gran Meliá Caracas (☎ 762-8111 ext 4103/4116/4306; www.granmeliacaracas.solmelia.com; gran.melia.caracas@solmelia.com; Av Casanova, Sabana Grande; d $275, 1-/2-/3-person apt $300/350/400, ste $660; P ✶ ▯ ▦) The opulent 660-room five-star Meliá is the largest and most luxurious hotel in Sabana Grande, and, indeed, Caracas. It has just about all the facilities you could wish for, including a gym, swimming pool, several restaurants and bars, and exceptionally slick service. All rooms come with added luxuries such as a Jacuzzi and even free slippers.

Lincoln Suites (☎ 762-8575, 762-6831; www.lincoln-suites.com.ve; Av Francisco Solano, Sabana Grande; d/ste incl breakfast & cocktail $68/73; P ✶ ▯) The 11-story, 125-room Lincoln Suites has cut its rates in recent years, but still has the same comfortable, spacious suites with full amenities, as well as a reasonably priced restaurant and bar. Excellent value.

Las Mercedes & Around Map p80✗

Want to stay closer to the restaurants and nightlife? Las Mercedes is an upmarket area, with very few budget and mid-range options but more top-end hotels to choose from.

BUDGET ✗

Hotel Nostrum (☎ 992-7646; fax 992-6646; Av Orinoco; d $20; P ✶) Hotel Nostrum is an unabashed 'love hotel,' but that need not bother heavy sleepers, especially given its clean new rooms, good bathrooms, and very reasonable price for the area. Bookings may not be respected on weekends.

TOP END

Radisson Plaza Eurobuilding (Map pp56-7; ☎ 902-1111; www.radisson.com; Final Calle La Guairita, Chuao; d/ste $126/368; P ✕ ✶ ▯ ▦) A landmark in eastern Caracas, the Eurobuilding can be seen from miles away thanks to its position behind a private airfield. Views from the hotel are similarly blessed, and rooms are also suitably comfortable and stylish.

Hotel Paseo Las Mercedes (☎ 993-9211; w .hotelpaseolasmercedes.com; Centro Comercial Paseo Las Mercedes, Las Mercedes; s/d $56/62, d/ste Mon-Fri $88/106; P ✶ ▦) Further up the luxury scale, there's the handy four-star Hotel Paseo Las Mercedes in the shopping mall of the same name. It hovers between mid-range and top-end prices, but has very light rooms, painted in a uniform pastel-pink color, and spiffy porters dressed in top and tails. You also have the pick of the local restaurants and nightlife at your doorstep. Breakfast is included on weekends.

Other recommendations:

JW Marriott (☎ 957-2222; www.marriott.com; Av Venezuela, El Rosal; d/ste $181/216; P ✶ ▯ ▦) This relatively new addition to Caracas' five-star club has facilities including gym and restaurant.

Tamanaco InterContinental Caracas (☎ 909-7111; www.intercontinental.com; Av Principal de Las Mercedes; d/ste $115/225; P ✕ ✶ ▯ ▦) Expect every amenity, including outdoor pool, a sauna and wheelchair access.

Altamira & Around Map p70✗

Altamira is an upmarket suburb, and it has some good, affordable mid-range accommodations that are well worth considering. It's an attractive and safe area based around a large bustling plaza and dotted with excellent restaurants and nightspots – all just 15 minutes from the center by metro.

MID-RANGE

Hotel Residencia Montserrat (☎ 263-3533; fax 261-1394; Av Avila, Altamira Sur; s/d/tr $28/31/34; P ✶) Just a few steps from the Altamira metro station, Montserrat is a responsible, solid-value hotel with soccer field–size rooms. True, its furniture and decoration are well worn in, but some rooms have great views. Get a room in the back to minimize street noise and score glorious vistas of La Estancia's gardens. But all is not lost if you're given a front-facing room – just fish out your earplugs and enjoy the oblique view of Plaza Altamira.

Hotel La Floresta (☎ 263-1955; hotellafloresta@ ✗ cantv.net; Av Ávila, Altamira Sur; s/d/ste/tr $29.50/32.50/39/41; ✶) Alternatively, you could try the more modern Floresta, just a few paces away from the Montserrat. Rooms here are much smaller, but they boast brighter – sometimes slightly lurid – furnishings, a reasonable choice of cable TV channels, and plenty of storage space. Some rooms

CARACAS

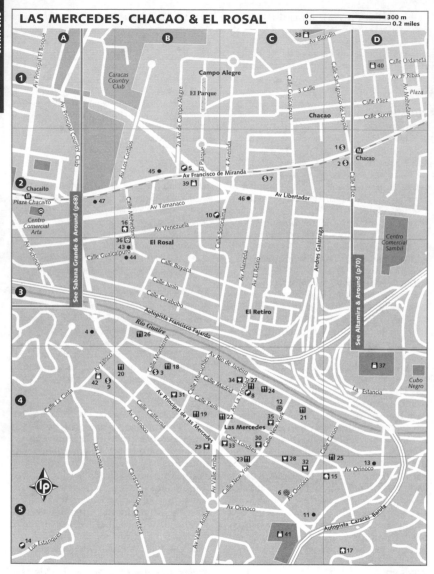

LAS MERCEDES, CHACAO & EL ROSAL

0   300 m
0   0.2 miles

have a small sofa for relaxing after a hard day's sightseeing.

Hotel Altamira (☎ 267-4284; hotelaltamira@telcel .net.ve; Av José Félix Sosa, Altamira Sur; d $28; P ✕) Positioned further away from the plaza on a quieter street, Hotel Altamira has fresh, white-washed rooms with bamboo furniture. Front-facing rooms have a small

balcony, which may not have picture-perfect views but do give an interesting angle on the city looking over a small, haphazardly built *barrio* to the skyscrapers and mountain beyond. Most rooms have cable TV. Some English is spoken.

Hotel Residencial El Cid (☎ 263-2611; Av San Felipe, La Castellana; s/d/tr $32/40/51; P ✕) Setting itself apart from the other options, this faded old hotel actually packs a surprising amount of character into its spacious apartments. Old-style heavy wooden furniture and fittings dominate the decor, and each apartment squeezes in a bedroom, salon with cable TV, and separate kitchenette.

TOP END
Hotel Continental Altamira (☎ 261-0644; reserv aciones@hotel-continental.org.ve; Av San Juan Bosco, La Castellana; s/d incl breakfast $70/77; P ✕ ✕ ✦) At first glance this large concrete three-star hotel can look past its sell-by date, but the ample, spacious rooms are very bright and comfortable and have cable TV, minibar, balcony and a huge closet as standard. Its position just a short walk from the metro is also a big plus.

Four Seasons Hotel (☎ 280-1000; www.fourseasons .com/caracas; Av Francisco de Miranda, Plaza Altamira;

P ✕ ✦ ✦) By the time you read this, the huge Four Seasons Hotel should be fully functioning, despite several delays in its grand opening. It's set to provide some of the ultimate luxuries Altamira has to offer – at a price, of course.

EATING
You could eat out three times a day for several years without ever visiting the same restaurant twice in Caracas. For more ideas *The Caracas Gastronomic Guide* (see p49) is a great resource for discovering the local cooking scene.

If you're on a budget, keep your eyes peeled for the *menú del día* or *menú ejecutivo* (set menu with two or three courses) for $2 to $5. Cheap chicken restaurants and *areperas* (restaurants selling *arepas* – small, thick corn pancakes) also abound. For breakfast, go to any of the ubiquitous

---

THE AUTHOR'S CHOICE

La Posada Corporativa (Map p70; ☎ 283-4817; gerdschad@cantv.net; 8a Transversal No 2, Los Palos Grandes; d/ste $70/90; P ✕ ✦ ✦) In a league of its own, this unique complex of cabins and small houses is loosely scattered through an extraordinary garden engulfed by huge old vine-draped trees and boasting exotic plants, fish-filled pools and ringing birdsong. The owner is a gifted carpenter, and his work fills the complex, from furniture to elevated wooden walkways. The historical building in the center houses a business room, several bars and plenty of cozy niches for relaxing.

This exclusive posada has just two double rooms and three double suites, so be sure to book well in advance, preferably for several nights as it is unlikely to accept visitors for a single night. There is no sign outside so it can be difficult to find: look for N2 painted on the wall.

panaderías (bakeries). In the evening, countless tascas come alive, particularly in La Candelaria and Sabana Grande.

Trendy suburbs such as Las Mercedes, Altamira and La Castellana boast dozens of upmarket restaurants that will serve you a worldwide range of delicacies. But be warned: Caracas restaurants are notorious for not including the 16.5% IVA tax in listed prices, and never the 10% service, so expect your dinner to cost 25% more (or 35% with the customary 10% tip).

The Center
& Parque Central   Map pp62–3

While it doesn't abound in chic restaurants, the center has plenty of low-priced eateries, many of which serve local fare known as comida criolla. The area east of Av Fuerzas Armadas, known as La Candelaria, is swamped with top-end tascas serving traditional Spanish dishes from tapas to seafood, and with long, lively bars for knocking back a wee dram or three.

BUDGET

Restaurant Las Vegas (☎ 563-1775; La Torre a Veroes; cachapas $1.50-2; 5am-7pm Mon-Sat) For a cheap feed on-the-go, this simple bar-like restaurant seems to have a constant line of office workers awaiting its freshly flipped cachapas (corncakes with toppings such as cheese, ham etc). It's located just off Plaza Bolívar.

El Salón del Sabor (☎ 564-9396; Ground fl, Edificio Iberia, Av Urdaneta, Esq Animas, La Candelaria; 3-course menú $4.50; 7am-4pm Mon-Fri) For a monstersized vegetarian lunch, just make your way to this canteen-style spot. It also does a meat-based menu for the same price.

Kafta (☎ 860-4230; Gradillas a San Jacinto; 3-course menú $4; noon-3:30pm Mon-Sat) The good-value lunch menu at this no-frills café situated above a busy market parade changes daily. There are some excellent Middle Eastern and Mediterranean dishes, from falafel to good ol' kebabs.

Lunchería Doña Agapita (La Cruz a Miguelacho; cachapas $1.25-3; 7am-7pm Mon-Sat) Excellent cachapa with ham and/or cheese can be had at this tiny no-nonsense spot off Plaza La Candelaria.

Restaurant Beirut (☎ 545-9367; Salvador de León a Socorrás; snacks & cakes $1.50-3, 2-course menú $3; 7am-6pm Mon-Sat) For a quick no-frills caffeine stop or good quality Arabic food with a Lebanese twist, this informal place does the trick.

Restaurant El Coyuco (☎ 572-9624; Av Urdaneta, Platanal a Candilito; mains $3-7; 9am-noon) Budget place for chicken and parrillas (mixed grill).

MID-RANGE & TOP END

Padre Sierra (☎ 482-9050; La Bolsa a Padre Sierra 18; mains $6-12; 7am-10:30pm) This bright and relatively swish option makes a good escape from the bustle of stalls outside. It offers extremely attentive service, and the long menu includes a bit of everything, including local fish and meat dishes plus pizza.

Café del Sacro (☎ 861-5814; Museo Sacro de Caracas, Plaza Bolívar; mains $6-13; noon-3pm Tue-Fri) Surely the best spot to escape the city rush, catch your breath and enjoy some home-style salads and sandwiches, washed down by a great espresso. It's situated in the serene open-air courtyard of Museo Sacro (p64), which once housed a cemetery – but don't let a couple of gravestones put you off your lunch!

Restaurant Les Grisons (☎ 564-2111; Plaza Catedral Hotel, Plaza Bolívar; mains $3-10; 8am-10pm Mon-Fri) You can sit with the whole plaza at your feet at this roof-top hotel restaurant. Its exalted position catches the breeze nicely, and the open-fronted terrace is strewn with trailing plants. A menu includes both local and international dishes, and some Swiss specialties also creep in. See p77 for accommodations here.

Tasca La Carabela (☎ 578-3020; Av Urdaneta, Esq Urupal; mains $9-14; 11am-late Mon-Sat;) No-holds-barred on the salty-dog decor here; sausages and hams hang from the rafters and one whole wall is filled with a protuberant ship relief that dominates the bustling little tasca. Squid dishes are recommended.

Casa Farruco (☎ 572-9343; Peligro a Puente República; mains $6-14; 11am-midnight;) This atmospheric old Spanish restaurant lies behind striking iron doors on Este 2. Within, it has a split personality – a rowdy bar and restaurant downstairs packed with local color and action, while upstairs there's a more tranquil ambience for family dining.

Tasca La Tertulia (☎ 572-9757; Alcabala a Urupal; mains $9-13; noon-11pm;) There's a dark, clandestine air as you enter the bar area of this two-level restaurant. It's lighter upstairs, where a large dining area has windows painted with crustaceans and other salty offerings. It offers a huge menu of seafood dishes, plus tapas and desserts.

Tasca Mallorca (☎ 572-5974; Alcabala a Puente Anauco; mains $7-13; ☯ 11am-11pm Mon-Sat; ☒) Another old tasca filled with character.

Sabana Grande & Around   Map p68

The Sabana Grande area boasts enough restaurants, cafés and snack bars to suit any taste, though with a particularly strong selection for budgeteers. Av Francisco Solano is the area's major culinary artery.

BUDGET

Centro de Comida Rápida Plaza Broadway (Blvd de Sabana Grande, Chacaíto; ☯ 11am-8:30pm) This budget food court features a collection of fast-food outlets serving everything from pizza to Chinese fried rice.

Centro Comercial El Recreo (Av Casanova, Sabana Grande; ☯ 10am-8pm) There is an upmarket food court in this flashy shopping center (see Shopping p89) – frequented by the well-heeled youth of the city.

Restaurant Da Marcelo (☎ 762-1451; Calle Coromoto, Sabana Grande; mains $3-5.50; ☯ 11:30am-3pm Mon-Fri) For quality Italian fare at the lower end of the price scale, check this unpretentious place hidden down a quiet street.

Restaurant El Arabito (☎ 761-0887; Av Casanova, Sabana Grande; snacks $1-2; ☯ 9am-9pm) This is the place for great Middle Eastern fast food, including tabbouleh, falafel and mouthwatering Arabian sweets.

Pastelería Heladería La Poma (☎ 762-4922; Blvd de Sabana Grande, Sabana Grande; ice-cream $1.25-2, cakes $0.60-1.50; ☯ 7am-10pm) This tempting cake shop has some of the best ice-cream and creative high-calorie pastries in Sabana Grande.

Restaurant Vegetariano Sabas Nieves (☎ 763-6712; Calle Pascual Navarro 12, Sabana Grande; buffet $3.25; ☯ 8am-6pm Mon-Fri, 8am-4pm Sat) The set menús change daily at this homely vegetarian spot. It serves great veggie _hallacas_ (maize dough and vegetables steamed in banana leaves) for $2 from September to December.

El Gourmet Vegetariano (☎ 730-7490; Av Los Jardines, La Campiña; buffet $4; ☯ 11:30am-2:30pm Mon-Fri; ☒) Tucked away one block north of Av Libertador is this bastion of vegetarian cooking. This place has been serving appetizing vegetarian buffets for half a century.

El Chalet Vegetariano (☎ 761-1658; Calle Los Manguitos, Sabana Grande; 3-course menú $3.25; ☯ 11am-3pm

---

> ### THE AUTHOR'S CHOICE   X
>
> **Gran Café** (Map p68; ☎ 763-1493; Blvd de Sabana Grande, Sabana Grande; 2-course menú $4.25; ☯ 6am-11pm Mon-Fri) Gran Café is an open-air café right in the thick of a bustling street market, alive with sharp-eyed urchins and energetic haggling. It is the perfect spot for people-watching or taking a breather over a coffee, pastry or meal-to-go.

Mon-Sat) Home-cooked vegetarian fare served in a cute, old chalet-style building near Hotel Plaza Palace.

MID-RANGE

Restaurant Urrutia (☎ 763-0448; Av Francisco Solano, Sabana Grande; mains $6-19; ☯ noon-11pm Mon-Sat, noon-5pm Sun; ☒) Situated in an unusual round building with curved dining areas and a slanting ceiling, Urrutia is one of the best Basque restaurants around. It has a bustling atmosphere full of business people relaxing over a meal, and its menu also includes a good list of _pasapalos_ (finger food).

Tasca Rias Gallegas (☎ 763-0575; Av Francisco Solano, Sabana Grande; mains $5-7; ☯ 11am-11pm) This is a delightful Spanish tasca with a horse-shoe-shaped bar, colourful tiles lining the walls and lines of arched windows. It's always brimming with lunching _caraqueños_.

Ristorante Da Guido (☎ 763-0937; Av Francisco Solano, Sabana Grande; mains $4.50-7; ☯ noon-9:30pm) Another old favorite for lovers of Italian food, Da Guido has a dark and mellow atmosphere, locked away up a creaky staircase and enclosed by dark murals, low curved ceilings, wooden fittings, and tiny stained-glass windows.

Pizzería Prosciutto (☎ 761-7449 ext 4025; Hotel Gran Meliá Caracas, Av Casanova, Sabana Grande; mains $7-14; ☯ noon-5pm) Posh pizza in flash surroundings. See p79 for accommodations.

Las Cancelas (☎ 763-6666; Calle de Bello Monte, Sabana Grande; 3-course menú $3.25, paella for two $13-15; ☯ 11:30am-11:30pm) Classic Spanish tasca with an extraordinarily long bar and some of the better paellas in town.

Las Mercedes   Map p80

Eating out is a passion for _caraqueños_, and nowhere else is that more obvious than in the fashionable dining district of Las

Mercedes. Competition here is fierce, with about a hundred international-style restaurants, bars and cafés closely packed into its streets. The zone's international flavor is even echoed by its streets, which sport names such as Calle Paris and Calle New York.

BUDGET

Restaurant Real Past (☎ 993-6702; Av Río de Janeiro; mains $2-5) While most restaurants in the area cater to a more affluent clientele, Real Past has some of the cheapest and most appetizing pasta and pizza around, though none of the swanky setting.

Doña Caraotica (☎ 993-0116; Av Principal de Las Mercedes; mains $3-7; ☺ 24hr) Cheap all-night *arepera* with every topping imaginable.

Pollo en Brasas Los Riviera (☎ 993-3607; Calle París; half-chicken and fries $3.50) Cheap-and-cheerful option for spit-roasted chicken and grills.

MID-RANGE & TOP END

Taiko (☎ 993-5647; Av La Trinidad; mains $6-18; ☺ noon-11pm Mon-Thu, 12:30pm-midnight Fri-Sun; ✺) One of the first sushi restaurants in Caracas, Taiko continues as a favorite for its haute cuisine of sushi in a super-swish minimalist setting.

Aranjuez (☎ 993-1326; Calle Madrid; parrillas $6-11; ☺ noon-11:30pm Mon-Sat, noon-10pm Sun; ✺) Other than a few token salads, this homely, old-style restaurant is totally dedicated to its *parrillas*, particularly its thick charcoal-grilled steaks. The ranch-style interior has a large bar and low wooden ceiling, and is usually buzzing with families and awash with the smell of sizzling steak.

La Romanissima (☎ 993-3334; Calle New York; mains $4.50-10; ☺ noon-11pm Mon-Sat, noon-5pm Sun; ✺) A small romantic location perfect for an evening tête-á-tête, La Romanissima serves quality home-style Italian pasta and risottos in a mellow, low-lit environment.

Avanti (☎ 993-7222; Av Principal de Las Mercedes; mains $5-10; ☺ 11am-midnight; ✺) Pizza and pasta are the specialties in this curvy, modern building. There's a castle-like playground for kids on the roof, and the concrete park outside rattles to the sounds of skateboard stunts.

El Granjero del Este (☎ 991-6619; Av Rio de Janeiro; mains $3-8.50; ☺ 24hr) For an all-night restaurant, El Granjero does a good job of avoiding

the ambience of a greasy-spoon café. It has a pleasant courtyard and fountain surrounded by tables, an open-fronted *arepa* counter, and a long menu offering good *parrillas*.

La Castañuela (☎ 992-6668; Av La Trinidad; mains $8-19; ☺ 11:30am-midnight; ✺) This decorative *tasca* is as much a feast for the eyes as the belly, smothered with colorful Andalucian-style tiling and pebbled walls. The interior is less extravagant, but it's always busy with people savoring its excellent Spanish seafood dishes. There's live music at weekends.

Other recommendations:

Maute Grill (☎ 991-5662; Av Rio de Janeiro; parrillas $6-10; ☺ noon-midnight; ✺) Delicious artery-clogging mixed grills heralded by a neon pair of horns outside.

Le Gourmet (☎ 909-7111 ext 7220; Tamanaco Inter-Continental Caracas; mains $9-15; ☺ noon-3pm & 7:30-11:30pm Mon-Fri, 7:30pm-11:30pm Sat; ✺) This restaurant inside the hotel Tamanaco InterContinental (p79) offers excellent French cooking.

Altamira & Around   Map p70

Altamira is another trendy area dotted with posh restaurants, hip cafés, discos and bars, along with its neighboring suburbs of La Castellana and Los Palos Grandes.

BUDGET

Restaurant El Presidente (3a Av, Los Palos Grandes; 3-course menú $5; ☺ 11:30am-3pm & 6-9pm Mon-Fri) This simple café is one of the few cheap options in Altamira, and is good for its home-style set-lunch menus.

La Ghiringhella Café & Deli (☎ 286-2501; Av Andrés Bello at 4a Transversal, Los Palos Grandes; breakfasts & snacks $1-2; ☺ 8am-6pm) Hidden from the road by a wall of palms and ferns, this shady,

---

THE AUTHOR'S CHOICE

Restaurant La Estancia (Map p70; ☎ 261-4223; Principal de la Castellana at Calle Urdaneta, La Castellana; parrillas $8-12; ☺ noon-midnight Mon-Sat, noon-11pm Sun) You mustn't leave Venezuela without indulging in one of the country's fabulous steaks. Famous for its grilled meats of every cut and style, La Estancia is one of the best spots in Caracas for meat-lovers. It's situated in a hacienda-style building filled with dark wooden ceilings and an overabundance of smartly dressed waiters.

open-air café is a great place for a *comida criolla* (typical Venezuelan cuisine) or an international breakfast of your choice.

El Mundo del Pollo (Av Mohedano, La Castellana; half-chicken & fries $3; 🕐 noon-midnight; ❌) You can also get a good feed without dipping too deeply into your wallet at this vast, cheerful fast-food restaurant.

Pollo en Brasas El Coyuco (☎ 286-0603; 3a Transversal, Los Palos Grandes; chicken & fries $4-5; 🕐 noon-10pm) Economical chicken-and-fries spot – look for the faux log-cabin front.

Plaza's Automercado (Centro Comercial Centro Plaza, Los Palos Grandes; 🕐 8am-9pm Mon-Sat, 8am-6pm Sun) Grocery shopping for the self-sufficient.

Also recommended is **Gran Pizzería El León** (see p86).

MID-RANGE & TOP END

Fritz & Franz (☎ 265-5724; Av San Juan Bosco at 3a Transversal, Altamira; mains $4.50-7; 🕐 noon-10:30pm Tue-Sat, noon-9pm Sun; ❌) Yep, you guessed right – this is a German restaurant with sausages galore, plus everything from goulash to sauerkraut. The mixed decor includes plenty of beer paraphernalia and a collection of German car-license plates.

El Barquero (☎ 261-4645; Av Luis Roche at 5a Transversal, Altamira; seafood $6-13; 🕐 noon-1am; ❌) Always busy with faithful clientele, El Barquero (the boatman) has been serving up a vast menu of excellent fish and seafood dishes for many a year. It has a good list of whiskey varieties to boot.

El Gran Charolais (☎ 263-5062; Av Principal de la Castellana, La Castellana; parrillas $8-12; 🕐 11:30am-midnight; ❌) There ain't much for vegetarians here: the huge model bull over the dark doorway proclaims a meat-lover's heaven, and as you walk through the dark entrance you'll be greeted by platters filled with hunks of temptingly juicy steak from which to choose your grill.

Other recommendations:

Spizzico (☎ 267-8820; Av Principal de la Castellana, La Castellana; snacks $1.50-3; pizza $5-9; 🕐 bakery from 7am, restaurant noon-midnight; ❌) Part self-service café, part pizzeria and with a bakery on the premises for just-out-of-the-oven freshness all day.

Chez Wong (☎ 226-5015; Plaza La Castellana, La Castellana; mains $9-13; 🕐 noon-midnight Mon-Sat, noon-8pm Sun; ❌) Chinese fare with Venezuelan influence.

Le Petit Bistrot de Jacques (☎ 263-8695; Av San Felipe, La Castellana; mains $6-12; 🕐 noon-10pm Mon-Sat) Authentic old-style French bistro.

THE AUTHOR'S CHOICE

Benihana (Map p70; ☎ 263-5183; Av San Juan de Bosco at 5a Transversal, Altamira; mains $9-16; ☎ noon-11pm Mon-Sat, noon-10pm Sun; ❌) Benihana deals in Caracas' three favorite S's: sushi, steak and seafood, but sushi is still the raison d'être of this trendy restaurant which has been instrumental in the rocketing popularity of Japanese food in the city. It's a good place to rub shoulders with well-heeled young *caraqueños* (inhabitants of Caracas).

El Hatillo ✗ COLOMBIA

The relatively recent explosion of eating outlets in the colonial village of El Hatillo means you can find almost any far-flung cuisine here, be it German, Thai or good ol' Venezuelan *comida criolla*.

Dulces Criollos (Plaza Bolívar; snacks $2-4; 🕐 10am-9pm) The sweet-toothed will have a field day in this candy shop on the plaza, which sells dozens of exotic and local fancies.

Betty Cróquer (☎ 961-4269; Av Bolívar; mains $6-10; 🕐 noon-midnight) This rooftop restaurant is packed with film-star paraphernalia and waxworks. Be sure to try the creamy rice drink Chicha Cróquer on the ground floor too.

La Gorda (☎ 963-7476; Calle Santa Rosalia 32; mains $5-8; 🕐 noon-3pm Mon-Fri, 8:30am-5pm Sat & Sun) La Gorda (literally, 'the fat woman') has been serving traditional Venezuelan dishes for decades.

Mauricio's (☎ 963-0789; 2nd fl, Los Aleros; fondue for two $19-26; 🕐 noon-midnight Tue-Sun) Swiss fondue restaurant with a view over the plaza.

DRINKING

For many, the Caracas nightlife is the best reason to come to the city at all. At the weekend, beautiful young things clad in designer labels swarm to Las Mercedes, El Rosal, Altamira and La Castellana. Check out the excellent website www.rumbacaracas.com (in Spanish) for up-to-the-minute trends, or get hold of the free monthly pamphlet distributed in bars and clubs.

Most bars open around 7pm but really liven up after 11pm, while clubs often open their doors later still. The days when most *caraqueños* come out to play are Thursday,

CARACAS

Friday and Saturday when you can expect the *rumba* (party) to roll till daybreak.

Bars & Pubs

Gran Pizzería El León (Map p70; ☎ 263-6014; Plaza La Castellana; ☼ daily) This is the most famous beer-guzzling spot in Caracas – mostly thanks to its cheap prices and good pizza. It's an open-air affair on a vast terrace below towering buildings. At the weekend, you'll find a large college crowd jovially debating over row upon row of beer bottles.

Greenwich Pub (Map p70; ☎ 267-1760; Av Sur de Altamira at José Felix Sosa, Altamira Sur; ☼ daily) This tiny, atmospheric English pub has gutsy rock bands and a variety of beer and *pasapalos* (finger food). Expect standing-room only when bands play.

Birras Pub & Café (Map p80; ☎ 992-4813; Av Principal de Las Mercedes at Av Valle Arribe; ☼ daily) Appropriately named with the Italian word for beer *(birras)*, this stubbornly rough-around-the-edges pavement bar has its priorities right, boasting the cheapest beers around, plus an emergency fridge devoted to energy drinks to keep the *rumba* rolling.

Boo Café (Map p80; ☎ 992-9354; Calle Londres at Calle New York, Las Mercedes; ☼ 5pm-late) This tiny bar is popular for its personable service and low prices. Soaking up some of the alcohol with the excellent food on offer is recommended.

Wassup (Map p80; ☎ 991-0686; Calle New York, Las Mercedes) This youthful American-style bar-cum-restaurant wins its numerous clientele through canny promotions on beer and a constantly changing entertainment program, with everything from joke competitions to 'daring parties.'

Tsunami (Map p80; ☎ 824-8399; Av Principal de Las Mercedes, Las Mercedes; ☼ 5pm-late Tue-Sun) Local bar flies gravitate toward this sharply triangular open-air bar, which has both open-air and indoor seating, plus a dance floor for when the mood takes you. Free entry and cheap beer before midnight.

Auyama Rumba (Map p80; ☎ 991-9489; Calle Londres, Las Mercedes; ☼ 5pm-late) This large, popular hangout has live rock bands and low prices to keep your thirst whetted.

Transnocho Lounge (Map p80; ☎ 993-1325; Edificio Itaca, Centro Comercial Paseo de Las Mercedes, Las Mercedes; ☼ Thu-Sun) Minimalist bar with low-key funk music and mirrored ceiling. Frequented by theater-goers.

Nightclubs

The hedonistic clubs of Caracas bear testament to the Venezuelans' religious devotion to having a good time. Most clubs open from Tuesday to Saturday, but the real action cranks from Thursday to Saturday after midnight. *Caraqueños* are famed for their inexhaustible energy, so don't plan on leaving before dawn.

The best areas for clubbing are the same as for bars (see earlier), and most bars also bring on the dancing when the beer has been flowing for long enough. The music generally hops between Latin Rock, alternative chillout, trance and plenty of Caribbean rhythms.

Cover charges usually include the cost of a few beers. Most discos won't let you in with sneakers or a T-shirt, so dress to impress.

Masai (Map p80; ☎ 265-4676; Centro Comercial San Ignacio, La Castellana; ☼ 11pm-late Mon-Sat) The resident DJ at this slick little bar-cum-club churns out all manner of danceable music from merengue to trance. There's more room to manoeuvre upstairs in a mellow seating area lit by lava lamps, and out on the outdoor terrace where the overheated crowd spills out to cool down.

Kazoo (Map p80; ☎ 993-3094; Av Principal de Las Mercedes, Las Mercedes; cover $6; ☼ 10pm-late Thu-Sat) The most fashionable *discoteca* (disco) in Las Mercedes, Kazoo plays a winning mix of electronic music and mainstream. It's a large, multilevel joint with a well-stocked bar, pool table and all the bells and whistles.

THE AUTHOR'S CHOICE

Loft (Map p80; ☎ 267-8998; Nivel Terraza, Centro Comercial San Ignacio, La Castellana; ☼ Tue-Sat) Easily the most spectacular club in the city, Loft sits high on the top of a multilayer shopping mall and boasts a retractable roof so you can party in the open air. Walkways above the dancefloor even divide into intimate 'floating' booths where nothing will lie between you and the stars. Unsurprisingly, the club attracts the cream of suave, young *caraqueños* (inhabitants of Caracas), and its sleek design and mellow chillout music add to the air of sophistication. Bring a heavily lined wallet and pray that it doesn't rain.

Ravens (Map p80; ☎ 993-1674; Calle Londres at Calle New York, Las Mercedes; ☺ 6pm-late Wed-Sat) Guest DJs each day produce a freestyle mix of musical choice at this fashionably swish choice built on several overlapping levels. Good deals on beer are another bonus.

Voga Bar (Map p80; ☎ 993-8053; Av La Trinidad at Madrid, Las Mercedes; ☺ 7pm-late Tue-Sat) Characterized by a kooky mixture of fake fur, drapes and oriental finery, this is another of the trendiest spots of the moment. There are live bands with retro music at weekends.

Gay & Lesbian Venues

Caracas has by far the most open (and the wildest) gay community in what is still a relatively conservative country. The local term to keep an eye out for is *'en ambiente.'* For more venues, check the websites www .republicagay.com, www.vengay.com and www.rumbacaracas.com (all in Spanish).

Brighton's (Map p70; ☎ 267-8613; Centro Comercial Bello Campo, Av Principal de Bello Campo, Bello Campo; ☺ Mon-Sat) This executive gay café-cum-bar close to Altamira has a cool, welcoming atmosphere as well as good international food and no-holds-barred company. If you stay late at the weekend, strippers, drag shows or other surprises are guaranteed. Thursday night belongs to the girls.

La Cotorra (Map p80; ☎ 992-0608; Centro Comercial Paseo Las Mercedes, Las Mercedes; ☺ 11pm-late) An old faithful on the Caracas scene, this was one of the first gay bars in the city. It's a dark, old-style pub with a barricaded door and a conspiratorial air. To find it, take the escalators one level up, turn right into the car park, then left along the perimeter. Once you've limbered up here, you can always go downstairs to the more youthful Zenon.

Zenon (Map p80; ☎ 993-8004; www.vengay.com in Spanish; Nivel Cine, Centro Comercial Paseo Las Mercedes, Las Mercedes; cover $6; ☺ 11pm-5am Thu-Sat) Expect a vanguard, open-minded spot behind the forbidding black door of this new, extravagant bar. It's on the cinema level in the car park, to the right and up a ramp – look for the purple neon lighting.

Tasca Pullman (Map p68; ☎ 761-1112; Edificio Ovidio, Av Francisco Solano, Sabana Grande; ☺ daily) This is one of the most frequented gay bars in Sabana Grande. Take care in the surrounding area after dark.

Copa's Dancing Bar (Map p80; ☎ 951-3947; Torre Taeca, Calle Guaicaipuro, El Rosal; ☺ Wed-Sat) Great spot for gays and lesbians alike, with a large, well-stocked bar, live DJs and risqué shows for the weekend crowd.

ENTERTAINMENT

The Sunday edition of *El Universal* carries a 'what's on' section called the 'Guía de la Ciudad.' It gives brief descriptions of selected upcoming events including music, theater, cinema and exhibitions.

Live Music

El Maní es Así (Map p68; ☎ 763-6671; Av Francisco Solano López at Calle El Cristo, Sabana Grande; ☺ Tue-Sun) This is one of the city's longest-standing and hottest salsa spots, where everything revolves around the dance floor and the live salsa bands. So what are you waiting for – grab a partner! Take taxis after dark as the area is not safe.

Juan Sebastián Bar (Map p80; ☎ 951-5575; Av Venezuela at Calle Mohedano, El Rosal; ☺ 5pm-2am Mon-Sat) A long-time stronghold of jazz in Caracas, Juan Sebastián Bar is still churning out the best after almost 30 years.

Little Rock Café (Map p68; ☎ 267-8337; 6a Av, Altamira; ☺ noon-2am) It's difficult to miss this wacky, cathedral-style den with a whirling sun motif in its center and a psychedelic motorcycle on top. It features rock bands at the weekend, and its stained-glass windows exalt not saints but rock icons like Jimi Hendrix and Jerry Lee Lewis. There's also a pool table, burgers and TexMex food on offer.

El Solar del Vino (Map p70; ☎ 266-2873; Av Blandín at Av El Avila, La Castellana; ☺ 4pm-3am Mon-Sat) This bustling tasca has live music (usually Caribbean salsa and other Caribbean rhythms) after 6pm from Wednesday to Saturday.

See also Classical Music & Ballet p88.

Cinemas

Films are generally shown with the original soundtrack and Spanish subtitles. Programs are listed in the local daily press (including the *Daily Journal*). A movie ticket costs $3 to $6.

The following cinemas show blockbuster international films:

Cines Unidos Sambil (Map p70; ☎ 709-7777; Centro Sambil, Av Libertador, Chacao)

El Recreo Cinex (Map p68; ☎ 200-2463; Centro Comercial El Recreo, Calle El Recreo, Sabana Grande)

CARACAS

For a mixture of art-house and mainstream films, also check the following:

Ateneo de Caracas (Map pp62-3; ☎ 573-4400; Bellas Artes) See p69 for more details.

Cinemateca Nacional (Map pp62-3; ☎ 576-1491; Galería de Arte Nacional, Bellas Artes)

Fundación Celarg (Map p70; ☎ 285-2721; Casa de Rómulo Gallegos, Av Luis Roche, Altamira)

Teatro Transnocho Cultural (Map p80; ☎ 993-1910; www.transnochocultural.com; Centro Comercial, Paseo Las Mercedes; tickets $9; (P))

Sports

Estadio de Béisbol (Baseball Stadium; Map p68; metro Ciudad Universitaria) *Béisbol* (baseball) is the local sporting obsession. Professional-league games are played from October to February at this stadium on the grounds of the Universidad Central de Venezuela. Tickets should be bought here early in the morning, particularly for games with the Leones de Caracas (Caracas Lions; www .leones.com).

Estadio Olimpico (Map p68; metro Ciudad Universitaria) This neighboring sports complex hosts major soccer matches between December and March, often on Saturday evenings.

Hipódromo La Rinconada (Map pp56-7; ☎ 681-9448) Caracas' excellent horse-racing track features racing on Saturday and Sunday afternoons starting at 1pm. The track is 6km southwest of the center, off the Autopista del Valle.

Theater

If you fancy catching a show, there are a dozen regular theaters in the city. They are usually open from Wednesday to Sunday, but some have performances only on weekends. Tickets cost between $3 and $10. If you visit during Caracas' Festival Internacional de Teatro in March/April of even-numbered years, you'll have a chance to see some of the best theater productions from Latin America and beyond. Festival performances are staged at theaters around the city.

Teatro Teresa Carreño (Map pp62-3; ☎ 800-673-7200; www.teatroteresacarreno.com; Complejo Cultural Teresa Carreño, Av México, Parque Los Caobos) and the Ateneo de Caracas (p69) almost always have something interesting showing, and you can see the productions of Rajatabla – Venezuela's best-known theater company – and La Compañía Nacional de Teatro.

Also check the schedules of the following:

Teatro Nacional (Map pp62-3; ☎ 484-5956; Av Lecuna)

Teatro Trasnocho Cultural (Map p80; ☎ 993-1910; www.trasnochocultural.com; Centro Comercial Paseo Las Mercedes, Las Mercedes) A hip new entertainment venue.

Classical Music & Ballet

The city's major stage for concerts and ballet is **Complejo Cultural Teresa Carreño** (p69). Also check the program of **Aula Magna** (☎ 605-4516; Universidad Central de Venezuela), which hosts performances by the symphony orchestra, usually on Sunday morning. Tickets can be bought from the Aula's ticket office directly before the concerts.

Other places that stage concerts include the Ateneo de Caracas (p69), Museo Sacro de Caracas (p64), Museo del Teclado (p69), Quinta Anauco (p67) and Centro Venezolano Americano (p58).

SHOPPING

Caraqueños adore shopping, and some don't stop until they drop or run out of money. La Candelaria, Sabana Grande, Chacaíto, Chacao and the historic center, are all tightly packed with stores, malls, stalls and ambulant vendors. There has also been an explosion of informal outdoor trading on the streets and in markets, which offer CDs, DVDs, clothes and everyday products at a fraction of shop prices.

Shopping Malls

To fully appreciate the national love affair with shopping, you need only visit a downtown shopping mall. Caracas has dozens and dozens of huge shopping malls, and new ones just keep popping up. The best place to experience Venezuelan's boutique lifestyle and apparently incurable obsession with shoe shops is **Centro Sambil** (Map p70; ☎ 267-9302; Av Libertador, Chacao; ⟨Y⟩ 9am-9pm, restaurants & cinema later; (P)). This mall opened in 1998, and since then has been packed with shoppers seven days a week. In fact, it's so popular that the powers that be had to introduce street barriers outside to control the crowds. It's hard to believe that this is a country in severe economic strife as you walk around the glitzy parades showcasing the latest designer trends and must-buys. Touted as South America's largest shopping mall, this vast five-level establishment comes complete with an aquarium, cyber-cafés, two multiplex cinemas, pool tables, video games, roof-top amphitheater, food court and a waterfall incorporated into the front wall of the building. But good luck finding them all: it's easy to get lost!

Other recommendations:

Centro Ciudad Comercial Tamanaco (Map p80; Autopista Francisco Fajardo, Chuao; P) Commonly known as CCCT, this older mall is yet another of the largest and most popular malls.

Centro Comercial Centro Plaza (Map p70; Av Francisco de Miranda, Los Palos Grandes; P)

Centro Comercial Chacaíto (Map p68; Plaza Chacaíto, Chacaíto)

Centro Comercial Concresa (Map pp56-7; Prados del Este; P) Located 2km south of Las Mercedes.

Centro Comercial El Recreo (Map p68; ☎ 761-2740; Av Casanova; ☼ 10am-8pm) Consistently draws crowds in Sabana Grande.

Centro Comercial Paseo Las Mercedes (Map p80; Av Principal de Las Mercedes, Las Mercedes; P)

Centro Comercial San Ignacio (Map p80 ☎ 263-0772; Av Blandín, La Castellana; ☼ 10am-8pm; P) Another flashy, exclusive mall.

Centro Lido (Map p80; Av Francisco de Miranda, El Rosal; P)

Markets

Caracas has a number of bustling markets, but don't expect picture-postcard South American bazaars full of traditionally dressed Indians. City markets mostly sell everyday products such as clothing, shoes, toiletries, watches and stationery. Some deal in food, including fruits and vegetables.

One of the most central markets is the shabby **Mercado de La Hoyada** (Map pp62-3; Av Fuerzas Armadas), near the metro station of the same name. A few blocks to the west is another **outdoor market** (Map pp62-3; Plaza Diego Ibarra), which has actually invaded – and now occupies – the plaza. Outside the center are **Mercado Guaicaipuro** (Map pp62-3; Av Andrés Bello, Sarria), and the **Mercado Chacao** (Map p80; 3 Calle, Chacao), which is three blocks north of the Chacao metro station.

Clothing & Footwear

Central markets are the cheapest areas to hunt for clothes and shoes. Alternatively, the area just east of Plaza Bolívar boasts a bewildering wealth of *zapaterías* (shoe shops) – indeed, nearly every third shop

is a one – confirming the susp[...] Venezuelans are shoe-crazy. T[...] evard of Sabana Grande is also li[...] economical stores and shopping m[...]. For up-to-the-minute fashions, comb some of the large shopping malls, particularly Centro Sambil and CCCT.

Crafts

To pick up those last-minute hammocks, papier-mâché devil masks or stuffed piran-has, check out the biggest craft shop of them all at **Hannsi** (☎ 963-5577; www.hannsi.com .ve in Spanish; Calle Bolívar 12; ☼ 9am-7pm Mon-Sat, 10:30am-7:30pm Sun), in El Hatillo (p73). The narrow, winding streets around Hannsi also house numerous high-quality craft stores, so take your time to dip into them all.

If you don't have time to get to El Hatillo, try the offerings at central **Maquita** (Map pp62-3; ☎ 576-8439; tiendamaquita@cantv.net; Tracabordo a Miguelacho 112, La Candelaria; ☼ 9:30am-7pm Mon-Sat), which has very good woodcarvings.

In the east, take a look at the family-run **Artesanía Altamira** (Map p70; ☎ 266-4727; Av Luis Roche, Altamira Sur; ☼ 9am-4pm Mon-Fri, 9am-1pm Sat), which has an assortment of hammocks and figurines, plus a veritable profusion of basket work. Also near Altamira, a high-quality store for carved furniture and wooden bowls is **Casa Curaba** (Map p70; ☎ 283-1857; Av Andrés Bello, Los Palos Grandes). And a focus on upmarket crafts from the Orinoco as well as other areas can be found in Las Mercedes at **Sotavento** (Map p80; ☎ 993-0974; Calle California at Jalisco).

On Sunday, artisans and artists set up stalls in front of the **Galería de Arte Nacional** (p69). This can be a great place to pick up bracelets, necklaces and popular crafts. Inside the gallery, there is also a pricier modern art and crafts store with some exquisite but expensive wares.

Jewelry

Venezuela is a major gold producer, so keen-eyed travelers can pick up some tempting bargains. The nucleus of Caracas' gold market is the legendary central **Edificio La Francia** (Map pp62-3; Plaza Bolívar; ☼ 9am-5pm Mon-Fri, 9am-2:30pm Sat), which boasts 10 stories of jewelry shops – about 100 shops in all. It's usually brimming with eager shoppers sporting a glint in their eye, and the streets outside ring with the cries of *compro oro*, *compro oro* (I buy gold, I buy gold). If you can't find what you want in La Francia, try the **Minicentro París** (Map pp62-3; Plaza Bolívar) or the **Multicentro Capitolio** (Map pp62-3; Plaza Bolívar), both just a few steps away.

Camping & Outdoor Equipment
Imported camping and trekking gear is increasingly available but expensive, while locally produced gear is cheaper and often of decent quality. Gas canisters for common camping stoves are easy to come by.

Corporación Verotex (Map p68; ☎ 951-3670; 2nd fl, Centro Comercial Arta, No 2-6, Plaza Chacaíto; ☽ 2pm-6pm Mon, 10am-1pm & 2-6pm Tue-Fri, 10am-2pm Sat) has a reasonable choice of camping, trekking and mountaineering equipment and is one of the cheapest retailers around. If it's shut, try the camping section in **Beco** (Map p68; ☎ 237-5011; Plaza Chacaíto; ☽ 8am-8pm) across the street, which has fuel, tents and other equipment on the 1st floor.

Even cheaper is **Loby** (Map pp56-7; ☎ 414-5930; Ground fl, Quinta Nenena, No 6, Calle Caurimare, Colinas de Bello Monte; ☽ 9am-5pm Mon-Fri), which makes backpacks, sleeping bags and high-mountain clothing, and imports mountaineering gear. It's also a great source of information on mountain guides.

GETTING THERE & AWAY
Air
The **Aeropuerto Internacional 'Simón Bolívar'** (www.aeropuerto-maiquetia.com.ve in Spanish) is in Maiquetía, near the port of La Guaira on the Caribbean coast, 26km from central Caracas. It's linked to the city by a freeway that cuts through the coastal mountain range with three tunnels, one as long as 2km. The airport has two terminals, one for international and the other for domestic flights, separated by 400m. There's a free shuttle service between the terminals.

The **international terminal** (☎ 303-1526) has a range of facilities, including a tourist office, car rental desks, three or four *casas de cambio*, a bank, three ATMs, post and telephone offices, a restaurant, several cafés, snack bars and a bunch of travel agencies. It even has a chapel, but at the time of writing lacked a left-luggage office (however one was planned for the future). Note that arriving passengers are not allowed to take luggage trolleys beyond the customs area.

The **domestic terminal** (☎ 303-1403) doesn't have money-changing facilities, but does have a tourist office called **Inatur** (☎ 355-1191; ☽ 7am-8pm), a cybercafé and a dozen desks for car rental companies, domestic airlines and tour operators, plus fast-food outlets.

For a list of international flight connections, see p335. For domestic connections and airline offices in Caracas, see p338. The fares for domestic flights given in the table below were a rough approximate at the time of research. Prices will vary depending on the airline, and are also subject to change.

DOMESTIC FLIGHTS & FARES
Destination	Single Airfare
Barcelona	$50-71
Barinas	$47-73
Barquisimeto	$48-68
Carúpano	$65-75
Ciudad Bolívar	$45-77
Coro	$54-68
Cumaná	$48-72
Las Piedras	$56-68
Maracaibo	$48-85
Maturín	$46-59
Mérida	$48-75
Porlamar	$30-82
Puerto Ayacucho	$68-93
Puerto Ordaz	$53-86
San Antonio del Táchira	$46-90
Valera	$61-78
Valencia	$34-50

At the time of writing, the international airport tax was a hefty $30 plus a further $13 departure tax. Domestic departures also incurred a $4.80 tax. Depending on the airline, taxes may be included in your ticket price so it's always worth checking beforehand. To check for any further increases, see the airport website earlier.

You can change your money upon arrival, but see the boxed text p331 for an explanation of official/black market exchange rates first. There are several *casas de cambio* in the main hall on the ground floor, including Italcambio, which changes cash and traveler's checks. It's open daily until the last flight. There is also a *casa de cambio* before customs, if you don't want to wait. Advances on Visa and MasterCard are given in the **Banco de Venezuela** (Upper Level;

8:30am-3:30pm Mon-Fri). Otherwise try the three ATMs (all on the upper level), but see the boxed text p330 for an explanation of why foreign cards do not always work in Venezuelan ATMs. Note that airport *casas de cambio* do not change bolívares back into foreign currencies.

For budget food, try **Cafetería Mocol** (snacks $1.25-2; 6am-10pm), well hidden on the basement level – look out for the stairs leading down behind the men's bathroom, roughly in the middle of the main hall.

Ignore any individuals who approach you claiming that they are from the tourist office (they're not) and offering help and information; they'll demand a hefty fee for anything they do. The genuine **Inatur office** (355-1060; 8am-midnight) is on the ground floor. To phone from the terminal, buy a phonecard at a newsstand. Maiquetía has the same area code as Caracas, so just dial the local Caracas number.

Boat

La Guaira, the port of Caracas, was affected by the disaster of December 1999 (see p94), but began operating normally again within a year. A ferry sometimes runs to Isa de Margarita from here. You can book tickets at the **Conferry** (Map p68; 709-0000; www.conferry.com in Spanish; Torre Banhorient, Av Casanova, Sabana Grande; 8am-11:30am & 2-5:30pm Mon-Thu, 8:30am-4:30pm Fri) offices, but always check schedules in advance because this ferry only runs when there is sufficient demand (see Isla de Margarita p233). There's no passenger service to Los Roques, only freight boats.

Bus

Caracas now has two modern intercity bus terminals and a central terminal for shorter journeys. The **Terminal La Bandera** (Map pp56-7), 3km south of the center, handles long-distance buses to anywhere in the country's west and southwest. The terminal is just 300m from La Bandera metro station, and you can walk the distance during the day, but take precautions at night when the area becomes unsafe. The terminal has good facilities, including computerized ticket booths, telephones, a **left-luggage office** (1st hr $0.55, per hr thereafter $0.15; 6am-9pm Mon-Sat, 7am-7pm Sun), an **information desk** (693-6607) and a plentiful supply of food outlets.

The city's other bus terminal, the **Terminal de Oriente**, is on the eastern outskirts of Caracas, on the highway to Barcelona, 5km beyond Petare (about 18km from Caracas' city center). It's accessible by numerous local buses from both the city center and Petare. A taxi from Altamira will cost about $4. The terminal features computerized ticket booths and a helpful **information desk** (243-2606). It handles all traffic to the east and southeast of the country. See the following bus table for standard fares and duration.

The upscale **Aeroexpresos Ejecutivos** (Map p70; 226-2364; www.aeroexpresos.com.ve; Av Principal de Bello Campo, Bello Campo) services several major cities including Maracay, Valencia, Barquisimeto, Maracaibo, Maturín and Puerto La Cruz in modern, comfortable buses. It's more expensive than other companies, but justifies it with extra security, air-conditioning, films, on-board toilet and a stewardess serving drinks.

Buses servicing regional destinations (La Guaira, Los Teques, Santa Teresa, Ocumare del Tuy etc) still depart from the chaotic and dirty old central **Nuevo Circo regional bus terminal** (Map pp62-3; Av Lecuna).

BUSES FROM CARACAS TO MAJOR DESTINATIONS

Destination	Distance	Fare	Time
Barcelona	310km	$7-11	5hrs
Barinas	512km	$10-14	8½hrs
Barquisimeto	341km	$7-10	5½hrs
Carúpano	521km	$11-16	8½hrs
Ciudad Bolívar	591km	$11-16	9hrs
Ciudad Guayana	706km	$13-18	10½hrs
Coro	446km	$10-13	7hrs
Cumaná	402km	$9-13	6½hrs
Guanare	427km	$9-13	7hrs
Güiria	663km	$14-19	12hrs
Maracaibo	669km	$13-17	10½hrs
Maracay	109km	$2-4	1½hrs
Maturín	518km	$11-16	8½hrs
Mérida	790km	$13-20	13hrs
Puerto Ayacucho	637km	$16-20	15hrs
Puerto La Cruz	320km	$7-11	5hrs
San Antonio del Táchira	865km	$17-22	14hrs
San Cristóbal	825km	$13-20	13hrs
San Fernando de Apure	398km	$8-12	8hrs
Tucupita	730km	$13-18	11hrs
Valencia	158km	$3-5	2½hrs
Valera	584km	$10-16	9½hrs

Car & Motorcycle

Driving into and out of Caracas is pretty straightforward. The major western access route is the Valencia–Caracas freeway, which enters the city from the south and joins Autopista Francisco Fajardo, the main east–west city artery, next to the Universidad Central de Venezuela. From anywhere in the east, access is by the Barcelona–Caracas freeway, which will take you directly to Av Francisco Fajardo.

To rent a car, make arrangements at home with international car rental companies such as Avis or Hertz. That way you can have a car waiting for you upon arrival. If you fly into Caracas without any previous arrangements, contact car rental companies at the Maiquetía airport. Operators in the international terminal include **Avis** (☎ 355-1190) and **Hertz** (☎ 355-1197), but they can't always provide a car on demand. You'll find more desks of local companies in the domestic terminal. Major rental companies also have desks in the lobbies of top-end hotels. For more information on car rental, see p341.

GETTING AROUND
To/From the Airport

There's a bus service between the Maiquetía airport and Caracas daily from 5:30am until 8pm. Buses are supposed to depart every half-hour, but they usually don't leave until they have enough passengers. In the city, the buses depart until 7pm from Calle Sur 17, directly underneath Av Bolívar, next to Parque Central. Stairs connect the two levels next to the Museo de los Niños; you can also get down to the buses by Calle Sur 17 from Av México (or Av Lecuna). At the airport, buses leave from in front of the domestic terminal. A shuttle bus runs from the international terminal to the domestic.

The bus fare to/from the airport is $1.60 on weekdays and $1.90 at weekends and holidays. It takes 30 to 50 minutes, depending on traffic. If you travel into the city during rush hour, it's faster to get off at the Gato Negro metro station and continue by metro.

The taxi fare from the airport to Caracas depends on which suburb you go to. Sample day fares (6am to 6pm) are to the center ($12) and Altamira ($16). Night tariffs are about 10% higher. The fares from the city

> **AIRPORT SCAMS**
>
> Armed robberies of newly arrived tourists by bogus taxi operators and other individuals offering unsolicited help are sadly becoming a frequent occurence at Maiquetía airport. Do not accept offers of assistance within the arrivals hall, only at the taxi rank or information office. Take licensed taxis with a clearly identifiable number, and if you are offered particularly low fares regard the taxi with suspicion. There is a taxi service using black Ford Explorers found directly outside the arrivals hall that is widely regarded as being the most reliable. Never allow the driver to bring along a second passenger, and never take a taxi that is parked in the airport's general car park rather than the regular taxi rank. Also, if you are expecting a pick-up service by a hotel or tour operator, where possible make a note of the driver's name in advance and check their *cédula* (national ID card) upon arrival.

back to the airport are generally 10% to 30% lower. They shouldn't charge extra for luggage.

Check the correct fare with the tourist office before boarding a taxi to avoid overcharging. Nonetheless, drivers sometimes charge exorbitant prices in the evening, after all the buses are gone, so try to book a flight that arrives reasonably early in the day.

If you only have an overnight stop in Maiquetía, you may prefer to skip the journey into Caracas and stay the night on the coast (see Litoral Central p94).

If you're arriving late at night in Maiquetía, don't venture outside the terminal further than the bus stop and taxi stand (both directly outside the building's doors). Hold-ups at gunpoint have been reported by travelers, and you wouldn't want to lose all your bags right after arriving; see the boxed text above.

Metro

The French-made metro system (www.metro decaracas.com.ve in Spanish) is the major means of getting around Caracas. It's fast, easy to use, clean and cheap, and it provides access to most major city attractions.

The metro has three lines, with a total length of 44km and 39 stations. The longest line, No 1, goes east–west all the way along the city axis. Line No 2 leads from the center southwest to the distant suburb of Caricuao and the zoo. The newest and shortest line, No 3, runs from Plaza Venezuela, past the university and southwest to El Valle. More lines are also planned for the future.

The system also includes a number of bus routes, called 'Metrobús,' which link some suburbs to metro stations. This means you can easily get to San Bernardino, Prados del Este, El Hatillo and other suburbs that are not reached directly by metro. For example, the Centro Ciudad Comercial Tamanaco (CCCT) is accessible by Metrobús No 211 (La Trinidad) from the Chacao station and No 201 (El Cafetal) from the Altamira station (ask the driver where to get off). Route No 202 goes to El Hatillo from Altamira on weekdays. All of the metro lines and Metrobús routes are marked on the Caracas maps posted in every metro station.

The metro operates daily from 5:30am to 11pm. The air-conditioned trains run every few minutes, but less frequently early in the morning and late in the evening. Yellow single-ride tickets cost $0.15 for a ride of up to three stations, $0.20 for four to seven stations, and $0.25 for any longer route. *Boletos de ida y vuelta* (roundtrip tickets) of any distance cost $0.35. The transfer ticket *(boleto integrado)* for a combined metro-plus-bus single journey costs $0.30.

Consider buying the *multiabono* ($1.55), an orange multiple ticket which is valid for 10 metro rides of any distance; not only do you save money, but you also avoid the seemingly interminable queues at the ticket counter every time you need to use the metro.

Put your ticket into the turnstile slot, which opens and flips it back out to you to use again at your destination. Bulky packages that obstruct other passengers are not allowed in the metro, especially during rush hours.

The metro is generally safe, though a few pickpockets operate in groups on the escalators of the busy stations. An example scenario might run as follows: the man in front of you drops something and bends down to retrieve it. His accomplices at the back push you, while the one directly behind you tries to pick your pockets. Be aware.

Bus

The extensive bus network covers all suburbs within the metropolitan area, as well as major neighboring localities. Carritos (small buses) are the main type of vehicle operating city routes. They run frequently but move only as fast as the traffic allows, sometimes getting trapped in traffic jams. However, they cost less than the metro ($0.5 to $0.15) and go to many destinations inaccessible by metro. It's also worth taking a carrito ride just to get a taste of local culture; the radio will be blasting pop and the driver undertaking breathtaking maneuvers when the traffic is flowing – a world apart from the smooth and silent metro ride.

Taxi

Identifiable by the 'Taxi' or 'Libre' sign, taxis are a fairly inexpensive means of getting around. None of the taxis have meters, so always fix the fare before boarding. It is recommended that you use only white cars with yellow plates and preferably those from taxi ranks, of which there are plenty, especially outside shopping malls. Alternatively, request one by calling any of the numerous companies that provide a radio service. Several companies, such as **Móvil-Enlace** (☎ 577-0922, 577-3344), service the entire Caracas area around the clock. Also try **Taxis El Rosal** (☎ 952-1019, 952-0079) and **Trini Taxis** (☎ 944-4665, 944-0553). Hotels will usually have reliable taxi companies on standby.

AROUND CARACAS

This section includes only what lies between the city and the coast. For other one-day destinations out of Caracas see the Central North chapter (p116).

PARQUE NACIONAL EL ÁVILA

This national park consists of a steep, verdant mountain that looms just to the north of Caracas. The park encompasses about 90km of the range, running east–west along the coast and separating the city from the sea. The highest peak is Pico Naiguatá (2765m).

The southern slope, overlooking Caracas, is virtually uninhabited but is crisscrossed with dozens of walking trails. The northern face, running down to the sea, is dotted

CARACAS

with hamlets and haciendas, yet few tourist trails are on this side. The park is crossed north to south by a few 4WD tracks and the teleférico (cable car).

Teleférico

Rising high above the city to the peak of El Ávila (2175m), the newly rebuilt **teleférico** (cable car; Map pp56-7; ☎ 793-7418; adult/child under 12/adult over 65 $9.50/5.50/5; ⏱ 8am-7:45pm Tue-Sun, 10am-7:45pm Mon) was opened with fanfare in 2002. Originally built by a German company (1956–7), the old teleférico line consisted of two routes: the now inoperable 7.5km run from El Ávila down to Macuto on the coast, and the recently reconstructed 4km run from Maripérez station (980m), next to Av Boyacá in Caracas, to Pico El Ávila.

The top offers breathtaking views of Caracas and the Valle del Tuy beyond, and toward the north is a stunning panorama of the coastline and Caribbean Sea stretching away to the horizon. There's a small mountaintop park where you can find fast-food stands, an ice rink, playground and regular dancing or performers.

The mountain's peak is itself crowned by the circular 14-story Hotel Humboldt, built in 1956, a fantastic landmark visible from almost every point in the city. It was closed when the cable car stopped running, but renovations are underway to open it once again. If you're curious and want to have a snoop inside, short tours cost $1.25.

Views are usually best before the mid- to late-afternoon clouds start snaking across the mountaintop, enveloping the complex in an eerie fog that hides objects within even a few meters. But when the views disappear and the cold sets in, there's always the new Swiss-style restaurant next to Hotel Humboldt to heat up your belly with hot fondues. Sweaters are recommended for those coming in the afternoon.

At the weekend, regular jeeps (to the left as you exit the teleférico) run to the tiny village of Galipan ($1, 12 mins), which has a cluster of cheaper restaurants. Irregular jeeps also run down to San Bernadino in Caracas.

A **camioneta** (truck; Map pp62-3; Sur 21) to Maripérez station runs from just north of Bellas Artes metro station, passing the teleférico station.

Hiking

Of all Venezuela's national parks, El Ávila provides the best infrastructure for walkers. There are about 200km of walking trails, most of them well signposted. Half a dozen camping grounds distributed around the park are equipped with sanitary facilities, and there are many more places designated for camping (but without facilities).

A dozen entrances lead into the park from Caracas; all originate from Av Boyacá, commonly known as 'Cota Mil' because it runs at an altitude of 1000m. Whichever route you choose, you'll have a short ascent before you get to a guard post, where you pay a nominal park entrance fee. The *guardaparques* (park rangers) may provide information and suggestions about routes. Before you come, however, buy the useful *Mapa para el Excursionista – Parque Nacional El Ávila* (scale 1:40,000), which has marked trails and camping facilities. Local maps can be found in most major bookstores, or enquire at the Inparque office (p61).

There are plenty of options for a half- or full-day hike, and at least four routes go up to Pico El Ávila. Start early, as it can get extremely hot by midmorning. For campers, one of the most scenic routes is the two-day hike to Pico Naiguatá. Take rain gear and warm clothes. Water is scarce, so bring your own, and don't forget plastic bags to bring all your rubbish back. The dry season is from December to April, but be prepared for a few showers in the upper reaches all the same.

LITORAL CENTRAL

The northern face of El Ávila park slopes steeply down to the sea, leaving only a narrow, flat strip of land between the foothills and the shore, referred to as the 'Litoral Central.' This strip has developed into a chain of coastal towns, including, from west to east, Catia La Mar, Maiquetía, La Guaira, Macuto, Caraballeda and Naiguatá. Sadly, most of the area was devastated by mudslides caused by torrential rains in December 1999.

The whole area from La Guaira to Naiguatá became a sea of ruins, and up to 50,000 people were buried under the mud. Macuto, Caraballeda and Naiguatá, once thrilling seaside resorts for *caraqueños*, were turned into ruined ghost towns, and remain much the same. It will take decades before the urban fabric is fully rebuilt, if ever.

Entire beaches are gone, complete with their infrastructure and facilities, and much of the colonial town of La Guaira was destroyed. A few hotels and restaurants have been reopening along the coast, but there's not currently much to see or do here.

Sleeping & Eating

Catia La Mar is now the most reliable choice of places to stay and eat near the airport. In general, it's an ugly town although the northern seaside suburb has a collection of modern residential towers and a small beach. Hotels are a tad overpriced for what they offer, taking advantage of the scarcity of lodging options elsewhere in the region.

All the places listed below are close to each other in the seaside suburb of Atlántida, in the northwestern part of town. The Hotel Puerto Viejo is located half a kilometer east of the other hotels near Av Principal Urb Puerto Viejod.

Hostal Tanausu (☎ 352-1704; Av Atlántida; s/tr $23/47, d $25-35; P 🞫) The newest and cleanest of local options, Tanausu is unmistakable with its colorful reliefs of animals plastering the exterior. There's also a similarly decorated small restaurant next door – look for the castle-style entrance.

Hotel de París (☎ 351-1248; Av Atlántida; d $12.50-16; 🞫) The entrance to this hotel is through an unpromising smoky bar with locals playing pool and downing beers. However, the basic rooms are some of the cheapest you'll find, and they're perfectly liveable, with low beds and minimalist bathrooms.

Luna Mar (☎ 351-1314; Av Club Náutico at Av Atlántida; d/tr/ste $19/28/25; P 🞫) Luna Mar has another unpromising entrance, this time through an indoor car park. But the entrance is belied by the rooms, which are spacious and clean with TV and respectable bathrooms. A couple of the rooms have sea views.

Hotel Aeropuerto (☎ 351-1145; aeropuertohotelsuites@hotmail.com; Av Club Nautico; d $22-25; P 🞫)

This hotel is an ugly concrete block of a building, with decent rooms, but corridor ceilings so low that tall folks will have to duck. It has a disco, a restaurant, and cable TV in the rooms.

Hotel Puerto Viejo (☎ 350-2500; bwreservas@telcel.net.ve; $81-91; P 🞫 🞫 🞫) Half a kilometer east of the other hotels is this upmarket alternative, right by the sea. It has no less than three swimming pools, each with beautiful views over the bay and full of sun worshippers. The light and airy rooms are spacious, with a salon, cable TV and a balcony. The hotel is near Av Principal Urb Puerto Viejod on an unsigned road.

Recommended options outside Catia La Mar:

Hampton Inn & Suites (☎ 331-7111; Av La Armada; s/d incl breakfast & airport shuttle $99/109; P 🞫 🖳 🞫) Flashy new upmarket alternative literally a stone's throw away from the airport, situated directly on the road departing from the terminal. Has a tennis court, gym and pool to while away long hours between flights. You may be able to negotiate half-day rates here too.

Posada Kiwa (☎ 515-5104; adanadventures@cantv .net; Calle La Clivera 9, Puerto Carayaca; d incl transport & breakfast $37) This basic posada in a small coastal village is about a 25-minute drive beyond Catia La Mar. There is little public transport, but with advance warning the English-speaking owner will ferry travelers to and from the airport (hence the higher price) and can organize regional tours on request. Rooms share a bathroom. There is a nice beach nearby.

Getting There & Away

Carritos leave regularly from Nuevo Circo regional bus terminal in Caracas for Catia La Mar via the airport, where you can catch them. To do this, leave the terminal through the passageway leading from the building's upper level to the parking lot, get to the main road and wave down a carrito ($0.15). Don't do it after dark. For the hotels listed for Catia La Mar, get off at the road fork next to the McDonald's and walk along Av Atlántida. It's a 10-minute walk to the Hotel de París, and another two minutes to most of the others.

The Central North

CONTENTS

Commonly referred to as 'El Centro,' the central north covers extensive areas of fresh woodland and comely hills, rolling down to the coastline. It lays claim to no fewer than six wildlife-rich national parks on the mainland, as well as the idyllic marine park of Los Roques, spreading its watery tentacles off the coast.

And more surprises lie hidden amid the mainland's hills and valleys. The 19th-century German town of Colonia Tovar is scattered prettily across a mountainside within reach of Caracas, and Venezuela's best hot-spring complex can be found further west at Las Trincheras. Here also lies the battlefield of Carabobo, a focal point of national pride, where national hero Simón Bolívar clinched Venezuelan independence.

The region also boasts some of the country's best festivals, heavily influenced by the days of African slavery. Spontaneous parties and impromptu jam sessions on the drums regularly light up small towns along the coast, and the coastline itself is riddled with remote coves and beaches accessible only by boat, ideal for those itching to leave civilization behind.

This is Venezuela's most developed and densely populated region: occupying less than 2.5% of the national territory, it is home to around 45% of Venezuela's inhabitants. Some places included in this chapter, such as Colonia Tovar, San Francisco de Yare and Parque Nacional Guatopo, are easy one-day trips out of Caracas.

THE CENTRAL NORTH

HIGHLIGHTS

- Snorkel and bask in the pristine waters of **Archipiélago Los Roques** (p99)
- Explore the former German mountainside colony of **Colonia Tovar** (p116)
- Dance to night-time drumbeats in coastal **Puerto Colombia** (p120)
- Hike through the ecological wonderland of **Parque Nacional Henri Pittier** (p122)
- Dance with the devils at **San Francisco de Yare** (p105)
- Soak in the therapeutic hot springs of **Las Trincheras** (p131)
- Visit the shrine to independence at **Campo Carabobo** (p130)

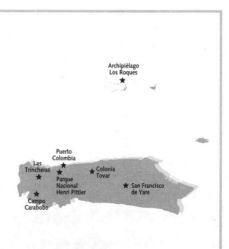

Archipiélago Los Roques ★

Puerto Colombia ★
Las Trincheras ★
★ Colonia Tovar
★ Parque Nacional Henri Pittier
★ San Francisco de Yare
Campo Carabobo ★

THE CENTRAL NORTH

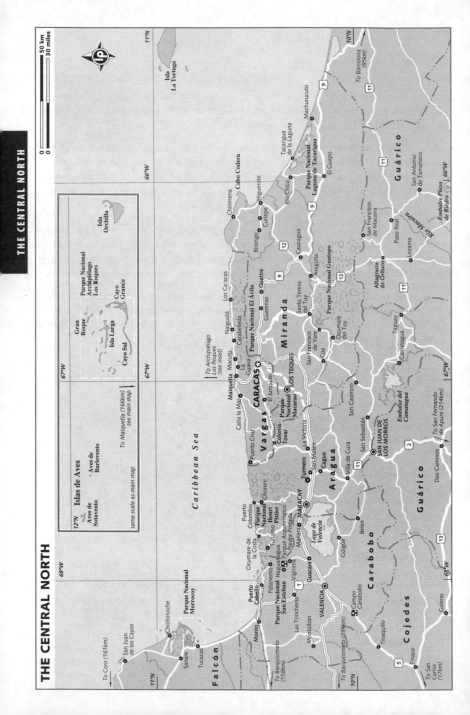

0   50 km
0   30 miles

Islas de Aves

same scale as main map

Aves de
Sotavento

Aves de
Barlovento

Isla
Orchilla

Parque Nacional
Archipiélago
Los Roques

Gran
Roque

Isla Larga

Cayo
Grande

Cayo Sal

To Maiquetía (166km)
see main map

To Archipiélago
Los Roques
(see inset)

Isla
La Tortuga

Caribbean Sea

Falcón

To Coro (161km)

San Juan
de los Cayos

Chichiriviche

Sanare

Tucacas

Parque Nacional
Morrocoy

Puerto
Cabello

Morón

Las Trincheras

Montalbán

Patanemo

To Barquisimeto (158km)

To Barquisimeto (139km)

Ocumare de
la Costa

Puerto
Colombia

Choroní

Parque
Nacional
Henri
Pittier

Parque Nacional
San Esteban

Naguanagua

Güigue

VALENCIA

Campo
Carabobo

Tinaquillo

Tinaco

To San
Carlos (17km)

Vigirima

Guacara

Mariara

Lago de
Valencia

Parque Arqueológico
Piedra Pintada

MARACAY

Belén

Carabobo

Cojedes

Galeras

Dos Caminos

Guárico

To San Fernando
de Apure (214km)

Embalse del
Camatagua

San Sebastián

Villa de Cura

San Juan de
Los Morros

Camatagua

Taguay

Altagracia
de Orituco

Lezama

Paso Real

San Francisco
de Macaira

San Antonio
de Tamanaco

Río Macaira

Embalse Playa
de Piedra

To Barcelona
(85km)

Parque Nacional Guatopo

Ocumare
del Tuy

San Casimiro

Cúa

San Francisco
de Yare

Santa Teresa
del Tuy

Magüita

El Guapo

Parque Nacional
Laguna de Tacarigua

Tacarigua
de la Laguna

Machurucuto

Río Chico

Cúpira

Higuerote

Chirimena

Cabo Codera

Curiepe

Birongo

Caucagua

Guatire

Guarenas

Parque Nacional El Avila

Miranda

LOS TEQUES

CARACAS

Parque
Nacional
Macarao

El Junquito

Colonia
Tovar

La Victoria

San Mateo

Cagua

Turmero

Aragua

Vargas

Maiquetía

Catia la Mar

Puerto Cruz

La
Guaira

Macuto

Naiguatá

Carabelleda

La
Sabana

Los Caracas

Inset labels:
10°N

11°N

11°N

11°N

10°N

68°W

67°W

66°W

67°W

68°W

67°W

66°W

12°W

Guárico

1

2

5

9

9

9

9

11

11

11

11

12

12

13

ARCHIPIÉLAGO LOS ROQUES

☎ 0237 / pop 1150

It's a cliché to call every other beach resort a tropical paradise, but few places merit the title more than Parque Nacional Archipiélago Los Roques. This stunningly beautiful collection of small coral islands, crisp white beaches and rich coral reefs is heaven for snorkelers, utopia for scuba divers and unadulterated bliss for sunbathers.

These idyllic islands are virtually unspoilt: no high-rise hotels, no nightclubs, and crime is virtually unheard of. The archipelago's only village is the tiny Gran Roque, while most islands are uninhabited and the silence is only broken by the occasional buzz of motorboats and splash of diving pelicans.

Los Roques lies about 160km due north off the central coast under a scorching sun and dazzlingly blue skies. Stretching 36km east to west, the archipelago consists of 42 islands big enough to bother naming, and about 250 other unnamed islets, sandbars and cays scattered around a crystal-clear, glittering lagoon brimming with marine life.

Gran Roque is the focal point of the archipelago, being home to virtually all of its population, accommodations and transportation. The whole archipelago, complete with the surrounding waters (2211 sq km), was made a national park in 1972. All visitors to Los Roques pay the $9.50 national park entry fee upon arrival ($5 for Venezuelans).

In order to preserve the habitat, protective zones have been created where tourists are not allowed or where access is limited to daytime visits. The only area with unrestricted access and the possibility of camping is the so-called **Zona Recreativa** (see map p100), which comprises Gran Roque and the nearby islands.

When to Go

Tourist peaks include late December and early January, Carnaval (first week of Lent), Semana Santa (Holy Week, culminating in Easter) and August. The slowest periods are May to July and September to November, when beaches are less crowded and bargains can sometimes be had.

The average temperature is about 28°C, with highs around 33°C in July and lows around 24°C in January. Rainfall is practically nonexistent, except for rare showers between September and January.

History

The archipelago has long been a stopping-off point for native Indians, sailors, pirates and explorers. It was used as much as a thousand years ago by Indians who temporarily inhabited the islands to catch fish, turtle and queen conch. Dos Mosquises was one of their major seats.

In colonial times, the islands saw a steady trail of foreigners, mostly from the Netherlands Antilles and England. In the 1920s, fishermen from Isla de Margarita were attracted by the abundance of fish and gradually settled the archipelago's main island, Gran Roque, pushing out the Dutch by the 1950s. Known as *roqueños*, the fisherman's descendants now make up the majority of the local population. Another recent influx of inhabitants is Italians, who seem to have a love affair with the islands. In fact, there are so many that speaking Italian is almost as useful as speaking Spanish here.

Flora & Fauna

The birds are a constant source of entertainment on the archipelago – from the continual rising and splashing falling of pelicans to mesmerizing gulls balancing like trapeze artists on undulating mooring ropes. Around 92 species of birds have been recorded on the islands, including 50 that migrate from North America. The only native mammal is the fishing bat, and there's also some reptiles, including four species of turtle and plenty of lizards, salamanders and iguanas. In terms of flora, the islands are sprinkled with grasses, thorny cacti, low bushes and mangroves.

But, if you find the flora and fauna above sea level interesting, just wait till you get underwater. The waters teem with riotously colorful fish, rays, barracudas, sea stars, mollusks, crabs, octopuses and lobsters, to name just a few. Any quick trip snorkeling around the archipelago's reefs will be rewarded by glimpses of everything from exquisite angelfish to the lumpish sea cucumber. And of course, the corals themselves are extraordinary, with names

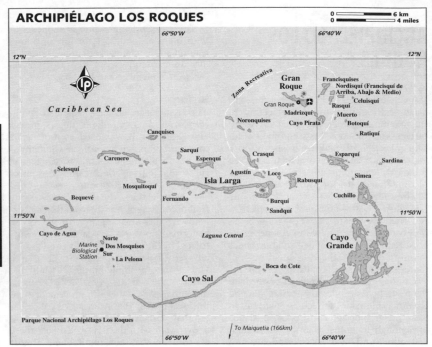

ARCHIPIÉLAGO LOS ROQUES

Caribbean Sea

Zona Recreativa

Gran Roque

Gran Roque

Francisquises
Nordisquí (Francisquí de Arriba, Abajo & Medio)
Celuisquí
Rasquí
Muerto
Botoquí
Ratiquí

Noronquises
Madrizquí
Cayo Pirata

Canquises

Sarquí
Espenquí
Crasquí
Esparquí
Sardina

Carenero
Selesquí
Agustín Loco
Simea
Rabusquí

Mosquitoquí
Isla Larga
Cuchillo

Bequevé
Fernando
Burquí
Sandquí

Cayo de Agua
Marine Biological Station
Norte
Dos Mosquises
Sur
La Pelona

Laguna Central
Cayo Grande

Cayo Sal
Boca de Cote

Parque Nacional Archipiélago Los Roques

To Maiquetía (166km)

THE CENTRAL NORTH

as exotic as their appearance, from the grooved brain coral to the orange elephant ear sponge and the devil's sea whip.

Los Roques is particularly famous for its delicious lobsters, though they have been overfished in recent years. There's now a ban on fishing lobster from May to October, but Los Roques still accounts for about 90% of national production.

Activities

The principal activity on Los Roques is relaxing: whether dozing in a hammock, cooling off in crystal-clear waters or soaking up the sun on pristine beaches. The longest uninterrupted strip of sand is on the island of Crasquí, while boat operators will most commonly drop passengers from Gran Roque at the islands of Francisquí de Arriba and Madrizquí. But you can also take your pick of many other beautiful spots. One word of warning: beaches on Los Roques are shadeless and the sun is relentless, made all the more powerful by reflection off the immaculately white sand. Sun block is a must, as are a hat and sunglasses.

SNORKELING & SCUBA DIVING

The archipelago is one of Venezuela's best areas for **snorkeling**. Among the most amazing places are the Boca de Cote and Noronquises, but there are other excellent sites closer to Gran Roque. The most popular spot is the so-called *piscina* (literally 'swimming pool') near Francisquí de Arriba, in a perfectly curved arc of beautiful corals. You actually don't even need to leave Gran Roque to find decent snorkeling waters – there's a good spot beyond the airstrip in the southeastern part of the island. You can rent snorkeling equipment in Gran Roque itself for about $5/10 a day with/without flippers.

Scuba diving is also fabulous here, and there's a wealth of good places to explore. Diving is organized by several companies, including **Sesto Continente** (☎ 0414-245-2225, in Caracas ☎ 0212-730-9080; www.scdr.com), which offers diving trips, PADI courses and equipment. Other outfits include **Ecobuzos** (☎ 221-1235; www.ecobuzos.com) and **Aquatics Dive Center** (☎ 416-0009, 0414-777-4894; www.scubavenezuela.com). Two dives generally cost $85 to $100.

WINDSURFING & KITESURFING

Los Roques is also a top-notch spot for windsurfing of all levels. It's organized by **Vela Windsurf Center** (www.velawindsurf.com) on the island of Francisquí de Abajo, which rents equipment ($20/35/50 per hour/half-day/day) and can provide lessons for beginners ($40 for two hours including equipment). Or for something different, ask here for **kayaks** and lessons in **kitesurfing**. For more information, inquire at **Oscar Shop** (☎ 414-5515; oscarshop@hotmail.com) by the Gran Roque airport.

OTHER ACTIVITIES

Los Roques is also renowned as one of the world's finest areas for **game fishing**, particularly for bonefish. These trips are expensive and require permits, so it's often best to arrange one in advance through a specialized company; for example, **Alpi Tour** (p74) in Caracas. In Gran Roque, **Posada Mediterráneo** (☎ 221-1130; www.posadamediterraneo.com) also organizes game-fishing stays.

You can also go **sailing** (per person per day $120-150) around Los Roques, on one of several sailing yachts that anchor off Gran Roque and wait for tourists. They have cabins equipped with berths and provide meals on board, and can take you for several days around the islands.

Finally, you can have a fantastic bird's-eye view of the islands from the **ultralight plane** (15-/25-min flight $40/70) parked at the airport.

Tours

The easiest way to visit the archipelago is on a one- or two-day tour. Tours are run by most of the small airlines with flights to Los Roques, and they all have their desks at the domestic or auxiliary terminals of the Maiquetía airport (see Los Roques Tour Operators p75). **Línea Turística Aereotuy** (LTA; in Caracas ☎ 212-763-8043; www.tuy.com/aereotuy.htm) is the biggest operator and has an office in central Caracas.

The all-inclusive one-day tour from Maiquetía normally costs $140 to $150, including the roundtrip flight, a boat excursion from Gran Roque to one or two of the nearby islands, lunch, soft drinks, one hour of snorkeling (equipment provided) and free time on the beach. Different operators may go to different islands and often have their own preferred snorkeling

---

CONSIDERATIONS FOR RESPONSIBLE DIVING

Please consider the following tips when diving, and help preserve the ecology and beauty of the archipelago's coral reefs:

■ Avoid touching living marine organisms with your body or dragging equipment across the reef. Polyps can be damaged by even the gentlest contact. Never stand on corals, even if they look solid and robust. If you must hold on to the reef, touch only exposed rock or dead coral.

■ Be conscious of your fins. Even without contact, the surge from heavy fin strokes near the reef can damage delicate organisms. When treading water in shallow reef areas, take care not to kick up clouds of sand. Settling sand can easily smother the delicate organisms of the reef.

■ Practice and maintain proper buoyancy control. Major damage can be done by divers descending too fast and colliding with the reef. Make sure that you are correctly weighted and that your weight belt is positioned so that you stay horizontal. Be aware that buoyancy can change over an extended trip: initially, you may breathe harder and need more weight; a few days later, you may breathe more easily and need less weight.

■ Resist the temptation to collect or buy corals or shells. Aside from the ecological damage, taking home marine souvenirs depletes the beauty of a site and spoils others' enjoyment.

■ Ensure that you take home all your rubbish and any litter you may find as well. Plastics in particular are a serious threat to marine life. Turtles can mistake plastic for jellyfish and eat it.

■ Resist the temptation to feed fish. You may disturb their normal eating habits, encourage aggressive behavior or feed them food that is detrimental to their health.

areas. LTA is the only company that runs trips in large catamarans (others have single-hull boats).

The two-day tour includes accommodations in Gran Roque and all meals, and it costs around $250 to $435, depending on the season, lodging standards and the number of people per room. Children are half price. An additional day costs another $140 to $220. Note that tour prices don't include the $9.50 entry fee to the national park.

Some operators, including LTA, also run tours from Isla de Margarita ($200 for a one-day tour, $340 to $500 for a two-day tour). LTA also offers fishing and scuba-diving packages.

A day tour is an enjoyable escape from Caracas, but it gives just a brief taste of what the archipelago has to offer. If this is all you want, the package is good value, as it's not much more expensive than the airfare. Two-day tours give a better insight but are far more expensive as the tour companies often use upmarket accommodations.

If you plan on staying two or more days, it's much better value to go it alone. Just buy a roundtrip ticket from one of the airlines and arrange all the rest in Gran Roque. **Oscar Shop** (☎ 414-5515; oscarshop@hotmail.com) provides boat transportation to the islands, organizes full-day boat tours, and rents out snorkeling equipment and beach chairs. Oscar can provide information on activities and recommend a *posada* (small, family-run guesthouse). His longest and most expensive excursion includes the magnificent Cayo de Agua, plus Dos Mosquises and its Marine Biological Station, and costs $20 per person, with a minimum of six passengers.

Try to avoid tourist peaks, when flights and accommodations are in short supply and prices can be stiff. Bargain for better accommodation prices in the slow season, and you can even try to haggle a few dollars off the flight back to Maiquetía (in which case consider buying a one-way ticket to Los Roques).

Getting There & Away

AIR
Airfares to Los Roques differ, so shop around. The Maiquetía–Los Roques one-way fare is about $50 to $75, and the round-trip fare ranges from $85 to $140. The flight takes about 40 minutes.

Línea Turística Aereotuy (LTA; in Caracas ☎ 212-763-8043; www.tuy.com/aereotuy.htm) occasionally offers budget one-way fares on its Friday afternoon flight from Maiquetía to Los Roques and morning flights back, so check out this possibility in advance.

LTA and **Rutaca** (☎ 212-576-0304) also fly to Los Roques from Isla de Margarita ($97 to $157 one-way). LTA occasionally offers cheaper fares on early morning flights, although it charges foreign nationals extra.

Normally, only 10kg of free luggage is permitted on flights to Los Roques, and you pay $0.30 for every additional kilogram.

BOAT
There are no passenger boats to Los Roques, only cargo boats, which depart two or three times a week (usually in the evening) from Muelle 7 in La Guaira port. They often take passengers for a small fee or sometimes even free of charge. However, these boats have no schedule, and it's virtually impossible to find out in advance the departure day and time. You have to personally go to the port and look for the captain. The trip itself normally takes about 12 hours and can be rough.

GRAN ROQUE
Lying on the northern edge of the archipelago, Gran Roque is the main island. On its southern side is a tiny picture-perfect fishing village of the same name, which accounts for the archipelago's biggest population: all 1100 of them.

The village's sandy streets are lined with flowers, shells and brightly painted houses, including just one bank, five grocery shops, a school, small police post but no less than 60-odd homely posadas. The only land vehicles you'll see are a few golf buggies that local bigwigs bounce around the island on, and a water and garbage truck. In contrast, the waterfront is packed with fishing boats, tour vessels and visiting yachts – all covered by a vast army of pelicans. Indeed, there are at least as many boats as there are families here. The island also has an airstrip by the village, which handles all tourist flights.

Unlike all the other islands, which are sandy and flat, Gran Roque has several massive rocky humps along its northwestern coast – the tallest is 110m – and cliffs that plunge vertically into the sea. Climb the hill crowned with an old lighthouse, known as the Faro Holandés, for sweeping views over the village, islands, coral reefs and the crystal-clear turquoise sea. The lighthouse itself was built in the 1870s and used until the early 1950s (there's now an iron beacon, further west).

Information

The island's only bank, **Banesco** (☎ 221-1265; Plaza Bolívar; ☯ 9am-noon & 2:30-5:30pm Mon-Fri, 10am-3pm Sat), arranges cash advances on Visa and MasterCard with a maximum of $500. Many establishments encourage payment in US dollars, though you may get a better deal in bolívares. **Inparques** (National Institute of National Parks; ☎ 0414-373-1004; ☯ 8am-noon & 2-6pm Mon-Fri, 8:30am-noon & 2:30-5:30pm Sat, 8:30am-noon Sun), at the far end of village, oversees the running of the national park and can give advice on places to camp and snorkel. **Oscar Shop** (☎ 414-5515; oscarshop@hotmail.com), by the airport, is a combination of shop, tour agency, boat operator and tourist office, all run by the knowledgeable Oscar. Upon arrival at Gran Roque, you will pass his kiosk by the airport. For Internet access, try **La Chuchera** (☎ 221-1417; Plaza Bolívar).

Sleeping

The explosion of posadas in the tiny village of Gran Roque over the last decade has been staggering. Locals have moved swiftly to transform their homes into hostels and there are now over 60 posadas providing some 500 beds (in 1995 there were just seven posadas). Most offer simple lodging and dining in a laid-back family environment, though they are expensive. The island has an electricity and desalination plant, though hot showers and air-con are still relatively rare luxuries. Food is also pricey, because everything except fish has to be shipped in from the mainland.

Many upmarket posadas offer packages, which include bed, all meals and boat trips to other islands, for $80 to $120 or more. Be warned that these packages are rarely good value, as trips include only the closest islands, usually Madrizquí or Francisquises (this boat trip costs just $5 to $6 per person with any boat operator). It's cheaper to stay in a budget posada and take boat trips separately, with Oscar or another boat operator.

All posadas offer single and double rooms, and most also have triples available. Prices vary from weekdays to weekends and depend also on demand.

BUDGET

Get ready to put your hands in your wallets. The bare minimum you'll pay for accommodation in Los Roques during the low season is about $20 per person (occasionally $16 after hard bargaining) for a bed, breakfast and supper. The following 'budget' choices reflect that norm.

Posada Roquelusa (☎ 0414-369-6401; r per person incl breakfast & dinner $25) You'll receive a well-trained greeting from the resident parrot when entering this old budget posada close to Inparques office at the far end of the village. It's a scruffier option than most, with a few rough edges and basic rooms, but friendly folks run it.

Doña Carmen (☎ 0414-291-9225; Plaza Bolívar; r per person incl breakfast & dinner $25-28) Doña Carmen has been going for over 30 years, the longest-running posada on the island. The concrete rooms are nothing special, though a couple face onto the beach, and all have a private bathroom and fan.

Doña Magalys (☎ 0414-373-1090; Plaza Bolívar; r per person incl breakfast & dinner $20) This authentic *roqueño* family home on the plaza has basic rooms with a mini-bathroom and fan, but lacks natural light. Magalys cooks up filling meals served in a homely atmosphere with other guests.

Posada El Botuto (☎ 0414-291-9194; r per person incl breakfast $30) Close to the Inparques office, this excellent little posada has some of the most personable service on the island. It has an open-fronted and sociable kitchen area shaded out the front by a large sail hung horizontally. The interior is similarly light, and five out of six of the neatly decorated rooms even have a tiny outdoor patio complete with their own shower. It costs $10 more in high season.

The cheapest option is to camp. Camping is allowed on all the islands within the recreation zone, including Gran Roque, and is free. After arrival go to the far end of the village to the **Inparques office** (☎ 0414-373-1004; ☯ 8am-noon & 2-6pm Mon-Fri, 8:30am-noon & 2:30-5:30pm Sat, 8:30am-noon Sun) for a free camping permit. The staff will tell you which islands are open for camping and snorkeling, and can give you other practical tips.

On Gran Roque, the camping site is next to the Inparques office, but it has no toilets or showers. The only public toilet (no shower) is at the airport on the opposite end of the village. Try to arrange access to the bath at a nearby posada for a price. You can buy bottled water in shops.

MID-RANGE

Posada La Lagunita (☎ 0414-291-9151; www.posada lagunita.com; Calle La Laguna; r per person incl breakfast/ all-inclusive $35/70) Edging out of the reach of budgeters, this new posada has spotless rooms and enthusiastic service. It also has a nice rooftop terrace, where the friendly staff mix up a free *Cuba libre* (rum and coke) for folks back from a hard day's sunbathing. Only one room has air-conditioning.

Piano y Papaya (☎ 0414-281-0104; www.pianoy papaya.com; r per person incl breakfast $50) Behind the church, this is a light, fresh and very welcoming posada that serves up some legendary fish dinners. English, French and Italian are all spoken.

Posada Guaripete (☎ 221-1368; posadaguaripete@ cantv.netr; r per person incl breakfast $45) You'll be welcomed by a burst of glorious pink flowers over the terraced passageway to this posada. Its rooms are largely unadorned but comfortable, and there's a long, shady terrace with strategically hung hammocks.

Posada del Recuerdo (☎ 221-1072; posadadelrec uerdo@cantv.net; Plaza Bolívar; r per person incl breakfast & dinner $32) This is a basic option with cheap but undistinguished rooms.

TOP END

Posada Acuarela (☎ 221-1456; www.posadaacuarela .com; Calle Las Flores; s/d incl breakfast $105/140; ❄) Designed and managed by architect and painter Angelo, this Mediterranean-style posada is one of the best on the island. It's filled with plants, open-topped patios and modern art, and there's an excellent rooftop terrace with hammocks and other seating on which to lounge in the breeze. Six rooms have air-conditioning, and there's one suite with its own private terrace above. English, French and Italian are spoken.

Posada Mediterráneo (☎ 221-1130; www.posada mediterraneo.com; Calle Las Flores; r per person incl breakfast & dinner $120; ❄ 🖵) This spotless, white-

washed posada comes highly recommended for its warm and friendly service. It has a great rooftop terrace and bar scattered with candles and seating. The rooms are simple but elegant with high ceilings and sparkling bathrooms. The posada offers big discounts from Monday to Friday.

Posada Natura Viva (☎ 221-1473; www.natura vivalosroques.com; s/d/tr per person incl breakfast $130/ 120/100; 🖵) One of the best *roqueño*-owned posadas, Natura Viva has a unique rooftop bar shaped as a ship, and a beautiful terrace scattered with parasols and looking directly over the sea. Down below, the stylishly decorated rooms are situated around a plant-filled courtyard and restaurant. There are several family rooms with mezzanine and fridge available. Prices go down significantly the longer you stay with them.

Also recommended:

El Paraiso Azul (in Caracas ☎ 0212-953-2707; www .gentedemar.com; r per person incl breakfast & dinner $80) Popular and often full. Look for the sunny yellow front.

Malibú (☎ 221-1274; posadamalibu@cantv.net; Calle La Laguna; s/d incl breakfast $117/180, air-con extra $20; ❄ 🖵) Cool and classy posada chockablock with plants.

Posada Arrecife (☎ 221-1066; arrecife@canv.net; r per person incl breakfast $75; ❄ 🖵) Jumble of styles, but with plenty of creature comforts and free-roaming parrots.

Posada La Terraza (☎ 221-1248; www.laterrazalosr oques.com; r per person incl breakfast $70; ❄) Behind the church, it has especially personal service with just two cozy rooms.

Eating

Since almost all posadas serve meals for their guests, there are few self-contained eating-places in Gran Roque.

Aquarena CaféTours Shop (☎ 277-5510; Calle Principal; snacks $5-10) At the entrance to town from the airstrip is this informal beachside café serving pizza, hamburgers, sandwiches, juices and delectable desserts. It has tables spilling out onto the beach and sells crafts.

Restaurant El Canto de la Ballena (☎ 225-2804; 3-course menu $15) This open-fronted option near the church also looks out to sea, and serves excellent seafood dishes. When lobster is in season, this is the place to get it.

La Chuchera (☎ 221-1417; Plaza Bolívar; mains $6.50-16; ☽ 11am-11pm; 🖵) This lively bar-cum-restaurant is splashed in primary colors and plays a constant soundtrack of upbeat music. Pizza (including a vegetarian option) is served from 4pm. Also on the menu are hamburgers, pasta and fish.

OTHER ISLANDS

The nearest island to Gran Roque is **Madrizquí**, about 1km to the southeast. It was the favorite island among affluent *caraqueños* (people from Caracas) who built their summer beach houses here before the archipelago was made a national park. Other nearby islands with dwellings are **Cayo Pirata** and **Crasquí**, which have fishing shelters known as *rancherías*, and **Francisquí** and **Rasquí**, which have posadas.

On the island of **Dos Mosquises Sur**, at the far southwestern edge of the archipelago, is the Marine Biological Station, run by the Fundación Científica Los Roques. The station, which can be visited, has breeding tanks where turtles and other endangered species are raised before being released around the archipelago; more than 5000 turtles have already been reared. There's also a small museum here displaying archaeological discoveries from the area.

Sleeping

Wherever you stay you'll never be far from a beach, but for that ultimate castaway feeling you can stay outside Gran Roque.

Camping is free: all you need is a permit from **Inparques** (☎ 0414-373-1004; 🕑 8am–noon & 2-6pm Mon-Fri, 8:30am–noon & 2:30-5:30pm Sat, 8:30am-noon Sun). Permits are available for the nearby islands of Madrizquí, Cayo Pirata and Francisquí. Further away, you can also camp on Noronquises and Crasquí. You must be self-sufficient with camping gear, food and water. Also don't forget to bring along snorkeling gear, insect repellent for small biting flies and good sun block.

Rancho Agua Clara (☎ 0414-247-3498; www .geocities.com/guayolosroques) This ranch on the island of Crasquí has a handful of beachside tents and toilet facilities. A one-night package costs around $60 to $75 per person, including the roundtrip boat ride, tents (with bedding provided), all meals, beach chairs and a shower. It costs less the longer you stay.

Arjona Tours (☎ 0414-373-1111; www.roques.net; 🗷) The most isolated non-camping option is an idyllically located two-cabin posada on the tiny Rasquí. See the website for a list of its all-inclusive packages that can be

> **NORDIS...QUE?**
>
> As you find your way around Los Roques, you may wonder about the islands' strange names. Many were first named by English explorers. Local fishermen preserved most of these original names but wrote them down phonetically. Then along came the linguistically correct cartographers, who changed the spelling to standard Spanish orthography. This is how Northeast Cay in English was recorded as 'Nordisky,' and eventually became 'Nordisquí.' Similarly, the Sails Cay went through 'Selesky' to 'Selesquí,' and St Luis Cay has become 'Celuisquí.'

combined with fishing, diving or windsurfing tours around the archipelago.

Campamento Francisquí (☎ 0414-337-3148) On Francisquí, there's also a basic, two-room posada. Ask for Marcos; phone for more details and prices, which include food and transfers.

Eating

There are a couple of fried-fish restaurants run by fisherfolk on Crasquí.

Restaurant Casamarina (mains $9-13, snacks $2-4.50) This is the only formal eating option outside Gran Roque and it is located on Francisquí de Arriba.

Getting There & Away

Oscar Shop or other boat operators in Gran Roque will take you to the island of your choice and pick you up at a prearranged time and date. Roundtrip fares per person are Madrizquí ($5), the Francisquises ($6), and Crasquí or Noronquises ($10).

MIRANDA STATE

SAN FRANCISCO DE YARE

☎ 0239 / pop 20,000

As you stroll around the colonial streets of this small, sleepy town, it's difficult to imagine the mayhem that reigns here annually during the Festival de Los Diablos Danzantes. This colorful festival sees visitors arrive in their thousands as the village is transformed into a huge mass of frenzied, costumed revelers in devil masks dancing to the hypnotic rhythm of drums and maracas.

This famous feast has been celebrated here annually since 1742, falling on Corpus Christi (the 60th day after Easter Day, in May or June and always on a Thursday). The date is not an official Venezuelan holiday, but it is very much so in San Francisco de Yare, which spends months gearing up for the festival.

San Francisco de Yare lies 70km by road southeast of Caracas. The town was founded in 1718 and boasts a fine mid-18th-century church, the Iglesia de San Francisco, and some well-preserved colonial architecture.

Festival de Los Diablos Danzantes

Easily one of Venezuela's most authentic and energetic festivals, the celebrations for the Festival de Los Diablos Danzantes (Festival of the Dancing Devils) begin at noon on the Wednesday, one day prior to Corpus Christi. Crowds of devil dancers don their colorful masks and red costumes, and depart from the Casa de Los Diablos Danzantes and take to the streets for the whole afternoon. In the evening, they go to El Calvario for the lengthy Velorio (Vigil), which lasts until dawn.

In the morning of Corpus Christi, the devils gather at the Casa de Los Diablos Danzantes to get the party rolling again with a short dancing session before heading for the local cemetery to pay respects to their predecessors. They then go to the parish church (but don't enter it) and continue in a joyful pageant to the Plaza de Los Diablos Danzantes, four blocks from the church, where they again take to frenzied dancing.

The frolicing only stops when a church procession bringing the bishop from Los Teques arrives. This is the symbolic climax

---

DANCING WITH DEVILS

The festival of the Diablos Danzantes (Dancing Devils) is a kaleidoscopic spectacle. Up to a thousand devil dancers clad in red costumes wearing monstrous masks strut around in everything from marching movements in double file to spasmodic squirms accompanied by the stirring clamor of drums. The devil dancers take to the streets on the Wednesday, one day before Corpus Christi, (held in honor of the Eucharist) and on the holy day itself. So, why do the devils come out on this holiest of days?

The ceremony manifests the struggle between evil and good, and the eventual triumph of the latter. No matter how profane the devil dances look, the devils come to the church to submit themselves to the Eucharist before returning to their whirling dances. Locals believe that the dance ritual will ensure abundant crops, welfare, prosperity and protection against misfortune and natural disasters. For the devils, the dance is their religion.

The festival blends Spanish and African traditions: its origins lie in Spain, where devils' images and masks featured in Corpus Christi feasts in medieval Andalusia. But when the festival was brought to the New World in colonial times, it found a fertile soil among the black slaves, who introduced the traditional African-style masks and the rhythm of drumbeats so characteristic of their homeland. Some saw this as an act of protest against the white god, a symbol of Spanish oppression and cruelty. But the profane and the divine gradually merged, producing a striking cross-cultural ritual.

While the ceremony's African roots are palpable, the dances are not performed exclusively by blacks. Devil dances have been preserved only in areas with the heaviest import of African slaves, including the towns of Naiguatá (Vargas); Cata, Chuao, Cuyagua, Ocumare de la Costa and Turiamo (Aragua); Canoabo, Guacara, Los Caneyes, Patanemo and Tocuyito (Carabobo); Tinaquillo (Cojedes); and San Francisco de Yare (Miranda). The celebrations in Chuao (p120) and San Francisco de Yare are best known.

Dances and costumes have their own characteristics in each community, especially the papier-mâché masks, which differ notably from town to town. San Francisco de Yare churns out large, elaborate masks depicting horned demons, monsters and fantastic animals painted in every color of the rainbow. Meanwhile, the masks from Chuao are smaller and painted with just three colors (white, black and red).

of the whole event, where good triumphs over evil for another year. A lengthy, solemn mass is celebrated on the square, with all the devils taking part. Once the mass is over, the ceremony of the Juramentación is held, in which young apprentices to devil dancers take a symbolic oath. The bishop gives God's blessing to the devils, and they all set off for the procession back to the church, carrying the image of the Holy Sacrament.

The multicolored hoards continue their dancing throughout the afternoon, wandering around the streets, stopping at makeshift street altars and visiting relatives before returning to the church at about 6pm for another procession, after which they head to El Calvario, where the celebrations conclude.

The script of the festivities differs slightly from year to year, but rest assured there will always be ritual devil dancing all over town.

Other Attractions

Corpus Christi is by far the best time to visit the town, but the ambience of the Diablos Danzantes is omnipresent, particularly in the weeks prior to the festival.

The **Casa de Los Diablos Danzantes** (Calle Rivas; admission free; ☼ 7am-noon & 2-4pm Tue-Fri, 7am-noon Sun), where the Corpus Christi celebrations begin, shelters a small museum with a collection of devil masks and photos from previous festivals. The family living in the house next door to the museum has the keys and can open it for you at other times.

You can stop by at several workshops manufacturing devil masks to see the production process and buy masks at good rates. One of the best is **Artesanía El Mocho** (☎ 222-9191; Calle Rivas), led by Manuel Sanoja. It's opposite the Monumento de Los Diablos Danzantes, above the Bodega San Antonio. **Artesanía Morgado** (☎ 222-9345; Calle Rivas 19), one block away on the same street, is run by another noted local artisan, Juan Morgado.

Sleeping & Eating

There are no regular hotels in San Francisco de Yare – the nearest reliable accommodation options are in Santa Teresa del Tuy and Ocumare del Tuy. There are several basic places to eat in San Francisco de Yare, including **Bar Restaurant El Deporte** (Plaza Bolívar; ☼ 2pm-11pm).

Getting There & Away

There's no direct transportation from Caracas to San Francisco de Yare, but you can get there easily with one connection from the Nuevo Circo regional bus terminal. Take one of the frequent buses to Ocumare del Tuy ($0.60, 1½ hours) or Santa Teresa del Tuy ($0.60, 1½ hours) and change at your destination. Buses shuttle between Ocumare and Santa Teresa every 15 minutes or so, and pass through San Francisco de Yare, providing convenient access.

PARQUE NACIONAL GUATOPO

Guatopo is an important biological enclave covered by lush rain forest in the otherwise heavily developed and populated hinterland of Caracas. Thanks to the wide range of elevations and copious rainfall, the park's vegetation is varied and exuberant, with huge trees up to 40m high, palms, ferns and orchids.

The rich mammal world includes jaguar, puma, tapir, armadillo and sloth, to name just a few. Guatopo is also good for birdwatching; macaws, parakeets, woodpeckers, hummingbirds, honeycreepers and dozens of other bird species are easily spotted in the forest canopy. But keep an eye on the ground as well – there are also some poisonous snakes, including the coral snake and (the most common and dangerous) macagua.

Established in 1958, Guatopo is about 100km by road (60km as the crow flies) southeast of Caracas. The park encompasses 1225 sq km of the rugged Serranía del Interior, a mountain range that splits off the Cordillera de la Costa and winds inland. The altitude in the park ranges between 200m and 1430m above sea level. The park is also a major water source for the region, since several dams have been built around the park, creating *embalses* (reservoirs).

The climate here is wet and warm. The rainiest months are October to December, while the driest ones are March and April, but rain gear is recommended any time of the year. Insects are also plentiful, so bring repellent. The temperature ranges between 25°C and 30°C, but drops to about 15°C on the highest peaks.

Orientation

The paved road between Santa Teresa del Tuy and Altagracia de Orituco winds

THE CENTRAL NORTH

through the middle of the park, passing all the recreational areas and starting points for walks. Public transportation from Caracas does travel along this road sporadically, but it's infrequent and dies in the afternoon. Given this, a one-day trip to the park from Caracas gives you a pretty limited time in the park. If you decide to do this, make an early start and go to Agua Blanca (p109) – a good starting point for walking. If you have your own transportation, you can easily visit several areas in the park and still have time for walking.

There are some basic lodging and camping facilities in the heart of the forest. The following section details the major stopovers on the route, from north to south (the exception being Hacienda La Elvira, which is accessible only from Altagracia de Orituco), along with their tourist facilities.

Sights & Activities
LOS ALPES DEL TUY
About 30km from Santa Teresa, **Parador Turístico Los Alpes** (snacks $0.50-2; ☼ 6am-6pm) is a

roadside cafeteria sitting on a Y-junction in lush surroundings, and serving hot snacks and drinks. Look out for the portly parrot fearlessly helping himself to customers' empanadas and beer.

The road branching to the south from here will take you to a viewpoint (3.5km from Los Alpes), then to another viewpoint (1km beyond). Five kilometers further on, you reach La Macanilla.

LA MACANILLA
At the time of writing, an Inparques visitors center was being built by the roadside in La Macanilla to house a small exhibition on the park's flora, fauna and geology. Once it's up and running, the *guardaparque* (park ranger) can give you information about the park. La Macanilla is the starting point for a beautiful 9km trail that winds through thick forest up to the mountain ridge, continues along the ridge, and comes back down to the road 4km from La Macanilla. However, the trail hasn't been maintained in recent years and was impassable at the time of writing.

PARQUE NACIONAL GUATOPO

AGUA BLANCA

Thirteen kilometers on, Agua Blanca is the park's major recreational area. There's an intriguing reconstructed *trapiche* or traditional **sugarcane mill** (admission adult/child $0.20/0.05; ☺ 7:30am-3pm Mon-Fri, 7am-4pm Sat & Sun) here, complete with its huge cauldrons and ladles, and you can take a bath in the *pozo* (pond) on the opposite side of the road.

From the pond, a steep and muddy 3km walking trail goes to Santa Crucita; allow up to 1½ hours to walk it at a leisurely pace. There's also another, shorter (1.5km) trail between Agua Blanca and Santa Crucita that takes just 45 minutes, running on the opposite, eastern side of the road – so you can take a roundtrip without returning the same way. See Santa Crucita (below) for more walks.

Agua Blanca attracts day-trippers on weekends, but is usually quiet on weekdays. It has a picnic area, toilets, a parking lot (guarded on weekends), a snack kiosk (open on weekends) and some accommodation options. Campamento Los Monos is a 26-bed dormitory that is reserved as a whole in advance through Caracas' **Inparques office** (☎ 285-4859; www.inparques.gov.ve in Spanish; Av Rómulo Gallegos, Caracas; ☺ 8am-noon & 1:30-4pm Mon-Fri). Bring your own sheets and blankets. There are also five **cabañas** (2-person $20), rustic timber structures on stilts, scattered around the forest. Bring mats, sheets, blankets or a sleeping bag. There's also a **camping ground** (per person $1.25). Bring your food if you come on weekdays.

SANTA CRUCITA

The next stop, Santa Crucita, is 1.5km from Agua Blanca. There is a small lagoon here, and you can pitch your tent at the grassy camping site. As well as the two trails coming here from Agua Blanca, there are two short local walking loops, one skirting around the lagoon (700m) and another one going through the nearby forest (800m).

EL LUCERO & QUEBRADA DE GUATOPO

The park's administrative center is El Lucero, 5.5km down the road from Santa Crucita. There's a large grassy camping ground here, plus park rangers to ply for information, but no food is available. Quebrada de Guatopo, 2km beyond El Lucero, has a picnic area, a creek and yet another camping ground. Again, bring your own food.

ALTAGRACIA DE ORITUCO

☎ 0238

Lying beyond the national park's boundaries, Altagracia de Orituco is 24km south of Quebrada de Guatopo. It's an ordinary town, but big enough to be a terminus for buses from Caracas and to have a collection of hotels and restaurants.

Buses to Caracas depart from the junction where the gas stations are located, 1km from Plaza Bolívar. Here you'll also find several hotels, including **Hotel Amazor** (☎ 334-1174; francidela@hotmail.com; Calle Pellón at Palacio 16; s/d/tr $14/19/25; P ☒), which has plain rooms with cable TV and warm water, plus a good restaurant. **Hotel Diamante** (☎ 334-1331; Av Ilustres Próceres; s/d $14/18; ☒) is a similar option recommended by locals.

HACIENDA LA ELVIRA

About 26km northeast of Altagracia, this charming old 19th-century coffee hacienda welcomes visitors. However, it's a tricky spot to get to. From Altagracia, you have to drive 8km east on the road to Paso Real and take the left turnoff north to San Francisco de Macaira. Follow this pothole-riddled road for 14km, and take the rough 4WD track branching off to the northwest and leading to La Elvira (4km). Getting anywhere nearby by public transportation is difficult. There are no accommodations, but camping is permitted. The administrative center in El Lucero is happy to give more information.

Getting There & Away

There are hourly buses from the Nuevo Circo regional terminal in Caracas to Altagracia de Orituco ($4.50, four hours), but they go via Cúa and San Casimiro along the road and don't pass through the park. There are also minibuses operating as por puestos to Altagracia. They run from about 5am to 2pm, depart when full and are faster than buses. They go via Santa Teresa and the park, and can let you off at any point on the road eg Agua Blanca ($3.50, two hours).

ARAGUA STATE

MARACAY

☎ 0243 / pop 605,000

Known as the Ciudad Jardín (Garden City), Maracay is the capital city of Aragua state.

There's almost nothing left of the colonial legacy in this 300-year-old city, but it does possess plenty of parks and leafy plazas, including the country's largest Plaza Bolívar. It's also the center of an important agricultural and industrial area, and has a palpable military presence, especially the air force.

Maracay is a frequent stopover en route to Parque Nacional Henri Pittier and its coastline. At an altitude of about 450m, the city has a hot climate (warmer than Caracas, but more pleasant than Maracaibo), with an average temperature of 25°C and most rain falling between April and October.

History

Founded in the mid-16th century, Maracay has long taken advantage of the valley's fertile soil, growing dozens of crops from cacao to sugarcane. However, it was a slow-growing town, and by 1900 the population had reached a mere 7000. Indeed, the city would have probably continued at this unhurried rate if it hadn't been for Juan Vicente Gómez (military dictators; p24), probably the most ruthless of all Venezuelan *caudillos*. He first came here in 1899 and fell in love with the town. After seizing power in 1908, he settled in Maracay and ruled both state and country from here until his death in 1935. He set about turning the town into a city worthy of being capital, building a grandiose bullring, opera house, zoo, splendid hotels and an air-force school that became the cradle of Venezuelan aviation.

After his reign, a second wave of city development came with the freeway linking Caracas with Maracay in the 1950s. Around this time, Venezuela also developed the most powerful air force in Latin America, much of it based in Maracay. The city is still an important military base, and the unsuccessful coup of 1992 (p25) began with the rebels' planes flying to Caracas from here.

Information

INTERNET ACCESS

There are Internet facilities in the Centro Comercial Paseo Las Delicias and Torre Sindoni.

Bibliotecas Virtu@les (Av Sucre; per hr $0.30; ☺ 9am-6:30pm Mon-Sat) Slow but extremely cheap.

Net Café (No 24, 1st fl,Centro Comercial La Capilla, Av Santos Michelana; per hr $0.80, per 15 min $0.30; ☺ 10am-6:30pm Mon-Sat) Much faster than Virtu@les.

MEDICAL SERVICES

Farmatodo (☎ 232-2049; Av 4a Las Delicias at Av Urb La Soledad) A large, well-stocked pharmacy north of the center.

MONEY

Banco de Venezuela (Calle Mariño)
Banesco (Av Páez)
Corp Banca (Calle Soublette)
Italcambio (☎ 235-6945; No 110-K, 1st fl, Centro Comercial Maracay Plaza, cnr Avs Aragua & Bermúdez; ☺ 8:30am-12:30pm & 1:30-5pm Mon-Fri, 9am-1pm Sat) Located 1.5km south of Plaza Bolívar.

POST

Ipostel (Av 19 de Abril; ☺ 9am-5pm Mon-Fri)

TELEPHONE

CANTV Calle Vargas (Internet per hr $0.65; ☺ 8am-8pm Mon-Sat, 9am-2pm Sun) Calle López Aveledo (☺ 8am-8pm Mon-Sat, 9am-2pm Sun) The Calle López Aveledo branch has no Internet.

TOURIST INFORMATION

Instituto Autónomo de Turismo de Aragua (Iatur; ☎ 242-2284; fondomixtoaragua@hotmail.com; Hotel de Golf Maracay, Av Las Delicias; ☺ 8am-4:30pm Mon-Fri) Located 2km north of the center.

Sights

PLAZA GIRARDOT

The historic heart of Maracay, Plaza Girardot (for once, not Plaza Bolívar), is crowned by a large obelisk topped with a bronze eagle, erected in 1897. It commemorates the North American volunteers who joined the independence war forces led by Francisco Miranda, but were captured and hanged in 1806 by the Spaniards.

The only colonial building left by the square is the handsome **cathedral** (☺ 6am-noon & 2:30-7pm Mon-Sat, 6am-7pm Sun), on its eastern side. The cathedral was completed in 1743 and not much has changed since. The white-washed exterior is particularly attractive when the late-afternoon sunlight strikes the facade.

MUSEO DE ARQUEOLOGÍA

An arcaded building erected by Gómez as the seat of government now houses the **archaeological museum** (☎ 247-2521; Plaza Girardot; ☺ 8am-3:30pm Tue-Fri, 9am-12:30pm Sat & Sun), featuring some interesting pre-Hispanic pottery and crafts of the diverse Indian groups living today.

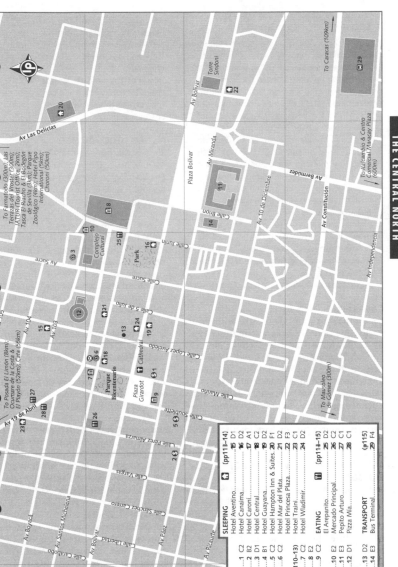

MARACAY

INFORMATION	
Banco de Venezuela................	1 C2
Banesco.................................	2 B2
Bibliotecas Virtu@les..............	3 D1
CANTV..................................	4 B1
Corp Banca...........................	5 C2
Net Café...............................	6 C2

SIGHTS & ACTIVITIES	(pp110–13)
Casa de Dolores Amelia..........	7 C2
Museo Aeronáutico................	8 E2
Museo de Arqueología...........	9 C2
Museo de Arte Contemporáneo..................	10 E2
Palacio de Gobierno...............	11 E3
Plaza de Toros Maestranza.....	12 D1
Santuario de Madre María de San José............................	13 D2
Teatro de la Opera................	14 E3

SLEEPING	(pp113–14)
Hotel Aventino......................	15 D1
Hotel Canaima......................	16 D2
Hotel Caroní..........................	17 A1
Hotel Central........................	18 C2
Hotel Guayana......................	19 D2
Hotel Hampton Inn & Suites..	20 F1
Hotel Mar del Plata...............	21 D2
Hotel Princesa Plaza..............	22 F3
Hotel Traini..........................	23 C1
Hotel Wladimir......................	24 D2

EATING	(pp114–15)
El Arepanito..........................	25 D2
Mercado Principal.................	26 C2
Pepito Arturo........................	27 C1
Pizza Mía..............................	28 C1

TRANSPORT	(p115)
Bus Terminal........................	29 F4

SELF-PRESERVATION SOCIETY

Juan Vicente Gómez was a feared military leader, and he was well aware of threats to his life (a consequence of his iron rule). It is said that he never slept in the same bed two nights in a row and that he built an elaborate system of escape tunnels from his office. He even constructed a road from Maracay over the mountains to the coast, in case he was forced to flee the country, and he surrounded himself with a strong military force, for which vast barracks were built. As if anticipating the worst, he also erected a grand mausoleum for himself within years of becoming ruler. But Gómez didn't only build tunnels for sudden flight – it's also said that a secret tunnel linked his office to the house of his favorite mistress, Dolores Amelia – so that's what he was really up to in those 'late nights at the office!'

CASA DE DOLORES AMELIA

Set on the northern side of Parque Bicentenario, this fine mansion was built in 1927 by Gómez for his favorite mistress, Dolores Amelia Núñez de Cáceres. Designed in the neo-Sevillan style, the building has been meticulously restored and is now sporadically occupied by companies. If you turn up during office hours, someone may show you around the patio, which is clad with glorious *azulejos* (ornamental tiles), reminiscent of the Alhambra in Granada.

SANTUARIO DE MADRE MARÍA DE SAN JOSÉ

The saintly **sanctuary** (admission free; 8:30am-11:30am & 2:30-5pm Tue-Sun), one block east of Plaza Girardot, is the most revered city site. Choroní-born Madre María (1875–1967) was beatified by papal decree in 1995. Her remains were exhumed and, to everybody's shock, the corpse was allegedly intact. You can see her diminutive body in a crystal sarcophagus in the Santuario (though the face and hands are covered with masks). See Choroní (p120) for more on Madre María.

PLAZA DE TOROS MAESTRANZA

Possibly the most stylish and beautiful bullring in the country, this large Spanish-Moorish construction was modeled on the one in Seville and built in 1933. It was originally called 'Calicanto,' but was then renamed in memory of César Girón, Venezuela's most famous matador, who tragically died in 1971. A monument of him fighting a bull stands in front of the ring. If you want to have a snoop inside, try getting in through the back door on the eastern side.

MUSEO AERONÁUTICO

This is the only **aeronautical museum** (233-3812; Av Santos Michelena; admission free; 9:30am-5pm Sat & Sun) in the country and well worth a look. There are about 40 aircraft on display, including four helicopters. Many are warplanes from the 1920s to the 1950s that once served in the Venezuelan air force. The collection's gem has to be a beautifully restored French Caudron G3 from the 1910s, reputedly still in perfect working order.

In the middle of the exhibition grounds is a statue of Juan Vicente Gómez: the first and only monument to the *caudillo*, unveiled amid great controversy in 1995.

The museum is only open on weekends. If you arrive on a weekday, inquire at the side gate at the end of Av Santos Michelena (best from 8am to 11am or 2pm to 3pm) and somebody may show you around. The soldiers at the gate may be unaware of this service, in which case politely ask them to call the supervisor (NCO).

MUSEO DE ARTE CONTEMPORÁNEO

The entire block opposite the aeronautical museum is occupied by the Complejo Cultural, including the **contemporary art museum** (237-8534; admission free; 8am-5pm Tue-Sun), which stages temporary exhibitions.

PLAZA BOLÍVAR

At three blocks long, this huge, tree-filled square is the largest Plaza Bolívar in the country and, quite possibly, Latin America. It was laid out by architect Carlos Raúl Villanueva and opened in 1930. The monument to Bolívar is identical to that in Caracas.

PALACIO DE GOBIERNO

This large edifice, on the southern side of Plaza Bolívar, was once the splendid Hotel Jardín. Inaugurated in 1930 by Gómez, this playground for the rich and beautiful overshadowed all other Venezuelan hotels of the day. The place witnessed many important episodes of the country's political, social and cultural life, and Carlos Gardel sang his nostalgic tangos here.

The hotel was closed down and remodeled as a government house in 1959, yet you can still feel the charm of the cloisters and interior gardens. If security guards refuse you entry at the front, try the back (south) gate from Av Páez.

TEATRO DE LA OPERA

Commissioned by Gómez in 1934, this theater (☎ 233-6043; fundtom@cantv.net; Av Miranda at Calle Brión) was intended to be the best in the country, to match the capital status of the city. An immense budget of two million bolívares was allotted for the structure alone. The theater was constructed swiftly, and by December 1935 (the month Gómez died) it was almost ready, missing only the imported ceiling and interior furnishings. Nonetheless, the new government halted work, and its decorations were moved to theaters in Caracas. It wasn't until 1973 that the theater finally opened. It can seat 860 people and stages a variety of visiting productions, from opera to folkloric dance.

MAUSOLEO DE GÓMEZ

In typical dictator style, once Gómez had taken a firm grip of Venezuela, he set about building himself a grandiose **mausoleum** (admission free; ⏰ 6am-3pm Tue-Sun) Finished in 1919, this rather pretentious pantheon structure is topped by a white Moorish dome, and houses the tomb of the general and members of his family. Curiously, the interior walls are covered with the kind of thanksgiving plaques normally reserved for saints, each reading 'Thanks for the favors,' and signed with initials.

Fresh flowers and lit candles are also frequently left at the tomb, evidence that Gómez is not forgotten. On the contrary, respect for Gómez has revived over recent years as a result of economic and political turmoil. Also referred to as the 'Panteón de Gómez,' the mausoleum is south of the city center, just behind the cemetery.

PARQUE ZOOLÓGICO

At the northern city limits, the sprawling **zoo** (Av Las Delicias; adult/child under 18 $0.30/0.10; ⏰ 9:30am-4:30pm Tue-Sun) is yet another of

Gómez' achievements, built on one of his own estates. It's a neat and well laid-out park with reasonable cage space for most of the animals. To get there from the city center, take the Castaño/Zoológico buseta, which goes all the way along Av Las Delicias and will deposit you right at the entrance.

Festivals & Events

The **Fiesta de San José**, Maracay's most important annual event, takes place over several days around March 19, the city's patron saint's day. The major *corrida* (bullfight) is celebrated during the feast, but other *corridas* are held on some Sundays during the year, mostly between Christmas and Easter.

Maracay's Teatro de la Opera invites some groups taking part in Caracas' International Theater Festival (p76) to perform here.

Sleeping

BUDGET

Hotel Mar del Plata (☎ 246-4313; Av Santos Michelena Este 23; s/d/tr $11/13/15; P 🐾) Appreciably better than the other central budget options is this peaceful hotel, which features clean, neat rooms and hot water.

Hotel Cristal (☎ 554-0668; Av Bolívar Oeste; d/tr $14/17; P 🐾) If you don't mind staying out of the center, this hotel has a large

---

THE AUTHOR'S CHOICE

Posada El Limón (☎ 283-4925; www.posada ellimon.com; Calle El Piñal 64; dm $10, d $35; P 🐾 💻 📞) A world apart from anything else listed here, this laid-back posada is situated in a tranquil residential suburb looking up to the lush mountains and lying next to a stream. Run by a personable Dutch guy, the complex is filled with colorful mosaics, leafy open patios and pre-Colombian decorative touches.

It provides beds or cheaper hammocks, meals, laundry, tours and transfers (for example, you can be picked up from Maiquetía airport and brought directly to the posada, for $100 for up to three people). The posada is in the suburb of El Limón, about 8km from the city center. There's no public transportation all the way to the gate; you can either take the El Limón buseta and then walk, or go by taxi ($3 from the center).

plant-filled hall and cool, spacious rooms with high tropical ceilings and cable TV. It's four blocks west of Av Ayacucho, easily accessible by countless buses running along Av Bolívar.

Hotel Traini (☎ 245-5502; Av 19 de Abril; d/tr/q $16/19/25; **P** **✖**) This reasonable central option above street level and behind a security grill is clean and good value, though it lacks personality.

Other possible choices:

Hotel Canaima (Av Bolívar; d $11; **✖**) Dingy spot near Plaza Bolívar.

Hotel Guayana (Av Bolívar; d with fan $6.25-8) Grim but quiet.

MID-RANGE

Hotel Aventino (☎ 245-7087; www.hotelaventino.com; 15 Calle López Aveledo; d $20-22, tr $24; **P** **✖**) This excellent choice looks a bit like an exotic birdcage as you enter through the extensive security bars draped with plants. Once in the neat rooms, look above the bed for five colorful buttons – these allow you to control the cable TV, air-con, various light switches, and cheesy, ambient music, all while lying flat on your back. There's a discount if you pay with cash.

Hotel Wladimir (☎ 246-1115; fax 246-2566; Av Bolívar Este; d/tr/q $22/31/35; **P** **✖**) The plain-looking Wladimir is well kept and central, has cable TV and is perfectly good for a decent night's kip. Street-front rooms can be noisy.

Hotel Caroní (☎ 554-4465; Av Ayacucho Norte 19; d/tr $19/23; **P** **✖**) This personable hotel is out of the center. It has attentive service, hot showers and cable TV, though rooms lack any distinguishing features.

Hotel Princesa Plaza (☎ 223-1008; www.hotelprincesaplaza.com; Av Miranda Este; d $34; **P** **✖**) Edging close to top-end quality, the large Princesa lies next to the 30-story brick-and-glass Torre Sindoni. It offers very good value (if a little bland) rooms with extra little comforts such as hairdryer and cable TV.

TOP END

Hotel Pipo International (☎ 241-3111; www.hotelpipo.com; Av Principal El Cestaño; d incl breakfast $60-65; **P** **✖** **▯** **▨**) This ageing four-star, high-rise hotel lies on the road to Choroní at the city limits. Rooms have cable TV, big bathrooms with a hairdryer, some good views and balconies.

Hotel Hampton Inn & Suites (☎ 200-1111; Centro Commercial Paseo Las Delicias; s/d $95/115; **P** **✖** **▯**) This brand spanking new hotel lies above a flashy new shopping mall filled with restaurants and boutiques. It has spacious, modern suite-apartments complete with a well-stocked kitchen, big bathroom and huge wide-screen TVs.

Eating

There are plenty of reasonably priced places to eat scattered throughout the city center. Some of the cheapest typical meals are to be found in the Mercado Principal, built by Gómez in 1921. There are plenty of upmarket restaurants along Av Las Delicias north of the city center.

El Arepanito (☎ 237-8621; Av 19 de Abril at Junín; arepas $1.25-2; ✥ 6-2am; **✖**) Open daily till late, this popular *arepera* has a pleasant plant-filled patio looking across the road to the planes in the aeronautical museum. It also serves good pizza and fruit juices.

Brasilandia (☎ 554-0398; Av Bolívar; mains $3-6.50; ✥ 11:30am-2am; **P** **✖**) From the outside, this large fast-food complex near Hotel Cristal looks like a cross between an airport hanger and a bingo hall. Inside, it serves up quality grills, chicken meals and excellent pizza, and is deservedly popular among locals for its low prices.

Las Terrazas del Vroster (☎ 832-9655; Av Las Delicias; mains $4-9; ✥ noon-11pm; **P**) A popular lunch stop for one and all, Vroster is an energetic restaurant covered by a low roof and supported on all sides by iron bars smothered by hanging baskets that let a refreshing breeze waft through. It serves a good range of pasta and pizza, as well as excellent seafood dishes.

Tasca El Riacho (☎ 241-8401; Av Las Delicias; mains $5-10; ✥ 11:30am-late; **P** **✖**) This cavernous tasca (Spanish-style bar-restaurant) has a huge curvaceous bar, large seating areas and a sophisticated, jazzy atmosphere that comes alive in the evening. You enter through a gimmicky false rock face and across a bridge.

El Bodegón de Sevilla (☎ 242-7914; Av Las Delicias; mains $5-8.50; ✥ 11:30am-late; **P** **✖**) Another traditional tasca, the mansion-style El Bodegón often has live Spanish music. It also has the typical low wooden ceiling, a vast menu including a bit of everything and, of course, an enormous, well-stocked bar for quaffing those essential aperitifs or nibbling on tapas.

Pepito Arturo (Av 19 de Abril; hamburgers $1.50-3; ☽ 10:30am-11:30pm) A down-to-earth, cheerful fast-food stop, Arturo's is the place to chow down on a cheap *parrilla* (mixed grill) washed down with a *batido* (fruit juice).

Pizza Mia (☎ 245-6010; Av 19 de Abril; pizza $3-13; ☽ 11:30am-10:30pm; ✖) This modern, family-friendly chain restaurant lies across the road from Pepito Arturo, and its long list of reasonably priced pizzas includes vegetarian options.

Getting There & Away

AIR

Maracay's civil airport is on the air-force base, 3km west of town. Avior has direct flights to Porlamar ($77 to $84, one hour, daily) and Mérida ($81, one hour, daily except Saturday).

BUS

The bus terminal is on the southeastern outskirts of the city center. It's within walking distance of Plaza Bolívar, but it's quicker to take any of the frequent city buses.

The bus terminal is vast and busy, with frequent transportation to most major cities. Ordinary buses to Caracas depart every 15 minutes or so ($2 to $4, 1½ hours), as do buses to Valencia ($0.65, one hour).

There are at least a dozen departures a day to Barquisimeto ($4 to $6, four hours), Maracaibo ($9 to $12, eight hours) and San Cristóbal ($11 to $14, 11 hours). Half a dozen buses run to San Antonio del Táchira ($14, 12½ hours), Coro ($8 to $10, 6½ hours) and Mérida ($11 to $14, 11 hours). There are direct buses to Puerto La Cruz ($9 to $12, seven hours) and Ciudad Bolívar ($19, nine hours); these buses bypass Caracas, saving time and money. Several ordinary buses per day go to San Fernando de Apure ($8, seven hours).

For transportation to El Playón and Puerto Colombia, see Getting There and Away (p124).

BOLÍVAR HACIENDA

The town of San Mateo, 20km east of Maracay, boasts a hacienda that once belonged to the Bolívar family. It was granted to them in 1593, after they came to settle in Venezuela from their native Spain. At the

beginning of the 18th century, the Bolívars built a sugarcane mill on their land and used African slaves to work the crops, a common practice throughout the region.

In 1814, Simón Bolívar set up a military camp on the hacienda, which became the target of fierce attacks by the royalist troops. Later on, Bolívar passed through San Mateo on various occasions, including a rest stop after the battle of Carabobo in 1821, when he freed the local slaves.

During the 19th century, the hacienda passed through the hands of various owners until Juan Vicente Gómez turned it into barracks in 1924.

Restored in the 1980s to its original state, the hacienda now houses two museums.

The **Museo de la Caña de Azúcar** (☎ 352-0341; ☽ 10am-4pm Tue-Sun) is centered on the original sugarcane mill. Exhibits include the mill itself and a variety of tools, implements and objects related to sugar production.

On the opposite side of the road is the affiliated **Museo Histórico Militar**. This finely restored historic house, on the top of a hill, features a collection of period armor, plus the usual Bolivariana, including documents and a number of portraits.

Getting There & Away

The Bolívar hacienda is located on the old Maracay–La Victoria road (not the freeway), a few kilometers east of San Mateo town. The road is serviced by frequent buses and por puestos, which will let you off at the hacienda entrance. Ask to be dropped off at El Ingenio de Bolívar, as the place is commonly known.

To get to San Mateo from Caracas, take a bus to La Victoria (from La Bandera terminal in Caracas) and from there catch a bus to San Mateo.

LA VICTORIA

☎ 0244 / pop 120,000

Founded in 1593, Nuestra Señora de Guadalupe de La Victoria was the capital of Aragua state until 1917, when Juan Vicente Gómez moved the title to Maracay, 30km to the west.

Today it's a busy city surrounded by factories, but its historic center, particularly the area around Plaza Ribas, retains some of its old architecture and flavor. Stroll around the central streets, between Plaza Ribas and Plaza Bolívar, which are five blocks apart. Both plazas boast a church – the large 18th-century neoclassical Iglesia de Nuestra Señora de la Victoria at Plaza Ribas, and the small Iglesia de Nuestra Señora de la Candelaria at Plaza Bolívar.

Sleeping & Eating

Hotel Hacienda El Recreo (☎ 321-0411; hotelelrecreo@hotmail.com; Av Rivas Dávila Oeste; d/tr/q $30/33/35; P 🍴 🏊) This converted sugar hacienda from 1724 is a haven of tranquility in sprawling grounds studded with huge palm trees and boasting a large swimming pool and restaurant (non-guests welcome). The hotel is on the road to San Mateo, within walking distance west of Plaza Ribas.

Getting There & Away

The bus terminal is 4km east of the historic center. Local por puestos shuttle between the terminal and center ($0.25).

There are frequent buses to Caracas, all running via the freeway ($2 to $4, 1¼ hours). Buses to Maracay go either via the freeway ($0.65 to $80, 30 minutes) or via the old road; the latter will drop you off at San Mateo ($0.50, 15 minutes). Por puestos to Colonia Tovar depart regularly and wind up along a spectacular 36km mountain road ($1.50, one hour). Sit on the right for better vistas.

COLONIA TOVAR

☎ 0244 / pop 9000

A little piece of old Germany lost in the Venezuelan cloud forest, this disorienting town of wood cabins lies scattered on a mountainside in the Cordillera de la Costa, about 60km west of Caracas. It was founded in 1843 by a group of 376 German settlers from the Schwarzwald (Black Forest), recruited by Italian Agustín Codazzi (see the boxed text p117).

Isolated from the outer world by the lack of roads and rules prohibiting marriage outside the colony, the village followed the mother culture, language and architecture for a century. It wasn't until the 1940s that Spanish was introduced as the official language and the ban on marrying outside the community was abandoned. Furthermore, it was not until 1963 that a paved road from Caracas reached Colonia Tovar, marking a turning point in the history of the tiny town.

Today, Colonia Tovar draws hordes of *caraqueños* on weekends, curious to glimpse the traditional architecture, chomp on German sausage, sweets or bread, and enjoy the delicious strawberries, apples, peaches and blackberries, which are cultivated locally. And the town thrives in its new role as a tourist attraction: the pretty buildings are decorated with ye olde Gothic script, waitresses sport frilly traditional garments and braided hair, and the streets are filled with fairy lights and stalls selling multicolored sweets, conserves and crafts.

Weekdays see the town deserted of tourists, but you can enjoy the town's lush surroundings and cordial inhabitants, some of whom are descendants of the original German settlers, at any time.

Whenever you come, bring warm clothing – the temperature drops in these upper reaches of the cordillera (the town is 1800m above sea level). Colonia Tovar's average temperature is 16°C, but it's much lower at night.

Information

The village has a few banks, though exchanging money at the weekend can be difficult. Tour agencies (see p117) will sometimes change money and give information about the locality. For Internet access try **Cyber X** (per hr $1; ⏰ 10am-6:30pm), five minutes up the road to Caracas, next to a pharmacy.

Sights & Activities

Stroll about the steep, winding streets to soak up the Christmassy atmosphere and see some fine examples of traditional German architecture. Call at the diminutive **El Museo de Historia y Artesanía** (☎ 0416-839-1062; admission $0.30; ☺ 9am-6pm Sat & Sun) to learn about the region's history, from antiquated swords to a fossilized crocodile.

Don't miss the quirky black-and-white **church**, a pretty L-shaped building with two perpendicular naves (one for women, the other for men) and the high altar placed in the angle where the naves join. From there, the patron saint of the town, San Martín de Tours, overlooks both naves.

For those sticking around, you might consider a trip down the hill to the **Spa Renacer Center** (☎ 355-1504, in Caracas 0212-985-2908; renacerspacenter@cantv.net), which appears to cater for stressed-out *caraquenos* escaping the city. A full day visit will set you back $30 to $55, including treatments and lunch.

There are various walking options around the town, including a hike up to **Pico Codazzi** (2425m), the highest peak in the area. To go there, you need to get first to the pass on the road to La Victoria, 5km out of Colonia Tovar (walk, hitch or take a por puesto to La Victoria), from where a path branches off to the right and leads up to the top (a half-hour walk).

Tours

Expediciones Rustic Tours (☎ 355-1908; rustic tours@cantv.net; Av Principal) Runs local sightseeing tours into the forest, mountains and down to the coast.

Regenwald Tours (☎ 355-1662; regenwald@cantv .net; Calle Bolívar) The best source of information on local activities such as hiking, paragliding and mountain biking.

Festivals & Events

Colonia Tovar hosts the annual chamber music event **Festival Internacional de Música de Cámara** (☎ 321-6240; www.festivalcoloniatovar.com.ve) at the end of November.

Sleeping & Eating

While Colonia Tovar is an easy day trip from Caracas, the town has more than a dozen hotels and cabañas, most with their own restaurants. Private bathroom and hot water are the norm, and some also have heated rooms. The accommodations are good and stylish, but don't come cheap by Venezuelan standards.

Hotel Selva Negra (☎ 355-1415; selvanegra@cantv .net; d $40, per extra person $9; **P**) Located to the right of the church through some big iron gates, Selva Negra (literally 'black forest') is the oldest and the best-known lodge in town. Opened in 1936, it is like a little village in itself, with about 40 tranquil, picturesque cabañas scattered along the grassy hillside, each sleeping two to six guests. They are all filled with old-style furniture and most have a balcony. The characterful, antique-style restaurant is in the original house with a café with good views alongside. And there's an outdoor playground to keep the kids happy.

A LIFE LESS ORDINARY

Swashbuckler, explorer, soldier, pirate, merchant and cartographer – it was the multitalented Italian Agustín Codazzi (1793–1858) who founded Colonia Tovar in 1843. Codazzi led an extraordinary life: at 17 he was fighting in the Napoleonic army, before he tried out international commerce and later took to managing a casino in Constantinople (now Istanbul).

When Codazzi heard that Bolívar was recruiting foreigners for a new Venezuelan army, he was the first to enroll. However, on his way south he met the French corsair Louis Aury, and together they landed on Providencia, a Colombian island. From there, they ransacked Spanish galleons, reaped huge rewards, and – as a bonus – contributed to the defeat of the Spaniards.

After the war, Codazzi was commissioned to draft maps of Venezuela. But after a while, the Venezuelan government began to look for European migrants eager to settle and work in Venezuela to help revive the devastated economy. Codazzi set about selecting a place with acceptable climatic conditions, then returned to Europe and collected a group of several hundred German peasants (the nationality he thought most adaptable), bringing them to Venezuela and founding Colonia Tovar. By then the Venezuelan authorities had lost enthusiasm for the program, and Codazzi dedicated himself to mapping. His excellent maps are now the pride of national archives in Venezuela and Colombia.

Cabañas Silkerbrunnen (☎ 355-1490; www.lacol oniatovar.net; d/tr/q/8-person $18/24/29/56, d/tr/q with kitchen $24/25/32) Some of the cheapest cabins in town are on offer at this friendly complex set into the hillside, in a *calle ciega* (blind alley) just below the church.

Cabañas Breidenbach (☎ 355-1211; Sector El Calvario; d/tr $19/25, d with kitchen & fireplace $22; P) With one of the best views in town, this large, well-tended hotel is situated on the mountainside above the town center. All rooms are large and modern, though if you can, it's worth splashing out on the doubles with kitchen, salon, and wood fireplace to ward off those chilly mountain nights and to toast your German sausages.

Hotel Restaurant Freiburg (☎ 417-5910; Calle Von Keller; d $32; P) A 15-minute walk away on the other side of the river valley is this old hotel and restaurant, still run by one of the town's original German families. However, the rooms are plain for the price. It has a fabulous old-style German restaurant with great views back up to the town center.

Hotel Restaurant Kaiserstuhl (☎ 355-1810; Calle Joaquín; d/tr $24/47; P) In the heart of town near the cemetery, Kaiserstuhl has comfortable rooms plus a good German restaurant with piped folk music and suitably buxom wait-resses in traditional dress and braided hair.

Other good choices:

Hotel Kafféé Mühle (☎ 355-1367; Sector El Calvario; d/tr $22/32, d cabaña with kitchen & fireplace $38) Has a good restaurant, motor-driven water wheel and small modern rooms.

Rancho Alpino (☎ 355-1470; www.hotelranchoalpino .com; Av Principal; d $26) Smart rooms, and restaurant serving German food and pizza.

Getting There & Away

The trip from Caracas requires a change at El Junquito. All carritos to El Junquito depart from Lecuna at San Juan Puerte Escondido in the center of Caracas ($0.40, 45 minutes to 1½ hours at the weekend). There are also large buses to El Junquito ($0.60); they don't have a terminal, but you can catch them on Av Lecuna or Av Universidad. From El Junquito, por puesto vans take you the remainder of the journey ($1, one hour).

If you don't want to go back the same way to Caracas (or want to continue further west), you can take an exciting ride south down to La Victoria. Over a distance of only 30km, the road descends about 1300m.

Por puestos depart regularly from Colonia Tovar ($1.50, one hour); grab a seat on the left side for better views.

PARQUE NACIONAL HENRI PITTIER
☎ 0243

Venezuela's oldest national park, created in 1937, Henri Pittier has something for everyone. There is a glistening coastline for beachgoers, a vast variety of species for bird-watchers, winding trails for hikers, colonial towns for architecture buffs and rolling Af-rican drumbeats for *rumba* (party) lovers.

Named for its founder, Swiss botanist Henri Pittier, the park covers 1078 sq km of the Cordillera de la Costa, the coastal mountain range (considered the northern continuation of the great Andean system). The Cordillera exceeds 2000m in some areas, then plunges down to the Caribbean coast in the north.

This mountainous region has a staircase of different zones: from Maracay, you ascend steeply through semi-dry decidu-ous woods to evergreen rain forest and, further up, to dense cloud forest – all over a remarkably short distance, taking just an hour by road. Over the crest and descend-ing for another hour northward to the sea, you get the same sequence in reverse, plus arid coastal scrub followed by beaches, mangroves and coconut groves at the base.

The park is famous for its birds. About 580 species have been identified in the park – that represents 43% of the bird species found in Venezuela and 7% of all the birds known in the world. Not bad for its puny size! Indeed, hardly any other park of this size in the world can match it. The animal world here is also rich and diverse, includ-ing tapir, deer, puma, agoutis, peccaries, ocelots, opossums, armadillos, monkeys, snakes, frogs and bats.

This extraordinary diversity is the combined result of the variety of habitats and their unspoiled condition. An added bonus is that Paso Portachuelo (1128m), the lowest pass in the mountain ridge, is on a natural migratory route for birds and insects flying inland from the sea from such distant places as Argentina and Canada.

Orientation

The park's highest point is Pico El Cenizo (2436m). From its east–west ridge, the cordillera rolls dramatically down north to the coast, and south to Maracay. Two roads, both paved, cross the park from north to south. Both originate in Maracay and go as far as the coast. The western road, the one built by Gómez as an escape route (see the boxed text p112), leads from Maracay to Ocumare de la Costa – via Paso Portachuelo – and on to El Playón on the beach, and then continues to Cata.

The eastern road heads from Maracay due north to Choroní and reaches the coast 2km further on, at Puerto Colombia. It's narrower, poorer and more twisting, but it climbs up to 1830m and is more spectacular. Both roads are about 55km long and are occasionally blocked by landslides

in the rainy season. There's no road connection between the coastal ends of these roads; a boat is the only way to get from one to the other.

The coast has rocky cliffs, interspersed with golden sandy bays filled with coconut groves – some almost totally virgin and undeveloped. The town of Puerto Colombia, at the end of the eastern road, is the major tourist destination offering the widest choice of hotels, restaurants and boat-rental facilities. El Playón, on the western road, is also developing into a popular tourist hangout.

Unless you are particularly interested in bird-watching in Rancho Grande (p121), it's better to take the eastern road, which

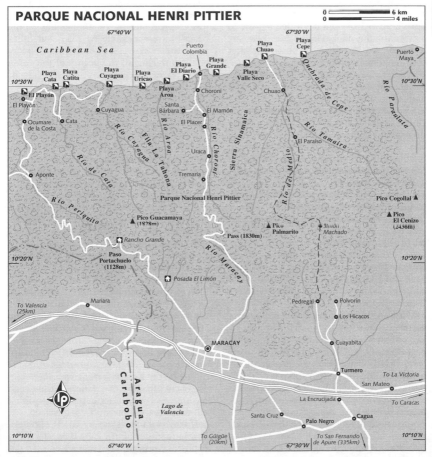

PARQUE NACIONAL HENRI PITTIER

provides access to more attractions and leads along a more spectacular route.

Sights & Activities
COLONIAL TOWNS
This section of coastline has been inhabited for centuries, and some colonial towns have survived on the national park boundaries. Interestingly, all these old towns are set well back from the waterfront; Ocumare de la Costa, Cuyagua, Cata, Choroní and Chuao were all founded several kilometers inland from the sea to protect themselves against the pirates who roamed the coast.

The tiny 385-year-old town of **Choroní** (p124) is the most charming. It comprises just a few narrow streets, but they're lined with fine pastel houses and a deeply shaded Plaza Bolívar. Madre María de San José was born here in 1875 and dedicated her life to service for the poor. The house where she lived and worked is on the plaza. She later continued her work with the poor in Maracay, where she founded a religious congregation. She died at the respectable age of 92 and was beatified in 1995.

On Choroní's plaza is a lovely parish church, Iglesia de Santa Clara, with a finely decorated ceiling. The wall over the high altar has been painted to look like a carved retable. The feast of Santa Clara, the patron saint of the town, is celebrated in August.

Puerto Colombia (p122), on the coast just 2km north of Choroní, was the local port. It has now developed into the region's biggest travelers' haunt – very hip with backpackers. Unlike the sleepy and nostalgic Choroní, Puerto Colombia is full of young crowds, posadas and restaurants. It's a great base for excursions to the national park and beaches, and the laid-back vibe is addictive. Many a traveler ends up delaying their departure.

Chuao (p124), about 8km east of Choroní as the crow flies, is a small old village, known for its cacao plantations and Diablos Danzantes celebrations (see the boxed text p105). Villagers live in almost complete isolation here: the only road is a rough 4km trail between the village and the sea. Access to Chuao is by boat from Puerto Colombia, followed by a walk along the trail.

Other old towns noted for their Diablos Danzantes traditions are **Ocumare de la Costa**, **Cata** and **Cuyagua**, though the celebrations here are not as famous as those in Chuao. All these towns are located in the western, coastal section of the park, and are connected to one another and to Maracay by road.

There was a big African population in all these towns, and their legacy has been preserved in the sensual culture and music. Drums have long been an integral part of life, and their pulsating beat immediately sparks dancing on weekend nights and holidays – particularly during the Fiesta de San Juan on June 23 and 24.

BEACHES
Some gorgeous and secluded beaches and coves surround the national park. The coastal bays are small, and the beaches short but wide and shaded from the relentless tropical sun by coconut palms. Some beaches are accessible by road, but other more solitary coves can only be reached by boat – offering all the beauty of the easily accessed beaches without the crowds or the litter.

The boat business is well developed, and can take you to any isolated beach you wish. The charge is by boat, not by passenger, so the fare depends on how many people go with you on the trip (usually up to 10 passengers). Competition between boat operators is fierce, so prices are negotiable: always try to bargain. Puerto Colombia is the busiest tourist-boat hub.

Before you go, decide which road to take, as you have to choose between the beaches of either the Cata or Puerto Colombia areas. Boats can transfer you from Cata to Puerto Colombia or vice versa, but this trip will cost around $65 per boat.

Puerto Colombia Area
Around Puerto Colombia, the most popular beach is **Playa Grande**, a five-minute walk by road east of town. It's about half a kilometer long and is shaded by coconut palms, but is busy and littered on weekends. There are several rustic shack restaurants at the entrance to the beach, serving mouth-watering fried fish. You can camp on the beach or sling your hammock between the palms, but don't leave your stuff unattended.

If Playa Grande is too crowded or littered, go to the undeveloped **Playa El Diario**, on the opposite (western) side of the town. To get there, take the side road, Calle El Cementerio, which branches off midway along the Choroní–Puerto Colombia road, next to a small bridge. The road passes a few hotels before it reaches the cemetery (500m from the turnoff), where the asphalt becomes concrete. Follow the road uphill for 200m and take a path branching off to the left. It climbs a bit, then goes down to the small and shadeless El Diario beach (a 25-minute walk from the cemetery). If you take the concrete road to its end on the mountaintop (crowned with a communication mast), a 10-minute walk from the cemetery, you'll get sweeping panoramic views.

Other beaches in the area are normally visited by boat, though some of them can also be reached on foot after a long, sweaty walk. Boats crowd at the river mouth in Puerto Colombia, and can take you to isolated beaches further down the coat, including **Playa Aroa** ($30 roundtrip per boat, 15 minutes one-way), **Playa Valle Seco** ($22, 20 minutes), **Playa Chuao** ($25, 30 minutes) and **Playa Cepe** ($32, 45 minutes). The boat can pick you up at any prearranged time. The trip may be quite rough if the waves are high; be prepared to get wet.

Cata Area
Further west, the first beach you can get to by road is **El Playón**, skirting the northern edge of the town of the same name. There are actually several small beaches here, the best of which is probably **Playa Malibú**, close to the Malecón.

Five kilometers eastward is the area's most famous beach, **Playa Cata**. Girls hang on to your bikinis – there's an unexpectedly strong backwash! The beach is a postcard crescent of sand bordering Bahía de Cata, and marred only by two ugly apartment towers looming over the beach. There are plenty of shack restaurants and one basic **posada** (d $9.50) on the western side.

Boats from Playa Cata take tourists to the smaller and quieter **Playa Catita**, on the eastern side of the same bay. It takes 10 minutes to get there, and the ride costs $1.60 per person in a group. You can also walk there, passing interesting xerophytic (adapted for minimal water conditions) vegetation on the way.

Further east is the unspoiled and usually deserted **Playa Cuyagua**, which is good for surfers. You can get there by a 2.5km sand trail from the town of Cuyagua. Alternatively, boats from Playa Cata can take you to the beach for about $19 roundtrip.

ESTACIÓN BIOLÓGICA RANCHO GRANDE
Far away from the coastal towns and beaches, this dilapidated **biological station** (in Maracay ☎ 0243-245-3470; admission $3, Inparques fee $0.20; ☺ 8am-4pm) is on the Maracay–Cata road, a few hundred meters before the Paso Portachuelo. Surrounded by cloud forest, this station sits at an altitude of 1100m just off the road; keep your eyes peeled for the sign.

The station is in an intriguing question-mark shaped building originally destined to be a posh country hotel, commissioned by Juan Vicente Gómez. The building was only half completed by the time Gómez died and it was deserted by the workers when they heard news of the dictator's death. Park founder Henri Pittier suggested establishing the new park's research station here; his proposal became a reality in the mid-1940s. The station is run by the Faculty of Agriculture of the Universidad Central de Venezuela, based at El Limón, the northwestern outer suburb of Maracay.

An ecological path known as the Sendero Andrew Field heads through the forest behind the station, and is open to the public. The path is named in memory of a young British botanist who tragically died here. The loop, which is easily walked in an hour, provides myriad opportunities to see the local flora and fauna, particularly birds.

For serious bird-watchers, it's feasible to see up to 400 species on a weeklong visit to the station. The best times for bird-spotting are early in the morning and late in the afternoon. December through to March is perhaps the best time for viewing migratory birds, though October and November are also good. You may also see monkeys, agoutis, peccaries, snakes and butterflies.

Adventurous travelers may want to hike to the top of Pico Guacamaya (see the following section). The station offers simple accommodations (see below), but no food. Bring reliable rain gear.

Sleeping
The biological station just has simple, dormitory-style accommodations, providing

about 40 beds. Though intended for visiting researchers, they're hardly ever all taken. Tourists are welcome to stay for $6 per head ($3 for students with an ISIC card). No camping is allowed and no food is provided, but you can use the kitchen facilities. Bring a sleeping bag, food and a flashlight.

HIKING

The national park has various rough paths linking villages scattered throughout the area and are used by locals. Some paths were originally traced centuries ago, but many were abandoned and eventually disappeared when the roads were built.

Coastal Routes

The area along the coast, where most of the villages are located, offers the best options for walkers and is relatively dry. It is possible, for example, to walk from Puerto Colombia west to Aroa (via Playa El Diario) or east to Chuao.

Various routes lead from the Choroní area to Chuao. One of the trails begins 6km south on the road from Choroní, at the place known as 'El Mamón;' the walk from here to Chuao will take five to seven hours. The route is confusing in parts because of various side paths, so consider taking a local guide (see Tours, this page).

Further up the mountains, the trails are few and far between. The terrain is covered by thick forest, and rainfall is high. The cordillera's northern slopes receive more rain than the southern ones, and the upper parts are pretty wet most of the year. The driest months are January to March.

Cross-Cordillera Routes

The trail going from Turmero, 14km east of Maracay, to Chuao is one of the few trails that traverse the cordillera. It is signposted and reasonably easy to follow, though its upper reaches can be very wet and muddy in the rainy season. This hike can be done in two days, but it may run to three.

Beginning from Turmero, take a taxi to the ranger's post in Pedregal ($4). From here, a 4WD trail goes northward to another ranger's post, Simón Machado (a five-hour walk), which is attended only in the tourist peak season. There's a water tank, but it's safer not to drink the water here, you are allowed to camp, but the scenery

isn't particularly impressive. The walking trail goes from here up to about 1950m on the crest (a three- to four-hour walk) and descends gradually over the northern slope to the hamlet of El Paraíso (a six-hour walk). The trail continues downhill to Chuao (a 1½-hour walk), from where a 4km dusty road (serviced by a few vehicles) goes down to the beach. The trip can also be done in reverse, from Chuao to Turmero.

Another challenging cross-cordillera trail links the Rancho Grande biological station with Pico Guacamaya (1828m). The path is faint and easy to lose; it will take you three to four hours uphill. Ask at the station for news on the condition of the trail.

TOURS

For hikes in the Choroní area (eg Choroní to Chuao), look for guides in Puerto Colombia, Choroní or one of the small villages up the road.

Virgilio Espinal (☎ 991-1106, 0416-431-6295, 0416-747-3833; senttovivi@hotmail.com) Virgilio Espinal is one of the good local guides for walks and bird-watching. He is English-speaking and commonly goes by the name 'Vivi.' If you ask locals in Choroní or Puerto Colombia, you will find him. Knowledgeable about the park, Vivi operates a rustic mountain refuge known as 'El Cocuy,' near the village of Uraca (on the Maracay–Puerto Colombia road), which serves as a base for tours ranging from two hours to several days and of any level of difficulty.

Osprey Expeditions (☎ 0416-496-5558, 0414-310-4491; ospreyvenezuela@yahoo.com) This is another small, up-and-coming agency with a tour guide named Ben; recommended by readers.

Sleeping & Eating

Accommodations and food are in good supply in Puerto Colombia and El Playón. You can camp at no cost on the beaches, but never leave your tent unattended.

PUERTO COLOMBIA

This tiny town has a score of places to stay – everything from rock bottom to luxury – and the number is growing swiftly. Be warned: prices rise by a whacking 30% on weekends and for major holiday periods (Christmas to early January, Carnaval, Holy Week, August). The rates listed in this section are for midweek off-peak times.

Restaurants, too, are numerous, so starving is improbable; fried fish is the local staple. Budget eating is provided by a cluster of simple restaurants near the pedestrian bridge leading to Playa Grande. On Playa Grande itself, there's a colony of rustic restaurants that cook inexpensive meals, mostly fried fish, for $3 to $5 per plate.

Hostal Colonial (www.choroni.net; Calle Morillo 37; d $9, d/tr with bathroom $10/12, q with kitchen $24) One of the cheapest places to stay is this ever-popular spot on the main access road, opposite the bus terminus. It's a sociable hostel with a wide variety of rooms, a courtyard at the back with a few hammocks, plus lockers, a kitchen and tours.

Posada Lemon Tree (☎ 991-1123; Calle José Maitín 3; d/tr $19/25, with air-con $22/28; 🌐 🖳) Recognizable by its brightly colored lemon paint job, this laid-back and welcoming German-run posada has an attractive enclosed courtyard and simple, good value rooms.

Posada La Casa de Las García (☎ 991-1056, in Caracas 0212-6622858; www.posada-garcia.rec.ve; Calle El Cementerio; d/tr/q incl breakfast $55/65/75; P 🌐) This centuries-old family hacienda is well worth the walk out of town. Its large, sprawling grounds contain meticulous gardens overflowing with flowers that attract hummingbirds, while the charming old-style rooms have characterful antique touches and hammocks hung outside. A newer extension at the back of the house has stylish, light rooms with air-con.

Posada Tom Carel (☎ 991-1220; www.posadatom carel.com; Calle Trino Rangel; d with fan $23, with air-con $25, q with fan & shared bathroom $25; 🌐) This colorful, characterful little family posada near Hostal Colonial has plenty of attention to detail with intricate mosaics and stenciling on the walls. Rooms are small and well kept – many with hammocks strung up over the beds.

Hostal Vista Mar (☎ 991-1250; vistamarchoroni@hotmail.com; Calle Colón; d/tr/q $16/19/22; P) This simple hostel is perched at the end of the seafront boulevard, and near a small park. Rooms are plain and a little dark, with cold-water bathrooms, but there's bamboo-shaded hammocks overlooking the sea on the breezy rooftop.

Posada Semeruco (☎ 991-1264; cataquero@cantv .net; Calle Morillo 65; d/tr $33/40; P 🌐) This elegant, upmarket posada is located further inland in a colonial-style building laid out around a flower-filled courtyard. Rooms have handsome old-style furniture and hammock chairs on the porch. Reservations

are mandatory: the email address is shared, so specify you want the Semeruco.

Hostal Casagrande (☎ 991-1251; www.hostalcasa grande.com; Calle Morillo 33; d/tr/q $60/79/97; P 🌐 🖳) Rooms in this stunning colonial-style hostel opposite the church have attractive wooden furniture and four-poster beds draped in gauzy mosquito nets to make you feel like royalty. The beautiful, shady courtyard contains several hammocks and a shallow birdbath-like pool for cooling off.

Posada La Parchita (☎ 991-1233; Calle Trino Rangel; d/tr/q $16/22/25; P) This cozy and quiet family-run posada is tucked away down a backstreet next to the river. It has a handful of simple, tidy rooms with fans set around a nice little patio.

Hacienda El Portete (☎ 991-1255; www.elportete .com; Calle El Cementerio; s/d/tr/q incl breakfast $38/47/57/63; P 🌐 🖳) A hundred meters up the road from Posada La Casa de Las Garcia is another part of what was once the same beautiful old cacao hacienda building. This colonial mansion has seen more extensive renovation, and contains its own restaurant, bar, games room and play area for kids. Each sparsely decorated room has its own hammock outside.

Hostal Piapoco (☎ 991-1108, in Caracas 0212-753-8790; Calle Morillo; d/tr $38/50; P 🌐 🖳) This is a large modern hostel on the main road at the entrance to the town. It has neatly kept rooms and a quiet, shadeless patio around the pool plus a few hammocks slung up by the restaurant.

Mesón Xuchytlán (☎ 991-1234; Plaza Bolívar at Calle Morillo 22; d with Jacuzzi $70, without Jacuzzi $60, q incl breakfast $125; 🌐) Stunning Mexican-style mansion near Plaza Bolívar.

Don Miguel (☎ 0416-447-1127; Calle Morillo; d $9.50; P) A cheap functional place with a rowdy cock-a-doodle-doo to wake you up in the morning.

Montañita (☎ 991-1132; Calle Morillo; d $16-19) This simple, friendly hostel has no sign; it is one block from the waterfront.

Bar Restaurant Araguaneyes (☎ 991-1137; Calle Los Cocos 8; mains $3-7; ☽ 8am-11:30pm) This lively restaurant-cum-drinking-hole is plastered with psychedelic beachbum murals and it has two nice terraces, one on the roof. It offers good international and criollo food including breakfasts, plus a fair list of cocktails ($1.25 to $2.50).

Tasca Bahia (☎ 0414-443-2654; Calle Los Cocos; mains $3.50-5; ◷ 8am-10pm) Great, down-to-earth spot for local seafood specialties.

CHORONÍ

An oasis of peace, Choroní is the place to escape the crowds of Puerto Colombia. The town has two pleasant colonial hotels located on the main street, but eateries are few and far between.

Hostería Río Mar (☎ 991-1038, in Caracas 0212-941-1945; riomar@cantv.net; Calle Miranda; d/tr/q $19/22/25; ✖ ▣) This attractive mustard-yellow house houses a good little hostel behind its heavy wooden door and colonial barred windows. It has a high bamboo roof, narrow corridors and simple but cheerful rooms.

Posada Colonial Choroní (☎ 0414-275-8419; www .mipagina.cantv.net/posadacolonial; Calle Miranda 34-1; d/tr/q $13/16/25) Backing onto the river just a few steps from Río Mar is this cheaper alternative. It is also in a high-ceilinged colonial building, though with a concrete courtyard and floors. Its relaxed, friendly host offers midweek discounts when it's not busy.

Hotel Hacienda La Aljorra (☎ 0414-798-1662; laljorra@hotmail.com; Carrera Maracay-Choroní km 49; d/tr $29/35, q $41-45; ℗) This huge, sprawling 18th-century cacao plantation has a charmingly renovated hacienda building 2km inland from Choroní, on the road to Maracay. The handsome, high-ceilinged rooms have fans and hot-water bathrooms, and the hotel has its own restaurant.

CHUAO

The little village of Chuao has a few simple but neat posadas with bunk beds and fans (but without private bathroom) for about $5 per person.

EL PLAYÓN

The counterpart of the eastern road's Puerto Colombia, El Playón is the major lodging center on the western road, sporting more than a dozen places to stay. The town is much larger than Puerto Colombia, but less attractive. Many places to stay are within two blocks of the waterfront. Prices given are midweek, but from Thursday to Sunday they rise by as much as 30%.

There are a few ramshackle restaurants in town and hotels will generally serve food on request.

Posada de La Costa Eco-Lodge (☎ 951-1006; www.ecovenezuela.com; Calle California 23; d/tr $22/28, d cabin $28; ▣ ▣) Set in a sunny garden facing the beach, the excellent de La Costa Eco-Lodge provides neat rooms with fan, cabañas, cold-water bathrooms, restaurant service, cable TV, boat trips, bike rental, snorkeling and scuba diving. It has a relaxed atmosphere and an enticing pool area with a fountain and sun loungers.

Posada Loley (☎ 993-1252; Calle Fuerzas Armadas; d/tr $13/16) This simple posada, one block back from the beach, is one of the cheapest and best budget options. It has a small garden and patio, laid-back host and meals are available for guests.

Hotel Costa de Oro (☎ 951-1010; Calle California 2; s/d/tr/q $19/25/35/40; ✖) Teetering on the edge of the sea, Costa de Oro offers spacious doubles with good hot-water bathrooms. Some rooms have great seafront views.

La Begoña (☎ 993-1971; Calle La Capilla; d/tr/q $25/32/38; ℗ ✖) Inland, this unimaginative but comfortable hotel block offers modern suites with good kitchens, huge fridges, cable TV and balconies.

Getting There & Away

The departure point for the park is the Maracay bus terminal. Buses to El Playón (marked 'Ocumare de la Costa') depart every hour from 7am to 5pm ($1.50, two hours). They can let you off at Rancho Grande but will charge the full El Playón fare. The last bus back to Maracay departs at 5:30pm.

There are also hourly minibuses from Maracay to El Playón, but they depart from El Limón, not the bus terminal. The advantage is that they run longer, until about 7:30pm. From El Playón, you can catch a carrito to Playa Cata ($0.65, 10 minutes).

To Puerto Colombia, buses leave from the bus terminal every one or two hours ($2, 2¼ hours). The last bus back to Maracay theoretically departs from Puerto Colombia at 5pm (later on weekends), but this departure time is not reliable.

CARABOBO STATE

VALENCIA

☎ 0241 / pop 1,060,000

Founded in 1555, Valencia is Venezuela's third-largest city, and played a crucial part in the fight for independence and its aftermath. It's a prosperous, bustling urban sprawl nestled in the north–south valley of the Río Cabriales and bordered by mountains. Much like its Spanish namesake, the Valencia region is famous for its orange groves and bullfighting. The city's Plaza de Toros Monumental is one of the largest in the Americas, seating an impressive 27,000 spectators. Set at an altitude of 480m, Valencia has an average temperature of about 25°C, with hot days ameliorated by the evening breeze that rolls down from the mountains.

History

Valencia has had a tumultuous and checkered history. It had not yet reached its seventh anniversary when Lope de Aguirre, the infamous adventurer obsessed with finding El Dorado, sacked the town and burned it to the ground. Twenty years later, the not-yet-fully-recovered town was razed by Carib Indians. Then in 1667 the town was seized and destroyed again, this time by French pirates. The town's proximity to Lago de Valencia didn't help either. The disease-breeding marshes brought about smallpox epidemics that decimated the population and scared away many survivors. Then in 1812, a devastating earthquake shook the Andean shell, leaving Valencia in ruins yet again.

And as if all that wasn't enough – the war for independence came to Valencia. Just two years after the earthquake, the town was besieged by royalist troops under the command of José Tomás Boves (fittingly known as 'the Butcher'). The ensuing slaughter left 500 people dead. Over the next seven years, no fewer than two dozen battles were fought around the town, only ceasing on June 24, 1821, when Bolívar's decisive victory at Carabobo secured Venezuela's independence.

The year 1826 saw Valencia become the first town to oppose Bolívar's sacred union, Gran Colombia. Its inhabitants called for Venezuelan sovereignty and, four years later, this demand became a reality. Congress decreed formal secession here and made Valencia the newborn country's capital, before switching it a year later to Caracas.

The town caught new economic wind in its sails after WWII, and today Valencia is Venezuela's most industrialized city. The city generates nearly a quarter of the country's national manufacturing production and is also the center of the most developed agricultural region.

Information

INTERNET ACCESS
Cybergest (Av Cedeño; per hr $0.50; ☺ 8.30am-7pm Mon-Sat)
Superchat (☎ 0414-423-4588; Callejon La Ceiba; per hr $0.50; ☺ 24hr) Located just off Av Bolívar Norte.

LAUNDRY
Mr Wash (Av Cedeño; ☺ 8am-noon & 2-6pm Mon-Sat)
Lavandería Lux (☎ 858-5419; Calle 103 Rondón; ☺ 8.30am-noon & 3-5.30pm Mon-Fri, 9am-1pm Sat)

MONEY
Corp Banca (Av 101 Díaz Moreno) Exchanges Amex traveler's checks.
Banco Mercantil (Calle 100 Colombia)
Banesco (Calle 99 Páez)
Banco de Venezuela (Av 101 Díaz Moreno at Calle 101 Libertad)
Italcambio (☎ 821-8173; No 12, Edificio Talía, Av Bolívar Norte, Urbanización Los Sauces) This *casa de cambio* (money-exchange office) is about 2km north of Plaza Bolívar.

POST
Ipostel (Calle 100 Colombia; ☺ 8am-4pm Mon-Fri, 8am-11am Sat)

TELEPHONE
CANTV (Calle 103 Rondón; Internet per hr $1; ☺ 8am-6.30pm Mon-Sat)

TOURIST INFORMATION
Dirección de Turismo de Carabobo (☎ 824-4231; Av Bolívar Norte, Torre Venezuela, 8th fl, No 8-A; ☺ 8am-noon & 2-5pm Mon-Fri) This tourist office is about 3.5km north of Plaza Bolívar.

Sights

PLAZA BOLÍVAR
The heart of the historic town, this plaza boasts the inevitable monument to Bolívar, though this one claims a certain novelty. The bronze figure, pointing toward Campo Carabobo, stands on a 10m-high white Italian marble column cut from a single block of stone. The monument was unveiled in 1889.

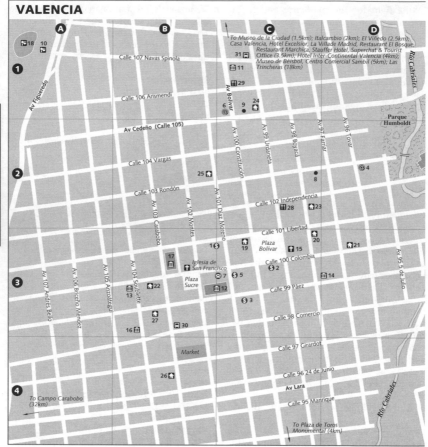

VALENCIA

To Museo de la Ciudad (1.5km); Italcambio (2km); El Viñedo (2.5km); Casa Valencia, Hotel Excelsior, La Villade Madrid, Restaurant El Bosque, Restaurant Marchica, Stauffer Hotel, Superchat & Tourist Office (3.5km); Hotel Inter-Continental Valencia (4km); Museo de Béisbol, Centro Comercial Sambil (5km); Las Trincheras (18km)

Calle 107 Navas Spinola

Calle 106 Arismendi

Av Cedeño (Calle 105)

Calle 104 Vargas

Calle 103 Rondón

Calle 102 Independencia

Calle 101 Libertad

Plaza Bolívar

Iglesia de San Francisco

Plaza Sucre

Calle 100 Colombia

Calle 99 Páez

Calle 98 Comercio

Calle 97 Girardot

Calle 96 24 de Junio

Av Lara

Calle 95 Manrique

Market

Parque Humboldt

Av Figueredo

Av Bolívar

Av 100 Constitución

Av 99 Urdaneta

Av 98 Boyacá

Av 97 Tamar

Av 96 Tovar

Av 95.5 de Julio

Av 101 Díaz Moreno

Av 102 Montes

Av 103 Carabobo

Av 104 Sublette

Av 105 Anzoátegui

Av 106 Briceño Méndez

Av 107 Andrés Bello

Río Cabriales

To Campo Carabobo (32km)

To Plaza de Toros Monumental (4km)

THE CENTRAL NORTH

CATEDRAL

The colonial **cathedral** (☎ 857-0979; Plaza Bolívar) is about 420 years old, though it has been altered by so many generations that today it's an eclectic hodgepodge of historical styles. The latest restoration was in the early 1950s, which saw the ceiling plastered with an intricate design resembling cake frosting.

The cathedral's most revered treasure, the figure of Nuestra Señora del Socorro, is kept in the chapel in the left transept on an elaborate red-and-gold stage. Carved in the late 16th century, the sorrowful Virgin in black has an expression of perpetual shock and sadness. She was the first statue in Venezuela to be crowned (in 1910) by Rome, and her original gold crown is encrusted with

so many precious stones it has to be stored in a safe.

The two large paintings, *The Last Supper* and *The Entry into Jerusalem*, that hang on each the chapel's side walls are the work of Antonio Herrera Toro, a well-known Valencia-born artist who painted murals in many local churches and buildings.

CASA PÁEZ

This beautifully preserved **historic mansion** (☎ 857-1272; Av 98 Boyacá at Calle 99 Páez; admission free; ⏰ 9am-noon & 3-5:30pm Tue-Fri, 9am-2pm Sat & Sun) is the former home of Venezuela's first president, General José Antonio Páez. He distinguished himself by forging a formidable army of *llaneros* (plainsmen) who

INFORMATION		
Banco de Venezuela	.1	B3
Banco Mercantil	.2	C3
Banco Mercantil	(see 7)	
Banesco	.3	C3
CANTV	.4	D2
Corp Banca	.5	C3
Cybergest	.6	C1
Ipostel	.7	C3
Lavandería Lux	.8	C2
Mr Wash	.9	C1

SIGHTS & ACTIVITIES	(pp125–8)	
Acuario	.10	A1
Ateneo de Valencia	.11	C1
Capitol	.12	C3
Casa de la Estrella	.13	B3
Casa Páez	.14	D3
Cathedral	.15	C3
Museo de Arte e Historia	.16	B3
Teatro Municipal	.17	B3
Zoológico	.18	A1

SLEEPING	🏠	(pp128–9)
Hotel Carabobo	.19	C3
Hotel Caracas	.20	C3
Hotel Caribe	.21	D3
Hotel Colón	.22	B3
Hotel Continental	.23	C2
Hotel Dinastía	.24	C1
Hotel Don Pelayo	.25	B2
Hotel El Diamante	.26	B4
Hotel Nacional	.27	B3

EATING	🍴	(p129)
Buffet Vegetariano	.28	C2
El Arepazo Criollo	.29	C1

TRANSPORT	(pp129–30)	
Buses to Campo Carabobo	.30	B3
Buses to Centro Comercial Sambil	.31	C1

fought under Bolívar, contributing greatly to the achievement of independence. In 1830, on the day Venezuela split from Gran Colombia, Páez took power as the first acting president and established his residence in the new capital. A year later, he was elected president of the republic and moved with the government to Caracas.

Restored and furnished with period fittings, the house is today a museum. The walls of the cloister lining the lovely central patio are graced with fascinating murals depicting the nine battles the general fought. The work was done by Pedro Castillo and supposedly directed by Páez himself. Ask the attendant to show you the tiny prison and torture room at the back of the house.

Wall paintings by unfortunate prisoners can still be seen here.

CAPITOL
Built in 1772 as a convent, this dazzlingly white building takes up half a block. The **Capitol** (Calle 99 Páez) became the government house a century later, when Guzmán Blanco pushed out the resident nuns – a bad habit of his, which he indulged at religious institutions throughout the country. Unfortunately guided visits were recently suspended due to political turmoil; call ☎ 857-1326 for news.

TEATRO MUNICIPAL
Modeled on the Paris Opera House and inaugurated in 1894, the stunning ceiling of this 640-seat **theater** (☎ 857-4276; Calle 100 Colombia) was painted by Antonio Herrera Toro. It depicts famous folk of music and literature, including Rossini, Shakespeare and Beethoven. To see it during the day, enter through the back door (from Calle Libertad), which leads onto the stage; the guards should switch the lights on for you.

MUSEO DE ARTE E HISTORIA
This small local-history **museum** (☎ 617-6867; Av 104 Soublette; admission free; ⏰ 9am-3:45pm Tue-Fri, 9am-noon Sat) is in the Casa de Los Celis, one of the most beautiful colonial mansions in the city, built in the 1760s and named after one of its owners. Unfortunately, the exhibits are scarce.

CASA DE LA ESTRELLA
The sovereign state of Venezuela was born in this **historic house** (☎ 874-3056; Calle 100 Colombia at Av Soublette; admission free; ⏰ 9am-5pm Tue-Sun) on May 6, 1830, when Congress convened here and decreed secession from Gran Colombia. Erected as a hospital around 1710 (thus being the city's oldest existing house), the building was remodeled after independence as a college, which later became the Universidad de Valencia. Extensively restored over recent years, the Casa is now a museum. The few exhibits on display include a brief history of Valencia's past posted on boards and a 15-minute video on the history of the house.

MUSEO DE LA CIUDAD
This curious orange-and-yellow brick **museum** (☎ 874-3056; Av Miranda at Calle Rojas Queipo;

admission free; 9am-5pm Tue-Fri, 10am-5pm Sat & Sun) is in the 19th-century palace-like Quinta La Isabela, better known as the Palacio de Los Iturriza, about 1.5km north of the center. The museum is dedicated to the city's history, though there's not much to see, except for changing exhibitions and the fine historic interior of the palace.

ACUARIO & ZOOLÓGICO

The favorite attractions for local inhabitants are undoubtedly the **aquarium** and **zoo** (857-4739; Av Fernando Figueredo; adult/child under 12 $1.90/1.25; 9am-5pm Tue-Fri, 10am-6pm Sat & Sun; P). The stars of the aquarium are the *toninas* (freshwater dolphins) kept in a large central pool. Shows are at 10am, noon, 2pm and 4:30pm Tuesday to Friday, and 11am, 2pm, 4pm and 5.30pm weekends. Next to the pool is the aquarium-terrarium, which showcases Venezuelan freshwater fish and snakes, including electric eels, piranhas and anacondas.

Beyond the aquarium is the small zoo, featuring Venezuela's most typical animal species, including the jaguar, tapir, Orinoco caiman, turtle and a variety of birds.

MUSEO DE BÉISBOL

This **museum** (841-1313; Centro Commercial Sambil, Mañongo; admission $2; 3pm-9pm Tue-Fri, 10am-9pm Sat, noon-6pm Sun; P), in the newly constructed Centro Comercial Sambil, 5km north of the city, is totally devoted to baseball fanaticism. It even has a pitching machine under the distinctive half-dome baseball roof of the shopping mall. Buses to Sambil run from the town center.

Festivals & Events

The two major local events are **Semana de Valencia**, in late March, and the **Fiestas Patronales de Nuestra Señora del Socorro**, in mid-November. The former features cultural events, an agricultural fair, parades, bullfights etc. The latter is a religious feast in honor of the city's patron saint, in which the crowned Virgin is taken out of the church and paraded in a procession.

In October of every year, the prestigious Salón Arturo Michelena opens in the **Ateneo de Valencia** (Av Bolívar) and goes on for three months until January. This is Venezuela's oldest visual-arts show, held every year since 1943. It presents a variety of styles

and forms, including painting, sculpture, performance, video and installations.

Sleeping

The cheapest accommodations are concentrated a few blocks around Plaza Bolívar, but these hotels are very basic and the area is unsafe at night. All the hotels listed have private bathrooms.

BUDGET

Hotel Continental (857-1004; Av 98 Boyacá No 101-70; d/tr $11/12.50;) This canary-yellow, colonial-style hotel is the best budget option in the center. It has good security and service compared with others in the area, and better kept rooms.

Hotel Carabobo (858-8860; Calle 101 Libertad No 100-37; d $14-15, tr/q $18/22;) Ideally located just off Plaza Bolívar, this hotel still has one foot in the 1970s with some lurid plastic furniture remaining and poor maintenance in places. However, it's a step above many budget places in the center with secure, clean rooms and good beds.

Hotel Colón (857-7105; Calle 100 Colombia No 103-37; d $16;) Styleless but secure hotel with hot-water bathrooms, TV and its own restaurant. The higher floors are lighter.

Hotel Nacional (858-3676; Calle 99 Páez No 103-51; d $6.50-9.50, d with air-con & TV $11-13, tr with air-con & TV $16;) This old building painted in startling pink-and-green paint houses a buzzing, unpretentious tasca restaurant. A courtyard out the back is surrounded by rooms that generally attract a pay-by-the-hour clientele. The air-conditioned rooms are better quality.

Hotel Caracas (857-1849; Av Boyacá No 100-84; d $6-9.50) Located just behind the cathedral, this place is literally falling apart at the seams, though its cool, plant-filled courtyard retains a certain 1920s charm in a not-been-touched-since-then way.

Hotel Caribe (857-1157; Calle 100 Colombia No 96-68; d with fan $9.50, d with air-con $12.50, tr with fan $12.50) Rusty-round-the-edges budget choice with open-air courtyard.

MID-RANGE & TOP-END

Hotel El Diamante (858-1595; Av 103 Carabobo; d with/without Jacuzzi $22/32; P) This diamond of a hotel is by far the best central option in its price range. There's a professional atmosphere with polite staff and piped music, plus the neat, freshly tiled rooms are sparklingly clean and have cable TV.

Hotel Dinastía (☎ 858-8139; hdinastia@cantv.net; Av 99 Urdaneta at Av Cadeño; d $33-34, tr/q/ste $36/38/39; P 🍴 🖥) This smart three-star hotel is easily one of best value options in the center. It has room service and a restaurant, plus large, comfortable rooms that include cable TV and a fridge.

Hotel Excelsior (☎ 821-4055; Av Bolívar Norte 129-30; d/tr/q $22/25/28; P 🍴) Stranded away north of the center, but in a safer area, is this reasonable hotel. It's a little worn around the edges but has friendly service, cable TV and hot-water bathrooms.

Hotel Don Pelayo (☎ 857-9378; Av 101 Díaz Moreno at Calle 103 Rondón; d $33; P 🍴) This fading but good high-rise hotel has a stylish Art Deco entrance up its curvy staircase, though it's much plainer inside. The well-fitted rooms have cable TV, and there is a hotel gym available.

Stauffer Hotel (☎ 823-5197; www.staufferhotel.com .ve; Av Bolívar Norte; s/d incl breakfast $44/48; P 🍴 🍸) This good-value hotel near the tourist office has no less than 17 floors, the top few of which have an excellent view of the city's soccer pitch and surrounding mountains. It also has an attractive outdoor swimming pool with nice views.

Hotel Inter-Continental Valencia (☎ 820-3100; www.interconti.com; Calle Juan Uslar, Urbanización La Viña; s/d/ste $139/149/250; P 🍴 🖥 🍸) This expensive five-star hotel, about 4km north of the city center, is the poshest place in town, with all the luxuries you would expect for the price.

Eating

The center has plenty of cheap feeds in the backstreets, where set meals can be found for just $2 to $3.50. However, the area is not renowned for quality dining, and restaurants here tend to close by 8pm, except for the tascas, which by that time turn into drinking venues. Better eating can be found north of the center along Av Bolívar Norte.

There's also a good choice of places to eat in El Viñedo, the area between Avs Sanda and Monseñor Adam to the west of Av Bolívar, about 2.5km north of the center. El Viñedo has become one of Valencia's trendiest spots, packed with restaurants, cafés and bars that draw in some of the more affluent local folks, particularly on weekend evenings.

Buffet Vegetariano (☎ 858-6550; Calle 102 Independencia at Av Urdaneta; 3-course menu $3; 🕒 7am-4pm Mon-Sat) For vegetarians and non-vegetarians alike, the best budget option in the center is this place, with hearty meat-free set meals, delicious cakes, fresh juices and salads.

El Arepazo Criollo (☎ 857-9921; Av Bolívar; mains $2-6; 🕒 24hr) Smart and popular joint serving a long list of arepas round the clock. You can point to your desired toppings on the buffet.

Also in the center, Hotel Don Pelayo, Hotel Nacional and Hotel Colón all have reasonably good and economical restaurants; Hotel Nacional is cheaper and serves an inexpensive lunchtime *menu del día* (daily menu).

La Villa de Madrid (☎ 823-6659; Av Bolívar Norte No 152-75; mains $6-8; 🕒 11am-late; 🍴) Paella is a specialty at this classy old-style Spanish restaurant with dark wooden pillars and a huge square bar hung with cured hams.

Casa Valencia (☎ 823-4923; Av Bolívar Norte; mains $5-13; 🕒 11am-late) Recommended by locals, this large, terracotta-colored traditional restaurant has attentive service, and serves up a good mixed grill.

Restaurant Marchica (☎ 825-3335; Av Bolívar Norte No 152-210; mains $6-14; 🕒 noon-11:30pm Mon-Sat, noon-9pm Sun; 🍴) This bustling old restaurant has a low and curving ceiling giving it the impression of being in a wine cellar. Customers can enjoy the traditional Spanish dishes and piano music.

Restaurant El Bosque (Av Bolívar Norte; 🕒 11am-midnight; 🍴) Recommended for low prices and great grills, this huge, drive-in joint has fast and filling food. Some dishes are served extra hot on a small charcoal barbecue left by your table.

Getting There & Away

AIR

The airport is about 7km southeast of the city center; a taxi from the center costs around $4. There are direct flights to Caracas ($34 to $50), from where you can continue to anywhere around the country. Other domestic destinations from Valencia are Barcelona ($57 to $76), Maracaibo ($38) and Porlamar ($57).

BUS

The bus terminal is about 4km northeast of the city center, in the Disneyland-style

Big Low Center, and is easily accessible by frequent local buses; alternatively, take a taxi for $2.50. The terminal is large and well organized and has a lot of facilities, including restaurants and snack bars.

Buses run regularly to most major cities. To Caracas ($3 to $5, 2½ hours), ordinary buses depart every 15 minutes or so; there are also frequent services to Maracay ($0.65, one hour). Half-hourly ordinary buses run to Puerto Cabello ($0.80, 50 minutes), Tucacas ($2.50, two hours) and Coro ($9, five hours). Hourly ordinary buses run to Barquisimeto ($3, three hours) and Chichiriviche ($2.80, 2½ hours).

A number of buses depart (mostly in the evening) to more distant destinations, including Maracaibo ($12 to $16, eight hours), San Cristóbal ($11 to $14, 10½ hours), San Antonio del Táchira ($13, 11½ hours) and Mérida ($11 to $16, 10 hours).

One of the most luxurious companies is **Aeroexpresos Ejecutivos** (☎ 871-5767; www.aeroex presos.com.ve) with services to Caracas, Puerto La Cruz, Barquisimeto and Maracaibo.

There are half a dozen buses a day to San Fernando de Apure ($8 to $9, eight hours), where you can change for the bus to Puerto Ayacucho.

CAMPO CARABOBO

For a taste of unadulterated Venezuelan patriotism, visit the **Carabobo Battlefield** (admission free; 😊 8am-4:30pm Tue-Fri, 9am-4:30pm Sat & Sun) 32km southwest of Valencia. This is the site of the great battle fought on June 24, 1821, in which Bolívar's troops decisively defeated the Spanish royalist army with help from the lancers of General Páez and British legionnaires. A milestone in Latin American history, the victory effectively sealed Venezuela's independence. To commemorate the event, a complex of monuments has been erected on the battle ground.

The wide entrance road turns into the **Paseo de Los Héroes**, a formal promenade lined with bronze busts of the battle heroes. The promenade leads to the huge **Arco de Triunfo** (Triumphal Arch) and the **Tumba del Soldado Desconocido** (Tomb of the Unknown Soldier). Two unflinching, deadpan soldiers guard the tomb and its flaming torch; their shockingly red gala period uniforms seem more suitable for a Siberian winter than for the baking sun of Carabobo. Fortunately for

them, the changing of the guard takes place every two hours.

A hundred meters beyond the arch is the impressive **Altar de la Patria**, a massive monument – the largest in Venezuela. Designed by a Spanish sculptor, Antonio Rodríguez del Villar, and unveiled in 1930, the monument depicts the main heroes and allegorical figures, all fashioned in stone and bronze. On the top is – you guessed it – an equestrian statue of Bolívar.

About 1km to the west is the **Mirador**, a viewpoint from which Bolívar commanded the battle. It has a large model of the battlefield and a panoramic view over the whole site. The diorama cubicle, to the right of the access road, screens historical films on the site.

You can either wander the site at will or latch onto one of the reverential guided tours (in Spanish) that run regularly throughout the day. The park has plenty of grassy expanses for picnicking and watching kids who often use the quiet back roads for skating and biking stunts.

Getting There & Away

The battleground is on the road to San Carlos. Frequent suburban buses (helpfully marked 'Campo Carabobo') go from Valencia to the battlefield ($0.45, one hour). In Valencia, they go east along Calle Comercio and turn south onto Av Carabobo. They will leave you in Carabobo, at the end of the entrance road.

PARQUE ARQUEOLÓGICO PIEDRA PINTADA

Mysterious stone petroglyphs are scattered throughout Carabobo state, the largest group of which is at the site known as Cerro Pintado or **Piedra Pintada** (admission free; 😊 9am-4pm Tue-Fri, 10am-4pm Sat & Sun; 🅿), 22km northeast of Valencia near the village of Tronconero. An important ritual center for pre-Hispanic communities, the site is covered by a jumble of weathered rocks and slabs scattered over a grassy slope.

Many of these stones bear shallow engravings of intriguing designs and figures, from owls to women giving birth, shamans and what is believed to be a sacred plan of the region. The exact age of the carvings is still a matter of discussion. Further on up the slope, there's an impressive group of upright megalithic stones; bring water and sturdy shoes to visit these.

The 12-hectare site, which was made an archeological park in 1996, has helpful Spanish-speaking guides on standby and there's a small museum in the visitors center.

Getting There & Away

To get to the park from Valencia, take the Maracay bus from the terminal and get off at Guacara ($0.65, 15 minutes), 13km east of Valencia (ask the driver to drop you at the Puente de Guacara). Go down the bridge and wave down the buseta marked 'Hospital-Tronconero,' which will bring you close to the Parque Arqueológico ($0.30, 20 minutes). Get off at the end of the line and walk for 10 minutes, following the signs.

LAS TRINCHERAS

☎ 0241 / pop 3000

Reputedly the second-hottest in the world, at about 92°C, the thermal springs of Las Trincheras (18km north of Valencia) are celebrated for their curative powers. Known for centuries, the springs have long attracted explorers and naturalists, among them Alexander von Humboldt, who famously used the waters to boil eggs in four minutes. In 1889, thermal baths and a hotel were built. In 1980, the old hotel was restored, a new one constructed beside it, and the murky-looking pools were remodeled. There are now three pools with temperatures ranging from 36°C to 48°C, as well as fountains, a sauna and a sociable mud bath where everybody slaps warm gloopy mud on each other and lets it cake in the sun.

The springs are renowned for their therapeutic properties and recommended for the treatment of a variety of ailments, including rheumatic, digestive, respiratory and allergic problems. They are also useful for losing weight, making the skin fresh and smooth, and helping with general relaxation.

You can either choose a **day pass** (admission $2.50; ☺ 7am-9pm Tue-Sun, 7am-4pm Mon, mud bath until 6pm) or stay in the on-site hotel, using the baths and other facilities at no extra cost. The hotel also has a pool exclusively for guests, plus a bewilderingly long list of health treatments on offer.

Sleeping & Eating

Centro Termal Las Trincheras (☎ 808-1502, in Caracas 0212-661-2703; www.trincheras.com; s/d/tr/ste/q $16/20/22/25/32; P ✗ ☎) The pleasant on-site hotel offers light, comfortable rooms with hot water and TV. The price includes use of the baths, sauna and other facilities. The restaurant offers all-day service for hotel guests and day visitors. It's usually easy to get a room during the week, but on weekends the hotel is full to bursting.

Opposite the entrance to the baths complex is **Manantial de Luz** (☎ 921-5052; d/tr/q $9.50/11/13; P), which has simple, basic rooms with fans and runs a great little **vegetarian restaurant** (set menu $3; ☺ 8am-9pm). The hotel price does not include entrance to the baths.

Getting There & Away

The center at the thermal springs has a **minibus** (☎ 0412-998-8151) to pick up customers from the Valencia bus terminal at prearranged times ($7.50 roundtrip); call in advance. Taxis cost $6.50 one-way.

You can also get to the baths from the Valencia bus terminal by catching any of the frequent buses to Puerto Cabello ($0.80). These buses go via the autopista (freeway) and charge the full fare to Puerto Cabello, but take only 20 minutes to get to Las Trincheras. They will put you down off the autopista, a 10-minute walk from the baths.

If you want to continue on from Las Trincheras north to Puerto Cabello, Tucacas or Chichiriviche, you'll have to wave down the appropriate bus on the autopista.

PUERTO CABELLO

☎ 0242 / pop 173,000

Puerto Cabello began life in the mid-16th century as a simple wharf built on the bank of a coastal lagoon. The site was a perfect natural anchorage, protected from wind and waves and connected to the open sea by a convenient strait. Indeed, there was hardly a better place for a port on the Venezuelan coast.

During the 17th century, the Dutch-run port grew fat on its contraband trade with Curaçao. It wasn't until 1730 that the Spanish took over the port, after the Real Compañía Guipuzcoana moved in. This company built an array of forts, and by the 1770s Puerto Cabello was the most heavily fortified town on Venezuela's coast.

Thus, during the War of Independence, it became an important royalist stronghold, and was the last place in Venezuela to be freed from Spanish rule.

Until recently the port handled 65% of the country's import and export cargo (excluding oil), though it has been hit hard by the recent economic crises. It has 34 docks, a dry dock, large warehouses and a naval base.

The partially restored colonial town center and two remaining forts are worth seeing, though the wider port wouldn't win any prizes for beauty. You can also visit the attractive surroundings, including beaches to the east and lush forests to the south.

Orientation

Puerto Cabello stretches westward for about 7km along the freeway, as far as the airport. The central area, at the eastern end of the city, can be clearly divided into two parts: the attractive colonial sector, to the north, and the uninspiring new center, to the south. Plaza Bolívar roughly marks the borderline between the two.

Information

The local tourist office is run by **Puerto Turistico** (☎ 362-1732; www.puertoturistico.com; Calle Puerto Cabello; ⏱ 8am-5pm Mon-Fri) in a new building constructed to provide passenger ferry services. For Internet connections, try **Urdaneta Center Net** (Calle 14 Urdaneta; per hr $1; ⏱ 8am-8:30pm Mon-Sat) outside the historic center.

Local banks that offer cash advances on Visa and MasterCard include **Banco de Venezuela** (Calle Colón) and **Banco Mercantil** (Plaza Bolívar), while **Corp Banca** (Av 2 Municipio) also changes Amex traveler's checks.

Spanish Forts

North of the old town, and separated from it by the entrance channel to the harbor, is colonial Fortín San Felipe, later renamed **Castillo Libertador** (admission free; ⏱ dawn-dusk). It's a fine-looking fort, though in a state of disrepair, and if you visit you'll have the sturdy ramparts all to yourself apart from the occasional vulture eyeing up the pigeons. The fort was constructed in the 1730s to protect the port and warehouses. During the War of Independence, the fort was for a time in the patriots' hands, but it was lost to the royalists in 1812. Francisco

de Miranda was jailed here before the Spanish sent him to prison in Spain. The fort was recovered in 1823, and later served General Gómez as a jail, mostly for political prisoners. Upon Gómez' death in 1935, the prison closed down and no less than 14 tons of chains and leg irons were thrown into the sea.

The fort is within the naval base, which operates a free hourly *bongo* (boat) across the channel from just below Plaza Flores, at the northern end of Paseo Malecón. The bongos are blue-and-white boats, some of which have 'base naval' printed on a tarpaulin. They will leave you near the naval-base entrance, from where the fort is a 10-minute walk west. En route, you could stop in the **Naval Museum** (☎ 360-1076; admission free; ⏱ 8am-noon & 1:30-4pm Tue-Fri) to get your fill of torpedoes and propellers.

On the 100m-high hill to the south of the city sits another fort, **Fortín Solano** (admission free; ⏱ dawn-dusk), built in the 1760s to secure commercial operations. Reputedly the last colonial fort built in Venezuela, it commands excellent views of the city and the harbor. The road to the fort branches off from the road to San Esteban on the outskirts of Puerto Cabello. Hence, you can combine a visit to the fort with the trip to San Esteban (p135). Even if you want to visit only the fort, take a San Esteban carrito to the turnoff to avoid walking through a shabby *barrio* (shantytown).

Old Town

The part of the old town to the west of Calle Comercio has been restored and the facades painted in bright colors. It's now a pleasant area to explore or watch the world go by from the open-air restaurants on the tree-shaded waterfront boulevard, **Paseo Malecón**.

Don't miss the two historic streets, **Calle de Los Lanceros** and **Calle Bolívar**. Note the overhanging balconies and massive doorways, including the fair-sized **Museo de Historia** (Calle Bolívar; admission free). Built in 1790 as a residence, this building has a graceful internal patio and facades over both streets. The museum has been closed since the early 1990s, but an association of local artists, complete with art gallery, now occupies the building. Have a snoop inside, and be sure to climb the tower for good views.

At the northern end of Calle de Los Lanceros is the **Iglesia del Rosario**, a handsome whitewashed church built in 1780. The bell tower is made of wood – unique in Venezuela. One block north of the church is the **Casa Guipuzcoana** (admission free; ☿ 8am-4pm Mon-Fri), built in 1730 as the office for the Compañía Guipuzcoana. Today it's a public library.

The library faces a triangular square with the **Monumento del Águila** (Eagle Monument) in the middle. This monument, a tall column topped by a condor, was erected in 1896 in memory of North Americans who gave their lives for Venezuelan independence. Recruited by Francisco de Miranda, in 1806 they sailed from New York to Ocumare de la Costa, north of Maracay. Upon dropping anchor, however, two boats with Americans aboard were surprised and captured by Spanish guard boats. Ten officers were hanged, and the remaining 50-odd recruits sent to prison.

Plaza Bolívar, at the southern edge of the colonial sector, boasts yet another fine equestrian statue of Bolívar. The massive, somewhat odd edifice built from coral rock and occupying the eastern side of the plaza is the **Catedral de San José**. It was begun in the mid-19th century and completed only some 100 years later.

Sleeping

Budget accommodations in town tend to double as shady love hotels (this is a port, after all). If you'd prefer to sidestep the town, see p134 for alternative accommodations along the coast.

Hotel Venezia (☎ 361-4380; Av Santa Bárbara No 13-36; d with fan $7.50, with air-con $10) One of the cheapest places is this small, simple Italian-run hotel opposite a large medical clinic.

Hotel El Fortín (☎ 361-4356; Calle Miranda; d $14-15, tr $19; P 😊) Located between Avs Bárbula and Carabobo this sparklingly clean and newly tiled, El Fortín is one of the better budget options in town. The uniform, white-washed rooms have cable TV, hot water and telephone.

Hotel Bahía Azul (☎ 361-4033; Av Santa Bárbara; d $16-17, tr $20, 6 people $28; P 😊) Bahía Azul is recommended for solid good value, with cable TV, spotless rooms and great attention to detail (you've never seen such intricately folded sheets!).

THE AUTHOR'S CHOICE

Posada Santa Margarita & Carmendal Rosario (☎ 361-7113, 361-4112; www.ptocabello.com; Calle Bolívar No 4-36; d without bathroom $25, d/tr with bathroom $40/57, d with bathroom & air-con $44; 😊 😊) Every once in a while, a posada pops up that has more character than all the other hotels in town put together. In Puerto Cabello, this is it. The posada actually consists of two separate houses, joined by a door and run by the same family. Prices include breakfast.

Located in the colonial town center, both houses are 270 years old. The right-hand house has been painstakingly renovated and still boasts the original walls of coral stone and sand, high ceilings, chandeliers and creaky old wooden floors. For an extra special location, ask for the rooftop room ($44), with a private bathroom in the lookout tower and its own terrace to watch the sun set.

Next door has more modern renovations and air-con rooms, as well as an *escalera caracol* (spiral staircase), internal patio, pool table and swimming pool that guests from both houses can use.

Hotel Isla Larga (☎ 361-3290; Calle Miranda; d $22; P 😊 😊) Fronting onto a square of scruffy wasteland near the bus terminal, this large, grey, slightly spooky building hums with the constant noise of a hundred air-con machines. It has professional service, small, neat rooms and its own tasca restaurant below.

Hotel Suite Caribe (☎ 364-2286; hotelscaribe@telcel.net.ve; Av Salom 21, Urb La Sorpresa; d old/new $44/50, tr $64; P 😊 😊 😊) For another step up the luxury ladder, try this tall, blockish hotel, on the freeway, 5km west of the city center (2km east of the airport). It has a great swimming pool and sunny patio, plus its own restaurant, gym and sauna.

Eating

The colonial sector has some good eateries on or just off Paseo Malecón.

Pizzería Da Franco (☎ 361-6161; Paseo Malecón; mains $3-7; ☿ 11am-10pm) This seafront spot has a family atmosphere and decent pizzas, with terrace seating outside.

Restaurant Los Lanceros (☎ 361-8471; Calle Lanceros No 3-90, Paseo Malecón; mains $5-13; ☯ 10am-10pm) Based in a characterful old colonial building with a sea view, this upmarket restaurant is hung with anchors and other nautical paraphernalia. It has a nice, little terrace on the malecón where you can catch the breeze and watch the occasional tanker rolling past.

Restaurant Briceño Ven (☎ 361-7392; Paseo Malecón; mains $5-13; ☯ 11am-midnight) Typical of restaurants running along the seafront malecón, this brightly painted joint has wooden colonial balconies, curvy iron-frame chairs and a terrace for coffee.

Restaurant La Fuente (☎ 361-6889; mains $4-7; ☯ 8am-10pm Mon-Sat) Above an ice-cream café and overlooking a leafy square, this Spanish tasca's strength is fish and seafood dishes. It has high stone arches with a small fountain in the center, and a good bar too.

The cheapest places in the area include the unpretentious **Lunchería Guipuzcoana** (off Calle Zea; mains $1.50-4; ☯ 10am-5pm Mon-Sat), opposite Monumento del Águila, and the lively little **Colonial Lunchería** (Calle Bolívar; set menu $2.50; ☯ 9am-6pm Mon-Sat).

Getting There & Away
AIR
The airport is 7km west of Puerto Cabello, next to the freeway, but there are no scheduled tourist flights.

BOAT
At the time of writing, a new **tourist port** (www.puertoturistico.com; Calle Puerto Cabello) had just been completed with the intention to provide future ferry services from Puerto Cabello to Curaçao, Isla de Margarita, Puerto la Cruz and La Guaira near Caracas. For up-to-date information, see the website or visit the tourist office.

BUS
The bus terminal is on Calle Urdaneta, about 800m west of Av Bolívar. Frequent carritos run between the terminal and the center, but you can walk it in 10 minutes. If you do decide to walk, never go via the Playa Blanca beach. It's notorious for the armed robbery of tourists, especially due north of the bus terminal.

Buses depart every 15 minutes to Valencia ($0.80, 50 minutes), where you change

for equally frequent buses to Caracas. There are regular buses to Tucacas ($1, 1¼ hours) and San Felipe ($1.50, 1¾ hours), and some less frequent departures to Chichiriviche ($1.50, 1¾ hours) and Barquisimeto ($2.50, three hours). For transportation to the nearby beaches and San Esteban, see Getting There & Away p135 and p136.

TRAIN
Puerto Cabello is the terminus of the railway line to Barquisimeto, but only handles freight transportation these days.

AROUND PUERTO CABELLO
Beaches
Several beaches lie to the east of Puerto Cabello, off the road to Patanemo. The closest ones is **Balneario Quizandal**, about 7km by road from the city. This beach is quite developed, with a parking lot, showers and restaurants, though it is not the best beach. However, boats from here can take you to **Isla Larga**, a beautiful, sandy island popular with beachgoers, swimmers and snorkelers. There are two wrecks near the island, a bonus attraction for snorkelers and divers. Several food stalls will be more than happy to stuff you with fish (open weekends and sometimes weekdays as well). Take good sun protection, as there is no shade. Many holidaymakers make the trip on weekends, so the two-way boat trip will cost just $3 per person, but during the week you'll have to pay the fare for the whole boat: $15 round-trip (negotiable).

The next exit off the Patanemo road, 1km beyond the one to Quizandal, leads to the small **Playa Huequito**. In the same place, another road branches off to the right and heads south to **Borburata**, the oldest town in Carabobo, founded in 1548. The town is widely known for its **Fiestas de San Juan** (June 23 and 24) and **San Pedro** (June 28). Borburata has some budget places to stay and eat, including basic bunk beds in the **Posada de Mi Tío** (☎ 421-7126; d & tr $9.50).

Back on the main road and continuing eastward from the junction, another road branches off to **Playa La Rosa** (admission $0.30, beach hut with bbq $2.50) one of the tidiest, best-maintained and safest beaches, as it lies next to a military area.

If you continue further eastward for about 1.5km, the road to Patanemo then

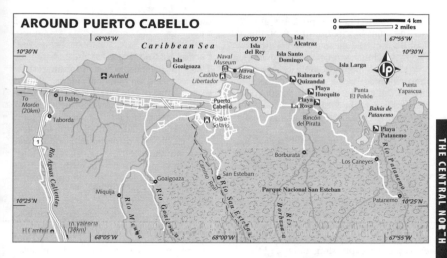

AROUND PUERTO CABELLO

brings you to the poor village known as **Rincón del Pirata**.

From this point, the road winds up a hill, then descends to yet another turnoff (6km beyond Rincón), which leads 1.5km to **Playa Patanemo**. This is the best beach in the area, wide and shaded by coconut palms. It tends to swarm with beachgoers on weekends but is fairly solitary on weekdays. It's lined with food outlets, including some more permanent *churuata*-style (thatched hut) restaurants with their owners residing on site; these open daily. You can pitch your tent anywhere amid the palms, but it's safer to camp next to one of the restaurants. There are mosquitoes at times – come prepared.

At the turnoff to the Patanemo beach is the rather rambling, overgrown **Campamento Turístico La Churuata** (☎ 0412-700-1599; cabañas d/tr $19/28; 🛏 🍽), with unadorned air-con rooms. Shortly beyond the turnoff, the road enters the village of **Los Caneyes**, which hosts several places to stay.

First comes the small and homely **Posada Natal Mar** (☎ 0412-536-7958; Av Principal Los Caneyes; d/tr $13/19; 🅿 🍽), which offers good old-fashioned value in a very friendly, down-to-earth environment. Locals and tourists alike recommend it, and the restaurant's economical fish suppers are legendary.

About 400m down the road you'll find the charming if unkempt **La Fortaleza** (☎ 0414-946-7576; Av Principal Los Caneyes; 6-/8-person cabañas $46/58), with two large, basic cabañas set in a vast garden.

Another 200m further down the road is **Casa de Playa El Edén** (☎ 0416-442-4955; Av Principal Los Caneyes; d/tr $40/50 q $57-63, 8-person cabin $82; 🛏 🍽), surely the pick of the bunch. It boasts a cool, open-air pizzeria, nice swimming pool and tropical gardens brimming with glorious flowers and fruits. Rooms have high tropical ceilings and beautiful polished-stone floors. This hostel is especially family friendly.

The road continues 1.5km to the village of **Patanemo**, noted for the Diablos Danzantes celebrations on Corpus Christi (60 days after Easter, in May or June) and for drumbeats on Fiesta de San Juan (June 23 and 24). At the entrance to Patanemo is **Posada La Chachita** (☎ 421-0198; Calle Bolívar de Patanemo; d with fan $13, with air-con $19; 🍽), which is more of a family home with a few rooms upstairs. It's relaxed and friendly, though it's further from beach. It can prepare meals for guests on request.

GETTING THERE & AWAY
Carritos run regularly between the Puerto Cabello bus terminal and Patanemo, and will put you down at any turnoff of your choice, within reasonable walking distance of the beach. The ride to Patanemo village takes half an hour and costs $0.60.

San Esteban
Seven kilometers south of Puerto Cabello, the pleasant village of San Esteban is surrounded by lush vegetation, and has a

cooler climate than the port. It's also the starting point for the Camino Real, the old Spanish trail leading south to Valencia (see Parque Nacional San Esteban following).

Walk south (600m from the bridge where the road ends) along a path on the same side of the river and you'll get to a large rock known as the **Piedra del Indio**, covered with petroglyphs. The rock is just next to the path, on your left.

San Esteban was the birthplace of Bartolomé Salom, one of the heroes of the War of Independence, who accompanied Bolívar all the way to Ayacucho. The **house** (admission free; ⏰ 9am-4pm) where he was born is 800m back along the road from the point where the carritos terminate. It has been left half ruined. Inside the main room is a life-sized statue of the general with an intense, concentrated expression, only slightly diminished by his somewhat bizarre position sitting in a hammock with a vase of flowers between his feet.

Further up the main road from Salom's house lies **Posada Mi Jaragual** (d/tr $13/16) alongside the river. This recently expanded posada is well kept, and the owner keeps a fascinating little collection of traditional liquors and medicines, bottled with everything from snakes to frogs. There are also a few simple places to eat in the village.

GETTING THERE & AWAY
Carritos to San Esteban depart regularly from the bus terminal in Puerto Cabello ($0.25, 25 minutes). They travel as far as the bridge in San Esteban, where the road ends.

Parque Nacional San Esteban

This national park, adjacent to the western part of Parque Nacional Henri Pittier, stretches from San Esteban southward almost to Valencia, on the northern outskirts of Valencia. Like its eastern neighbor, the park protects a part of the Cordillera de la Costa, noted for its rich and diverse flora and fauna.

There's a popular trail in the park known as the 'Camino Real.' In colonial times, it was the main route linking Puerto Cabello with Valencia, along which goods were transported. The trail leads from north to south, passing over the ridge at an altitude of about 1400m. You can still see traces of the cobbled Spanish road and will even encounter the original Spanish bridge, the 1808 Puente de Los Españoles. The trail is relatively easy, though side paths joining it can be confusing. Although the walking time between San Esteban and Naguanagua is about eight hours, count on two days to take it at a leisurely pace. There have been problems reported at the southern end, as the northern suburb of Naguanagua, Bárbula, is noted for armed robbery.

Many walkers departing from the northern end (San Esteban) make it just a one-day roundtrip by only going as far as the Spanish bridge. It's about a three-hour walk up and a two-hour walk back down. The tourist office in Puerto Cabello can help you to find a guide, should you need one.

The Northwest

CONTENTS

Venezuela's northwest is a tropical wonderland blessed with a stunning diversity of natural features – coral islands and beaches, rain forests and deserts, caves and waterfalls, and South America's largest lake. You can enjoy this variety at the region's nature reserves and 12 national parks. Culturally, the northwest combines the traditional with the contemporary, from the living Guajiro indigenous culture and splendid heritage of Coro to the slick modernity of Maracaibo.

On the northwest coast, Parque Nacional Morrocoy attracts visitors with its colorful reefs and powdery sands, and the peaceful city of Coro, a gem of colonial architecture. Further west along the coast, Maracaibo is perhaps not the top spot on travelers' lists, but it's a city with character and a great festival held in the name of the state's patron saint. The city's environs also have a lot to show visitors.

The inland portion of the northwest is less traveled, yet it's also noted for its natural beauty and cultural attractions. Here you can see charming colonial towns, buy some of Venezuela's finest crafts, sample the country's best wine and discover the holy shrines of the mysterious María Lionza cult.

HIGHLIGHTS

- Enjoy the sandy beaches and coral reefs of the **Parque Nacional Morrocoy** (p152)
- Stroll about the charming colonial streets of **Coro** (p139)
- Explore remote wonders of the **Península de Paraguaná** (p144)
- Join the crowds celebrating the Feria de la Chinita in **Maracaibo** (p167) in November
- Marvel at the unique lightning phenomenon of **Catatumbo** (p177)

FALCÓN STATE

CORO

☎ 0268 / pop 160,000

Set at the base of the Península de Paraguaná, Coro is the capital of Falcón state and a pleasant, peaceful city. Thanks to a large university, it has a noticeably cultured air. More importantly, Coro features some of the best colonial architecture in all of Venezuela and boasts a few good museums.

Since Coro's historic center was declared a national monument in the 1950s, a number of the old houses have been restored. The cobblestone Calle Zamora, where most of the historic mansions are located, is one of the loveliest colonial-style streets in the country. In 1993, Coro was included on Unesco's World Heritage list.

Once in Coro, it's worth visiting the arid Península de Paraguaná (p144) and the lush, mountainous Sierra de San Luis (p150), two interesting and completely different regions. You can explore them on your own or take a tour (see Tours, p143).

Orientation

Coro's center, where you are likely to spend just about all your time in town, is small and compact, and pleasant for leisurely strolls about the streets. Conveniently, here are all but one of the important sights and a lion's share of hotels and restaurants, and even the airport, which is rarely the case in the cities. Probably your only trip away from the center (and a recommended one) will be a visit to the Médanos de Coro.

Information

EMERGENCY

Ambulance (☎ 251-2409)
Fire (☎ 251-9923)
Police (☎ 251-9856)

INTERNET ACCESS

Internet access in Coro is cheap: $0.40 to $0.80 an hour. Several facilities listed below are in the historic center and close at 8pm or earlier. If you need to use the Internet late in the evening, some of the following cybercafés, located away from the center, are open till late:

ATC Micro Suply (Calle Falcón)
Centro de Navegación Internet (cnr Av Manaure & Calle Zamora)
Ciudad Bitácora (cnr Calle Zamora & Calle Jansen; ☺ 7am-2am) The largest and fastest cybercafé in town, five blocks east of Av Manaure. Take a sweater – it's cold!
El Triángulo Azul (Castillo Don Leoncio; Av Manaure; ☺ 9am-midnight) Seven blocks south of Calle Falcón, near Banesco.
L&D Sistemas (Calle Zamora)
P&P Connections (Plaza Falcón)

THE NORTHWEST

UPS & DOWNS OF VENEZUELA'S FIRST CAPITAL

Founded by Juan de Ampiés in 1527, Santa Ana de Coro is one of the oldest towns on the continent and the first capital of colonial Venezuela. In the same year, King Carlos I of Spain leased the city and the entire province to the Welsers of Germany to conquer, settle and exploit. The king was forced to sign the contract because he was heavily in debt to German banking firms for loans he had used to buy the title of Holy Roman Emperor Karl V (Charles V) in 1519. On the other hand, the Germans were eager to share in the reputedly fabulous riches of the newly discovered continent. The church was quick to follow, and in 1531 it established the Episcopal See in Coro, the first archdiocese founded in the New World.

Despite this promising start, Coro's development was bogged down from the beginning. The town was little more than a jumping-off point for expeditions in search of treasure, but El Dorado never materialized. In 1546 the contract with the Welsers was canceled and the administrative seat of the province moved to El Tocuyo, 200km to the south. The church was more patient, but finally relocated the archdiocese to Caracas in 1637.

Having suffered from looting and burning by pirates on various occasions throughout the 16th and 17th centuries, Coro struggled hard to survive and was revived only by contraband trade with Curaçao and Bonaire during the 18th century. Most of the historic buildings date from that time, and it's no surprise that their architectural detail is influenced by the Dutch baroque.

THE NORTHWEST

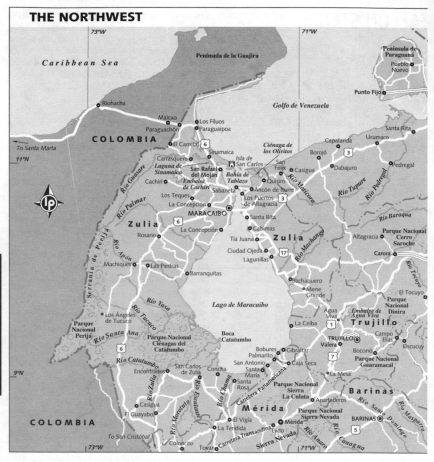

MEDICAL SERVICES

Clínica Nuestra Señora de Guadalupe (☎ 252-6011; Av Los Médanos)

Hospital Universitario Dr Alfredo van Grieken (☎ 252-5700; Av El Tenis)

MONEY

Banco de Venezuela (Paseo Talavera)

Banco Mercantil (Calle Falcón) Two blocks east of Av Manaure.

Banesco (Av Manaure) Eight blocks south of Calle Falcón.

Corp Banca (Calle Zamora) Three blocks east of Av Manaure.

Italcambio (airport) Changes cash and traveler's checks.

TELEPHONE

Telcel (Calle Falcón)

TOURIST INFORMATION

Secretaría de Turismo (☎ 251-8033; Paseo La Alameda; ⏱ 8am-noon & 2-6pm Mon-Thu, 8am-4pm Fri) The office is on the central pedestrian mall just north of Plaza Bolívar.

Sights

HISTORIC MANSIONS & MUSEUMS

All of the city's interesting museums are in restored colonial buildings. The **Museo de Arte de Coro** (☎ 251-5658; Paseo Talavera; admission free; ⏱ 9am-12:30pm & 3-7:30pm Tue-Sat, 9am-4pm Sun), in a beautiful 18th-century mansion, is a branch of the Caracas Museo de Arte Contemporáneo and, like its parent, features thought-provoking and well-presented temporary exhibitions.

Diagonally opposite, in another great historic mansion, the **Museo de Arte Alberto Henríquez** (☎ 252-5299; Paseo Talavera; admission free; 🕒 9am-noon & 3-6pm Tue-Sat, 9am-noon Sun) also has modern art – shows change regularly but are always worth a visit. At the back of the mansion is an old synagogue, founded in 1853. This is the first synagogue in Venezuela, though the present furnishings are all replicas.

For an insight into the colonial past, go two blocks north to the **Museo Diocesano Lucas Guillermo Castillo** (☎ 251-5645; Calle Zamora; admission $0.50; 🕒 9am-noon & 3-6pm Tue-Sat, 9am-2pm Sun), named after a local bishop. Accommodated in 15 rooms of a 17th-century Franciscan convent, the museum boasts an extensive collection of religious and secular art from the region and beyond, including Venezuela's oldest tempera painting and some extraordinary statues of Madonna carved in wood. It's one of the best collections of its kind in the country. All visits are guided (in Spanish only), and the tour takes about 45 minutes.

A short walk west is the **Casa de los Arcaya** (☎ 251-0023; Calle Zamora) with its attractive, tile-roofed balconies. The mansion houses the **Museo de Cerámica Histórica y Loza Popular** (admission free; 🕒 9am-noon & 3-6pm Tue-Sat, 9am-1pm Sun), a small but interesting museum of antique pottery and ceramics from all over the world.

The **Casa de las Ventanas de Hierro** (Calle Zamora; admission $0.30; 🕒 9am-noon & 3-6pm Tue-Sat, 9am-2pm Sun) is noted for a splendid 8m-high plaster doorway and the wrought-iron grilles (brought from Seville, Spain, in 1764) across the windows. It now shelters a private collection of historic objects, collected by the family over generations. Nearby, the **Casa del Tesoro** (Calle Zamora) houses an art gallery, while the **Casa de los Soto** (Calle Zamora) is a private residence and cannot be visited but is worth looking at from the outside.

COLONIAL CHURCHES

The massive fortress-like **Catedral** (Plaza Bolívar) was begun in the 1580s and finished half a century later, making it the oldest surviving church in Venezuela. There are no remainders of its early history inside, but the 1790 baroque main retable is a good example of late-colonial art.

Two blocks north, the 18th-century **Iglesia de San Francisco** (Calle Zamora) was closed for restoration at the time of research, but is likely to be reopened by the time you visit. The cupola of the 1760s Capilla del Santísimo Sacramento, at the top of the right aisle, is a very fine piece of Mudejar art, showing the strong influence of Moorish style in medieval Spain.

Just a stone's throw to the west of San Francisco is another 18th-century church, the **Iglesia de San Clemente** (Calle Zamora). It was laid out in a Latin cross plan and is one of the very few examples of its kind in the country. Note the anchor hanging from the middle of the ceiling, which commemorates St Clement's martyrdom (he was drowned after being weighed down with an anchor).

THE NORTHWEST

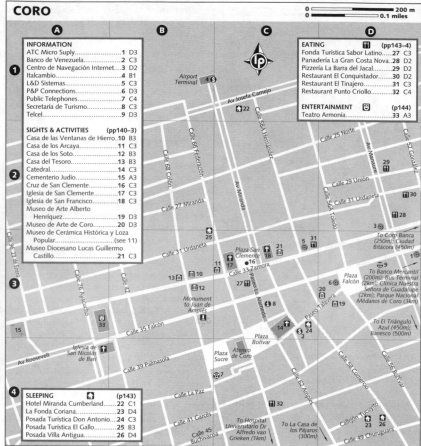

CORO

0 ———————————— 200 m
0 ———————————— 0.1 miles

INFORMATION
ATC Micro Suply......................1 D3
Banco de Venezuela..................2 C3
Centro de Navegación Internet....3 D2
Italcambio..............................4 B1
L&D Sistemas..........................5 C3
P&P Connections......................6 D3
Public Telephones....................7 C4
Secretaría de Turismo................8 C3
Telcel...................................9 D3

SIGHTS & ACTIVITIES (pp140–3)
Casa de las Ventanas de Hierro..10 B3
Casa de los Arcaya..................11 C3
Casa de los Soto.....................12 B3
Casa del Tesoro......................13 B3
Catedral...............................14 C3
Cementerio Judío.....................15 A3
Cruz de San Clemente..............16 C3
Iglesia de San Clemente...........17 C3
Iglesia de San Francisco...........18 C3
Museo de Arte Alberto
  Henríquez...........................19 D3
Museo de Arte de Coro............20 D3
Museo de Cerámica Histórica y Loza
  Popular.............................(see 11)
Museo Diocesano Lucas Guillermo
  Castillo.............................21 C3

EATING 🍴 (pp143–4)
Fonda Turística Sabor Latino.....27 C3
Panadería La Gran Costa Nova..28 D2
Pizzería La Barra del Jacal.........29 D2
Restaurant El Conquistador.......30 D2
Restaurant El Tinajero..............31 C3
Restaurant Punto Criollo...........32 C4

ENTERTAINMENT 🎭 (p144)
Teatro Armonía......................33 A3

SLEEPING 🛏 (p143)
Hotel Miranda Cumberland.......22 C1
La Fonda Coriana....................23 D4
Posada Turística Don Antonio...24 C3
Posada Turística El Gallo..........25 B3
Posada Villa Antigua...............26 D4

Airport Terminal
Av Josefa Camejo
Calle 66 Federación
Calle 68 Colón
Calle 58A Hernández
Calle 25 Norte
Av Manaure
Calle 57 González
Av Miranda
Calle 27 Miranda
Calle 29 Unión
Calle 56A Toledo
Calle 31 Urdaneta
Calle 26 23 de Enero
Calle 76 Fy Ayacucho
Calle 72
Calle 31 Urdaneta
Plaza San Clemente
Calle 33 Zamora
Paseo Los Alamedas
Paseo Talavera
Plaza Falcón
Monument to Juan de Amplíes
Calle 35 Falcón
Plaza Bolívar
Calle 58 Comercio
Calle 56 Bolívar
To Corp Banca (250m); Ciudad Bitácora (450m)
To Banco Mercantil (200m); Bus Terminal (2km); Clínica Nuestra Señora de Guadalupe (2km); Parque Nacional Médanos de Coro (3km)
To El Triángulo Azul (450m); Banesco (500m)
Av Roosevelt
Iglesia de San Nicolás de Bari
Calle 39 Palmasola
Plaza Sucre
Ateneo de Coro
Calle 62 Ampíes
Calle La Paz
Calle 41 Garcés
To Hospital Universitario Dr Alfredo van Grieken (1km)
Calle 45 Buchivacoa
To La Casa de los Pájaros (300m)
Callejón Tucuyito
Calle 49 Churuguara

THE NORTHWEST

In the barred pavilion on the plaza between the two churches is the **Cruz de San Clemente** (Plaza San Clemente). This is said to be the cross used in the first mass celebrated after the town's foundation. It's made from the wood of the *cují* tree, a slow-growing species of acacia that is found in this arid region.

CEMENTERIO JUDÍO

Established in the 1830s, this is the oldest **Jewish cemetery** (cnr Calle Zamora & Calle 23 de Enero) still in use on the continent. It's normally locked and the keys are kept in the Museo de Arte Alberto Henríquez (p141). Inquire there, and a guide will accompany you and show you around the graveyard.

Jews came to Coro from Curaçao in the early 19th century, a period of intensive trade with the Dutch islands. In the course of time, they formed a small but influential commercial community, despite persecution by the post-independence caudillo governments. Today there are perhaps a dozen Jews still living in Coro.

The cemetery was founded by Joseph Curiel, a rich Jewish merchant who met Simón Bolívar in Angostura and offered him the help of the Venezuelan Jewish community in the cause of independence. Curiel's tomb is one of the most elaborate, while the grave of his 10-year-old daughter, dated 1832, is the oldest tomb in the cemetery.

PARQUE NACIONAL MÉDANOS DE CORO
Just northeast of the city is a spectacular desert landscape, dominated by sand dunes up to 30m high, giving an impression of being in the middle of the Sahara. The **Médanos de Coro** (admission free; ⏰ 7am-7:30pm) is today a national park, created in 1974 to protect this unique environment on the isthmus of the Península de Paraguaná.

To get to the park from the city center, take the Carabobo bus from Calle Falcón and get off 300m past the large Monumento a la Federación. From here it is a 10-minute walk north along a wide avenue to another public sculpture, the Monumento a la Madre. A few paces north there is nothing but sand.

Tours
Budget full-day **tours** (per person $25-30) to Península de Paraguaná and the Sierra de San Luis are organized by the managers of the **Posada Turística El Gallo** (☎ 252-9481; posadae lgallo2001@hotmail.com; Calle Federación No 26) and **La Casa de los Pájaros** (☎ 252-8215; rstiuv@cantv.net; Calle Monzón No 74).

Sleeping
Posada Turística El Gallo (☎ 252-9481; posadaelgallo 2001@hotmail.com; Calle Federación No 26; s/d/tr with fan $10/12/16) This is one of the cheapest options in town, run by a friendly Frenchman who rebuilt the place from a colonial ruin. It's simple and lacks private bathrooms, but is otherwise clean, pleasant and perfectly acceptable. The seven rooms are arranged around a leafy patio and guests can use the kitchen facilities. The owner provides good tourist information.

La Casa de los Pájaros (☎ 252-8215; rstiuv@cantv .net; Calle Monzón No 74; dm $5, d with bathroom & fan $12, with air-con $16; 🅿 🖳) This is a pleasant and friendly private home, which welcomes travelers to its three small rooms and one four-bed dorm. Guests can use the kitchen and Internet (30 minutes free access per day).

Posada Turística Don Antonio (☎ 253-9578; Paseo Talavera No 11; d/tr $16/20; 🖳) Rebuilt in a colonial style, Don Antonio is a brand new posada right in the city's heart. It has nine comfy matrimoniales and three triples, all equipped with bathroom and air-conditioning.

Posada Villa Antigua (☎ 0414-682-2924; Calle Comercio No 46; d $12-16; 🖳) The six old-fashioned rooms here are arranged around a small patio and provide bathrooms and noiseless air-conditioning. It's a pretty place and has an inexpensive restaurant.

La Fonda Coriana (☎ 0414-684-7021; Callejón Tucuyito; d $12-15; 🖳) Just around the corner from Villa Antigua, La Fonda is another likable six-room posada, which also has its own restaurant.

Hotel Miranda Cumberland (☎ 252-3022, 252-3344; www.hotelescumberland.com; Av Josefa Camejo; s/d/tr/ste $40/44/48/56; 🅿 🖳 🖳 🖳) Diagonally opposite the airport terminal, Cumberland is the best place to stay in town, with spacious air-conditioned rooms and still better suites, all with safe boxes and Internet connections. The hotel has its own restaurant, bar and a bean-shaped swimming pool surrounded by coconut palms. Room prices include buffet breakfast.

Eating
Fonda Turística Sabor Latino (Paseo La Alameda; breakfasts $2, lunches $2-3; ⏰ 8am-8pm; 🖳) Nestled in the central pedestrian mall, this is a good spot for some of the cheapest meals in town (including 14 different set breakfasts) in a simple interior or at the shaded tables outside. The menu features staples of Venezuelan cuisine, including *arepas* (stuffed corn pancakes).

Restaurant El Tinajero (Calle Zamora; mains $2-4) El Tinajero is an enjoyable inexpensive eatery serving popular Venezuelan fare on two tiny patios of a rustic historic house.

Restaurant Punto Criollo (☎ 252-2043; Calle Federación; breakfasts $2-3, lunches $3-4; ⏰ 7am-3pm Mon-Sat) This simple eight-table place gets packed completely with patrons at lunchtime, and deservedly so. It also offers filling breakfasts.

Pizzería La Barra del Jacal (☎ 252-7350; Calle Unión; mains $3-6) Don't be misled by its name – this attractive open-air restaurant offers more than just pizzas and gets particularly busy in the evening when a gentle breeze dissipates the heat of the day.

Restaurant El Conquistador (☎ 252-6794; Calle Urdaneta; mains $4-10; 🖳) Satisfactory food, prompt service and tastefully decorated interior make El Conquistador one of the best eateries in town. Go for *parrilla aire*, *mar y tierra* or *paella valenciana*, which are among their specialties.

Panadería La Gran Costa Nova (☎ 252-6680; Av Manaure; meals $2-4; ⏰ 6am-9pm) Costa Nova has been fully refurbished (adding 'Gran' to its name in the process) and now has tables inside and out, plus a lunch menu. It offers good breakfasts, lunches and snacks, and is as popular as ever.

Entertainment

Cine en la Calle (Paseo Talavera) A free open-air cinema on the Paseo Talavera every Tuesday at 7pm. It focuses on Venezuelan and Latin American films.

Teatro Armonía (Calle Falcón) The city's main performing arts venue. Classical music concerts by the local philharmonic orchestra (considered to be the best in the country) are held every Thursday at 7pm (tickets cost just $0.75).

Getting There & Away

AIR

The **Aeropuerto Internacional José Leonardo Chirinos** (☎ 251-5290; Av Josefa Camejo) is just a five-minute walk north of the city center. **Avior** (☎ 253-1689) has daily flights to Caracas ($54 to $68), where you need to change for other destinations. **Aerocaribe Coro** (☎ 252-1837) flies light planes to Curaçao ($160 for a 30-day roundtrip ticket).

BUS

The **Terminal de Pasajeros** (☎ 252-8070; Av Los Médanos) is about 2km east of the city center, and is accessible by frequent city transport. There are ordinary buses to Punto Fijo ($2, 1¼ hours, 90km), Maracaibo ($5.50, four hours, 259km) and Valencia ($7, five hours, 288km) leaving every half-hour until about 6pm. Most of the direct buses to Caracas ($10 to $13, seven hours, 446km) depart in the evening, but you can easily take one of the buses to Valencia and change. Several direct buses go nightly to Mérida ($12 to $18, 13 hours, 782km) and to San Cristóbal ($12 to $17, 12 hours, 698km); all these buses depart in the evening and go via Maracaibo.

Within the region, there are buses to Adícora ($1.25), on the eastern coast of Península de Paraguaná, as well as por puesto jeeps to Curimagua ($2), in the Sierra de San Luis.

PENÍNSULA DE PARAGUANÁ

☎ 0269

With a geography quite different from the mainland, and a history influenced by the Netherlands Antilles, the Península de Para-

guaná is an intriguing anomaly. Shaped vaguely like a human head, the peninsula stretches about 60km from north to south and 50km from east to west. Covering an area of about 2500 sq km, Paraguaná is Venezuela's largest peninsula. It was once an island, but wind and waves gradually built up a sandbar, linking it to the mainland.

Paraguaná is flat except for an unusual mountain, the 830m Cerro Santa Ana, which juts up from the middle of the peninsula. The lowland vegetation features semi-desert plant species, the most noticeable of which is the *cardón*, a columnar cactus tree. Only in the upper reaches of the mountain is the plant life lusher, including some rain forest species.

The climate is generally dry, with a period of light rain extending from October to December. On average, there are only 40 rainy days per year. There are no permanent rivers on the peninsula and the region was never densely populated because of the scarcity of fresh water.

The peninsula offers a variety of attractions and activities, including colonial towns, nature reserves, beaches, windsurfing, hiking and flamingo watching, plus the general feeling of traveling through a remote semidesert outback.

HISTORY

The original inhabitants of Paraguaná were the Amuay, Guaranao and Caquetío Indians, all belonging to the Arawak linguistic family, but today these people are extinct. Europeans first saw Paraguaná in 1499, when Alonso de Ojeda landed at Cabo de San Román, on the northern tip of the peninsula. Some 130 years later, the Dutch settled the nearby islands of Curaçao, Aruba and Bonaire, and since then there has been a steady mix of Spanish, Dutch and indigenous cultural influences.

The earliest colonial towns emerged not on the peninsular coast, but inland, close to Cerro Santa Ana, as it provided the only source of fresh water. Some of the towns' old urban fabric remains, including several churches.

Things began to change with the oil boom. In the 1920s an oil terminal was built in Punto Fijo to ship oil overseas from Lago de Maracaibo. Refineries were constructed in the 1940s, and Punto Fijo

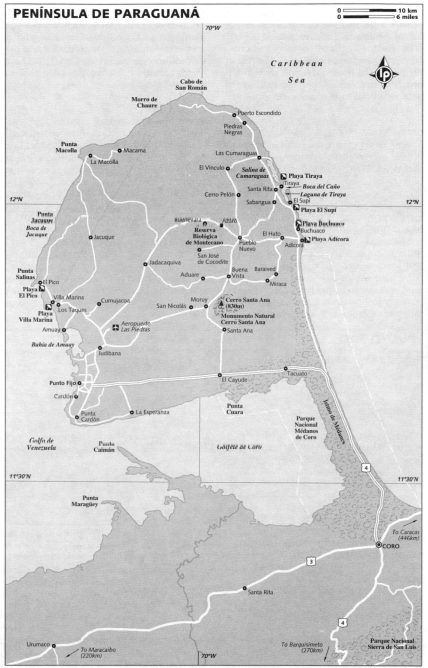

PENÍNSULA DE PARAGUANÁ

0 — 10 km
0 — 6 miles

70°W

Caribbean Sea

Cabo de San Román

Morro de Chaure

Puerto Escondido

Piedras Negras

Punta Macolla
La Macolla
Macama

Las Cumaraguas

El Vínculo
Salina de Cumaraguas
Playa Tiraya
Tiraya
Boca del Caño
Santa Rita
Laguna de Tiraya
Cerro Pelón
Sabarigua
El Supí
Playa El Supí

12°N

Buenevad
Azaro
Reserva Biológica de Montecano
Pueblo Nuevo
El Hato
Playa Buchuaco
Buchuaco
Adicora
Playa Adicora

Punta Jacuque
Boca de Jacuque
Jacuque

San José de Cocodite
Jadacaquiva
Aduare
Buena Vista
Baraived
Miraca

Punta Salinas
Playa El Pico
El Pico
Villa Marina
Los Taques
Cumujacoa
San Nicolás
Moruy
Cerro Santa Ana (830m)
Monumento Natural Cerro Santa Ana
Santa Ana

Playa Villa Marina
Amuay
Aeropuerto Las Piedras

Bahía de Amuay
Judibana

Punto Fijo
Cardón
El Cayude
Tacuato

Punta Cardón
La Esperanza
Punta Cuara

Parque Nacional Médanos de Coro

Golfo de Venezuela
Punta Caimán
Golfete de Coro

Istmo de Médanos

4

11°30'N
11°30'N

Punta Maragüey

To Caracas (446km)
CORO

3

Santa Rita

4

To Maracaibo (220km)
Urumaco
70°W
To Barquisimeto (270km)
Parque Nacional Sierra de San Luís

THE NORTHWEST

embarked on a boom that continues today, rapidly becoming the largest urban center on the peninsula. The area around the city is dominated by the oil industry and criss-crossed by multilane highways. The rest of the peninsula, however, hasn't rushed into progress and modernity. It's still dotted with small old towns and their tiny colonial churches.

ORIENTATION

There's an array of paved roads on the peninsula, except in the almost uninhabited northwest. Having an independent means of transportation is a great advantage here, because buses and por puestos are not frequent, but they do service most of the larger localities, including Punto Fijo, Santa Ana, Moruy, Pueblo Nuevo and Adícora.

The usual springboard for the peninsula is Coro, from where buses go to Adícora and Punto Fijo, the only places with a reasonable choice of accommodations and food. Punto Fijo is much better serviced by public transportation, but otherwise it's an unremarkable place. It's better to go to the more pleasant Adícora and use it as a base for further excursions, such as viewing flamingos at Laguna de Tiraya or hiking up Cerro Santa Ana. Day tours around the peninsula organized from Coro (p143) are worth considering if you want just a quick taste of Paraguaná.

Punto Fijo

Punto Fijo appeared on maps in 1925, following the construction of an oil terminal serving Lago de Maracaibo. The building of two refineries, in Amuay and Punta Cardón, boosted the development of the young town. Today it's an industrial city of about 140,000 inhabitants, approaching the size of Coro, the state capital, but it's busier, with more active commerce and a faster pace of life.

The only city on the peninsula, Punto Fijo has a good range of hotels and restaurants – establishments that are scarce elsewhere on Paraguaná. You may need to stay overnight here en route to or from the Netherlands Antilles, but the city itself is of marginal interest.

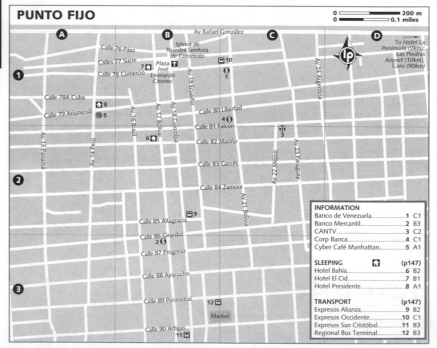

PUNTO FIJO

INFORMATION	
Banco de Venezuela	1 C1
Banco Mercantil	2 B3
CANTV	3 C2
Corp Banca	4 C1
Cyber Café Manhattan	5 A1

SLEEPING	(p147)
Hotel Bahía	6 B2
Hotel El Cid	7 B1
Hotel Presidente	8 A1

TRANSPORT	(p147)
Expresos Alianza	9 B2
Expresos Occidente	10 C1
Expresos San Cristóbal	11 B3
Regional Bus Terminal	12 B3

ORIENTATION & INFORMATION

The downtown is based on two north–south streets, Av Bolívar and Av Colombia, along which many stores, hotels, restaurants and banks are located. Useful banks include **Banco de Venezuela** (cnr Av Bolivia & Calle Comercio), **Banco Mercantil** (cnr Av Bolívar & Calle Girardot) and **Corp Banca** (cnr Calle Falcón & Av Bolivia). **Cyber Café Manhattan** (cnr Av Perú & Calle Arismendi) is one of several central Internet facilities, or use the Internet at **CANTV** (cnr Calle Falcón & Av Méjico).

SLEEPING & EATING

Punto Fijo has a few places to stay and most have their own restaurants.

Hotel Presidente (☎ 245-8964, 245-5156; cnr Av Perú & Calle Arismendi; s $15, d $17-18, tr/ste $20/25; ❄) This modern establishment has reasonable rooms and hot water. Triples and suites are better value than doubles and singles.

Hotel El Cid (☎ 245-5245; fax 245-8165; cnr Calle Comercio & Av Bolívar; s $16, d $19-22, tr $28; P ❄) This large, impersonal place has good-sized, clean rooms, a bar, a restaurant and a disco.

Hotel Bahía (☎ 245-5743; fax 245-8254; cnr Calle Mariño & Av Bolívar; s $10, d $13-14, tr $16; ❄) One of the cheapest options in the center, this hotel can be particularly interesting for budget solo travelers, as it offers low rates for singles. Rooms are rather small and dim but otherwise OK.

Hotel La Península (☎ 245-9734, 245-9776; hotel peninsula@eldish.net; Calle Calatayud; d $40-45, tr/ste $55/70; P ❄ ▨) On Punto Fijo's southeastern outskirts, La Península is one of the city's top offerings, with comfy rooms, two restaurants, swimming pool, gym and pool tables.

GETTING THERE & AWAY

Air

Punto Fijo's airport, **Aeropuerto Internacional Josefa Camejo** (☎ 246-0278), is about 10km northeast of the city and is labeled in all the air schedules as 'Las Piedras,' not 'Punto Fijo.' There are no public buses to the airport; a taxi from the city center will cost $5. There are daily flights to Caracas ($56 to $68) and Maracaibo ($48 to $60).

Dutch Caribbean Airlines (☎ 247-5358, 247-4434) has daily flights to Curaçao ($105 round-trip), whereas **Aerocaribe Coro** (☎ 415-5555) flies daily to Aruba ($95 roundtrip).

Bus

Punto Fijo has not yet built a central bus terminal; bus companies have their own offices scattered throughout the city center. **Expresos Occidente** (cnr Calle Comercio & Av Bolivia), **Expresos Alianza** (cnr Calle Altagracia & Av Colombia) and **Expresos San Cristóbal** (cnr Calle Artigas & Av Colombia) service long-distance routes, including Caracas ($12 to $16, 8½ hours, 536km), Maracaibo ($7.50 to $11, 5½ hours, 349km), San Cristóbal ($14 to $19, 14 hours, 788km) and Mérida ($14 to $20, 15 hours, 872km).

Regional buses depart from the market square. Buses to Coro ($2, 1¼ hours, 90km) run every half-hour until about 6pm. There are also hourly buses to Pueblo Nuevo via the freeway and Santa Ana, and busetas to Pueblo Nuevo via Judibana and Moruy.

Santa Ana

The sleepy little town of Santa Ana is renowned for its colonial church – one of the prettiest country churches in Venezuela. It's also a convenient starting point for a hike to the top of the dramatic Cerro Santa Ana.

The town is reputed to have existed since at least the 1540s, originally as a Caquetío Indian settlement, and was once Paraguaná's major urban center. The church, on the eastern side of Plaza Bolívar, was built in the 16th century – thus being the first church on the peninsula – and was extended and remodeled at the end of the 17th century. The unusual bell tower was built around 1750, and at the same time the main retable was added – it's an amazing piece of popular art graced with naive elements. The church is often open during the day, but if you find it locked, go to the Casa Parroquial, on the northern side of Plaza Bolívar, and somebody may open it up for you.

Santa Ana has several basic places to eat, but nowhere to stay overnight. The Inparques office is one block north of the church. Buses between Pueblo Nuevo and Punto Fijo pass on the main road every hour or so.

Moruy

Another lovely colonial church is in the small village of Moruy, 6km northwest of Santa Ana. Built around 1760, the church is modest in internal furnishing and decoration, but is beautifully proportioned and has a charming facade. The village (along with the nearby hamlet of San Nicolás) is noted for the manufacture of *silletas paraguaneras*, chairs made from the cactus wood of the *cardón*, and you can see and buy them on roadside stalls.

Moruy is a popular starting point for hikes up Cerro Santa Ana. There's nowhere to stay overnight in the village and only a couple of places for a meal. Busetas and buses run regularly to Punto Fijo, Pueblo Nuevo and Santa Ana.

Cerro Santa Ana

Rising 830m above the plains, this mountain is visible from almost any point on the peninsula. It actually has three peaks; the highest is the westernmost and looks dramatic from almost every angle. The mountain, along with its environs (19 sq km altogether), has been decreed a natural monument and is under the control of Inparques. The mountain's vegetation varies from xerophytic species at the base to a type of cloud forest above 500m. There are even some orchids and bromeliads in the upper reaches.

Two ways lead to the top. The main route begins at Moruy and heads eastward for 800m along an unpaved road to the Inparques post and a bivouac area. From here, a proper trail heads to the highest peak. It's about a three-hour walk up to the summit (two hours back down).

Another starting point is the town of Santa Ana, from where a rough road from the Inparques office heads north to another bivouac site (a 30-minute walk). The trail that begins here leads to the lowest, eastern peak, then continues up westward along the crest to the main peak. This route is not clear at some points, so you should be careful not to get lost.

Both Inparques posts allow hikers to start uphill until about 9am. You should register before departure at the respective post, but there's no charge. Hikers need to return by 3pm and mark their return on the list.

The peak is always windy and frequently shrouded in cloud. Occasionally it rains in the upper reaches, especially between September and January, the wet months. Take along a sweater, waterproof gear and proper shoes – the path near the top can be muddy.

Pueblo Nuevo

Home to about 8000 people, Pueblo Nuevo is the largest town in the inland portion of Paraguaná. It still contains some fine colonial houses and a church dating from 1758, although the latter was remodeled in the 20th century.

SLEEPING & EATING

Posada de Luis (☎ 988-1072; Calle Falcón; d/tr $16/22) This likeable, neat, 10-room posada, 300m west of Plaza Bolívar, is so far the only reliable place to stay.

   Restaurant Popular (☎ 988-1133; Calle Falcón; mains $2-3) It's indeed popular, serving straightforward, tasty meals at low prices. Try *chivo* (goat), the local specialty.

GETTING THERE & AWAY

There are frequent buses, busetas and por puestos to Punto Fijo (via Moruy) and Adícora, and two busetas a day direct to Coro.

Reserva Biológica de Montecano

This small wooded area, only 16 sq km, is the only remaining lowland forest on the peninsula. Amazingly, it provides a habitat for 62% of the plant species of Falcón state and attracts a great variety of birds. The **Montecano biological reserve** (admission $0.75; 8am-5pm) is about 7km west of Pueblo Nuevo. It is run by Infalcosta, a Coro-based institute established in 1995 for the development and conservation of Falcón's arid coastal areas.

The reserve's visitors center is on a narrow road leading to the village of San José de Cocodite, which branches off from the Pueblo Nuevo–Buena Vista road 2km south of Pueblo Nuevo. There's no public transportation on this side road; you can hitch or walk 5km from the turnoff. From the visitors center, a guide will take you on a trip along a looped path that winds up and down through the reserve. It's an easy 1½-hour walk through an unusual habitat full of amazing plants and birds, and you'll even find a small lake on the way. The best times to see the birds are early in the morning and late afternoon, and you avoid the burning heat of midday. The admission fee includes guide service.

Adícora

The small town of Adícora, on Paraguaná's eastern coast, features a fine beach, some well-preserved 18th-century architecture, fabulous windsurfing and kitesurfing opportunities, plus a reasonable choice of accommodations and restaurants. It's the most popular tourist destination on the peninsula.

Founded on a small headland jutting into the sea, Adícora was used in the 18th century by the Compañía Guipuzcoana as one of its trading bases, turning it into a prosperous town. Strolling around the streets, you'll still find brightly colored Dutch-Caribbean houses characterized by barred windows on pedestals, topped with decorated caps.

ACTIVITIES

Adícora has gained international fame as a **windsurfing** center, with some of the best wave and wind conditions on Venezuela's coast. The winds are the strongest and the most consistent from January to May, and the calmest from September to November. The windsurfing is safe because the breeze is always onshore, and the place is virtually untouched by big tourism, so it's beautifully unspoiled, informal and inexpensive.

Over recent years, **kitesurfing** has become hugely popular, perhaps even more so than windsurfing. There are a few local operators, all on the Playa Sur (South Beach), offering windsurfing/kitesurfing courses, equipment rental and simple accommodations. They include the following:

Adícora Kitesurfing (☎ 0414-697-5457; www.adicora kitesurf.com) Run by Carlos and offers kitesurfing courses (no windsurfing), including three-/seven-day packages complete with accommodations and meals. It's only open on weekends in low season.

Archie's Kite & Windsurfing (☎ 988-8285; www .kitesurfing-venezuela.de) A German-run school open December to May only.

Windsurf Adícora (☎ 988-8224, 0416-769-6196; www.windsurfadicora.com) The biggest and most reliable facility, open year-round. It offers both windsurfing and kitesurfing, plus good rooms with air-con and bathroom.

SLEEPING & EATING

Adícora has a better choice of places to stay than most other towns on the peninsula. Prices are higher on weekends, when tourists come. Some locals rent out rooms in their homes, which can make for some of the cheapest and safest forms of lodging – ask around. On the other hand, don't rent unattended cabañas or beach houses; these places are easy prey for robbers. There are restaurants in the buildings along the beach, though most of them are only open on weekends.

Posada La Carantoña (☎ 988-8173; Calle Comercio; d with fan $16, air-con $22; 🕳) In a fine old house, one block back from the beach, this enjoyable place offers rustic, but stylish rooms arranged around a patio, plus a budget restaurant.

Posada Casa Rosada (☎ 988-8004; El Malecón; tr/q $22/25; 🕳) This beachfront, four-room proposition has its own restaurant attractively decorated with crafts.

Campamento Vacacional La Troja (☎ 988-8048, 415-5030; mamaluz17@hotmail.com; Calle Santa Ana; r per person $20; P 🕳) Occupying an entire block in the middle of town, this walled complex, built in the traditional style and set in a lush garden (quite unusual on the arid peninsula), provides comfortable and stylish accommodations and food. Spacious rooms have a fan and bathroom and the price includes breakfast.

GETTING THERE & AWAY

Adícora is linked to Coro ($1.25, one hour) by eight buses a day, the last departing at around 5pm. There are also por puestos to Pueblo Nuevo and busetas to Punto Fijo.

Lagunas & Salinas

Flamingos feed at **Laguna de Tiraya**, about 6km north of Adícora. Peak season is November to January, but you can be pretty sure of finding some birds almost year-round. The lagoon is accessible by the paved road to Santa Rita (which skirts the western shore of the lagoon), but there is no public transportation on this road. You can walk or try to hitch (the traffic is mainly on weekends; at other times it's sporadic), or take a taxi from Adícora.

The flamingos may be quite close to the western shore or off in the distance, on the eastern side of the lagoon. As a rough rule, they come to the western shore in the afternoon after doing their morning fishing on the eastern side.

Further north, between Santa Rita and Las Cumaraguas, is the **Salina de Cumaraguas**, where salt is mined using rudimentary methods. The lagoon is noted for the amazingly beautiful color of its water, which ranges from milky pink to deep purple.

THE NORTHWEST

If you have your own transportation, you can explore the region further north as far as **Cabo de San Román**, which is the northernmost point in Venezuela. If not, there are irregular por puestos ($1) on a paved road from Las Cumaraguas to Pueblo Nuevo via El Vínculo. Be prepared for the heat: take sufficient water, sunscreen, sunglasses and a hat.

Beaches

The beaches on Paraguaná don't match those of Morrocoy or Henri Pittier, and the dearth of coconut palms means that they usually lack shade. Like all other beaches in Venezuela, Paraguaná's beaches are quiet on weekdays and swamped on the weekends.

The beaches on the eastern coast stretch almost all the way from Adícora to Piedras Negras. **Adícora** is the most popular beach resort, though **El Supí** and **Buchuaco**, further north, have arguably finer beaches. **Tiraya** is less popular with holidaymakers because it's harder to reach. On the western coast, the popular beaches include **Villa Marina** and **El Pico**, both serviced by local transportation from Punto Fijo.

SIERRA DE SAN LUIS

☎ 0268

This belt of verdant mountains boasts picturesque towns, waterfalls, about 20 caves and a dozen *simas* – deep vertical holes in the earth. The Sierra de San Luis stretches south of the arid Coro coast and offers a fresh, pleasant climate, exotic forests full of birds, and a good choice of walking paths. There's an array of hotels and restaurants and reasonable public transportation.

The Sierra is a vital source of water for the whole coastal area, including the Península de Paraguaná. About 200 sq km of this rugged terrain was made into a national park in 1987. Elevations within the park range from 200m up to 1501m on Cerro Galicia, the park's highest point. Average temperatures range between 25°C and 15°C, according to altitude. Annual rainfall is moderate, not exceeding 1500mm, and the wettest months are October to December.

Orientation

San Luis, Cabure and Curimagua are the major towns of the Sierra, all of which are accessible by public transportation from

Coro. Curimagua is the closest to Coro (45km) and is the only one regularly serviced. Curimagua and its environs also have the best choice of accommodations and provide the most popular and convenient base for visiting the region. You can go there on your own and stay in a posada, from where you can explore the Sierra. Many of the posada owners will offer visitors excursions around area sights, or at least provide them with information on what to see and how to get there. However, the most popular form of visiting the Sierra is a day tour from Coro (p143), which covers most of the sights listed below.

Sights

Of the three main towns, **San Luis** is possibly the most picturesque. Founded in 1590, it's the oldest Spanish settlement in the area and has preserved some of its colonial architecture, including a fine church. Of the waterfalls, the **Cataratas de Hueque**, northeast of Cabure, is the largest and the most spectacular.

Among the caves, the **Cueva de Zárraga** and the **Cueva del Nacimiento** are the most frequent tourist destinations. Both are accessible from the **Camino de Los Españoles**, an old Spanish trail between Cabure and La Negrita; its best-preserved part is near Acarite, where there is a brick Spanish bridge dating from around 1790.

The **Haitón de Guarataro**, midway between Curimagua and San Luis, is the most impressive local *sima*. It's 305m deep, but the mouth is only about 12m in diameter.

Sleeping & Eating

The places to stay in the region are clean, pleasant and friendly. They don't offer excessive luxuries, but are adequate, comfortable and inexpensive. Most are small, family-run posadas managed by the owners. All places listed here have rooms with private bathrooms and provide meals.

CURIMAGUA & AROUND

Hotel Turístico Gran Apolo (☎ 416-1202; hotelgran apolo@cantv.net; d/tr/q $18/25/33; P ⌘) Right in the center of Curimagua, this is the biggest place to stay (14 rooms), and has some useful extras, including a reasonable restaurant, a rooftop terrace with long vistas, and a fair-sized swimming pool.

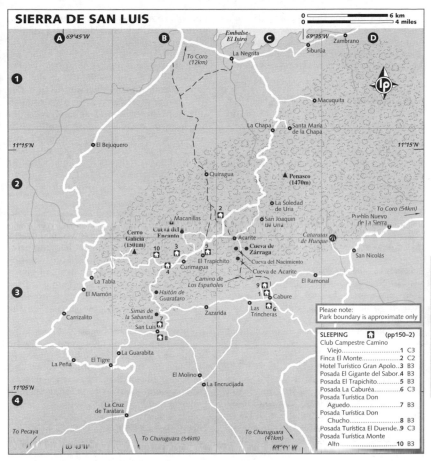

SIERRA DE SAN LUIS

SLEEPING 🏠 (pp150–2)
Club Campestre Camino
Viejo.................................1 C3
Finca El Monte.......................2 C2
Hotel Turístico Gran Apolo...3 B3
Posada El Gigante del Sabor.4 B3
Posada El Trapichito............5 B3
Posada La Caburéa..............6 C3
Posada Turística Don
Aguedo.............................7 B3
Posada Turística Don
Chucho..............................8 B3
Posada Turística El Duende..9 C3
Posada Turística Monte
Alto..................................10 B3

THE NORTHWEST

Posada El Gigante del Sabor (☎ 416-0992; d/tr $8/10) At the western end of town, the Giant of Taste is very basic, but look at the prices! It also serves some of the cheapest meals.

Posada Turística Monte Alto (☎ 416-0835; d $18, cabañas $30-35) About 2km west of Curimagua, this agreeable posada, stuck to a steep hillside, offers five comfy matrimonial rooms, two cabañas (for four to five guests) providing great views, and a no-nonsense restaurant.

Posada El Trapichito (☎ 416-1989; d/tr $10/14) About 2km northeast of Curimagua, off the road to Coro, this is another good address and one of the cheapest deals. It too, has an inexpensive restaurant and the portions are generous.

Finca El Monte (☎ 416-0622; fincaelmonte@yahoo .com; s/d/tr $10/13/16) El Monte is a nine-hectare farm owned and run by a friendly Swiss couple, Ernesto and Ursula. It has just three rooms for guests, can prepare meals on request and organizes hikes in the area. It's 5km northeast of Curimagua, on the road to Coro.

SAN LUIS
Posada Turística Don Aguedo (☎ 666-3073; Calle Principal; d/tr $13/16) This charming place at the foot of the mountain has four perfectly acceptable rooms with bathroom and fan, and a rustic restaurant serving filling meals. It's an oasis of tranquility, except for early morning cockcrow.

Posada Turística Don Chucho (☎ 666-3053; d/tr $16/20; (P)(≊)) Don Chucho has reasonable rooms with bathroom and fan, a refreshing small pool, its own restaurant, and a bar on a terrace with great views over the valley.

CABURE

Posada Turística El Duende (☎ 661-1079; d/q $16/24) The loveliest place to stay, about 1.5km up a steep, rough road from the town. Charmingly rustic and informal, the posada has five simple rooms, plus an appealing restaurant. Have a look at the great 300-year-old ceiba next to the house.

Club Campestre Camino Viejo (☎ 661-1016; d $20-24, cabañas $30-40; (P)(X)(≊)) Next to the local cemetery, the Country Club occupies spacious grounds and offers the most complete facilities, featuring cabins, chalets, restaurant, bar, swimming pool and disco on weekends.

Posada La Cabureña (☎ 661-1093; Calle Bolívar; tr $20; (X)) Next to the church, this new five-room place provides neat, homely rooms with air-con, bathroom and hot water. The sheer number of pictures on the walls makes you feel as if you are in a provincial museum.

Getting There & Away

The usual point of departure for the Sierra is Coro. Por puesto jeeps to Curimagua (via La Chapa) depart from 5am until mid-afternoon ($2, 1½ hours, 45km). There are also infrequent carritos to Cabure (via Pueblo Nuevo de La Sierra), some of which continue up to San Luis.

PARQUE NACIONAL MORROCOY

One of the most spectacular coastal environments in Venezuela, Parque Nacional Morrocoy comprises a strip of mainland, and an offshore area dotted with islands, islets and cays. Some islands are skirted by white-sand beaches and surrounded by coral reefs. At the eastern edge of Falcón state, Morrocoy is one of the most popular parks with those looking for beaches and snorkeling.

The park is also well known for its variety of water birds, including ibis, herons, cormorants, ducks, pelicans and flamingos. They permanently or seasonally inhabit some of the islands and coastal mangroves, especially the Golfete de Cuare, which is

one of Venezuela's richest bird-breeding grounds and has been declared a wildlife refuge.

Venezuelan beachgoers come en masse on holidays and weekends and leave the islands littered. The fragile island environment is unfortunately beginning to suffer from human interference, though you can still enjoy deserted and apparently virgin beaches on weekdays. More significantly, some of the coral has died, purportedly the result of a 1996 chemical leak. Independent biologists claimed that up to half of the hard coral was dead. It has begun to rebound, but it's likely to take decades for the full recovery.

Orientation

The park lies between the towns of Tucacas and Chichiriviche, which are its main gateways. Both have well-organized boat services to the islands, as well as an array of places to stay and eat. You can use them as a base for day trips to the islands, but if you have a tent or a hammock you can stay on the islands themselves.

The most popular island is Cayo Sombrero, which has fine coral reefs and some of the best beaches. It's more exposed to the open sea than most other islands, and the breeze means that it has fewer insects. Other places good for snorkeling include Playuela and Boca Seca.

Sleeping & Eating

Camping is officially permitted on four islands: Cayo Sal, Cayo Muerto, Cayo Sombrero and Cayo Paiclás. If you plan on staying in a hammock, make absolutely sure you take along a good mosquito net. All four of the islands have beach restaurants and/or food kiosks, but some of them may be closed on weekdays in the slow season.

Before you go camping, you need to contact the Inparques office in Tucacas (see following) and shell out a camping fee of $1 per person per night, payable at the Banesco in Tucacas.

When camping on the islands, take sufficient water, some food to save on predictably overpriced beach eateries, snorkeling gear, good sun protection and a reliable insect repellent. The insects here – small biting gnats known locally as *puri-puri* –

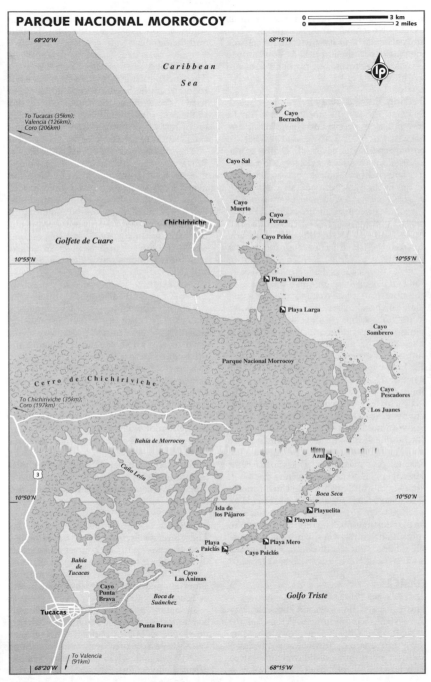

PARQUE NACIONAL MORROCOY

0   3 km
0   2 miles

68°20'W

Caribbean
Sea

68°15'W

Cayo
Borracho

To Tucacas (35km);
Valencia (126km);
Coro (206km)

Cayo Sal

Cayo
Muerto

Chichiriviche

Cayo
Peraza

Cayo Pelón

Golfete de Cuare

10°55'N

10°55'N

Playa Varadero

Playa Larga

Cayo
Sombrero

Parque Nacional Morrocoy

Cerro de Chichiriviche

Cayo
Pescadores

To Chichiriviche (35km);
Coro (197km)

Los Juanes

Bahía de Morrocoy

Azul

Caño León

3

Boca Seca

10°50'N

10°50'N

Isla de
los Pájaros

Playuelita

Playuela

Playa
Paiclás

Playa Mero

Cayo Paiclás

Bahía
de
Tucacas

Cayo
Las Ánimas

Cayo
Punta
Brava

Boca de
Suánchez

Golfo Triste

Tucacas

Punta Brava

68°20'W

To Valencia
(91km)

68°15'W

THE NORTHWEST

are most annoying in windless months, usually November and December. They are particularly nasty early in the morning and late in the afternoon. You can use gas camping stoves, but no open fires are permitted.

Getting There & Away
Boats to the islands normally take up to seven or eight people and charge a flat rate per trip. Prices to all islands and beaches are posted next to the ticket office close to the loading dock in Tucacas. They are round-trip fares per boat, not per person. The fare to the farthest islands, such as Cayo Sombrero or Cayo Pescadores, is around $38. Closer destinations include Playa Paiclás ($23), Playa Mero ($25), Playuela ($26) and Playa Azul ($30). The boat will pick you up from the island in the afternoon or at a later date, depending on when you want to return. On weekdays during the off-season, you can usually bargain down the price.

Before you decide to go to one particular island or beach, check for excursions with stops on various islands, organized by some boat operators and hotel managers. They may be an interesting proposition and not so expensive. For example, a full-day boat trip organized by **Posada Amigos del Mar** (☎ 812-3962, 0414-484-7570; Calle Nueva) costs about $10 per person.

Chichiviriche has two piers: the Embarcadero Playa Norte, near the eastern end of Av Zamora; and the Embarcadero Playa Sur, about 1km southwest. Boat fares are the same at both piers. As in Tucacas, the boat takes a maximum of seven to eight passengers, and the fare given is per boat. Popular shorter trips include Cayo Muerto ($10), Cayo Sal ($13) and Cayo Pelón ($14), whereas Cayo Sombrero ($38) is the leading further destination. The return time is up to you, and haggling over the price is also possible. Some hotels and posadas (including the Caribana Hotel) organize boat trips.

TUCACAS
☎ 0259 / pop 25,000
This ordinary, hot town on the Valencia–Coro road, has nothing to keep you for long. But with the Parque Nacional Morrocoy just a stone's throw away, the town has developed into a holiday center dotted with hotels and restaurants. Plenty of new

developments are springing up toward the south of town, between the Morón road and the beach.

Orientation
The town's lifeline is Av Libertador, a 1km road stretching between the Morón–Coro road in the west and the bridge to an island in the east. Many hotels and restaurants are on or just off this street. Buses stop at the intersection of the two roads.

The island across the bridge, Cayo Punta Brava, is part of the national park. A 15-minute walk from the bridge along the paved road will bring you to the beach, which is shaded with coconut palms; more beaches lie further east on the same island, accessible by road. To visit other islands in the park, go to the *embarcadero* (landing dock), close to the bridge, which is packed with pleasure boats waiting for tourists.

Information
Tucacas has no reliable tourist office – try the staff at your hotel or scuba-diving operators. The office of **Inparques** (☎ 812-2176; Av Libertador; ☉ 8am-12:30pm & 2-5pm), which you need to contact if you want to camp on the islands, is close to the bridge. Pay your camping fee at **Banesco** (Av Libertador), which also gives cash advances on Visa and MasterCard (from the cashier, not the ATM). **Banco Provincial** (Carretera Coro-Morón) has a useful ATM, but it's 2km south of the center. Both diving schools will be happy to accept your cash dollars and may take your traveler's checks as well.

Tucacas has several Internet facilities, including the fast **CANTV** (Centro Comercial Morrocoy, Carretera Coro-Morón), 300m south of the bus stop.

Activities
There are two scuba diving operators in town. Both offer diving courses and guided dives run by professional licensed instructors, and both have shops selling diving and snorkeling equipment, some of which can be rented.

Submatur (☎ 812-0082, 812-1051; morrocoysub matur@cantv.net; Calle Ayacucho No 6) is owned and managed by Mike Osborn from Guyana. With 40 years' experience, it is one of the oldest diving schools in the country. Sample prices include a four-day open water NAUI course for $300 and a two-dive day trip for $60. Two-day and longer diving trips in a sailing boat to Bonaire and Islas Las Aves can be organized ($125 per day).

Amigos del Mar Divers (☎ 812-1754; amigos-del -mar@cantv.net; Calle Democracia No 1), near the embarcadero, is cheaper then Submatur. It's owned by a Belgian, André Nahon, one of the former instructors of Submatur.

Sleeping

Posada Amigos del Mar (☎ 812-3962, 0414-484-7570; Calle Nueva; s/d/tr $7/8/12; P) This simple, pleasant 10-room posada is run by André of the diving school of the same name. It has spacious rooms with bathroom and fan overlooking a leafy garden, and guests can use the kitchen. The posada is beyond the Ambulatorio Urbano, a three-minute walk from the bus stop.

Posada El Ancla (☎ 812-0253; posadaelancla@cantv .net; Calle Páez; d/q $16/20; P 🗙) El Ancla is a friendly, family-run, four-room place, two blocks south of Av Libertador. Rooms don't have private facilities but there are four shared bathrooms, exactly one per room.

Posada Náutica (☎ 812-2559; Calle Falcón; B&B $22; 🗙 🖲) This pretty, three-story house shelters seven rooms, a pleasant restaurant downstairs and a small pool.

Posada d'Alexis (☎ 812-3390; Calle Falcón; d $19-20, q $28; P 🗙 🖲) Next door to Posada Náutica, this is another nice small guesthouse with its own restaurant. Rooms are arranged around a pool with a waterfall and amazing weeping willows.

Posada de Carlos (☎ 812-1493; Av Libertador; d/tr $10/16) Named after the owner, this small hotel has eight rooms with bathroom and fan, and you can use the kitchen. The establishment's name isn't posted, but the place is recognizable by the 'sí hay habitación' inscription on the door.

Posada Balijú (☎ 812-1580; www.posadabaliju.com; Calle Libertad; package $55; P 🗙) Right on the waterfront, this is one of the most charming places around, providing tranquility, stylish surroundings and a family atmosphere. It's available by package only, which includes bed, breakfast, lunch, dinner and boat excursions.

Posada Venemar (☎ 812-2669; www.venemar.com; Av Libertador; d $30-35, ste $45; 🗙) Near the bridge, Venemar offers good-quality matrimoniales and suites – all with sea views – plus a fine

restaurant, which is one of the best places in town for a seafood dinner.

Aparto Posada del Mar (☎ 812-3587; www.aparto posadadelmar.com; Av Silva; d/tr/ste $40/46/90; P 🗙 🖲) This spacious waterfront compound offers reasonable rooms (great suites with sea views), adequate restaurant, fair-sized swimming pool, kitchen for guests, own pier and beach, and a sauna, should you need to warm yourself in this steamy climate.

Eating

Restaurant El Timón (☎ 812-0783; Av Libertador; mains $5-8; 🗙) El Timón offers solid, satisfying food – particularly seafood – at good prices, and you can eat it inside or at the tables outside.

Arepera La Esperanza (Av Libertador; arepas $1; ☾ 24hr) No matter if it's midday or midnight, this is an important stop to grab one (or more) *arepas*, which come with 15 different fillings.

Restaurant El Funchal (☎ 812-2478; Av Libertador; mains $5-10) Set on the 1st-floor terrace in the same building where the Arepera La Esperanza is located, El Funchal is rustic and informal, and has a skillful chef specializing in *mariscos* (seafood).

Panadería La Reina De Mar (Av Libertador; breakfast $2-3, lunch $2-4) This is the best of the local *panaderías*, with tables inside and out. It serves fresh, tasty sandwiches, chicken, lasagna, cakes and excellent coffee.

Getting There & Away

Tucacas sits on the Valencia–Coro road, so buses run frequently to both Valencia ($2, 1½ hours, 91km) and Coro ($5.50, 3½ hours, 197km). Buses from Valencia pass through regularly on their way to Chichiriviche ($0.75, 40 minutes, 35km).

CHICHIRIVICHE

☎ 0259 / pop 12,000

Chichiriviche is the northern gateway to Parque Nacional Morrocoy, providing access to half a dozen neighboring cays. Accommodations, food and boats are in good supply here. The town is smaller than Tucacas, but just as unattractive, apart from the waterfront, which is crammed with old colorful fishing boats.

Access to the town is from the west, by the 12km road that runs along a causeway through mangrove swamps. The area lining

THE NORTHWEST

this road is a favorite feeding ground for flamingos, which gather here mostly between August and January; however, a small community can remain up to March or even April, as long as there's sufficient water. November is usually the peak month, when up to 5000 birds are in the area.

Orientation

Upon entering the town proper, the access road divides. Its main branch, Av Zamora (also called Av Principal), continues straight ahead to the bus terminus and the town's center, ending at the waterfront next to the northern pier. This area boasts a number of hotels, restaurants and other businesses. The southern branch, Vía Fábrica de Cemento, goes to the cement plant south of town, providing access to the southern pier on the way.

Information

In the absence of a tourist office you can ask hotel managers for local information. The **Banco Industrial de Venezuela** (Av Zamora) gives advances on Visa, but that's about all it can do for you; it doesn't accept MasterCard. Internet access is provided by several cybercafés, including **Bit Manía** (Paseo Bolívar), **Comunications City** (Av Zamora), near the bus stop, and **Morrocoy @ Services** (Av Zamora). Chichiriviche has no diving schools.

Sleeping

Villa Gregoria (☎ 818-6359; aagustinm@yahoo.es; Calle Mariño; d with fan $13, with air-con $20; P 🌂) This Spanish-run and Spanish-looking posada, near the bus terminus, has good rooms with bathrooms. Choose a room on the upper floor – they are brighter and more attractive – and relax in a hammock or an armchair on the great terrace. The owner organizes car tours to Coro and Puerto Cabello.

Morena's Place (☎ 815-0936; posadamorenas@hot mail.com; Sector Playa Norte; r per person $5) This inviting five-room posada, in a fine old house near the waterfront, is one of the cheapest in town. It's run by friendly English-speaking Carlos, who also offers laundry service, budget meals and tours, and rents out two kayaks ($12 a day).

Hotel Capri (☎ 818-6026; hotel_capri@cantv.net; Av Zamora; d $16-20, tr $24; 🌂) Capri is not going to gain many stars, but nonetheless is an ad-

equate inexpensive option a stone's throw from the waterfront.

Posada Milagro (☎ 815-0864; Av Zamora; d $13) Just 50m back from the seashore, the Milagro has seven simple matrimoniales with bathrooms, fans and sea views. Ask for a room in the Licorería Falcón and choose one on the top floor for better vistas.

Caribana Hotel (☎ 818-6837; Paseo Bolívar; d $22-25, tr $48; 🌂) Refurbished over recent years, Caribana now offers neat rooms with fine tile work and comfortable beds, and organizes tours. It's just off Av Zamora.

Hotel La Garza (☎ 818-6711; hotellagarza@cantv .net; cnr Av Zamora & Vía Fábrica de Cemento; d $30-40; P 🌂 🏊) At the entrance to the town, 1km back from the waterfront, La Garza has a long-standing tradition and maintains its reasonable standards and facilities, including its refreshing swimming pool and adjacent restaurant. Rooms vary in size and quality, so it's best to have a look before checking in.

Hotel Mario (☎ 818-6811; hotelmariovzla@cantv.net; Av Zamora; d/tr/ste $42/52/80; P 🌂 🏊) Across the road from La Garza, the Hotel Mario has a large pool, a large restaurant and 130 large rooms. Room prices include breakfast.

Coral Suites Hotel & Spa (☎ 815-1033; www .hotelcoralsuites.com; Vía Fábrica de Cemento; ste $60-100; P 🌂 🏊) A big, modern five-star affair, this is a touch of Miami in Chichiriviche. Enjoy a vast swimming pool with water slides, plus tennis courts, two restaurants, a conference room for up to 1000 people, and beds wide enough to sleep across – all that at modest Venezuelan prices.

Eating

Restaurant Txalupa (☎ 818-6056; El Malecón; mains $8-12; 🕐 noon-10pm) This Basque-run, respectable establishment does good fish and seafood at good prices. It's on the 1st floor, providing views of the fishing boats on the shore and the islands on the horizon. Upstairs is a tasca with plenty of drinks and still better views.

Ristorante Il Faro (☎ 416-0066; Calle La Marina; mains $6-15; 🕐 noon-10pm) Set in a beautiful colonial-style mansion, Il Faro has some of the best food in town, and not only Italian as its name would suggest. Take a table on the spacious upper-floor terrace with wide vistas over the sea, and enjoy the *parrillada de mariscos* (seafood grill $12) or a lobster ($20) – both local specialties.

Restaurant El Rincón de Arturo (Av Zamora; breakfasts $2.50, set lunches $3) Budget travelers are likely to appreciate the straightforward tasty meals in this tiny, rustic place.

Getting There & Away
Chichiriviche is about 22km off the main Morón–Coro highway and is serviced by half-hourly buses from Valencia ($2.80, 2½ hours, 126km).

There are no direct buses to Chichiriviche from Caracas or Coro. To get there from Caracas, take any of the frequent buses to Valencia ($2.50, 2½ hours, 158km) and change there for a Chichiriviche bus. From Coro, take any bus to Valencia, get off in Sanare ($5, 3¼ hours, 184km), at the turnoff for Chichiriviche, and catch the Valencia–Chichiriviche bus.

LARA & YARACUY STATES

BARQUISIMETO
☎ 0251 / pop 800,000
It's said that every inhabitant of Barquisimeto sings or plays a musical instrument – the city is known as Venezuela's musical capital. It's a modern city dotted with shady parks and plazas, where you'll see plenty of musical bands and ensembles rehearsing in public, and a conspicuous number of locals walking the streets carrying bulky black cases with their precious tubas and cellos.

Barquisimeto has a few attractions worth visiting and a delightful warm and dry climate with a mean temperature of 24°C. It's also a jumping-off point for the surrounding region – a beautiful land of arid hills, colorful crafts and mysteries of María Lionza.

Originally founded in 1552, Barquisimeto moved three times before eventually being established at its present-day location in 1563. Its growth was slow, as the indigenous tribes in the region were fierce in defending their territory. It wasn't until the 20th century that the city really developed to become a thriving commercial and industrial center and the capital of Lara state. Today, it's Venezuela's fourth-largest city, after Caracas, Maracaibo and Valencia.

Orientation
Barquisimeto's center, spreading to the north of Plaza Bolívar, has a regular grid pattern, which is easy to navigate. Its main commercial street is Av 20, heavily packed with shopping centers and stores. The area around Plaza Bolívar is quieter, but becomes a ghost town after dark, so don't plan on night walks. More attractive and relaxing is the city's eastern sector, along Av Lara and Av Los Leones, about 3km east of the center. The area is dotted with spanking new shopping malls, well-appointed restaurants and trendy night spots – a destination for the city's beautiful people.

Information
EMERGENCY
Fire (☎ 231-9131)
Police (☎ 231-0111)

INTERNET ACCESS
Internet access in Barquisimeto is fast and cheap ($0.50 to $0.80 an hour), and there are plenty of cybercafés all across the center. The **Centro Comercial Capital Plaza** (cnr Av Vargas & Av 20) alone has around 10 cybercafés, and it's a good point to start if you are nearby. Other central places include the following:
D&G Website Internet (Centro Comercial BarquiCenter, Av 20 btwn Calles 22 & 23)
formula1.com (Calle 23 btwn Carreras 18 & 19)
Internet y Copias (cnr Carrera 19 & Calle 24)

MEDICAL SERVICES
Clínica Luis Razetti (☎ 232-7111, 231-9011; Calle 27 btwn Carreras 21 & 22)
Hospital Central Dr Antonio María Pineda (☎ 251-3846; cnr Av Las Palmas & Av Vargas)
Policlínica de Barquisimeto (☎ 254-0044; cnr Av Los Leones & Av Madrid) Northeast of town.

MONEY
Banco de Venezuela (cnr Av 20 & Calle 31)
Banco Mercantil (cnr Carrera 19 & Calle 29)
Banco Provincial (cnr Av 20 & Calle 31)
Banesco (cnr Carrera 19 & Calle 27)
Corp Banca (cnr Av 20 & Av Vargas)
Italcambio Airport (☎ 443-1910; ⏱ 7am-7pm); City (☎ 254-9790; Centro Empresarial Barquisimeto, Av Los Leones; ⏱ 8:30am-5pm)

POST
Ipostel (cnr Carrera 17 & Calle 25)

BARQUISIMETO

SIGHTS & ACTIVITIES	(pp158–9)
Iglesia de Barquisimeto	13 A1
Iglesia de la Concepción	14 B3
Iglesia de San Francisco	15 C3
Museo de Barquisimeto	16 B3

SLEEPING	(p159)
Hotel del Centro	17 B2
Hotel Lido	18 B3
Hotel Príncipe	19 C2
Hotel Yacambú	20 D2

EATING	(pp159–60)
El Bodegón del Centro	21 C2
Restaurant Marisquería Rio Mar.	22 D3
Restaurant Vegetariano Natural Food Center	23 B2

ENTERTAINMENT	(p160)
Ateneo de Barquisimeto	24 C3
Teatro Juárez	25 B2

| SHOPPING | (p157) |
| Centro Comercial Capital Plaza | 26 D2 |

INFORMATION	
Banco de Venezuela	1 A2
Banco Mercantil	2 B2
Banco Provincial	3 A2
Banesco	4 B2
CANTV	5 B2
Clínica Luis Razetti	6 B2
Corp Banca	7 D2
D&G Website Internet	8 C2
formula1.com	9 C2
Internet y Copias	10 C2
Ipostel	11 B3
Telcel	12 C2

TELEPHONE
CANTV (Carrera 19 btwn Calles 25 & 26)
Telcel (Carrera 19 btwn Calles 24 & 25)

TOURIST INFORMATION
Dirección de Turismo (☎ 255-7544, 255-9321; Edificio Fundalara, Av Libertador; 8am-noon & 1:30-3:30pm Mon-Fri) It's over 2km northeast of the center, near the Complejo Ferial. To get there, take Ruta 12 bus from anywhere along Carrera 19 in the center. The office operates information desks in the bus terminal and at the airport.
Inparques (☎ 254-2933, 254-8118; Parque del Este; Av Libertador; 9am-noon & 2-5pm Mon-Fri) The office provides information about the national parks in the region, Yacambú and Terepaima, and books accommodation in the parks.

Sights
The lovely **Plaza Bolívar**, full of splendid tall palm trees, is the birthplace of the city. The pretty **Iglesia de la Concepción** (Plaza Bolívar), on the square's southern side, was Barquisimeto's first cathedral, but it was destroyed in the earthquake of 1812 and rebuilt 30 years later in a different style.

A few steps south of the church is the **Museo de Barquisimeto** (☎ 717-1022; Carrera 15 btwn Calles 25 & 26; admission $0.50; 9am-5pm Tue-Fri, 10am-5pm Sat & Sun) in an imposing historical building with a rectangular courtyard centered on a chapel. It was built in the 1910s as a hospital, and later used for other purposes, until authorities decided to demolish it to make way for modern buildings. Thanks to public protests, though, it was restored and turned into a museum, and it's a beautiful structure in itself. Its rooms house various temporary exhibitions, usually interesting and well displayed, and always a surprise.

The tiny **Plaza Lara**, two blocks east of Plaza Bolívar, is the city's only area with colonial character, thanks to the restored historic buildings lining the square. It's no doubt the finest historic plaza in town and is charmingly shaded with old trees. On the northern side of the plaza is the **Ateneo de Barquisimeto** (☎ 232-4655; cnr Carrera 17 & Calle 23), a busy center for cultural activities. Go in and check what's on.

The handsome **Iglesia de San Francisco** (Plaza Lara), on the southern side of the plaza, was built in 1865 and carried the distinction of being Barquisimeto's second city cathedral, until the modern **Catedral de Barquisimeto** (cnr Av Venezuela & Av Simón Rodríguez) was constructed in the 1960s. It's a bold, innovative design noted for its parabolic concrete roof and a centrally located high altar. The cathedral is open only for mass (normally at 6pm weekdays, with more services on Sunday), so plan accordingly.

Parque Zoológico y Botánico Bararida (☎ 252-4774; cnr Av Los Abogados & Calle 13; admission $1; ☺ 9am-5pm), 1.5km northeast of the center, features the botanical and zoological gardens. It's a large, relaxing park with an artificial lake and cafés, and it's worth coming here to have a close look at some of Venezuela's typical animals, such as the tapir, jaguar and capybara.

Festivals & Events
The city's biggest annual event is the **Fiestas Patronales de la Divina Pastora**. The patron saint's day is January 14, and its central feature is a solemn procession parading the image of the Virgin Mary from the shrine in Santa Rosa village into the city. The celebrations go for several days before and after the saint's day, and include agricultural fairs, concerts and sports events held in the Complejo Ferial (fairgrounds).

Sleeping
Most visitors will want to stay in the city center for good accommodations that are close to the main sights. The eastern suburbs offer the city's best lodgings, but little in the way of budget accommodations. If you're in transit and looking for a place to crash for a night, you can choose from half a dozen basic hotels in an unattractive area on the northern side of the bus terminal. But do yourself a favor and check out a few before settling in – they differ significantly in standards and rates.

Hotel del Centro (☎ 808-0378; Av 20 btwn Calles 26 & 27; d/tr with fan $8/9, d/tr/q with air-con $8/10/11; 🕮) Hidden among dozens of shoe shops, the Hotel del Centro is really central and just about the cheapest acceptable option in the area. Rooms are basic but all have private bathrooms. Some of the rooms on the upper floors provide excellent bird's-eye views of the busy commerce on the street below.

Hotel Lido (☎ 231-5568; Carrera 16 btwn Calles 26 & 27; d $10-12, tr $14; P 🕮) Just one block from Plaza Bolívar, this small place is not a Sheraton, but all rooms have air-con and bathrooms, and it isn't expensive. It's also used *por ratos* (by the hour), so don't be surprised that couples come and go.

Hotel Yacambú (☎ 251-3229; Av Vargas btwn Carrera 19 & Av 20; d/tr/ste $24/28/30; 🕮) Nestled on a busy avenue, Yacambú has already passed its years of glory, yet it still does a rife business. Grab one of the two suites – they are noticeably better than the ordinary rooms and have balconies. The hotel has an enjoyable, inexpensive restaurant.

Hotel Príncipe (☎ 231-2111, 231-2544; fax 231-1731; Calle 23 btwn Carreras 18 & 19; d/tr $34/38; P 🕮 🕮) Aptly named the 'Prince,' this is a respectable four-star 150-room establishment right in the heart of the city. It's well maintained and provides most of the facilities you'd wish for, such as a reliable restaurant, cozy bar and a fair-sized swimming pool at the back where you have a feeling of being outside the city.

Posada La Segoviana (☎ 252-8669; lasegoviana@ terra.com.ve; Calle 7 btwn Carreras 2 & 3, Urbanización Nueva Segovia; d/tr/q/ste $30/34/38/48; P 🕮) This is Barquisimeto's first (and so far the only) posada, set in a quiet residential eastern suburb, about 2km from the city center. With just nine rooms, it provides personalized service and cozy ambience, but it's often full, so book well in advance.

Hotel Barquisimeto Hilton (☎ 256-4110; www .barquisimeto.hilton.com; Carrera 5 btwn Calles 5 & 6, Urbanización Nueva Segovia; d $140; P 🕮 🕮 🕮) In the same suburb as La Segoviana, the five-star Hilton provides Barquisimeto's ultimate luxuries, including a gym.

Eating
The city center is packed with places to eat, particularly Av Vargas and its environs and, to a lesser extent, Av 20. The best restaurants, though, are in the eastern suburbs.

El Bodegón del Centro (☎ 231-6556; cnr Carrera 19 & Calle 21; mains $4-8) This tasca-style restaurant with a large bar in the middle and dark-wood furniture does solid food, including *churrasco* (rib steak) and trout, at affordable prices.

Restaurant Marisquería Río Mar (☎ 252-9104; Calle 17 btwn Carreras 17 & 18; mains $6-10; ☺ 11:30am-9pm) Río Mar is one of the best fish and seafood eateries in town. The interior looks pretty ordinary, but the food is first class and fresh. Try the *canoa de mariscos* (seafood with pineapple; $8) or *paella marinera* ($14 for two persons).

Maranello Bar & Grill (☎ 715-0786; Centro Comercial Churún Merú, Av Lara; salads $5-7, pasta $5-7, mains $6-10; ☻ noon-1am) Opened by a Ferrari fan, the place is swamped with all kinds of Ferrari Formula One paraphernalia, and you can buy some of the stuff in a small shop at the back. As for the food, it's a fine choice of tasty pasta, salads, grilled beef and a couple of Tex-Mex dishes.

Círculo Restaurante (☎ 254-0975; Centro Empresarial Proa, Urbanización El Parral; mains $5-10; ☻ noon-3pm & 7-11pm Mon-Sat) This smart restaurant, with a modern, scarcely decorated interior, offers nouvelle cuisine combining Italian and French specialties, and has a sushi bar.

D'elpunto Restaurant (☎ 254-8367; Urbanización Nueva Segovia, cnr Carrera 1 & Calle 4; mains $8-12; ☻ noon-3pm & 7-10:30pm Mon-Sat, noon-4:30pm Sun) D'elpunto comes with what they call *comida creativa* (creative food). The waiters will be happy to explain the intricacies, but if you still have doubts about what to choose, probably the best bet is to order the *menú de degustación* ($10), which features samples of seven different creations by the chef.

Restaurant Vegetariano Natural Food Center (cnr Carrera 18 & Calle 26; meals $2-3; ☻ 11am-4pm Mon-Sat) This popular and central vegetarian spot serves straightforward set lunches and snacks.

Entertainment

Ateneo de Barquisimeto (☎ 232-4655; cnr Carrera 17 & Calle 23), on Plaza Lara, is a busy center of cultural activities, including musical works and changing art exhibitions.

Teatro Juárez (☎ 231-6743; cnr Carrera 19 & Calle 25) The city's main theater scene, but hosts other cultural events as well, including music performances.

Getting There & Away

AIR

The **Aeropuerto Jacinto Lara** (☎ 441-9940; Av Vicente Landaeta) is 4km southwest of the center. The Ruta 7 city bus runs between the bus terminal and the airport, or take a taxi ($3). Flights to and from Barquisimeto are serviced by **Aeropostal** (☎ 231-1176, 442-4317), **Avior** (☎ 443-3985) and **Santa Bárbara** (☎ 443-1224).

There are several departures a day to Caracas ($48 to $68) and one or two direct flights to Maracaibo ($54 to $75). To other destinations, you need to go via either Caracas or Maracaibo.

BUS

Barquisimeto straddles an important crossroads, with roads (and, accordingly, buses) leading in all directions. The large and busy **Terminal de Pasajeros** (☎ 442-2189; cnr Av Rómulo Gallegos & Carrera 24), 2km northwest of the center, is linked by frequent city buses to the center and other districts.

Buses depart regularly throughout the day to Valencia ($3 to $4, three hours, 183km), Maracaibo ($6.50, five hours, 328km), Barinas ($5.50, 4½ hours, 258km), Guanare ($4.50, 3½ hours, 173km), Valera ($4.50, four hours, 243km) and Caracas ($7 to $10, 5½ hours, 341km). Half a dozen buses depart nightly to Mérida ($10 to $13, eight hours, 449km) and San Cristóbal ($11 to $14, nine hours, 521km). Buses to Coro ($9, seven hours, 387km) go every two to three hours. Buses within the region (to Quíbor, El Tocuyo, Sanare, Chivacoa) run frequently.

CHIVACOA
☎ 0251 / pop 52,000

Chivacoa, 58km east of Barquisimeto on the road to Valencia, is the jumping-off point for Cerro de María Lionza, the holy mountain that is home to the cult of María Lionza (see the boxed text p161). As such, Chivacoa boasts a number of *perfumerías* selling everything imaginable related to the cult. Don't miss browsing through these shops to get a taste of the phenomenon – it's a unique and striking experience! Note the huge amounts of cigars and candles – indispensable ritual accessories – and hundreds of strange essences, perfumes and lotions. Have a look at the books and brochures dealing with magic, witchcraft and foretelling, and get familiar with the cult's pantheon, as every *perfumería* has a complete stock of plaster figures of the deities in every size and color.

Sleeping & Eating

In Chivacoa there a few places to stay and most have their own restaurants.

Hotel El Lusitano (☎ 883-0366; cnr Calle 10 & Av 12; d with fan $6, d with air-con $9-10, tr with air-con $12; ☒)

This is one of the cheapest options and not a bad choice. The rooms have private bathrooms and are well maintained, and the hotel has a reasonable tasca-style restaurant.

Hotel Abruzzese (☎ 883-0419; Av 9 btwn Calles 10 & 11; d with fan $7-10, d with air-con $10-13; P) One block from Plaza Bolívar, Abruzzese has neat rooms with private facilities, and a Chinese restaurant.

Hotel Venezia (☎ 883-0544; Centro Comercial Venezia, cnr Calle 12 & Av 9; s/d/tr $7/12/15; P) Marginally better than the other two hotels, Venezia has all rooms with bathrooms and air-con. They are all on the upper floor, around the courtyard of the shopping center. The hotel restaurant serves budget food, including pizza.

Getting There & Away

Plenty of buses run between Barquisimeto and Valencia or San Felipe, all of which will let you off on the main road on Chivacoa's northern outskirts, a 10-minute walk to Plaza Bolívar.

There are also direct buses from Barquisimeto to Chivacoa (marked 'Chivacoa Directo') that will deposit you in the town's center ($1, one hour, 58km), as well as por puestos ($1.50, 45 minutes). In Chivacoa, por puestos to Barquisimeto park on Calle 9 next to the church, while buses depart from Av 7 between Calles 13 and 14.

CERRO DE MARÍA LIONZA

Although the cult of María Lionza is practiced throughout Venezuela, its most sacred area and the focus for pilgrimages is the mountain range referred to as the Cerro de María Lionza, south of Chivacoa. Devotees come here year-round, mostly on weekends, to practice their rites. The biggest celebrations, which attract thousands, are held on October 12 (Discovery of America) and during Semana Santa (Holy Week).

The followers have built several sanctuaries along the northern foothills of the mountains, where they flock before heading up the slopes. The most important of these are Sorte and Quiballo (or Quibayo). Both have their own altar mayor (high altar), where the initial celebrations are performed, before the group and its medium head off to the shrine of their choice – one of many that are scattered over the forested rugged land. It's at these shrines where the

---

CULT OF MARÍA LIONZA

A striking amalgam of native indigenous creeds, African voodoo and Christian practices, the cult of María Lionza involves magic, witchcraft, esoteric rites and trance rituals.

The cult is pantheistic and involves a constellation of deities, spirits and other personalities with very diverse origins. At the top of the hierarchy is María Lionza, a female deity usually portrayed as a beautiful woman riding a tapir. One story of her origin tells of a woman from a dark-skinned tribe who gave birth to a light-skinned, green-eyed girl of surpassing beauty. The girl grew up to be venerated by her tribe and, eventually, by the surrounding peoples. As the years passed, her life became the stuff of legends, and ever since she has been revered by her devoted followers.

Often referred to as La Reina (Queen), María Lionza is followed by countless divinities – historical and legendary personages, saints and powers of nature – usually grouped into *cortes* (courts). The list of the most popular deities includes Cacique Guaicaipuro, the Virgen de Coromoto, Negro Felipe and Dr José Gregorio Hernández, and you'll even find Simón Bolívar.

Few serious studies of the cult have been conducted, so many of its aspects, such as its origins or doctrines, are still obscure. What is clear, however, is that the cult attracts more and more followers every year, and spiritual centers proliferate in cities throughout the country. The 'guides,' or intermediaries, who run these centers claim to be able to communicate with deities and spirits, heal the sick, tell the future and the like.

---

proper rites are performed, which may last the whole night or longer and usually include a trance séance.

Cerro de María Lionza is part of a much larger mountain formation known as the Macizo de Nirgua. Covered with thick rain forest, the range is rich in endemic species. In 1960, Inparques declared the 117-sq-km area as the Monumento Natural María Lionza, in an attempt to protect the region from overuse by the cult's followers. However, the religious significance of the place overshadows its natural wealth.

Quiballo

Not really much of a town, Quiballo is just a collection of several dozen shabby shacks that are either *perfumerías* or basic places to eat. The high altar, on the riverbank, shelters a bizarre collection of images – figures of Bolívar, various Indian caciques, and numerous statues of María Lionza herself. The faithful sit in front of the altar, smoke cigars and light candles. The Inparques office is behind the altar.

Quiballo is far larger than Sorte (so it has more frequent transportation) and seems to be more accustomed to casual visitors. However, it's not a tourist spot by any definition. Behave sensibly and modestly, and don't openly use your camera, which may easily arouse hostile reactions from cult believers.

Hiking up the Cerro

From the Quiballo altar, a path goes over the bridge to the opposite bank of the river (in which the faithful perform ritual ablutions) and then splits into a maze of paths that wind up the mountain, some climbing to the very top. All along the paths are *portales* (literally 'gates'), shrines dedicated to particular deities or spirits. On the top are Las Tres Casitas (Three Little Houses) of María Lionza, Negro Felipe and Cacique Guaicaipuro. Technically, the trip to the top can be done in less than three hours. In practice, though, it may take far, far longer, for various reasons.

Followers of the cult point out that the trip is full of drawbacks and dangers. At each portal you have to ask the appropriate spirit for permission to pass. This is done by smoking cigars, lighting candles and presenting offerings. Permission may or may not be granted. Various devotees commented that they had tried on various occasions and hadn't succeeded. Those who continue on without permission may be punished by the spirits. Some, local stories claim, have never returned.

The Inparques staff members have a far more pragmatic standpoint. They don't recommend the trip to the top because of muddy paths, snakes and the possibility of getting lost.

An additional problem is that, like any other place with crowds of people, this one attracts thieves. Robberies have been reported by visitors. Try not to venture too far on your own, and keep your wits about you. If you're desperate to go to the top, consider taking a guide, for both safety and orientation. Some locals in Quiballo may accompany you. The question of to what degree you comply with the spirits' wishes is up to you.

Wandering around, especially on weekends, you may come across a group of faithful practicing their rituals. Keep away unless you're invited or unless you are with a guide who will introduce you.

Sleeping & Eating

There are no hotels in either Sorte or Quiballo, but you can camp in a tent or sling a hammock on the river bank as the pilgrims do. If this is the case, never leave your tent and belongings unattended. It's much better to hang your hammock in a *cabaña* in Quiballo for a small fee. You won't starve at the shack restaurants, but their offerings are mostly basic.

Getting There & Away

Jeeps and vans to Quiballo ($0.50, 20 minutes, 8km) depart when full from Chivacoa's Plaza Bolívar. They run regularly on weekends, but there may be only a few departures on weekdays. Jeeps to Sorte ($0.50, 15 minutes, 6km) are even less frequent. The jeeps travel 4km south on a paved road to the María Lionza roadside altar, then turn right onto a rough road and continue through sugarcane plantations for another 4km to Quiballo. The road to Sorte branches off to the left 1km past the altar.

QUÍBOR

☎ 0253 / pop 60,000

A swiftly growing satellite town of Barquisimeto, 35km southwest of the state capital, Quíbor is a thriving folk art and craft center. It's also worth stopping here to have a look at the region's pre-Columbian indigenous heritage.

Sights

The **Cementerio Indígena de Quíbor** (cnr Av 8 & Calle 12), just off the Plaza Florencio Jiménez, is a pre-Hispanic cemetery accidentally discovered in 1965. Numerous tombs and more than 26,000 pottery pieces have been excavated in what is thought to be a burial ground for tribal elders of an aboriginal community that lived here around the 3rd century AD. It's Venezuela's most important discovery of this kind.

Most of the finds from the graveyard are now on display in the **Museo Antropológico de Quíbor** (☎ 491-3781; cnr Calle 12 & Av 10; admission $0.75; ✆ 9am-noon & 3-5pm Tue-Fri, 10am-5pm Sat & Sun), two blocks north of Plaza Bolívar. The collection includes Indian tombs, funerary urns, mortuary offerings and a lot of pottery.

One of the oldest colonial relics, dating from the town's foundation in 1620, is the **Ermita de Nuestra Señora de Altagracia** (Calle 13 btwn Av 19 & Av 20), a fortress-like church on the northern edge of Quíbor. The large **Iglesia de Nuestra Señora de Altagracia** (Plaza Bolívar) is also named after the patron saint, but was only built in 1808 and was reconstructed after the earthquake of 1881.

The best place to see (and buy) crafts is the **Centro de Acopio Artesanal** (cnr Av Rotaria & Cubiro road; ✆ 9am-5pm), a large craft center 1km southeast of Quíbor. The center stocks crafts made in Quíbor and in the nearby towns and villages, such as Tintorero, Guadalupe, Cubiro and Sanare.

Sleeping & Eating

Quíbor has two places to stay and one of them has its own restaurant.

Hostería Valle de Quíbor (☎ 491-0601; cnr Av 5 & Calle 7; d $19-20, tr $22; P 🍽 🖻) Four blocks southeast of Plaza Bolívar, this is the best place to stay in town. Occupying large grounds that give a feeling of a country location, the Hostería offers 33 comfortable rooms in a two-story hotel building and a further 40 rooms in bungalows. All rooms have private bathrooms, hot water and air-conditioning, and you can have tasty, inexpensive meals at the hotel's prepossessing restaurant beside the pool.

Hotel El Gran Duque (☎ 491-0149; Av Florencio Jiménez; d with fan $7-9, d with air-con $10-12; 🖻) Next to La Ceiba gas station, at the entrance to the town from Barquisimeto, this inexpensive hotel does not have a romantic location, but otherwise is OK, and all its 22 rooms have private facilities.

Getting There & Away

Buses between Barquisimeto and Q run frequently from 6am to 6pm ($0. 45 minutes, 35km). There are also por puestos ($1, 30 minutes). In Barquisimeto, they depart from the bus terminal; in Quíbor, they line up at the corner of Av 6 and Calle 12, one long block south of Plaza Bolívar. Buses to El Tocuyo run along Av 7, lining Plaza Bolívar.

EL TOCUYO

☎ 0253 / pop 50,000

The glorious days of El Tocuyo, 30km southwest of Quíbor, are still palpable in the ruins of colonial churches, in the museums, and in the stories of old inhabitants. Referred to as the 'Mother City of Venezuela,' this was once a wealthy town and Venezuela's capital. Devastated by a quake in 1950, El Tocuyo is today not much more than an ordinary modern city, yet it's worth coming to see what's left of the past.

History

Founded in 1545 in a verdant valley of the Río Tocuyo, Nuestra Señora de la Pura y Limpia Concepción del Tocuyo swiftly developed into one of Venezuela's most important towns. It was established 200km back from the coast, but had access to the sea via a navigable river. Just two years after its foundation, the authorities moved the seat of government here from Coro, and the town became the province's capital for the next 30 years. Splendid colonial churches and mansions popped up and the city was a starting point for expeditions to explore and settle the colony. Barquisimeto and Caracas were founded from El Tocuyo.

In 1577 the capital was transferred to Caracas, but El Tocuyo continued to expand, taking advantage of its fertile soil that's ideal for growing sugarcane and a variety of vegetables. It was here that the Spanish first introduced sugarcane to the continent, and the crop could be harvested year-round thanks to favorable climatic conditions.

Unfortunately, a serious earthquake in 1950 ruined all seven colonial churches and a good number of opulent public buildings. The job was completed by Colonel Marcos Pérez Jiménez, Venezuela's dictator at the time. On his orders, most of the damaged structures were demolished and a new town

El Tocuyo is now a
ust a handful of re-
d historic buildings.

eñora de la Concepción
.... ~... ~alles 17 & 18) is the town's most
important monument. The church was
badly damaged in the 1950 earthquake and,
like most other buildings, it was bulldozed –
despite the fact that it could have been
repaired. It was later reconstructed and
its whitewashed exterior is noted for its
unusual bell tower and fine facade. Inside,
the extraordinary retable from the 1760s
(which miraculously survived the earthquake) takes up the whole wall behind the
high altar. Like almost all altarpieces of the
period, it was carved entirely out of wood
but, unusually, was not painted or gilded;
it's the only one of its kind in the country.
The church is open only for religious services, normally held at 6pm on weekdays,
with more masses on Sunday. If you can't
make it to the service, go to the Casa Parroquial beside the church, and someone is
likely to let you in.

None of the other colonial churches was
restored or reconstructed, but two were left
in ruins, untouched from the day of the
earthquake: the **Iglesia de Santo Domingo** (cnr
Carrera 10 & Calle 19), and the **Iglesia de Belén** (Carrera
12 btwn Calles 15 & 17). One of the few buildings
that somehow withstood the quake is the
Convento de San Francisco (Plaza Bolívar), though
the adjacent church didn't make it. Today
the building is occupied by the Casa de la
Cultura. Do go inside to see its spacious
two-story arcaded courtyard.

El Tocuyo has two small museums, both
related to the town's history. The **Museo
Arqueológico JM Cruxent** (Plaza Bolívar; admission
free; 🕘 8am-4pm Mon-Fri) has a small collection
of pre-Hispanic pottery, photos depicting
the damage by the 1950 earthquake, and
regional crafts. Note the remains of a 30m-
long steam riverboat from around 1850,
proving that the Río Tocuyo was navigable
for large vessels.

The **Museo Lisandro Alvarado** (Calle 17 btwn
Carreras 10 & 11; admission free; 🕘 9am-noon & 2-5:30pm
Mon-Fri), named after the locally born politician, doctor and anthropologist, features old
maps, documents, paintings and etchings
and a variety of historic objects. Watch out

for an amazing old bell from the no-longer-
existing San Francisco Church.

Sleeping & Eating
El Tocuyo has a few places to stay and the
Posada Colonial has its own restaurant.

Posada Colonial (☎ 663-0025; Av Fraternidad btwn
Calles 17 & 18; d $14-16, tr/q $18/20; Ⓟ 🏽 🏊) The
most enjoyable and central place to stay,
a stone's throw from Plaza Bolívar, this
colonial-style posada has 24 neat rooms, a
restaurant, and a pool in the garden which
is populated with coconut palms. Ask for a
room upstairs, which has balconies.

If the posada can't accommodate you
for some reason, there are two marginally
cheaper but less attractive options:

Hotel Venezia (☎ 663-1267; cnr Calle Comercio &
Carrera 9)
Hotel Nazaret (☎ 663-2434; Av Fraternidad btwn
Calles 7 & 8)

Getting There & Away
Buses between Barquisimeto and El Tocuyo
($1, 1¼ hours, 65km) run at least every
half-hour until about 6pm. There are also
por puestos ($1.50, one hour).

SANARE
☎ 0253 / pop 18,000
With its steep streets winding over hillsides,
Sanare is a charming town with a noticeable mountain appearance and atmosphere.
Founded in 1620, it boasts some fine historic
architecture around the central streets and
a handsome parish church, the three-nave
Iglesia de Santa Ana. Surrounded by forested hills and pretty verdant in itself, the
town has been nicknamed the 'Garden of
Lara,' and is a gateway to the Parque Nacional Yacambú. Sanare enjoys a fresh climate with an average temperature of 20°C.

Information
The **Oficina de Turismo Municipal** (Av Bolívar btwn
Calles 13 & 14; 🕘 8am-noon & 2-5pm Mon-Thu, 8am-3pm
Fri) is two blocks east of Plaza Bolívar.

Sleeping & Eating
Sanare has at least half a dozen places to
stay and most have their own restaurants.

Posada Turística El Cerrito (☎ 449-0016; Calle
Providencia; s/d/tr/q $10/16/18/20) About 500m
south of Plaza Bolívar (take Calle 17 from
the square), this is a charming and stylish

place. Built in a colonial style, the posada has 14 rooms (with bathrooms) lining a patio, plus a budget restaurant.

Hotel Taburiente (☎ 449-0148; Av Miranda; d $12-14, tr $18) Nestled right behind the church, this neat and very central 21-room hotel is a good deal and it, too, has its own restaurant.

Hotel La Fumarola (☎ 449-0754; Sector Palo Verde; tr $24) Probably the most comfortable option, La Fumarola is 3km north of Sanare on the road to Quíbor. It has cabañas, a restaurant and a pool.

Getting There & Away
Minibuses run regularly between Barquisimeto and Sanare ($1.25, 1¼ hours, 57km) until mid-afternoon.

PARQUE NACIONAL YACAMBÚ
At the northern end of the Andean massif, this park reaches elevations of up to 2200m and has Venezuela's only active volcano, locally called La Fumarola after the cloud of smoke that floats over it. This park protects a 270-sq-km chunk of the mountain range known as the Sierra de Portuguesa, southeast of Sanare.

Most of the area is covered with cloud forest with plant species typical of the Andes, many of which are endemic. About 60 species of orchid have been recorded. There haven't been any detailed studies of the fauna, but it is remarkably rich and includes rare, endangered mammals such as the *oso frontino* (spectacled bear) and jaguar. The park is particularly good for bird-watchers.

Yacambú is an important water resource for the region, and there's a large reservoir, the Embalse Yacambú, formed by a dam built just south of the park. The rainy period is from April to November; in higher areas the mean annual rainfall reaches 3000mm.

Orientation
Access to the park is from Sanare by the 30km road that goes to the dam. This road crosses the park and passes near the Inparques administrative center at El Blanquito, about 20km from Sanare. The rangers here can give you information about the walks and sights, including *miradores* (viewpoints), waterfalls and the Cañón de Angostura, the gorge formed by the Río Negro.

Sleeping
The park provides accommodations in 12- and 14-bed cabins (bring your own sheets) in El Blanquito, but you need to pay for the whole cabin ($12), not just the beds you're going to use. Camping is allowed for $2 per tent. You should book cabins several days in advance at the Inparques office (p158) in Barquisimeto. Payment for both cabins and camping has to be made at a bank before you go – Inparques will give you details.

Getting There & Away
There doesn't seem to be a regular form of public transportation to the park other than occasional por puestos from Sanare. Negotiate the ride with drivers in Sanare.

CARORA
☎ 0252 / pop 95,000
Founded in 1569 on the bank of Río Morere, Carora has experienced several serious floods (the last in 1973), but has preserved much of its colonial architecture. The historic center has been restored and is a charming place, particularly Plaza Bolívar, which is one of Venezuela's most amazing plazas.

Carora's other reason for pride is its wine – Venezuela's best – and you can visit the vineyards and winery, and see the whole production process. Though commercial production only began in 1990, the wine has already won international medals.

Information
INTERNET ACCESS
Ciber Café Carora (cnr Av Francisco de Miranda & Calle 21B)
Fotocopiado-e-Internet (Calle Comercio btwn Carreras El Calvario & Contreras)
Zona Ciber (cnr Av Francisco de Miranda & Calle 22)

MONEY
Banco de Venezuela (cnr Av Francisco de Miranda & Calle 20)
Banco Provincial (cnr Av 14 de Febrero & Carrera Lara)
Banesco (cnr Carrera Lara & Calle Rivas)
Corp Banca (Av Francisco de Miranda & Calle 19)

TELEPHONE
CANTV (Av 14 de Febrero btwn Carreras Lara & Bolívar)

TOURIST INFORMATION
Centro de Información y Atención Turística (Av Francisco de Miranda; ☯ 9am-noon & 2-5pm Thu-Sat, 9am-1pm Sun) It's in a kiosk in front of the bus terminal.

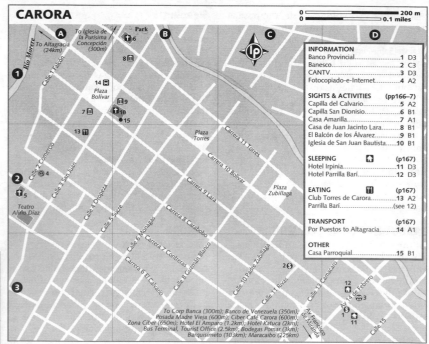

CARORA

INFORMATION
Banco Provincial.....................1 D3
Banesco.................................2 C3
CANTV..................................3 D3
Fotocopiado-e-Internet...........4 A2

SIGHTS & ACTIVITIES   (pp166–7)
Capilla del Calvario.................5 A2
Capilla San Dionisio................6 B1
Casa Amarilla........................7 A1
Casa de Juan Jacinto Lara.........8 B1
El Balcón de los Álvarez...........9 B1
Iglesia de San Juan Bautista....10 B1

SLEEPING   (p167)
Hotel Irpinia........................11 D3
Hotel Parrilla Barí.................12 D3

EATING   (p167)
Club Torres de Carora.............13 A2
Parrilla Barí........................(see 12)

TRANSPORT   (p167)
Por Puestos a Altagracia.........14 A1

OTHER
Casa Parroquial....................15 B1

Sights

The historic quarter, centered on the post-cardlike Plaza Bolívar and populated with elegant tall palm trees, is neat, well kept and colonial in style, even though not all the buildings date from that period. Have a look at the mid-17th-century **Casa Amarilla** (Plaza Bolívar), Carora's oldest surviving building, now a public library, and **El Balcón de los Álvarez** (Plaza Bolívar), a two-story 18th-century house where Bolívar stayed in 1821. The **Casa de Juan Jacinto Lara** (cnr Calle San Juan & Carrera Torres) is the birthplace of the hero of the War of Independence, who gave his name to the state.

The town has some fine colonial churches. The main one, the mid-17th-century **Iglesia de San Juan Bautista** (Plaza Bolívar) shelters an amazing, richly gilded main retable dating from 1760. The church is only open in the late afternoon, but if you turn up at any other reasonable time of the day, inquire in the Casa Parroquial, right behind the church, and someone is likely to open it for you.

The **Capilla San Dionisio** (cnr Carrera Torres & Calle Comercio) dates from 1743. It's used only for special ceremonies, such as funerals, and is closed at other times. About 300m northeast of San Dionisio, in the middle of arid woodland, is the striking ruin of the **Iglesia de la Purísima Concepción**, commonly referred to as the 'Portal de la Pastora.' You'll get a good view of the ruin from the dike at the end of Calle Comercio.

The **Capilla del Calvario** (cnr Carrera El Calvario & Calle Comercio) has a beautiful facade, a fine example of local baroque. Its simple interior features an interesting main retable, plus two side retables on both walls. The chapel is often open in the morning, but if it's locked, the keys are kept in Casa Parroquial.

Venezuela has almost no wine tradition, but this may change with the **Bodegas Pomar** (☎ 421-2191, 421-2225; www.bodegaspomar.com.ve; Carretera Lara-Zulia), 3km south of the city center, where the country's best wine is produced. It comes in 17 varieties and is marketed under the Viña Altagracia label for distribution throughout the country.

Bodegas Pomar features the facilities where the whole production process takes place, everything from sorting the grapes to packing the final product into cardboard boxes. Grapes come from the 125-hectare vineyard in the village of Altagracia (hence the wine's brand name), 24km northwest of Carora. Altagracia's climate features a harmonious blend of low humidity, good sunlight, warm days and fresh nights year-round, so the crop can be harvested twice a year (in March and September).

You can visit Bodegas Pomar, but arrange this a few days in advance. Guides will take you on a tour around the installations and show you the whole production process, but only in March and September (in other months all you can see is the machinery). The tour takes anywhere from 45 minutes to 1½ hours (commentary is in Spanish only), and so far is free, but they plan to introduce a fee. Bodegas Pomar can also organize a visit to the vineyards in Altagracia in your transportation. If you don't have any, you can go on your own by por puesto, but contact the Bodegas before to arrange your visit. Por puestos to Altagracia depart infrequently from Plaza Bolívar.

Sleeping

Hotel Parrilla Barí (☎ 421-6745; Av 14 de Febrero; d/tr with fan $7/10, with air-con $9/12; P ⋈) One of the cheapest central shelters, Barí is basic but acceptable and all of its 13 rooms have private facilities. Choose a room away from the busy road.

Hotel Irpinia (☎ 421-6362; cnr Carrera Lara & Av 14 de Febrero; s/d/tr $12/14/17; P ⋈) Another convenient place in the center, Irpinia has 36 neat, spacious rooms with bathrooms and air-con; take one facing the inner courtyard – they are quieter.

Posada Madre Vieja (☎ 421-2590; Av Francisco de Miranda; d/tr/q $22/25/28; P ⋈) Set in the spacious garden-like grounds, Madre Vieja offers 16 fair-sized rooms in a two-story building away from the noisy road, and has an enjoyable restaurant in a palm-leaf thatched *churuata* (traditional hut).

Hotel Katuca (☎ 421-3310; Av Francisco de Miranda; d $18-20, tr $25; P ⋈) Just 300m from the bus terminal, Katuca is convenient for buses, but not much more. Otherwise, it's a pleasant place, with a large leafy garden, 34 decent rooms and its own restaurant.

Hotel El Amparo (☎ 421-2537; Carretera Lara-Zulia; d/tr $20/23; P ⋈) Roughly midway between

the Madre Vieja and Katuca, this is the newest addition to Carora's accommodation offer, much in the class of the other two.

Eating

Parrilla Barí (☎ 421-6745; Av 14 de Febrero; meals $2-4) The restaurant of Hotel Parilla Barí looks extremely basic, yet the food is OK, portions are generous and none of its 40-plus dishes costs more than $5.

Club Torres de Carora (☎ 421-3410; Calle San Juan btwn Carreras Carabobo & Lara; mains $4-6; ⏱ noon-3pm Mon-Fri) Most facilities (including a swimming pool) in this great rambling colonial mansion are for members only, but the restaurant is open to all and is excellent value.

Getting There & Away

Carora lies about 3km north off the Barquisimeto–Maracaibo freeway. The **Terminal de Pasajeros** (Av Francisco de Miranda) is on the southeastern outskirts of town, about 600m northwest off the freeway. The terminal is linked to the town's center by city minibuses.

Carora has half-hourly buseta connections with Barquisimeto ($2, 1½ hours, 103km), and there are also por puestos ($3, 1¼ hours). It's an interesting trip on a good autopista (freeway) across arid, hilly countryside. Ordinary buses to Maracaibo ($5.50, 3½ hours, 225km) come through from Barquisimeto every hour. To Caracas ($9 to $13, seven hours, 444km), buses come through from Maracaibo; it may be faster to go to Barquisimeto and change there.

ZULIA STATE

MARACAIBO

☎ 0261 / pop 1.5 million

Hot as hell and rich with oil, Maracaibo is Venezuela's second largest urban center after Caracas. It's a mostly modern city with tall tower blocks, wide streets and a few shady parks. Visibly prosperous, Maracaibo becomes a ghost town in the middle of the day when the scorching heat drives everyone indoors for three hours or more of air-conditioned siesta.

In sharp contrast to the urban modernity are the many Guajiro women in their long colorful dresses, and sometimes even with their faces painted with a dark pigment. The Guajiros, who inhabit the region, are

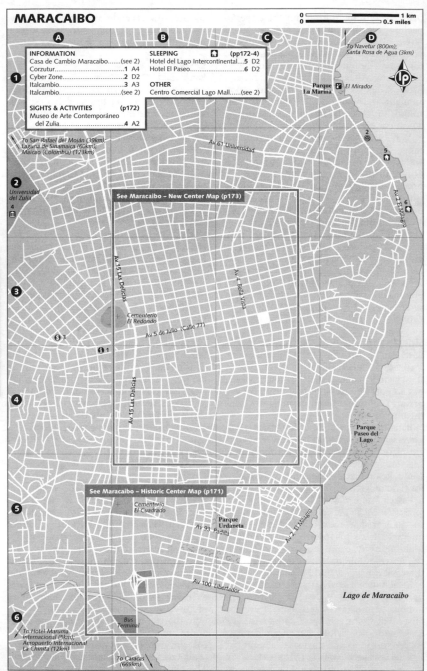

MARACAIBO

0 ————— 1 km
0 ————— 0.5 miles

INFORMATION
Casa de Cambio Maracaibo......(see 2)
Corzutur.....................................**1** A4
Cyber Zone................................**2** D2
Italcambio..................................**3** A3
Italcambio..............................(see 2)

SIGHTS & ACTIVITIES (p172)
Museo de Arte Contemporáneo
del Zulia...............................**4** A2

SLEEPING 🏠 (pp172–4)
Hotel del Lago Intercontinental....**5** D2
Hotel El Paseo..........................**6** D2

OTHER
Centro Comercial Lago Mall......(see 2)

To Navetur (800m);
Santa Rosa de Agua (3km)

Parque
La Marina 🚶 El Mirador

To San Rafael del Moján (39km);
Laguna de Sinamaica (60km);
Maicao (Colombia) (123km)

Av 67 Universidad

Universidad
del Zulia
4 🏛

See Maracaibo – New Center Map (p173)

Av 15 Las Delicias

Av 4 Bella Vista

Cementerio
El Redondo

🛈 **3**

Av 5 de Julio (Calle 77)

🛈 **1**

Av 15 Las Delicias

Parque
Paseo del
Lago

See Maracaibo – Historic Center Map (p171)

Cementerio
El Cuadrado

Parque
Urdaneta

Av 93 Padilla

Av 2 El Milagro

Av 100 Libertador

Lago de Maracaibo

Bus
Terminal

To Hotel Maruma
Internacional (5km);
Aeropuerto Internacional
La Chinita (12km)

To Caracas
(669km)

THE NORTHWEST

among the most traditional indigenous groups in the country, and Maracaibo is Venezuela's only city with such a conspicuous presence of aboriginal communities.

Founded as a trading post in 1574, Maracaibo was a backwater on the shores of the vast Lago de Maracaibo, until 1914, when drillers struck oil. By the late 1920s Venezuela came to be the world's largest exporter of oil, the Saudi Arabia of South America, while Maracaibo developed into the country's oil capital, with two-thirds of the nation's output coming from beneath the lake. Today, it's the capital of Zulia, Venezuela's richest state, and an important port. The Maracuchos, as local inhabitants are called, feel they are producing the money that the rest of the country is spending.

Maracaibo is a sweltering stop for travelers on the way to or from Colombia's Caribbean coast. Stay a day or two to visit some of the city's icons, including the old holy basilica and the brightly painted restored houses on Calle Carabobo. With a few more days, it's well worth exploring the city environs noted for a colorful mix of tradition and modernity. In particular, be sure to make a detour to see the old *palafitos* on the shores of Laguna de Sinamaica. Five hundred years ago, Spanish sailors saw these over-water houses on stilts and named the place 'Little Venice' – Venezuela.

Orientation

Maracaibo is a big metropolis with vast suburbs, but (as is usually the case) the tourist focus of attention is on the central districts. Generally speaking, these encompass the historic center to the south and the new center to the north. Getting between the two is easy and fast, so it doesn't really matter much where you stay. The new center, however, offers a far better choice of hotels, restaurants and other facilities, and it's safer at night. The old quarter boasts more sights, but they can all be visited on one or two leisurely daytime trips.

Information

EMERGENCY
Fire (☎ 723-7707)
Police (☎ 722-3644)

INTERNET ACCESS
Cyber Place (Map p173; Av 8 btwn Calles 72 & 73)
Cyber Zone (Map p168; Local PNC 17A, Centro Comercial Lago Mall, Av El Milagro)
en red cyber cafe (Map p173; Av 5 de Julio btwn Avs 3H & 3Y)
Postnet (Map p173; Av Bella Vista btwn Calles 69 & 70)

MEDICAL SERVICES
Hospital Central (Map p171; ☎ 722-6404; Av El Milagro btwn Calles 94 & 95)

MONEY
Major banks in Maracaibo have plenty of branches and the city also has a few *casas de cambio* (money-exchange offices).
Banco de Venezuela Historic Center (Map p171; cnr Av 5 & Calle 97); New Center (Map p173; cnr Av Bella Vista & Calle 74)
Banco Mercantil New Center (Map p173; cnr Av Bella Vista & Calle 67)
Banco Provincial Historic Center (Map p171; cnr Av El Milagro & Calle 97); New Center (Map p173; cnr Av Bella Vista & Calle 74)

THE LARGEST LAKE, THE LONGEST BRIDGE & A MINI-MANHATTAN

About 120km wide and 200km long, the 12,800-sq-km Lago de Maracaibo is by far South America's largest lake. It is also the richest – enormous deposits of oil beneath the lake bed have made Venezuela a major oil exporter.

Maracaibo sits on the strait linking Lago de Maracaibo to the Caribbean Sea. The strait is spanned by the Puente Rafael Urdaneta, a bridge named after the greatest local hero. It was built in the early 1960s in order to provide road access to and from the rest of the country, and it was the first pre-stressed concrete bridge in the world. Measuring 8679m, it is the longest bridge in South America.

Entering Maracaibo from anywhere in the east or southeast, you'll cross the bridge and be able to see the vast expanse of the lake while traveling high above the water. Sit on the right side of the bus to catch a great view of the city, with its forest of high-rise blocks along the lakeside vaguely reminiscent of New York's Manhattan skyline.

Banesco New Center (Map p173; cnr Av Bella Vista & Calle 71)

Casa de Cambio Maracaibo New Center (Map p173; ☎ 797-2576; Av 9B btwn Calles 77 & 78); Av El Milagro (Map p168; ☎ 792-2174; Centro Comercial Lago Mall, Av El Milagro).

Corp Banca Historic Center (Map p171; cnr Av Libertador & Av 14); New Center (Map p173; cnr Av Bella Vista & Calle 67)

Italcambio Airport (☎ 736-2513); Av 20 (Map p168; ☎ 783-2040; Centro Comercial Montielco, cnr Av 20 & Calle 72); Av El Milagro (Map p168; ☎ 793-2983; Centro Comercial Lago Mall, Av El Milagro)

TELEPHONE
CANTV (Map p171; Local 43, Centro Comercial Plaza Lago, Av Libertador)

Telcel (Map p171; Local 52-53, Centro Comercial La Redoma, Av Libertador)

TOURIST INFORMATION
Corpozulia (Map p173; ☎ 794-9424; Edificio Corpozulia, Av Bella Vista btwn Calles 83 & 84; ☺ 8am-4pm Mon-Fri) Located 2km north of the historic center, accessible by the Bella Vista por puestos.

Corzutur (Map p168; ☎ 783-4928; Edificio Lieja, cnr Av 18 & Calle 78; ☺ 8am-4pm Mon-Fri) Also found 2km northwest of the historic center.

Sights
HISTORIC CENTER   Map p171
The historic center boasts most of the tourist sights, a short walk from each other. The axis of this sector is the **Paseo de las Ciencias**, a seven-block-long greenbelt laid out after the demolition of the colonial buildings that formed the core of Maracaibo's oldest quarter, El Saladillo. This controversial plan, executed in 1973, effectively cut the very heart out of the old town. The only structure not pulled down was the blue-colored neo-Gothic **Iglesia de Santa Bárbara** (cnr Av 8 & Calle 95).

At the western end of the Paseo is the **Basílica de Chiquinquirá**, which features opulent interior decor. In the high altar is the venerated image of the Virgin of Chiquinquirá, affectionately referred to as La Chinita. Legend has it that the image of the Virgin, painted on a small wooden board, was found in 1709 by a humble *campesina* (peasant) on the shore of Lago de Maracaibo. Upon being brought to her home, the image began to glow. It was then taken to the church, and miracles started to happen. In 1942 the Virgin was crowned as the patron saint of Zulia.

The image of the Virgin Mary, accompanied by San Andrés and San Antonio, is hardly recognizable from a distance, but special access is provided to allow you to get close to it. Note the large crown above the image, made of gold and encrusted with precious stones. Pilgrims gather here year-round, but the major celebrations (p172) are held in November.

The eastern end of the Paseo de las Ciencias is bordered by the **Plaza Bolívar** and the 19th-century **Catedral** (cnr Av 4 & Calle 95). The most revered image in the cathedral is the Cristo Negro or Cristo de Gibraltar, so called as it was originally in the church of Gibraltar, a town on the southern shore of Lago de Maracaibo. The town was overrun and burned by Indians in 1600, but the crucifix miraculously survived, even though the cross to which the statue was nailed was incinerated. Blackened by smoke, Cristo Negro is also known, like La Chinita, for his miraculous powers, and attracts pilgrims from the region and beyond. The image is in the chapel to the left of the high altar.

The arcaded mid-19th-century **Palacio de Gobierno** (Plaza Bolívar) is also called the Palacio de las Águilas (Palace of the Eagles) for the two condors placed on its roof. Next door is the late 18th-century Casa Morales, better known as **Casa de la Capitulación** (☎ 725-1194; Plaza Bolívar; admission free; ☺ 8am-noon & 1-6pm Mon-Fri), for it was here that the Spaniards who were defeated in the naval battle of Lago de Maracaibo signed the act of capitulation on August 3, 1823, sealing the independence of Gran Colombia. This is the only residential colonial building left in the city. It has been restored, fitted with period furniture and decorated with paintings of heroes of the War of Independence.

Across the street from the casa is the mighty, art deco **Teatro Baralt** (p175), which you can tour.

A short walk north from the center is **Museo Urdaneta** (Calle 91A No 7-70; admission free; ☺ 8:30am-3pm Mon-Fri), which is dedicated to Maracaibo-born General Rafael Urdaneta, the city's greatest independence hero. Built on the site of Urdaneta's birth, it features a collection of objects, documents, paintings and other memorabilia related to the general and the events of the period.

Calle 94, better known as **Calle Carabobo**, has been partly restored to its former

MARACAIBO – HISTORIC CENTER

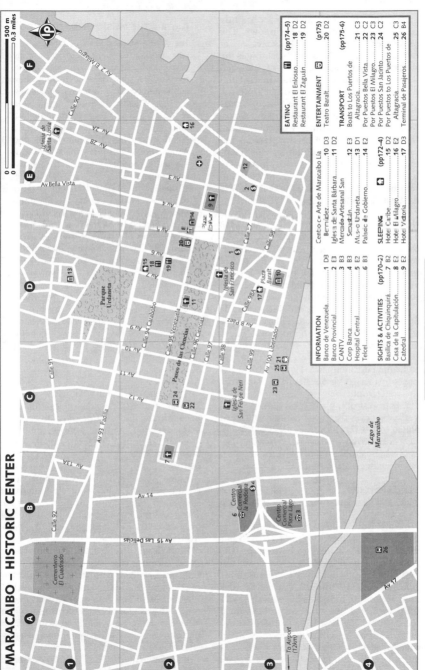

THE NORTHWEST

INFORMATION
Banco de Venezuela	1 D3
Banco Provincial	2 E3
CANTV	3 B3
Corp Banca	4 B3
Hospital Central	5 E2
Telcel	6 B3

SIGHTS & ACTIVITIES (pp170-2)
Basílica de Chiquinquirá	7 B2
Casa de la Capitulación	8 E2
Catedral	9 E2
Centro de Arte de Maracaibo Lía Bermúdez	10 D3
Iglesia de Santa Bárbara	11 D2
Mercado Artesanal San Sebastián	12 E3
Museo Urdaneta	13 D1
Palacio de Gobierno	14 E2

SLEEPING (pp172-4)
Hotel Caribe	15 D2
Hotel El Milagro	16 E2
Hotel Victoria	17 D3

EATING (pp174-5)
Restaurant El Enlosao	18 D2
Restaurant El Zaguán	19 D2

ENTERTAINMENT (p175)
Teatro Baralt	20 D2

TRANSPORT (pp175-6)
Boats to Los Puertos de Altagracia	21 C3
Por Puestos Bella Vista	22 C2
Por Puestos El Milagro	23 C3
Por Puestos San Jacinto	24 C2
Por Puestos to Los Puertos de Altagracia	25 C3
Terminal de Pasajeros	26 B4

appearance, and is notable for its brightly colored facades and grilled windows. The most spectacular part of the street is between Avs 6 and 8. Also worth visiting is the **Mercado Artesanal San Sebastián** (cnr Av El Milagro & Calle 96), a colorful Guajiro craft market full of beautiful hammocks and other crafts.

The sector south of the Paseo de las Ciencias is a wonder of heat, dirt and chaos. Many streets are crammed with stalls, making the area feel like a market. Here is the imposing old market-building, which operated as the Mercado Principal from 1931 to 1973. It has been wholly remodeled and refurbished, and opened as the **Centro de Arte de Maracaibo Lía Bermúdez** (p175).

NORTHERN SUBURBS   Map p168
The lakeshore **Parque La Marina** (cnr Av El Milagro & Av Bella Vista), 5km north of the center, features **El Mirador**, a lookout on the top of a 50m-high tower, which provides a good view over the city and the lake. It was closed for restoration at the time of research.

About 3km further north is **Santa Rosa de Agua**, once a small lakeside village, today a suburb within the city boundaries. There are some *palafitos* on the shore that might be worth a visit if you don't plan on a trip to Laguna de Sinamaica. Have a look at the bust of Amerigo Vespucci, on the plaza near the waterfront.

Northwest of the city center, on the university's grounds, the strikingly modern **Museo de Arte Contemporáneo del Zulia** (☎ 759-4866; Av Universidad; admission free; ◷ 9am-5pm Tue-Sun) stages temporary displays of modern art in its huge exhibition halls.

Special Events
Maracaibo's major annual event is the **Feria de la Chinita**, which springs to life around November 10 and continues until the coronation of the Virgin on November 18. Apart from religious celebrations, the weeklong festival includes various cultural and popular events such as bullfights, *toros coleados* (rodeo with bulls), street parades and, obviously, music – above all the *gaita* (see the boxed text this page), the typical local genre. The best time to listen to the gaita is on the eve of November 18, when musical groups gather in front of the basilica to play the *Serenata para la Virgen* (Serenade for the Virgin).

GAITA – THE MUSIC OF MARACAIBO

The *gaita* is Maracaibo's musical identity – what tango is to Buenos Aires. It's a lively percussion- and voice-based sound, performed by a small band, with lyrics often improvised on religious or political themes. A classical *gaita* ensemble includes the *cuatro* (a small, four-stringed guitar), *tambora* (large wooden drum) and *furruco* (another drum-based instrument). Ricardo Aguirre (1939–69), nicknamed 'El Monumental,' is considered one of the greatest *gaita* singers.

Gaita is most popular from October to January, peaking during the Christmas season, when it can be heard everywhere – in bars and buses, on the street and on the beach. Plenty of restaurants and bars across town stage live *gaita* music in that period.

Most musicologists agree that *gaita* has Spanish origins, but it evolved in Maracaibo's central quarter of El Saladillo, part of which was razed for the Paseo de las Ciencias. *Gaita* hasn't been overshadowed by the nationwide *joropo*; on the contrary, it has made its way well outside Zulia to become the second most popular national beat.

The Feria de la Chinita marks the beginning of the Christmas celebrations, reflected in the illumination of Av Bella Vista and a general Christmas atmosphere.

Sleeping
BUDGET

It's most convenient to stay in the historic center, though it doesn't offer anything special in the way of accommodations. The northern suburbs are a bit safer and provide better lodgings, yet you'll be away from most of the major sights.

Hotel Victoria (Map p171; ☎ 722-9697; Plaza Baralt; ✜) Victoria is certainly a place with character and style, and is attractively located overlooking the old market-building, but for decades it was left unkempt and rundown. It was closed for refurbishing when we were there. Most likely, it will remain inexpensive. Choose a room with a balcony and a view over the plaza.

Hotel Caribe (Map p171; ☎ 722-5986; Av 7 No 93-51; d with bathroom $11-12, tr with bathroom $13; ✜)

MARACAIBO – NEW CENTER

0 ———— 500 m
0 ———— 0.3 miles

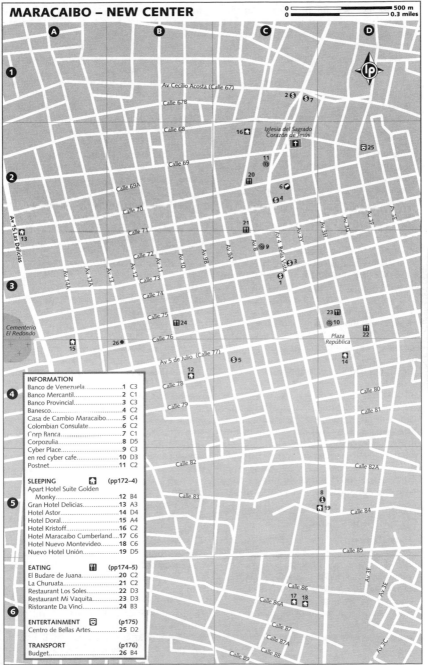

INFORMATION
Banco de Venezuela	1 C3
Banco Mercantil	2 C1
Banco Provincial	3 C3
Banesco	4 C2
Casa de Cambio Maracaibo	5 C4
Colombian Consulate	6 C2
Corp Banca	7 C1
Corpozulia	8 D5
Cyber Place	9 C3
en red cyber cafe	10 D3
Postnet	11 C2

SLEEPING (pp172–4)
Apart Hotel Suite Golden Monky	12 B4
Gran Hotel Delicias	13 A3
Hotel Astor	14 D4
Hotel Doral	15 A4
Hotel Kristoff	16 C2
Hotel Maracaibo Cumberland	17 C6
Hotel Nuevo Montevideo	18 C6
Nuevo Hotel Unión	19 D5

EATING (pp174–5)
El Budare de Juana	20 C2
La Churuata	21 C2
Restaurant Los Soles	22 D3
Restaurant Mi Vaquita	23 D3
Ristorante Da Vinci	24 B3

ENTERTAINMENT (p175)
Centro de Bellas Artes	25 D2

TRANSPORT (p176)
Budget	26 B4

THE NORTHWEST

Just two blocks from the Plaza Bolívar, the 60-room Caribe has a new section at the back. These new rooms have noiseless, central air-con that can be pretty efficient, but there's no way to switch it off or to graduate the temperature. Be prepared to get that sweater out of the bottom of your backpack.

Hotel El Milagro (Map p171; ☎ 722-8934; Av El Milagro No 93-45; d with bathroom $10-12, tr with bathroom $13; ℗ 🔀) El Milagro is acceptable, but don't expect miracles despite its name – its rooms are a little on the small side and it has a similar pesky central air-con system as the Caribe.

Hotel Astor (Map p173; ☎ 791-4510, Plaza República; s $9, d $10-11; 🔀) One of the cheapest hotels at one of the best locations, the Astor is basic, yet passable. It's attractively positioned in a hip and safe area, with a dozen trendy restaurants within a 200m radius.

Hotel Nuevo Montevideo (Map p173; ☎ 722-2762; Calle 86A No 4-96; d $10-12, tr $14; ℗ 🔀) Set in an old rambling mansion, this tranquil place has 13 large rooms with high ceilings, air-conditioning and private facilities.

Nuevo Hotel Unión (Map p173; ☎ 793-3278; Calle 84 No 4-60; d $10-11, tr $14; 🔀) Just a few steps from the Corpozulia tourist office, this is another small budget spot with a touch of style and personalized attention.

MID-RANGE

There are no mid-priced or upmarket hotels in the old city center; they've all opted for more elegant, new districts, mainly in the northern part of the city.

Hotel Maracaibo Cumberland (Map p173; ☎ 722-2944; www.hotelescumberland.com; Calle 86A No 4-150; s/d/ste $34/38/52; ℗ 🔀) Roughly midway between the old and new centers, this three-

star 87-room hotel is a good compromise between quality and price, and has a breezy rooftop terrace.

Hotel Doral (Map p173; ☎ 797-8385; cnr Av 14A & Calle 75; d $20-24; 🔀) One of the cheapest in this price bracket, this small 22-room hotel isn't anything particularly memorable, yet it has quiet, acceptable air-con rooms and an adjacent no-nonsense steak restaurant.

Gran Hotel Delicias (Map p173; ☎ 797-6111; hotel delicias@telcel.net.ve; cnr Av Las Delicias & Calle 70; s/d/ste $32/35/44; 🔀 🖳 🖥) The Delicias provides reasonable standards and facilities, and is one of the cheapest hotels in town that has its own pool – a bonus you'll surely appreciate in this steamy climate.

Apart Hotel Suite Golden Monky (Map p173; ☎ 797-3285; goldenmonky@hotmail.com; Calle 78 No 10-30; s $27, d $32-38, tr $42; ℗ 🔀 🖥) Central and convenient, Monky offers a spread of rooms, suites and studios, and a restaurant, and it doesn't cost a fortune.

TOP END

Hotel Kristoff (Map p173; ☎ 797-2911; hkristoff@cantv .net; Av 8 No 68-48; s $43-58, d $65-80, ste $145; ℗ 🔀 🖳 🖥) Frequently used by business people, Kristoff is a busy, respectable four-star establishment that has a wide range of facilities, including a restaurant and a gym.

Hotel del Lago Intercontinental (Map p168; ☎ 792-4222, 794-4222; www.intercontinental.com; Av El Milagro; s/d $135/150; ℗ 🔀 🖳 🖥) Opened in 1953, this large lakeside five-star hotel is Maracaibo's institution. It offers 368 rooms, two restaurants, a sizeable swimming pool, sauna and its own beach, though you are advised not to bathe because the water in the lake is polluted.

Eating

Most upmarket restaurants have nestled in the northern sector of the city, in particular in the new center around Av Bella Vista. The historic center hosts a lot of cheap eateries, but nothing really posh or classy.

Restaurant El Enlosao (Map p171; Calle 94; mains $2-4) Set in a charming historic mansion, the Casa de los Artesanos, El Enlosao serves unpretentious but tasty Venezuelan food at low prices. The *parrilla* (grill) is so copious that you may struggle to finish it, but if you're after something small, ask for the *sopa del día* (soup of the day) for just $1.25.

THE AUTHOR'S CHOICE

Hotel El Paseo (Map p168; ☎ 792-4422; elpaseo@iamnet.com; cnr Av 1B & Calle 74; d $80; ℗ 🔀 🖳 🖥) This attractive waterfront high-rise hotel has 59 unusually large rooms (be sure to choose one with the lake views), all with private bathrooms, hot water, silent air-conditioning, cable TV and a fridge. Downstairs is a business center with Internet access and a small pool.

THE NORTHWEST

THE AUTHOR'S CHOICE

Restaurant El Girasol (mains $6-12; ☺ noon-3pm & 7pm-midnight) is the only revolving restaurant in the country – an entire circle takes about two hours and 20 minutes and the floor-to-ceiling windows all around provide for great views. It offers international cuisine, including a fair choice of pasta, fish and seafood.

Restaurant El Zaguán (Map p171; ☎ 717-2398; cnr Calle 94 & Av 6; mains $4-6) A few paces away from El Enlosao, this inviting restaurant serves hearty local and international cuisine, and has a delightful open-air café shaded by two beautiful old ceibas.

Restaurant Mi Vaquita (Map p173; ☎ 791-1990; Av 3H No 76-22; mains $7-12; ☺ noon-11pm) Founded in the early 1960s, Mi Vaquita is arguably the best known steak house in town and does a great job. It has a warm timber-decked interior and a lively bar to the side.

La Churuata (Map p173; ☎ 798-9685; cnr Calle 72 & Av 8; mains $7-12; ☺ noon-midnight) Another trendy steak house, La Churuata combines delicious food with enjoyable decor, and it too, has an adjacent bar.

Ristorante Da Vinci (Map p173; ☎ 798-8934; Av 11 btwn Calles 75 & 76; mains $6-12) With a mock Renaissance fountain in front of the restaurant, Da Vinci is, predictably, an Italian affair, and is consistently popular with locals for its fine food and relaxed atmosphere.

Restaurant Los Soles (Map p173; ☎ 793-3966; Av 5 de Julio No 3G-09; mains $5-10) Run by a Mexican family, this bright, airy new spot brings some authentic Mexican flavor to town. You can have your tacos and enchiladas either in the colorful interior or at the alfresco tables.

El Budare de Juana (Map p173; ☎ 798-3219; cnr Av 8 & Calle 70; arepas $2, juices $1; ☺ 7am-11pm) This clean and efficient *arepera* offers 25 different kinds of delicious *arepas* and a dozen freshly made juices to wash the food down.

Entertainment

Have a look in *Panorama*, Maracaibo's major daily paper, for what's going on in the city.

Centro de Arte de Maracaibo Lía Bermúdez (Map p171; ☎ 723-1355, 723-0166; Av Libertador btwn Avs 5 & 6) The center has an auditorium where it hosts musical events, theater and arthouse films. It also stages temporary exhibitions.

Centro de Bellas Artes (Map p173; ☎ 791-2950; Av 3F No 67-217) Bellas Artes has a multipurpose auditorium used for concerts, arthouse films and theater performances. It's also home to the Orquesta Sinfónica de Maracaibo and the Danza Contemporánea de Maracaibo.

Teatro Baralt (Map p171; ☎ 722-3878; cnr Calle 95 & Av 5) Inaugurated in 1932, this is the main central venue for theater performances, but it also stages other events. Half-hour guided tours are run 9am to noon weekdays, if there are no other activities in the theater.

Getting There & Away

AIR

The **Aeropuerto Internacional La Chinita** (☎ 735-8094; Av El Aeropuerto), about 12km southwest of the city center, is not linked by city buses; take a taxi ($6). Maracaibo is serviced by most major airlines, including **Aeropostal** (☎ 735-1490), **Aserca** (☎ 735-3607), **Avior** (☎ 735-1910), **Laser** (☎ 735-3001) and **Santa Bárbara** (☎ 735-1193).

There are more than a dozen flights daily to Caracas ($48 to $85), serviced by all the listed airlines. Aeropostal and Santa Bárbara fly direct to San Antonio del Táchira ($58 to $82), and Avior and Santa Bárbara go direct to Mérida ($42 to $64). For other destinations you usually have to change planes in Caracas.

BUS

The large and busy **Terminal de Pasajeros** (Map p171; ☎ 722-1443; Av 15) is about 1km southwest of the historic center. City buses link the terminal to the center and other districts.

Within Venezuela

Ordinary buses to Coro ($5.50, four hours, 259km) and Valera ($5, four hours, 238km) run every half-hour. Buses to Barquisimeto ($6.50, five hours, 328km) depart every hour and stop en route in Carora ($5.50, 3½ hours, 225km). There are regular departures to Caracas ($13 to $17, 10½ hours, 669km), though most buses depart in the evening. Four or five buses depart nightly for San Cristóbal ($10 to $13, eight hours, 439km) and five to six buses go to Mérida ($10 to $14, nine hours, 523km).

THE NORTHWEST

To/From Colombia

Three bus companies – Bus Ven, Expreso Brasilia and Expresos Amerlujo – run air-conditioned buses to Cartagena via Maicao, Santa Marta and Barranquilla (all in Colombia). **Bus Ven** (☎ 723-9084; bus terminal) has one early morning departure daily from Maracaibo's bus terminal (and is cheaper than its competitors): Santa Marta ($32, seven hours, 374km), Cartagena ($38, 11 hours, 597km). The buses cross the border at Paraguachón (you actually change buses there) and continue through Maicao, the first Colombian town.

It is cheaper to go by por puesto to Maicao ($8, 2½ hours, 123km) and change there. Por puestos depart regularly from about 5am to 3pm and go as far as Maicao's bus terminal. From there, several Colombian bus companies operate buses to Santa Marta ($9, four hours, 251km) and further on; buses depart regularly until about 5pm.

All passport formalities are done in Paraguachón on the border. Venezuelan immigration charges a $13 *impuesto de salida* (departure tax), paid in cash by bolívares by all tourists leaving Venezuela.

You can change bolívares into Columbian pesos at the Maracaibo terminal or in Paraguachón or Maicao, but don't take them further into Columbia. They are very difficult to change beyond Maicao. Wind your watch back one hour when crossing from Venezuela to Columbia.

CAR & MOTORCYCLE

Maracaibo has all the major car rental companies. Most have desks at the airport, but some also maintain offices in the city.
Aco Rent a Car (☎ 735-3610; Airport)
Budget Airport (☎ 735-1256); City (Map p173;
☎ 797-0107; Calle 76 No 13-08)
Hertz Airport (☎ 735-0832); City (Map p171; ☎ 736-2357; Hotel Maruma Internacional, Av Circunvalación 2)
Thrifty (☎ 735-1631; Airport)

Getting Around

City transportation is serviced by buses and por puesto cars. You are most likely to need them to get between the historic center and the northern suburbs, which are linked to each other by three main roads: Av El Milagro, Av Bella Vista and Av Las Delicias. El Milagro por puestos depart from Av Libertador (Map p171). The Bella Vista por puestos leave from the corner of Av 12 and Calle 96 (Map p171). From the same corner depart San Jacinto por puestos, which run north along Av Las Delicias.

AROUND MARACAIBO
Los Puertos de Altagracia

Called either Los Puertos or Altagracia for short, this town faces Maracaibo from the opposite side of the strait. It has preserved some of its old architecture, particularly the charming, typical houses painted in bright colors. The most interesting area is around Plaza Miranda, the square just one short block up from the lakefront. A stroll about the town, together with a pleasant boat trip from Maracaibo, justifies a half-day tour.

GETTING THERE & AWAY

Boats from Maracaibo to Altagracia ($1, 40 minutes) depart every two hours until about 6pm from the wharf off Av Libertador (Map p171). In Altagracia, the boats anchor at the pier 100m southwest of Plaza Miranda.

There are also por puestos that leave when full from next to the wharf in Maracaibo and arrive at Altagracia's bus terminal ($1.25, 40 minutes). The ride is via the Rafael Urdaneta Bridge. Boats are the more pleasant means of transportation, but sometimes break down, leaving por puestos as the only option.

Ciénaga de los Olivitos

Lovely pink flamingos live year-round at Ciénaga de los Olivitos, about 20km northeast of Altagracia, the only place in Venezuela where they have built nests. The mangroves are home to many other bird species as well – about 110 species have been recorded in the region. The 260-sq-km area covering the lagoon and its environs was decreed a wildlife reserve in 1986 and is administered by Profauna. Before you set off to the marshes, contact the office of **Profauna** (☎ 761-4959, 761-4547) in Maracaibo for information.

GETTING THERE & AWAY

The Ciénaga de los Olivitos is not easy to get to, as it is inaccessible by road. Take a bus or por puesto from Altagracia to Quisiro, get off in the village of Ancón de

Iturre and talk to the local fishers. Better still, negotiate a taxi in Altagracia to take you to the Profauna post.

Isla de San Carlos

San Carlos Island is famed for its impressive, massive fort, the Castillo de San Carlos, which was built in the 1670s to guard the lake entrance from pirates. Even though the mouth was largely protected by a sandbar, many marauders were eager to cross over and sack Maracaibo. The fort was in Spanish hands until the 1823 battle of Lago de Maracaibo, and after their defeat it passed to the republicans.

In 1903 the fort was bombarded by a fleet of warships sent by Germany, Italy and Great Britain to blockade Venezuelan ports after the country failed to pay its foreign debts. During the dictatorship of Juan Vicente Gómez, the fort served as a jail for political prisoners, after which it was used as an arms depot. Finally decreed a national monument, it was extensively restored in the late 1980s to become a tourist attraction.

Castillo de San Carlos is built on a four-pointed-star plan, with circular watchtowers at each corner and a square courtyard in the middle. San Carlos Island is about 45km north of Maracaibo, and with its fine white-sand beaches and the castle, it makes a great day trip.

GETTING THERE & AWAY

The fort is accessible by boats from the town of San Rafael del Moján. San Rafael, 39km north of Maracaibo, is serviced by a number of buses and por puestos from the city's bus terminal.

On Saturday and Sunday, you can also go to San Carlos by boat direct from Maracaibo. **Navetur** (☎ 741-5035, 741-5047) operates a pleasure boat, departing from the pier at Puntica de Piedra at 9am and returning at 4pm. A roundtrip ticket is $10. Puntica de Piedra is 800m northeast of Parque la Marina (see Map p168), but the access is through a poor suburb, so it's better to go by taxi instead of walking.

Laguna de Sinamaica

The most popular tourist sight around Maracaibo, Laguna de Sinamaica, is noted for the *palafitos* – houses built on piles

along the lakeshore. Reputedly it was here that the Spanish explorers Alonso de Ojeda and Amerigo Vespucci saw native people living in *palafitos* in 1499, and gave Venezuela its name (see History p20).

Today, pleasure boats take tourists for trips around the lagoon and its side water channels to see the famous *palafitos*. Some houses are still traditionally built of *estera*, a sort of mat made from a papyrus-like reed that grows in the shallows. If you ignore the TV antennas sticking out from the roof of almost every house, they probably don't look much different from their predecessors 500 years ago. Many houses, though, are now built from modern materials, including timber, brick and tin.

GETTING THERE & AWAY

Laguna de Sinamaica, 60km north of Maracaibo, makes for an easy day trip from the city. Take a bus heading to Guana or Los Filuos from the Maracaibo bus terminal and get off in the town of Sinamaica ($1.75, two hours, 60km). From there, por puestos do a short run on a side road to Puerto Cuervito ($0.30, 10 minutes, 5km), on the edge of the lagoon.

In Puerto Cuervito, a fleet of pleasure boats waits all day long to take tourists around the lagoon. A boat takes up to six passengers and charges $13 per boat. Since there are very few tourists coming these days, it usually takes a lot of time to collect six passengers. Come on the weekend, when more visitors turn up, but even then be prepared for a long wait or bargain down the fare and go. The standard tour takes about an hour, but you can go for a longer trip for a small extra charge. There's a restaurant in Puerto Cuervito.

Parque Nacional Ciénagas del Catatumbo

The (literally) striking feature of this area is the lightning (see the boxed text p178) which continues almost uninterrupted without any claps of thunder. The phenomenon, referred to as Relámpago de Catatumbo (Catatumbo Lightning) or Faro de Maracaibo (Maracaibo Beacon), can be observed at night all over the region, weather permitting, from as far away as Maracaibo and San Cristóbal. Traveling by night on the Maracaibo–San Cristóbal or San Cristóbal–Valera roads,

MYSTERIES OF CATATUMBO LIGHTNING

The 1937 tourist brochure *Venezuela Turística* includes the Catatumbo Lightning as one of the country's unique tourist attractions. It says that the natural phenomenon is found nowhere else on earth and that its cause is unknown. Both of these statements remain true today.

Centered on the mouth of the Río Catatumbo at Lago de Maracaibo, the phenomenon consists of frequent flashes of lightning with no accompanying thunder, which gives an eerie sensation. Even though the luminosity and frequency of the lightning have diminished over recent decades and it can stop for some days, on clear dry nights you are in for an unbelievable and shocking experience. You will even be able to read this guidebook by the light of the lightning!

Various hypotheses have been put forth to explain the lightning, but so far none have been fully proven. The theory that stands out is based on the topography of the region, characterized by the proximity of 5000m-high mountains (the Andes) and a vast sea-level lake (Lago de Maracaibo) – a dramatic configuration found nowhere else in the world. The clash of the cold winds descending from the freezing highlands with the hot, humid air evaporating from the lake is thought to produce the ionization of air particles responsible for the lightning.

you'll get a glimpse of it, but the closer you get, the more impressive the spectacle becomes. Towns on the southern shores of Lago de Maracaibo (such as San Antonio, Bobures or Gibraltar) all provide good views, as do some of the towns up on the Andes slopes (including several viewpoints near La Azulita). Tours organized from Mérida (p186) are a good and comfortable way to see the Catatumbo lightning close-up. The national park also features the rich vegetation and wildlife of the vast wetlands bordering Lago de Maracaibo to the north of the Río Catatumbo.

The Andes

CONTENTS

Here is a world of towering peaks, rocky cliffs and icy lakes – alpine scenery at its best. South America's spinal column, the Cordillera de los Andes is the longest mountain chain on earth, running the whole length of the continent from Tierra del Fuego to the Caribbean Sea. Venezuela shares the 400km-long northern end of the Andes, topped by the country's tallest peak, Pico Bolívar (5007m). Further down are long, lush mountain valleys, rugged cloud-forest carpets, cascading creeks and waterfalls, and charming old mountain villages accessible by narrow winding roads.

Mérida state is in the heart of the Andes – it has the highest mountains and the best-developed tourist facilities. The city of Mérida is a real adventure sports capital, offering everything from trekking and paragliding to rafting and canyoning. It's the most popular travelers' destination in Venezuela, and shouldn't be missed.

The two other Andean states, Trujillo and Táchira, also provide great adventure travel opportunities, but are almost untouched. Trujillo has some gorgeous colonial gems set in splendid mountain scenery, while Táchira boasts wild, unexplored mountains protected by four national parks.

THE ANDES

HIGHLIGHTS

- Take a trip on Mérida's famous **teleférico** (cable car; p186)

- Hike to the remote mountain village of **Los Nevados** (p194)

- Try white-water rafting down wild Andean rivers, organized from **Mérida** (p196)

- Go mountain trekking up to **Pico Bolívar** and **Pico Humboldt** (p193), Venezuela's highest peaks

- Watch the mysterious Good Friday Passion play in **Tostós** (p204)

THE ANDES

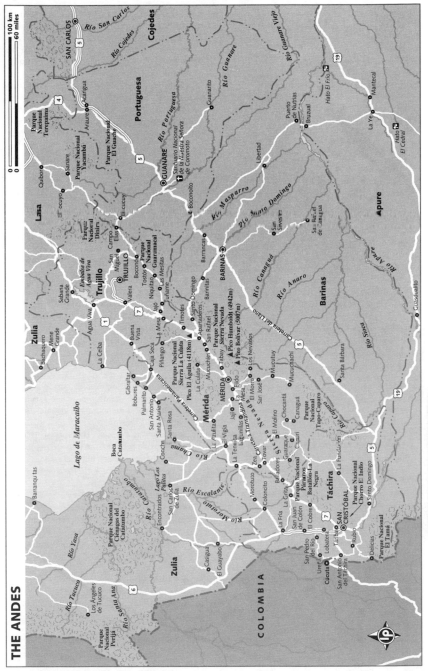

MÉRIDA STATE

MÉRIDA
☎ 0274 / pop 310,000

Very popular with travelers, Mérida has an unhurried and friendly atmosphere, plenty of tourist facilities and beautiful mountains all around, including the 5007m-high Pico Bolívar just 12km away. It's also home to the famous *teleférico,* the world's highest and longest cable-car system, and is Venezuela's major center for adventure sports and outdoor activities.

The Universidad de Los Andes (Venezuela's second-oldest university, now teaching about 46,000 students in different campuses throughout the city) gives Mérida a sizable academic community and an atmosphere that is both cultured and bohemian. The city is inexpensive and reasonably safe by Venezuelan standards, and enjoys a pleasant, mild climate, with an average temperature of 19°C (66°F).

History
Founded deep in the heart of the Andes and separated by the high mountains from both Colombia and Venezuela, nothing much happened in the tiny town of Mérida during its 250 years under the Spanish domination. In 1812 an earthquake devastated the center, further hindering its development.

After Venezuela's independence, the isolation that had retarded Mérida's progress suddenly proved to be its ally. During the federation wars in the mid-19th century, when Venezuela was plunged into full-blown civil war, the city's solitude attracted refugees fleeing the bloodshed, and the population began to grow. It was not, however, until the 1920s that access roads were constructed and later paved, which smoothed the way for Mérida's subsequent development. Its transition from a town into a city really took place only over the last few decades.

Orientation
Mérida sits on a flat *meseta,* an alluvial terrace stretching for about 12km between two parallel rivers, its edges dropping abruptly to the riverbanks. The historic quarter is at the northeastern end of the plateau, easily recognized by the typically Spanish

---

THE ANDES

MÉRIDA'S ILLEGITIMATE BIRTH

In 1558 Captain Juan Rodríguez Suárez led an expedition from Pamplona (in present-day Colombia) into the Sierra Nevada of what is now Venezuela. Upon entering a deep long valley bordered by two towering mountain ranges he founded a town and named it Mérida, after his birthplace in Spain.

At that time Pamplona was an important political and religious center in the Spanish viceroyalty of Nueva Granada, and a number of official expeditions had set out from there to explore the region and found new settlements (including San Cristóbal and Barinas). But this expedition was different because Rodríguez Suárez was in search of gold and was not authorized to found new cities, which could only be done by a royal decree from the Spanish Crown.

As soon as the governor of Pamplona learned that someone had been traveling around Nueva Granada founding cities without proper authority, he sent out an expedition to track down Rodríguez Suárez and bring him to justice. He was caught, arrested for 'usurpation of Royal prerogative,' and was found guilty. His sentence – to be dragged from the tail of his horse around the streets of Bogotá until he was dead, then his body was to be 'quartered' and left to rot, no burial allowed.

But Rodríguez Suárez was able to flout Spanish authority once again – with the help of a local bishop and a few old friends he escaped from the jail where he was awaiting his grisly fate. Suárez fled to Trujillo (Venezuela) where he was granted political asylum, becoming the first political refugee in the New World. In a petty revenge of the colonial bureaucracy, a certain Juan de Maldonado was sent out again from Pamplona, with all his paperwork in order, and re-founded Mérida in 1560, legally. Posterity, however, has judged in favor of the adventurer, and Rodríguez Suárez is recognized as the founder of the city, and 1558 as the year of Mérida's true, if illegitimate, birth.

chessboard street layout. Having filled the *meseta* as densely as possible, Mérida is now expanding beyond it, sprawling past the rivers.

The airport is just 2km southwest of the center, while the bus terminal is a little further west. Both are linked to downtown by frequent city buses.

Information

EMERGENCY
Fire (☎ 266-3612)
Police (☎ 263-8471)

INTERNET ACCESS
Mérida has plenty of Internet facilities and they are probably the cheapest in Venezuela,

MÉRIDA

0 ——————— 1 km
0 ——————— 0.5 miles

INFORMATION
Clínica Mérida...............................1 B4
Cormetul.......................................2 D1
Corp Banca....................................3 B4

SIGHTS & ACTIVITIES (pp184–6)
Jardín Botánico..............................4 C1
Parque Zoológico Chorros de Milla...5 B1
Venusa...6 B5

SLEEPING (p189)
Hotel El Serrano............................7 A4

DRINKING (pp190–1)
La Cucaracha Café.....................(see 9)
La Cucaracha Racing Bar...........(see 9)
La Cucaracha.................................8 A5

SHOPPING (p191)
Centro Comercial Alto Prado.........9 B3
Giros......................................(see 9)
Mercado Principal.........................10 B4

TRANSPORT (p191)
Airport..11 B4
Bus Terminal................................12 A4

OTHER
Perigeo..13 B4

To Los Aleros (24km); Mucuchíes (48km); San Rafael (55km); Barinas (157km); Valera (160km)

See Central Mérida Map (p185)

To La Venezuela de Antier (14km); Jají (38km)

To San Cristóbal (224km)

THE ANDES

at $0.40 to $0.70 per hour. Following are some central locations:

Ciber Café El Russo (Map p185; Av 4 No 17-74)
Conection Center (Map p185; Av 2 No 17-40)
Cyber Sp@ce (Map p185; Calle 21 btwn Avs 2 & 3)
La Abadía (Map p185; Av 3 No 17-45) Internet in the restaurant of the same name; see the boxed text p189.

LAUNDRY

Some posadas offer laundry service; if not, there are many central facilities.

Lavandería Andina (Map p185; Av 7 No 22-45)
Lavandería Ecológica (Map p185; cnr Av 4 & Calle 16)
Lavandería Marbet (Map p185; Calle 25 No 8-35)
Lavandería Yibe (Map p185; Av 6 No 19-25)

MEDICAL SERVICES

Clínica Albarregas (☎ 244-8101, 244-7283; Calle Tovar No 1-26)
Clínica Mérida (Map p183; ☎ 263-0652, 263-6395; Av Urdaneta No 45-145)

MONEY

Banco de Venezuela (Map p185; Av 4 btwn Calles 23 & 24)
Banco Mercantil (Map p185; cnr Av 5 & Calle 18)
Banesco (Map p185; Calle 24 btwn Avs 4 & 5)
Corp Banca (Map p183; Av Las Américas)
Italcambio (Map p183; ☎ 263-2977; Airport, Av Urdaneta)

POST

Ipostel (Map p185; Calle 21 btwn Avs 4 & 5)

TELEPHONE

CANTV (Map p185; cnr Calle 26 & Av 3)
Telcel (Map p185; Calle 20 No 4-64)

TOURIST INFORMATION

Cormetur (www.cormetur.com in Spanish) Main tourist office (Map p183; ☎ 263-5918, 263-4701, 800-637-4300; cnr Av Urdaneta & Calle 45; ☺ 8am-noon & 2:30-6pm Mon-Fri); Airport (Map p183; ☎ 263-9330; Av Urdaneta; ☺ 8am-6pm); Bus terminal (Map p183; ☎ 263-3952; Av Las Américas; ☺ 9am-4pm); Mercado Principal (Map p183; ☎ 262-1570; Av Las Américas; ☺ 9am-4pm Mon & Wed-Sat, 7am-2pm Tue & Sun); Teleférico (Map p185; Parque Las Heroínas; ☺ 8am-3pm Wed-Sun)
Inparques (Map p185; Teleférico, Parque Las Heroínas) Permits for Parque Nacional Sierra Nevada.

Sights

The city center is pleasant for leisurely strolls, even though it has little in the way of colonial architecture or outstanding sights. The leafy **Plaza Bolívar** (Map p185) is the city's heart, but it's not a colonial square. Work on the monumental **Catedral Metropolitana** was begun in 1800, based on the plans of the 17th-century cathedral of Toledo in Spain, but it was not completed until 1958, and probably only then because things were sped up to meet the 400th anniversary of the city's founding.

Next to the cathedral, the **Museo Arquidio-cesano** (Map p185; ☎ 252-1238; Plaza Bolívar; admission $0.75; ☺ 9am-noon Tue-Sat) features a fine collection of religious art. Note the Ave María bell cast in AD 909, thought to be the world's second-oldest surviving bell. It must have been brought from Spain by the missionaries and somehow ended up in the church of Jajó. By the early 20th century, though, it was unused and intended to be melted for reuse. Luckily, a priest from Valera sent it to Mérida for a closer inspection, thus saving it from destruction.

Across the plaza is the **Casa de la Cultura Juan Félix Sánchez** (Map p185; ☎ 808-3255; Plaza Bolívar; admission free; ☺ 9am-noon & 3-6pm Mon-Sat). Rooms on the upper floor are used for temporary exhibitions of work by local artists and craftspeople. On the ground level, there's a craft shop (see Shopping, p191).

The building of the Universidad de Los Andes, just off the plaza, houses the **Museo Arqueológico** (Map p185; ☎ 240-2344; cnr Av 3 & Calle 23; admission $0.50; ☺ 8am-11:30am & 2-5:30pm Tue-Sun), which has a collection related to the pre-Hispanic times of the region.

The large, modern Centro Cultural Tulio Febres Cordero shelters the **Museo de Arte Moderno Juan Astorga Anta** (Map p185; ☎ 252-4380; Calle 21 btwn Avs 2 & 3; admission free; ☺ 8am-noon & 2-6pm Tue-Fri, 10am-2pm Sat & Sun). It stages changing exhibitions of modern art by Venezuelan artists.

Set in a beautiful 300-year-old mansion with a courtyard, the **Museo de Arte Colonial** (Map p185; ☎ 252-7860; cnr Av 4 & Calle 20; admission $0.50; ☺ 9am-4pm Tue-Fri, 9am-1pm Sat & Sun) has a small but carefully assembled collection of sacred art, dating mostly from the 18th century.

The small Parque de Las Cinco Repúblicas boasts Venezuela's oldest **Bolívar monument** (Map p185; Calle 13 btwn Avs 4 & 5), dating from 1842. The small bust sitting atop a high, massive column looks totally out of proportion.

Visit the **Parque Zoológico Chorros de Milla** (Map p183; ☎ 244-3864; Av Chorros de Milla; admission $2;

CENTRAL MÉRIDA

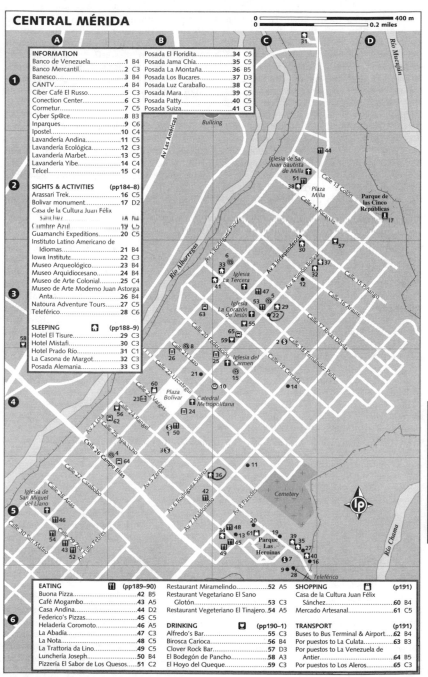

| 0 | 400 m |
| 0 | 0.2 miles |

INFORMATION
Banco de Venezuela......................1 B4
Banco Mercantil...........................2 C3
Banesco......................................3 B4
CANTV..4 B4
Ciber Café El Russo......................5 C3
Conection Center.........................6 C3
Cormetur.....................................7 C5
Cyber Sp@ce...............................8 B3
Inparques....................................9 C6
Ipostel......................................10 C4
Lavandería Andina......................11 C5
Lavandería Ecológica..................12 C3
Lavandería Marbet......................13 C5
Lavandería Yibe.........................14 C4
Telcel.......................................15 C4

SIGHTS & ACTIVITIES   (pp184–8)
Arassari Trek.............................16 C5
Bolívar monument......................17 D2
Casa de la Cultura Juan Félix
  Sánchez..............................18 B4
Cumbre Azul............................19 C5
Guamanchi Expeditions..............20 C5
Instituto Latino Americano de
  Idiomas...............................21 B4
Iowa Institute...........................22 C3
Museo Arqueológico..................23 B4
Museo Arquidiocesano...............24 B4
Museo de Arte Colonial..............25 C4
Museo de Arte Moderno Juan Astorga
  Anta...................................26 B4
Natoura Adventure Tours............27 C5
Teleférico.................................28 C6

SLEEPING   (pp188–9)
Hotel El Tisure.........................29 C3
Hotel Mistafi...........................30 C3
Hotel Prado Río........................31 C1
La Casona de Margot.................32 C3
Posada Alemania.......................33 C3

Posada El Floridita.....................34 C5
Posada Jama Chía......................35 C5
Posada La Montaña....................36 B5
Posada Los Bucares....................37 D3
Posada Luz Caraballo..................38 C2
Posada Mara.............................39 C5
Posada Patty.............................40 C5
Posada Suiza.............................41 C3

EATING   (pp189–90)
Buona Pizza..............................42 B5
Café Mogambo..........................43 A5
Casa Andina.............................44 D2
Federico's Pizzas........................45 C5
Heladería Coromoto....................46 A5
La Abadía.................................47 C5
La Nota....................................48 C5
La Trattoria di Lino....................49 C5
Lunchería Joseph.......................50 B4
Pizzería El Sabor de Los Quesos....51 C2
Restaurant Miramelindo..............52 A5
Restaurant Vegetariano El Sano
  Glotón..................................53 C3
Restaurant Vegeteriano El Tinajero..54 A5

DRINKING   (pp190–1)
Alfredo's Bar.............................55 C3
Birosca Carioca.........................56 B4
Clover Rock Bar........................57 D3
El Bodegón de Pancho................58 A3
El Hoyo del Queque...................59 C3

SHOPPING   (p191)
Casa de la Cultura Juan Félix
  Sánchez..............................60 B4
Mercado Artesanal.....................61 C5

TRANSPORT   (p191)
Buses to Bus Terminal & Airport....62 B4
Por puestos to La Culata.............63 B3
Por puestos to La Venezuela de
  Antier..................................64 B5
Por puestos to Los Aleros............65 C3

THE ANDES

(☾ 8am-5pm Tue-Sun) on the northern outskirts of the city, 4km from the center. Set on a mountain slope along the Río Milla and named after the waterfalls in the park, the small, scenic zoo features a selection of local fauna, including the jaguar, condor, anaconda, capybara, tapir, and capuchin and spider monkeys. Don't miss walking uphill along the creek to see the waterfalls.

Not far from the zoo is the **Jardín Botánico** (Map p183; ☎ 416-0642; Av Alberto Carnevali; admission free; ☾ 8am-5pm). Inaugurated in 2000, the botanical garden is still young and has a long way to develop. Of its total 44-hectare area, only 4 hectares are as yet open to the public. It's worth coming anyway, particularly on Saturday or Sunday, when an unusual 'aerial path' is open for visitors. You 'walk' using ropes between platforms built atop four tall trees. The 'trip' takes 1½ hours and costs $3.50.

TELEFÉRICO DE MÉRIDA

The highlight of any visit to Mérida is the **teleférico** (Map p185; ☎ 252-1997, 252-5080; www .telefericodemerida.com in Spanish; Parque Las Heroínas), the world's highest and longest cable-car system, now running again after various periods of being out of order. It was constructed in 1958 by a French company and runs 12.5km from the bottom station of Barinitas (1577m) in Mérida to the top of Pico Espejo (4765m), covering the ascent in four stages. The three intermediate stations are La Montaña (2436m), La Aguada (3452m) and Loma Redonda (4045m).

The cable car normally operates Wednesday to Sunday, though in tourist season it runs daily. The first trip up is at 7:30am and the last at noon (7am and 1pm, respectively, in peak season). The last trip down is about 2pm (4pm in peak season). The roundtrip ticket from Mérida to Loma Redonda costs $13, and the last stage from Loma Redonda to Pico Espejo is another $3; no student discounts are available. Large backpacks are $2 extra.

The ascent to Pico Espejo takes about 1½ hours if you go straight through. It's best to go up as early as possible, as clouds usually obscure views later in the day. You can then take some short walks around Pico Espejo and/or Loma Redonda before going back. Don't forget to take warm clothes and sunblock.

Apart from splendid views during the trip itself, the cable car provides easy access for high-mountain hiking, saving you a day or two of puffing uphill. Bear in mind, however, that acclimatization problems can easily occur by quickly reaching high altitudes.

Activities

The region provides excellent conditions for a range of activities as diverse as rock climbing, bird-watching, paragliding, horse riding and rafting, and local operators have been quick to make them easily accessible for visitors – see Tours below for tour companies, and Around Mérida (p193) for more details.

Courses

Mérida is a great place to study and practice Spanish. In the Andes, Spanish is spoken more slowly than in other parts of the country, so you are likely to find it easier to understand. The city has several language schools and the prices of language courses tend to be lower here than just about anywhere else in the country. There are also plenty of students and tutors offering private lessons – inquire at popular traveler hotels and tour companies. The major institutions offering Spanish courses include:

Instituto Latino Americano de Idiomas (Map p185; ☎ 262-0990; latinoamericano@cantv.net; Edificio Don Atilio, cnr Av 4 & Calle 21)

Iowa Institute (Map p185; ☎ 252-6404; www.iowainstitute.com; cnr Av 4 & Calle 18)

Venusa (Map p183; ☎ 263-8855; Edificio Tibisay, Av Urdaneta No 49-49)

Tours

There are plenty of tour companies in Mérida, and prices are generally reasonable. Understandably, mountain trips figure prominently on tour-company agendas and include treks to Pico Bolívar and Pico Humboldt; expect to pay about $30 to $50 per person per day, all-inclusive.

The village of Los Nevados is probably the most popular destination among those who don't attempt to climb the peaks. Most companies offer trips there, but you can easily do it on your own. The tour companies listed in this section will give you the details on how to do it.

The Parque Nacional Sierra de la Culata is another attractive destination, available as a tour from most agents. It's a two- to three-day trip and costs around $30 to $50 per person per day, all-inclusive.

A recommended excursion out of Mérida is a wildlife safari to Los Llanos, and most companies offer this trip, usually as a four-day tour for $100 to $160.

Other special-interest tours readily available in Mérida focus on mountain biking, paragliding, rafting, canyoning, rock climbing, fishing and horseback riding. Some companies handle rental of mountaineering equipment, camping gear and bikes; if you just need equipment, not a guide or a tour, check **Cumbre Azul** (Map p185; ☎ 416-3231; Calle 24 No 8 153), which specializes in rental.

As elsewhere in the country, Mérida's tour companies will normally accept cash payment for their services in US dollars. Most will accept traveler's checks, but not credit cards. Following are the best-established and most reliable local tour companies:

Arassari Trek (Map p185; ☎ /fax 252-5879; www .arassari.com; Calle 24 No 8-301) Run by Swiss polyglot Tom Evenou and his wife Raquel, the company has a wide range of tours, including trekking, horseback riding and mountain biking, as well as some of the most adventurous rafting and canyoning trips. It also offers great Los Llanos tours and Catatumbo trips to see the unique Catatumbo lightning (p177). Arassari has some of the best guides, including Alan Highton (wildlife and bird-watching) and Roger Manrique (bird-watching). It also sells domestic/international airline tickets.

Guamanchi Expeditions (Map p185; ☎ 252-2080; www.guamanchi.com; Calle 24 No 8-86) One of Mérida's largest and longest-operating companies, owned and managed by John Peña, it offers a choice of well prepared tours up the mountains and down to Los Llanos, and runs rafting and kayak trips. It has bicycles for rent, bike tours and information about do-it-yourself bike trips. It has a posada at the same address.

MÉRIDA – A LAND OF FIESTAS

The **Feria del Sol** is Mérida city's main annual bash, full of music, popular dance, sports events, bullfights and a beauty pageant. It runs for nearly the whole week preceding Ash Wednesday. This apart, the city and the region are rich in festivities, many of which are confined to a particular small area or a single town. Given the strong traditional character of the region, it comes as no surprise that many events have religious roots and are linked to the religious calendar. You can take it for granted that every village will be holding a celebratory feast on the day of its patron saint. There are frequent local buses to all the following destinations; inquire at the tourist information for details.

Jan – Paradura del Niño Game in which villagers 'steal' the infant Jesus from his crib, then search for him and celebrate his 'finding;' it's popular throughout the region for the entire month.

Jan 6 – Los Reyes Magos (Epiphany) Particularly solemn carol-singing ceremony in the town of Santo Domingo.

Feb 2 – Los Vasallos de La Candelaria Ritual dances in La Parroquia, Mucuchíes, Bailadores and La Venta.

Easter – Semana Santa (Holy Week, leading up to Easter) Observed in many towns and villages, including particularly La Parroquia, Lagunillas, Santo Domingo, Chiguará and La Azulita.

May 15 – Fiesta de San Isidro Labrador Sort of agrarian rite in honor of the patron saint of farmers, celebrated with processions featuring domestic animals and crops; it's most elaborate in Apartaderos, Mucuchíes, Tabay, Bailadores and La Azulita.

Jul 25 – Fiesta de Santo Apóstol Held in Lagunillas, Ejido and Jají.

Sep 30 – Los Negros de San Gerónimo Celebrated in Santo Domingo.

Oct 24 – Fiesta de San Rafael Patron saint's day feast in San Rafael.

Dec 8 – Fiesta de la Inmaculada Concepción Spectacular display of some 20,000 candles, which are lit in the evening in the main plaza of Mucurubá.

Dec 29 – Fiesta de San Benito Event held in honor of Venezuela's only black saint, in which the locals take to the streets in red-and-black costumes and sometimes black-colored faces, and spend the day dancing to the rhythm of drums and parading from door to door; observed in Timotes, La Venta, Apartaderos and Mucuchíes.

Dec 31 – Despedida del Año Viejo (Farewell to the Old Year) Midnight burning of life-size human puppets, often stuffed with fireworks, which have been prepared weeks before and placed in front of the houses; celebrated regionally.

THE ANDES

Natoura Adventure Tours (Map p185; ☎ 252-4216; www.natoura.com; Calle 24 No 8-237) Managed by José Luis Troconis, this company is particularly good for mountain trekking and climbing, though it runs a range of other tours as well, including bird-watching in the Mérida region and beyond. It conducts its tours in small groups and uses good-quality camping and mountaineering equipment. It also sells domestic/international airline tickets.

All three companies consistently receive good reports from travelers, and their prices are comparable. There are plenty of other tour operators in town, many of which nestle around Parque Las Heroínas and along Calle 24. They may be reliable and will cost much the same or even less than those listed. Shop around, talk to other travelers and check things thoroughly before deciding.

Sleeping

Mérida has heaps of places to stay all across the center. Most of these are posadas, which are small, inexpensive family-run guesthouses usually with a friendly atmosphere. Many have hot water and provide laundry facilities, and some allow guests to use the kitchen.

Most travelers are perfectly satisfied with the standards offered by the posadas, but should you prefer a conventional hotel, Mérida has a choice of these in every price bracket, although there's nothing really very posh or very expensive in town.

BUDGET

Posada Los Bucares (Map p185; ☎ 252-2841; losbucarespos@hotmail.com; Av 4 No 15-05; s/d/tr $12/15/18; P) This fine historic mansion is an enjoyable place to stay. It has cozy rooms set around a tiny patio, plus a tiny restaurant.

Posada Mara (Map p185; ☎ 252-5507; Calle 24 No 8-215; d/tr $8/12) Mara is a modern, well-kept hotel that offers 11 cozy, spotless rooms distributed on two floors – good value.

Posada El Floridita (Map p185; ☎ 251-0452; Calle 25 No 8-44; r per person $4) This Cuban-run, nine-room guesthouse is one of the cheapest options with private facilities, and it's not a bad choice. Take a room on the upper floor – they are brighter.

Posada Jama Chía (Map p185; ☎ 252-5767; Calle 24 No 8-223; r per person without bathroom $4) If you can live without a private bathroom, this is a good option. The rooms are clean and tidy and the guests can use the kitchen.

Posada Patty (Map p185; ☎ 251-1052; Calle 24 No 8-265; r per person without bathroom $3) This is an informal and friendly home that has some of the cheapest beds in towns. The rooms (five in all) are spartan and don't have private facilities, but look at the price! You can use the kitchen and the fridge. Patty also offers some of the cheapest laundry services around, and not just for the guests.

La Casona de Margot (Map p185; ☎ 252-3312; Av 4 No 15-17; d $13-15, tr $20) Next door to Los Bucares and quite similar in style and atmosphere, Margot is another small posada, which provides enjoyable and stylish accommodations and doesn't cost a fortune. It has a small patio, pretty rooms and an old-world feel to it.

Posada Luz Caraballo (Map p185; ☎ 252-5441; fax 252-0177; Av 2 No 13-80; s/d/tr/q $10/14/20/25; P) Facing the tree-filled Plaza Milla, Luz Caraballo has 36 rooms spread over three floors. The rooms are fair-sized and well maintained, and there's a good hotel restaurant downstairs, serving inexpensive meals.

Posada Suiza (Map p185; ☎ 252-4961; cnr Av 2 & Calle 18; s/d/tr without bathroom $7/10/13, with bathroom $10/13/17) This friendly place has a choice of 10 rooms with and without private facilities, arranged around a colonial-style courtyard, and has a quiet terrace with hammocks at the back, providing lovely views of the mountains. You can use the kitchen free of charge, and have a great buffet breakfast for $3. The manager runs a tour agency.

Posada Alemania (Map p185; ☎ 252-4067; Av 2 No 17-76; s/d/tr without bathroom $7/12/16, with bathroom $10/14/20) Managed by a German, the 'German Guesthouse' is, predictably, particularly popular with German travelers. Like most other posadas, this one also occupies a historic building, so it has a style and feel

---

✱
THE AUTHOR'S CHOICE

Posada La Montaña (Map p185; ☎ 252-5977; posadalamontana@icnet.com.ve; Calle 24 No 6-47; s/d/q $12/16/25) One of the great favorites at a budget level, La Montaña is a beautiful, old-fashioned, two-story house that has a lot of colonial charm and atmosphere. All of its 17 rooms have bathrooms with hot water, and safety boxes. The tastefully decorated hotel restaurant serves hearty fish, pasta and steaks.

> **THE AUTHOR'S CHOICE**
>
> **Hotel El Serrano** (Map p183; ☎ 266-7447; hotelserrano@telcel.net.ve; Av Los Próceres; s/d/tr/q/ste $27/32/35/38/50; P 🍽 🖳 🛍) About 4km southwest of the center, El Serrano is a smart, 52-room, three-star hotel with a swimming pool. It has large, comfortable rooms and, still better, suites (for up to four persons), and there are plenty of flowering plants all around the place – indoor and out – that make you feel like you're in a garden. Excellent value.

of times gone by. Guests can use the well-equipped kitchen with fridge, and relax in hammocks.

MID-RANGE & TOP END

Hotel Mistafi (Map p185; ☎ 251-0729; hotelmistafi@cantv.net; cnr Av 3 & Calle 15; d/tr $25/28; P 🍽 🖳) You probably won't find anything better in the center than this one. Mistafi is a new, comfortable hotel with ample rooms, good beds and its own restaurant. Some rooms have air-conditioning, though you'll hardly need it in this mild climate. Choose a room at the back for both the tranquility and mountain views.

Hotel El Tisure (Map p185; ☎ 252-6072; fax 252-6061; Av 4 No 17-47; s/d/tr/ste $18/22/25/32; P) Built in colonial style but offering modern facilities, El Tisure is an inexpensive central option offering 30 spacious rooms, an enjoyable bar and a no-frills restaurant.

Hotel Prado Río (Map p185; ☎ 252-0633; www.hotelpradorio.com.ve; Av 1; d $35-45, tr $55; P 🖳 🛍) Set in vast, walled-in grounds, a short walk north of the center, Prado Río is an attractive proposition. Besides a hotel building with 13 spacious rooms, there's a colony of whitewashed cabañas arranged in the form of a Mediterranean town with a further 84 rooms. The complex is well maintained and adorned with flowers, and has its own restaurant, bar and a large swimming pool.

Eating

Lunchería Joseph (Map p185; ☎ 252-3956; Calle 23 btwn Avs 4 & 5; breakfast $2, lunch $2-3; ⏰ 6am-3:30pm Mon-Sat) Just off Plaza Bolívar, Joseph is one the best budget eateries, offering a selection of set breakfasts and lunches to choose from. It looks pretty ordinary, but the food is tasty,

portions generous and the service prompt. It's so popular that you may have to stand in line at the door during lunchtime.

Restaurant Vegetariano El Sano Glotón (Map p185; Av 4 No 17-84; set lunch $2; ⏰ noon-9pm) A tiny street-corner two-level place, this is one of the most popular veggie restaurants in town.

Restaurant Vegetariano El Tinajero (Map p185; Calle 29 No 3-54; set lunch $2-3;) Another veggie stronghold, El Tinajero is recommended, but it's open for lunch only.

Federico's Pizzas (Map p185; ☎ 416-3963; Pasaje Ayacucho; pizza & pasta $3-4, mains $4-5) This lovely two-level spot with pastel-colored walls, tasteful decoration and quiet background music, serves pasta and pizza, as well as an assortment of meat and fish dishes.

La Trattoria da Lino (Map p185; ☎ 252-9555; Pasaje Ayacucho; mains $4-7) If you are after a fine Italian dinner, you won't do wrong coming to this well-appointed restaurant with a delicate Mediterranean touch and savory, authentic home-cooked Italian food.

La Nota (Map p185; ☎ 252-9697; cnr Calle 25 & Av 8; snacks $2-3, mains $3-5) Nicknamed 'Mérida's McDonald's,' La Nota does indeed have burgers, but also a choice of palatable mains, which make a filling lunch or dinner.

Casa Andina (Map p185; ☎ 252-4811; Av 2 No 12-30; set menú $2.50, mains $3-5) Set in a red-tiled, whitewashed historic house, the friendly Casa Andina is a combination of restaurant and museum. The restaurant, serving popular Venezuelan fare, is in the patio and is adorned with crafts and antiques. A few front rooms house a collection of pre-Hispanic stone and pottery pieces.

Pizzería El Sabor de Los Quesos (Map p185; Plaza Milla; pizza $2-4) Some of the town's cheapest

> **THE AUTHOR'S CHOICE** ✳
>
> **La Abadía** (Map p185; ☎ 251-0933; Av 3 No 17-45; mains $4-8; ⏰ noon-11pm) This meticulously reconstructed colonial mansion has several different dining spaces, both indoor and alfresco, plus a cybercafé. Delightfully decorated throughout, this is easily one of the loveliest places to eat in town, serving great salads, meats and pastas. And while you're waiting for your meal, or after you've finished it, you can use the Internet free of charge for up to 30 minutes.

THE ANDES

THE AUTHOR'S CHOICE

Heladería Coromoto (Map p185; ☎ 252-3525; Av 3 No 28-75; ice-cream $1-3; 🕑 2:15pm-9:45pm Tue-Sun) You shouldn't miss this – the most famous ice-cream parlor on the continent, appearing in the *Guinness Book of Records* for the largest number of ice-cream flavors. The place offers more than 900 flavors, though not all are available on an average day. Among the more unusual varieties, you can try Polar beer, shrimp, trout or chicken with spaghetti. You can even have the Lonely Planet flavor (which appears under its Spanish name, Planeta Solitario).

pizzas can be found in this charming rustic colonial house with two patios, and they aren't bad at all!

Buona Pizza (Map p185; ☎ 252-7639; Av 7 No 24-46; pizza $3-4) Convenient, central and open till late, this is another recommended budget pizza outlet; takeaway is available.

Café Mogambo (Map p185; ☎ 252-5643; cnr Calle 29 & Av 4; light meals $3-5) This trendy modern bistro serves snacks and light dishes including salads, sandwiches and burritos. The main music theme is jazz, as you can tell by the instruments and photos of jazz stars hanging on the walls. Live jazz (or sometimes salsa) is played on Friday nights.

Restaurant Miramelindo (Map p185; ☎ 252-9437; Calle 29 btwn Avs 4 & 5; mains $6-12) One of the best restaurants in the center, Miramelindo serves international fare, including some Basque dishes, and has a sushi bar.

Drinking & Dancing

El Hoyo del Queque (Map p185; ☎ 252-4306; cnr Av 4 & Calle 19) Arguably the best bar in the center, this trendy, charming spot consistently fills up with patrons every evening, sometimes well beyond its capacity, until the friendly French manager tries to close it at 1am. Rock videos run on a large screen and, while the atmosphere is reaching its peak, the crowd rushes to dance between the tables.

Alfredo's Bar (Map p185; cnr Av 4 & Calle 19) This bar has long been one of the most popular watering holes with young revelers, largely due to its incredibly cheap beer, reputedly the cheapest in Venezuela (about $0.20 per

bottle until 7pm, $0.40 after that). On weekend nights, it's so completely packed that it's impossible to get in, let alone sit or dance.

Clover Rock Bar (Map p185; ☎ 416-5570; Av 4 btwn Calles 14 & 15) Clover is a lively, smoky bar that plays loud rock and salsa and sometimes has live music. It's frequented by students and young folks and is often packed solid, particularly after 1am when El Hoyo patrons move here.

Birosca Carioca (Map p185; ☎ 252-3804; Calle 24 No 2-04) This is the most popular central disco-bar, great for drinking and dancing in a 'student' atmosphere. Set in a historic building, in which the covered patio is now a dance floor, this rustic place has a lot of charm, good old rock music, cheap beer and, usually, a great atmosphere. Live music is staged on some weekends.

El Bodegón de Pancho (Map p185; ☎ 244-9819; Centro Comercial Mamayera, Av Las Américas) Within walking distance from the center, El Bodegón is one of the oldest discos in town, and it continues to draw crowds. The timber-decked ground-level hall has the charm of an old tavern and vibrates with Latin rhythms, with bands usually playing on Friday. Upstairs is a large dance floor, which blasts with hip-hop, trance and the like.

La Cucaracha (Map p183; Centro Comercial Las Tapias, Av Andrés Bello) For those who want it loud, this is the place – Mérida's largest and loudest discotheque. The music level is actually so high that it continuously triggers off the alarms of cars parked outside. The 10-year-old place has a few different musical ambiences, with the main dance room blasting with techno music and Latin-Caribbean rhythms playing downstairs. Over 1000 revelers can turn up and squeeze inside on a good weekend night.

La Cucaracha Café (Map p183; Centro Comercial Alto Prado, Av Los Próceres) A new creation of La Cucaracha's owner, this is a vast modern nightclub rather than a café, with two large bars and live Latin music at the weekend. This is upmarket territory frequented by beautiful people.

La Cucaracha Racing Bar (Map p183; Centro Comercial Alto Prado, Av Los Próceres) Up the stairs from the café, this is the newest addition to the La Cucaracha family, and the most impressive one. It's again a large cool place with tables and two bars. Racing is the theme here; there are life-sized racing boats and bikes and a

Porsche hanging from the ceiling, and two reputedly original Formula-One crates – a red Ferrari and a blue Williams – sitting atop the bars.

Shopping

Mérida is a good place to buy local crafts.

Casa de la Cultura Juan Félix Sánchez (Map p185; ☎ 808-3255; Plaza Bolívar; ❧ 9am-noon & 3-6pm Mon-Sat) Large, well-stocked craft shop on ground level.

Mercado Artesanal (Map p185; Parque Las Heroínas; ❧ 9am-6pm) Small arty crafts market, home to a dozen stalls selling crafts and some more artistic fare.

Mercado Principal (Map p183; ☎ 262-0437, 262-1570; Av Las Américas; ❧ 7am-4pm) Vast, busy and colorful main city market with dozens of stalls selling food and crafts.

Giros (Map p183; ☎ 244-1313; Centro Comercial Alto Prado, Av Los Próceres; ❧ 2pm 10pm Mon Fri, 10am-10pm Sat, 4pm-10pm Sun) The best CD shop in town. Run by a friendly Argentinean and Uruguayan staff, it has a wide choice of Latin rhythms, Venezuelan *gaita* and *joropo*, jazz and classics, and you can listen to it while sipping delicious coffee from a small café at the back.

Getting There & Away

AIR

The **Aeropuerto Alberto Carnevali** (Map p183; ☎ 263-1612, 263 7804; Av Urdaneta) is right inside the city, 2km southwest of Plaza Bolívar, accessible by buses from the corner of Calle 25 and Av 2. **Avior** (☎ 244-2454) and **Santa Bárbara** (☎ 263 4170) fly daily to and from Caracas ($48 to $75). There are also direct flights to Maracaibo ($45 to $58) and San Antonio del Táchira ($42 to $54).

BUS

The **Terminal de Pasajeros** (Bus Terminal; Map p183; ☎ 263-0051; Av Las Américas) is 3km southwest of the city center; it's linked by frequent public buses, which depart from the corner of Calle 25 and Av 2.

A dozen buses run daily to Caracas ($13 to $20, 13 hours, 790km) and half a dozen to Maracaibo ($10 to $14, nine hours, 523km). Small buses to San Cristóbal depart every 1½ hours from 5:30am to 7pm ($7, five hours, 224km) – all go via El Vigía and La Fría, not via the Trans-Andean (Carretera Transandina) route.

Four buses daily run to Valera ($5.50, five hours, 160km) via the Trans-Andean highway, and five buses go to Barinas ($4.50, four hours, 157km). Both roads are spectacular. Regional destinations, including Apartaderos and Jají, are serviced regularly throughout the day.

CAR & MOTORCYCLE

Four car-rental companies have their desks at the airport, but three will only rent a car to travel within the region. A small car rented by the local companies will cost around $40 to $50 daily, including insurance and unlimited mileage.

Alquil-Auto (☎ 263-1440) Travel restricted to Mérida state.

Budget (☎ 262-2728) No restrictions, but much more expensive than the three local companies.

Dávila Tours (☎ 263-4510) Restricted to Mérida and Barinas states.

Visbal Rental Car (☎ 416-0185) Restricted to Mérida state.

Getting Around

The city is well serviced by small buses and minibuses, but they stop running around 8pm to 9pm, leaving taxis as the only alternative. Taxis are cheap, so you may prefer to move around by taxi anyway. They are particularly convenient for trips to and from the bus terminal and airport, when you're carrying all your bags with you. The taxi trip between the city center and the bus terminal or airport will cost about $2 each way.

Línea Tele-Cars (☎ 263-9589, 263-8834) is a reliable taxi company with radio service. Apart from services within the city, the company organizes taxi trips around the region, including Jají, El Águila, Mucuchíes and San Rafael and the theme parks.

AROUND MÉRIDA
Sights

The region that surrounds Mérida offers plenty of attractions, both natural and cultural. Many sights are accessible by road, so you can get around by public transportation. This is particularly true of the towns and villages on the Trans-Andean highway (Carretera Transandina) and surrounding mountain slopes and valleys. Many of them have preserved their historic architecture and old-time atmosphere.

THE ANDES

Exploring the region is quite easy, as transportation and accommodations along the Trans-Andean highway are in good supply. Virtually every sizable village on the road has at least one posada or hotel, and there are plenty of roadside restaurants.

JAJÍ & AROUND

Extensively reconstructed in the late 1960s to become a handsome, typical *pueblo andino* (Andean town), Jají is probably the best known of the region's traditional mountain towns. Its delightful Plaza Bolívar is surrounded by a whitewashed church and old balconied houses that now host craft shops. Jají has a few posadas and restaurants, should you like to linger longer. You can also visit an old coffee hacienda on the town's outskirts.

The town is about 38km west of Mérida, easily accessible by buses from the bus terminal ($0.80, 50 minutes). A bonus attraction is the spectacular access road from Mérida, which winds through lush cloud forest.

About 8km before Jají, beside the road, is the Chorrera de Las González, a series of five waterfalls. You can stop here to bathe in the falls' ponds, or just to have a look. Instead of returning by bus straight back to Mérida, you can walk 1.5km along the road (toward Mérida) to a junction, take a right turn and walk another 7km to La Mesa, a fine old town. Por puestos from La Mesa will take you to the larger town of Ejido, where you change for Mérida. It's a great day trip out of Mérida.

MUCUCHÍES & AROUND

The 400-year-old Mucuchíes is another lovely *pueblo andino*, proud of its beautiful parish church facing Plaza Bolívar. Stroll about the adjacent streets to see the lovely little houses; some of them are craft shops, offering attractive handmade textiles, particularly ponchos woven on archaic looms. You may need to buy a poncho if you stay for a while – it gets a bit chilly at night. The town has plenty of accommodations, just take your pick.

About 7km further up the road is the village of San Rafael, noted for its amazing, small stone chapel built by a local artist, Juan Félix Sánchez, who died in 1997 and is buried inside. This is his second chapel; the first, in similar style, was built two dec-

ades ago in the remote hamlet of El Tisure, inaccessible by road. You can walk there in five to six hours or rent a mule.

Any bus to Valera, Barinas or Apartaderos will drop you at Mucuchíes or San Rafael. Alternatively, inquire at Mérida's tour operators or tourist information about transport to Mucuchíes.

CIDA ASTRONOMICAL OBSERVATORY

North of San Rafael, at an altitude of about 3600m, is the **Centro de Investigaciones de Astronomía** (CIDA; ☎ 0274-271-2780, 271-3883; www .cida.ve in Spanish), an astronomical observatory with four telescopes and a museum of astronomy. It's normally open to the public only on weekends, but in peak holiday seasons (Christmas, Carnaval, Easter, August) it's open daily. CIDA is off the main road, and there is no public transportation on the access road to the observatory, but tours are organized from Mérida by **Perigeo** (Map p183; ☎ 0274-263-9896; Centro Comercial Glorias Patrias, cnr Av Urdaneta & Calle 37). Tours ($15 per person) depart on Saturday at 2pm (daily in high season) from Parque Las Heroínas and return around midnight.

THEME PARKS

Three theme parks have been opened in the vicinity of Mérida by a local entrepreneur, Alexis Montilla. They have become favorite attractions for Venezuelan tourists, though they may look somewhat tacky to foreign travelers. Put aside at least three hours to visit each park and go on weekends or during holiday periods to experience a touch of Venezuelan popular culture. Don't go if it's raining, because much of the action takes place outdoors.

Los Aleros (☎ 0274-808-1503; www.losaleros.net in Spanish; admission $12.50; ◷ 9am-6pm, ticket office closes 4pm), on the road to Mucuchíes, 24km from Mérida, was opened in 1984. It's a re-creation of a typical Andean village from the 1930s, complete with its Plaza Bolívar, church, school, post office, cinema, shops, bakery, restaurant and a working radio station. It's brought to life with period events, music, crafts and food, plus a few extra surprises. Everything really looks and feels as it did 70 years ago, except for the prices. Por puestos from the corner of Calle 19 and Av 4 in Mérida will take you there ($1, frequent departure).

La Venezuela de Antier (☎ 0274-808-1500; www.la venezueladeantier.net in Spanish; admission $15; ☺ 9am-7pm, ticket office closes 3pm) opened in 1991. It's a sort of Venezuela in a capsule, reproducing the country's landmarks, costumes and traditions. You'll find replicas of the bullring of Maracay, the Urdaneta bridge of Maracaibo and Mérida's oldest monument to Bolívar. You'll see Amazonian Indians in their palm-leaf thatched *churuatas* (traditional huts), Guajiro women dressed in their traditional *mantas*, and General Juan Vicente Gómez will show up in full uniform. Dancing devils from San Francisco de Yare will dance in their monstrous masks, and cockfights are held at the weekend. There's also an impressive collection of vintage cars. The park is 14km from Mérida on the Jají road; take a por puesto from Calle 26 between Av 3 and Av 4.

La Montaña de Los Sueños (☎ 0275-414-2262; admission $15; ☺ 4pm-midnight, ticket office closes 8pm), 52km west of Mérida, is Montilla's most recent creation, opened in 2002. This is a Venezuelan Hollywood, revolving around the movie theme, featuring film- and cinema-related paraphernalia, plenty of archaic cine cameras, movie studios and two cinemas screening old films. You'll also find a lot of vintage cars and an unbelievable collection of amazing old jukeboxes – no doubt South America's record. And, of course, there's a good supply of bars and restaurants to eat and drink in till late. To get to La Montaña, take the Chiguará bus from Mérida's bus terminal. For a late return, the park's attendants can call a taxi for you ($15).

Activities

HIKING & MOUNTAINEERING

The most popular high-mountain trekking area is the **Parque Nacional Sierra Nevada**, east of Mérida, which has all of Venezuela's highest peaks, including Pico Bolívar (5007m), Pico Humboldt (4942m) and Pico Bonpland (4883m). Climbing these peaks shouldn't be attempted without a guide unless you have climbing experience. Guided trips are offered by most of Mérida's tour operators (p186).

Pico Bolívar, Venezuela's highest point (5007m), is one of the most popular peaks to climb. Given the country's mania for Bolívar monuments, it's no surprise that a bust of the hero has been placed on the summit. The climb requires a rope, and ice and snow equipment in the rainy season, which will be provided by your guide. What you can do without a guide is hike along the trail leading up to Pico Bolívar. It roughly follows the cable-car line, but be careful walking from Loma Redonda to Pico Espejo – the trail is not clear and it's easy to get lost.

Venezuela's second-highest summit, **Pico Humboldt** (4942m) is also popular with high-mountain trekkers. There's not much here in the way of mountaineering, but the hike itself is marvelous. The starting point for the trek is La Mucuy, accessible by road from Mérida. A four- to six-hour walk from La Mucuy will take you up to the small **Laguna La Coromoto** (3200m), where trekkers normally camp the first night. The next day, it's a four-hour walk to reach **Laguna Verde** (4000m), one of the largest lakes in the area. Some hikers stay here the second

---

ANDEAN CLIMATE & WEATHER

As a general guide, the Venezuelan Andes enjoy a dry season from December to April. May and June is a period of changeable weather, with a lot of sunshine, but also frequent rain (or snow at high altitudes). It is usually followed by a short, relatively dry period from late June to late July before a long, really wet season begins. August to October are the wettest months, during which hiking can be miserable. The snowy period – June to October – may be dangerous for mountaineers.

The weather changes frequently and rapidly, even in the dry season. Rain (or snow, at upper reaches) can occur any time, and visibility can drop dramatically within an hour, leaving you trapped high up in the mountains for quite a while. Be careful and hike properly equipped, with good rain gear and warm clothing, as well as some extra food and water. Particular care should be taken on remote trails, where you may not meet anyone for days. Also keep in mind the risk of altitude sickness.

THE ANDES

night, or you can walk for another hour to **Laguna El Suero** (4200m), a tiny lake almost at the foot of the glacier. It gets freezing at night, so have plenty of warm clothes. Pico Humboldt is a two- to four-hour ascent, depending on the weather. You reach the snowline at about 4850m. Further up, crampons and an ice axe are recommended, and keep an eye out for crevasses. Again, this climb is best done with an experienced local guide, particularly in the rainy (snowy) season.

Back at Laguna El Suero, you can return the same way to La Mucuy or continue along the route known as **La Travesía** to the cable-car top station at Pico Espejo (4765m). After an initial 500m ascent from

the lake, the trail to Pico Espejo (four to six hours) goes for most of the way at roughly the same altitude of nearly 4700m. You can then climb Pico Bolívar before returning to Mérida by foot or teleférico. The whole loop normally takes four to six days.

An easier destination is **Los Nevados**, a charming mountain village nestled at about 2700m (simple accommodations and food are available). The trip is normally done as a two-day loop that includes rides by cable car, mule and jeep. The usual way is to go by cable car up to Pico Espejo, have a look around and go down (also by cable car) to Loma Redonda. Then walk (five to six hours) or ride a mule ($5, four to five hours) to Los Nevados for the night. The

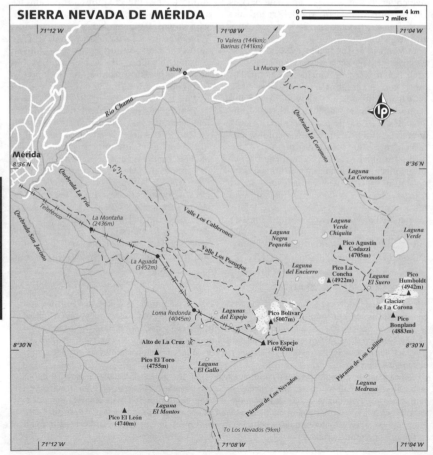

SIERRA NEVADA DE MÉRIDA

next day, take a jeep to Mérida ($40 for up to five people, four to five hours, 63km) along a breathtaking, cliffside-hugging track.

The **Parque Nacional Sierra La Culata**, to the north of Mérida, also offers some amazing hiking territory, and is particularly noted for its desert-like highland landscapes. Take a por puesto to La Culata (departing from the corner of Calle 19 and Av 2), from where it's a three- to four-hour hike uphill to a primitive shelter known as El Refugio, at about 3700m. Continue the next day for about three hours to the top of **Pico Pan de Azúcar** (4660m). Return before 4pm, the time the last por puesto tends to depart back to Mérida.

Some guided tours don't return the same way, but instead descend southeast through an arid moonscape-like terrain to a chain of mountain lakes and on down to Mucuchíes via natural hot springs. Trails are faint on this route, and it's easy to get lost if you don't know the way; don't wander too far unless you're an experienced trekker.

Another interesting area for hiking is further east, near **Pico El Águila** (4118m). Take a morning bus to Valera and get off at Venezuela's highest road pass, **Paso del Cóndor** (4007m), about 60km from Mérida. Bolívar marched this way on one of his campaigns, and a statue of a condor was built here in his honor (hence the name of the pass).

There's a roadside restaurant where you can have a hot chocolate before setting off. Take the side road up to Pico El Águila (a 20-minute walk), crowned with a communications mast, to reach a beautiful *páramo* (open highland) filled with *frailejones* (espeletia) and great panoramic views.

Back at the pass, walk 5km south to **Laguna Mucubají** (3540m). The path leads through another splendid *páramo*, before descending to the Barinas road and the lake, one of the largest in the region. There is an Inparques post here that will provide information about the area. From here, it's an hour's walk through reforested pine woods to **Laguna Negra**, a small, beautiful mountain lake with amazingly dark water. A 45-minute walk further uphill will bring you to another fine lake, **Laguna Los Patos**.

A trail from Laguna Mucubají leads 7km south up to the top of **Pico Mucuñuque**

(4672m), the highest peak in this range, which is known as the Serranía de Santo Domingo. The roundtrip will take a good part of the day. It's a rather difficult hike, as the trail is not clear in the upper reaches and you have to ascend over 1100m from the lagoon. Ask for detailed instructions at the Inparques post by Laguna Mucubají.

Some of Mérida's tour operators can provide information about these and other do-it-yourself tours. Don't ignore their comments about safety measures. If you are going to stay overnight in the Parque Nacional Sierra Nevada you need a permit from Inparques (so far, La Culata doesn't require permits). Permits are issued on the spot by Inparques outlets at the park's entry points, including one next to the cable car station (see p184), one in La Mucuy and another one by Laguna Mucabají (you have to show your passport and pay $1 per person per night for Mucabají). Permits should be returned after completing your hike – this is to make sure nobody is left wandering lost in the mountains.

MOUNTAIN BIKING

Several tour companies in Mérida organize bike trips and rent bikes. Shop around, as bicycle quality and rental prices may differ substantially between the companies. One of the popular bike tours is the loop around the remote mountain villages south of Mérida known as Pueblos del Sur. Ask for recommended bike trips to do on your own. Bike rental is around $8 to $10 a day.

PARAGLIDING

Most visitors glide on tandem gliders with a skilled pilot, so no previous experience is necessary. The usual starting point for flights is Las González, an hour-long jeep ride from Mérida, from where you glide for 20 to 30 minutes down 850 vertical meters. The cost of the flight ($40 to $50) includes jeep transportation.

You can also take a paragliding course that takes four to seven days, covering theory (available in English) and practice (including solo flights); the cost is $250 to $350. The course allows you to fly solo, but you'll still have to rent a paraglider ($50 a flight, $200 a week, plus the cost of transportation).

Paragliding is offered by most all-round Mérida tour companies (p187), which either

THE ANDES

have their own pilots or will contract one for you.

RAFTING & CANYONING
Rafting is organized on some rivers on the southern slopes of the Andes. It can be included in a tour to Los Llanos or done separately as a two-day rafting tour ($80 to $100 per person). It's normally a wet-season activity, but some rivers allow for year-round rafting.

The newest craze, described by travelers as 'awesome, terrifying, beautiful, insane but amazing' or 'quite possibly the maddest thing you can do without getting killed,' is canyoning – climbing, rappelling and hiking down a river canyon. Full-day, all-inclusive canyoning tours go for around $50. Arassari Trek offers the most adventurous rafting and canyoning tours (see p187).

WILDLIFE WATCHING
The best wildlife-watching destination is Los Llanos, an immense plain savannah south of the Andes. Los Llanos is Venezuela's great repository of wildlife, particularly birds, but it's also excellent ground to get a close touch with caimans, capybaras, piranhas and anacondas, to name just a few. Several ecotourist camps in Los Llanos offer wildlife-watching tours on their ranches (see Hatos p224), but they are expensive ($80 to $150 per person per day). Mérida's tour companies (p186) provide similarly fascinating excursions for $30 to $40 per day. They are normally offered as four-day all-inclusive packages.

FISHING
Anglers may be interested in trout fishing. The most popular places to fish are Laguna Mucubají and the nearby **Laguna La Victoria**, and, to a lesser extent, **Laguna Negra** and **Laguna Los Patos** (see p195 for details on how to get there). The fishing season runs from mid-March to the end of September. You need a permit from the **Ministerio de Producción y Comercio** (☎ 263-9152, 263-5258) in Mérida. The permit costs $12 and allows angling in Mérida state's national parks. Bring your own fishing equipment. You can buy some gear in Mérida, but don't rely on renting the stuff from tour companies or anywhere else.

TRUJILLO STATE

VALERA
☎ 0271 / pop 145,000

Surrounded by mountains and blessed with warm, invigorating weather, this pleasant town is the northern gateway to the Andes and a springboard for traveling around the region. Conveniently, Valera is an important transportation hub, providing regular bus connections within the region and beyond, and has the state's only airport. While the fresh mountain air carries the scent of adventures ahead, the town itself is worth a quick look.

Founded in 1820, Valera began to grow rapidly after the construction of the Trans-Andean highway was completed in the 1920s. Today it's the largest and most important urban center in Trujillo state and the state's only real city – far larger and more populous than the state capital, Trujillo.

Information

INTERNET ACCESS
Cybermax (cnr Av Bolívar & Calle 8)
Cybertek (Centro Comercial Edivica, Av Bolívar btwn Calles 8 & 9)
motorway.net (Centro Comercial Iglio, cnr Av Bolívar & Calle 7)

MEDICAL SERVICES
Hospital Central de Valera (☎ 225-8976; Final Calle 6)

MONEY
Banco de Venezuela (Plaza Bolívar)
Banco Provincial (cnr Av Bolívar & Calle 9)
Banesco (cnr Av Bolívar & Calle 6)
Corp Banca (cnr Av Bolívar & Calle 5)

POST
Ipostel (cnr Av 11 & Calle 7)

TELEPHONE
CANTV (Centro Comercial Edivica, Av Bolívar btwn Calles 8 & 9)
Telcel (Calle 9 btwn Avs 9 & 10)

TOURIST INFORMATION
Centro de Información Turística (☎ 225-4286; Av Bolívar btwn Calles 10 & 11; ☷ 8am-noon & 2-5pm Mon-Fri)

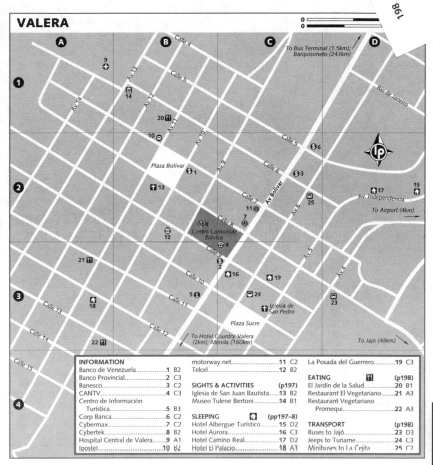

VALERA

To Bus Terminal (1.5km);
Barquisimeto (243km)

Río de Janeiro

Plaza Bolívar

Av Independencia
To Airport (4km)

Centro Comercial
Bolívia

Iglesia de
San Pedro

Plaza Sucre

To Hotel Country Valera
(2km); Mérida (160km)

To Jajó (48km)

INFORMATION		
Banco de Venezuela	1	B2
Banco Provincial	2	C3
Banesco	3	C2
CANTV	4	C3
Centro de Información		
Turística	5	B3
Corp Banca	6	C2
Cybermax	7	C2
Cybertek	8	B2
Hospital Central de Valera	9	A1
Ipostel	10	B2

motorway.net	11	C2
Telcel	12	B2

SIGHTS & ACTIVITIES	(p197)	
Iglesia de San Juan Bautista	13	B2
Museo Tulene Bertoni	14	B1

SLEEPING	(pp197–8)	
Hotel Albergue Turístico	15	D2
Hotel Aurora	16	C3
Hotel Camino Real	17	D2
Hotel El Palacio	18	A3

La Posada del Guerrero	19	C3

EATING	(p198)	
El Jardín de la Salud	20	B1
Restaurant El Vegetariano	21	A3
Restaurant Vegetariano		
Promequi	22	A3

TRANSPORT	(p198)	
Buses to Jajó	23	D3
Jeeps to Tuname	24	C3
Minibuses to La Cejita	25	C2

THE ANDES

Sights

Erected in 1925, the neo-Gothic **Iglesia de San Juan Bautista** (Plaza Bolívar) takes pride in being the tallest church in the Venezuelan Andes, its twin towers rising up to 44m. The interior is illuminated through large, colorful stained-glass windows commissioned in Germany.

The **Museo Tulene Bertoni** (cnr Av 13 & Calle 6; admission free; 8am-5:30pm Mon-Fri) has a varied collection related to the history of the city and the region, including pre-Hispanic pottery, religious paintings from the colonial era, and old weapons and furniture. Note the fossils of mollusks dating back to the period when the region was a seabed, about 80 million years ago.

Sleeping

La Posada del Guerrero (231-2062; Calle 9 No 5-38; d with fan $8-10, with air-con $10-12;) Nestled in a quiet street, yet very central, this small hotel has well-kept rooms and its own budget restaurant. It's one of the best backpacker options.

Hotel Aurora (231-5675; Av Bolívar btwn Calles 9 & 10; d/tr $11/13;) This is not a memorable establishment, but it's cheap, and has clean rooms and an inexpensive restaurant. Check the air-con – it can be pretty noisy.

Hotel Albergue Turístico (225-5016, 415-0216; Av Independencia; d/tr $15/18;) Albergue is good value: 20 spacious rooms with newly revamped bathrooms and lots of hot water, and a simple restaurant.

Hotel El Palacio (☎ 225-2923; Centro Comercial Miami Center, Calle 12 btwn Avs 10 & 11; d $22-24, tr/ste $27/28; P 🐱) A palace it is not, but nonetheless it's a reasonable 45-room hotel with a restaurant, overlooking a colorful and lively street market area.

Hotel Camino Real (☎ 225-2815, 221-4817; Av Independencia; d $30; P 🐱) This three-star, 13-story hotel, its exterior painted in an abstract geometric style, has 60 cozy rooms, an inexpensive restaurant and an attractive rooftop bar with large soft armchairs, ice-cold beer and great panoramic vistas.

Hotel Country Valera (☎ 231-5612, 231-0377; Av Bolívar; s/d/ste $20/26/32; P 🐱) On the outskirts of the city, 2km southwest of the center, the Country Valera is a comfortable modern place and a good choice if you don't mind staying away from the downtown. It has its own restaurant.

Eating

The city center is packed with eating outlets, though there's nothing really to write home about. Take note, that all the hotels listed above have their own restaurants. Vegetarians have quite a choice as well, including:

El Jardín de la Salud (Av 11 No 6-24; set menú $2-3; 🌣 lunch Mon-Fri)

Restaurant El Vegetariano (Calle 11 No 11-21; set menú $2-3; 🌣 lunch Mon-Fri)

Restaurant Vegetariano Promequi (Calle 13 No 8-77; set menú $2-3; 🌣 lunch Mon-Fri)

Getting There & Away

AIR

The **Aeropuerto Antonio Nicolás Briceño** (☎ 244-1378) is about 4km northeast of the city center. A taxi will cost about $4, or you can take a La Cejita minibus from the corner of Av 6 and Calle 6. **Avior** (☎ 244-0055) has four flights daily to Caracas ($61 to $78), from where you can continue to other cities.

BUS

The **Terminal de Pasajeros** (☎ 225-5009; Av México) is about 1.5km northeast of the center. To get there, take the northbound city bus marked 'Terminal' from Av Bolívar.

There are a dozen buses a day to Caracas ($10 to $16, 9½ hours, 584km); most depart in the evening, and all go via Barquisimeto, Valencia and Maracay. Ordinary buses to Barquisimeto ($4.50, four hours, 243km) run every one to two hours. Expresos Valera

has half-hourly departures to Maracaibo ($5, four hours, 238km).

Transporte Barinas has four buses daily to Mérida ($5.50, five hours, 160km) along the spectacular Trans-Andean highway. The road winds almost 3500m up to Paso del Cóndor (at 4007m it is the highest road pass in Venezuela), before dropping 2400m down to Mérida. There are also por puesto taxis to Mérida ($8, four hours).

Por puesto minibuses to Trujillo ($0.75, 40 minutes, 35km) depart every 10 to 20 minutes from the bus terminal, and to Boconó ($2.50, 2¼ hours, 106km) every 30 minutes.

Buses to Jajó ($1, 1½ hours, 48km) depart from the corner of Calle 8 and Av 4 (locally known as Punto de Mérida) every 40 minutes from 7am to 5pm.

Two or three jeeps a day to Tuñame ($1.50, two hours, 74km) depart from Av 6 between Calles 9 and 10.

TRUJILLO

☎ 0272 / pop 52,000

The capital of Trujillo state, Trujillo is noted for its attractive setting, agreeable climate, fine colonial architecture and the unhurried air of days gone by. It's a peaceful town, 450-years-old, just 35km northeast of Valera. A huge statue of the Virgin Mary watches over Trujillo, and provides visitors with bird's eye views of the town, the state and the mountains beyond.

Trujillo was the first town to be founded in the Venezuelan Andes (in 1557), but the continuous hostility of the local Cuica indigenous group caused it to be moved several times. It was called the 'portable city' because seven different locations were tried before the town was permanently established at its present site in 1570.

Located in a long narrow valley, El Valle de los Cedros, Trujillo has an unusual layout – it's only two blocks wide but extends more than 2km up the mountain gorge. Despite new suburbs at the foot of the historic sector, Trujillo remains a small and provincial place, in both appearance and spirit.

Information

INTERNET ACCESS

Ciber Café Los Balcones (Plaza Bolívar)

DMT Sistemas (Edificio Almendrón, cnr Av Bolívar & Calle Candelaria)

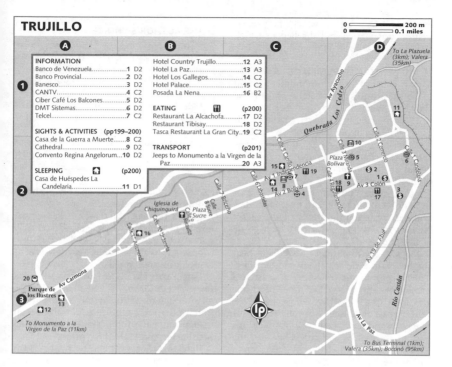

TRUJILLO

0 — 200 m
0 — 0.1 miles

INFORMATION
Banco de Venezuela...............1 D2
Banco Provincial.....................2 D2
Banesco.................................3 D2
CANTV..................................4 C2
Ciber Café Los Balcones..........5 D2
DMT Sistemas.......................6 D2
Telcel..................................7 C2

SIGHTS & ACTIVITIES (pp199–200)
Casa de la Guerra a Muerte......8 C2
Cathedral...............................9 D2
Convento Regina Angelorum...10 D2

SLEEPING (p200)
Casa de Huéspedes La
Candelaria.......................11 D1

Hotel Country Trujillo.............12 A3
Hotel La Paz.........................13 A3
Hotel Los Gallegos.................14 C2
Hotel Palace.........................15 C2
Posada La Nena.....................16 B2

EATING (p200)
Restaurant La Alcachofa.........17 D2
Restaurant Tibisay.................18 D2
Tasca Restaurant La Gran City..19 C2

TRANSPORT (p201)
Jeeps to Monumento a la Virgen de la
Paz....................................20 A3

To La Plazuela
(3km); Valera
(35km)

To Monumento a la
Virgen de la Paz (11km)

To Bus Terminal (1km);
Valera (35km); Boconó (95km)

MONEY
Banco de Venezuela (cnr Av Colón & Calle Comercio)
Banco Provincial (Av Bolívar btwn Calle Comercio
& Calle Miranda)
Banesco (Av 19 de Abril)

TELEPHONE
CANTV (cnr Av Bolívar & Calle Carrillo)
Telcel (cnr Av Independencia & Calle Carrillo)

TOURIST INFORMATION
Corporación Trujillana de Turismo (☎ 236-1455,
236-1277; ☺ 8am-noon & 1-4pm Mon-Fri) The office is
in La Plazuela (see p200).

Sights
OLD TOWN
Trujillo's historic quarter stretches along
two parallel east–west streets, Av Independencia and Av Bolívar. In the eastern
part of the sector is the leafy **Plaza Bolívar**,
the town's historical heart and still the nucleus
of the city's life today. The mighty **Catedral**
(Plaza Bolívar), completed in 1662, has a lovely
whitewashed facade and some charming
old altarpieces inside.

There are some graceful historic buildings around the plaza, including the **Convento Regina Angelorum** (cnr Av Independencia & Calle
Miranda). Built in the early 17th century as a
convent, it's now the public library. Do go
inside to see its splendid courtyard. You'll
find more surviving colonial houses west
of the plaza, on Av Independencia and Av
Bolívar. The best approach to sightseeing is
to take either of the two streets uphill and
return down by the other one. They merge
10 blocks further up to become Av Carmona, but the best architecture is within a
few blocks of the plaza.

The **Casa de la Guerra a Muerte** (☎ 236-6879;
Av Independencia No 5-29; admission free; ☺ 9am-5pm
Mon-Fri, 9am-noon Sat & Sun), also known as the
Centro de Historia, houses an interesting
history museum. Exhibits include old maps,
armor, period furniture, pre-Columbian
pottery and even a fully equipped kitchen
with an historic stove. It was in this house
on June 15, 1813, that Bolívar signed the
controversial Decreto de Guerra a Muerte
(Decree of War to the Death), under which
all captured royalists were to be summarily

THE ANDES

executed. The table on which the proclamation was signed and the bed in which Bolívar slept are part of the exhibition.

MONUMENTO A LA VIRGEN DE LA PAZ

This gigantic, 47m-high monument is said to be the world's tallest **Statue of the Virgin Mary** (admission $0.75; ☺ 9am-5pm). Inaugurated in 1983, the massive, concrete statue stands on a 1700m-high mountaintop overlooking Trujillo, 11km southwest of the town. The internal elevator and staircase provide access to five *miradores* (viewpoints), the highest of which peeks out through the Virgin's eyes. You can enjoy views over much of Trujillo state, and on a clear day, you can even see the peaks of the Sierra Nevada de Mérida and a part of Lago de Maracaibo.

Jeeps to the monument leave from next to the Parque de los Ilustres in Trujillo. They depart upon collecting at least five passengers and charge $0.80 per head one way for a 20-minute trip. On weekdays the wait may be quite long, but you can pay for five seats and have the jeep to yourself. It's best to start early, as later in the day the Virgin is often shrouded by clouds, even in the dry season. If you feel like some exercise, the monument is a two- to three-hour walk uphill from town.

LA PLAZUELA

This tiny colonial quarter, 3km north of Trujillo on the Valera road, was once a town in its own right, but is now Trujillo's distant suburb. Partially rebuilt and restored to its former glory, La Plazuela is not much more than one cobbled street, complete with a church, and red-tiled whitewashed houses, which now shelter a few shops and the tourist office. Enjoy a cup of coffee at an outdoor table in this timeless little plaza.

Getting to La Plazuela is easy – just get off the Valera–Trujillo por puesto there. Getting away may be a bit harder, as most por puestos come through full and won't stop.

Sleeping

Casa de Huéspedes La Candelaria (Calle Candelaria; d $10-13; P ☺) Two blocks downhill from Plaza Bolívar, this inviting, 15-room new hotel is excellent value. Rooms are spotless

---

THE AUTHOR'S CHOICE

Hotel Country Trujillo (☎ 236-3942, 236-3646; Av Carmona; d $21-27, tr $33; P ☺ ☎) The Country is definitely the best place in town, offering spacious air-conditioned rooms that have wide, comfortable beds, fridges and stylish furniture. It has a fair-sized swimming pool (which can be used by nonguests for $4), and a relaxed restaurant by the pool that serves both local and international cuisine.

---

and quiet and have fridge and private bathrooms with hot water.

Posada La Nena (☎ 236-7009; Calle Arismendi; tr $9; ☒) Owned and managed by a friendly naive-style painter, La Nena has five neat rooms and it's one of the very few specifically nonsmoking places.

Hotel Palace (☎ 236-6936; cnr Av Independencia & Calle Carrillo; s/tr $5/9, d $7-8) The name might be an overstatement to say the least, but the hotel has rooms with fans, set around an enchanting patio full of flowers and drying bedsheets. And look at the prices!

Hotel Los Gallegos (☎ 236-3193; Av Independencia No 5-65; s/d with fan $9/10, d with air-con $12-14; ☒) Convenient location, adequate standards and budget rates make this 32-room hotel a reasonable choice.

Hotel La Paz (☎ 236-4864, 236-5157; cnr Calle 15 & Av Carmona; d/tr/q $15/18/22; P ☒) This seven-story edifice, a bit out of proportion for this site, offers 28 spacious suites, though they are rather on the basic side and pretty worn out.

Eating

Restaurant Tibisay (cnr Calle Regularización & Av Colón; mains $2-4) Just behind the cathedral, Tibisay is consistently popular among locals for its straightforward, cheap, tasty meals.

Restaurant La Alcachofa (Av Colón btwn Calle Comercio & Calle Miranda; set menú $2; ☺ lunch) Simple and modest, this is the only vegetarian spot in town, serving a filling *menú ejecutivo* (set meal) at lunch only.

Tasca Restaurant La Gran City (☎ 236-5254; Av Independencia; set menú $2.50, mains $4-7) Perhaps nothing particularly special by Caracas standards, but here it's one of the best eateries in town, and it also offers a solid *menú ejecutivo* for $2.50, something which is hard to get in Caracas for this price.

Getting There & Away

The **Terminal de Pasajeros** (Av La Paz) is 1km northeast of the town's center, beyond Río Castán, and is accessible by urban minibuses. The terminal is rather quiet, and the only really frequent connection is with Valera ($0.75, 40 minutes, 35km). A few night buses go to Caracas ($10 to $14, 9½ hours, 589km). Transportation to Boconó ($2.50, two hours, 95km) is infrequent and thins out in the early afternoon. You may need to go to Valera, from where minibuses to Boconó depart regularly until about 5pm.

BOCONÓ

☎ 0272 / pop 48,000

Boconó is a handsome, tranquil town nestled on the bank of the Río Boconó amid verdant hills. Simón Bolívar named the place the 'Garden of Venezuela,' and it indeed lives up to its name. Enjoying fertile soil and a mild climate (with a mean temperature of around 20°C), Boconó is famed for its lush natural vegetation and cultivation of a variety of crops, including coffee, fruit and vegetables. The town is 95km southeast of Trujillo, and the journey there, via a winding mountain road, is a spectacular attraction in itself.

Boconó is an important regional craft center, known particularly for its weaving, basketry and pottery, and there are plenty of home workshops and craft shops in town. The surrounding region is dotted with pretty little towns such as San Miguel, Tostós and Niquitao (see p203), for which Boconó is a convenient jumping-off point.

Boconó was founded in 1560 on one of the sites chosen for Trujillo, but when the state capital made one of its several moves, some of the inhabitants decided to stay on. Isolated for centuries from the outside world, Boconó grew slowly and remained largely self-sufficient. It wasn't until the 1930s that the Trujillo–Boconó road was built, linking the town to the state capital and the rest of the country, although a sense of isolation is still palpable around the place.

Information

INTERNET ACCESS

Café Cibertzion (Centro Comercial Doña Blanca, Calle Vargas)

MEDICAL SERVICES

Hospital Rafael Rangel (☎ 652-2513; Av Rotaria)

MONEY

Banco de Venezuela (Av Sucre btwn Calle Bolívar & Calle Jáuregui)
Banco Provincial (cnr Av Independencia & Calle Vargas)
Banesco (cnr Av Independencia & Calle Vargas)

POST

Ipostel (cnr Calle Bolívar & Av Sucre)

TELEPHONE

CANTV (Plaza Bolívar)
Telcel (cnr Calle Vargas & Av Independencia)

Sights

The **Museo Trapiche de los Clavo** (☎ 652-3655; Av Rotaria; admission free; 9am noon & 3 6pm Mon-Fri, 10am-6pm Sat & Sun) occupies the walled-in compound of a 19th-century sugarcane hacienda. The core of the museum is the original sugarcane mill *(trapiche)* and exhibits related to traditional sugar production, but there's more to see here. One of the buildings features temporary exhibitions, while another shelters several craft shops. In the southwestern corner is a pleasant open-air restaurant, whereas in the northern end are craft workshops – look for the textile workshop, where you can see artisans weaving rags and blankets on their archaic rustic looms.

The **Ateneo de Boconó** (☎ 652-2592; Calle Páez) is another place where you can see local weavers at work in their textile workshop on the upper floor. The Ateneo runs arts-and-crafts exhibitions from time to time. Down the road from the Ateneo is the **Paseo Artesanal Fabricio Ojeda** (cnr Calle Páez & Av Cuatricentenario), a craft market featuring a collection of craft stands.

The small **Museo Campesino Tiscachic** (☎ 652-3313; Calle Tiscachic; admission free; 9am-3pm Mon-Fri) has quite an interesting exhibition of crafts – mostly woodcarving, pottery and basketry – fashioned by local artisans. It's in the Centro de Servicios Campesinos Tiscachic, 150m northeast of town past the bridge and off the road to Valera. The center hosts a lively food market on Saturday.

Sleeping

Posada Machinipé (☎ 652-1506; Calle Bolívar No 6-49; d/tr/q $12/16/18) The Machinipé is a tastefully

THE ANDES

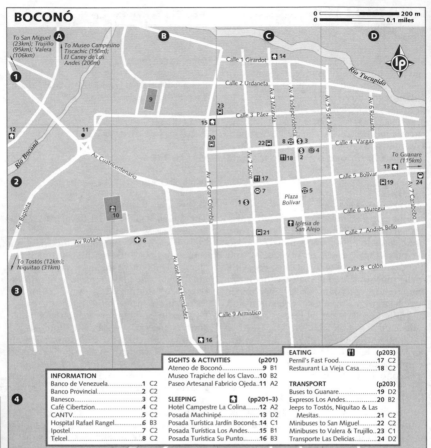

BOCONÓ

0 _____ 200 m
0 _____ 0.1 miles

To San Miguel (23km); Trujillo (95km); Valera (106km)

To Museo Campesino Tiscachic (150m); El Caney de los Andes (200m)

Río Tucupido

Calle 1 Girardot

Calle 2 Urdaneta

Calle 3 Páez

Av 3 Miranda

Av 4 Independencia

Av 5 5 de Julio

Av 6 Ricaurte

Río Boconó

Av Cuatricentenario

Av 2 Sucre

Calle 4 Vargas

To Guanare (115km)

Calle 5 Bolívar

Av 7 Carabobo

Av 1 Gran Colombia

Calle 6 Jáuregui

Plaza Bolívar

Av Baptista

To Tostós (12km); Niquitao (31km)

Av Rotaria

Iglesia de San Alejo

Calle 7 Andrés Bello

Calle 8 Colón

Av José María Hernández

Calle 9 Armístico

INFORMATION	
Banco de Venezuela	1 C2
Banco Provincial	2 C2
Banesco	3 C2
Café Cibertzion	4 C2
CANTV	5 C2
Hospital Rafael Rangel	6 B3
Ipostel	7 C2
Telcel	8 C2

SIGHTS & ACTIVITIES	(p201)
Ateneo de Boconó	9 B1
Museo Trapiche del los Clavo	10 B2
Paseo Artesanal Fabricio Ojeda	11 A2

SLEEPING	(pp201–3)
Hotel Campestre La Colina	12 A2
Posada Machinipé	13 D2
Posada Turística Jardín Boconés	14 C1
Posada Turística Los Andes	15 B1
Posada Turística Su Punto	16 B3

EATING	(p203)
Pernil's Fast Food	17 C2
Restaurant La Vieja Casa	18 C2

TRANSPORT	(p203)
Buses to Guanare	19 D2
Expresos Los Andes	20 B2
Jeeps to Tostós, Niquitao & Las Mesitas	21 C2
Minibuses to San Miguel	22 C2
Minibuses to Valera & Trujillo	23 C1
Transporte Las Delicias	24 D2

decorated family home that offers five small rooms to guests. The friendly owners are knowledgeable about the town and state, and can provide information. They can also organize tours around the regional attractions.

Posada Turística Los Andes (☎ 652-1100; Calle Páez No 1-08; s/d/tr/q without bathroom $6/7/8/10, with bathroom $7/8/10/12) A tip for the cheapest-place-in-town hunters, this is a very rustic yet acceptable spot and even has hot water. It offers absolute bargain rates for all kinds of rooms.

Posada Turística Su Punto (☎ 652-1047; Av José María Hernández; d/tr $10/16; P) This new posada has four spotless rooms in two bungalows, and a good restaurant that specializes in

chicken and is decorated with antiques and crafts.

Hotel Campestre La Colina (☎ 652-2695; www .hotel-lacolina.com.ve; Vía Las Guayabitas; d $22; P) Set on a slope next to the river, this relaxing

---

THE AUTHOR'S CHOICE

Posada Turística Jardín Boconés (☎ 652-0171; Calle Girardot No 3-05; d/tr/q $10/12/13) This restored 100-year-old house has a leafy central garden shaded by two old mango trees – it's no doubt a romantic place. It has eight cheerful, tranquil rooms, all with private bathroom and hot water. Meals are available on request.

THE ANDES

place with a countryside feel has a colony of chalets scattered over its spacious grounds, a hotel building overlooking the river, and its own restaurant. It's an ideal place for motorists, but will also perfectly suit travelers without their own wheels.

Eating

Restaurant La Vieja Casa (Av Miranda No 4-29; mains $3-6) This atmospheric old-fashioned restaurant is tastefully adorned with antiques, and you'll even find an old piano in one of its four cozy rooms. It serves hearty Venezuelan food.

Pernil's Fast Food (cnr Calle Bolívar & Av Sucre; snacks $2-4) This smart, modern new corner spot has already conquered local stomachs thanks to its tasty sandwiches, hamburgers, *arepas* (filled maize pancake) and *shawarmas* (Arab sandwich with pieces of beef/chicken served in pitta bread).

El Caney de Los Andes (Calle Tiscachic; mains $3-6) Come to eat, drink and maybe dance in this huge rustic hut thatched with palm leaves, right behind the Museo Campesino Tiscachic. It has become popular for its delicious *carne en barra* (beef grilled on a stick), but it's equally good for a drinking session, particularly at the weekend, when there's live music (*joropo, gaita*, mariachi) till late, sometimes till dawn.

Getting There & Away

The bus terminal is being built in the southern part of Boconó, but it may still be a while before it opens. So far, transportation companies have their own offices scattered throughout the central streets, from where their vehicles depart.

Minibuses to Valera ($2.50, 2¼ hours, 106km) depart from Calle Páez as soon as they're full (roughly every half-hour) until about 5pm. From the same spot, there are minibuses to Trujillo ($2.50, two hours, 95km), but they are not as regular and stop running earlier.

There are a few nightly buses to Caracas ($9.50 to $13, 10 hours, 542km), operated by two companies: Transporte Las Delicias, Calle Bolívar, and Expresos Los Andes, Av Colombia. They all go via Guanare. Buses to Guanare ($3, 3½ hours, 115km) also depart from Av Ricaurte until 3pm. If you miss the last one, you can catch a Caracas-bound bus. Minibuses to San Miguel ($0.75,

40 minutes, 27km) depart from Calle Vargas every hour or so.

Jeeps to Niquitao ($1, 50 minutes, 31km) depart from Av Sucre about every 30 minutes until 5pm or 6pm weekdays. At the weekend, they leave when full (every one to two hours). The Niquitao jeeps don't enter Tostós, but there are direct jeeps to Tostós ($0.50, 20 minutes, 12km) departing from the same stop. Also from this stop are jeeps to Las Mesitas ($2, 1½ hours, 44km), beyond Niquitao. In theory, three jeeps run per day, at 1pm, 3pm and 5pm, but only the first two are reliable.

SAN MIGUEL

The tiny town of San Miguel is famous for its colonial church, the **Iglesia de San Miguel** (☽ 9am-noon & 2-5pm Mon-Fri, 9:30am-noon Sat, 11am-2pm Sun), an austere, squat structure dating from around 1760. Its unusual features include roofed external corridors on both sides and a Latin-cross layout, a design rarely used in Venezuela. However, the church's star attraction is its extraordinary 18th-century retable in the high altar. Painted with decorative motifs in bright colors in a charming naive style, this is one of the most beautiful, folksy retables in the country. Even if you're not a great fan of churches, this one is worth a detour – San Miguel is just 27km north of Boconó through bucolic countryside.

There's more to see in the church, including two side retables in the transept, made in the same style as the main one, though a bit more modest. And don't miss the statue of the blind Santa Lucía holding her eyes on a plate, on the left side of the arch leading to the chancel. It's a singularly impressive sight. Use the opening hours as guidelines only and ask around for the priest if you find the church locked.

The town's main event is the **Romería de los Pastores y los Reyes Magos** (Pilgrimage of the Shepherds and Magi), celebrated annually from January 4 to 7.

Sleeping & Eating

Opposite the church, the **Hostería San Miguel** (☎ 0416-772-8398; Plaza Bolívar; d $10-12, tr $14) is the only place to stay in town. It's pretty modest, but comfortable and not without charm. All its eight rooms have bathrooms with hot water, and the rooms upstairs also have balconies. Meals may be available by prior arrangement, though probably only in the high season.

Getting There & Away
San Miguel lies 4km off the Boconó–Trujillo road. The narrow, paved side road to the town branches off 23km from Boconó. Minibuses to Boconó ($0.75, 40 minutes, 27km) run every hour or so.

TOSTÓS
During Holy Week, diminutive Tostós is the focus of nationwide attention for its celebrations of **Vía Crucis Viviente**, a stunning Passion play re-enacting the last days of Christ's life. This blend of religious ceremony and popular theater, performed by locals who play the parts of Jesus, the apostles and Roman soldiers, is held on Good Friday. On that day the town fills up, and the crowd's emotions become almost hysterical when Christ is crucified. The rest of the year, Tostós is as it has been for 380 years: a sleepy town picturesquely tucked into the hillside.

The town is 12km southwest of Boconó and can be easily reached by regular por puesto jeeps ($0.50, 20 minutes).

NIQUITAO
☎ 0271 / pop 5000
Niquitao is another pretty colonial town, spectacularly set in a long valley surrounded by mighty mountains. Founded in 1625, it still has much of its historic fabric in place, particularly around Plaza Bolívar. The town sits at an altitude of nearly 2000m and has a typical mountain climate, with warm days and chilly nights – come prepared. It's a good base for excursions (see Around Niquitao this page).

Sleeping & Eating
Niquitao has a few posadas to stay in and most can provide meals.

Posada Turística Guirigay (☎ 885-2149; Av Bolívar; d $7-8, tr $10; P) Just one block south of the plaza, Guirigay is arguably the best value in town, providing reasonable comfort at very low rates, and a restaurant. Its five rooms are set around a central patio, and all have bathrooms and hot water.

Posada Mamá Chepy (☎ 885-2173; Calle Páez; r per person $3.50) About 400m south of Plaza Bolívar, the friendly Mamá Chepy is the cheapest and most basic place. It has five very rustic rooms – two with bathrooms, three without – and can prepare meals on request.

Posada Turística Niquitao (☎ 885-2042; Plaza Bolívar; d $20-28, q $32; P) Set in a meticulously restored historic mansion, reputedly almost 400 years old, the Niquitao is the most stylish and elegant lodging option. Its rooms are comfortable and spotless, and its own restaurant specializes in local cuisine.

Getting There & Away
Jeeps (taking up to 12 passengers) service Niquitao from Boconó ($1, 50 minutes, 31km) every 30 minutes on weekdays and every one to two hours at the weekend.

From Niquitao there is a 13km road (partly paved but in bad shape) winding uphill to Las Mesitas. Jeeps service this route from Boconó (p203). Beyond Las Mesitas, a rough road leads to the town of Tuñame (transportation is scarce on this stretch), from where a better road continues downhill to Jajó. Tuñame has a couple of basic posadas and a jeep link to Valera.

AROUND NIQUITAO
Niquitao is a convenient base for trips to the surrounding mountains, including Trujillo state's highest peak, **La Teta de Niquitao** (4006m). You can walk there from Niquitao, but it will take two days roundtrip, so be prepared for camping. You can also go by jeep; the day trip to the top will include a two- to three-hour jeep ride uphill via Las Mesitas to the Llano de la Teta, followed by an hour's walk to the summit.

Another possibility is to climb **Pico Guirigay** (3870m). It's also a long, hard hike, or an easy day trip by jeep plus an hour's walk to the top. Jeep excursions can be arranged through hotel managers in Niquitao, who can also suggest other interesting destinations in the region. A jeep taking up to 10 persons will cost roughly $70 to $100 for a full-day trip (check tour prices offered by Posada Machinipé in Boconó p201). Horse-riding trips can also be arranged in Niquitao.

For shorter excursions around Niquitao you won't need a jeep or a guide. One good day trip is to **Viaducto Agrícola**, a spectacular old iron bridge over the lush Quebrada El Molino. You can go down to the stream

THE ANDES

of El Molino, 80m below the bridge, and take a refreshing bath. The bridge is on the Niquitao–Las Mesitas road, a 30-minute walk from Niquitao.

In the same area, a bit further up the road, is the site of the **Batalla de Niquitao**, which took place on July 2, 1813, and was one of the important battles of the War of Independence. The battlefield is a memorial site, with busts of the battle heroes.

Another easy trip out of Niquitao is to **Las Pailas**, scenic waterfalls in the Quebrada Tiguaní that are a leisurely walk uphill from the town. You can bathe here too, though the water is pretty cold.

JAJÓ
☎ 0271 / pop 4000

Set amid gorgeous green mountains, Jajó is one of the finest small colonial towns in Trujillo state. Established in 1611, the town has preserved much of its old architecture and atmosphere – its prettiest part lies just north of Plaza Bolívar.

Sleeping & Eating
In the region Jajó there a few places to stay and they either have their own restaurants or are willing to provide meals.

Posada Pueblo Escondido (☎ 0414-971-7841; Plaza Bolívar; r $10) This two-story colonial building, next to the church, has four simple rooms with bathroom, to sleep up to four persons. The friendly owners can provide information about the region and will be happy to cook for you if you wish.

Posada de Jajó (Plaza Bolívar; d/tr $9/10) Set in another colonial building on the plaza (recognizable by its balcony), this six-room place is on the basic side but has much olde-worlde charm. Señora Amparo, who runs the posada, can provide home-cooked meals, but let her know in advance.

Hotel Turístico Jajó (☎ 0416-771-1127; Plaza Bolívar; d $9-10, tr $12) The only modern building on the square, this three-story, 17-room hotel spoils the appearance of the plaza but is otherwise OK, and provides good vistas over the square from its front rooms – be sure to ask for one of them. It has its own restaurant, which serves good trout.

Posada Marysabel (☎ 0416-871-3233; Calle Páez; d $10-13, tr/q $16/19; [P]) Two short blocks north of Plaza Bolívar, the eight-room Marysabel offers reasonable standards, though some

rooms don't have windows – have a look around the place and choose the room. It too has its own restaurant, conveniently open for breakfast as well.

Getting There & Away
The usual point of departure for Jajó is Valera ($1, 1½ hours, 48km). Buses run every 40 minutes till about 5pm in both directions.

Jajó is linked by an interesting but rough mountain road to Boconó (via Tuñame, Las Mesitas and Niquitao) that climbs nearly as high as 3800m. There are jeeps to Tuñame from Valera, but no regular transportation further on to Las Mesitas. See Valera (p196) and Niquitao (p204) for further information.

TÁCHIRA STATE

Táchira is as yet rarely visited by travelers, just transited. Its national parks are relatively unexplored and don't have facilities, and there were no tours to them at the time of research.

SAN CRISTÓBAL
☎ 0276 / pop 350,000

Spread over a mountain slope at an altitude of about 800m, San Cristóbal has a scenic location and agreeable climate. Called 'La Ciudad de la Cordialidad' (Cordial City), it's a lively, modern city with steep streets, leafy plazas, cordial inhabitants and some tourist attractions. Stop here for a day to have a quick look around the place, or stay longer in January, when the city goes mad for two weeks celebrating its Feria de San Sebastián.

Founded in 1561 by Juan de Maldonado, the town was ruled from Nueva Granada (present-day Colombia) for more than 200 years, but didn't grow any bigger than an obscure hamlet. In 1777 it came under Venezuelan administration, but remained small and linked to Colombia because of the lack of roads to anywhere in Venezuela. A trip to Caracas was at least a two-week boat expedition by river down to Lago de Maracaibo and then by sea along the coast. It wasn't until 1925 that the winding Trans-Andean road reached San Cristóbal from Mérida, and it was only in the 1950s that the Pan-American highway was completed,

THE ANDES

SAN CRISTÓBAL

0 — 200 m
0 — 0.1 miles

INFORMATION
Banco de Venezuela...............1 C3
Banco Provincial.....................2 B1
Banesco...................................3 C4
CANTV....................................4 B4
Centro de Contacto Atelcom...5 C2
Corp Banca.............................6 B3
Cybercafé Dinastía...................7 C1
Ipostel...............................(see 12)
Punto Net Cyber Café.............8 C4
Telcel......................................9 C3

SIGHTS & ACTIVITIES (p207)
Ateneo del Táchira.................10 C3
Cathedral...............................11 B4
Edificio Nacional....................12 A4
Museo de Artes Visuales y del
    Espacio.............................13 B4
Palacio de Gobierno...............14 D4

SLEEPING (pp207–8)
Hotel Horizonte......................15 B3
Hotel Parador del Hidalgo.......16 C4
Suite Ejecutivo Dinastía..........17 C1

EATING (p208)
El Bistrot del Gordo Barón.......18 B4
Restaurant La Bologna.............19 C4
Tienda Naturalista Tropical......20 B4
Tostadería Grecón..............(see 10)

To Hotel Grecón,
Tostadería Grecón
(100m); Puente
Libertador (5km)

To Barrio Obrero, Hotel
Valle de Santiago,
Posada Los Pirineos (1.5km); Cotatur, Posada
El Remanso (2.5km); Castillo de la Fantasía
(3km); Complejo Ferial (4km); Museo del
Táchira (5.5km)

Calle 15
Calle 14
Calle 13
Calle 12
Calle 11
Calle 10A
Calle 10
Calle 9
Calle 8
Calle 7
Calle 6
Calle 5
Calle 4

Plaza Páez
Iglesia La Ermita
(San Juan Bautista)

Plaza Galviras
Plaza San Carlos
Plaza La Libertad
Plaza Bolívar
Plaza Urdaneta
Plaza Maldonado
Plaza Bicentenario
Plaza Sucre

Carrera 1
Carrera 2
Carrera 3
Carrera 4
Carrera 6
Carrera 8
Carrera 9
Carrera 10
Carrera 11
Carrera 12

Av 5 Francisco de Hevia
Av 7 Isaías Medina Angarita

Centro Cívico
Iglesia de San José
Iglesia de San Antonio
Colegio María Auxiliadora

To Ciudad Bitácora
To Bus Terminal (2km);
Santo Domingo (38km)

To Posada Turística Don Manuel
(600m); Inparques (1km)

Palacio Episcopal

providing the city with a fast, lowland link to the center of the country.

Today, San Cristóbal is the capital of Táchira state and a thriving commercial center fueled by the proximity of Colombia, just 40km away. It's an important transit point on the Pan-American route between Venezuela and Colombia; you'll pass through if you are traveling to/from anywhere in Colombia except the Caribbean coast.

Orientation

San Cristóbal's historic quarter is centered on a triangle of three squares – Plaza Maldonado, Plaza Bolívar and Plaza Sucre – but the city has expanded in all directions far beyond its downtown area. The focus of the

new development has moved to the east and north, with Barrio Obrero (literally, 'Working Class Suburb'), 1.5km northeast of the center, becoming a trendy, upmarket district, not exactly what its name would suggest. Here is the cream of city's restaurants and nightclubs. The tourist office, Cotatur, is 1km further to the northeast.

Information

INTERNET ACCESS

Most cybercafés are in Barrio Obrero, with a couple in the city centre.

Centro de Contacto Atelcom (cnr Av 7 & Calle 12)
Ciudad Bitácora (Calle 11 btwn Carreras 21 & 22, Barrio Obrero; 9am-2am) Located in Barrio Obrero, this is the largest and oldest cybercafé.

THE ANDES

Cybercafé Dinastía (cnr Av 7 & Calle 14)
Punto Net Cyber Café (Calle 5 No 8-60)

MONEY
Banco de Venezuela (cnr Calle 8 & Carrera 9)
Banco Provincial (cnr Av 5 & Calle 15)
Banesco (cnr Av 7 & Calle 5)
Corp Banca (cnr Av 5 & Calle 8)

POST
Ipostel (Edificio Nacional, Calle 4 btwn Carreras 2 & 3)

TELEPHONE
CANTV (cnr Av 5 & Calle 5)
Telcel (Av 7 No 9-97)

TOURIST INFORMATION
Cotatur (☎ 357-9655, 357-9578; cnr Av España & Av Carabobo; 8am-noon & 2-5.30pm Mon-Fri) The tourist office is 2.5km northeast of the city center, accessible from the bus terminal or from buses in the center; look for the Línea Intercomunal white bus with green stripes. Cotatur has desks at the airport terminals of Santo Domingo and San Antonio, open during flight times only.
Inparques (☎ 347-8347; Parque Metropolitano, Av 19 de Abril; 8am-12:30pm & 2-6pm Mon-Fri) Just south of town, Inparques provides information about the national parks in the region.

Sights

San Cristóbal began its life around what is now Plaza Maldonado. The monumental, twin-towered **Catedral** was completed in the early 20th century, after the previous church had been wrecked by an earthquake. It houses the venerated statue of San Sebastián, the city's patron saint. Next door to the cathedral is the fine, neocolonial **Palacio Episcopal**. On the northern side of the plaza is the massive, late-19th-century **Edificio Nacional**, the city's largest historic building, today home to public offices, courts of law and the post office.

Plaza Bolívar is not a colonial square either. The oldest building here is the stylish **Ateneo del Táchira** (☎ 342-0536), built in 1907 as the Sociedad Salón de Lectura. Today it hosts a cultural center with its own art gallery and an auditorium staging theater performances and screening arthouse movies. Do go inside to see what's on.

There are more historic buildings on and around Plaza Sucre, including the large **Palacio de Gobierno**. Also known as the Palacio de los Leones, because of the stone lions on its roof, this palace-like edifice was built in the 1910s as a government house.

The new **Museo de Artes Visuales y del Espacio** (☎ 343-3102; cnr Carrera 6 & Calle 4; admission free; 9am-1pm & 3-7pm Tue-Sat), set in a beautiful 100-year-old, 14-room mansion, features changing exhibitions of painting and sculpture by local artists.

The **Complejo Ferial** (cnr Av España & Av Universidad), 4km northeast of the center, is a large fairground and sports complex, complete with exhibition halls, a stadium, a velodrome and Venezuela's second-largest bullring. About 1.5km north of the complex is the **Museo del Táchira** (☎ 353-0543; Final Av Universidad; admission free; 8am-5:30pm Tue-Fri, 10am-6pm Sat & Sun). Accommodated in a spacious old coffee and sugarcane hacienda, the museum features interesting exhibitions on the archaeology, history and ethnography of the region.

San Cristóbal's curiosity is the **Puente Libertador**, an old suspension bridge across the Río Torbes, constructed by the same company that built the Eiffel Tower. This intricate iron structure was brought from Europe and assembled in the 1920s, and has carried vehicular traffic ever since. The bridge is off Av Antonio José de Sucre, 5km north of the center; to get there, take any bus to Táriba, Cordero or Palmira.

Festivals

San Cristóbal's major annual bash is the **Feria de San Sebastián**, held in the second half of January. It includes agricultural and industrial fairs, bullfights, bicycle races and other sports events, a crafts fair, popular music, dances and parades, plus a lot of food and drink. Many events take place at the Complejo Ferial.

Sleeping

For upmarket accommodations, head to the northeastern suburbs, beyond Barrio Obrero. The city center has a good choice of inexpensive lodging but nothing really upscale.

Hotel Horizonte (☎ 341-9077; cnr Calle 7 & Carrera 4; s/d/tr $12/14/15) It's not a new hotel, but it's well maintained and reasonably clean, and all rooms have a fan and hot water.

Hotel Parador del Hidalgo (☎ 343-2839; Calle 7 No 9-35; s/tr, $7/12 d$8-10) This is an offer for rock-bottom budget travelers – 26 spartan yet acceptable rooms with a fan at a convenient central location.

Hotel Grecón (☎ 343-6017; Av 5 btwn Calles 15 & 16; d $12-18; ﹇❄﹈) One of the cheapest options for those who need air-con, Grecón, 100m north of the center, is a small hotel offering 20 spotless rooms.

Suite Ejecutivo Dinastía (☎ 343-9530; cnr Calle 13 & Av 7; s/d/tr $16/20/22; ﹇P﹈ ﹇❄﹈) An offspring of the more expensive Hotel Dinastía, one block to the north, this small place provides comfortable and quiet rooms (not suites as its name would suggest).

Posada Turística Don Manuel (☎ 347-8082; Carrera 10 No 1-63; s/d/tr $10/13/16) This is the cheapest of San Cristóbal's half a dozen posadas, and the one closest to the center – it's just a 10-minute walk south of the center. It's a family home with four simple rooms rented out to tourists. Guests can use the kitchen and fridge.

Posada El Remanso (☎ 342-1587; Av Principal de Pueblo Nuevo, Los Naranjos; d $20-22; ﹇❄﹈) This new small posada, in a quiet residential suburb close to the tourist office, has six rooms and can provide meals for guests.

Posada Los Pirineos (☎ 355-6528; posadapirineos@cantv.net; Av Francisco Cárdenas, Pirineos Parte Baja; d $40-52; ﹇❄﹈) San Cristóbal's best posada, Los Pirineos is a pretty, friendly place, conveniently set just a few blocks from Barrio Obrero. It has 15 plush rooms with wide beds and serves meals on request.

Hotel Valle de Santiago (☎ 342-5090; www.hotel-valledesantiago.com; Av Las Pilas, Santa Inés; d $70-75, ste $95; ﹇P﹈ ﹇✕﹈ ﹇❄﹈ ﹇🖵﹈) This is arguably the city's best hotel, set in a stylish brick building 1.5km northeast of the center. Modern,

small (25 rooms) and comfortable, it provides most facilities you'd wish for, including a well-appointed restaurant, lobby bar, gym, Internet access and nonsmoking rooms. Room rates include breakfast.

Eating

The city's main dining quarter is Barrio Obrero, which has loads of restaurants, including some of the best in town. A good place to start is Carrera 20, sarcastically nicknamed by the locals the 'Calle del Hambre' (Street of Starvation). The center also has lots of restaurants, though mostly budget ones, including numerous greasy spoons serving set lunches for $1.50 to $2.

Restaurant La Bologna (☎ 343-4450; Calle 5 No 8-54; mains $3-5) La Bologna serves solid economical food, for which it's consistently popular with locals, and deservedly so.

El Bistrot del Gordo Barón (☎ 353-3458; Carrera 4 No 5-34; pasta $3-5, mains $5-10; ﹇◷﹈ 11:30am-5pm Mon-Sat) This inviting bright locale with neat white tablecloths has an international menu (including fine seafood), but if you want to keep it on the cheap, go for the delicious pasta.

Tienda Naturalista Tropical (☎ 343-7481; Carrera 6 No 6-11; set menú $2) An oasis for vegetarians, Tropical serves hearty budget set-price meals at lunchtime, and snacks later during the afternoon.

Tostadería Grecón (☎ 343-6017; Av 5 btwn Calles 15 & 16; arepas $1-2) Come here for some of the best *arepas* in town, and what a choice of fillings!

Getting There & Away

AIR

San Cristóbal's airport, **Aeropuerto Base Buenaventura Vivas** (☎ 234-7013), is in Santo Domingo, about 38km southeast of the city, but not much air traffic goes through there. The airport in San Antonio del Táchira (p211) is far busier and just about the same distance from San Cristóbal.

BUS

The vast and busy **Terminal de Pasajeros** (☎ 346-5590; Av Manuel Felipe Rugeles, La Concordia) is 2km south of the city center and linked by frequent city bus services.

More than a dozen buses daily go to Caracas ($13 to $20, 13 hours, 825km). Most depart in the late afternoon or evening for

---

THE AUTHOR'S CHOICE

Castillo de la Fantasía (☎ 353-0848; www.castillodelafantasia.com; Av España, Pueblo Nuevo; s/d $60/65, ste $70-80; ﹇P﹈ ﹇❄﹈ ﹇🖵﹈) The 'Fantasy Castle' is an opulent eclectic mansion with much character and style. Built only in 1988, it will take you back in time a century or more with its 18 old-fashioned rooms (each different and individually named), stylish furniture and ancient statues. Yet it has most of the modern amenities, including noiseless air-conditioning and Jacuzzi. Breakfast is included in the room rates.

an overnight trip via El Llano highway. Ordinary buses to Barinas ($7, five hours, 313km) run every hour or so between 5am and 6:30pm.

Buses to Mérida ($7, five hours, 224km) go every 1½ hours from 5:30am to 7pm, but they may depart before their scheduled departure time if all seats are taken. The 7pm bus is unreliable if fewer than 10 passengers show up. Five buses depart nightly for Maracaibo ($10 to $13, eight hours, 439km).

Por puesto minibuses to San Antonio del Táchira ($1.25, 1¼ hours, 40km), on the Colombian border, run every 10 or 15 minutes; it's a spectacular but busy road.

SAN PEDRO DEL RÍO
☎ 0277 / pop 5000

The tiny town of San Pedro del Río is Táchira's little architectural gem. With its narrow cobblestone streets lined with red-tile roofed, single-story whitewashed houses, it looks like a typical old Spanish town straight out of a picture postcard. It has been extensively restored and is well cared for and clean. Particularly lovely is Calle Real, the town's central nerve, along which most craft shops and restaurants have nestled.

San Pedro has become a popular weekend haunt for Venezuelans from the region, mostly from San Cristóbal, 40km away. On these days, food and craft stalls open and the town blossoms. During the rest of the week, by contrast, San Pedro is an oasis of peace and solitude.

Sleeping
Posada Turística Mi Vieja Escuela (☎ 291-3720; cnr Calle Real & Carrera Calanzancio; s $10-12, tr/q $14/18) Set in a fine vintage house that was once a school, the Escuela has nine neat rooms with fans and all the charm of times gone by. A filling breakfast is available on request for $2.

Posada Turística Paseo La Chirirí (☎ 291-0157; Calle Los Morales No 1-27; d 10-13, tr/q $16/18) One block west of Plaza Bolívar, La Chirirí doesn't have the yesteryear's air of the Escuela, but has equally clean rooms and a craft shop.

Eating
Dining spots have mushroomed since tourists began to come, but most of them open only on weekends. Local specialties include the *gallina* (boiled and roasted hen) served with yucca, rice and salad, which can be found on the menu of most restaurants. The whole bird with accompaniments ($20) will feed four to six persons.

La Casona de los Abuelos (☎ 291-4830; cnr Calle Real & Carrera General Márquez; mains $3-7) Open more regularly than most other restaurants, this is a large, colonial-style mansion that serves typical local fare, including the *gallina*.

Other restaurants worth trying (on weekends only) include **Río de Las Casas** (Calle Real), **El Balcón** (Calle Real) and **El Refugio de San Pedro** (Plaza Bolívar).

Getting There & Away
From San Cristóbal, take the half-hourly Línea Colón bus to San Juan de Colón and ask the driver to let you off at the turnoff to San Pedro ($1.50, 1¼ hours, 40km), from where it's a 10-minute walk to the town. To return from San Pedro to San Cristóbal, take the Expresos Ayacucho bus to San Juan de Colón ($0.40, 20 minutes, 9km) and change for the Línea Colón bus to San Cristóbal ($1.50, 1½ hours, 49km). There may be one or two direct buses a day from San Pedro to San Cristóbal.

If you are coming from the north (eg from Mérida or Maracaibo), get off at the turnoff to San Pedro, about 9km past San Juan de Colón (the driver will know where to let you off). Going to Mérida from San Pedro involves a few changes. Take the Expresos Ayacucho bus to San Juan de Colón and change for one of the frequent buses to La Fría ($1, 50 minutes), where you get a bus to El Vigía, and change again there for a Mérida bus.

SAN ANTONIO DEL TÁCHIRA
☎ 0276 / pop 60,000

San Antonio is a Venezuelan border town, sitting on a busy San Cristóbal–Cúcuta road and living off trade with neighboring Colombia. You will pass through it if taking this route between the two countries, but otherwise there's no other reason to visit. Wind your watch back one hour when crossing from Venezuela to Colombia.

Information
IMMIGRATION
DIEX (Carrera 9 btwn Calles 6 & 7; ◷ 6am-10pm) This office puts exit or entry stamps in passports. All tourists

THE ANDES

SAN ANTONIO DEL TÁCHIRA

INFORMATION
Banco de Venezuela..................1	B2
CANTV....................................2	C3
CompuNet Cybercafé...............3	C2
DAS Office (Colombian	
Immigration).....................4	A1
DIEX......................................5	C2
Infoplanet Cybercafé..............6	C1
Ipostel...................................7	B3
Telcel....................................8	C1
Turismo Internacional.............9	B1
Turismo Turvinter..................10	C1
Turismo Uribante..................11	C1

SLEEPING (pp210–11)
Hotel Adriático.....................12	C1
Hotel Colonial......................13	B3
Hotel Terepaima...................14	B2

TRANSPORT (p211)
Buses to Ureña.....................15	C3
Buses to Ureña.....................16	C1
Expresos Los Llanos..............17	C1
Expresos Mérida....................18	C1
Expresos Occidente...............19	C1
Expresos San Cristóbal...........20	B1
Por puestos to Cúcuta...........21	C2
Por puestos to San Cristóbal...22	D2

leaving Venezuela are charged a $13 *impuesto de salida* (departure tax). You need to buy stamps for this amount in a shop (open till 5pm only) across the road from DIEX. Nationals of most Western countries don't need a visa for Colombia, but all travelers must get an entry stamp from DAS (Colombian immigration). The DAS office is just past the bridge over the Río Táchira (the actual border), on the right.

INTERNET ACCESS
CompuNet Cyber Café (Calle 6 No 8-28)
Infoplanet Cybercafé (Calle 4 No 3-45)

MONEY
There are plenty of *casas de cambio* in the center, particularly on Av Venezuela and around the DIEX office. They all change cash, but none will touch your traveler's checks. You can change bolívares to Colombian pesos (and vice versa) here or in Cúcuta – the rates are pretty much the same.
Banco de Venezuela (cnr Calle 3 & Carrera 9)

POST
Ipostel (cnr Carrera 10 & Calle 2)

TELEPHONE
CANTV (cnr Calle 4 & Carrera 13)
Telcel (cnr Av Venezuela & Calle 4)

TOURIST INFORMATION
Tourist information desk (Airport) Open only during flight times; 2km northeast of town.

TRAVEL AGENCIES
Turismo Internacional (☎ 771-5555; Av Venezuela No 4-04)
Turismo Turvinter (☎ 771-0311; Av Venezuela No 6-40)
Turismo Uribante (☎ 771-1779; Av Venezuela No 5-59)

Sleeping & Eating
San Antonio del Táchira has three decent places to stay and each has it its own restaurant.

Hotel Adriático (☎ 771-5757; hoteladriatico@hotmail.com; Calle 6 No 5-51; s/d/tr $13/20/25; P 🍴) Possibly the best place to stay in the center, the Adriático offers fair-sized rooms with new, silent air conditioners. Some rooms have balconies, if you want to watch the world go by. The hotel restaurant is reasonable and not expensive.

Hotel Colonial (☎ 771-2679; Carrera 11 No 2-51; d with fan $7-8, with air-con $10-11, tr with fan $9, with air-con $12; 🍴) One of the cheapest hotels in town, the Colonial is a small, family-run affair with its own restaurant serving inexpensive set lunches. The rooms are basic, but acceptable and all have private facilities.

Hotel Terepaima (☎ 771-1763; Carrera 8 No 1-37; d/tr with fan $8/10, with air-con $10/13; P 🍴) This is another small family-managed place with 14 very simple rooms upstairs and a rustic restaurant providing simple breakfasts and lunches.

Getting There & Away

AIR

The **Aeropuerto Juan Vicente Gómez** (☎ 771-2692), 2km northeast of town, can be reached by Ureña buses. They depart from Plaza Miranda, but if you don't want to go that far, you can catch them on the corner of Calle 6 and Av Venezuela.

Aeropostal, Aserca and Rutaca have daily flights to Caracas ($46 to $90). Aeropostal and Santa Bárbara fly direct to Maracaibo ($58 to $82). Santa Bárbara also flies to Mérida ($37 to $47). Airlines have their desks at the airport, but you can book and buy tickets at the central travel agencies (see Information p210). Shop around – their prices differ.

There are no direct flights to Colombia from San Antonio; go to Cúcuta across the border, from where you can fly to Bogotá, Medellín and other major Colombian cities.

BUS

The bus terminal is midway to the airport. Half a dozen bus companies operate buses to Caracas ($17 to $22, 14 hours, 865km), with a total of seven buses daily. All depart between 4pm and 7pm and use El Llano route. Most of these bus companies also have offices in the town center: **Expresos Los Llanos** (☎ 771-2690; Calle 5 No 4-26), **Expresos Mérida** (☎ 771-4053; Av Venezuela No 6-17), **Expresos Occidente** (☎ 771-4730; cnr Carrera 6 & Calle 6), and **Expresos San Cristóbal** (☎ 771-4301; Av Venezuela No 3-20). They all sell tickets, but then you have to go to the terminal anyway to board the bus.

No direct buses run to Mérida; go to San Cristóbal and change there. Por puestos to San Cristóbal leave frequently from the corner of Av Venezuela and Carrera 10 ($1.25, 1¼ hours, 40km).

To/From Colombia

Buses ($0.40) and por puestos ($0.60) run frequently to Cúcuta in Colombia (12km). You can catch buses on Av Venezuela, but remember to get off at DAS just behind the bridge for your Colombia entry stamp (or walk from San Antonio across the bridge to DAS) and than take another bus. Buses go as far as the Cúcuta bus terminal, passing through the center. You can pay in bolívares or pesos.

The Cúcuta terminal is dirty, busy and unsafe – one of the poorest in Colombia – so watch your belongings closely. You may be approached by well-dressed, English-speaking characters who will offer help in buying your bus ticket. Ignore them – they are con artists. Buy your ticket directly from the bus office.

From Cúcuta, there are frequent buses to Bucaramanga ($10, six hours, 201km) and two dozen buses daily to Bogotá ($29, 16 hours, 630km). If you plan on staying in Cúcuta, don't go all the way to the terminal, just get off in the center.

THE ANDES

Los Llanos

Venezuela's geographical heart, Los Llanos (The Plains) is a billiard-table-flat savanna that makes up one third of the national territory – the entire central area from the Andes down to the Río Orinoco. These hot, eerie grasslands stretch as far as the eye can see in an almost hypnotic vista, and provide a unique off-the-beaten-track travel experience.

The region's main attraction is its wildlife – Los Llanos is Venezuela's biggest repository of wildlife and because of the open landscape the animals are relatively easy to watch. In fact, nowhere else will you see so many caimans, birds and capybaras in their natural habitat.

Los Llanos is also Venezuela's spiritual heart, where the country's patron saint, the Virgen de Coromoro, miraculously appeared 350 years ago. A stunning church has been built in the middle of the plains in homage to the Virgin, and it's now a landmark that draws pilgrims from every corner of the country.

Los Llanos' contribution to Venezuelan culture is *joropo* music, the fast-paced rhythm that is now the national beat. It can be heard all over the country, yet it's here that you can enjoy it in its most authentic and spontaneous form, played by small home-bred local bands in every village.

HIGHLIGHTS

- Venture out on a wildlife safari amid caimans, dolphins and birds, organized from the **hatos** (p224)

- Join the pilgrims at the **Santuario Nacional de Nuestra Señora de Coromoto** (p220)

- Feel the pulsating rhythms of **joropo music** (p218)

- Explore the spiritual capital of **Guanare** (p219)

Guanare
Santuario Nacional ★
de Nuestra Señora
de Coromoto
Hato Piñero ★
★ Hato La Fe
★ Hato El Frío
Hato El Cedral ★
★ Hato Doña Bárbara

Geography

Los Llanos is a low-lying flat savanna covering about 300,000 sq km of Venezuela (plus another 250,000 sq km in Colombia). It's mostly covered by grass, with ribbons of gallery forest along the rivers, and scattered islands of woodland here and there.

Rivers are numerous and, in the wet season, voluminous. The main ones are the Apure, Meta, Arauca and Capanaparo, all of which are left-bank (south) tributaries of the Orinoco.

Climate

The climate is extreme in both wet and dry seasons, resulting in either floods or droughts. The wet period lasts from May to November and brings frequent and intense rains. The rivers overflow, turning much of the land into lagoons. In the dry season, December to April, the sun beats down upon the parched soil, and winds blow the dust around.

Getting Around

You can fly into Barinas, but you'll have to rely on land transport to take you into the heart of the savanna. Roads, however, are few and far between. San Fernando de Apure is accessible by paved roads from Maracay/Caracas in the north, and Barinas/Guanare in the northwest. There's also a paved road from San Fernando southward to Puerto Páez, on the Colombian border.

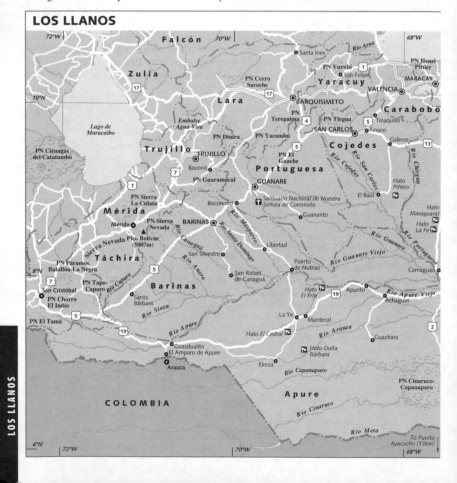

LOS LLANOS

BARINAS

☎ 0273 / pop 250,000

Set on the northwestern edge of Los Llanos, Barinas is the region's biggest city and the capital of Barinas state. It's a thriving center of a vast agricultural and ranching region, which is also rich in oil, and an important transportation hub, making it a convenient base for adventures into Los Llanos. The city has a prosperous and turbulent past, the relics of which can still be seen today. It's a likable place sporting a compact, lively downtown and large leafy suburbs.

History

Barinas' long and checkered history began in 1577 when it was founded by Spanish conquerors from Pamplona in Nueva Granada (now Colombia). At the beginning of the 17th century, tobacco gave the town an economic base and overseas fame, as Barinas was the only region in the colony that the Spanish Crown allowed to grow tobacco. Other crops, including sugarcane, bananas and cacao, were subsequently introduced to the region, as was raising cattle. By the end of the 18th century, Barinas was Venezuela's largest and wealthiest town after Caracas.

The civil wars that plagued Venezuela during the 19th century affected the development of the town and the state, but afterwards a steady revival began. Agriculture and the cattle industry were joined by a

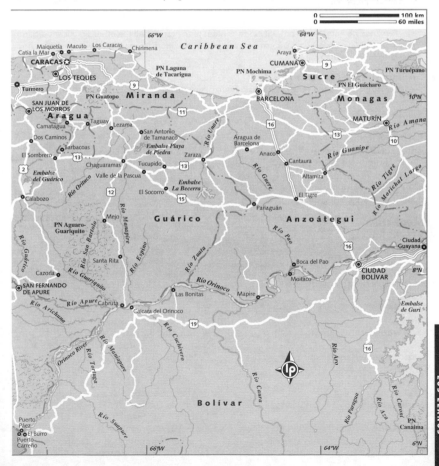

QUICK FACTS ABOUT LOS LLANOS

People

Los Llanos is inhabited by the *llaneros,* Venezuelan 'cowboys', who are a fiercely independent, tough and resilient people used to a hard life. It was not coincidence that Bolívar enlisted *llaneros* in his army to fight against the Spaniards, with great success.

Culture

The *llaneros* have developed their own distinctive culture and folklore. One of the favorite pastimes is *coleo* or *toros coleados,* a sort of rodeo. Its aim is to bring down a bull by grabbing its tail while riding a galloping horse. The region's most successful cultural export is *joropo* music (see the boxed text, p218).

Economy

Cattle raising is the principal activity and the region is Venezuela's major beef producer. It also produces dairy products and agricultural crops, and provides the country with river fish. Since the discovery of oil reserves in Anzoátegui and Barinas states, Los Llanos has become an important oil producer.

Cities

San Fernando de Apure is the only city in the center of the region. All the other significant urban centers, including Barinas and Guanare, developed in the more hospitable environment at the northern fringe of the plains.

Administrative Divisions

Los Llanos comprises the states of Barinas, Apure, Portuguesa, Cojedes and Guárico. Sometimes the southern part of Anzoátegui is included.

---

short-lived timber industry, which took advantage of the extensive tropical forest in the region, chopping it down rapidly and indiscriminately. Meanwhile, oil was discovered in the region south of Barinas, and is today pipelined to the coast near Morón.

Information

INTERNET ACCESS
You Ciber.com (cnr Av Briceño Méndez & Calle Cedeño)

MONEY
Banco de Venezuela (cnr Av Marqués del Pumar & Calle Plaza)
Banco Mercantil (cnr Av Marqués del Pumar & Calle Bolívar)
Banco Provincial (cnr Av Marqués del Pumar & Calle Carvajal)
Banesco (cnr Av Marqués del Pumar & Calle Cruz Paredes)
Corp Banca (cnr Av Libertad & Calle Camejo)

POST
Ipostel (Calle Carvajal btwn Av Montilla & Av Libertad)

TELEPHONE
Telcel (cnr Av Marqués del Pumar & Calle Arzobispo Méndez)

TOURIST INFORMATION
Corbatur (☎ 552-8162; Palacio del Marqués, Plaza Bolívar; ⓨ 8am-noon & 2-6pm Mon-Fri)

Sights

The unusual, two-block-long Plaza Bolívar still boasts buildings dating from the city's fat days. The pastel-colored, graceful **Cathedral** was built in the 1770s, except for the bell tower, which was added in 1936.

Across the plaza is the imposing **Palacio del Marqués**, occupying one entire side of the square. Commissioned by the Marqués de las Riberas de Boconó y Masparro as his private residence and constructed in the 1780s, the palace reflected the owner's wealth and Barinas' prosperity at the time. It was partly ruined during the Wars of Federation in the mid-19th century, but was later restored. It now houses governmental offices, including the tourist office.

Also set on the plaza is the colonial-style **Casa de la Cultura** (☎ 552-3643), built in the 1780s as the town hall and jail. José Antonio Páez, a republican hero, was imprisoned here but managed to escape, liberating 115 of his fellow prisoners in the process.

The building was the town jail until 1966, but today it houses a cultural center, staging art exhibitions and various cultural events. An auditorium for the local theater was being built at the back at the time of research.

Named after a local poet, the **Museo Alberto Arvelo Torrealba** (☎ 532-4984; cnr Calle de Julio & Av Medina Jiménez; admission free; ☺ 9am-noon & 3-6pm Tue-Sun) is set in a splendid 200-year-old mansion with a charming patio and a tree-shaded garden. It features an exhibition related to the history of the city and the region.

The **Museo de Arte Colonial y Costumbrista San Francisco de Asís** (☎ 533-4641; Av Medina Jiménez btwn Calle Pulido & Calle Bolívar; admission free; ☺ 2pm-5pm Mon, 8:30am-11:30am & 2-5pm Tue-Fri) has a bizarre 30,000-piece private collection of old objects, including kerosene lamps, hospital beds, jukeboxes, crucifixes, chamber pots, fire extinguishers, wedding dresses, surgical instruments, turtle shells – you name it. It's stunning. The friendly attendants, accompanied by the owner's six dogs, will show you around and have stories about every single exhibit. Note the first street gas lamps from Plaza Bolívar.

In the vast grounds of the Universidad Nacional Experimental de Los Llanos Ezequiel Zamora (Unellez), 3km southwest of the center, the **Jardín Botánico** (☎ 546-4555; Av Alberto Torrealba; admission free; ☺ 8am-3pm Mon-Fri) has many beautiful trees, a plant nursery and a small zoo featuring local species.

Sleeping & Eating

There are a variety of accommodation choices and half a dozen cheap hotels around the bus terminal.

Posada Turística Doña Delfina (☎ 533-4648; Av Briceño Méndez btwn Calle Arismendi & Calle Pulido; s/d/tr/q $10/13/19/25; P ☒) One of the best budget places in the center, the new, eight-room Delfina is quiet, pleasant and friendly, and has an inexpensive restaurant serving hearty home-cooked meals and beer. The surrounding courtyard has plenty of room to breathe.

Hotel Internacional (☎ 552-2343, 552-3303; Calle Arzobispo Méndez; d $16-20, tr/q $23/25; P ☒) The 48-room, three-star Internacional is the oldest hotel in town and great value. Built in the early 1950s (when there was still no

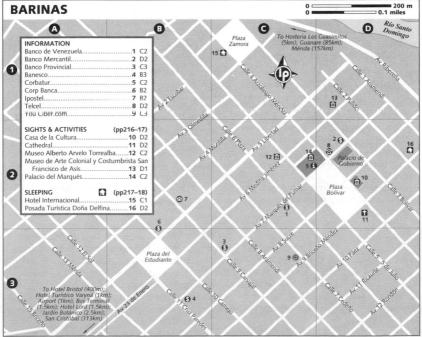

BARINAS

0 ———————— 200 m
0 ———————— 0.1 miles

INFORMATION	
Banco de Venezuela	1 C2
Banco Mercantil	2 D2
Banco Provincial	3 C3
Banesco	4 B3
Corbatur	5 C2
Corp Banca	6 B2
Ipostel	7 B2
Telcel	8 D2
You Ciber.com	9 C3

SIGHTS & ACTIVITIES	(pp216–17)
Casa de la Cultura	10 D2
Cathedral	11 D2
Museo Alberto Arvelo Torrealba	12 C2
Museo de Arte Colonial y Costumbrista San	
Francisco de Asís	13 D1
Palacio del Marqués	14 C2

SLEEPING	(pp217–18)
Hotel Internacional	15 C1
Posada Turística Doña Delfina	16 D2

Plaza Zamora

To Hostería Los Guasimitos (5km); Guanare (85km); Mérida (157km)

Río Santo Domingo

Av Ribereña

Av 2 Escobar
Av 3 Olmedilla
Calle 4 Arzobispo Méndez
Calle 1 Arismendi
Calle 2 Pulido
Calle 4 Montilla
Calle 6 Plaza
Av 5 Libertad
Av 6 Medina Jiménez
Palacio de Gobierno
Plaza Bolívar
Calle 3 Bolívar
Av 7 Marqués del Pumar
Calle 5 5 de Julio
Av 8 Sucre
Calle 8 Arismendi
Av 9 Briceño Méndez
Calle 10 Páez
Calle 6 Camejo
Plaza del Estudiante
Calle 12 El Sol
Calle 13 Mérida
Calle 9 Carvajal
Calle 11 Ricaurte
Calle 7 Cedeño
Calle 15 Bricño
Av 23 de Enero
Calle 11 Cruz Paredes
Calle 10 Camejo
Calle 12 Rondón

To Hotel Bristol (400m); Hotel Turístico Varyná (1km); Airport (1km); Bus Terminal (1.5km); Hotel Lord (1.5km); Jardín Botánico (2.5km); San Cristóbal (313km)

LOS LLANOS

reliable road connection with Caracas), it has large rooms, high ceilings, spacious common areas and a no-nonsense restaurant serving copious meals. Ask for a room overlooking the lovely courtyard with a fountain.

Hotel Lord (☎ 532-1866; Callejón 5; d/tr with fan $7/8, d/tr with air-con $8/10; ✖) If you're looking for a budget room around the bus terminal, try this first – it's one of the cheapest options and good value for money. Simple but acceptable, Hotel Lord has 15 rooms with bathrooms and a budget restaurant, all managed by a helpful family.

Hotel Turístico Varyná (☎ 533-2477; hotelvarynat@ cantv.net; Av 23 de Enero; d $30-35, tr $40; P ✖) Close to the airport, Varyná has a colony of 10 single-story cabins, plus a restaurant facing the street. Each cabin has four rooms with a bathroom and hot water. The hotel is a bit faded, but neat and tidy, and gives a refreshing feel of being far away from the city.

Hotel Bristol (☎ 552-0911; hotelbristol@cantv.net; Av 23 de Enero; s/d/tr $42/45/55; P ✖) Occupying a nine-story block 1km southwest of the center, Bristol is a busy modern hotel popular with businesspeople. It's a comfy (if a bit soulless) place, and has a bar and restaurant.

Hostería Los Guasimitos (☎ 546-1546; guasimit os@cantv.net; d $20-24, tr $28; P ✖ ▯ ▣) Travelers with their own transportation may be interested in this country-style motel off the road to Guanare, about 5km northwest of the city center. The complex features 100 spacious rooms with fridge, bathroom and hot water. There is also a gym, Internet café, large swimming pool, bar and a restaurant serving typical regional food.

Getting There & Away

AIR
The airport is 1.5km southwest of Plaza Bolívar. **Avior** (☎ 532-1203) and **LAI** (☎ 533-2780) have several flights daily to Caracas ($47 to $73).

BUS
The **Terminal de Pasajeros** (Av Cuatricentenaria) is 2km west of Plaza Bolívar and is serviced by local buses. Barinas has regular buses southwest to San Cristóbal ($7, five hours, 313km) and northeast to Caracas ($10 to $14, 8½ hours, 512km). Buses to Guanare ($1.50, 1¼ hours, 85km) run every half-hour from 4am to 6pm.

Transporte Barinas has five departures a day to Mérida ($4.50, four hours, 157km). Unión Táchira has por puestos to Mérida, which depart as soon as all seats are taken (roughly every one to two hours). The road, which winds up the mountain slopes, is spectacular. Sit on the right for more dramatic views.

JOROPO – MUSICAL PULSE OF LOS LLANOS

Once you arrive in Los Llanos you'll hear these fast-paced, harp-led rhythms everywhere. Every second inhabitant of the plains sings or plays one of the *joropo* instruments, and every village has at least one *joropo* ensemble. You can love it or hate it, but you can't escape it. In any case, it is likely to be a new musical experience, since *joropo* is almost unknown outside Venezuela and Colombia.

Also known as the *música llanera* (local music), the *joropo* is believed to have its origins in the Spanish flamenco, but it has changed considerably over the centuries in its new home. It's usually sung and accompanied by a small band that normally includes the *arpa llanera* (a local harp), a *cuatro* (four-string small guitar) and maracas (gourd rattles). There's a dance form of *joropo* as well.

The harp came over from Spain during the colonial period, but it was not until the 20th century that it made its way into *joropo* music. By that time, it had evolved into quite a different instrument, smaller and less elaborate than its European parent. Normally associated with lyrical salon music, the harp has found a totally new form of expression in *joropo*. Presumably reflecting the hard life of the *llaneros* (inhabitants of Los Llanos), it sounds clear and sharp, often even wild.

The harp is sometimes replaced by the *bandola*, another European offspring. It's a mandolin derivative, with a pear-shaped body and four nylon strings. The *cuatro* accompanies the melody played by the harp or the *bandola*. The *cuatro* is also of European origin and has gradually changed in the New World.

Several companies, including Expresos Los Llanos and Expresos Zamora, operate buses southeast into Los Llanos, with half a dozen departures daily to San Fernando de Apure ($9 to $13, nine hours, 469km). It's a hypnotic (some would say monotonous) way to travel right across the best part of Los Llanos.

GUANARE
☎ 0257 / pop 140,000

Guanare is Venezuela's spiritual capital, famous for its Virgen de Coromoto (or Nuestra Señora de Coromoto), the country's patron saint. It was around here in 1652 that the Virgin miraculously appeared before an Indian chief and left him an image of herself (see the boxed text, p221). The site became a destination for pilgrims from around the region. The canonization in 1942 of the Virgin as the patron saint of Venezuela contributed to even larger floods of the faithful; today it's Venezuela's major pilgrimage center, attracting half a million visitors a year.

The focus of pilgrimages has moved to the exact place of the Virgin's apparition, 25km south of Guanare, where a huge sanctuary has been built, yet Guanare continues to pull in pilgrims as the Virgin's traditional home and the only city around.

Information

INTERNET ACCESS
Invermega (Carrera 6 btwn Calles 17 & 18)
Sistemas Integrales (Carrera 5 btwn Calles 13 & 14)

MONEY
Banco de Venezuela (cnr Carrera 6 & Calle 15)
Banco Mercantil (cnr Carrera 5 & Calle 6)
Banco Provincial (cnr Carrera 5 & Calle 20)
Banesco (cnr Carrera 6 & Calle 16)

TELEPHONE
CANTV (Carrera 6 btwn Calles 16 & 17)
Telcel (Carrera 5 btwn Calles 10 & 11)

TOURIST INFORMATION
Corpotur (☎ 251-0324; Pabellón de Exposiciones, Av IND; 8am-noon & 2-6pm Mon-Fri) The office is opposite the Instituto Nacional de Deporte, 1.5km southwest of the center.

Sights

By far the most important religious monument is the **Basílica Catedral de Nuestra Señora de Coromoto** (Plaza Bolívar; 6:30am-noon & 2-7pm Mon-Fri, 6:30am-7:30pm Sat & Sun). It was constructed in 1710–42, but the 1782 earthquake almost completely destroyed it. The holy image of the Virgin, which had been kept inside, was saved and returned to the reconstructed church. It resided here until 1999, when it was taken to the new santuario (p220).

Once inside the church, your eyes will immediately be caught by a three-tier main retable, an excellent piece of colonial baroque art made in 1739. It later took 16 months to gild. In front of the retable stands the elaborate 3.4m-high *sagrario* (tabernacle), made entirely of silver in 1756. A painting on the dome over the high altar depicts the legend of the Virgen de Coromoto. The colorful stained-glass windows were commissioned in Munich, Germany.

The mid-18th-century **Convento de San Francisco** (☎ 251-6483; cnr Carrera 3 & Calle 17) no longer serves its original purpose as a convent. In 1825, Venezuela's first college was opened here. Today, the building accommodates the offices of the Universidad Nacional Experimental de Los Llanos. You can enter its spacious courtyard, which has retained much of its old style and charm. The adjacent church is now used for university meetings and symposiums.

Opposite the church is a splendid two-story colonial mansion, one of the few buildings remaining from the Spanish period. It's now home to the **Museo de la Ciudad de Guanare** (☎ 253-0832; cnr Carrera 3 & Calle 17; admission $0.50; 8am-4pm Tue-Fri, 8am-2pm Sat), and features exhibits related to the town's history. Don't miss visiting the rooms on the upper floor, which shelter a small but fine collection of historic religious art.

Two blocks north is **Parque Los Samanes** (cnr Carrera 1 & Calle 16; admission $0.20; 8:30am-5pm Tue-Sun), named after the species of spreading tree that grows in the park. You'll find an impressive specimen in front of the entrance. Bolívar's troops reputedly camped here in 1813.

There are several monuments dedicated to the Virgen de Coromoto in the town center, including the 1928 statue on **Plaza Coromoto**, seven blocks east of Plaza Bolívar along Carrera 5. On the same square you'll find a charming sculptured scene depicting the miraculous appearance of the Virgin to the Indian cacique and his family.

Outside the center, just 500m west of the tourist office, is the **Museo de Los Llanos** (☎ 253-0102; Complejo Ferial José Antonio Páez; admission free; ⏰ 8:30am-12:30pm & 2:30-5:30pm Tue-Sun), which has an archeological collection from the region.

Festivals & Events

As might be expected, Guanare's annual celebrations revolve around the Virgen de Coromoto. Most pilgrims flock to the city in time for the Fiesta de la Virgen de Coromoto on September 8, the anniversary of the Virgin's appearance.

Guanare is also noted for its Mascarada, a three-day-long colorful Carnaval celebration that culminates in a parade of *carrozas* (floats).

Sleeping

Hotel Italia (☎ 253-1213, 251-4277; Calle 20 btwn Carreras 4 & 5; d $12-14, tr $14-16; P ☒) Run by an Italian family, this is a decent central hotel that would suit any budget traveler. Some of the hotel's 87 rooms have been revamped and now have hot water, while others don't but are cheaper. The hotel restaurant offers tasty food at low prices.

Posada del Reo (cnr Calle 16 & Carrera 3; d/q $16/22; ☒) The posada is on the site that was once occupied by the city jail. To make you aware of this, the rooms are labeled 'cells'. This central lodging was closed for refurbishing at the time of research but once reopened it should make for a very comfortable stay. Call Corpotur tourist office, which administers the posada.

Motel La Góndola (☎ 253-1480, 251-2802; cnr Carrera 5 & Calle 3; d $15-17, tr $22; P ☒) Another central accommodation, 400m west of Plaza Coromoto, La Góndola is enjoyable and quiet, and good value. Its 42 fair-sized rooms are arranged around two spacious courtyards, while the cozy restaurant serves palatable food at economic prices.

Hotel Mirador (☎ 253-4520, 253-5320; cnr Av Circunvalación & Av IND; d $18-20, tr $22; P ☒ ☒) A new and expanding hotel complex 200m south of the tourist office, the Mirador has 60 large rooms, all with hot water and fridge, plus a reasonable restaurant.

Eating

Papa Boris Restaurant (☎ 253-3035; cnr Carrera 6 & Calle 13; set menú $2, mains $4-8; ⏰ 11am-9:30pm; ☒) Papa Boris gives you an option to eat inside or out – both are cool and lovely. As for food, you have quite a choice, but go for the specialty – *batea* – which is a *parrilla*-type dish served on a wooden board. The *batea mixta* ($9) comes with pork, chicken, beef and all the accompaniments, and will normally feed two people, unless you are very hungry.

El Bodegón de Pedro Miguel (☎ 251-4358; cnr Calle 15 & Carrera 8; mains $4-6) This is a long-standing tasca-style restaurant, with a long menu, moderate prices and a dim interior. It's fine to eat the seafood.

Getting There & Away

The **Terminal de Pasajeros** (Av UNDA) is 2km southeast of the city center, and is serviced regularly by local transportation. To get there from the center, take the eastbound busetas No 12 or 24 from Carrera 5.

Guanare sits on El Llanos highway, so there is a fair bit of traffic heading southwest to San Cristóbal ($8 to $12, 6½ hours, 398km) and northeast to Caracas ($9 to $13, seven hours, 427km). There are hourly buses to Barquisimeto ($4.50, 3½ hours, 173km) and several departures a day to Boconó ($3, 3½ hours, 115km). Buses to Barinas ($1.50, 1¼ hours, 85km) run frequently until 6pm. If you are heading to Mérida, go to Barinas and change.

SANTUARIO NACIONAL DE NUESTRA SEÑORA DE COROMOTO

☎ 0257

The **Santuario Nacional** (☎ 251-0333, 251-5071; ⏰ 8am-6pm) is the holy site where the Virgen de Coromoto (see the boxed text, p221) allegedly appeared in 1652. A cross was placed here after the event, and was later replaced with a chapel, but the site was isolated and rarely visited. Instead, the pilgrims flocked

---

THE AUTHOR'S CHOICE

Posada del Cabrestero (☎ 253-0102; Complejo Ferial José Antonio Páez; d/tr $16/20; ☒) The most charming place to stay in town, this 15-room colonial-style posada is next door to the Museo de Los Llanos. Rooms have wide comfy beds, silent air-conditioning, a fridge and a tiny patio at the back. Breakfast is available on request.

A VENEZUELAN MIRACLE

One sunny day in 1652, as Indian Chief Coromoto and his wife were crossing a stream near their hut, a radiant lady of incredible beauty appeared and walked over the water toward them. While they stared at the divine creature, she started talking to them in their own language. She urged the chief to go with his tribe to the white men to have holy water poured over their heads so that they could go to heaven.

Astonished and confused, the chief promised to comply. He told the story to the Spaniard who owned a nearby plantation, and with his permission the whole tribe soon moved onto the settler's land and built their huts. They were put to work on the plantation and given religious instructions.

As months passed, though, the chief was increasingly unhappy with the indoctrination and wanted to return to his native pastures. One day he refused to assist in religious acts and went back to his hut. While he tried to rest and calm his anger, the beautiful lady suddenly appeared again, radiating with rays of light more dazzling than the midday sun.

This time the chief was not in a peaceful mood. He grabbed his bow and arrows, but the shining vision moved quickly around. He then tried to catch her in his hands but the dazzling creature vanished. When he opened his hand all he found was a small image of the divine lady.

Angry and irritated, he threw the image down and ran into the dark night. While he was madly running through the woods, he was bitten by a venomous snake. Only then, moments before his death, did he ask to be baptized, and he told his tribe to do likewise.

The radiant lady, named after the Indian chief the Virgen de Coromoto, is today the patron saint of Venezuela, while the tiny image he found in his hand is the object of devotion by millions of Venezuelans.

to Guanare's church, which for centuries boasted the holy image and effectively acted as the Virgin's shrine.

In 1980 the construction of a huge church at the actual site of the apparition commenced and was completed for the papal visit in February 1996, when 300,000 faithful attended a mass. The holy image of the Virgin has been brought to the site from Guanare.

The church is monumental, stunningly modern and truly powerful. What is equally striking is the church's solitary location amid vast plains. It looms like a gigantic beacon in the middle of a wilderness, guiding pilgrims to the end of their journey.

Designed by the Venezuelan architect Erasmo Calvani, it's a bold, irregular concrete structure topped with two unequal bell towers, 76m and 68m high. Its central nave has been laid out on a floor plan of an 80m-by-80m heart. The nave has no columns, which gives the impression of great volume and space. The wall behind the high altar is graced with marvelous stained-glass windows depicting the history of the apparition – the work is by another Venezuelan artist, Guillermo Márquez.

The high altar is believed to be at the exact location where the Virgin appeared. The holy image is in an elaborate reliquary right behind the altar. You can get close and see the image through the magnifying glass. It's an oval painting measuring 22mm by 27mm. Today its colors are almost totally washed out, and the picture is pretty faint and indistinct.

You can go up to a viewing platform at 36m which is built between the two towers and provides vast panoramic views; the platform is accessible by elevator for a nominal fee. A museum in the basement of the church features religious paraphernalia related to the Virgin and a collection of votive offerings.

Getting There & Away

The Santuario is 25km south of Guanare – 10km by the main road toward Barinas, and then a further 15km by the paved side road branching off to the south. Small buses, operated by Línea Los Cospes, depart every 15 minutes from the corner of Carrera 9 and Calle 20 in Guanare, and will deposit you right at the church's entrance ($0.40, 40 minutes).

SAN FERNANDO DE APURE

☎ 0247 / pop 140,000

The capital of Apure state, San Fernando is an old river port hundreds of miles away from any sizable urban centers. The remoteness, the river and the lazy pace of life give the city a certain charm, but most visitors come to San Fernando on their way to the *hatos* (p224) in the surrounding region, which boast some of the best wild-life-watching Los Llanos has to offer.

San Fernando started as a missionary outpost at the end of the colonial era. Sitting on the bank of the large Río Apure, in the very heart of Los Llanos, the town developed into an important trading center,

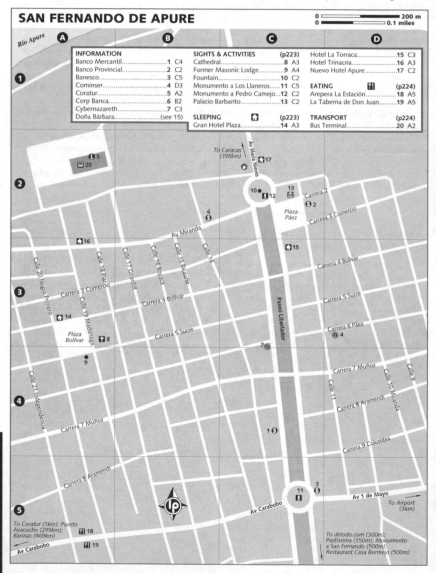

SAN FERNANDO DE APURE

INFORMATION		SIGHTS & ACTIVITIES	(p223)	Hotel La Torraca.............................15 C3
Banco Mercantil....................1 C4		Cathedral...............................8 A3		Hotel Trinacria............................16 A3
Banco Provincial...................2 C2		Former Masonic Lodge.........9 A4		Nuevo Hotel Apure.......................17 C2
Banesco................................3 C5		Fountain...............................10 C2		
Cominser..............................4 D3		Monumento a Los Llaneros......11 C5		EATING 🍴 (p224)
Coratur.................................5 A2		Monumento a Pedro Camejo...12 C2		Arepera La Estación.....................18 A5
Corp Banca...........................6 B2		Palacio Barbarito...................13 C2		La Taberna de Don Juan.............19 A5
Cybernazareth......................7 C3				
Doña Bárbara...................(see 15)		SLEEPING 🏠 (p223)		TRANSPORT (p224)
		Gran Hotel Plaza...................14 A3		Bus Terminal...........................20 A2

growing rich on the trade in heron and egret feathers, and caiman skins. By the early 20th century, it was Venezuela's second largest river port, after Ciudad Bolívar. Today, cattle raising is the major activity in the region, followed by crop farming. Crops and livestock are funneled through San Fernando and trucked north to Caracas and the central states of Aragua, Carabobo and Miranda.

Information

INTERNET ACCESS

Cominser (cnr Carrera Páez & Calle 11)
Cybernazareth (cnr Carrera Páez & Paseo Libertador)
detodo.com (Av Libertador btwn Calle Carabobo & Av Fuerzas Armadas)

MONEY

Banco Mercantil (Paseo Libertador btwn Carrera Aramendi & Carrera Colombia)
Banco Provincial (Plaza Páez)
Banesco (cnr Paseo Libertador & Av 1 de Mayo)
Corp Banca (cnr Av Miranda & Calle 14)

TOURIST INFORMATION

Coratur Bus Terminal Desk (☎ 514-7292; ☾ 8am-noon & 2:30-5:30pm Mon-Fri); City Main Office (☎ 342-9912, 342-9963; Calle Rodríguez Rincones, Urbanización Tamarindo; ☾ 8am-noon & 2:30-5:30pm Mon-Fri);

TRAVEL AGENCIES

Doña Bárbara (☎ 341-3463, dbarbara@cantv.net; Edificio Hotel La Torraca, Paseo Libertador) Essentially an outpost of its own Hato Doña Bárbara, but it can also provide information about other *hatos* in the region, including La Fe, El Frío and El Cedral.

Sights

Walk along Paseo Libertador, the city's main thoroughfare. At its northern end is a circular plaza, its large **fountain** adorned with six charmingly kitsch concrete caimans. Beside the fountain is the **Monumento a Pedro Camejo**, a bronze equestrian statue of one of the bravest lancers to have fought in Bolívar's army. Camejo, who died in the battle of Carabobo, is known as Negro Primero, as he was the first black person to distinguish himself in the War of Independence.

Just east of the fountain is the ornate, two-story **Palacio Barbarito**, built by the Barbarito brothers from Italy at the turn of the 19th century. At that time the Río Apure used to pass by just a few meters from the palace pier, and boats came directly from Europe up the Orinoco and Apure. The brothers made a fortune on heron and egret feathers during the 1910s bonanza, but later on, when the business deteriorated, they sold the palace and left. It then passed through the hands of various owners who divided and subdivided it repeatedly, so much of the original internal design has been lost.

About 600m south along Paseo Libertador is the **Monumento a Los Llaneros**, dedicated to the tough and brave people who made up the backbone of Bolívar's army. Another 600m down the Paseo is the huge **Monumento a San Fernando**, an allegorical monument to the city presented by the city itself.

The Plaza Bolívar, six blocks west of Paseo Libertador, boasts a modern tentlike **cathedral** and an old **masonic lodge**, and is pleasantly shaded with trees.

Sleeping

Hotel La Torraca (☎ 342-2777, 342-2676; Paseo Libertador; d $15-17, tr/ste $19/22; **P** ⊠) The reception desk doesn't look very promising, but don't worry – the 48 rooms, distributed over three floors, are airy, bright and good value. Most of them look at the back and are quiet, but if you want some action, take a front room with a balcony and watch the world go by on the busy Paseo Libertador.

Hotel Trinacria (☎ 342-3578, 342-3778; Av Miranda; d $14-16, tr/q $18/20; **P** ⊠) Trinacria is not the most romantic place on earth, but it has unusually large rooms with private facilities and noiseless air-conditioning, and is within spitting distance from the bus terminal – perfect for those very early buses.

Nuevo Hotel Apure (☎ 341-4483, 342-2214; Av María Nieves; d $26; **P** ⊠) This motel-style 30-room establishment provides reasonably comfy and quiet accommodations and has its own no-nonsense restaurant.

Gran Hotel Plaza (☎ 342-1504, 342-1255; Plaza Bolívar; s/d/tr $25/30/35; **P** ⊠) This is possibly San Fernando's top bet, though don't expect any Sheraton-like luxuries. It has fairly reasonable rooms with views over the peaceful and leafy plaza, and is just about the only hotel in town that has hot water, if you really need it in this steamy, sticky climate.

Eating

Restaurant Casa Bermejo (☎ 342-7613; Paseo Libertador; mains $3-7) Set at the foot of the giant Monumento a San Fernando, this inviting, cozy place does an excellent job, as you can tell by the number of patrons. The restaurant offers pasta, steaks and seafood, but try *bagre* or *dorado*, a yummy river fish, that is not often seen on local menus.

Pastissima (cnr Paseo Libertador & Av Fuerzas Armadas; pasta $3-4) As its name suggests, this is a pasta affair, offering 15 fresh, home-made varieties in the tiny, four-table spot. You may like to go for the *pastissima*, which is a combination of four pastas.

La Taberna de Don Juan (☎ 342-6259; Av Carabobo; mains $6-9) Don Juan is a respectable, slightly upmarket restaurant, which hosts discos and sometimes live music on weekend nights. As for food, it has the international cuisine sporting the *paella valenciana* ($16 for two persons) as one of the specialties.

Arepera La Estación (Av Carabobo; arepas $1.50; ☾ 5:30pm-3:30am) This is a food kiosk, serving great *arepas* (stuffed corn pancakes) with 20 different fillings till late.

Getting There & Away

AIR

San Fernando has its airport 3km east of the city center, but there were no flights when we were there.

BUS

The bus terminal is on the northern outskirts of the city, near the river. You can either walk there (five minutes from Plaza Bolívar) or take a taxi ($1).

There are several departures a day to Caracas ($8 to $12, eight hours, 398km), or you can go by any of the half-hourly buses to Maracay ($8, seven hours, 319km) and change there. Half a dozen buses a day travel to Barinas ($9 to $13, nine hours, 469km) on a remote road across the heart of the plains. Watch out for animals.

Six buses a day (all in the morning) set off for another interesting ride, south to Puerto Ayacucho ($10, seven hours, 299km) via Puerto Páez. The road is now paved all the way and traversable year-round, but the bridges over the Capanaparo and Cinaruco are incomplete, so the trip includes *chalana* (ferry) crossings across these two rivers and, obviously, across the Orinoco between Puerto Páez and El Burro. It's a very enjoyable trip.

HATOS

Most of Los Llanos is divided into large ranches known as *hatos*. They are principally dedicated to cattle raising, as they have been for a century or more, but some of them have turned to ecotourism. The owners have built *campamentos*, lodges equipped with tourist facilities, and run excursions to show guests the local wildlife. Some *hatos* have taken a serious approach to environmental issues, introducing the protection of wildlife within their ranches, installing research stations and contributing to ecological funds.

Excursions are basically photo safaris in a jeep or boat. There's usually one trip in the morning and another in the afternoon – the best times to observe the wildlife and to avoid the unbearable midday heat. Boat trips are more common in the rainy period, while jeep rides prevail in the dry season. Visitors are taken deep into wilderness areas where animals, and especially birds, are plentiful and easy to see. Among the mammals and reptiles, capybaras and caimans are particularly common (see the boxed text, p226). Piranha-fishing is also an activity offered by all the *hatos*.

Visits to some *hatos* are available only on an all-inclusive package, which has to be booked and paid beforehand, usually in Caracas. Packages are normally three-day, two-night visits that include full board and one or two excursions each day. Other *hatos* are more flexible, allowing visitors to come without pre-payment, stay a day or two and pay accordingly.

Tours in most *hatos* cost between $100 and $130 per person per day, which adds up to some $300 to $400 for a three-day tour. Cheaper wildlife safaris in Los Llanos are available from Mérida (p182), where several local tour companies have put together their own llanos circuits. They don't use the ecotourist ranches' services; rather, they have their own *campamentos* or arrangements with local families and utilize their lodging and eating facilities. Conditions are usually rustic, and the whole trip is more casual, but you will see nearly the same abundance of wildlife for roughly a third of the *hatos'* tour price.

Following are some of the best-known *hatos*. Their approximate locations are shown on the Los Llanos regional map (p213).

Hato El Frío

The Spanish-run **Hato El Frío** (☎ 0240-808-1004, 0414-743-5329; www.elfrioeb.com) occupies about 800 sq km on both sides of the Mantecal–San Fernando road, in what is known as Llano Bajo (Lower Plain). It's home to 45,000 head of cattle, an estimated 10,000 capybaras and 15,000 spectacled caimans. The *campamento*, 2km north of the road, features a lodge with 10 double rooms, an enchanting dining room and a biological station where caimans, turtles and other endangered species are bred. Boats and jeeps are available to take visitors for four-hour excursions in the morning and the afternoon. There's a choice of about 10 excursions in the dry season and five in the wet season.

When there are vacancies, El Frío accepts individual travelers turning up without bookings, but does recommend an advance call. The price is $110 per person per day in the high season (November 15 to April 30) and $80 the rest of the year.

The entrance to El Frío is 187km west of San Fernando (42km east of Mantecal) and is easily accessible by public transportation. The San Fernando–Barinas buses will drop you off at the main gate, from here it's a 20-minute walk to the *campamento*.

Hato El Cedral

Another Llano Bajo ranch, about 65km southwest of El Frío, **Hato El Cedral** (Map p68; in Caracas ☎ 781-8995; www.hatocedral.com; 5th fl, Edificio Pancho, No 33, Av La Salle, Los Caobos, Caracas) covers 530 sq km and has around 15,000 head of cattle. More than 300 bird species have been recorded on the ranch, as well as 20,000 capybaras and numerous other species. The *campamento*, 7km west off the road, provides comfortable lodging in 25 double rooms, all equipped with private bathrooms with hot water, and there is also a tiny pool. Half a dozen different excursions are offered, by boat or specially prepared minibus.

El Cedral stringently requires advance booking in Caracas. The price in the high season (November 15 to April 30) is $170 per person a day in a double room. In the off-season, it's $140. The ranch is accessible by infrequent San Fernando–Elorza buses, but if you prefer, the *hato* can provide a car from Barinas ($120 roundtrip for up to four persons).

Hato Doña Bárbara

Part of La Trinidad de Arauca cattle ranch, **Hato Doña Bárbara** (dbarbara@cantv.net) is close to El Cedral but is accessible only via a roundabout route through Elorza. In the dry season, it can be reached by road, but in the wet season, the only access is by river (two hours from Elorza).

With 360 sq km, Doña Bárbara is smaller than El Frío and El Cedral, but its wildlife is equally rich and diverse, except for capybaras, which are not so numerous here. Instead, there's quite a number of ant-eaters. The *campamento* has 21 double rooms with bathrooms and offers two excursions a day, by boat, jeep and on horseback. Reservations should be made through the Doña Bárbara travel agency (p223) in

---

WHEN TO GO ON A WILDLIFE SAFARI IN LOS LLANOS

Wildlife is abundant in both rainy and dry seasons. The main difference is that in the dry season most animals flock to scarce sources of water, which makes them easy to watch. In the wet season, on the other hand, when most of the land is half-flooded, animals are virtually everywhere, but are harder to spot because they are not concentrated in certain areas.

The dry season is considered the high season. This is a good time to come, as you can expect good weather and more trip options because more land is accessible. The closer to the end of the dry season you come, the better. In late April or early May, just before the first rains, the crowds of caimans or capybaras can be unbelievable! In most *hatos*, the high season also means higher prices.

If you go in the dry season, take a hat, sunglasses and sunblock. They may also be useful in the wet season, and you'll need wet-weather gear as well. Whenever you come, don't forget a flashlight, mosquito repellent, good binoculars and plenty of film.

LOS LLANOS

THE WILDLIFE OF LOS LLANOS

Apart from the legendary anacondas and piranhas, Los Llanos is most famous for the myriad birds that gather seasonally to breed and feed, or live permanently on the grassy plains and wetlands. About 360 bird species have been recorded in the region, which accounts for a quarter of all the bird species found in Venezuela. Waterbirds and wading birds predominate, and the list includes ibis, herons, cormorants, egrets, jaçanas, gallinules and darters. The *corocoro*, or scarlet ibis *(Eudocimus ruber)*, noted for its bright red plumage, appears in large colonies in the dry season. Three-quarters of the world's corocoro population lives in Venezuela.

As for mammals, the most common local species (apart from the omnipresent cattle, of course) is the *chigüire*, or capybara *(Hydrochoerus hydrochaeris)*. This is the world's largest rodent, growing up to about 60kg, and has a face like a guinea pig and a coat like a bear's. It's equally at home on land and in the water, feeding mainly on aquatic plants. Other local mammals include armadillos, peccaries, opossums, anteaters, tapirs, ocelots and the occasional jaguar. Two interesting aquatic mammals are the *tonina*, or freshwater dolphin *(Inia geoffrensis)*, and the *manatí*, or manatee *(Trichechus manatus)*, which inhabit the large tributaries of the Orinoco. Both are endangered species, but numbers of the latter are dangerously low.

Also threatened with extinction is the largest American crocodile, the caimán del Orinoco *(Crocodylus intermedius)*. These huge reptiles once lived in large numbers and grew up to 8m from head to tail but the population was decimated by ranchers, who killed them for their skins. Far more numerous is the *baba*, or the spectacled caiman *(Caiman crocodylus)*, the smallest of the family of local caimans, growing up to 3m in length.

San Fernando de Apure. A minimum three-day stay is required. Price is $125 per person per day year-round, all inclusive.

The *campamento* was named after Rómulo Gallegos' classic novel, for which the *hato* provided the setting and principal character. The grave of Francisca Vásquez de Carrillo (the real name of the ranch's owner, on whom Doña Bárbara was based) is here. Today the ranch is run by the Estrada family.

Hato La Fe

One of the smallest, cheapest and most accessible *hatos* is **Hato La Fe** (☎ 0414-468-8749, 0414-946-1419; soreliafranco@yahoo.es; ☒) It's in Guárico state, in what is called the Llano Medio (Middle Plain), about 74km north of San Fernando de Apure. It covers just 10 sq km, so understandably there are fewer animals here than at the large ranches. There are not many capybaras, but you'll find spectacled caimans, anteaters, capuchin monkeys, iguanas and plenty of birds. Excursions are organized both inside and outside the ranch, including one to the neighboring Hato Masaguaral with its biological station breeding Orinoco caimans.

A beautiful colonial-style mansion, next to the road, provides the base for excursions.

It has seven rooms (three with and four without bathrooms) and a rustic restaurant, and there's a pool at the back. The prices are $70 per day in the high season (November 1 to April 30) and $65 the rest of the year, all-inclusive except for long trips outside the ranch. You can lower the cost if you camp in your tent or sling your hammock. The ranch is friendly to casual visitors, but call ahead to check the availability of rooms. You can also book with Piedras Vivas travel agency (p75) in Caracas, but make sure they don't charge you more than the ranch would.

La Fe is in Corozo Pando, roughly midway ($1.50, 1½ hours) between San Fernando de Apure and Calabozo; buses on this road run every half-hour. Get off at *alcabala* (road checkpost), which is next to the ranch's gate.

Hato Piñero

The best-known ranch in the Llano Alto (Upper Plain), **Hato Piñero** (Map pp56-7; in Caracas ☎ 991-1135, 992-4413; www.hatopinero.com; Biotur Hato Piñero, 6th fl, Edificio General de Seguros, No 6-B, Av La Estancia, Chuao, Caracas) is in Cojedes state, close to the town of El Baúl. It's accessible by road from the central states. If you are coming from Caracas, head to Valencia, from here it's about 210km south.

Given its location, Piñero has a somewhat different spectrum of wildlife from that of the ranches in the Llano Bajo. The topography of this 800-sq-km ranch is more diverse, and forests cover part of the terrain. The wet season comes later (in late May or early June) and ends earlier (in September). Although capybaras and caimans are not ubiquitous here, there is a large variety of other animals, including ocelots, monkeys, anteaters, agoutis, foxes, tapirs and iguanas. This is largely the effect of hunting and logging bans, which were introduced as early as the 1950s.

The tourist facilities accommodate about 25 guests in rooms with private bathrooms, and packages should be booked in Caracas. The package, including full board and excursions, will cost $95 a day in the low season (May to November) and $130 from December to April. The ranch can provide transportation from Caracas ($190 round-trip for up to four persons).

The Northeast

Venezuela's northeast is a diverse mosaic of natural marvels. Encompassing sun-drenched islands and golden Caribbean beaches, rich coral reefs, fresh mountains and verdant valleys, this is the classic destination for get-away-from-it-all holidays of sunbathing and water sports. One of the most famous island destinations in the Caribbean, Isla de Margarita alone attracts more international holidaymakers than anywhere else in Venezuela. And the coast features many more idyllic stretches, including the dazzling islands and beaches of Parque Nacional Mochima, and the off-the-beaten-path beaches and coves hidden away in remote stretches of the coastline beyond Río Caribe.

However, popular as they are, the northeast isn't just about its beaches. This region also boasts Venezuela's best cave, and is home to fascinating wildlife, rugged peninsulas, little-trodden hiking trails and a scattering of historical forts, towns and churches where the Spanish conquered and settled. Plus there's plenty more to discover: salt pans, cacao plantations, hot springs and vast ranches of water buffalo. Once you've spent time in the northeast, you'll understand what prompted Columbus to whimsically declare the region as 'paradise on earth.'

HIGHLIGHTS

- Sun worship at the ever-popular beaches of **Isla de Margarita** (p242)
- Splash out at the picturesque islands of **Parque Nacional Mochima** (p251)
- Skinny dip at the secluded beaches east of the **Río Caribe** (p265)
- Explore underground in Humboldt's magnificent **Cueva del Guácharo** (p275)
- Get off the beaten track in the remote **Parque Nacional Península de Paria** (p271)

THE NORTHEAST

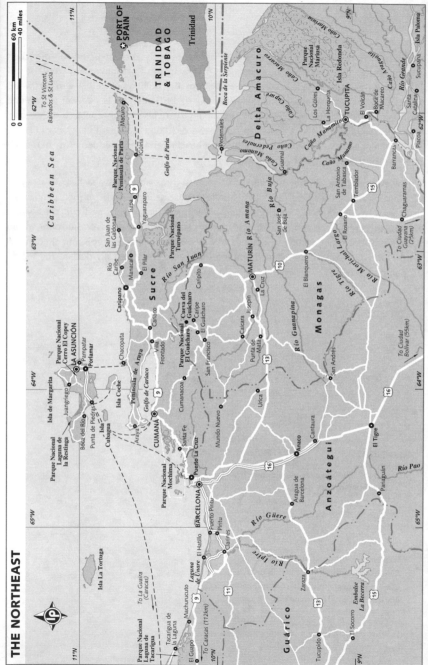

ISLA DE MARGARITA

☎ 0295 / pop 350,000

Sun seekers and bargain hunters are drawn en masse to Isla de Margarita for its beautiful beaches and duty-free prices. As well as being a prime destination for Venezuelans, the island also caters for large numbers of charter-flight international holidaymakers looking for white sand and blue sea within reach of a comfy bed, plenty of shops, bars and a nicely chilled Margarita cocktail.

But the island offers much more than just sand, sun and spending. It boasts a rich and colorful spectrum of habitats, from mangrove swamps to mountainous cloud forest and extensive semidesert. It features two fine Spanish forts, one of the oldest churches in the country plus a sprinkling of little old towns, some of which are vivid centers of craftwork. And the well-developed tourist structure means that there are all kinds of activities on offer – from snorkeling trips to world-class windsurfing.

With an area of 1071 sq km, Isla de Margarita is Venezuela's largest island, 69km from east to west and 35km from north to south. Lying some 40km off the mainland, it is composed of what were once two islands, now linked by a narrow, crescent-shaped sandbank, La Restinga. The island houses five major nature reserves, among them two national parks.

The eastern section is the more fertile and contains 95% of the island's population and towns, connected by a well-developed array of roads. The western Península de Macanao is, by contrast, arid and sparsely populated, with just 20,000 people living in a dozen villages dotted along the coast.

The island's typically Caribbean climate is glorious year-round: temperatures between 25°C and 28°C, mitigated by evening breezes. The rainy period lasts from November to January, with rain falling mostly during the night. Peak seasons include Christmas, Easter and the August holiday period. May, June and October are the quietest months.

Getting There & Away

AIR

The island is a lucrative market, so almost all the major national airlines fly into **Aeropuerto Internacional del Caribe General Santiago Mariño** (☎ 0295-269-1027). There are about 20 flights a day to Caracas with various carriers, including Aeropostal, Aserca and Avior. The normal one-way fare is $56 to $82, but discounted fares – sometimes as low as $30 – are occasionally available, so shop around. There are scheduled direct flights to Barcelona ($25 to $45), Carúpano ($33), Cumaná ($34), Maracay ($77 to $84), Valencia ($57 to $76) and Maturín ($29 to $50) among others, and indirect flights to just about anywhere else in the country. Aereotuy and Rutaca fly to Los Roques ($97 to $157). Avior flies direct to Port of Spain, Trinidad ($188 roundtrip) and Rutaca goes via Maturín for $107 three times weekly.

ISLAND TOP TEN

There's plenty more to do on Isla de Margarita after soaking up the tropical rays on its famous beaches. Following are some highlights:

- Hire some **wheels** (p239) and discover Margarita's remote villages and hilltops
- Try your hand at windsurfing or kitesurfing off **Playa El Yaque** (p243)
- Drift down Parque Nacional La Restinga's mangrove tunnels (see p242)
- Catch the sunset with an ice-cold beer at **Juangriego** (p241)
- Dive or snorkel around the **Archipelago Los Frailes** (p243)
- Sample the glitzy shopping and nightlife of **Porlamar** (p238)
- Tickle a starfish's underbelly at Boca de Río's **Museo Marino** (p242)
- Escape the crowds to the remote **Macanao Peninsula** (p244)
- Explore the island's best restored colonial **fortresses** (p239)
- Pay your respects to her holiness the **Virgen del Valle** (p240) in her pilgrimage site in El Valle

ISLA DE MARGARITA

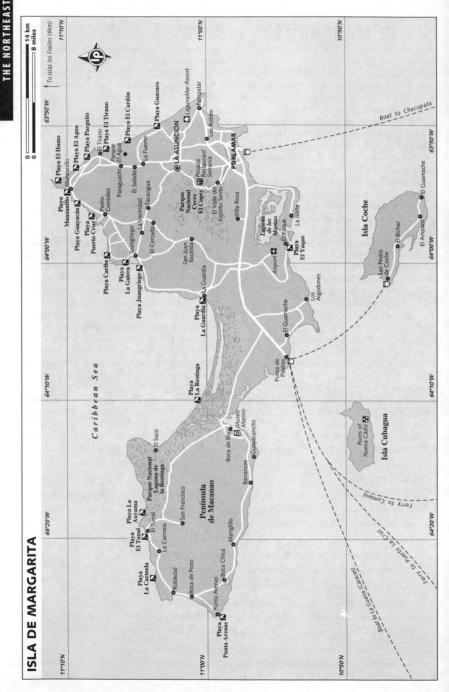

0 ─────── 14 km
0 ─────── 8 miles

To Islas los Frailes (4km)

Caribbean Sea

Playa El Humo
Playa El Agua
Playa Parguito
Playa El Tirano
El Tirano
Parque
El Agua
Playa El Cardón
Playa Guacuco
Manzanillo
Playa
Manzanillo
Playa Guayacán
Playa
Puerto Cruz
Pedro
González
La Fuente
La Vecindad
Paraguachí
El Salado
LA ASUNCIÓN
LagunaMar Resort
Pampatar
La Tacarigua
Posada
Restaurant
Serranía
Boat to Chacopata
Playa Caribe
Playa
La Galera
Playa Juangriego
Juangriego
El Cercado
Parque
Nacional
Cerro
El Copey
El Valle del
Espíritu Santo
PORLAMAR
San Juan
Bautista
Villa Rosa
Laguna
de los
Mártires
La Isleta
La Guardia
Playa
La Guardia
Airport
Playa
El Yaque
Playa El Yaque
Isla Coche
El Guamache
Los
Algodones
El Guamache
El Bichar
El Guamache
San Pedro
de Coche
El Ampato
Playa
La Restinga
Punta de
Piedras
El Saco
Museo
Marino
Boca de Río
Guayacancito
Ruins of
Nueva Cádiz
Isla Cubagua
Parque Nacional
Laguna de
la Restinga
Barrancas
San Francisco
Playa La
Auyama
El Tunal
La Carmela
Península
de Macanao
Playa
La Carmela
Robledal
Boca de Pozo
Manglillo
Boca Chica
Ferry to Cumaná
Punta Arenas
Playa
Punta Arenas
Ferry to Puerto La Cruz
Boat to La Guaira (Caracas)

63°50'W
64°00'W
64°10'W
64°20'W

11°10'N
11°00'N
10°50'N

The following airline offices are located in Porlamar:

Aeropostal (☎ 263-9374; www.aeropostal.com; Centro Comercial Galerías, Av 4 de Mayo)

Aereotuy (LTA; ☎ 263-2211; www.tuy.com/aereotuy.htm; Av Santiago Mariño)

Aserca (☎ 261-6186; www.asercaairlines.com; Centro Comercial Galerías, Av 4 de Mayo)

Avior (☎ 263-8615; www.avior.com.ve; Av 4 de Mayo)

Laser (☎ 269-1429; www.laser.com.ve; Calle Zamora)

Rutaca (☎ 263-9236; www.rutaca.com.ve; Calle Cedeño)

BOAT

Isla de Margarita has links with the mainland via Puerto La Cruz and Cumaná from the ferry terminal, Punta de Piedras (29km west of Porlamar), and also has small boats to Chacopata from Porlamar itself. Busetas and *micros* (small buses) regularly shuttle between Punta de Piedras and Calle Mariño in Porlamar.

Tickets for the **Conferry** (☎ 239-8148) ferries can be bought at the **Porlamar office** (☎ 239-8339; www.grancacique.com.ve; Av Santiago Mariño) or at the Punta de Piedras ferry terminal. Tickets for Gran Cacique are also available in the Porlamar office and in **Punta de Piedras** (☎ 239-8339). Frequent small buses ($0.50) run between Punta de Piedras and Porlamar; taxis charge $6.

An international ferry service between Pampatar and Trinidad, St Vincent, Barbados and St Lucia, operated by Windward Lines, may come back to Margarita in the future (see Güiria p271).

From Puerto La Cruz

The Puerto La Cruz route is operated by **Conferry** (☎ 261-6780; www.conferry.com; Calle Marcano, Porlamar; ⏱ 8am-noon & 2-5pm Mon-Fri, 8am-noon Sat) car/passenger ferries, with three to four departures daily. Passenger fares are $9/4.50 for adults/child under seven and seniors in 1st class, and $6/3.20 in 2nd class. Cars go for $16 to $19. The trip takes about 4½ hours. Conferry also operates its modern *Margarita Express* on this route, which takes up to 500 passengers and 150 cars and runs at up to 36 knots. It sails twice a day and takes just two hours, costing $26/13 per adult/under 7s or over 65s in VIP class and $17.50/9.50 in 1st class.

Additionally, the route is operated by the passenger-only *Gran Cacique Express* hydrofoil, with two departures a day at 10am and 7pm (adult/child under seven $15/8, two hours).

From Cumaná

The Cumaná route is serviced by *Gran Cacique II*, which shuttles twice a day (1st class adult/child under seven $13/9, tourist class $10/6, two hours). Naviarca also sometimes runs large ferries to Cumaná ($9, 3½ hours, twice daily). In Isla de Margarita, tickets for Naviarca ferries are only sold in Punta de Piedras.

In the off-season, there may be fewer departures than listed.

From La Guaira

In the high season only, Conferry also runs boats from La Guaira, near Caracas, for adult/child under seven $48/25 in VIP class and $35/19 in 1st class.

From Peninsula de Araya

The cheapest route to Isla de Margarita is the passenger-only boat service which ferries between Chacopata and the breakwater near the old lighthouse in central Porlamar. Boats run from 8am until about 4pm, approximately every two hours or when full. The schedule is infrequent – if there are few passengers around, some departures may be canceled. Boats vary in size, capacity (from about 30 to 70 passengers) and quality – some look ready to sink at any moment. The trip takes one to 1½ hours ($4.50).

Getting Around

Margarita's airport is in the southern part of the island, 20km southwest of Porlamar, and can be reached by por puestos ($2). A taxi on this route will cost about $10.

Conferry (☎ 261-6780; www.conferry.com; Calle Marcano, Porlamar; ⏱ 8am-noon & 2-5pm Mon-Fri, 8am-noon Sat) runs a ferry service between Punta de Piedras and Isla de Coche, operated daily at 5pm and returning at 6am next day (adult/under 7s or over 65s $0.80/0.45, one hour).

Porlamar is the island's transportation hub, from where frequent small buses (called *micros* or busetas) service towns and beaches around the eastern part of the island. Public transportation on the Península de Macanao is poor.

Renting a car or scooter is cheap and rewarding. There are at least a dozen car-rental companies opposite the airport's international terminal, and many have offices in Porlamar. You can get a small car for as little as $15 to $30 per day. Scooters and bicycles can be hired at several places in Porlamar from around $12 per day.

For more laid-back sightseeing, plenty of travel agencies will happily show you around. They offer general-interest tours, specific trips (eg Laguna de La Restinga) and activities (horse riding, fishing, snorkeling, scuba diving). The Archipiélago Los Frailes, northeast of Margarita, has become a popular destination for snorkeling.

PORLAMAR
☎ 0295 / pop 102,000

Porlamar is the largest and busiest urban center on the island and is likely to be your first stop when you arrive from the mainland. It's a bustling city replete with enticing shopping centers, hotels and restaurants. Tree-shaded Plaza Bolívar is Porlamar's historic center, but the city is rapidly expanding eastward, with new suburbs and tourist facilities being built all the way along the coast as far as Pampatar.

Information

EMERGENCY
Police (☎ 261-4919; Av Losada)

IMMIGRATION
DIEX (☎ 263-4766; Calle Arismendi No 7-85; 🕑 9am-noon & 2-5pm Mon-Fri) This is the place to get visa or tourist-card extensions. Ask here or at the tourist office for foreign-consulate representatives in Margarita.

INTERNET ACCESS
Cabinas Telefónicas Privadas (Calle Malavé; 🕑 9:30am-1pm & 2-6pm Mon-Sat)
Café Utopia (Centro Comercial Costa Azul, Av Bolívar; 🕑 11am-late)
Cyber Café (Ciudad Comercial Jumbo; 🕑 9am-9pm Mon-Sat)
Cyber Café (Calle Mariño; 🕑 8:30am-6:30pm Mon-Sat)
Digicom (Calle Fermín; 🕑 9am-12:30pm & 2-8pm Mon-Sat)
Tel.com (Plaza Bolívar; 🕑 8:30am-7pm Mon-Sat)
Virus C@fe (Calle Tubores; 🕑 9am-12:30pm & 3-7pm Mon-Fri)

LAUNDRY
Lavandería Divino Niño (☎ 264-7783; Calle Cedeño; per 5kg $2.50; 🕑 8:30am-6pm Mon-Sat)

Lavandería Edikö's (☎ 0416-695-2480; Calle Fermín; per machine $1; 🕑 8am-7pm Mon-Sat, 8:30am-1pm Sun)
Lavandería La Burbuja (Calle Maneiro; per kg $0.65; 🕑 7am-6pm Mon-Sat) There is also another branch at Calle Fajardo.

MEDICAL SERVICES
Clínica La Fe (☎ 262-2711; Av Jóvito Villalba, Los Robles) A good clinic outside the center.
Farmacias SAAS (☎ 263-8080; Centro Comercial Galerías, Av 4 de Mayo; 🕑 24hr) Well-stocked pharmacy.
Hospital Central Dr Luis Ortega (☎ 261-1101, 261-6508; Av 4 de Mayo) The most convenient central clinic.

MONEY
Stores will accept cash dollars for payment using the official exchange rate. Credit cards are widely accepted in shops, up-market hotels and restaurants. Banks that handle credit-card advances on Visa and MasterCard:
Banco de Venezuela (Blvd Guevara)
Banesco (Av 4 de Mayo)
Corp Banca (Centro Comercial Galerías, Av 4 de Mayo) There are also branches at Av Santiago Mariño and Calle Velázquez.

There are *casas de cambio* (money exchange office) in the airport and in the city. Those that change cash and traveler's checks include:
Cambios Cussco (☎ 264-1102; Calle Velázquez)
Italcambio (☎ 263-3240; Ciudad Comercial Jumbo, Nivel Ciudad)
Triple casa de cambio (☎ 261-0458; Edificio Tiffany Palace, Av 4 de Mayo)

POST
Ipostel (☎ 263-4577; Calle Maneiro; 🕑 8am-5pm Mon-Fri)

TOURIST INFORMATION
Corpotur (☎ 262-2322; corpoturmargarita@cantv.net; Centro Artesanal Gilberto Menchini, Av Jóvito Villalba, Los Robles; 🕑 8:30am-12:30pm & 1:30-5:30pm Mon-Fri) This government-run tourist office is midway between Porlamar and Pampatar.
Cámara de Turismo (☎ 262-0683; caturmar@cantv .net; Quinta 6, Av Virgen del Valle, Urb Jorge Coll; 🕑 8am-12:30pm & 2-5pm Mon-Fri) This private tourist-information corporation is in a residential district beyond Corpotur.

Sights & Activities
One of Porlamar's few tourist sights is **Museo de Arte Contemporáneo Francisco Narváez**

PORLAMAR

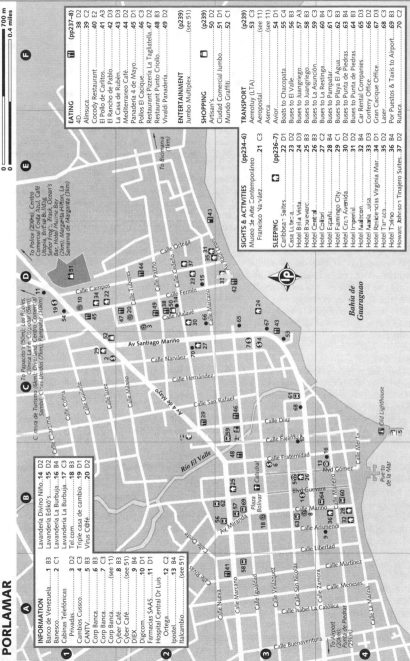

(☎ 261-8668; Calle Igualdad at Calle Díaz; ☽ 8:30am-3:30pm Mon-Fri, 10am-3:30pm Sat & Sun) in a large, modern building in the town center. On the ground floor is a large collection of sculptures and paintings by the Margarita-born artist Narváez (1905–82), while the upper floor is used for temporary exhibitions.

The theme park **Diverland** (☎ 262-0813; Av Jóvito Villalba; ages 10-34 $7.50, ages 35-64 $4; ☽ 6pm-midnight Fri-Sun) has a modest collection of roller coasters and other attractions. One of the biggest draws within this complex is the separately run **Waterland** (☎ 262-5545), which – by reservation only – lets you swim with dolphins and seals in the attached swimming pool. All sorts of packages can be organized from the basic $50 deal including a video, briefing and 30 minutes with the dolphins, to full training courses.

Sleeping

Porlamar has stacks of hotels for every budget. As a general rule, prices and standards rise from west to east. Prices given are for the low season, expect to pay 20% to 30% more when visiting from mid-July to mid-September or mid-December to mid-January.

BUDGET

Most cheap hotels lie in the older, western side of Porlamar, while budget accommodations in the new center are few and far between. However, if you can, it's worth spending a few extra dollars for nicer surroundings, better restaurants, cybercafés, bars and security. All the hotels listed in this section have private bathrooms, unless indicated otherwise.

Hotel Tamaca (☎ 261-1602; tamaca@unete.com.ve; Av Raúl Leoni; s/d with fan $11/13.50, s/d with air-con & hot water $14/17, tr with air-con & hot water $21-24; ☒) This is the most popular backpacker shelter in the more upmarket Eastern side of Porlamar – and deservedly so. It has a wide variety of basic rooms, and the hotel has its own bar-cum-restaurant surrounded by trees and lit with multicolored lights in the evening.

Hotel Residencias Virginia Mar (☎ 261-2373; Calle Fermín; s/d/tr $9.50/11/12.50; ☒) Also in the modern eastern section of town, though not so recommendable, this gringo haunt has uninterested staff and beaten-up, though spacious and livable, rooms near the main street.

Hotel Malecón (☎ 263-8888; Calle La Marina; s/d $6.50/7.50) If you'd rather save your bolívares and stay in the cheaper Colonial side of town, this is one of the friendliest places you could choose. It has quirky narrow passageways, and light but simple doubles, some overlooking the sea.

Hotel Central (☎ 264-7162; Blvd Gómez; d/tr $9/12.50; ☒) This budget option is located on the old town's bustling Blvd Gómez and has a large balcony from which to watch the world go by. It's a quiet, family-run affair that sees few travelers. Rooms have little natural light.

Other budget choices:

Hotel Torino (☎ 261-7186; Calle Mariño No 7-33; s/d/tr $7.50/9/10; ☒) Fine if you don't mind cold-water showers or the occasional *cucaracha* (cockroach).

Hotel Boulevard (☎ 261-0522; Calle Marcano; d/tr/q $17/19/22; ☒ ▢) Bland but comfortable enough for a low to middle-range budget.

Hotel Gran Avenida (☎ 261-7457; Calle Cedeño; d/ste $17/25; ☒) Styleless central option lacking natural light, but with fridge and TV.

Hotel España (☎ 261-2479; Calle Mariño; s/d $4.50/6, d with bathroom $7) Cheapest but scuzziest option near the waterfront.

MID-RANGE

All the following hotels have private, hot-water bathrooms.

Hotel María Luisa (☎ 261-0564; fax 263-5978; Av Raúl Leoni; s/d/tr/q $21/23/28/29; ℗ ☒ ▣) While this white three-star hotel doesn't scream personality, it's very nice and good value for money, with clean rooms, cable TV, a patio-bar and a cute private swimming pool. It's also within easy strolling distance of the best seafront restaurants.

Hotel Imperial (☎ 261-6420; Av Raúl Leoni; d/tr/q $19/23/27.50; ℗ ☒) If the María Luisa is full, this older place is just a few steps away is also relatively good, though it lacks the same airy atmosphere. For both hotels, ask for a room in one of the upper floors with a view over the sea. English is spoken.

Casa Lutecia (☎ 263-8526; Calle Campos; d incl breakfast $19; ☒) This is one of very few homely posada-style places to stay in high-rise-happy Porlamar. And it's a very pretty little spot with a relaxed atmosphere and a shady terrace encompassed by tropical flowers and hanging vines. The pleasant rooms have mosquito nets and cable TV.

Hotel Flamingo City (☎ 264-5564; Av 4 de Mayo; d/tr $19/22.50; ☒) Strategically placed on the main shopping street, Flamingo City has uniform, carpeted rooms with one double and one single bed, hot-water bathrooms, a fridge and a safe. It's recognizable by the bright-blue paint job, and its position in the shadow of an enormous bank building next door.

Hotel Colibrí (☎ 261-6346; hotelcolibri@starmedia .com; Av Santiago Mariño; s/d/tr/q incl breakfast $24/32.50/ 41/53; ☒) This pleasant, upmarket hotel is distinguished by its professional English-speaking service, sparklingly clean rooms (with cable TV) and corridors decorated with mosaics, art and pastel-pink paint. It has a small terrace on the roof.

Howard Johnson Tinajero Suites (☎ 263-8380; www.howardjohnson-ve.com; Calle Campos; s/d/tr/q $32/ 39/44/47; P ☒ ☒) Though not as swanky as the giant top-end hotels, this apartment hotel has a very comfortable collection of family-friendly suites equipped with a kitchenette, fridge, microwave and coffee-maker, plus all the pots and pans – everything you need to be independent. The cost is about $25 more in the high season.

Caribbean Suites (☎ 264-2120; carsuites@hotmail .com; Calle Fermin; d/tr $25/37; P ☒) This budget option is a well-equipped hotel with family-oriented suites.

TOP END
Porlamar has plenty of hotels in this category. Virtually all of them are in the eastern part of the city, from Av Santiago Mariño eastward toward Pampatar.

Hotel Marina Bay (☎ 262-5211; www.hotelmarina bay.com; Calle Abancay, Costa Azul; s/d $60/75; P ☒ ☒) This is an aging but good choice by the sea and close to Porlamar's nightlife. It has glass lifts, fully equipped rooms with balcony, most looking down over the central swimming pool.

Hotel Bella Vista (☎ 261-7222; www.hbellavista .com; Av Santiago Mariño at Calle Igualdad; d/tr with city view $70/82, swimming pool view $78/90, sea view $87/99; P ☒ ☒) Smack in the middle of coastal Porlamar is this large high-rise four-star hotel, which offers most of the amenities you'd wish for, including large open-plan tropical gardens strewn with palm trees and bordering the sea. All prices include breakfast.

Margarita Hilton (☎ 262-0810; www.margarita .hilton.com; Calle Los Uveros, Costa Azul; s & d $177, superior $208, luxury $240, extra luxury $312, ste $300-468; P ☒

☒ ☒) An oldie but a goodie, the Hilton has been setting the standard in Porlamar for many years, and still can't be beaten for luxury. It's got the glitziest casino in town, and the garden-filled complex is packed with so many other boutiques, bars, restaurants and other features that it can be easy to get lost. A highlight is the pool area, which has waterfalls, islands, volleyball and fountains.

La Samanna de Margarita (☎ 262-2222; habit aciones@lasamannademargarita.com; Av Bolívar; d $103; P ☒ ☒ ☒ ☒) Let's face it – we're all looking for some serious R&R in Margarita, be it feet up on the beach or being pampered rotten in a health spa. Well this hotel, 2km east of central Porlamar, offers everything from facials to massages, reflexology and a large Jacuzzi pool (price list at reception). The hotel itself also boasts a breezy pool, fresh airy rooms with four-poster beds and beautiful ceramic-decorated bathrooms that give you the choice to bathe in either salty or fresh water.

Eating
Porlamar is jam-packed with restaurants catering for every price range. Most of the restaurants pitched at tourists are in the eastern sector of the city, east of Av Santiago Mariño.

CAFÉS & QUICK EATS
Panadería 4 de Mayo (Calle Fermín at 4 de Mayo; snacks & sandwiches $0.60-1; ☒ 7am-10pm) Of several bustling *panaderías* (bakeries) in the vicinity, this invariably popular spot comes up trumps. It also has beautiful pastries, sandwiches and cakes with as much cream and strawberries as you can eat, and its terrace has to be Porlamar's top people-watching spot.

Vivaldi Panadería (☎ 263-0452; Calle Patiño at Calle Malavé; ☒ 7am-10pm; ☒) A more tranquil spot for frothy cappuccinos, excellent pastries and a morning newspaper, Vivaldi's bakery has a pleasant little terrace or air-con interior to choose from.

4D (☎ 261-5805; Calle Malavé; ice-cream $2-5; ☒ 9am-midnight) Opposite Vivaldi, the chic 4D has a large, shaded terrace where you can cool off with one of the bucket-sized tubs of ice-cream in 27 flavours from passion fruit to tiramisu.

Alinsuca (Calle Cedeño; mains $2.50-4; ☒ noon-4pm Mon-Sat) Hearty low-budget pasta outfit that also has pizzas; you can take away or eat in.

El Pollo de Carlitos (Calle Marcano; mains $2-3; ☺ noon-1am Mon-Sat) This rustic restaurant does chicken and does it well. Half a chicken with *hallaca* (chopped meat in maize dough, steamed in banana leaves) and salad costs just $2.

Pollos El Cacique (Calle Igualdad; mains $2-5; ☺ 11am-10pm) Another reasonably good-value chicken affair, this time in a modern, fast-food environment with identically uniformed staff.

RESTAURANTS

Cocody Restaurant (☎ 261-8431; Av Raúl Leoni; mains $9-13; ☺ 6pm-late Thu-Tue; ☒) The best part of this cozy, night-time venue is the romantic, beachfront terrace lit only by candles, spot-lit palms and the pinpricks of light visible from across the bay. It proffers up fine French food including some drop-dead gorgeous fish dishes.

El Rancho de Pablo (☎ 263-1121; Av Raúl Leoni; mains $5-9; ☺ 8am-11pm) The biggest and best of a clutch of beachfront restaurants in the area, this shady spot sees all manner of folk enjoying seafood, fish and grills while watching the beachgoers at play.

Restaurant Pizzería La Tagliatella (☎ 264-1096; Calle Fermín; pizzas $5-8; ☺ 11:30am-11pm Mon-Sat; ☒) This snug little restaurant serves beautiful Italian pasta, pizzas, risotto and grills. It also has a far-ranging wine list to enjoy.

Restaurant Punto Criollo (☎ 263-6745; Calle Igualdad 19; mains $3-6; ☺ 8am-midnight; ☒) Deservedly popular with locals for its solid Venezuelan food and budget prices, this large, no-nonsense restaurant has a lengthy bit-of-everything menu, smartly bow-tied waiters and a long drinks list to linger over.

Hotel Tamaca (☎ 261-1602; Av Raúl Leoni) Tamaca's tiny garden bar sees plenty of backpackers devouring pizza and downing a beer in the evening. There's a pool table to one side to distract you from belly rumblings while waiting for your food.

La Casa de Rubén (☎ 263-7964; Final Av Santiago Mariño; mains $4-9; ☺ 11:30am-11pm Mon-Sat) Somewhat hidden from the road, this homestyle restaurant serves all the typical Margariteña *pescado y mariscos* (fish and seafood) dishes you could wish for. Add your thoughts to

the growing collection of customer's scribbles on the walls.

Mediterraneo Café (☎ 264-0503; Calle Campos; pasta $6-10; ☺ 11:30am-3:30pm & 7-11pm Mon-Sat; ☒) This smart Italian restaurant sets course for a nautical theme, and serves delicious local and Mediterranean dishes both on an outdoor terrace and in an air-con interior.

Drinking & Dancing

Bars appear and disappear at lightning speed in Margarita, so check locally for the latest hotspots. There's always a collection of rustic shacks, well stocked with cold beers, on the beach. Most of the trendy nightclubs and bars are outside the city center.

British Bulldog (☎ 267-1527; Centro Comercial Costa Azul, Av Bolívar; ☺ 9pm-late Thu-Sat, Tue-Sat in high season) Margarita's first and only British-style pub, with a cheerful British-Venezuelan running the show behind the bar. It often has live rock music at weekends.

Café Utopia (Centro Comercial Costa Azul, Av Bolívar; ☺ 11am-late) This fresh modern café has a spacious outdoor terrace, an indoor bar and Internet booths set into a line of glass-top tables. It's an equally good spot for a leisurely daytime java or for limbering up for a big night in the local clubs.

El Rancho de Pablo (☎ 263-1121; Av Raúl Leoni) Lulled by the sound of waves and with the sea breeze in your hair, it's hard not to slip into a mellow holiday mood at this beach-side bar and restaurant. There are several smaller huts and bars nearby.

Papacito's (Av 4 de Mayo; ☺ 8pm-late Wed-Sat) This wood-decked pub and Mexican restaurant is hidden behind a wall of cacti and bamboo 200m beyond Centro Comercial Jumbo Plaza. The rustic outdoor bar and dance floor has a happening atmosphere once a crowd gathers – bring on the tequila!

Señor Frog's (☎ 262-0451; Centro Comercial Costa Azul, Av Bolívar; ☺ 6pm-late Tue-Sun) This hard-to-miss lurid-yellow building covered with Muppet-like plastic figures of upside-down cows and track-suited frogs is a gimmicky family restaurant by day and a thumping Latin-pop-orientated *discoteca* (disco) by night.

Track (Top fl, Centro Comercial Costa Azul, Av Bolívar; ☺ Thu-Sun) An edgier crowd tend to frequent this more exclusive club, where DJs pump out hip-hop, house, chillout and trance.

Ocean's Bar (Centro Comercial Costa Azul, Av Bolívar; ⓨ Thu-Sat) Another option at the ever-popular Costa Azul center, this VIP-style bar has to be the most stylish of the bunch. Don't expect the 'in' crowd to arrive before 11pm.

Entertainment

Many of the bigger hotels give a nod to Las Vegas with their showy casinos filled with beeps, flashes and short-skirted hostesses. If you want to join in, try the casino hall at the Margarita Hilton (see p237), which is one of the best.

Recommendations for cinemas:

Cines Unidos (☎ 262-1568; Centro Comercial Sambil, Los Robles; admission $3)

Jumbo Multiplex (☎ 264-6665; www.cinex.com.ve; Centro Comercial Jumbo Plaza; admission $2)

Shopping

Oh yes, ask Venezuelans and they'll all agree that Porlamar is a great place for shopping. Several sparkling malls dot Porlamar and Pampatar, packed with imported duty-free goods, from clothes and jewelry to electrical knick-knacks. In many cases, the prices given are only a few dollars less than on the mainland, but there are frequent sales and plucking up the nerve to ask for *'su mejor precio'* (your best price) will often knock a fair few bolívares off the cost – even in boutiques.

The most elegant and expensive shopping areas are on and around Avs Santiago Marino and 4 de Mayo. Here you'll find jewelry, imported spirits, fashionable clothing, computers etc. For clothes, check **Mundo Graffiti** (☎ 263-9242; Av Santiago Mariño at 4 de Mayo; ⓨ 10am-7:30pm Mon-Sat, 10am-3pm Sun), which is one of the largest and most economical retailers around. And don't miss combing the huge six-level **Ciudad Comercial Jumbo** (Av 4 de Mayo at Calle Campos). Or catch a bus out to **Centro Comercial Sambil** (Av Bolívar; ⓨ 10am-9pm Mon-Sat, noon-8pm Sun; Ⓟ), which is the shiniest and newest of the island's shopping malls.

The old center has some of the cheapest shops. Many of these nestle in two central pedestrian malls, Blvd Guevara and Blvd Gómez, south of Plaza Bolívar.

For crafts, one of very few specialized outlets is **Artisan's** (☎ 261-9626; Calle Malavé; ⓨ 9am-4pm Mon-Fri, 9am-1pm Sat). In the after-noon, craft and souvenir stalls also mushroom along Av Santiago Mariño, selling their wares until 9 or 10pm.

Getting There & Away

Porlamar is the main base for international and national routes to Isla de Margarita; see p233 for airline office details.

There's frequent transportation to most of the island, including Pampatar, La Asunción and Juangriego, operated by small buses, which leave from different points in the city center; the departure points for some of the main tourist destinations are indicated on the map p235.

Getting Around

There are several car-rental companies in front of the Hotel Bella Vista, but you'll find plenty more cheap places throughout the town. Many also hire out scooters (see p233 for prices). For sportier visitors, **Bicimania** (☎ 262-9116; bicimania@cantv.net; Centro Comercial AB; ⓨ 9am-1pm & 4:30-7pm Mon-Fri, 9am-3pm Sat), east of town, rents out bicycles.

PAMPATAR
☎ 0295 / pop 35,000

Pampatar is 10km northeast of Porlamar, but the two urban centers are gradually merging into a single sprawling conurbation. Founded in the 1530s, Pampatar was one of the earliest settlements on Margarita, and within 50 years it grew into the largest shipping center in what is now Venezuela. It still shelters some colonial buildings and a nostalgic hint of bygone days, but it's increasingly circled by new constructions.

Sights

Pampatar's fort, the **Castillo de San Carlos Borromeo** (admission free; ⓨ 9am-noon & 2-5pm Tue-Sun), is in the center of town, on the waterfront. It was built from 1662 to 1684 on the site of a previous stronghold that was destroyed by pirates. It's the best-preserved fort on the island, and a classic example of Spanish military architecture.

Opposite the fort is the **parish church**, a sober whitewashed construction from the mid-18th century. Go inside to see the crucifix, Cristo del Buen Viaje, over the high altar. Legend has it that the ship that carried the crucifix from Spain to Santo Domingo called en route at Pampatar, but d~

repeated efforts it couldn't depart until the Christ image had been unloaded. It has remained in Pampatar since.

The beach extends for a kilometer east of the fort, and exudes old-world charm, with rustic boats anchored in the bay playing host to a colony of pelicans, and fishers repairing nets on the beach. Unfortunately the beach is not for swimming, owing to water pollution.

The cape at the far eastern end of the bay is topped by another fort, the ruined **Fortín de la Caranta**, which provides sweeping views.

Courses

Centro de Lingüística Aplicada (CELA; ☎ 262-8198; www.cela-ve.com; Calle Corocoro, Quinta Cela, Urbanización Playa El Ángel) offers intensive Spanish language courses of different levels, with optional accommodations and meals in family homes. Excursions and cultural activities also run.

Sleeping & Eating

La Posada de Aleja (☎ 262-7044; laposadadealeja@ hotmail.com; Calle Nueva Cadiz; s/d/tr/q $16/19/22/25; ✖) Brightly decorated in rainbow colors, this cheery guesthouse is run by a friendly family and just a short hop from the beach. Rooms are spotless and good value. Prices rise by 30% in high season.

Aparthotel Don Juan (☎ 262-3609; Calle Almirante Brión 10; d/tr $11.50/12.50; ✖) This simple no-frills hotel offers straightforward value with clean rooms, many with bunk beds, near to the seafront.

Posada La Bufonera (☎ 262-9977; Calle Almirante Brión; d/tr $19/22; P ✖) Across the street from Don Juan, this is the most attractive spot in Pampatar. Its cozy suites house two to three people with a hot-water bathroom and rustic one-hob, small-fridge kitchen. Its positioned right on the beach, so you can wake up to the morning catch of fish. Prices rise by $6 in high season.

Hotel Flamingo Beach (☎ 262-4822; flamingo@ enlared.net; Calle el Cristo; s/d $40/64; P ✖ ✿) Further east from the others is this upstanding three-star choice with a glass lift running front face, an outdoor pool, tennis nd small private beach. Try to score vith a sea view.

you're hungry, head for the line tched shacks on the beach, each

with a powerful sound system and good supply of cold beer and fried fish.

LagunaMar Resort (☎ 262-1117; www.lagunamar .com.ve; Sector Apostadero; s/d per person incl 3 meals $80/ 70, children under 12 incl 3 meals $20; P ✖ 💻 ✿) You'll need a map to navigate your way around this enormous, sprawling resort 3km north of Pampatar. Its impressive list of facilities include four swimming pools (one with wave machine, another with a waterslide pool), a kids' club, casino, a private lagoon for water sports including kayaking and water-skiing, floodlit tennis courts, volleyball… the list is endless. If you'd rather not stay, a day pass of $25 includes use of the facilities, drinks and lunch.

Getting There & Away

Buses running between Porlamar and Pampatar make the trip every five to 10 minutes ($0.25, 20 minutes).

EL VALLE DEL ESPÍRITU SANTO

☎ 0295 / pop 12,000

Commonly called 'El Valle' (Valley), this small town is Margarita's spiritual capital, home to the island's patroness, the miraculous Virgen del Valle. Her image, kept in the mock-Gothic church on the plaza, draws pilgrims from all around eastern Venezuela year-round – particularly on September 8, the Virgin's day. El Valle is the first Marian religious sanctuary in the Americas.

Sights

The fanciful, gingerbread-house–like **Basílica de Nuestra Señora del Valle**, standing out in all its pink-and-white glory on the central plaza, was built from 1894 to 1906 and is the current home to the Virgin. According to local history, the image of the Virgin was brought to the town around 1510. Her statue is to the right of the high altar, usually surrounded by a huddle of devotees. You can buy rosaries, amulets, crafts – oh, and a few hundred images of the virgin – from a crowd of religious stalls next to the church. Shops around the main plaza can also be a good place to buy crafts, especially hammocks and hats.

The **Museo Diocesano** (admission free; ☾ 9am-noon & 2-5pm Tue-Sat, 9am-1pm Sun), behind the church, features objects related to the Virgin plus votive offerings from the faithful.

In a different vein, diagonally opposite the church is the **Casa Museo Santiago Mariño** (admission free; ⏰ 8am-1pm & 3-6pm Mon-Sat, 8am-1pm Sun), the house where its namesake hero of the War of Independence was born in 1788. The sizable country mansion has been painstakingly reconstructed and fitted with vintage furniture and period memorabilia.

Getting There & Away
Buses between Porlamar and El Valle shuttle frequently ($0.25, 15 minutes).

LA ASUNCIÓN
☎ 0295 / pop 20,000
Although Porlamar is by far the largest urban center on the island, the small, sleepy town of La Asunción is the state capital of Nueva Esparta. This tranquil spot is set in a fertile, verdant valley.

Sights
Built in the second half of the 16th century, the **Catedral** (Plaza Bolívar; ⏰ open for services 6-10am & 6-8pm), on the attractive, tree-shaded Plaza Bolívar, is one of the oldest surviving colonial churches in the country, widely thought to be the second oldest after Coro's cathedral. It has an unusual bell tower and a delicate Renaissance facade portal.

On the northern side of the plaza is the **Museo Nueva Cádiz** (Plaza Bolívar; admission free; ⏰ 9am-4pm Tue-Sun), named after the first Spanish town in South America, which was established around 1500 on Isla Cubagua, south of Margarita. An earthquake in 1541 completely destroyed the town. The museum displays a small collection of exhibits related to the region's history.

Just outside town, a 10-minute walk southward up the hill, is the **Castillo de Santa Rosa** (admission free; ⏰ 9am-5pm Tue-Sun) one of seven forts built on the island to protect it from pirate attacks. It provides great views and has some old armor on display.

Sleeping & Eating
Hotel de la Asunción (☎ 242-0666; Calle Unión; d $9-11.50, tr $16; Ⓟ 🅿️) Two blocks east of Plaza Bolívar, this run-of-the-mill budget hotel is one of the very few places to stay.

Getting There & Away
Buses from Porlamar will let you off on Plaza Bolívar ($0.50, 20 minutes). After looking around, you can return or continue on to Juangriego ($0.50, 20 minutes).

PARQUE NACIONAL CERRO EL COPEY
If you have your own wheels and want to leave the crowds behind, you might want to head up into the fresh, hilly Parque Nacional Cerro El Copey southwest of La Asunción. The old road climbs up through cool, scented woodland before descending to El Valle on the other side. It passes some beautiful viewpoints and picnic stops, or you can stop for a meal at the idyllic hilltop **Posada Restaurant Serrania** (☎ 242-8864; Carrera La Asunción–El Valle; mains $3-6; ⏰ 11am-7pm Tue-Sun; 🅿️), 3km southwest of La Asunción. The posada also has good little rooms, with bathroom, fridge and TV for $22 for a double or $28 for a family room. But it's the view over treetops and down to the sea that you'll remember.

JUANGRIEGO
☎ 0295 / pop 24000
Set on the edge of a fine bay in the northern part of Margarita, Juangriego is a relaxing backwater famous for its fabulous sunsets. The place to hang is the beach along the bay, with rustic fishing boats, visiting yachts and pelicans. Far away on the horizon, the peaks of Macanao are visible, and are spectacular when the sun sets behind them.

Crowning the hill just north of town is the **Fortín de la Galera** (admission free; ⏰ dawn-dusk). These days little remains of the colonial fort (destroyed by royalists in 1817) other than some stone walls with a terrace and a refreshment stand, but it sees a steady trail of hand-holding couples arriving in the late afternoon for a sweeping view of the sunset.

If you're coming from La Asunción (see earlier) consider stopping off in Santa Ana to see its church, which is similar to the La Asunción cathedral but two centuries younger. In the nearby village of El Cercado, typical Venezuelan pottery is made.

Sleeping
Juangriego is increasingly catering to tourism. Prices rise by 25% in high season.

Hotel Nuevo Juangriego (Calle La Marina; d with bathroom & fan $14, with air-con $20; 🅿️) This small hotel is smack in the middle of the beach, and the five rooms facing the bay have balconies from where you can enjoy a postcard snap of the sunset.

Hotel-Restaurant Patrick's (☎ 253-6218; Calle El Fuerte; d/tr $12.50/19; 🅿️) About 200m north along the beach, this secure French-run hotel offers nine good rooms, with TV, hot water, and a restaurant offering – you guessed it – French dishes (and pretty darn good ones at that).

El Caney (☎ 253-5059; Calle Guevara 17; d/tr $10/15) This is a colorful little Peruvian-run posada. Nice touches include a palm-thatched terrace out front, and a pool table out back.

Posada Los Tucanes (☎ 253-1716; Calle El Fuerte; d with bathroom $18; ⚠) Next door to Hotel Patrick's is this simple and quiet, four-room place.

Just back from the beach, in the Centro Comercial Juangriego, on Calle La Marina, are two uninspiring but cheap hotels:

Hotel Gran Sol (☎ 253-3216; d $9.50; ⚠)
Hotel La Coral (☎ 253-2463; d $9; ⚠)

Eating
Restaurants and bars line the beachfront, all perfectly positioned to keep sunset-watchers fed and watered with romantic suppers and cold beer. They include the recommended **El Viejo Muelle** (Calle La Marina; mains $4-8) and **El Búho** (☎ 239-8340; Calle La Marina; ⚠).

Getting There & Away
Frequent buses run between Porlamar and Juangriego ($0.80, 40 minutes) via La Asunción.

PARQUE NACIONAL LAGUNA DE LA RESTINGA
The national park of **Laguna de la Restinga** (in Porlamar ☎ 242-0306; admission $0.30, boats extra; ⚠ 8am-4:30pm) covers the lagoon and a large mass of mangroves riddled with narrow, labyrinthine channels at its western end. This is a habitat for a variety of birds, including pelicans, cormorants and scarlet ibis.

Buses from Porlamar go regularly to La Restinga ($0.50) and will deposit you at the entrance to the embarkation pier. From there, five-seat motorboats will take you on a trip (half-hour/hour per boat $9.50/ 12.50) drifting along the interconnecting *caños* (channels) that cut through the mangroves. Note the romantic caño names like *mi dulce amor* (my sweet love), *túnel de los enamorados* (tunnel of lovers).

The boats can also take you to a fine shell beach, where you can grab fresh fried fish in an open-air restaurant before returning (half-hour/hour trip and pick up $12.50/16

per boat). In the low season, be prepared for long waits, or pay for the empty seats.

MUSEO MARINO
This new **Marine Museum** (☎ 291-3231; www.fpol ar.org.ve/museomarino; Blvd El Paseo, Boca del Río; adult/ child $2.50/1.25; ⚠ 9am-4:30pm) is worth the trip across the island, especially for families. It has a shallow pool of safe-to-handle starfish, snails and other underwater fauna that will thrill the kids. But don't stick your hands in the outdoor turtle pool as there are a couple of small sharks sharing their water! The museum also has a small aquarium of other colorful marine life and large exhibitions of coral, shell and photography. Travel agents often combine visits to La Restinga with a trip to the museum.

BEACHES
Isla de Margarita has 167km of world-famous coastline endowed with some 50 beaches big enough to bear names, not to mention countless smaller stretches of sandy coast. Many beaches have become highly developed tourist magnets with swish hotels, beachside restaurants, bars, and deck chairs and sunshades for rent. However, though the island is no longer a virgin paradise, with a little legwork you can still find relatively deserted strips of sand too.

Margarita's beaches have little shade, and some are virtually barren. Those on the northern and eastern coasts are generally better than those skirting the southern shore of the island. You can camp on the beaches, but don't leave your tent unattended. Swimmers should be aware of the dangerous undertows on some beaches, including Playa El Agua and Playa Puerto Cruz.

Playa El Agua
This wonderful 3km-long stretch of white sand has become Margarita's trendiest beach, full of Venezuela's beautiful and arty people, their chocolate bodies contrasting with lobster-colored gringos. During short holiday peaks, bathing here can prove a sardine-can experience, but at other times it's a welcoming and wonderfully laid-back spot.

The shoreline is shaded with coconut groves, and densely dotted with palm-leaf-thatched restaurants and bars that offer a good selection of food, cocktails and music.

The northern, less developed part of the beach tends to have fewer crowds.

ACTIVITIES

Travel agencies along the beach offer trips to **Los Frailes**, a small archipelago of coral islands northeast of Margarita. It's a great place for **scuba diving** ($80 for two dives) or **snorkeling** ($35 for day). Various other beach and water sports services are available, including **jet skiing** ($22 for 30 minutes) and in high-season there's sometimes **bungee-jumping** nearby for $30. Flights along the coast in ultra-light planes were suspended recently following an accident.

Parque El Agua (☎ 234-8559; www.parqueelagua .com; Av 31 de Julio; over 1.21m tall $6.25, under 0.79m tall free admission, after 2pm $5; ☼ 10am-5pm Thu-Sun, daily during high season), near Playa El Cardón, is a large family-friendly waterpark with water shutes and a large outdoor Jacuzzi. The park is a short taxi-ride south of Playa El Agua.

SLEEPING & EATING

Behind the beach is a swathe of mostly mid-range to luxury top-end hotels and holiday homes. The following prices are for low season: expect tariffs to rise by 10% to 20% in high season. For eating, there are several shacks and restaurants sitting directly on the beach.

Chalets de Belén (☎ 249-1707; Calle Miragua 3; d with fan $16, with air-con $19, 6-person cabin with fan $32; P ☒) For neat, cozy rooms at one of the lowest prices in town, this tiny little family-run spot comes highly recommended. Its affable host and her flock of small, white dogs are exceptionally welcoming, and the chalets are only a short walk from the beach.

Hotel Costa Linda Beach (☎ 249-1303; hotelcosta linda@cantv.net; Calle Miragua; s/d/tr incl breakfast $34/38/ 44; P ☒ ☒) Readers consistently recommend this warmly decorated, rustic ranch-style bungalow run by personable owners. It has shady terracing, several hammocks and a sunny pool surrounded by grassy gardens. There's also a bar and restaurant. It's a five-minute walk to the beach.

Hostería El Agua (☎ 249-1297; www.hosteriahotel .com; d/tr incl breakfast $16/28; P ☒) This place on the Manzanillo road, 350m back from the beach, is one of the cheapest places around though some bemoan it being a long haul from the beach. It also offers a friendly bar, tours, and bicycle and motorcycle rental.

Hotel Miramar Village (☎ 249-1797; www.mira marvillage.com; Calle Miragua; d $22; ☒ ☒) This OK-value hotel is situated right on the beach.

La Isla Restaurant (☎ 249-0035; mains $5-10; ☼ 11am-11pm) This is an excellent thatched-roof spot right on the beach.

GETTING THERE & AWAY

The beach has regular bus transportation from Porlamar ($0.80, 45 minutes), so you can easily come for the day if you can't afford to stay overnight.

Playa El Yaque

Playa El Yaque, south of the airport, has tranquil waters and steady winds, perfect for **windsurfing**. It has already gained an international reputation and is a hangout for the windsurfing community from Venezuela and Europe (don't be surprised to see prices in Euros). Several professional outfits on the beachfront offer windsurf rental (per hour/day/two days $15/45/75). They also offer lessons at $35 per hour, or $150 for an advanced course of 10 hours. Another upcoming new craze is **kitesurfing**. You can find lessons here for $39 for an hour and a half, or $180 for six hours. Just rental costs for kitesurfing cost $165 for 10 hours.

SLEEPING

El Yaque Motion (☎ 263-9742; www.elyaquemotion .com; s/d $20/25, with bathroom $25/30) One of the cheaper options, this laid-back place has clean, simple rooms and a sociable kitchen terrace. German and English are spoken. Try bargaining for lower prices out of season. Campers can enquire about staying behind this building for a small fee.

Surfhotel Jump'n Jibe (☎ 263-8396; www.jumpn jibe.com; Av Principal El Yaque; s/d incl buffet breakfast $24/ 48, s/d with terrace incl buffet breakfast $42/60; P ☒ ☒) Of several mid-range hotels fronting onto El Yaque beachfront, this cool relaxed choice is surely one of the best. It has clean sparking rooms, a palm-filled garden, and terrific sea views (even better if you can afford a terraced room). Prices rise from November to March.

Other Beaches

Other top beach destinations include **Playa Guacuco** and **Playa Manzanillo**. One of Margarita's finest beaches is **Playa Puerto Cruz**, which has arguably the widest, whitest stretch of sand and still isn't too overdeveloped. **Playa Parguito**, next to Playa El Agua, has strong waves good for surfing. If you want to escape from people, head for the largely unpopulated **Macanao Peninsula**, which is the wildest part of the island – and so are some of its beaches (which are mostly shadeless and deserted). A reasonable road skirts right around the barren peninsula so travelers with their own transport can easily explore the whole coastline; hiring your own car or scooter is the best way to explore. Take plenty of water.

ANZOÁTEGUI STATE

BARCELONA

☎ 0281 / pop 320,000

The yesteryear feel still lingers within the old town of Barcelona, a large coastal city and capital of the Anzoátegui state. The colonial center is a pleasant place, with leafy plazas and a mishmash of historic architecture. The city was founded in 1671 by a group of Catalan colonists and it hasn't rushed into modernity at quite the frenetic pace of its more youthful neighboring city, Puerto La Cruz, with which Barcelona is gradually merging into a single urban sprawl.

Information

INTERNET ACCESS

Centro de Navegación (Centro Comercial Marinelli, Av 5 de Julio)

MONEY

Banco de Venezuela (Plaza Boyacá) Will give cash advances on Visa and MasterCard.

Banesco (Carrera 9 Páez) Offers the same services as Banco de Venezuela.

Corp Banca (Plaza Bolívar) Will give credit-card advances and change Amex traveler's checks.

Barcelona's airport, 2km south of town, has two *casas de cambio*:

Italcambio (☎ 275-3882; ☽ 6am-8pm Mon-Fri & other flight times)

Oficambio (☎ 277-3843; ☽ 6am-8pm Mon-Fri & other flight times)

POST

Ipostel (☎ 275-7652; Carrera 13 Bolívar; ☽ 8am-noon & 2-5pm Mon-Fri) Near the plaza.

TELEPHONE

CANTV (☎ 274-9719; Centro Comercial La Llovizna, Av 5 de Julio) This center has phones and good Internet access.

TOURIST INFORMATION

Corporación de Turismo del Estado Anzoátegui (Coranztur; ☎ 275-0474; www.corporaciondeturismo anzoategui.com; Av 5 de Julio; ☽ 8am-noon & 2-5pm Mon-Fri) The main tourist office, located on the ground floor of the Gobernación building.

Dirección de Turismo (☎ 274-9601; dinformatica@ alcaldiabarcelona.gov.ve; Carrera 13 Bolívar; ☽ 8am-noon & 2-5:30pm Mon-Fri) Just off Plaza Boyacá, though far less helpful than Coranztur.

Sights

The city's historic center is **Plaza Boyacá**, which boasts a statue of General José Antonio Anzoátegui, the Barcelona-born hero of the War of Independence after whom the state is named. On the western side of this tree-shaded plaza stands the **Catedral**, built a century after the town's founding. The most venerated object in the church is the glass reliquary in a chapel off the left aisle, where the embalmed remains of Italian martyr San Celestino are kept. The richly gilded main retable dates from 1744.

On the southern side of the plaza is the fascinating little **Museo de Anzoátegui** (☎ 416-1941; admission free; ☽ 9am-noon & 2-5:30pm Tue-Fri, 9am-3pm Sat, 9am-1pm Sun). Housed in the oldest surviving building in town (built in 1671), where the likes of General Páez and Guzmán Blanco once trod, the museum features a variety of objects related to Barcelona's history. The highlight is the surreal collection of puppet-like religious statues equipped with movable limbs. Only their faces, hands and feet have been properly finished as they were originally dressed in robes and their arms and legs adjusted to place them in the appropriate pose.

An annex to the museum is housed in the **Ateneo de Barcelona** (☎ 277-2687; Calle 1 San Félix at Carrera 12 Juncal; admission free; ☽ 9am-noon & 2-5pm Mon-Fri), two blocks east. On the 1st floor of this colonial-style building is a 44-piece collection of art (most of which date from the 1940s and 1950s) by prominent modern Venezuelan artists, including Jesús Soto. There's a small handicraft shop attached, but a better selection of crafts is offered by **Gunda Arte Popular** (☎ 276-0767; Carrera

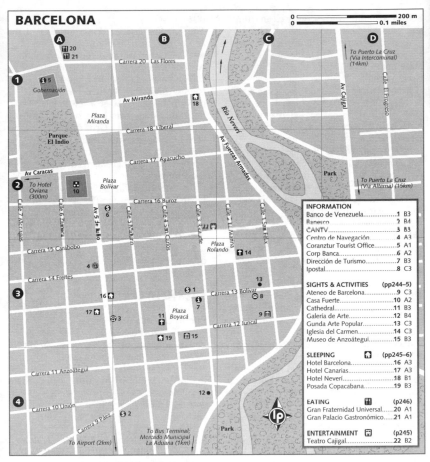

BARCELONA

0 ———————— 200 m
0 ———————— 0.1 miles

INFORMATION
Banco de Venezuela.................1 B3
Banesco.....................................2 B4
CANTV.......................................3 B3
Centro de Navegación...............4 A3
Coranztur Tourist Office............5 A1
Corp Banca...............................6 A2
Dirección de Turismo.................7 B3
Ipostal......................................8 C3

SIGHTS & ACTIVITIES (pp244–5)
Ateneo de Barcelona.................9 C3
Casa Fuerte.............................10 A2
Cathedral................................11 B3
Galería de Arte........................12 B4
Gunda Arte Popular.................13 C3
Iglesia del Carmen...................14 C3
Museo de Anzoátegui..............15 B3

SLEEPING (pp245–6)
Hotel Barcelona......................16 A3
Hotel Canarias........................17 A3
Hotel Neverí............................18 B1
Posada Copacabana................19 B3

EATING (p246)
Gran Fraternidad Universal......20 A1
Gran Palacio Gastronómico......21 A1

ENTERTAINMENT (p245)
Teatro Cajigal.........................22 B2

Bolívar 1-24; ⏰ 8:30am-noon & 2:30-6:30pm Mon-Sat), which has everything from devil masks to Christmas decorations.

Plaza Rolando is flanked by the **Iglesia del Carmen** and the **Teatro Cajigal**, both dating from the 1890s. The latter is an enchanting, small theater still used for stage performances and concerts (see the entrance board for current listings). The security guards can let you in during the day.

Further to the northwest, Plaza Bolívar is occupied by the **Casa Fuerte**, which was once a Franciscan hospice, but was destroyed by the royalists in a heavy attack in 1817. Over 1500 people who took refuge here, defenders and civilians alike, lost their lives in the massacre that followed. The surviving parts of the walls have been left in ruins as a memorial.

Sleeping

Barcelona has nothing upmarket – for this you need to go to Puerto La Cruz.

Hotel Canarias (☎ 277-1034; Carrera 13 Bolívar; d with fan $9, with air-con $11; ❄) This is a quirky, little budget hotel with a mini wishing-well, plastic birds, antique-style chairs and potted plants. It has plain rooms of different standards and prices, so have a look at a few before booking in.

Hotel Oviana (☎ 276-4147; Av Caracas; d/tr $25/ 29; ❄) This is one of Barcelona's better options, though a longer hop from the center. The hotel is five blocks west of Plaza

Bolívar. Its uniform rooms are clean, simple and have good hot-water bathrooms.

Posada Copacabana (☎ 277-3473; Carrera Juncal; d/tr with bathroom $16/24; 🕮) A new inviting place next to the cathedral with 11 rooms. Great value.

Hotel Barcelona (☎ 277-1076; Av 5 de Julio; d/tr $19/22; 🕮) This high-rise hotel has a good position overlooking a pedestrianized boulevard. Rooms are bland but serviceable, though bathrooms lack hot water.

Hotel Neverí (☎ 277-2376; Av Fuerzas Armadas at Av Miranda; d/tr $13.50/15; 🕮) Recognizable by the vivid mural of tropical flowers and birds coating the outside, this place has a deceptively grand staircase, large no-frills rooms and its own restaurant. Can be noisy.

Eating

Again, dining out is better in Puerto La Cruz, but there are some good, cheap places to eat.

Mercado Municipal La Aduana (🕒 6am-2pm) This is right next to the bus terminal, 1km south of town. It has more than a dozen popular restaurants serving a variety of typical food.

Gran Fraternidad Universal (☎ 277-5045; Av 5 de Julio; 🕒 8am-1pm Mon-Fri; set menu $2.50) There's always service with a smile at this friendly vegetarian restaurant and natural-products shop. You'll often find simple breakfasts available from 8am.

Gran Palacio Gastronómico (Av 5 de Julio; 🕒 7am-8pm) This down-to-earth self-service restaurant serves all the usual Venezuelan favorites from *arepa* to roasted chicken, and is normally chockablock with local officials from the Gobernación building.

Getting There & Away

AIR

The airport is 2km south of the city center. Buses going south along Av 5 de Julio pass within 300m of the airport ($0.25). Several carriers have daily flights to Caracas ($50 to $71). **Avior** (☎ 276-1465) flies to Puerto Ordaz ($78). **Aserca** (☎ 274-1240) services Maracaibo ($100) and San Antonio del Táchira ($100) via Caracas. **Santa Barbara** (☎ 274-0444) flies to Barquisimeto ($84) and Mérida ($95) via Caracas. Several airlines, including Avior and **Rutaca** (☎ 276-7090), fly direct to Porlamar on Isla de Margarita ($25 to $45). Prices listed are one-way.

BUS

The bus terminal is 1km southeast of the city center, next to the market. Take a buseta ($0.20, 10 minutes) going south along Av 5 de Julio, or walk for 15 minutes.

The terminal handles mostly regional routes, including hourly buses to Píritu ($1) and Clarines ($0.80). Few long-distance buses originate from here, but occasionally buses from Puerto La Cruz call here on their way to Caracas and Ciudad Bolívar. The terminal in Puerto La Cruz is far busier, so it's better to go there instead of waiting in Barcelona.

To Puerto La Cruz, catch a buseta going north on Av 5 de Julio ($0.30, 45 minutes). They use two routes, Vía Intercomunal and Vía Alterna. Either will set you down in the center of Puerto La Cruz. There are also faster por puesto minibuses ($0.40), which depart from Av 5 de Julio 2½ blocks south of Banesco.

PUERTO LA CRUZ
☎ 0281 / pop 207,000

Puerto La Cruz is the major gateway to the nation's favorite getaway, Isla de Margarita, and a jumping-off point to the beautiful Parque Nacional Mochima (p251), which stretches just north and east of the city. Taking advantage of its position, it has grown into Venezuela's major water-sports center, with half a dozen marinas and yacht clubs, yacht rental, diving and fishing tours.

But until the 1930s Puerto La Cruz was no more than an obscure village. It boomed after rich oil deposits were discovered to the south, and port facilities were built just east of town and serve as a main terminal to ship oil overseas. Nowadays, this city is a youthful, dynamic and quickly expanding place.

The city itself is not noted for its beauty, though it features a lively 10-block-long waterfront boulevard, Paseo Colón, packed with hotels, agencies, bars and restaurants. This seafront area comes to life in the late afternoon and evening, when craft stalls open and a gentle breeze sweeps away the heat of the day.

Information

EMERGENCY

Policia Estado Anzoategui (☎ 266-1937; Calle Los Cocos) The local police station, near Parque Andrés Eloy Blanco.

INTERNET ACCESS

Austrian Online Center (AOC; ☎ 268-6010; Centro Comercial Cristoforo Colombo, No 15, upper fl, Paseo Colón; ⏰ 9am-9pm Mon-Sat)

Café Digital (Centro Comercial Cristoforo Colombo, No 29, upper fl, Paseo Colón; ⏰ 9am-9pm Mon-Sat)

LAUNDRY

Lavandería Libertad (☎ 265-5204; Calle Libertad No 100; per 3kg $2; ⏰ 8am-noon & 2-7:30pm Mon-Fri, 7:30am-8pm Sat)

Lavandería Margarita (Calle Bolívar; per machine $0.40; ⏰ 8am-noon & 2-7:30pm Mon-Sat)

MEDICAL SERVICES

Farma Santa Barbara (☎ 268-5560; Calle Freites; ⏰ 8:30am-7:30pm Mon-Sat) A central pharmacy.

MONEY

Most major banks are within a few blocks south of Plaza Colón:

Banco de Venezuela (Calle Miranda)
Banco Mercantil (Calle Arismendi)
Banesco (Calle Freites)
BBVA (Calle Carabobo)
Corp Banca (Av 5 de Julio)

You'll find *casas de cambio* in top-end hotels on the Paseo, including Hotel Gaeta, or try **Italcambio** (☎ 265-3993; Centro Comercial Paseo del Mar, Paseo Colón; ⏰ 8:30am-5pm Mon-Fri, 9am-1pm Sat).

POST

Ipostel (☎ 268-5355; Calle Freites; ⏰ 8am-noon & 2-5pm Mon-Fri)

PUERTO LA CRUZ

0 — 400 m
0 — 0.2 miles

INFORMATION	
Austrian Online Center..........(see 32)	
Banco de Venezuela................1 D3	
Banco Mercantil.....................2 D2	
Banesco...................................3 C3	
BBVA..4 D2	
Café Digital.........................(see 32)	
CANTV......................................5 C3	
Corp Banca..............................6 D3	
Farma Santa Barbara...............7 C3	
Ipostel.....................................8 C3	
Italcambio...............................9 C3	
Lavandería Libertad...............10 B4	
Lavandería Margarita.............11 B4	

SIGHTS & ACTIVITIES	(p248)
Aquatic Adventures...............12 D2	
Explosub............................(see 14)	

SLEEPING	(pp248-50)
Cristina Suites.......................13 D4	
Hesperia Puerto La Cruz........14 D2	
Hotel Caribbean Inn...............15 D3	
Hotel Comercio......................16 C3	
Hotel Cristal Park...................17 C3	
Hotel Europa..........................18 C3	
Hotel Gaeta............................19 C3	
Hotel Guayana.......................20 C3	
Hotel Margelina.....................21 B3	
Hotel Montecarlo...................22 B3	

Hotel Neptuno......................23 B3
Hotel Rasil............................24 B4
Hotel Riviera.........................25 C2
Hotel Sorrento......................26 D3

EATING 🍴	(p250)
Centro Naturalista La Colmena..27 C2	
Lunchería Ali Miranda.............28 D3	
Mister Pollo...........................29 C3	
Restaurant Chic e Choc...........30 B3	
Ristorante O'Sole Mio............31 B3	

SHOPPING 🛍	(p247)
Centro Comercial Cristoforo Colombo.................32 C3	

TRANSPORT	(pp250-1)
Bus Terminal.........................33 C4	
Excursion Boats.....................34 C2	
Excursion Boats.....................35 B3	
Minibuses to Barcelona..........36 C3	
Minibuses to Santa Fe............37 C4	
Por Puestos to Guanta...........38 D3	

Caribbean Sea

Plaza Colón

Plaza Bolívar

Iglesia de Santa Cruz

To Santa Fe (36km); Cumaná (72km)

To Centro Commercial Plaza Major, Complejo Turístico El Morro, Trattoria El'Ancora (4km); Hostería El Morro (4.5km); Golden Rainbow Maremares Resort & Spa, Maniquí (5km); Barcelona (15km)

To Ferry Terminals & Aeroexpresos Ejecutivos (1km)   Parque Andrés Eloy Blanco

TELEPHONE
CANTV (Paseo Colón; ⊙ 9am-10pm Mon-Sat, 10:30am-4pm Sun) Telephones and good Internet access.

TOURIST INFORMATION
The **Coranztur** tourist office was closed due to Paseo Colón's reconstruction at the time of research (and may not reopen). The closest office is in Barcelona.

Complejo Turístico El Morro

This large and modern complex on the waterfront, 4km west of the city center, is one of the most ambitious urban projects ever to be carried out in the country. Set on a coastal stretch of land, roughly in the form of a 1.5km by 2km rectangle, the complex is a model residential retreat for stressed-out urbanites, designed and built entirely from scratch. The area has already been crisscrossed by a maze of canals, on the banks of which a whole city of apartment blocks and houses is springing up. Houses have their own piers and slipways. The complex boasts commercial centers, hotels, parks, gardens and golf courses.

The project began in the 1970s, and some areas and hotels are completed. There are two flashy shopping malls including Centro Comercial Plaza Mayor on the southern side of the complex, which has two multi-screen cinemas. **Night boat excursions** (per person incl drinks $6; ⊙ 5:30pm Sat & Sun) around the canals are organized on weekends from here.

To get to the complex from either Puerto La Cruz or Barcelona, take the Av Intercomunal and get off one block north of the Crucero de Lecherías, where five 20-story residential towers, known as the Conjunto Residencial Vistamar, loom. From there, por puestos go north, skirting the western, then northern side of the complex and take you to the marina.

Tours

A score of travel agents can be found on Paseo Colón, nestled in handicraft shops and hotel lobbies. They offer regional tours around Parque Nacional Mochima (p251) as well as further afield. These tours usually include snorkeling (equipment provided), and may also feature fishing, scuba diving and other water sports. Boat trips are also organized from Santa Fe (p254) and Mochima (p254), and may be cheaper there.

Boat excursions to the nearby islands of Mochima depart regularly every morning from piers on either end of Plaza Colón. They are either transportation-only trips or more complete tours that may include snorkeling, lunch and drinks.

Some of the most popular destinations are Playa El Saco and Playa Puinare (both on Isla Chimana Grande), as well as Playa El Faro (on Isla Chimana Segunda), which all have nice beaches and food facilities. Playa El Faro also has iguanas and good snorkeling grounds.

Note that Playa El Saco, Playa Puinare and Playa El Faro all have boat services that run to and fro, so you don't need to take a formal tour. Boats depart between 8am and noon from the city waterfront and return in the afternoon between 2pm and 5pm. The roundtrip fare to El Faro or El Saco is $4.50 to $6 per person. Campers can pay $6 to arrange for pick-up on a later date (camping costs $1 per person a night on the main beaches). There may also be some boats to Isla de Plata, but you can get there more cheaply from Guanta (see p253).

When there are enough tourists, a transport-only tour can be arranged to Playa El Saco and Playa Puinare and Playa El Faro. The trip costs a few dollars more than the roundtrip fares to a single beach, but varies according to the number of people going: inquire at the marina.

Another popular tour goes further, to Islas Arapo and Arapito, and includes an hour's snorkeling (equipment provided) in La Piscina – a wildlife-rich coral reef between the two islands. The boats depart from Puerto La Cruz' waterfront from 9am to 10am and return about 5pm; tours cost $18 to $25 per person, including lunch and soft drinks.

Aquatic Adventures (previously Lolo's Diving Center; ☎ 267-3963, 0414-806-3744; www.aquaticadven.com; Marina Puerto La Cruz) and **Explosub** (☎ 267-3256 ext 5524; www.puntonet.com.ve/explosub; Hotel Hesperia Puerto La Cruz) are major local diving schools that organize diving courses and tours. A two-dive trip costs about $75.

Sleeping

Puerto La Cruz is an expensive place to stay by Venezuelan standards, and hotels fill up fast in season. Many hotels have gathered on Paseo Colón and the adjoining streets, and this is the most lively area to stay. All the hotels listed below have private bathrooms.

BUDGET

Hotel Neptuno (☎ 265-3261; fax 265-5790; Paseo Colón at Calle Juncal; s/d/tr $14/19/22; 🗶) The Neptune has corridors painted in a lurid yellow and green paint job and similarly canary-colored 'Hotel Neptuno Football Club' shirts and other gear on sale in reception. Rooms are good value with hot-water bathrooms and cable TV, while the hotel's biggest attraction is its open-sided restaurant with sweeping views out to sea.

Hotel Europa (☎ 268-8157; Plaza Bolívar at Calle Sucre; d/tr $13/15; P 🗶) Pass through the car-park entrance to reach the entrance to this sparsely adorned hotel, whose only extravagance is a neon-lit image of the Virgin Mary at the top of the stairs. Rooms are plain but spacious, with a basic bathroom. Very friendly staff.

Hotel Margelina (☎ 268-7545; Paseo Colón; s/d/tr $9.50/12/14; 🗶) While none of the bare-bones hotels in Puerto La Cruz can claim style, the creaky beds and wonky corridors of Margelina do retain character. And if you don't expect luxury from the hotel, you should also be pleased with the position bang on the seafront and near several restaurants.

Other recommendations:

Hotel Guayana (☎ 265-2175; Plaza Bolívar; s with fan $9.50, s/d with air-con $12/14; 🗶)

Hotel Montecarlo (☎ 268-5677; 119 Paseo Colón; d $9.50-12.50, apt $16; 🗶)

MID-RANGE

Hotel Comercio (☎ 265-1429; Calle Maneiro No 9-D; d/tr $16/18; 🗶) If you can dip a little deeper into your cash stash, this well-kept block is a better choice. True, its uninterested staff are less personable than Europa, but rooms have cable TV, a higher level of security and downstairs rooms also have hot water.

Hotel Sorrento (☎ 268-6745; Av 5 de Julio No 60; s/d/tr/q/ste $16/20/26/30/36; 🗶) This orange-brick, relatively new hotel has a welcoming atmosphere. Rooms are comfortable though nothing to write home about. Cable TV is provided and family rooms have fridges.

Hotel Cristal Park (☎ 267-0744; fax 265-3105; Calle Libertad at Calle Buenos Aires; d/tr $23/28; 🗶) This compact, well-furnished hotel makes up for its inland position and lack of good

sea views by offering very clean, good value rooms, all with hot-water bathrooms and cable TV. It has friendly, young staff and good security.

Hotel Gaeta (☎ 265-0411; gaeta@telcel.net.ve; Paseo Colón at Calle Maneiro; d without sea view $27, with sea view $34, tr $34; P 🗶) Smack in the middle of the seafront boulevard, this old hotel keeps its rooms in very good nick. Sea-view rooms cost more, but are also bigger and better. All rooms have hot-water bathrooms and cable TV, and are freshly decorated, and light-filled, with wickerwork furniture.

Hotel Caribbean Inn (☎ 267-4292; h_caribbean@ convergence.com.ve; Calle Freites; d/tr/q $38/45/52; P 🗶 🖾) Still more comfortable is this big, impersonal but professional three-star hotel towering over Calle Freites. It offers ample doubles with hot-water bathrooms and cable TV.

Hotel Rasil (☎ 267-2422; rasilplc@hotmail.com; Calle Monagas at Paseo Colón 6; d without sea view $32, with sea view $34; P 🗶 🖾) This 25-floor, four-star hotel is one of the poshest on the waterfront though a short walk from the action. It has balconies from which to enjoy the panoramic sea views, only slightly marred by an ugly patch of wasteland in front of the hotel. Rooms are pleasantly furnished with wickerwork furniture, and have hot-water bathrooms, cable TV and fridge.

Hostería El Morro (☎ 281-1312; fax 281-4226; Av Americo Vespucio, El Morro; d/tr $24/29; P 🗶 🖾) One of the cheapest options in the upmarket area of Complejo Turístico El Morro, this hotel has access to the beach and offers comfortable rooms (with national TV), hot-water bathrooms and a restaurant and bar.

You could also try **Hotel Riviera** (☎ 267-2111; hotel-riviera@cantv.net; Paseo Colón 33; d without sea view $30, with sea view 32, tr $35; 🗶).

TOP END

Hesperia Puerto La Cruz (☎ 500-3666; hotel@hesperia -puertolacruz.com; Paseo Colón; d $85 incl breakfast; P 🗶 🖵 🖾) This ship-shaped five-star option is the best in the town center, and located just a short walk from the marina. Almost all rooms have beautiful sea views (with balcony), plus there is a private beach below. The Hesperia has a casino, spa and good wheelchair accessibility.

Golden Rainbow Maremares Resort & Spa (☎ 281-1011, in Caracas 0212-959-0148; www.maremares .com; d & tr incl breakfast $103; P 🗶 🖵 🖾) The newest and most classy hotels are mostly in the Complejo Turístico El Morro, including this vast sprawling complex with its own spa, tennis courts, sauna and a positively gigantic 3000-sq-meter swimming pool, complete with wave machine. And only a short putt away is a new nine-hole golf course.

Cristina Suites (☎ 418-7777; www.cristinasuites .com; Av Municipal; d/tr incl breakfast $59/63; P 🍴 🕹) Cramming no less than 250 identical suites into its two looming towers, Cristina Suites lies several blocks further back from Paseo Colón. It has an outdoor pool below the towers, and the spacious suites each have a kitchen, salon and eating area.

Eating

The cream of the city's restaurants are along Paseo Colón. This area stays alive well into the evening, when fresh breezes alleviate the heat and people gather in the establishments overlooking the beach. It's essentially an upmarket area, but it also shelters some half a dozen cheap Middle Eastern fast food eateries serving set lunches for about $3.

Centro Naturalista La Colmena (☎ 265-2751; Paseo Colón 27; 3-course menu $3; 🕙 11:45am-2pm Mon-Fri) This lunch-only vegetarian café and natural products shop has flowery tables and a tiny covered terrace looking out across the boulevard to the sea. It serves recommended budget set lunches.

Restaurant Chic e Choc (☎ 265-2551; Paseo Colón; mains $5-15; 🕙 11:30am-2:30pm & 7-11pm Mon-Sat; 🍴) Characterized by the shiny chrome tubing outside and low curvy booths in a low-lit setting within, this restaurant is recommended for its French cuisine: everything from duck à l'orange to jumbo-shrimps flambéed 'à la pirate' ($12).

Hotel Neptuno (☎ 265-3261; Paseo Colón at Calle Juncal; mains $3.50-8) In the same area is this restaurant towards the top of the Hotel Neptuno. Its dishes are filling and relatively cheap, but the principal attraction is the wide-ranging view out to sea (great when the sun is low).

Lunchería Ali Miranda (☎ 266-2591; Calle Miranda; 3-course menu $3; 🕙 7:30am-4pm Mon-Sat) Offering a wide choice of cheap set meals and a hearty *desayuno criollo* (typical breakfast), this down-to-earth spot has friendly efficient service, tasty food, generous portions and low prices. Consistently popular with locals.

Trattoria L'Ancora (☎ 281-5266; Centro Comercial Plaza Mayor; pizzas $5-9.50, pasta $4-6; 🕙 noon-11pm; 🍴) This well-positioned restaurant overlooks the canals of El Morro, where you can watch expensive boats glide past as you chow down on tasty pizza and pasta dishes. You can relax in its open-air terrace or indoor glass-walled area with air-con.

You could also try the following:

Centro Comercial Plaza Mayor (El Morro) Has a food court serving a variety of fast food from sushi to coconut ice-cream.

Mister Pollo (Calle Sucre off Paseo Colón; mains $2.50-4; 🕙 11am-9pm Mon-Sat) Tasty chicken at low prices.

Ristorante O'Sole Mio (Paseo Colón; mains $3-5.50) An affordable Italian restaurant.

Entertainment

The city's nightlife is to be found principally in El Morro.

Maniqui (☎ 280-3472; Level C3, Centro Comercial Caribbean Mall, Av Américo Vespucio; admission $0.60 Thu-Fri, men/women incl drinks $6/3 Sat; 🕙 10pm-late Thu-Sat) is accepted by most as *lo mejor rumba* (the best party) in town.

There are several cinema complexes in El Morro's Centro Comercial Plaza Mayor:

Cines Plaza Mayor (☎ 281-3903; admission $2)

Cines Unidos (☎ 281-6764; admission $2)

Getting There & Away

AIR

The nearest airport is in Barcelona (see p246).

BOAT

Puerto La Cruz is the major departure point for Isla de Margarita, with services offered by **Conferry** (☎ 267-7847; www.conferry.com; Sector Los Cocos) and **Gran Cacique Express** (☎ 263-0935; www .grancacique.com.ve; Sector Los Cocos). Smaller excursion boats leave from the small piers in town. See p233 for fare details and travel times.

The ferry terminals are accessible by por puesto from the center or a taxi will cost $2. Go in the daytime – it's a spectacular journey between the islands of Parque Nacional Mochima.

BUS

The busy bus terminal is just three blocks from Plaza Bolívar. Frequent buses run west to Caracas ($7 to $11, five hours) and east to Cumaná ($2.50, 1½ hours); many of the latter continue east to Carúpano ($4 to $7, four hours) and some go as far as Güiria ($8, 6½ hours). If you go eastward (to Cumaná or further on), grab a seat on the left side of the bus, as there are some spectacular views over the islands of Parque Nacional Mochima. Por puesto cars also run to Caracas ($12, four hours), Maturín ($6, 2½ hours) and Cumaná ($4, 1¼ hours).

Buses to Ciudad Guayana run roughly every two hours ($7 to $10, six hours), and all go via Ciudad Bolívar ($6 to $9, four hours). There are also buses to Maturín ($4 to $6, three hours), a few of which continue on to Tucupita ($8 to $11, 6½ hours).

Por puesto jeeps to Los Altos depart regularly from the southern corner of the terminal ($0.65, 40 minutes). Por puesto minibuses to Santa Fe park just outside the western corner of the terminal ($0.65, 45 minutes).

To Barcelona, take a city bus from Av 5 de Julio. They go by either Av Intercomunal or Vía Alterna ($0.30). Both will deposit you in Barcelona's center in 45 minutes to one hour, depending on the traffic. There are also por puesto minibuses to Barcelona, which are faster.

Aeroexpresos Ejecutivos (☎ 267-8855) has one of the best services to Caracas, leaving from the ferry terminal west of town.

CLARINES & PÍRITU

The small towns of Clarines and Píritu, both by the Caracas–Barcelona highway, have two of the best-restored and most interesting small-town colonial churches in the region.

Founded in 1694, **Clarines** is an old colonial town about 1km south of the highway. Its church, **Iglesia de San Antonio** (☸ 9:30-11:30am & 3-6pm), is at the upper end of the historic town. Built in the 1750s, the church is a massive, squat construction laid out in a Latin-cross floor plan, and is one of only a few examples of its kind in Venezuela. Twin square towers border the austere and muck-encrusted facade. The most unusual features of the structure are the two external arcades running between the towers and the transepts on both sides of the church. The single-nave interior is topped with a wooden cupola and is refreshingly well balanced in proportion. Over the high altar is a three-tier main retable from around 1760. It is placed against the wall, which

still bears its original painting depicting a curtain.

Sixteen kilometers east of Clarines, **Píritu** lies just north of the highway (but the access road branches off from the highway 2km before the town and rejoins it 2km beyond). The town was founded in 1656, and about half a century later, the fortress-like **Iglesia de Nuestra Señora de la Concepción** (admission free; ☸ 8am-11am & 5-6:30pm) was built. This three-nave church has quite a number of remarkable colonial altarpieces. The main retable and the two side retables date from about 1745 and are richly gilded.

Scattered around each town center are small local restaurants serving cheap set meals.

Getting There & Away

Clarines and Píritu are usually visited as a daytrip from Barcelona or Puerto La Cruz. As both towns are just off the Caracas–Barcelona highway, access is easy. Apart from the long-distance buses running between these two cities, there are hourly buses from Barcelona to both Píritu ($1) and Clarines ($0.80).

PARQUE NACIONAL MOCHIMA
☎ 0293

About three dozen picturesque islands dot the clear, warm waters of Mochima, a beautiful 950-sq-km national park covering the offshore belt of the Caribbean coast between Puerto La Cruz and Cumaná. Most of the islands are barren and spectacularly rocky in parts, but some also have fine beaches for soaking up the tropical sun. Coral reefs and good snorkeling also surround a few of the islands.

Roughly bisected by the border of Anzoátegui and Sucre states, the park also includes a strip of mountainous hinterland lined with appealing bays and beaches. The area offers year-round warmth and the waters are usually calm, abounding with marine life. Tranquility seekers will be happy midweek, when only a handful of beachgoers are to be found on the more far-flung islands.

Orientation

The off-shore part of the park can be reached only by boat. Trips are organized by boat operators from Puerto La Cruz (p248),

THE NORTHEAST

PARQUE NACIONAL MOCHIMA

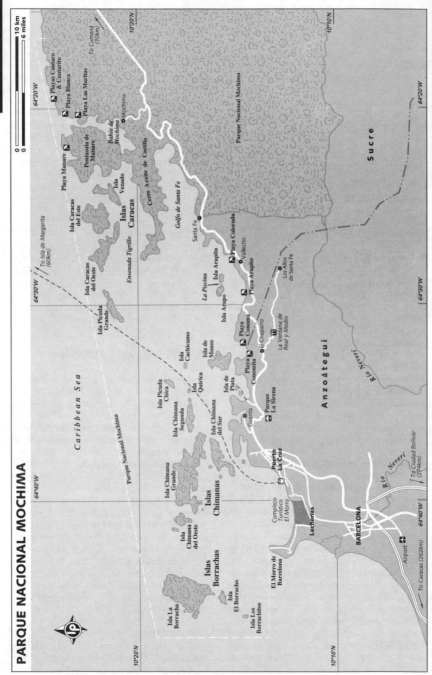

Santa Fe (p254) and Mochima (p254), of which Santa Fe is probably the cheapest. The main groups of islands include, from west to east, Islas Borrachas, Islas Chimanas and Islas Caracas. There are also a number of islands closer to the mainland, such as Isla de Plata and Isla de Monos.

The mainland park lies along the Puerto La Cruz–Cumaná road, serviced frequently by buses and por puestos, with lots of accommodations and food facilities. A dozen beaches lie off the road, the most popular of which is the palm-studded Playa Colorada, 27km east of Puerto La Cruz. Be warned that deserted beaches can be unsafe, particularly at night. There have been reports from campers of robberies on both island and mainland beaches.

About 8km east of Playa Colorada is the town of Santa Fe, which has become a backpacker haunt with fair tourist facilities. Another 15km east along the Cumaná road, a side road branches off 4km downhill to the village of Mochima, a jumping-off point for nearby beaches.

For panoramic views of the park, take a trip to Los Altos de Santa Fe, a mountain village 30km east of Puerto La Cruz. Or another, completely different visual approach is by the ferry between Puerto La Cruz and Isla de Margarita, which sails between some of the park's islands.

Isla de Plata

This is one of the most popular islands among Venezuelans, thanks to the beach and coral reefs, as well as its proximity to the mainland. There are food and drink stalls on the island but no drinking water. It also has a startling, surreal view of the huge cement plant nearby.

Isla de Plata is about 10km east of Puerto La Cruz and is accessible by frequent boats from the pier at Pamatacualito, the eastern suburb of Guanta. This suburb is serviced by regular por puestos from Puerto La Cruz ($0.30, 10 minutes). Boats run regularly, especially during weekends, taking 10 minutes to get to the island ($2.50 roundtrip). Excursion boats from Puerto La Cruz are more expensive and less regular.

Playa Colorada

This small, narrow beach has fine orange sand shaded with coconut groves. One of the top coastal destinations for locals, it has been populated with a colony of cubic tin kiosks and a line of rustic restaurants built at the back of the beach.

On weekends, it swarms with a young crowd looking to party and enjoy the spectacular sunset. You may also find boats willing to take you out to La Piscina (see p248). The beach is just 200m off the road, and you'll get a good view of it approaching by road from the east.

SLEEPING & EATING

There's quite a choice of places to stay close to the beach:

Posada Nirvana (☎ 0414-824-5607; Calle Marchán; s without bathroom $5, d/tr with bathroom $10/12.50, ste with bathroom & kitchen $16) Delightfully informal Swiss-run guesthouse. The garden houses a few hammocks and an outdoor Jacuzzi. The owner also prepares fabulous breakfasts ($4). Guests can use the kitchen. The posada is on Calle Marchán, 500m uphill from the coastal road.

Quinta Jaly (☎ 0416-681-8113; Calle Marchán; s/d/tr $11/12.50/16; ☒) Opposite Posada Nirvana, this neatly maintained country home stay is run by an affable French-Canadian. Here, too, guests have free access to the kitchen, and an optional breakfast is available for $2.50. The tidily trimmed gardens also contain a few hammocks for kicking back with a book.

Posada Edgar Lemus (☎ 0416-482-7133; d/tr $12.50/19) If you don't feel like walking uphill after a hard day's beach-going, check out this simple family posada, just off the main road. It has four spacious, clean rooms hidden behind an overgrown garden.

Hotel Tucusito (☎ 0416-681-6365; d/tr/q $25/28/32; ☒ ☒) Midway from the main road to the Posada Nirvana and Quinta Jaly is the upmarket, though slightly run-down, Tucusito, which offers spacious rooms, and two-bedroom trailers with kitchenette.

Santa Fe

This outwardly drab fishing town has become hip with the international backpacker crowd for its relaxed vibe and proximity to the islands of Mochima. It's the place to spend mornings meditating in a hammock, days taking launches to nearby beaches, and nights drinking fruity *merengadas* (f milkshake) and cold beer on the all without breaking the budget

This is thanks to the grassroots initiative of some residents, inspired by journalist and writer, José Vivas, to make the place a small ecotourist resort. The project went ahead with such enthusiasm and determination that there are now a dozen posadas along the kilometer-long beach, many owned and managed by foreigners. The conditions are simple, prices modest, and activities such as Spanish lessons, boat excursions and snorkeling are available. And there's even an international public phone on the beach.

The beach itself is nothing special, but it's regularly cleaned and the water is clear and sheltered. Bring insect repellent.

TOURS

Most posada and hotel managers organize tours and excursions. A standard full-day boat trip ($6.50 to $8) will normally feature La Piscina and the Islas Caracas, calling at two or three beaches and stopping for snorkeling (equipment provided). The Posada Café del Mar offers some of the cheapest boat trips – about $6.50 per person, with a minimum of four people.

SLEEPING & EATING

All but one of the places listed here are along the beach, just a stone's throw from each other. Each has rooms with fan and bathroom, unless otherwise specified.

Posada Café del Mar (☎ 231-0009; d $9) Entering the beach, the first place you'll reach is this German-run café and posada. It's one of the best-value budget haunts, offering 14 simple rooms with fans and hot water on upper levels, and good budget food. There's also a breezy rooftop terrace hung with hammocks, and the manager offers cheap boat tours.

La Sierra Inn (☎ 231-0042; cooperativasantafedemisamores@hotmail.com; d & tr $12.50; P 💻) A little further along is this pioneer hotel managed by José Vivas himself. It has simple rooms, several outdoor terraces and barbecue possibilities .... rak rental and tours are avail-

te Delfines (☎ 431-4166; lossietede il.com; d/tr/q $9.50/12.50/16) More ie a bit further down the this rosy-colored posada, s and a rooftop pool table nmended by readers.

Hotel Las Palmeras (☎ 231-0008; tr with fan $16, with air-con $22, apt with air-con $38; 🆇) If you can't survive without your air-con and hot showers, check out this elegant spot 100m back from the beach. It has friendly staff and a sizeable garden.

Playa Santa Fe Resort & Dive Center (☎ 0414-773-3777; www.santaferesort.com; d without bathroom $12.50, seafront d/tr with bathroom $44, upper-story d/tr with bathroom $38; P 💻) Don't be put off by the title of 'resort;' this is a smallish upper-end posada with vine-shaded gardens and highly varied rooms including some seafront options that are deliciously light and breezy. It also offers a range of activities, including scuba diving ($60 for two dives), snorkeling ($16), rafting (half-day $16), fishing and biking. English is spoken.

Hotel Cochaima (☎ 416-4294; s/d $6.50/9) This sizable but basic hotel has a cheap beach-facing restaurant, pool tables and is managed by a very cheery local family.

Bahía del Mar (☎ 231-0073; d $10) More stylish is the seven-room posada in the neighboring house to Hotel Cochaima, which is run by a friendly French Canadian. Nab the room upstairs if you can – it's the best.

GETTING THERE & AWAY

Regular buses and por puestos from Puerto La Cruz and Cumaná will deposit you on the highway at Santa Fe's main junction. Walk 1km through the town to the market on the seafront. Turn left to reach the beach, which is lined with posadas.

Mochima

The small village of Mochima has no beach of its own, but it is a jumping-off point to half a dozen isolated mainland beaches inaccessible by road. The beaches are beautiful though shadeless, and are solitary except during major holiday peaks. Only the more visited Playa Blanca and Playa Las Maritas have food facilities open daily year-round.

TOURS

Transportation to the beaches is provided from the wharf in the village's center, where boats anchor and *lancheros* (boatmen) sit on the shore and wait for tourists. They can take you to any beach, among them Playa Las Maritas ($12.50), Playa Blanca ($12.50), Playa Manare ($16), and Playas Cautaro and Cautarito ($16). The listed figures are roundtrip fares per boat (up to seven passengers), and you can be picked up whenever you want. Don't hesitate to bargain!

Some hotel managers provide transportation for their guests, which can work out cheaper than *lancheros*. Some also organize trips around several islands, eventually leaving travelers for most of the day on a selected one. Longer tours, which can include cruises to Islas Caracas, La Piscina and Playa Colorada, plus snorkeling, are also available (see p248). Nené of the **Posada Villa Vicenta** (☎ 416-0916) offers some of the cheapest tours.

Mochima has two scuba diving operators: **Aquatics Diving Center** (☎ 430-1649, 0414-777-0196; aquaticsdc@cantv.net) and **La Posada de Los Buzos** (☎ 416-0856, in Caracas 0212-961-2531, 0414-242-6143; faverola@cantv.net). Both organize diving courses, dives and excursions, and handle snorkel rental; the latter also runs rafting trips on the Río Neverí.

SLEEPING & EATING
Mochima has a fair choice of accommodation and food facilities. Locals also rent out rooms and houses if there is demand.

Posada Gaby (☎ 0414-773-1104; 1–3-person r with air-con incl breakfast & boat to beach $32, with fan only $25; ❷) This yellow-daubed house, on the sea brink at the far end of the village, is the largest and best place to stay. The clean, tiled rooms are pleasant and there's a large open-fronted common area by the sea, filled with rainbow-style seating.

Posada Villa Vicenta (☎ 416-0916; s/d/tr $9/10/12.50; ❷) Located one block back from the wharf, this posada is the highest building in town. It has four levels stepping their way back up the hillside, each with a mini terrace boasting fine vistas over the bay (better on the higher floors). The rustic, stone-walled rooms have fans and cold-water bathrooms.

Posada Doña Cruz (☎ 0414-993-2690; 1–3-person r with TV $16, without TV $12.50; ❷) This colorful, though impersonal, little posada near the wharf has half a dozen small rooms with private bathroom. The owners do not live in the same building, but in front of the village car park.

Posada El Mochimero (☎ 0414-773-8782; tr with fan $11, with air-con $16; ❷) This hostel, opposite the restaurant of the same name, has plain rooms with cold-water bathrooms.

Those situated upstairs are much lighter and better tiled.

El Mochimero (☎ 416-2229; Calle La Marina; mains $4-9; ❤ 11am-9pm) Sitting on a platform over the sea and looking out towards the national park, this simple restaurant and bar has a scrumptious specialty of – surprise, surprise – fish dishes.

GETTING THERE & AWAY
Jeeps departing from Cumaná will bring you to the village's center ($0.65, 35 minutes), next to the wharf. There's no direct transportation from Puerto La Cruz.

Los Altos de Santa Fe
The mountain village of Los Altos is accessible by a winding paved road from the coast and is serviced regularly throughout the day by jeeps from Puerto La Cruz ($1.25, 40 minutes). Sitting at an altitude of about 900m, it has a fresh climate that's wonderfully cool compared to the coast. Los Altos is a typical one-street village, snaking up and down the rugged terrain for almost 5km without any pronounced center. It's surrounded by verdant highlands sprinkled with coffee and cacao haciendas.

Although Los Altos is only 4km back from the coast as the crow flies, it doesn't provide many panoramic views of the coast and the islands beyond. The best vistas are from the access road, as you approach the village. Once you enter it, about 7km from

---

THE AUTHOR'S CHOICE

Long before you get to Los Altos, just 1.5km from the coastal highway, you'll pass by a delightful spot named **La Ventana de Real y Medio** (Map p252; ☎ 431-4620; mains $3-8; ❤ 9am-late). The terrace restaurant serves *comida criolla* (typical cuisine) and provides spectacular views over the glistening waters and story-book islands of the Parque Nacional Mochima. What's more, it's an amazing place in itself, decorated with folksy objects and quirky bric-a-brac, which the owner calls the 'Museo de la Tradición y del Humor.' The restaurant has a few air-con suites for four, five and six guests to stay overnight for $19 a double and $5 for each additional person.

THE NORTHEAST

the turnoff at the coastal highway, the road gradually descends inland. Jeeps continue for about 5km to their terminus on the opposite end of the village.

SLEEPING & EATING

Los Altos itself has just one place to stay, other than seasonal posadas and fields available for camping (at about $3 per person).

Posada del Paraíso (☎ 416-9752; d/tr $9.50/11; P), 2km into the village, offers 10 relatively basic matrimonial rooms and three doubles in a hillside cabin smothered in orange and avocado trees. Simple but agreeable, it has its own café on a cool terrace at the back with a view of lush green mountains. Some rooms have balconies.

About 700m inland from Posada del Paraíso, **Il Picolit** (☎ 0416-693-3059; mains $4.50-9.50; 11:30am-7pm Sat & Sun) serves quality Italian fare in a snug little open-air restaurant covered with a pergola. It's only open at weekends.

For amazing views of Mochima, hunt for **Restaurant Chepina** (☎ 416-9829; mains $2.50-4.50; 11am-4pm) a little further down the road from Il Picolit on the left-hand side, but without a sign. This hilltop café serves typical food like *mondongo* (seasoned tripe in bouillon with vegetables) and freshly squeezed orange juice.

SUCRE STATE

CUMANÁ

☎ 0293 / pop 305,000

Founded by the Spaniards in 1521, Cumaná takes pride in being the oldest existing town on South America's mainland. Although there's not much historic architecture left, due to several devastating earthquakes in the town's history, you can still see the large fort crowning a hillock above the town center and a few streets that retain their colonial charm. Today the city is both the capital of Sucre state and an important port for sardine fishing and canning.

Cumaná is noted more for its attractive environs than for the city itself. There are some beaches nearby, the closest being Playa San Luis, southwest of the city. More beaches are in the Parque Nacional Mochima, a little further down the coast. Cumaná is also one of the gateways to Isla de Margarita and a convenient jumping-off point for the Península de Araya, Santa Fe, the village of Mochima and the Cueva del Guácharo.

Information

Tourist police (☎ 416-4376; 9am-noon & 3-6pm Mon-Fri, 4pm-7pm Sat & Sun) Based at the Museo de Arte Contemporáneo de Cumaná.

INTERNET ACCESS

Pacho's Café (☎ 431-1777; Calle Sucre; 9am-8pm Mon-Sat)

MONEY

The only *casa de cambio* is **Oficambio** (☎ 433-1626; Calle Mariño; 8am-noon & 2:30-6pm Mon-Fri), 600m west of Plaza Miranda. It changes cash and traveler's checks. Most major banks are on Calle Mariño and Av Bermúdez, including:
Banco de Venezuela (Calle Mariño at Calle Rojas)
Banco Mercantil (Av Bermúdez at Calle Gutierrez)
Banesco (Calle Mariño at Calle Carabobo) Gives cash advances on Visa and MasterCard.
Corp Banca (Av Bermúdez at Av Aristides Rojas) One kilometer west of Plaza Miranda.

POST

Ipostel (☎ 432-2616; Calle Paraíso) For snail mail.

TELEPHONE

Telcel (Calle Paraíso; 9am-8:30pm Mon-Sat, 10:30am-2pm Sun) Telephones and good Internet access.

TOURIST INFORMATION

Dirección de Turismo (director ☎ 0414-840-0581; Calle Sucre; 8am-noon & 2:30-5:30pm Mon-Fri) Offers a limited service in the city center, close to Iglesia de Santa Inés. There's also a tourist stand at the airport.

Sights

The grandest and best-restored colonial structure in town is the coral-rock **Castillo de San Antonio de la Eminencia** (☎ 431-5303; fun dacastillosa@hotmail.com; admission free; 7am-7pm), overlooking the city and coastline from a hill just southeast of the center. Constructed in 1659 on a four-pointed-star plan, it has survived repeated pirate attacks and destructive earthquakes. Ask the guards on duty to show you photos of the damage caused by the 1929 earthquake.

There were originally four such forts in the area, and the remains of nearby **Castillo**

CENTRAL CUMANÁ

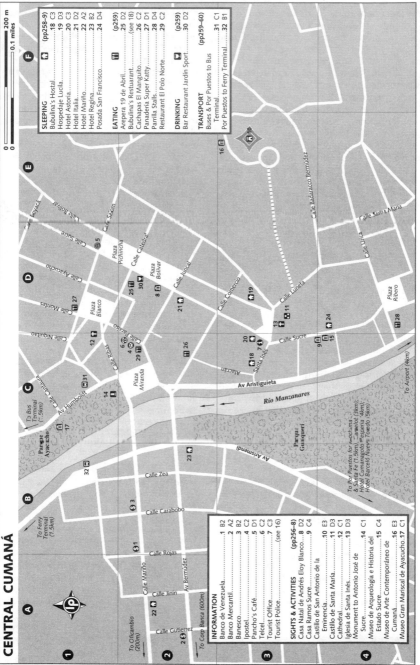

INFORMATION
Banco de Venezuela.....................1	B2
Banco Mercantil............................2	A2
Banesco.......................................3	B2
Ipostel..4	C2
Pancho's Café..............................5	D1
Telcel...6	C2
Tourist Office................................7	C3
Tourist Police................(see 16)	

SIGHTS & ACTIVITIES   (pp256–8)
Casa Natal de Andrés Eloy Blanco....8	D2
Casa Ramos Sucre.........................9	C4
Castillo de San Antonio de la	
Eminencia................................10	E3
Castillo de Santa María..................11	D3
Cathedral....................................12	C1
Iglesia de Santa Inés.....................13	D3
Monument to Antonio José de	
Sucre.......................................14	C1
Museo de Arqueología e Historia del	
Estado Sucre.............................15	C4
Museo de Arte Contemporáneo de	
Cumaná....................................16	E3
Museo Gran Mariscal de Ayacucho..17	C1

SLEEPING   (pp258–9)
Bubulina's Hostal...........................18	C3
Hospedaje Lucila...........................19	D3
Hotel Astoria.................................20	C3
Hotel Italia....................................21	D2
Hotel Mariño.................................22	A2
Hotel Regina.................................23	B2
Posada San Francisco.....................24	D4

EATING   (p259)
Arepera 19 de Abril........................25	D2
Bubulina's Restaurant...........(see 18)	
Cachapas El Manguito.....................26	C2
Panadería Super Katty.....................27	D1
Parrilla Stalls.................................28	D4
Restaurant El Polo Norte..................29	C2

DRINKING   (p259)
Bar Restaurant Jardín Sport..............30	D2

TRANSPORT   (pp259–60)
Buses & Por Puestos to Bus	
Terminal....................................31	C1
Por Puestos to Ferry Terminal..........32	B1

THE NORTHEAST

de Santa María (built in 1669) are within the grounds of Santa Inés church – sweet talk the priest and he may let you through to have a peek at what remains.

Next to Castillo de San Antonio is the small concrete-and-glass **Museo de Arte Contemporáneo de Cumaná** (☎ 416-4376; admission free; ☺ 9am-noon & 3-6pm Mon-Fri, 4pm-7pm Sat & Sun). It stages changing exhibits of modern art, and some freestanding sculptures are scattered around its grounds.

The streets around the **Iglesia de Santa Inés** have retained their colonial appearance. The church itself dates from 1929 and has few objects from earlier times inside, apart from the 16th-century statues of *El Nazareno* (Christ with the Cross) and the patron saint Santa Inés, both are in the chapels in the right-hand aisle. The **Catedral**, on Plaza Blanco, is also relatively young and has a hodgepodge of altarpieces in its largely timbered interior.

The city has more museums, though they are pretty modest. The **Casa Natal de Andrés Eloy Blanco** (president ☎ 0414-777-8555; Plaza Bolívar; admission free; ☺ 9am-noon & 3-6pm Mon-Fri) is a historic house where one of Venezuela's most extraordinary poets was born in 1896 (see p37). **Casa Ramos Sucre** (☎ 431-3777; Calle Sucre No 29; admission free; ☺ 9am-noon & 3-6pm Mon-Fri) is dedicated to another local poet, José Antonio Ramos Sucre, born here in 1890. Sucre's poetry was well ahead of its time, and it was only in the 1960s that his verses attracted the attention of scholars, publishers and finally readers. Long before that, he committed suicide at the age of 40. The well-preserved house is stuffed with beautiful period furniture.

Next door to the Casa Ramos Sucre, the **Museo de Arqueología e Historia del Estado Sucre** (Calle Sucre; admission free; ☺ 8:30am-noon & 2:30-5:30pm Mon-Fri) has a small archaeological collection though it was closed for renovations in late 2003.

The **Museo Gran Mariscal de Ayacucho** (☎ 432-1896; Av Humboldt; admission free; ☺ 8:30am-noon & 2:30-6pm Tue-Sat) is dedicated to the Cumaná-born hero of the War of Independence, General Antonio José de Sucre (1795–1830), who liberated Peru and Bolivia.

Sleeping

Many budget places are conveniently located in the city center, within a few blocks of Plaza Bolívar, while top-end places are to be found further outside town. All the hotels listed have rooms with private bathroom. They all are pretty simple and dark but inexpensive.

Bubulina's Hostal (☎ 431-4025; Callejón Santa Inés; d $16; ✗) An altogether more stylish option is this one-story historical building down a narrow colonial street. The interior is a totally new construction, but retains a cozy charm and airiness. The 12 *matrimoniales* and doubles all have TV, hot-water bathrooms, flowery decorations and curvy ironwork furniture. There's a nice little attached restaurant too (p259).

Hotel Astoria (☎ 433-2708; hotelastoria_7@hotmail.com; Calle Sucre 51; s/d/tr $9/10/12.50; P ✗) This is the best central option for those on a strict budget. Though nothing fancy, it has an ever-smiling host, comparatively good-sized and well-lit rooms, fans, and air-con that's switched on from 7pm to the morning.

Hotel Regina (☎ 432-2581; Av Arismendi; d $15; P ✗) This professional but plain place has recently smartened up its act. Handily, it has its own restaurant and a separate little bar. Choose an east-facing room on the top floor for views over the city center, including its two churches and the fort.

Hotel Barceló Nueva Toledo (☎ 451-8118; ntoledo@telcel.net.ve; Final Av Universidad; s/d/tr $44/49/66; P ✗ ☎) This huge apartment hotel is a good choice for the price, given its large swimming pool complete with fountains, and modern suites containing a lounge, kitchen and cable TV. It's not far from the

---

THE AUTHOR'S CHOICE

Posada San Francisco (☎ 431-3926; posadasanfrancisco@hotmail.com; Calle Sucre 16; d $22; ✗) This beautiful posada is different from anything else listed. It's in a renovated old *casona* (large house) – surely one of the loveliest colonial mansions in town – and it has eight ample rooms with mile-high cane ceilings, cable TV, safe, private bathroom and ceiling fan. The rooms are all arranged around a tranquil, palm-filled patio of traditional-style tiles and surrounded by an overhanging roof. The posada also has an attractive bar, a good restaurant and a pool table on which to while away the evening.

beach either, though 5km from the town center.

Hotel Cumanagoto Hesperia (☎ 430-1400; www .hotelcumanagoto.com; Final Av Universidad; d with view of pool/golf course $116/103; P ⧉ ▣ ⧐) The rather flash Hotel Cumanagoto provides some of the best luxuries in town, with plenty of mod-cons including tennis courts, a large pool and a neighboring golf course. It's about 4km from the center.

There are several other cheapies in town:

Hospedaje Lucila (☎ 431-1808; Calle Bolívar; d $7.50) Basic little homestay with small rooms around a courtyard strewn with family washing.

Hotel Italia (☎ 433-3678; Calle Sucre; s/d/tr $8.50/10/11; ⧉) A dark and rambling building that's a shade on the decrepit side, but with a few better but little air-con rooms out the back.

Hotel Mariño (☎ 432-0751; Calle Mariño; s/d/tr $11/12.50/15; P ⧉) High-rise with good views.

Eating

The city center has few upper-range establishments for eating, but budget travelers will be spoilt for choice. Some of the cheapest grills can be found at the *parrilla* stalls off Plaza Ribero, one long block south of Iglesia Santa Inés.

Restaurant El Polo Norte (☎ 0414-795-5689; Calle Paraíso at Calle Juncal; set menú $2-3; ⧖ 9am-9pm Mon-Sat) Large, inexpensive meals can be had at this humble hideaway, cocooned away from the busy street via a narrow passageway. It serves a long list of *criollo* favorites on tables blasted by overworked fans (hold on to your napkins).

Cachapas El Manguito (Calle Comercio; ⧖ noon-6pm Mon-Sat) This simple open-fronted spot resembles an indoor market stall more than a restaurant, but it serves filling *cachapas* (corn pancake) for just $1.25 a go. Can't argue with that.

Bubulina's Restaurant (☎ 431-4025; Callejón Santa Inés; set menú $2.50; ⧖ noon-10pm) For a step up in the quality stakes, head for this simple but very good restaurant in the hostel of the same name. It whips out tasty national lunches such as *pabellón criollo* (shredded beef, rice, black beans, cheese and plantain) on tables topped by frilly doilies and surrounded by garden-style iron chairs.

Posada San Francisco (☎ 431-3926; Calle Sucre; mains $5-9; ⧖ 8am-9pm) The quiet open-air patio restaurant at the colonial Posada San Francisco makes for a romantic atmosphere in the evening, when lights are left low and the stars are visible above. The posada hasn't always welcomed non-guests to its restaurant, so double-check in advance.

Also worth a peek:

Arepera 19 de Abril (Calle Catedral; arepas $2-3) Fast and filling *arepas*.

Panadería Super Katty (☎ 431-2955; Plaza Blanco; ⧖ 6am-10pm) Bakery with great pastries and enough frosted cakes to cater for a dozen weddings.

Drinking

Bar Restaurant Jardín Sport (Plaza Bolívar; beer $0.30; ⧖ 6am-midnight) The locals' favorite for chatting the day away is this informal open-air bar in a courtyard off Plaza Bolívar. It has a few pool tables and serves inexpensive snacks, but it's essentially the cheap beer that keeps the punters coming back for more.

Entertainment

Camelot (⧖ Thu-Sat) The queues don't lie: this is one of the area's most popular nightclubs. It's located off Av Universidad about 3km along the road towards Puerto La Cruz, before you reach the Hotel Cumanagoto Hesperia. There's another club fittingly named Drunkard's next door.

Getting There & Away

AIR

The airport is about 4km southeast of the city center. There are frequent flights to Caracas ($48 to $72) with Avior and other airlines, and to Porlamar, on Isla de Margarita ($34) with Rutaca and others.

BOAT

All ferries and boats to Isla de Margarita depart from the docks next to the mouth of the Río Manzanares and go to Punta de Piedras. Operators are **Gran Cacique II** (☎ 432-0011) and **Naviarca** (☎ 431-5577; naviarca@ telcel.net.ve); see p233 for departure times and fare details.

Naviarca also operates a ferry to Araya on the Península de Araya, although it's often easier to go by the small boats called *tapaditos* (see p262 for details).

The area around the ferry docks in Cumaná is not famous for its safety, so take a por puesto ($0.30) from just north of the bridge, or take taxi ($1.25).

THE NORTHEAST

BUS

The bus terminal is 1.5km northwest of the city center and is linked by frequent urban buses along Av Humboldt.

There are regular services to Caracas ($9 to $13, 6½ hours). All buses go through Puerto La Cruz ($2.50, 1½ hours), and there are also frequent por puestos to Puerto La Cruz ($3, 1¼ hours).

Half a dozen buses depart daily for Ciudad Bolívar ($8 to $12, six hours) and a few less to Güiria ($6, five hours). Buses to Carúpano run regularly throughout the day ($2.50 to $3, 2½ hours), as do por puestos ($4.50, four hours).

To Caripe, there is one departure daily, theoretically at 12:30pm ($4, 3½ hours). More reliable, however, may be a private minibus, which is supposed to depart at 3pm ($5, three hours). They all pass the Cueva del Guácharo shortly before arriving at Caripe and can let you off at the cave's entrance.

Por puesto cars to Santa Fe ($1, 45 minutes) depart from near the Mercadito, one block off the Redoma El Indio. Jeeps to Mochima ($0.65, 35 minutes) depart from the same street.

PENÍNSULA DE ARAYA

☎ 0293 / pop 30,000

Lying just across the deep and intensely blue Gulf of Cariaco from Cumaná, the Península de Araya comprises a 70km-long and 10km-wide finger of strikingly barren land characterized by arid red sands and scrubby dunes. Punta Arenas, on the peninsula's end, is just 5km northwest of Cumaná as the crow flies, but it's some 180km by road. The peninsula's sparse population is scattered through a handful of coastal villages on the northern coast, along which the solitary and rather rough road runs.

Araya

The peninsula's two major attractions – a huge colonial fort and the vast *salinas* – are both near the town of Araya, at the western end of the peninsula. Araya, the largest settlement on the peninsula, is easy to get to by boat or ferry from Cumaná (see p262). The town sits on the Bahía de Araya,

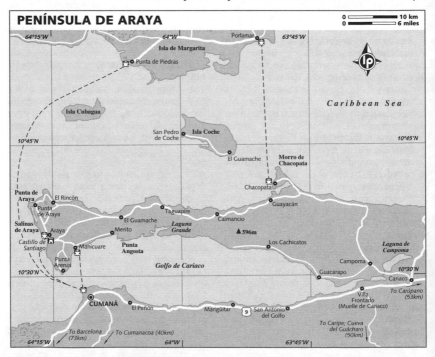

A PINCH OF SALT

For such a lifeless stretch of land, Araya has a compelling history. The Spaniards first claimed the peninsula in 1499. After the discovery of fabulous pearl fisheries offshore, they sailed down to the western tip of the peninsula to find another, quite different treasure – extensive *salinas*, or salt pans.

Salt, an essential means of preserving food, was an increasingly valuable commodity in Europe. However, it was the Dutch that took advantage, and rather cheekily set about extracting the salt from under the Spaniards noses. The Spanish, on the other hand, blindly concentrated on their pearl harvesting and it wasn't until the pearl beds were wiped out in the mid-16th century that they realized their mistake. By that time, the *salinas* were being furtively exploited not only by the Dutch but also by opportunistic English, and there wasn't a lot the Spanish could do about it. Various battles were fought, but plundering of the salt continued.

In exasperation, the Crown set about constructing a mighty fortress in 1618. However, it took almost 50 years to be completed thanks to pirate raids, storms and heat so fierce that the men mostly worked during the night. The fortress became the most costly Spanish project to be realized in the New World to that time, but once equipped with 45 cannons and defended by a 250-man garrison, La Real Fortaleza de Santiago de León de Araya repelled all who attempted to take it.

However, the fort's fortunes changed again in 1726 when a wild hurricane threw up a tide that broke over the salt lagoon, flooding it and turning it into a gulf. With the salt reserves lost, the Spanish abandoned the peninsula. Before leaving, they set about blowing up the fort to prevent it from falling into foreign hands. Despite igniting all the available gunpowder, however, the sturdy structure resisted. Damaged but not destroyed, the mighty bulwarks still proudly crown the waterfront cliff.

Meanwhile, the *salinas* slowly returned to their previous state, and mining was gradually re-introduced. Today they are Venezuela's largest *salinas* and produce about half a million metric tons per year.

with its pier in the middle. The fort is 750m to the south, while the *salinas* (salt pans) spread outward to the north.

SALINAS DE ARAYA

This sprawling salt-extraction site includes three areas: the *salinas naturales* (natural salt lagoon; referred to as Unidad 1), *salinas artificiales* (artificial salt pans; Unidad 2) and the main complex, where salt is sorted, packed and stored.

The *salinas naturales*, about 1km east of town, consist of a strikingly pink salt lagoon, from which the salt is dragged to the shore by specially constructed boats, cleaned and then left to dry in enormous glistening heaps.

On the other hand, the *salinas artificiales*, a few kilometers north of the town, are a colorful array of rectangular pools filled with salt water. The intense strength of the sun evaporates this water, leaving behind pure salt, which is then dragged out, the pool refilled and the process begun again. Numerous pools in different stages

of evaporation create an incredible variety of color tones, from rich creamy pinks to deep purple. You may ask, why pink? Well, the water coloration has a lot to do with *artemia*, a microscopic saltwater shrimp found in the water.

A poorly maintained old *mirador* (lookout) is on the hill to the east of the *salinas*, providing a good view over this chessboard of pools. It's on the road to Punta de Araya, 2km north of Araya.

The government company that runs the operation, **Sacosal** (☎ 437-1123), doesn't conduct official tours. However, you may strike it lucky by turning up early (ideally between 8am and 10am) and sweet-talking the attending officials. If somebody's free and willing, you may score a short free tour (Spanish only) around Unidades 1 and 2, hitching lifts with company pickup trucks. Don't depend on such VIP treatment however, as they're a busy lot.

Even without a tour, you can still see a good bit of the *salinas*, including the mirador, from outside the installations and restricted areas. Start early in the morning and be prepared for baking heat. Don't forget to take plenty of water, sunscreen, sunglasses and a hat.

CASTILLO DE SANTIAGO
This, the biggest and oldest colonial fort in the country (see the boxed text, p261), is commonly referred to as *El Castillo* (Castle). The four-pointed structure stands on the waterfront cliff at the southern end of the bay, a 10-minute walk along the beach from the wharf. Although damaged, the gargantuan coral-rock walls are an awesome sight and give a good impression of how the fort must have once looked. You can wander freely around the site, as there's no gate.

Sleeping & Eating
Posada Araya Wind (☎ 437-1132; Calle El Castillo; d/tr with air-con & bathroom $12.50/16, d/tr/q with fan & shared bathroom $9.50/11/12.50; ❄) The most stylish of the five or six rustic posadas in the town, Araya Wind lies so close to the fortress that its practically sitting in its shadow. It's also a short hop from a quiet little beach. Inside, the neatly decorated posada has good rooms, cane roofing and furniture, plus a scattering of antique-style wooden chairs.

Posada Helen (☎ 437-1101; Calle El Castillo; d/tr with air-con $11/12.50, d with fan $9.50; ❄) A stone's throw away from Araya Wind is this homely posada, which has a variety of comfortable, slightly frilly rooms with TV.

Restaurant Araya Mar. (☎ 437-1382; mains $3-4; ❄ 8am-11pm) Eating places in the same area include this open-fronted café that catches the breeze. It also has new air-con *matrimonial* rooms for $11.

You'll find more posadas on the opposite side of the village, around Plaza Bolívar.

Getting There & Away
Naviarca runs a ferry service between Cumaná and Araya ($2.20, one hour), but its schedule is, as they say, 'flexible.' In theory, the ferry is scheduled to leave from Cumaná at 7am, noon and 4:30pm on weekdays, and 5pm on weekends. It returns from Araya at 6am, 10am and 3pm on weekdays, and at 10am on weekends.

Small *tapadito* boats are more frequent, faster and more reliable. They shuttle between Manicuare and Cumaná ($0.80,

20 minutes) every 20 to 30 minutes until 4pm or 5pm, and the remaining Araya–Manicuare leg is covered by frequent por puestos ($0.30, 10 minutes).

Although there's a paved road between Araya and Cariaco (95km), there's little traffic traveling along it. There are occasional por puestos from Araya to Cariaco, but you can't rely on them. Traffic dies completely after 3pm.

There's also a boat service between Chacopata and Porlamar, on Isla de Margarita. See p233 for details. There's a por puesto service between Chacopata and Cariaco ($2.20, 45 minutes), and direct por puestos between Chacopata and Carúpano ($4.50, 1½ hours).

CARÚPANO
☎ 0294 / pop 110,000
Set on the coast 137km east of Cumaná, Carúpano is the last city of any size on Venezuela's Caribbean coast. It's an active port for cacao, cultivated in the region before being shipped overseas, and the city provides a stepping-stone to the far northeastern beaches and other attractions.

Information
INTERNET ACCESS
WC C@fé (Centro Comercial Olas del Caribe, Av Independencia; ❄ 9am-8pm Mon-Sat)

MONEY
Banco de Venezuela (Av Independencia) Gives credit-card cash advances.
Banesco (Plaza Colón) Offers similar services.
Corp Banca (Plaza Colón) Changes Amex traveler's checks.

POST
Ipostel (☎ 331-1149; Av Carabobo; ❄ 9am-5:30pm Mon-Fri)

TELEPHONE
CANTV (☎ 331-9555; Av Juncal; ❄ 8am-7pm Mon-Sat) Telephones and good Internet access.

TOURIST INFORMATION
Corpomedina (☎ 331-5241, 331-3917; playamedina@ cantv.net; Carúpano Airport) Provides information and booking for its *cabañas* (holiday cabins) at Playa Medina (p268) and Playa Pui Puy (p268).
Dirección de Turismo (Edificio Rental Fundabermudez, 1st fl, Av Independencia No 8; ❄ 8am-noon & 2-5pm Mon-Fri) Has free maps.

CARÚPANO

0 _____ 500 m
0 _____ 0.3 miles

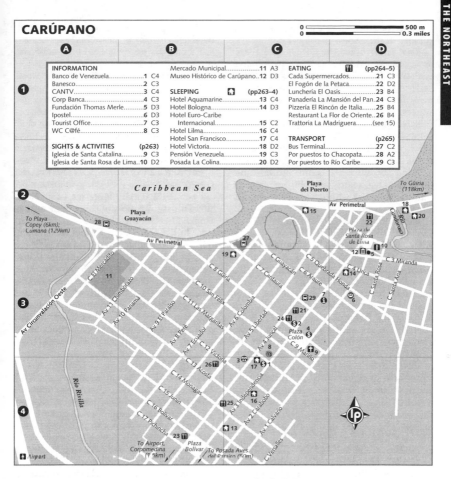

INFORMATION
Banco de Venezuela.................1 C4
Banesco.....................................2 C3
CANTV......................................3 C4
Corp Banca.............................4 C3
Fundación Thomas Merle........5 D3
Ipostel....................................6 D3
Tourist Office.........................7 C3
WC C@fé..................................8 C3

SIGHTS & ACTIVITIES (p263)
Iglesia de Santa Catalina.......9 C3
Iglesia de Santa Rosa de Lima..10 D2

Mercado Municipal.................11 A3
Museo Histórico de Carúpano..12 D3

SLEEPING (pp263–4)
Hotel Aquamarine..................13 C4
Hotel Bologna........................14 D3
Hotel Euro-Caribe
    Internacional.....................15 C2
Hotel Lilma.............................16 C4
Hotel San Francisco................17 C4
Hotel Victoria.........................18 D2
Pensión Venezuela.................19 C3
Posada La Colina....................20 D2

EATING (pp264–5)
Cada Supermercados..............21 C3
El Fogón de la Petaca.............22 D2
Lunchería El Oasis..................23 B4
Panadería La Mansión del Pan..24 C3
Pizzería El Rincón de Italia......25 B4
Restaurant La Flor de Oriente..26 B4
Trattoria La Madriguera.........(see 15)

TRANSPORT (p265)
Bus Terminal..........................27 C2
Por puestos a Chacopata.........28 A2
Por puestos a Río Caribe.........29 C3

Fundación Thomas Merle (☎ 331-3370; merle@ telcel.net.ve; Plaza de Santa Rosa de Lima) Can book for and give information about Hacienda Aguasana and Hato Río de Agua (p267). Posada La Colina (p264) may also give information.

Sights

Despite its regular chessboard layout, a reminder of the town's colonial origins in 1647, the town has no outstanding historic monuments. However, you might want to visit the two main churches, **Iglesia de Santa Catalina** (Plaza Colón) and **Iglesia de Santa Rosa de Lima** (Plaza de Santa Rosa de Lima), the modest **Museo Histórico de Carúpano** (Plaza de Santa Rosa de Lima; admission free; ◱ 8:30am-noon & 2:30-6pm Mon-Fri); and the unusually large **Mercado Municipal**.

Festivals & Events

Carúpano springs to life for the four days (Saturday to Tuesday) before Ash Wednesday, when **Carnaval** is held and there are dances, parades and lots of rum.

Sleeping
TOWN CENTER

Posada Aves del Paraíso (☎ 332-2001; Av Independencia No 251; d with bathroom $12.50, without bathroom $9.50) This welcoming four-room home stay is 1½ blocks southwest of Plaza Bolívar. It's one of the best budget places around, arranged in a historic house with a palm-filled garden to one side. There's no sign.

Hotel Bologna (☎ 331-1241; Av Independencia No 47· d/tr $9.50/16; ☒) This hotel has an unpromis⸱

entrance but there are clean and good value rooms out the back with cable TV.

Hotel San Francisco (☎ 331-1074; fax 331-5176; Av 4 Juncal 87A; d $16; P ☒) If you can't live without your air-con, check out this style-less but accommodating hotel, which also throws in cable TV, but has no hot water.

Hotel Lilma (☎ 331-1341; Av Independencia No 161; d $14-16, tr $18; P ☒) For much the same price as San Francisco, the similarly characterless Lilma swaps the advantages round by offering hot-water bathrooms but no cable TV. It also has a fairly good little restaurant and a smoky bar with its TV permanently tuned into sports.

Hotel Victoria (☎ 331-1554; fax 331-1776; Av Perimetral; d/tr/q $22/25/28; P ☒) Marginally better is this old hotel, a 10-minute walk east of the bus terminal on the seafront boulevard. It combines hot-water bathrooms with cable TV but its rooms are a bit rough around the edges.

Hotel Euro-Caribe Internacional (☎ 331-3911; fax 331-3651; Av Perimetral; d $36-47, ste $94; P ☒ ▣) Another luxurious place, this high-rise hotel peers down on the seafront. Its impressive list of amenities includes rooms with cable TV and king-size beds, plus a cyber café, gym, bar and a restaurant. Paying with credit cards pushes up the room cost by 12%.

THE AUTHOR'S CHOICE

Posada La Colina (☎ 332-2915; merle@tel cel.net.ve; Av Boyaca 51; s/d/tr/q incl breakfast $25/30/34/38; P ☒ ▣) Far and away the most characterful hotel in town, the exquisitely kept Posada La Colina is perched on a small hillock above the town, just behind the hotel Victoria. It's in a renovated old mansion that combines rustic character with comfort, and is filled with shady palm gardens and patios. The spacious rooms are good value, with hot-water bathrooms and cable TV, and there is an excellent restaurant open till 10pm daily. However, the focal point of the whole building is its beautiful open-air pool and b‒‒ rea that has a wonderful view span‒ the town, the surrounding hills and ι sea. Surely the ideal spot to catch nset.

Other options in the center:

Hotel Aquamarine (☎ 332-0898; Av Independencia No 185; d $9; ☒) Entrance through harem-like bamboo arches and swing-doors.

Pensión Venezuela (☎ 0414-774-7726; Calle Cantaura No 49; d/tr without bathroom $6.50/7.50) Cheapest bet around the bus terminal.

OUTSIDE CARÚPANO

There are some good posadas on Playa Copey, about 6km west of the city (taxi $2.50 one-way).

Posada Nena (☎ 331-7297; www.posadanena.com; Calle Principal, Playa Copey; s/d with fan $8, d upstairs $15, d/tr with air-con $15/18, 3-/4-person apt $35; ☒ ▣) This is how most of us imagine a small tropical beach hotel. It's set in a sandy garden dotted with palms, bright flowers and hammocks. Plus it has a games room, bar and is only a brief walk from the beach. When busy prices rise by 15% to 20%.

Posada Casa Blanca (☎ 331-6896; Calle Principal, Playa Copey; d/tr/q $12.50/19/25; P ☒) With a back gate leading directly onto the beach, this family house has a few quirky rooms available, a couple of which are decorated lavishly. Bathrooms have cold water only.

Eating

There are plenty of small eateries scattered throughout the city.

Mercado Municipal (Calle El Mercadito) If you're pinching pennies, this market place is one of the best options for unsophisticated local dishes.

Panadería La Mansión del Pan (Av Juncal; ☼ 7am-9pm; ☒) Easily the best central *panadería*. People flock here for breakfast and daytime snacks: join them for the *pasteles* (pastries), *cachitos* (hot filled croissant) and a thimble-sized cup of coffee.

El Fogón de La Petaca (☎ 331-4277; Av Perimetral No 1; mains $4.50-7.50; ☼ 11:30am-10pm; ☒) This upper-crust joint on the seafront boulevard mixes together several cultures, decor and cuisines, with a good wine list to boot. There are separate smoking and non-smoking rooms: a rarity in Venezuela.

Pizzería El Rincón de Italia (☎ 331-3459; Av Juncal; ☼ 11:30am-11pm) For Italian food (including some very passable pizzas), hit this friendly restaurant, located in a pretty open-air courtyard, studded with potted plants.

Restaurant La Flor de Oriente (Av Libertad; mains $1.50-4; ☼ 10:30am-9pm Mon-Sat) Large old-school café with plastic-topped tables and hearty *comida criolla* – especially *arepas* – for just a few bucks.

Lunchería El Oasis (☎ 0414-780-5307; Plaza Bolívar; ☺ 6pm-late) This is a tiny Middle Eastern cubby-hole fronting a leafy plaza and serving beautiful falafel, kafta and the like. Only comes alive latish.

Other recommendations:

Cada Supermercados (Av Juncal; ☺ 8am-7pm Mon-Sat) For do-it-yourself picnics.

Trattoria La Madriguera (Hotel Euro-Caribe Internacional; mains $5-9; ☺ 11am-3pm & 6-10pm Tue-Sun; 😶) Delicious pastas at good prices.

Getting There & Away
AIR
The airport is 1.5km west of the city center. There are daily flights to Porlamar, on Isla de Margarita ($33), and Caracas ($65 to $75).

BUS
The bus terminal is a short walk north of the center, on Av Perimetral. Buses to Caracas depart mostly in the morning and evening ($11 to $16, 8½ hours), and they all run via Cumaná ($2.50 to $3, 2½ hours) and Puerto La Cruz ($4 to $7, 4 hours). There are also frequent por puestos to Cumaná ($4.50, two hours).

Half a dozen buses run to Güiria ($3.50, 2½ hours) coming through from Caracas/Puerto La Cruz; por puestos also go to Güiria regularly ($4.50, two hours). Three or four buses go daily to Ciudad Guayana ($9 to $12, seven hours).

To Río Caribe, you can go either by por puesto ($0.80, 30 minutes), departing from Av Juncal near the corner of Calle Cantaura, or by buses ($0.50, 45 minutes) from the same area, which also pass along Av Perimetral.

For Isla de Margarita, the shortest and cheapest way is via Chacopata. Direct por puestos to Chacopata depart from Av Perimetral near the market ($4.50, 1½ hours), where you change for a boat to Porlamar ($4.50, one to 1½ hours). See p233 for more details.

RÍO CARIBE
☎ 0294
Río Caribe is a seaside town 25km east of Carúpano. It's an old port that grew fat on cacao export, and the air of the former splendor is still palpable in the wide, tree-shaded Av Bermúdez with its once resplendent, now mostly decadent mansions.

It's a pleasant, peaceful town popular with holidaymakers, and can be a useful springboard for beaches further east. If you come, visit the 18th-century church on Plaza Bolívar.

Information
Mareaje Tours (☎ 646-1931; mareajetours@cantv.net; Av Bermúdez 72) and an infrequently manned **tourist booth** on Plaza Sucre can provide some information about the town and the region. Mareaje offers a couple of machines with unreliable Internet access, as does **Parian@Café** (Av Bermúdez; ☺ 5:30pm-11pm Mon-Sat). The **police station** (☎ 414-6910) is on Calle Junín.

Tours
Mareaje Tours (☎ 646-1931; mareajetours@cantv.net; Av Bermúdez 72) organizes boat and car trips around the region, as do most of the posadas, including **Posada Caribana** (☎ 646-1242; www.caribana.com.ve; Av Bermúdez 25) and **Posada de Arlet** (☎ 646-1290; Calle 24 de Julio 22). Shop around, as routes, services and prices vary. Day tours include a boat trip to three beaches (about $19), the buffalo ranch and hot springs ($22), Playa Uva and the Bukare cocoa plantation ($19) and various combinations of the above. All prices include lunch.

Sleeping
The town has a good range of accommodations, including several posadas.

Villa Antillana (☎ 646-1413; antilla99@cantv.net; Calle Rivero 32; s/d/tr/q $19/24/35/42) Set in a restored 19th-century mansion, the quiet Villa Antillana has a handful of attractive *matrimoniales* and suites around a pretty tiled courtyard. All rooms have been painstakingly reconstructed and decorated by the owner-architect with bags of character. There are also good modern amenities, comfortable mattresses, fans and hot-water bathrooms.

Posada Caribana (☎ 646-1242; www.caribana .com.ve; Av Bermúdez 25; s/d/tr/q with fan $40/35/40/50, s/d/tr with air-con $45/39/45; 😶) The more upmarket Posada Caribana is another picture-postcard Caribbean *casona* (mansion) from the 19th century. It has 11 good sized rooms that line an immacu

THE NORTHEAST

maintained, traditional-style patio. The price also includes breakfast. It also has its own restaurant, and runs a full package of regional tours.

La Posada de Arlet (☎ 646-1290; Calle 24 de Julio 22; s/d/tr $16/19/28) Owned and managed by a polyglot Swiss woman, this place is a more modest but homely option with neat compact rooms and nicely kept cold-water bathrooms.

Hotel Mar Caribe (☎ 416-6197; Final Av Gallegos; d/tr incl breakfast $22/28; ✖ ☀) Lying under enormous palm trees near the waterfront, this large hotel must once have been the pride of the town. It's now a distant shade of its former self, but still boasts 50 spacious rooms, a bar and restaurant.

Pensión Papagayos (☎ 646-1868; Calle 14 de Febrero; s/d $5/10) This tiny family home rents out four well-kept rooms sharing two bathrooms, and you can use the kitchen and fridge. The doorstep is usually overrun with kids from the town's school, which lies just a few steps away.

Posada Don Chilo (☎ 646-1212; Calle Mariño No 27; d/tr $6.50/9.50) Cheapest and most basic in town; all rooms share a bathroom.

Eating

Tasca Mi Cocina (Calle Juncal; mains $2-7; ✖ 11am-10pm; ✖) This popular hideaway for good food at good prices is on a side street off Av Bermúdez near Plaza Sucre.

Restaurant Doña Eva (Calle Girardot at Plaza Miranda; mains $2.50-6; ✖ 11am-11pm) Another down-to-earth choice, Doña Eva serves hearty pasta, chicken and fish dishes. Set back from the road on a simple terrace, this is where locals relax with an ice-cold beer.

Parian@Café (Av Bermúdez; ✖ 5:30pm-11pm Mon-Sat; 💻) Popular with foreign travelers for food typical of the region and a hip, casual atmosphere.

Getting There & Away

Por puestos depart frequently to Carúpano from Plaza Bolívar ($0.80, 30 minutes), and there are also buses marked 'Ruta Popular' ($0.50).

‚equent por puesto pickup trucks the villages of Medina ($1), Pui 50) and San Juan de Las Galdonas v don't get as far as the beaches and Pui Puy: you need to walk he way, about a half-hour trip

in either case. Otherwise, you'll need to rent the vehicle, which costs 10 times more than the por puesto fare. Trucks depart from the southeastern end of Río Caribe, opposite the gas station. Traffic thins in the early afternoon.

AROUND RÍO CARIBE
☎ 0294

The coast east of Río Caribe has some of the country's loveliest beaches. There are perhaps two dozen pocket-sized and larger beaches on the 50km coastal stretch between Río Caribe and San Juan de Unare, the last seaside village accessible by road. The best known is Playa Medina, closely followed by Playa Pui Puy, but you can find other amazing patches of sand.

The hinterland behind the beaches features a picturesque coastal mountain range rolling down into the vast plains that stretch to the south. The mountains and the plains shelter hot springs, a buffalo ranch and cacao haciendas. There are a dozen posadas scattered across the region, but roads are few and in bad shape, and transportation is infrequent (see Getting There & Away earlier).

On the one hand this makes getting around tricky, but on the other, it means that the region is, in general, blissfully free of tourists.

Orientation

Most travelers come to the region to discover its many secluded beaches, accessible via rough country roads, along which the locals leave cacao to dry in the sun.

The first beaches worth visiting east of Río Caribe are side-by-side **Playa Loero** and **Playa de Uva**. They lie 6km from Río Caribe by the road to Bohordal, then another 6km by a paved side road that branches off to the left. Back on the main road, 8km beyond the turnoff to Playa Loero is the **Hacienda Bukare**, a working cacao plantation open to visitors.

Proceeding east, a paved road branches off 4km beyond Bukare and goes 5km to the village of Medina then northward for 1km to a fork. The left branch goes for 2km to the picture-postcard crescent-shaped **Playa Medina**. The right branch leads 6km over a potholed road to the village of Pui Puy and continues for 2km to the beautiful **Playa Pui Puy**.

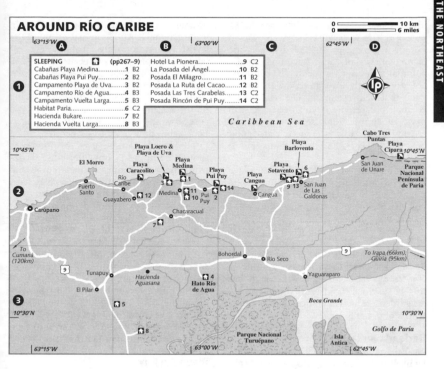

AROUND RÍO CARIBE

| 0 | 10 km |
| 0 | 6 miles |

SLEEPING (pp267–9)		
Cabañas Playa Medina..............1	B2	Hotel La Pionera.......................9 C2
Cabañas Playa Pui Puy...........2	B2	La Posada del Ángel.................10 B2
Campamento Playa de Uva......3	B2	Posada El Milagro....................11 B2
Campamento Rio de Agua........4	B3	Posada La Ruta del Cacao.......12 B2
Campamento Vuelta Larga.......5	B3	Posada Las Tres Carabelas.......13 C2
Habitat Paria............................6	C2	Posada Rincón de Pui Puy.......14 C2
Hacienda Bukare......................7	B2	
Hacienda Vuelta Larga.............8	B3	

Few travelers venture further to the east, though beaches dot the coast as far as the eye can see. The seaside village of **San Juan de Las Galdonas** has especially fine beaches. Its main access road is a wholly paved 23km stretch that branches off the Río Caribe–Bohordal road 6.5km beyond the turnoff to Medina. Another access is by a potholed 22km road that branches off the Bohordal–Yaguaraparo road in the hamlet of Río Seco, 4km east of Bohordal (serviced by infrequent por puestos). Both roads wind spectacularly up and down over the mountain range.

From San Juan de Las Galdonas, a dirt road (serviced by sporadic transportation) goes for 20km to the village of San Juan de Unare. An hour's walk east by a rough road brings you to Playa Cipara, one of the longest beaches in the area. From just east of here, the Parque Nacional Península de Paria (p271) stretches 100km along the coast to the eastern tip of the peninsula. A path to the park's nearest village, Santa Isabel, runs from Playa Cipara.

There are more attractions further inland, south of the Carúpano–Güiria high-way, used by all the buses and por puestos. Beginning from Bohordal and heading west for 10km, you'll find the entrance to **Hato Río de Agua**, a vast buffalo ranch. Another 8km down the road, you'll reach the hot springs of **Hacienda Aguasana**.

Proceeding west for another 5km, you'll pass through the town of Tunapuy. About 2.5km further west, a paved side road branches off to the south and goes for 1km to **Campamento Hacienda Vuelta Larga**. The road runs another 7km to the hacienda proper. East of here stretches the wild **Parque Nacional Turuépano.**

The following sections feature information about the major attractions highlighted above, complete with their facilities. You can explore the region on your own or take advantage of a wealth of tours on offer. Tours are organized mostly by hotels and posadas in Río Caribe (see p265).

Playa Loero & Playa de Uva

At the end of the 6km access road, which goes up and over some tight curves and hills, is the minuscule Playa de Uva and its idyllic **Campamento Playa de Uva** (☎ 416-6284; www.caribana.com.ve; s/d/tr/q incl 3 meals $50/83/113/139) in a grassy, palm-shaded cove. The camp consists of four charmingly rustic colonial-style houses, with 12 comfortable rooms with hot-water showers, plus a palm-thatched restaurant. The beach itself is small but serene. If you need a restful place in almost total isolation from the outside world, this is a pretty darn good bet. Booking is via Posada Caribana (p265) in Río Caribe .

Just to the west of Playa de Uva, Playa Loero is another pleasant, though less memorable, beach. It has no facilities, but you can string your hammock under the roof of the *churuata*.

There are several other cheaper posadas back in the village of Guayabero before the turnoff to the beach. Try the beautiful **Posada La Ruta del Cacao** (☎ 0414-994-0115; Via Playa Medina; d incl breakfast $11; **P**), which has hugely spacious cabins dotted amid tropical gardens, as well as conical thatched huts with a pool table, a bar and hammocks.

Hacienda Bukare

Near the small village of Chacaracual, 14km from Río Caribe, this old **cacao hacienda** (☎ 808-1505, 0414-777-1147; bukare@cantv.net; s/d/tr/q incl breakfast $25/32/34/38 July-Sept, $32/38/41/44 Dec–mid-Jan; **⚑**) is still in operation, albeit on a small scale. Hour-long tours ($3.20 per person) from 10am to noon and 3pm to 5pm, are conducted around the grounds, including a demonstration of processing cocoa and – not to forget – the all-important tasting. The handsome historic house offers rooms for visitors, a small plunge pool and a stylish cozy restaurant. You can also stay in the single cabaña across the road ($30 double without breakfast), or in a hammock with use of the bathroom facilities ($10 per person). The owner is an experienced and knowledgeable guide, and he organizes a variety of tours around the region. He also rents out bicycles.

Playa Medina

With a reputation as one of the most beautiful beaches on the Venezuelan coast, this golden 400m-long beach is set in a glorious deep bay shaded with a forest of coconut palms. And despite the soft sand, cleanliness and sheltered location, the isolated Playa Medina rarely gets overrun by beachgoers. Amid the palms are seven stylish reservation-only cabañas and a restaurant, all operated by **Corpomedina** (☎ 0294-331-5241, 331-3917; playamedina@cantv.net; Carúpano Airport). Packages including cabins and two meals cost $41 to $50 per adult, depending on the season. Children up to 10 years old cost 50%, and infants under three are free. Each cabin houses up to six people.

The beach can be used by anybody, though camping is not allowed. Señoras from the surrounding hamlets come and serve basic meals and snacks (such as fried fish and empanadas) for day-trippers.

Some budget accommodation options lie within walking distance of the beach. The family-run **Posada El Milagro** (☎ 0416-694-5291; r per person incl breakfast & dinner $16), 2km up the road from the beach, offers simple, rustic rooms mostly with bunk beds, cane ceilings, bathroom and fan.

One kilometer further inland, in the middle of the village of Medina, is the colorful 19-room **La Posada del Ángel** (☎ 0416-794-7477; d $16, with breakfast & dinner $19; **⚑**), with its own budget restaurant and thatched-roof bar.

Playa Pui Puy

Another of the best beaches around, Pui Puy is a 1.3km-long stretch of fine white sand shaded by coconut groves. The sea is less sheltered here, and waves can get big enough for bodysurfers. It also has a colony of 16 holiday cabañas and a restaurant operated by **Corpomedina** (☎ 0294-331-5241, 331-3917; playamedina@cantv.net; Carúpano Airport; adult/child under 10 incl 3 meals $22/11 Mon-Thu, $25/13 Fri-Sun). The restaurant serves budget meals for guests and nonguests alike.

A cheaper option is the newly built **Posada Rincón de Pui Puy** (☎ 0416-894-1488; Playa Pui Puy; d $19), sitting on the brink of the sea at the far end of the beach, with a panoramic view of the bay from its patio. The cramped rooms have a toilet, but showers are separate.

Camping on this beach is permitted for $2 per tent, and you pay $0.20 for using the bathroom. It may be possible to rent a hammock for $3 per night. If you come with your own, sling it under the roof for a nominal fee. Mosquitoes and sand flies appear in the mornings and evenings, particularly during the rainy season, so bring repellent, mosquito nets and long-sleeved shirts.

San Juan de Las Galdonas

Tiny San Juan is an authentic old port of about 1500 inhabitants that continues living its own lethargic life. The fine beaches around the village are enough to keep you hooked, but local tour operators can also take you just about anywhere in the region and beyond.

The cheapest place to stay, the Spanish-owned and -managed **Posada Las Tres Carabelas** (☎ 0416-894-0914; Eudilis2001@latinmail.com; d incl breakfast & dinner $16), sits spectacularly on top of a cliff high above the beach, providing gorgeous views over the sea. Run by a friendly Spaniard, the posada offers 13 rooms with bathroom, fan and mosquito net. It also runs the restaurant, which features some Spanish dishes. The owner takes travelers on budget hiking trips up the mountains of the Parque Nacional Península de Paria, while boat trips are organized by **Botuto** (☎ 0416-785-0166), who lives close by.

Off the far eastern end of the village is the Mediterranean-style **Habitat Paria** (☎ 0414-779-7955; www.habitatparia.vzla.org; d/tr/q $19/25/30; **P**), which has a gate onto the Playa Barlovento. It's overrun by tropical gardens hung with shells, and offers 12 simple rooms with bathroom and fan, a restaurant and tours. There's also a plunge pool and volleyball net.

The towering, five-level **Hotel La Pionera** (☎ 331-5101; www.hotellapionera.com; d/tr/q $22/25/30; **☾**) looms over the beach, and would fit better in Miami than this tiny, mostly single-story community. It offers more luxuries than anything else around the region. Owned and managed by a Frenchman, the hotel has its own restaurant, bar, Jacuzzi and a fair-sized swimming pool. Richard offers a thick package of upmarket tours within the region and beyond.

Hato Río de Agua

This buffalo ranch, which occupies a 200-hectare chunk of marshland to the south of the El Pilar–Bohordal road, has 540 water buffalo as well as abundant bird life. The ranch's usual occupation has been the production of buffalo meat and cheese, but it has also turned to tourism. An attractive **campamento** (☎ 0416-794-7412; d incl breakfast, dinner & excursions $38), consisting of five conical cabañas and a thatched restaurant, sits 2km off the road. Longer excursions can also be arranged for about $12.50. Pack-

ages are booked by the **Fundación Thomas Merle** (☎ 0294-331-3370; merle@telcel.net.ve; Plaza de Santa Rosa de Lima) in Carúpano.

Day visits (without accommodations and meals) are also possible between 7am and 6pm daily; they cost $2 per person. The visit includes a brief look around the ranch, a short trip in a dugout canoe, the chance to sit on top of a water buffalo, a soft drink or fruit juice and a piece of the distinctively tangy buffalo cheese.

Hacienda Aguasana

This hacienda has a long trail of mineral-rich **aguas termales** (hot springs; ☎ 414-7087; elsygo erke@cantv.net; adult/child under 10 incl drink $3.20/1.50; **☾** 8:30am-6pm). There are 17 ponds of various sizes and with water of different temperatures scattered around the hacienda's grassy lands and linked by paths. Some ponds are natural, while others have been shaped. There are also bubbling hot-mud pools for you to achieve that instant elephantine look. Bring your bathing suit and a towel.

Other services, such as acupressure and mud massage ($16), are available. The hacienda also has a few simple double rooms to rent for $16 including breakfast. The hacienda is operated by the **Fundación Thomas Merle** (☎ 0294-331-3370; merle@telcel.net.ve; Plaza de Santa Rosa de Lima) in Carúpano.

Hacienda Vuelta Larga

Operated by Klaus Müller, this **hacienda** (☎ 666-9052; vueltalarga@cantv.net; d per person incl breakfast & dinner $28) is a 10-sq-km ecological ranch with water buffalo, and about 230 bird species. The hacienda has a *campamento*, about 7km north of the ranch, which provides lodging and hearty traditional food. Birding trips are conducted by Klaus' son, Daniel, who is an experienced bird-watcher. A half-day excursion costs $11.

Parque Nacional Turuépano

The 726-sq-km Turuépano national park is a wild marshland crisscrossed by a maze of natural water channels and populated by a wealth of wildlife, mainly birds and fish. The habitat is similar to that of the Delta del Orinoco, characterized by high temperature and humidity, and a significant tide that gives rise to a peculiar type of vegetation.

The park lacks tourist facilities and is rarely visited. Talk to Richard of Hotel La

Pionera and Billy of Hacienda Bukare, who are the most experienced in the subject.

IRAPA
☎ 0294

Irapa is an old port on the Golfo de Paria that flourished on cacao shipments overseas. Today it's a sleepy place that still bears traces of glory and large houses influenced by the spiky, multi-layered Trinidadian architectural style. The town doesn't see much through traffic and has an air of isolation and tranquility.

Sleeping
Posada Tierra de Gracia (☎ 989-7863; Calle Bermúdez; d $9; P ⚡) Recognizable by the pre-Colombian reliefs on its terracotta-colored walls, this good little posada has well-kept rooms around a wide central courtyard. You'll find it a block back from the beach.

Getting There & Away
Por puestos depart from the town's center to Carúpano ($4.50, 1½ hours) and Güiria ($1.25, 40 minutes).

GÜIRIA
☎ 0294 / pop 30,000

This town marks the easternmost point on Venezuela's coast reachable by road, 275km from Cumaná. It's the largest town on the Península de Paria and an important fishing port. The town itself is rather ordinary, though the rugged neighboring Parque Nacional Península de Paria, stretching along the peninsula's northern coast, is attractive.

Güiria is a major transit point on the Venezuela–Trinidad route. Although the ferry no longer operates, a passenger-boat service has taken its place.

Information
Banco Mercantil (Calle Bolívar at Calle Juncal) and **Banesco** (Calle Bolívar) can give advances on Visa and MasterCard. For Internet access, try **Conexiones Buz3** (Calle Valdez; ⊙ 9am-8pm Mon-Sat, 11am-5pm Sun).

Sleeping & Eating
Hotel Plaza (☎ 982-0022; Calle Vigirima at Plaza Bolívar 18; d $12.50; ⚡) This traveler's favorite has a new extension upstairs with small but

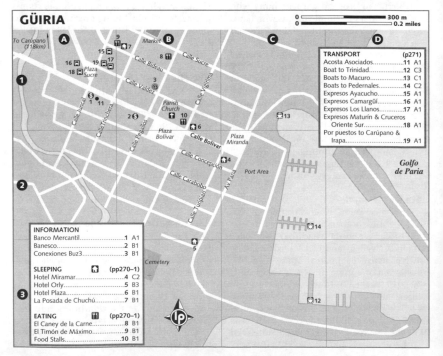

GÜIRIA

| 0 | 300 m |
| 0 | 0.2 miles |

To Carúpano (118km)

Market

Golfo de Paria

Port Area

Plaza Bolívar

Plaza Miranda

Parish Church

Cemetery

TRANSPORT (p271)
Acosta Asociados...............11 A1
Boat to Trinidad.................12 C3
Boats to Macuro................13 C1
Boats to Pedernales...........14 C2
Expresos Ayacucho............15 A1
Expresos Camargüi............16 A1
Expresos Los Llanos..........17 A1
Expresos Maturín & Cruceros
    Oriente Sur....................18 A1
Por puestos to Carúpano &
    Irapa............................19 A1

INFORMATION
Banco Mercantil...................1 A1
Banesco...............................2 B1
Conexiones Buz3.................3 B1

SLEEPING (pp270–1)
Hotel Miramar.....................4 C2
Hotel Orly............................5 B3
Hotel Plaza..........................6 B1
La Posada de Chuchú............7 B1

EATING (pp270–1)
El Caney de la Carne.............8 B1
El Timón de Máximo.............9 B1
Food Stalls..........................10 B1

freshly decorated rooms with cold-water bathrooms. The posada has its own cheap eatery downstairs.

La Posada de Chuchú (☎ 982-1266; Calle Bideau 35; d $12.50; 🔀) Alternatively, this posada has larger, beige-colored rooms with cable TV, a writing desk and plentiful hot water. It's also situated directly above the best restaurant in town, El Timón de Máximo (see following).

Hotel Miramar (☎ 982-0732; Calle Turipiari; d $7.50; 🔀) To save more bolívares, you can stay in this primitive little place further toward the port. It has dark but neatly kept rooms out the back.

Hotel Orly (☎ 982-1830; Av Pária; d/tr $16/22; 🔀) This is the most professional hotel in town. It's fitted with a polished-stone staircase and walls painted in a luridly colorful marble effect. The modern rooms have cable TV and hot-water bathrooms.

El Timón de Máximo (Calle Bideau; mains $6-10; 🕒 noon-3pm & 6-11pm Mon-Sat, noon-3pm Sun) frequently sees off-duty naval officers piling in for fish specialties and fresh fruit juices laced with Angostura bitters.

El Caney de la Carne (☎ 0414-784-1776; Calle Pegallos; mains $5-7; 🕒 11am-2am) On Sundays, the swing doors of this little grill restaurant open to a scene of local ladies munching on meaty platters, playing cards and gambling with corn chips.

You'll find more eating outlets around the central streets, including cheap and filling food stalls alongside church.

Getting There & Away
BOAT
Windward Lines used to operate a ferry on the Güiria–Trinidad–St Vincent–Barbados–St Lucia route. However, the Güiria to Trinidad leg was suspended in 2000. Windward Lines planned to eventually replace the suspended routes with a Puerto La Cruz–Isla de Margarita–Port of Spain weekly service.

These days, Windward Lines' representative, **Acosta Asociados** (☎ 982-0058; grupoacosta@cantv.net; Calle Bolívar 31; 🕒 9am-noon & 3-5pm Mon-Fri), operates the *Sea Prowler*, a comfortable and air-conditioned passenger boat that runs between Güiria and Chaguaramas, near Port of Spain, Trinidad. It is supposed to arrive every Wednesday at noon and depart back to Chaguaramas at 3pm (3½ hours) – be there at 1:30pm. Fares are

$73 one-way, and $121 roundtrip including port tax on the outward journey (for those returning from Trinidad there is an additional port tax of $12).

Peñeros (fishing boats) leave from the northern end of Güiria's port to Macuro. Irregular fishing and cargo boats (a few per week) go to Pedernales, at the mouth of the Delta del Orinoco. The trip takes four to five hours and the fare is negotiable; usually around $7 per person. From Pedernales, riverboats go south to Tucupita.

BUS
Several bus companies servicing Güiria have their offices close to each other, around the triangular Plaza Sucre, where the Carúpano highway enters the town.

There are six buses a day to Caracas, departing in the early morning and late afternoon ($14 to $19, 12 hours). They all go via Cumaná ($6, five hours) and Puerto La Cruz ($8, 6½ hours). Por puestos run frequently to Carúpano ($5, two hours) and Irapa ($1.25, 40 minutes) from Plaza Sucre.

MACURO
☎ 0294 / pop 2000
Macuro is a remote fishing village near the eastern tip of the Península de Paria. Its claim to fame is that Columbus reputedly landed somewhere here in August 1498, though no records state the exact landing site. What is known is that this was the only place on South America's mainland where Columbus came ashore.

Although Macuro is a poor place, it has bags of character. If you decide to come, visit the little history museum and consider a hike to Uquire (see Walking Trails p272). There are several very basic posadas, including friendly **Posada Beatriz** (Calle Mariño; d $6.50).

Boats from Güiria depart daily except Sunday, somewhere between 10am and noon ($2.50, 1½ to two hours). Boats depart Macuro for Güiria early in the morning, between 5am and 6am. At the time of writing, there was no overland access, though a road link eastward from Güiria has been in the works for years.

PARQUE NACIONAL PENÍNSULA DE PARIA
This 375-sq-km park stretches for 100km along the northern coast of the peninsula,

right up to its eastern tip. It encompasses a coastal mountain range, which looms up almost right from the sea and reaches its maximum elevation point at Cerro Humo (1257m). The coast is graced with many coves, in which tiny fishing villages have nestled.

The mountain is largely covered with forest, and the higher you go, the wetter it is. The upper reaches of the outcrop (roughly above 800m) form a typical cloud-forest habitat that is largely unexplored and intact, with rich and diverse wildlife. On the other hand, the southern foothills are being increasingly cleared by local farmers. An additional threat is the discovery of offshore oil, the exploitation of which may alter this remote bucolic peninsula completely.

Orientation

The park has no tourist facilities and access is not straightforward. The villages on the northern coast are best (or only) accessed by boat, the closest points of departure being Macuro and San Juan de Unare. However, boat trips are irregular and expensive. Access from the south is from the Carúpano–Güiria highway, but there are few gateways here leading into the park.

A few trails cross the park north to south, and these are the best way to get deeper into the wilderness. Ideally, you should hire a guide, because the trails are not always easy to follow.

Walking Trails

One of the trails goes between the villages of Manacal and Santa Isabel, in the western end of the park. The rough road to Manacal branches off the Carúpano–Güiria highway 20km east of Yaguaraparo and winds uphill to the village at 750m. There are few vehicles along this road, so you may need to walk (three hours). There are no hotels in Manacal, but informal accommodations can usually be arranged. If you have a hammock, you may be allowed to sling it under somebody's roof.

The trail from Manacal winds to the hamlet of Roma and then uphill to the 1000m crest, before descending to Santa Isabel, on the coast. Guides can be found in Manacal, and the hike will take five to seven hours. Stuck to the hillside high above the bay and dotted with rocky islets, Santa Isa-

bel is a tiny fishing village. It shelters the rustic **Posada de Cucha** (d incl 2 meals $19), which offers beds and meals and a marvelous view over the rugged coast from its balcony.

There are no roads from the village, but a path goes westward to Boca del Río Cumaná (two to four hours), then along the shore to Playa Cipara (one hour) and onward to San Juan de Unare (one hour). The first part of the trail is faint, so a guide is recommended (available in Santa Isabel). Otherwise, negotiate for a boat to San Juan de Unare, then continue to San Juan de Las Galdonas.

On the opposite, eastern end of the park is a path from Macuro to Uquire on the northern coast (a five- to six-hour walk). Uquire has a good beach, and you may be able to arrange a room or hammock for the night. You can either walk back or hunt for a boat to return you to Macuro around the peninsula's tip.

If you don't fancy walking, hire a boat in Macuro to take you to Uquire and other nearby places, such as Don Pedro and San Francisco. The roundtrip fare won't be much more than the one-way trip. Tours along the coast are organized from San Juan de Las Galdonas (see p269).

MONAGAS STATE

MATURÍN

☎ 0291 / pop 340,000

Founded in 1760 as a Capuchin mission, the thriving commercial city of Maturín has grown into a hub of the agro-industrial development of the eastern Llanos. Large deposits of oil exploited in the region have augmented the city's status. Maturín is also a busy regional transport hub, connecting routes from the northeastern coast to the Delta del Orinoco and the Gran Sabana.

Information

The tourist office **Cormotur** (Corporacion Mona-guense de Turismo; ☎ 643-0798; www.cormotur.gov.ve; Hacienda Sarrapial, Av Alirio Ugarte Pelayo; 🕑 8am-noon & 3-6pm Mon-Fri) is 5km north of the city center on the Caripito road in a colonial-style hacienda dating from 1823. To get there, take the Ruta 4 carrito from the center.

Most major banks are on Av Bolívar. Corp Banca is on the traffic circle on Av Bolívar at Calle 8. For changing money or traveler's checks there's the nearby **Italcambio** (☎ 642-2901; No 34, Centro Comercial Porto Fino, Av Bolívar at Carrera 8; ☺ 8am-12:30pm & 2:30-6pm). For Internet access try **Postweb** (☎ 643-3249; Calle Piar No 38; ☺ 8am-noon & 2-7pm Mon-Sat), near Hotel La Trinidad.

Tours

One of the major operators offering tours along the Río Morichal Largo (see later) is **El Centro del Mundo** (☎ 641-3501; cdmundo@cantv.net; Centro Comercial Fiorca, Planta Baja, Av Libertador No 13). All-inclusive full-day tours include transport, a boat trip and lunch, and cost $125/85 per person in groups of three/10 people. The company also runs tours in the Río Buja area, where it has its own Boca de Tigre *campamento*. A two-day, all-inclusive tour costs $125 per person, with a minimum of four people ($90 for each additional night).

Sleeping

Budget hotels around the central Plaza Ayacucho are easily accessible from the bus terminal by frequent city buses; you can also take a taxi ($2).

Hotel La Trinidad (☎ 642-2476; Calle 18 No 6; d $9.50-12.50, tr/q $16/19; ☒) This friendly, clean spot is arguably the best cheapie in town. Most of the tiled rooms have cable TV and hot water. The hotel is well managed, and it has two similar branches just around the corner.

Hotel Ayacucho Plaza (☎ 641-3080; Plaza Ayacucho; s $9.50, d $10-11; ☒) This friendly, busy hotel on the plaza is tucked away behind several layers of security bars. It has plain but good rooms with cable TV. There's a slightly cheaper hotel of more or less the same ilk next door.

Hotel Monagas Internacional (☎ 651-8811; fax 651-8727; Av Libertador at Orinoco; d $21; P ☒ ☒) This formerly top-end hotel comes in very handy thanks to its position by the bus station. It's a high-rise affair with spacious, good value rooms with cable TV.

Hotel Colonial (☎ 642-1175; fax 642-5316; Av Bolívar 58; d/tr $22/25; P ☒) Alternatively, for a more personal environment and a central position near the cathedral, try this popular option. It's got homely rooms, with fridges and hot-water bathrooms, and there's a restaurant to boot.

Hotel Morichal Largo (☎ 651-4222; www.moricha llargo.com.ve; Av Bella Vista; s/d $52/56; P ☒ ☒ ☒)

This top-end option has luxurious rooms, large grounds, a couple of tennis courts, sauna and a gym. It's 3km out of town on the road to Puerto La Cruz.

Stauffer (☎ 643-1111; www.stauffer-hotel.com.ve; Av Alirio Ugarte Pelayo; d incl breakfast $102; P ☒ ☒ ☒) This hotel has all the comfort of a five-star hotel, and is located 3km north of town.

Getting There & Away

AIR

The airport is 2km east of the city center; eastbound buses Nos 1 and 5 from Av Bolívar will let you off near the terminal. **Aeropostal** (☎ 643-8470) operates flights to Caracas ($46 to $59), while **Rutaca** (in Caracas ☎ 576-0304) and **Avior** (☎ 643-2626) fly to Porlamar ($29 to $50). Rutaca has three flights a week to Port of Spain, Trinidad ($93 one-way, $107 for a seven-day roundtrip).

BUS

The bus terminal is on Av Libertador near Av Orinoco, 2km southwest of the city center. It is linked to the city center by frequent urban transportation.

Several buses run to Caracas daily, mostly in the evening ($11 to $16, 8½ hours). There are buses to Ciudad Guayana ($5, 3½ hours), Tucupita ($5, four hours) and Caripe ($2, three hours); all these regional routes are also serviced by por puestos for nearly double the bus fare.

For the Cueva del Guácharo (p275), take the Caripe bus or por puesto, get off at the turnoff to Cariaco at the village of El Guácharo (9km before Caripe) and walk or hitch to the cave (2.5km).

The most luxurious service to Caracas costs $14 to $16 with **Aeroexpresos Ejecutivos** (☎ 0291-651-3695; Av Libertador), which has a terminal half a kilometer from the main bus station.

RÍO MORICHAL LARGO

The lower course of the Río Morichal Largo, southeast of Maturín near the Delta del Orinoco, has beautiful lush vegetation, rich wildlife and Warao Indian settlements. The tourist infrastructure includes a pleasure-boat service down the river. The embarkation point is on the highway to Ciudad Guayana, about 90km southeast of Maturín, where excursion boats wait for tourists.

The boat trips give a taster of wildlife and Indian communities typical of the Delta del Orinoco; they're a shorter alternative to the delta tours out of Tucupita. Tour companies in Maturín (see p273) and elsewhere offer tours along the river. You can go direct to the embarkation point and negotiate a trip with the boat operators, but be prepared to wait or pay for the empty seats.

The village of San José de Buja, 85km southeast of Maturín, is another springboard for a delta-like experience down along the Río Buja.

CARIPE

☎ 0292 / pop 12,000

Set in a verdant mountain valley midway between Maturín and the Caribbean coast, Caripe is an easygoing town renowned for its agreeable climate, coffee and orange plantations, and its proximity to Cueva del Guácharo, Venezuela's most magnificent cave.

Caripe makes for an inviting weekend escape for Venezuelans from the steamy lowlands, and will often fill up during its elaborate Easter celebrations. The village itself is little more than two parallel streets, on which most activities and services are centered.

Information

Banesco (Av Guzmán Blanco) gives cash advances on Visa and MasterCard. For Internet access, head to the telecommunications office **Telsenet** (8am-8:30pm Mon-Sat, 8am-1pm Sun), located off Plaza Bolívar.

Sights & Activities

Save for a beautiful colonial high altar in the modern parish church, there's not much to see in town, but the rugged surroundings are ripe for exploration and hiking. The number-one attraction in the region is the Cueva del Guácharo, 12km from the town (see p275).

El Mirador (1100m), to the north of the town, commands sweeping views over the Valle del Caripe. It's an hour's walk from town; you can also get there by road. Among the other sights are two beautiful waterfalls: the 30m-high **Salto La Payla**, near the Cueva del Guácharo, and the 80m-high **Salto El Chorrerón**, an hour's walk from the village of Sabana de Piedra. Further away

are the **Puertas de Miraflores**, a spectacular river canyon; and the **Mata de Mango**, which features 22 caves, including the impressive Cueva Grande and Cueva Clara.

Tours

Oscar Gregori, manager of Hotel Samán, can offer guidance on organizing tours and finding guides around the region. Also in the town is **Naur Tours** (☎ 0416-874-3549; naur -tours@cantv.net; Calle Manzana Nueve No 35, Sector La Orquidia) near the bus terminal. Alternatively, the guides at the Cueva del Guácharo are always keen for more work guiding guests to other local attractions.

Sleeping & Eating

Though many have shut in recent years, Caripe still has a few central hotels and there are plenty of upmarket chalets scattered around the surrounding countryside. Prices may rise on weekends.

TOWN CENTER

Hotel Samán (☎ 545-1183; Av Chaumer No 29; s/d/tr $12.50/15/19) This long-running hotel is still the best in town. It has comfortable rooms, a stream running beneath the building and a courtyard packed with plants, plus puppets and models peering out from the windowsills. The knowledgeable manager can put you in touch with local guides and also offers special rates for backpackers. Prices drop in low season.

Mini Hotel Familiar Nicola (☎ 545-1489; Av Gusmán Blanco; d/tr $12.50/16) Further out on the road to Maturín is this snug little family house, which rents out a few clean, modern rooms with hot-water bathrooms.

La Posada (☎ 0416-892-4130; Av Enrique Chaumer; d without bathroom $5) You get what you pay for in this bare-bones posada behind a grubby restaurant and opposite the town church. It's a clapped out old-timer with very basic rooms, but it's the cheapest place to stay.

Trattoria Da Stefano (☎ 414-6107; Calle Cabello; mains $2-4; noon-6pm Mon-Wed, noon-9pm Thu-Sun) Mouth-watering pasta at low prices – ask for the homemade ones. A bona fide Italian, who is also helpful and knowledgeable on the area, runs this outfit.

Restaurant Mogambo (☎ 545-1021; Av Chaumer; mains $5-9; 8am-11pm Wed-Mon; P) A few steps on from Hotel Samán is this little gem of a restaurant. Set in a pink chalet-style building, it has a nice terrace, children's playground and an indoor dining room and bar, stacked with an impressive collection of miniature liqueur bottles. It has good *criollo* food.

AROUND CARIPE

There are more places to stay outside town, particularly along the road between Caripe and the village of El Guácharo. Some have cabañas that work out cheaply if you are in a large party.

Cabañas La Floresta (☎ 414-8878; Sector La Peña; d/tr $13/17; 6-/8-/10-person cabañas $25/32/38; P) Down a pretty flower-covered lane and across a stream lies this hillside holiday camp in a neatly trimmed lawn scattered with orange and mango trees. The larger cabañas are fitted with well equipped kitchens and outdoor barbeques. It's located 2km from the town center on the road to Maturín.

Pueblo Pequeño Vacation Villas (☎ 545-1843; pueblopequeno1@cantv.net; Sector Amanita off Via Cocollar; d/tr $22/25, d/tr cabaña $32/44; P ⊠) This upmarket holiday village is not unlike La Floresta, though it also has a reliable restaurant open daily, a children's playground, sauna, laundry service and a swimming pool. It's a few hundred meters closer to Caripe than La Floresta.

Getting There & Away

The bus terminal is at the northeastern end of the town, behind the market. There's an evening bus to Caracas via Cumaná at 6pm ($10, nine hours). Buses to Maturín depart every 1½ hours until about 5:30pm ($2, three hours), and there are also por puestos ($3.50, two hours).

Another daily bus runs to Cumaná in the morning ($4, 3½ hours), and a private minibus also goes at 6am ($5, three hours). They all pass the Cueva del Guácharo en route. An infrequent bus from Caripe passes the cave ($0.20, 10 minutes). A roundtrip taxi from Caripe to the cave only costs $1.25 if you tell them to come back in two hours. If they wait for you, it will cost $10. Some tour operators and hotels also organize trips.

CUEVA DEL GUÁCHARO

Venezuela's longest, largest and most magnificent cave, the **Guácharo Cave** (in Maturín ☎ 0292-641-7543; adult/student $5/2; ⊙ 8am-4pm; P), is 12km from Caripe on the road toward the coast. The eminent scientist Alexander von Humboldt penetrated 472m into the cave in September 1799, and it was he who first classified its namesake inhabitant, the *guácharo*, or oilbird (see the boxed text following).

Apart from this unique bird, the cave houses fish, crabs, spiders, ants, centipedes and bats. Keep your eyes peeled for the rodents that scamper boldly across your path. The cave also shelters a maze of stalactites and stalagmites that shine with calcium crystals. Highlights include a formation called the 'piano,' a column with deep niches that it's possible to tap out a tune on (though don't expect too much from the guide's rendition of chopsticks). And if you finish the full tour, you'll be treated to a peek at the well-rounded rock formations in the *Sala de Los Senos* (Room of the Breasts). If you get one of the cheekier guides, expect more x-rated interpretations

---

THE GUÁCHARO

The eerie shrieking and flapping that echoes in the high galleries of the Cueva del Guácharo is made by a curious, reddish-brown species of bird that is the only one of its kind in the world. The *guácharo*, or oilbird *(Steatornis caripensis)*, is a nocturnal, fruit-eating bird that inhabits caves in various tropical parts of the Americas, living in total darkness and leaving the cave only at night for food. It has a radar-location system (similar to bats) that enables it to navigate. It has a curved beak and enormous whiskers, and grows to about 60cm long, with a wingspan of a meter.

This colony is by far the biggest in Venezuela. From August to December, the population in this single cave is estimated at 10,000 birds, and occasionally up to 15,000. In the dry season the colony diminishes, but at least 8000 birds remain in March and April. The birds inhabit only the first chamber of the cave, 750m-long Humboldt's Hall. And the name of the first chamber following this area, *El Silencio* (Silence), echoes the relief felt by explorers to leave the birds' unsettling screeches behind.

of rock formations when the kids aren't listening.

The cave was declared Venezuela's first natural monument in 1949 and the 627-sq-km area around the cave was decreed the Parque Nacional El Guácharo in 1975.

All visits to the cave are by guided tours in groups of up to 10 people; tours take about 1½ hours. A 1200m portion of the total 10.2km length of the cave is normally visited, though occasionally water rises in August and/or September limiting sightseeing to half a kilometer. Bring non-slippery shoes for tramping over the mud and guano (droppings). The reception building also has a small museum and cafeteria. Bags must be left by the ticket office. Cameras with flash can be used only beyond the guácharos gallery.

You can camp at the entrance to the cave after closing time; it costs $3.50 per tent and the bathroom is open 24 hours. If you do camp, watch the hundreds of birds pouring out of the cave mouth at around 6:30pm and returning at about 4am. You can also take a short trip to the waterfall of Salto La Payla, a 25-minute walk from the cave.

Getting There & Away

Possible jumping-off points for the cave include Cumaná (p259), Caripe (p275) and Maturín (p273). See those sections for transportation details.

Guayana

CONTENTS

GUAYANA

GUAYANA

Home of Venezuela's greatest natural attractions, including the world's highest waterfall, Angel Falls, Guayana encompasses the whole of Venezuela's southeast – the vast Delta del Orinoco and all the land south of the river. It covers the states of Delta Amacuro, Bolívar and Amazonas, comprising half of the country's land area, yet is home to just 6% of Venezuela's population.

Here is Venezuela at its best, wildest and most fabulous: the great Delta del Orinoco – a maze of islands separated by water channels and populated by traditional Indian communities and rich wildlife; a chunk of the Amazon basin – a thick green carpet of rain forest, some of it virtually untouched by humans; and, perhaps most spectacular, the mysterious world of the tepuis, with their moonscape scenery and unique endemic flora – from one of these giant table mountains spills Angel Falls, an unforgettable sight from either boat or plane, and climbing a tepui is the ultimate wilderness adventure.

Travelers looking for cultural fare will enjoy the enchanting old river port of Ciudad Bolívar and the region's mosaic of indigenous communities. Guayana is home to the majority of Venezuela's Indian groups, including the Warao, Pemón and Yanomami, which constitute about 10% of the region's total population.

HIGHLIGHTS

- Marvel at the awe-inspiring **Angel Falls** (p300)
- Explore the unique table mountain of **Roraima** (p309)
- Savor the old-time charm of **Ciudad Bolívar** (p284)
- Embark on a boat trip into the **Delta del Orinoco** (p279)
- Travel up the **Río Caura** (p291) to Salto Pará

DELTA DEL ORINOCO

Covering nearly 30,000 sq km – the size of Belgium – this is one of the world's great river deltas and a fascinating region to explore. The Río Orinoco reaches a width of 20km in its lower course before splitting into about 40 major channels (and perhaps 250 smaller ones), which flow out along 360km of Atlantic coast. The southernmost channel, Río Grande, is the main one and is used by ocean-going vessels sailing upriver to Ciudad Guayana.

The delta is a vast labyrinth of islands, channels and mangrove swamps. The land is largely covered by mixed forest that includes a variety of palms, of which the *moriche* is the most typical of the region. The palm has traditionally provided the staple food for the delta's inhabitants, the Warao Indians, as well as material for their dwellings, crafts, tools, household implements and wine.

The climate of the delta is hot and humid, with an average temperature of around 27°C throughout the year, though nights can be quite cool. Annual rainfall varies from 1500mm to 2500mm, and the closer you get to the coast the more it rains. The driest period is from January to March. The water level is usually at its lowest in March and highest from August to September when many parts of the delta become marshy or flooded.

GUAYANA

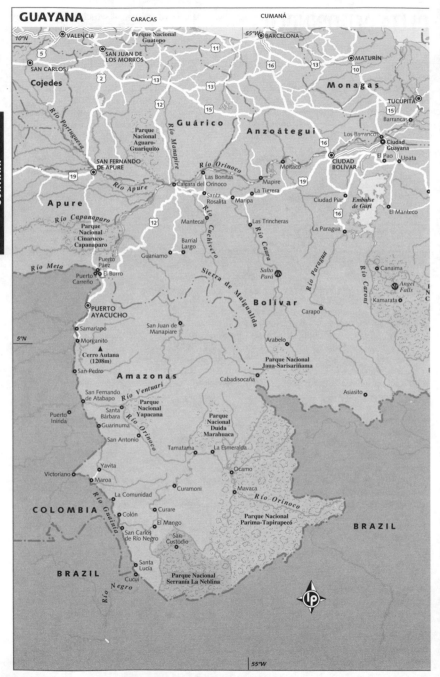

GUAYANA

CARACAS

CUMANÁ

10°N

VALENCIA

Parque Nacional Guatopo

55°W BARCELONA

5

SAN JUAN DE LOS MORROS

11

MATURÍN

SAN CARLOS

16

13

10

Cojedes

2

13

Monagas

TUCUPITA

12

15

Guárico

Anzoátegui

15

Barrancas

Parque Nacional Aguaro-Guariquito

Río Manapire

Los Barrancos

16

Ciudad Guayana

SAN FERNANDO DE APURE

Río Orinoco

Moitaco

CIUDAD BOLÍVAR

El Pao

Upata

19

Calcara del Orinoco

Las Bonitas

La Tigrera

19

Río Apure

Santa Rosalita

Maripa

Ciudad Piar

Embalse de Guri

Apure

Río Capanaparo

Mantecal

Las Trincheras

16

El Manteco

Parque Nacional Cinaruco-Capanaparo

12

Barrial Largo

Río Cuchivero

Río Caura

La Paragua

Río Meta

Guaniamo

Sierra de Maigualida

Salto Pará

Río Paragua

Canaima

Puerto Páez

Puerto Carreño

El Burro

Bolívar

Carapo

Río Caroní

Angel Falls

PUERTO AYACUCHO

San Juan de Manapiare

Kamarata

Samariapó

Arabelo

5°N

Morganito

Cerro Autana (1208m)

San Pedro

Amazonas

Cabadisocaña

Parque Nacional Jaua-Sarisariñama

Asiasito

San Fernando de Atabapo

Río Ventuari

Parque Nacional Yapacana

Puerto Inírida

Santa Bárbara

Parque Nacional Duida Marahuaca

Río Orinoco

Guarinuma

San Antonio

Tamatama

La Esmeralda

Victoriano

Yavita

Ocamo

Maroa

Curamoni

Mavaca

La Comunidad

Río Orinoco

COLOMBIA

Río Guainía

Colón

Curare

Parque Nacional Parima-Tapirapecó

BRAZIL

El Mango

San Carlos de Río Negro

San Custodio

BRAZIL

Santa Lucía

Cucui

Parque Nacional Serranía La Neblina

Río Negro

55°W

55°W

The best time to the see the wildlife in the delta is in the dry season, when wide, orange, sandy beaches emerge along the shores of the channels. In the rainy months, when rivers are full, boat travel is easier, but the wildlife disperses and is more difficult to see.

Curiously enough, the state that encompasses the delta is not named after the Orinoco, but after the Amacuro, a small river that runs along part of the Guyana border and empties into Boca Grande, the Orinoco's main mouth. Tucupita is the state capital and a base for Delta del Orinoco adventures.

TUCUPITA

☎ 0287 / pop 70,000

The capital of the Delta Amacuro state is a hot, steamy river port and the only sizeable town in the Delta del Orinoco. You can take a pleasant stroll around the central streets and along Paseo Mánamo, the riverbank esplanade, but the town is mainly visited as a base for exploring the delta.

Tucupita sits beside the westernmost channel of the Delta del Orinoco, Caño Mánamo, which flows northward for 110km and empties into the Golfo de Paria near the town of Pedernales. Caño Mánamo has been blocked by a dike 22km south of Tucupita, erected in the 1960s as part of a flood-control program aiming to make land in the northern delta usable for farming. The road that runs atop the dike is Tucupita's only overland link with the rest of the country.

Tucupita evolved in the 1920s as one of a chain of Catholic Capuchin missions founded in the delta to convert the indigenous peoples. The missions established social programs that focused on providing Indians with education and health services; they opened up the region for both governmental activities and *criollo* (Creole) colonists and, ultimately, for tourism.

Information

INTERNET ACCESS

Compucenter.com (Centro Comercial Delta Center, Plaza Bolívar)
Copicom (Calle Petión)
Gos's Computer (Calle Petión)

MONEY

Banco de Venezuela (Calle Mánamo)
Banesco (Calle Petión)
Mi Casa (Plaza Bolívar) Convenient ATM on the main plaza.

GUAYANA

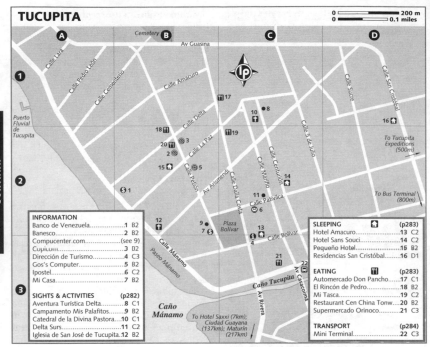

INFORMATION
Banco de Venezuela...............1 B2
Banesco.................................2 B2
Compucenter.com.............(see 9)
Cupicom................................3 B2
Dirección de Turismo...........4 C3
Gos's Computer....................5 B2
Ipostel..................................6 C2
Mi Casa.................................7 B2

SIGHTS & ACTIVITES   (p282)
Aventura Turística Delta.........8 C1
Campamento Mis Palafitos.......9 B2
Catedral de la Divina Pastora...10 C1
Delta Surs.............................11 C2
Iglesia de San José de Tucupita.12 B2

SLEEPING   🛏   (p283)
Hotel Amacuro......................13 C2
Hotel Sans Souci....................14 C2
Pequeño Hotel......................15 B2
Residencias San Cristóbal........16 D1

EATING   🍴   (p283)
Automercado Don Pancho......17 C1
El Rincón de Pedro................18 B2
Mi Tasca...............................19 C2
Restaurant Cen China Tonw...20 B2
Supermercado Orinoco..........21 C3

TRANSPORT   (p284)
Mini Terminal.......................22 C3

POST
Ipostel (Calle Pativilca)

TOURIST INFORMATION
Dirección de Turismo (Oficina 18, Piso 2, Edificio San Juan, Calle Bolívar; ☽ 8am-noon & 2-5pm Mon-Fri)

Sights
The **Iglesia de San José de Tucupita** (Calle Mánamo), the Capuchin mission church built in 1930, is the oldest building in town. It served as a parish church until the massive **Catedral de la Divina Pastora** (Av Arismendi) was completed in 1982, after nearly three decades of construction.

Tours
All local tour operators focus on trips into the delta. These tours usually consist of all-inclusive two- to four-day excursions and you can expect to pay between about $40 to $80 per person per day, depending on the company, the routes and conditions, and particularly on the number of people in the group. With the exception of Delta Surs, all the following agencies listed

offer tours to the northern part of the delta toward Pedernales. All the companies have *campamentos* (camps) that serve as a base for trips around the area.

Aventura Turística Delta (☎ 721-0835; a_t_d _1973@hotmail.com; Calle Centurión) The most popular company with travelers, and probably the cheapest. The facilities are simple and its two basic camps have hammocks and.

Campamento Mis Palafitos (☎ 721-1733; www .deltaorinocomispalafitos.com; Centro Comercial Delta Center, Plaza Bolívar)This operator is not very cheap, but has a comfortable 32-cabin camp providing rooms with bathroom, two hours by boat from Tucupita. Excursions cater mostly to Venezuelan families and travelers may find it too relaxed – unless that's what you want.

Delta Surs (☎ 721-3840; cnr Calles Mariño & Pativilca) The oldest local tour company, operating since 1987, and the only one that offers tours to the far eastern part of the delta. Its Campamento Maraisa, in San Francisco de Guayo, has cabañas with beds and bathrooms.

Tucupita Expeditions (☎ 721-0801; www.orinoco delta.com; Calle Las Acacias) Just 700m east of the centre, this is possibly the most expensive agency. It works principally with organized groups and generally doesn't focus on individual travelers.

Even in peak season, the number of tourists coming through Tucupita is fairly low. As a result, the local tour business is pretty lazy and you may need to wait a while before the group is collected, or pay more and go in a small party. Some travelers buy delta tours in Ciudad Bolívar (p288), which may not be much more expensive, but will save you time and money in the long run. Also consider Sacoroco River Tours (p296) in Ciudad Guayana, which organizes reasonably priced trips to the southern delta. Some of Ciudad Bolívar's tour agencies use Sacoroco services, but are likely to charge more than you'd pay by booking directly. In any case, it may be a good idea to check various options and contact agents before rushing to Tucupita.

Sleeping

Hotel Amacuro (☎ 721-0404; Calle Bolívar; d/tr with fan $10/14, with air-con $14/20; ✴) Just off Plaza Bolívar, Amacuro is nothing particularly special, but it has reasonably clean, good-sized rooms, and a large terrace to sit, sip cold beer and relax.

Residencias San Cristóbal (☎ 721-4529; Calle San Cristóbal; d $8-9, tr $10; P) Not really central and without air-con, the 40-room San Cristóbal is otherwise cheap and good value. It has

---

INDEPENDENT GUIDES

Independent guides (called *piratas* by the registered companies) will descend like vultures as soon as you arrive at Tucupita. Their tours may be cheaper, though you never actually know what you'll get for your money. Lonely Planet has received very mixed (even totally contradictory) comments about their services.

If you decide to go on a tour with one of these guides, clarify all the details of the trip (duration, places to be visited, food and lodging etc) and have a look at the boat before you commit yourself. Make sure the boat has two engines (required by law) and preferably a roof, and that mosquito nets are provided for hammocks. After you and your guide agree on a price, you should insist on paying only the money necessary for predeparture expenses (gasoline and food), and pay the remaining part upon your return.

---

revamped private bathrooms and new mattresses. Choose a room upstairs.

Pequeño Hotel (☎ 721-0523; Calle La Paz; d with fan $6-8, with air-con $8-10, tr with fan $10, with air-con $12; ✴) The family-run Pequeño Hotel has dim rooms and lumpy beds, but is just about the cheapest place in town and has a homely atmosphere. The señora locks the door at 10pm and goes to bed, so don't be late.

Hotel Sans Souci (☎ 721-0132; Calle Centurión; s/tr with fan $5/10, with air-con $7/13, d with fan $6-8, with air-con $9-11; ✴) Also on the basic side and a bit rundown, Sans Souci is waiting for some refurbishing, which is likely to upgrade standards and prices. Meanwhile, inspect a few rooms and choose because some are much better then others.

Hotel Saxxi (☎ 721-2112; Zona Paloma; d $22-30, tr $40; P ✴ ☎) About 7km south of Tucupita, Saxxi is the largest and best place to stay in the area. It has 96 rooms with hot water, a restaurant and bar. Check if there is a disco on Friday or Saturday night – unless you plan to join the dancing party, these are probably not the best days to stay there. The hotel is accessible by buses from the Mini Terminal, or take a taxi ($2.50).

Eating

In the evening food stalls open along Paseo Mánamo, turning it into a lively spot where locals gather to meet friends, eat, drink and have fun. There's also a choice of regular restaurants in town.

Mi Tasca (☎ 721-0428; Calle Dalla Costa; mains $3-6) Ask anybody where to go for a lunch or dinner, and most locals will send you to Mi Tasca. Now enlarged and revamped, the place remains Tucupita's best eatery, with a varied menu, good prices, generous portions and quick service. Try the *lau lau* (catfish) – it's delicious.

El Rincón de Pedro (Calle Petión; mains $2-3) 'Pedro's Corner' is a tiny family-run spot serving unpretentious meals at proletarian prices.

Restaurant Cen China Tonw (Calle Petión; mains $2-4) This is perhaps not the most authentic Chinese cuisine in your life, but not the most expensive either.

Should you need food provisions for a delta trip:

Automercado Don Pancho (Calle Dalla Costa)
Supermercado Orinoco (Calle Tucupita)

GUAYANA

THE CANOE PEOPLE OF DELTA DEL ORINOCO

The Delta del Orinoco is inhabited by the Warao (or Guarao) Indians, who have lived here from time immemorial. Today numbering about 25,000, they are Venezuela's largest indigenous group after the Guajiro of Zulia. Two-thirds of the Waraos live in the eastern part of the delta, between the Caño Mariusa and the Río Grande, where they are distributed across about 250 tiny communities.

The Waraos dwell along the small channels, constructing their open-sided, wooden huts on stilts on riverbanks and living mostly off fishing. Water is pivotal in their lives, as indicated by the tribe's name; in the local language *wa* means 'canoe' and *arao* means 'people.' They are excellent boat builders, making their dugout canoes from logs of large trees, using fire and simple axes.

Only half the Waraos speak Spanish. Most of the indigenous community still use their native language, officially classified as 'independent' because it doesn't belong to any of the major linguistic families. Linguists have not yet determined the origins of the language.

The Waraos are skillful craftspeople, renowned for their basketry and woodcarvings, especially animal figures carved from balsa wood. Their *chinchorros* (hammocks), made from the fiber of the *moriche* palm, are widely known and sought after for their quality and durability, and are sold at markets and craft shops across the country.

Getting There & Away

The **Terminal de Pasajeros** (cnr Carrera 6 & Calle 10) is 1km southeast of the center; walk or take a taxi ($1). The **Mini Terminal** (Calle Tucupita) handles local and suburban bus traffic.

Five buses nightly make a run to Caracas ($13 to $18, 11 hours, 730km) via Maturín. Expresos La Guayanesa has two buses daily to Ciudad Guayana ($4, 3½ hours, 137km), but faster por puestos ($6, 2½ hours) serve this route regularly. The trip includes a ferry ride across the Río Orinoco from Los Barrancos to San Félix (no extra charge).

For Caripe and Cueva del Guácharo, take a bus to Maturín ($5, four hours, 217km), or one of the more frequent and faster por puestos ($8, three hours), and change.

LOWER ORINOCO

The Lower Orinoco is the industrial heart of Guayana. It's the most densely populated part of the region, and is the only area with a road network to speak of. Guayana's only two cities are here – Ciudad Bolívar and Ciudad Guayana – both situated on the right (south) bank of the Río Orinoco, in Bolívar state.

While Ciudad Bolívar is a colorful colonial city with preserved historic architecture, Ciudad Guayana is a modern urban sprawl graced with charming riverside parks. Either of the two cities makes a convenient starting point for exploring the region.

CIUDAD BOLÍVAR

☎ 0285 / pop 350,000

An old Spanish port on the Orinoco, about 420km upstream from the Atlantic, Ciudad Bolívar is one of Venezuela's most popular destinations, partly for the city itself, and partly to access the natural attractions in the region, primarily Angel Falls. During modern times the town has expanded greatly, yet its historic core has retained the flavor of an old river town and conserved its colonial era architecture. Add to this a few good museums and a lively annual festival, and you will find Ciudad Bolívar a very enjoyable spot to hang out for a while.

History

Founded in 1764 on a rocky elevation at the river's narrowest point, the town was named Santo Tomás de la Guayana de Angostura – *angostura* means 'narrows.' It grew as a lonely beacon on a great river hundreds of miles away from any major cities, and within 50 years was already a thriving port and trade center. Then, suddenly and unexpectedly, Angostura became the spot where much of the country's (and the continent's) history was forged.

Libertador Simón Bolívar came here in 1817, soon after the town had been liberated from Spanish control, and set up the base for the military operations that led to the final stage of the War of Independence. The town was made the provisional capital of the yet-to-be-liberated country. It was

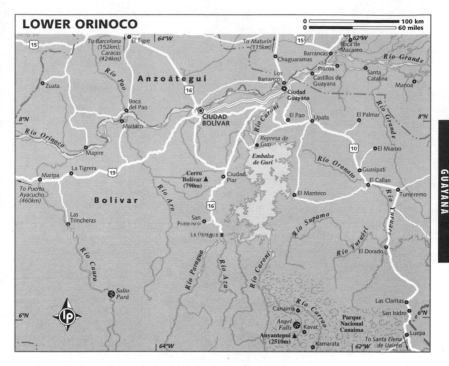

LOWER ORINOCO

GUAYANA

in Angostura that the British Legionnaires joined Bolívar before they all set off for the battle of Boyacá in the Andes, which secured the independence of Colombia. The Angostura Congress convened here in 1819 and gave birth to Gran Colombia, a unified republic comprising Venezuela, Colombia and Ecuador. The town was renamed 'Ciudad Bolívar' in 1846, in honor of the hero of the independence struggle. Today, it's the capital of Bolívar state, Venezuela's largest state, occupying over a quarter of the country's territory.

Orientation

The peaceful historic quarter is perched on a hillside overlooking the mighty Orinoco. Most of the sights are in this colorful old central area and, conveniently, there's a good choice of accommodations here as well. Along the riverbank is the bustling Paseo Orinoco, the city's lifeline, while the modern suburbs further south are home to the tourist office, the good Museo de Arte Moderno Jesús Soto, the bus terminal and the airport.

Information

EMERGENCY
Fire (☎ 632-8980)
Police (☎ 632-4357)

INTERNET ACCESS
Dispanaca (Map p287; cnr Calles Dalla Costa & Bolívar)
Estrella de Oriente (Map p287; cnr Calle Bolívar & Calle Igualdad)
Galaxia.com (Map p287; Centro Comercial Abboud Center, Paseo Orinoco btwn Calles Piar & Roscio)
Gallery Computer (Map p286; cnr Avs República & Jesús Soto; ☒ 24hr)

LAUNDRY
Lavandería Woo Lee & Co (Map p287; Calle Zea btwn Calles Piar & Roscio)

MEDICAL SERVICES
Hospital Ruiz y Páez (Map p286; ☎ 632-0077; Av Germania)

MONEY
Banco de Venezuela (Map p287; cnr Paseo Orinoco & Calle Piar)

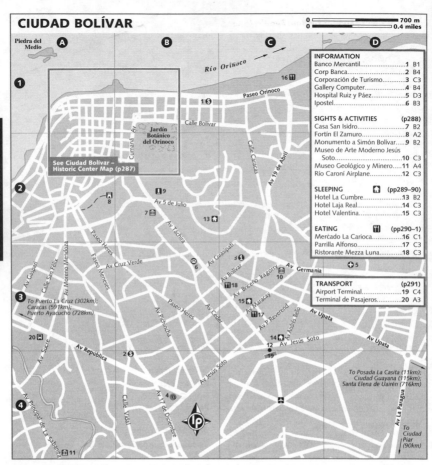

CIUDAD BOLÍVAR

See Ciudad Bolívar –
Historic Center Map (p287)

INFORMATION
Banco Mercantil.......................1 B1
Corp Banca...............................2 B4
Corporación de Turismo..........3 C3
Gallery Computer.....................4 B4
Hospital Ruiz y Páez.................5 D3
Ipostel......................................6 B3

SIGHTS & ACTIVITIES   (p288)
Casa San Isidro.........................7 B2
Fortín El Zamuro.......................8 A2
Monumento a Simón Bolívar....9 B2
Museo de Arte Moderno Jesús
    Soto.....................................10 C3
Museo Geológico y Minero.....11 A4
Río Caroní Airplane.................12 C3

SLEEPING   (pp289–90)
Hotel La Cumbre.....................13 B2
Hotel Laja Real.......................14 C3
Hotel Valentina.......................15 C3

EATING   (pp290–1)
Mercado La Carioca................16 C1
Parrilla Alfonso.......................17 C3
Ristorante Mezza Luna............18 C3

TRANSPORT   (p291)
Airport Terminal......................19 C4
Terminal de Pasajeros.............20 A3

Banco Mercantil (Map p286; cnr Paseo Orinoco &
Calle Zaraza)
Banesco (Map p287; cnr Calles Dalla Costa & Venezuela)
Corp Banca (Map p286; cnr Paseo Meneses & Calle
Vidal)

POST
Ipostel (Map p286; Av Táchira btwn Avs Cruz Verde &
Guasipati)

TELEPHONE
CANTV (Map p287; cnr Paseo Orinoco & Calle Dalla Costa)

TOURIST INFORMATION
Corporación de Turismo (Map p286; ☎ 632-2362;
Quinta Yeita, Av Bolívar; ☻ 8am-noon & 2-5:30pm
Mon-Fri)

Sights
PASEO ORINOCO   Map p287
This lively waterfront boulevard is lined
with arcaded houses. Midway along the
Paseo is the **Mirador Angostura**, a rocky headland that juts out into the river at its narrowest point. If you happen to be here in
August, when the water is at its highest, the
river will be just below your feet. This is also
the time to watch fishermen with their *atar-
rayas* (circular fishing nets) catching a delicious fish called *sapoara* (or *zapoara*), which
appears only during this short period. In
March, by contrast, the water level is likely
to be lower by 15m or more.

The lookout commands good views up
and down the Orinoco. About 5km upriver

you'll see a suspension bridge, **Puente de Angostura**, the only bridge across the Orinoco along the river's entire 2140km length (a second bridge is being constructed near Ciudad Guayana). This 1678m-long bridge, with its central, highest section 45m above the river (in the low-water season), was built over a five-year period and opened in 1967. Pedestrians are not allowed on the bridge – you'll need a motor vehicle in order to make the crossing.

Close to the lookout is a restored 18th-century prison building that functioned as a jail until 1952. It's now home to the **Instituto Cultural del Orinoco** (☎ 632-8801; cnr Paseo Orinoco & Calle Igualdad), which has an exhibition of crafts from Indian communities in Venezuela's south, but was closed at the time of writing.

In a spacious colonial residence known as the Casa del Correo del Orinoco, two blocks west along the Paseo, is the **Museo de Ciudad Bolívar** (☎ 632-4121; Paseo Orinoco; admission $0.20; ☒ 9am-noon & 2-5pm Mon-Fri). It was here that the republic's first newspaper was published, from 1818 to 1821, and you can see the original press on which it was printed, plus a collection of local modern paintings.

COLONIAL QUARTER   Map p287
The historic heart of the city is on a hillside to the south of the river; it's an oasis of tranquility, a world apart from the bustle of Paseo Orinoco. Most facades lining the steep streets are painted in bright colors – anything from pink to pistachio – and look lovely. It's a great place for a leisurely stroll along random streets without looking at a map.

The quarter is centered on the finely restored **Plaza Bolívar** which, apart from the usual monument to the hero, sports five allegorical statues personifying the five countries Bolívar liberated. To the east looms the massive **Catedral**, begun right after the town's founding and completed 80 years later.

Half of the plaza's western side is taken up by the **Casa del Congreso de Angostura** (admission free; ☒ 9am-5pm Tue-Sun), built in the 1770s. In 1819 it was home to lengthy debates by

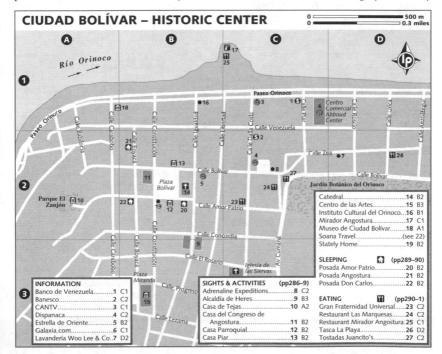

CIUDAD BOLÍVAR – HISTORIC CENTER

0   500 m
0   0.3 miles

INFORMATION	
Banco de Venezuela	1 C1
Banesco	2 C2
CANTV	3 C1
Dispanaca	4 C2
Estrella de Oriente	5 B2
Galaxia.com	6 C1
Lavandería Woo Lee & Co.	7 D2

SIGHTS & ACTIVITIES	(pp286-9)
Adrenaline Expeditions	8 C2
Alcaldía de Heres	9 B3
Casa de Tejas	10 A2
Casa del Congreso de Angostura	11 B2
Casa Parroquial	12 B2
Casa Piar	13 B2
Catedral	14 B2
Centro de las Artes	15 B3
Instituto Cultural del Orinoco	16 B1
Mirador Angostura	17 C1
Museo de Ciudad Bolívar	18 A1
Soana Travel	(see 22)
Stately Home	19 B2

SLEEPING ⌂	(pp289-90)
Posada Amor Patrio	20 B2
Posada Angostura	21 B2
Posada Don Carlos	22 B2

EATING ⛔	(pp290-1)
Gran Fraternidad Universal	23 C2
Restaurant Las Marquesas	24 C2
Restaurant Mirador Angostura	25 C1
Tasca La Playa	26 D2
Tostadas Juancito's	27 C2

GUAYANA

the Angostura Congress, and you can still sense the air of those days while strolling about the formal rooms, wide corridors and elegant courtyards.

On the northern side of the plaza is the **Casa Piar** (admission free; 9am-5pm Tue-Sun), where General Manuel Piar was kept prisoner in October 1817 before being stood against the cathedral wall and executed by firing squad. Piar liberated the city from Spanish control, but rejected Bolívar's authority and was sentenced to death in a controversial and much criticized trial. The plaque on the cathedral's wall marks the spot where he was shot dead, while Bolívar watched the execution from the Casa del Congreso de Angostura.

The 18th-century **Casa de los Gobernadores** and **Casa Parroquial**, next to each other on the upper side of Plaza Bolívar, are other fine historic buildings, but are not open to the public.

One block south you'll see the **Alcaldía de Heres** (cnr Calles Igualdad & Concordia), a pair of fine old buildings on both sides of the street, linked by an intriguing aerial walkway.

Don't miss visiting **Parque El Zanjón**, a most unusual city park, full of massive *lajas* (boulders). The lovely red-tile roofed **Casa de Tejas**, picturesquely set on one of the boulders, houses a small art gallery.

On the southern edge of the colonial sector is the delightfully tree-shaded **Plaza Miranda**. A sizable building on its eastern side was constructed in 1870 as a hospital, but it never served that purpose. It has had a bizarre list of tenants instead, having been used as a prefecture, theatre, army barracks and police station. Eventually, after extensive refurbishing, it opened in 1992 as the **Centro de las Artes** (630-1306; admission free; 9am-5pm Tue-Sun) and stages temporary exhibitions of modern art.

OUTSIDE THE HISTORIC CENTER   Map p286

The **Fortín El Zamuro** (admission free; 9am-5pm Tue-Sun) is a small fort built in the late-18th-century atop the highest hill in the city, just south of the colonial quarter. It provides fine views over the old town. The entrance is from Paseo Heres.

The **Casa San Isidro** (Av Táchira; admission free; 9am-5pm Tue-Sun) is a lovely colonial mansion set in a coffee hacienda that once stretched as far as the airport. Bolívar stayed here for a few months, during which he reputedly composed his vehement speech for the Angostura Congress. The house's interior is maintained in the style of Bolívar's era.

Diagonally opposite San Isidro is the gigantic **Monumento a Simón Bolívar** (cnr Av Cumaná & Av 5 de Julio). Founded in 1999, this 10m-high bronze statue is by far the tallest monument to the hero ever built in Venezuela, and looks a bit apocalyptic.

The **Museo de Arte Moderno Jesús Soto** (632-0518; cnr Av Germania and Av Briceño Iragorry; admission free; 9:30am-5:30pm Tue-Fri, 10am-5pm Sat & Sun) has an extensive collection of kinetic works by Soto, as well as works by other national and international modern artists. Born in Ciudad Bolívar in 1923, Jesús Soto is Venezuela's most internationally renowned contemporary artist. Have a look at Soto's large sculpture (you can actually go inside it) in the museum's internal garden.

It is worth visiting the airport to see the legendary **Río Caroní airplane** (Av Jesús Soto), proudly parked in front of the terminal building. This is the original plane in which Jimmie Angel landed atop Auyantepui in 1937 (see the boxed text, p300). The plane was removed from the tepui in 1970, restored in Maracay, and brought here.

In the southwestern suburb of La Sabanita is the **Museo Geológico y Minero** (Av Principal de La Sabanita; admission free; 9am-noon & 2-5pm Mon-Fri), which introduces Guayana's mines, mining techniques and machinery.

Tours
ANGEL FALLS

Ciudad Bolívar is the main gateway to Angel Falls, and tours to the falls are the staple of virtually all the tour operators in the city. One of the most popular tours, offered mainly in the dry season, is a one-day package that includes a roundtrip flight to Canaima, a flight over Angel Falls, lunch and a short boat excursion in Canaima, and a walk to other nearby falls. Tours depart from Ciudad Bolívar between 7am and 8am and return between 4pm and 5pm, costing about $150 to $200 per person.

Another popular offer is a three-day package that includes a boat trip to the foot of Angel Falls instead of a flight over it ($160 to $240). These trips are normally run in the rainy season only, but with the recent climatic anomalies they have been operating for most of the year with just a few months break sometime between January and April.

Some agents offer tours to Angel Falls via La Paragua, a small town midway to Canaima, accessible by road from Ciudad Bolívar. Instead of flying all the way from Ciudad Bolívar to Canaima (70 minutes), tourists are taken overland to La Paragua, from where they take a 25-minute flight to Canaima, cutting down the flight's cost and ultimately the tour price by up to $40.

Most agents will offer a variety of other tours that include Angel Falls (eg Angel Falls and Kavac), and may tailor tours to suit your particular requirements. For example, if you don't want to come back to Ciudad Bolívar but would rather continue to Santa Elena de Uairén, the tour operators can replace the Canaima–Ciudad Bolívar return portion with the Canaima–Santa Elena ticket, charging the difference in airfares.

Tour companies use the services of small local airlines, all of which are based at the airport. There are half a dozen of them, including Rutaca, Ciaca, Transmandú and Aerobol. The luggage allowance limit is 10kg. These airlines can fly you to Canaima ($50 to $60 one-way), and can include a flight over Angel Falls for $40 to $50 extra. You can buy tickets directly from the airlines or from tour operators.

OTHER TOURS

All the tour companies offer a range of other tours, of which trips to the Gran Sabana are possibly the most popular with travelers – though they will cost less if bought in Santa Elena de Uairén. These tours are usually offered as four-day jeep trips for about $200 to $250 all-inclusive.

Another tour appearing on the itinerary of various operators is Río Caura, normally scheduled as a five-day trip costing $180 to $250. Also on offer is the trek to the top of Roraima, which costs roughly $240 to $300 for a six- to seven-day tour. It's cheaper to go by bus to Santa Elena de Uairén (p313) and buy this tour there. Some agencies also sell Delta del Orinoco tours ($180 to $300 for a three- to four-day tour). The prices listed are only ballpark figures; they may vary among the companies and largely depend on the number of people in the group.

TOUR COMPANIES

There are plenty of tour operators in the city. Some may wait for you at the bus terminal, but don't buy any tour on the street. Check the offer of several companies, as prices and programs may vary widely. Most tour operators have their offices either in the airport terminal or in the historic quarter. The usual form of payment is cash, preferably US dollars. Some agents will also accept traveler's checks, but most won't touch plastic money, or if they do, they'll charge about 10% more.

Recommended operators:

Adrenaline Expeditions (Map p287; ☎ 632-4804, 0414-385-2812; adrenalinexptours@hotmail.com; Centro Comercial Roque Center, Calle Bolívar) One of the cheapest operators, with plenty of tours on offer, including the budget Angel Falls package via la Paragua.

Gekko Tours (Map p286; ☎ 632-3223, 0414-854-5146; www.gekkotours-venezuela.de; Airport Terminal) Run by Pieter Rothfuss of Posada La Casita, Gekko is a responsible agency offering a wide range of quality tours.

Sapito Tours (Map p286; ☎ 632-7989, 0414-854-8234; www.sapitotours.com; Airport Terminal) Representative of Bernal Tours from Canaima (p303).

Soana Travel (Map p287; ☎ 632-6017, 0414-854-6616; soanatravel@gmx.de; Posada Don Carlos; cnr Calles Boyacá & Amor Patrio) Based at the posada and run by its German owner, Martin Haars, Soana specializes in Río Caura tours.

Tiuna Tours (Map p286; ☎ 632-8697, 0414-893-3003; tiunatours@hotmail.com; Airport Terminal) Ciudad Bolívar's office of the major Canaima operator (p303).

Turi Express Dorado (Map p286; ☎ 632-7086, 0414-893-9576; turiexpress@cantv.net; Airport Terminal) Long-standing, respectable company with good offers and reasonable prices.

Festivals & Events

The city's major annual bash is the **Feria del Orinoco**, held in late August to correspond with the massive appearance of the *sapoara* in the river. The celebrations include – you guessed it – a *sapoara* fishing competition, tons of *sapoara* on the local menus, aquatic sports, an agriculture fair, and a range of cultural and other popular events. The **Fiesta de Nuestra Señora de las Nieves**, the patron saint of the city, is held on August 5.

Sleeping

Ciudad Bolívar has four lovely posadas and all four are recommended; coincidentally, all of them are managed by Germans.

There's also a choice of hotels, but nothing really upmarket or expensive.

Posada Amor Patrio (Map p287; ☎ 632-8819, 0414-854-4925; plazabolivar@hotmail.com; Calle Amor Patrio; s/d/tr $10/15/20) The most popular backpacker shelter, right behind the cathedral, Amor Patrio has five tastefully decorated rooms with fans and shared bathrooms. If all rooms are taken you can stay in a hammock ($4) on a top-floor terrace with views over Río Orinoco. The posada has a kitchen, which can be used by guests free of charge, and offers an inexpensive laundry service. The manager can provide information and organize tours.

Posada Don Carlos (Map p287; ☎ 632-6017, 0414-854-6616; soanatravel@gmx.de; Calle Boyacá; d with fan $15, with air-con $25; P 🖳 🖳) This brand new posada, set in a meticulously restored, grand, historic mansion with two ample patios, is one of the most amazing places to stay, ideally combining modern facilities with olde-worlde charm and a great antique German bar. Breakfast is available on request and guests can use Internet free of charge.

Posada Angostura (Map p287; ☎ 632-4639; Calle Boyacá; s/d/tr $25/28/32; 🖳) Another colonial house with character, Angostura has seven rooms distributed over two floors, all with bathroom, fan and air-con. It may soon have an extension in an imposing historic residence half a block down the road, which was in the process of major rebuilding at the time of research.

Posada La Casita (☎ 617-0832, 0414-854-5146; www.gekkotours-venezuela.de; Urbanización 24 de Julio; s/d/tr $10/12/15; P 🖳) Here is something different – a country estate on the city outskirts, 11km east of the center. Occupying spacious grounds, La Casita has bungalows and cabins with bathroom, or you can sleep in a hammock ($4) or camp in your tent ($2 per person). Delicious meals ($4) are available on request, and you can bathe in the pool and practice your Spanish with the resident macaws. The owner, who also runs Gekko Tours, provides a free 24-hour pickup service from the bus terminal and airport, and shuttle transfers between the posada and the city center a couple of times a day.

Hotel Valentina (Map p286; ☎ 632-2145, 632-7253; Av Maracay; s/d/tr/q $18/20/22/24; P 🖳) Nestled in a quiet residential suburb, the 45-room Valentina is a five-minute walk from the air-

port. The rooms are quite big, and the hotel restaurant is famed for its *lau lau* (catfish).

Hotel Laja Real (Map p286; ☎ 632-7911, 632-7944; www.lajareal.com; cnr Avs Andrés Bello & Jesús Soto; s/d/tr $22/28/30; P 🖳 🖳) One of the best hotels in town, just near the airport terminal, the Laja Real has 65 fair-sized neat rooms with fridge and hot water. The hotel has a swimming pool, which is accessible to non-guests ($3), and a restaurant.

Hotel La Cumbre (Map p286; ☎ 632-7709; lacumbre@cantv.net; Av 5 de Julio; r $28; P 🖳 🖳) Set atop a hill in the middle of town, La Cumbre provides good views of the city and Río Orinoco, and at the same time gives an impression of being well outside the city. The hotel has 24 spacious rooms, which sleep up to four persons (the same price for one or four persons), a rustic restaurant and a bean-shaped pool.

Eating

Mercado La Carioca (Map p286; Paseo Orinoco; mains $2-4; 🕑 lunch) Popularly called 'La Sapoara,' this market at the eastern end of the Paseo Orinoco has several rustic restaurants lining the riverfront and serving inexpensive meals. The fish comes straight from the river and is delicious.

Tasca La Playa (Map p287; ☎ 632-0231; cnr Calles Urica & Zea; mains $4-7) Don't be deterred by the smoky, dim interior – La Playa serves satisfying steaks and seafood at reasonable prices. It's also a good place for a beer or five.

Gran Fraternidad Universal (Map p287; cnr Calles Amor Patrio & Dalla Costa; set meals $2.50; 🕑 lunch Mon-Fri) Vegetarians should appreciate this tiny dining room that provides tasty veggie meals. Get there soon after noon, as it runs out of food quickly.

Restaurant Mirador Angostura (Map p287; Paseo Orinoco; mains $1.50-2.50) This large, open-sided *churuata* (traditional palm-thatched circular hut), set right on the Orinoco bank, serves basic meals and beer for next to nothing. It's one of cheapest places in town at one of the best locations.

Restaurant Las Marquesas (Map p287; Av Cumaná; set menú $2, mains $2-4) Run by a Colombian family, Las Marquesas has copious home-cooked meals and a few popular Colombian specialties.

Tostadas Juancito's (Map p287; ☎ 632-6173; cnr Av Cumaná & Calle Bolívar; set menú $2-3, arepas $1; 🕑 6:30am-6:30pm) This popular *arepera*, which has been sitting on this busy street corner from time immemorial, has *arepas* with a dozen different fillings.

Parrilla Alfonso (Map p286; ☎ 632-2034; Av Maracay; mains $5-8; ☺ noon-3pm & 6-11pm Mon-Sat) Alfonso is a charming informal spot with old timber tables scattered in the garden. It has some of the best *parrillas* (mixed grills) in town, but also offers rich *lau lau*.

Ristorante Mezza Luna (Map p286; ☎ 632-0524; cnr Av Táchira & Bolívar; pasta & pizza $5-7, mains $7-10) This enjoyable airy restaurant, with seating both indoors and outdoors, offers satisfying Italian food.

Shopping

Ciudad Bolívar is an important center for the gold trade, and it may be worth checking local jewelers if you plan on buying gold. Many of the gold shops nestle in two passageways in the historic quarter – Pasaje Bolívar and Pasaje Trivigno-Guayana – both of which are in the block between Paseo Orinoco and Calle Venezuela, and between Calle Dalla Costa and Calle Piar.

Getting There & Around

AIR

The **Aeropuerto Ciudad Bolívar** (Map p286; ☎ 632-4978; Av Jesús Soto) is 2km southeast of the river-front and is linked to the city center by local transport. Avior and Rutaca fly daily to Caracas ($45 to $77). There are plenty of tour operators with flights to Canaima (see Tours, below).

BUS

The **Terminal de Pasajeros** (Map p286; cnr Avs República & Sucre) is 1.5km south of the center. To get there, take the westbound buseta marked 'Terminal' from Paseo Orinoco.

Plenty of buses go to Caracas ($11 to $16, nine hours, 591km); most of them depart in the evening. There are also direct buses to Maracay ($11 to $16, 9½ hours, 627km) and Valencia ($12 to $17, 10½ hours, 676km), which don't go through Caracas, but via the shorter Los Llanos route. These are the buses to take if you want to go to Venezuela's northwest or the Andes and avoid connections in Caracas.

Buses to Puerto La Cruz ($6 to $8, four hours, 302km) run every hour or two. A dozen buses a day go to Puerto Ayacucho ($10 to $13, 10 to 12 hours, 728km). To Ciudad Guayana ($1.50, 1½ hours, 115km), buses depart every 15 to 30 minutes.

Several bus companies, including Turgar, Expresos San Cristóbal, Expresos Los Llanos and Expresos Caribe, operate buses to Santa Elena de Uairén ($11 to $19, 10 to 12 hours, 716km), with a total of eight departures daily. Expresos Caribe is the fastest and most comfortable, but also the coldest and most expensive.

CAR & MOTORCYCLE

There is a **Budget** (Map p286; ☎ 632-7413, 632-7431) car rental at the airport terminal.

RÍO CAURA

The right-bank (south) tributary of the Río Orinoco, about 200km southwest of Ciudad Bolívar, the picturesque Río Caura offers a variety of natural and cultural experiences few other rivers can match. It's graced with islands, beaches and huge granite boulders, and cut by rapids and waterfalls, of which Salto Pará is one of the most spectacular. For a good part of its course, the Caura flows through wildlife-rich rain forest, with riverbanks inhabited by indigenous communities. The major local group is the Yekuana, particularly renowned for its fine basketry.

Boat trips on the Caura can be run year-round, unlike excursions on some other rivers, which are only possible during the rainy season. It's also one of Venezuela's least-polluted rivers, as yet unaffected by gold mining, though prospectors have been combing the region for a while. Finally, the Caura is a 'black river' (see the boxed text, p295), so mosquitoes are scarce.

Tours

Various travel operators in Caracas (eg Akanán Tours), Ciudad Bolívar (eg Soana Travel) and other cities offer Río Caura tours. These are most often a five-day package costing $40 to $60 per day all-inclusive (accommodations in hammocks). Tour operators in Ciudad Bolívar are the cheapest.

The usual starting point for Río Caura tours is Ciudad Bolívar, from where tourists are driven west for 205km along the Puerto Ayacucho road, then along a small side road branching off to the south and running for about 50km to Las Trincheras. There are several *campamentos* in the area,

GUAYANA

where tours stay the first and last nights. On the second day, boats take tourists 130km upriver (a five- to six-hour ride) to a vast sandbank known as El Playón, where the night is spent. The following day, a two-hour walk uphill takes visitors to the amazing Salto Pará, consisting of five 50m-high falls.

CIUDAD GUAYANA

☎ 0286 / pop 700,000

Ciudad Guayana has beautiful parks graced with waterfalls, plus well-developed tourist facilities, including upmarket hotels, fancy restaurants and cool bars. It sits strategically in the middle of three major tourist destinations – Delta del Orinoco, Ciudad

Bolívar and the Gran Sabana, so it's a convenient base. It's also the major transportation hub for eastern Venezuela.

This fast-paced, young metropolis is one of the richest cities in the country. Not yet 50 years old, it's already twice the size of the state capital, Ciudad Bolívar, and is growing fast. It's Venezuela's heavy industry center and the place where big money is generated – and quickly and easily spent. Ciudad Guayana has ritzy shopping malls, vibrant nightclubs and plenty of fast cars – a lifestyle Ciudad Bolívar can only dream about. A city with almost no past, but a bright future, Ciudad Guayana is a strange, intriguing urban sprawl, which you may want to see and experience for yourself.

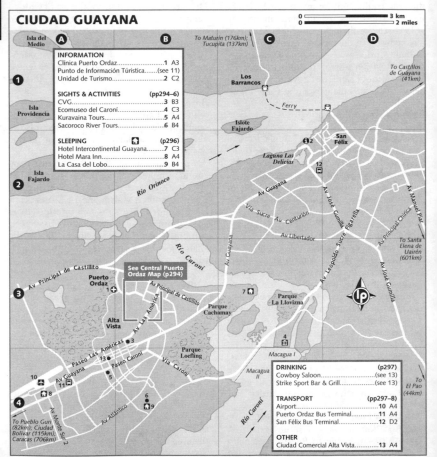

CIUDAD GUAYANA

0 ——— 3 km
0 ——— 2 miles

INFORMATION
Clínica Puerto Ordaz.........................1 A3
Punto de Información Túristica.......(see 11)
Unidad de Turismo...........................2 C2

SIGHTS & ACTIVITIES (pp294–6)
CVG...3 B3
Ecomuseo del Caroní.........................4 C3
Kuravaina Tours................................5 A4
Sacoroco River Tours.........................6 B4

SLEEPING (p296)
Hotel Intercontinental Guayana........7 C3
Hotel Mara Inn.................................8 A4
La Casa del Lobo..............................9 B4

DRINKING (p297)
Cowboy Saloon.............................(see 13)
Strike Sport Bar & Grill..................(see 13)

TRANSPORT (pp297–8)
Airport...10 A4
Puerto Ordaz Bus Terminal...............11 A4
San Félix Bus Terminal.....................12 D2

OTHER
Ciudad Comercial Alta Vista............13 A4

PUERTO ORDAZ VERSUS SAN FÉLIX

Set on the Río Orinoco at its confluence with the Río Caroní, Ciudad Guayana is an unusual city. Officially 'founded' in 1961 to serve as an industrial center for the region, it embraced into its metropolitan boundaries two very distinct urban components – the colonial town of San Félix, on the eastern side of the Caroní, and the nine-year-old iron ore port of Puerto Ordaz, on the opposite bank.

At the time of its founding, the total population of both areas was 40,000. Today the two parts have merged into a 20km urban sprawl that is home to 700,000 people. It's Venezuela's fastest-growing city and is likely to remain so until the population reaches the government's target of one million people.

Three bridges across the Río Caroní link the two sections of the city, which still can't come to terms with the 'Ciudad Guayana' name: the inhabitants persistently refer to their hometown as either 'San Félix' or 'Puerto Ordaz,' depending on which side of the river they are talking about. And don't look for 'Ciudad Guayana' in air and bus schedules, because there's no such destination – the airport and the bus terminals appear under the name of the sector where they are located.

San Félix was founded in the 16th century, but there's nothing really colonial about the place. The town's center is a busy, dirty commercial sector, parts of which resemble a street bazaar. It's essentially a working-class suburb and some neighborhoods can be unsafe, especially after dark.

Puerto Ordaz is an entirely different story; modern and well planned, it has wide avenues, modern shopping malls and smartly dressed folks walking its clean sidewalks. It's basically the executive zone, as you can easily tell from the people, their cars and the general atmosphere.

Orientation

Ciudad Guayana's two parts, Puerto Ordaz and San Félix, are linked by Av Guayana, the east–west thoroughfare that runs right across the city. San Félix, on the east bank of Río Caroní, has little to attract travelers, apart from its large, busy bus terminal, which you are likely to use arriving or departing. About 1km north of the terminal, overlooking the Orinoco, is San Félix's old center.

Puerto Ordaz, on the west bank of Río Caroní, is far more attractive and has the lion's share of facilities, including hotels, restaurants, tour agencies and cybercafés. Its center is close to Río Caroní, at the eastern end of Puerto Ordaz. About 2km southwest is Alta Vista, a modern district centered on a huge shopping mall, Ciudad Comercial Alta Vista. Another 2km southwest is Puerto Ordaz's airport. Further west is a vast industrial zone known as Matanzas, and beyond it, a bridge across the Orinoco is being built, planned to be opened in 2004. The city's main attractions, its three scenic parks, are on the banks of Río Caroní.

Information

EMERGENCY

Fire (☎ 951-1592)

Police (☎ 922-2740)

IMMIGRATION

Brazilian Consulate (Map p294; ☎ 923-5243; Edificio Amazonas, Av Las Américas)

INTERNET ACCESS

Puerto Ordaz has plenty of Internet facilities and they are usually fast and cheap ($0.60 to $0.80):

Ciberlibrería S@las (Map p294; Centro Comercial Topacio, Carrera Upata, Puerto Ordaz)

Ciudad Comercial Alta Vista (Map p292; Av Guayana, Alta Vista) There are dozens of cybercafés here.

Cyber Café Continental (Map p294; Av Principal de Castillito, Puerto Ordaz)

Navigator (Map p294; Torre Loreto, Av Las Américas, Puerto Ordaz)

Punto Shop (Map p294; Calle Guasipati, Puerto Ordaz)

Sala Web La Red.com (Map p294; Calle San Cristóbal, Puerto Ordaz)

MONEY

Banco de Venezuela (Map p294; cnr Avs Las Américas & Monseñor Zabaleta)

Banco Mercantil (Map p294; cnr Av Ciudad Bolívar & Vía Venezuela)

Banco Provincial (Map p294; cnr Av Ciudad Bolívar & Carrera Upata)

Banesco (Map p294; Vía Caracas btwn Calle Guasipati & Av Las Américas)

Corp Banca (Map p294; cnr Calle Urbana & Carrera Ciudad Piar)
Italcambio (Map p292; ☎ 951-7266; airport terminal, Av Guayana)

MEDICAL SERVICES
Clínica Puerto Ordaz (Map p292; ☎ 923-9630, 923-8556; Vía Venezuela)

TELEPHONE
CANTV (Map p294; Carrera Padre Palacios, Puerto Ordaz)
Telcel (Map p294; Torre Loreto, Av Las Américas, Puerto Ordaz)

TOURIST INFORMATION
Punto de Información Turística (Map p292; ☎ 717-5733; Puerto Ordaz bus terminal; ☼ 7am-8pm)

Unidad de Turismo (Map p292; ☎ 0414-868-6825; cnr Calle Orinoco & Carrera Ribas, San Félix; ☼ 8am-noon & 1-4pm Mon-Fri)

Sights
The wooded 52-hectare riverside **Parque Cachamay** (Map p292; Av Guayana; admission $0.30; ☼ 9am-5pm Tue-Sun) is a relaxing spot to walk, but its showpiece is the view of the Río Caroní, which turns into a series of rapids and eventually into a spectacular 200m-wide line of waterfalls. For safety reasons, don't venture into remote corners of the park; stay close to where most visitors are – along the waterfront. The park is 2km southeast of Puerto Ordaz' center; take a bus or taxi ($1.50) to get there.

CENTRAL PUERTO ORDAZ

0 500 m
0 0.3 miles

INFORMATION
Banco de Venezuela...........................1 D2
Banco Mercantil................................2 B3
Banco Provincial...............................3 B2
Banesco..4 D1
Brazilian Consulate...........................5 C4
CANTV..6 C3
Ciberlibrería S@las...........................7 C2
Corp Banca......................................8 D2
Cyber Café Continental......................9 D2
Navigator.......................................10 B4
Punto Shop....................................11 C3
Sala Web La Red.com........................12 A2
Telcel..(see 10)

SLEEPING (p296)
Hotel Dos Ríos................................13 C4
Hotel Embajador..............................14 D2
Posada Turística Kaori......................15 A3
Posada Turística Salto Ángel..............16 A1
Residencia Ambato 19.......................17 B4
Residencias Tore (extension).............18 A1
Residencias Tore.............................19 A1

EATING (pp296–7)
Boulevar de la Comida Guayanesa...20 C1
El Bigote del Abuelo.........................21 C4
Fuente de Soda La Fuente..................22 C2
Pasta Fresca Caroní..........................23 D2
Pastapoli.......................................24 D2
Pastelería ChiQuito's........................25 D2
RicArepa.......................................26 C2
Ristorante La Romanina.....................27 D2
Tasca Restaurant Jai-Alai..................28 C4
Trattoria Da'Giulio..........................29 D2

DRINKING (p297)
El Ají..30 C2

Adjoining the Cachamay from the southwest is the much larger **Parque Loefling** (Map p292; Av Guayana; admission free; ☺ 9am-5pm Tue-Sun). It has a small zoo featuring native wildlife, with some animals in cages and others (including tapirs, capybaras and capuchin monkeys) wandering freely. The park was named after a Swedish botanist, Peter Loefling, who came to Venezuela in 1754 to study Guayana's plants, but died of yellow fever two years later at the age of just 27.

Another park noted for its falls, the 160-hectare **Parque La Llovizna** (Map p292; Av Leopoldo Sucre Figarella; admission free; ☺ 9am-5pm Tue-Sun) is on the other (eastern) side of the Río Caroní. It's spectacularly on 26 islands separated by narrow water channels and interconnected by 36 footbridges. The park's highlight is the 20m-high Salto La Llovizna, which produces the *llovizna* (drizzle) after which both the waterfall and park are named. Several vantage points provide views over the falls. The park is accessible from Av Leopoldo Sucre Figarella, which crosses over the Río Caroní next to the gigantic Macagua hydroelectric scheme, but no urban buses service this route. A taxi from either Puerto Ordaz or San Félix shouldn't cost more than $4.

Close to Parque La Llovizna is the **Ecomuseo del Caroní** (Map p292; ☎ 960-4464; Av Leopoldo Sucre Figarella; admission free; ☺ 10am-9pm Tue-Sun). Adjacent to the Macagua dam, the museum features an art gallery, a photo exhibition tracing the history of the dam construction and a collection of pre-Hispanic pottery found during the construction work. A balcony provides a view over the huge turbine room.

If you decide to visit **San Félix**, walk to the Río Orinoco bank, just off Plaza Bolívar, and watch the river, which at this point is 7km downstream from its confluence with the Caroní. You'll notice the river has two distinct colors: the waters closer to your bank (originating from the Caroní) are conspicuously darker than the more distant waters of the Orinoco proper. The phenomenon is also visible from the San Félix–Los Barrancos ferry.

Tours

Travelers can visit some of the city's huge industrial establishments, including the steel mill and aluminum plant. For information about the tours, contact the headquarters of **CVG** (Corporación Venezolana de Guayana; Map p292; ☎ 966-1530; Edificio CVG, Av Cuchivero, Alta Vista Norte).

Virtually all local tour operators are based in Puerto Ordaz and focus on Guayana's highlights such as Angel Falls, Gran Sabana and Delta del Orinoco. Most of these tours can be arranged more cheaply in Ciudad Bolívar, but if you happen to be here anyway, check the offers and prices before shopping elsewhere. Some companies can organize half-day trips to the Castillos de Guayana (p298) and to Represa de Guri (p298).

BLACK RIVER, WHITE RIVER

The color of rivers ranges from light grey or yellow (the so-called *ríos blancos*, literally 'white rivers') to dark coffee or even inky black (*ríos negros*, literally 'black rivers'). The color is a result of a number of factors, including the flora along the banks and the chemical components of the rock and soil of the riverbed. Generally speaking, a dark color results from a low organic decomposition, usually caused by poor nutrient levels in the soils (such as in the case of the Amazon rain forest). Black rivers are almost free of mosquitoes and other insects, and caimans are virtually unknown. In contrast, all these creatures abound in white rivers.

Most of the right-bank (southern) tributaries of the Orinoco, including the Caroní, Caura and Sipapo, are dark rivers, while most of the rivers of Los Llanos, such as the Apure and Arauca, are white rivers. The color of Río Orinoco itself largely depends on the colors of its tributaries, but generally, the lower its course, the lighter the color.

The most interesting place to see the color differences is at the confluence of a black river and a white river. The waters of the tributary don't usually mix with the main river immediately, but tend to form two parallel flows of different colors. This is clearly visible at the confluence of the Caroní and Orinoco at Ciudad Guayana, where dark- and light-colored waters flow side by side for more than 10km.

GUAYANA

Ivarkarima Expediciones (☎ 922-2619, 0414-386-4913, 0414-868-1537; ivarka@telcel.net.ve) Small, two-person company offering tours around the regional highlights at reasonable prices. It has new vehicles, which it uses for its Gran Sabana tours.

Kuravaina Tours (Map p292; ☎ 717-4463, 0414-872-3623; kuravaina@telcel.net.ve; Edificio Manantial, Av Paseo Caroní, Alta Vista Sur) Has a similar tour itinerary and prices to Ivarkarima; the two companies sometimes work together.

Sacoroco River Tours (Map p292; ☎ 961-5526; sacoroco@yahoo.com; Calle Gahna No 19, Villa Africana, Manzana 32) This one-man agency offers tours to the southern part of the Delta del Orinoco, in the Río Grande area. The owner, Roger Ruffenach, speaks English, German and French, and personally guides all the boat trips. Two- to four-day tours are available for $45 to $50 per day. Good value.

Sleeping

Puerto Ordaz has a much better choice of hotels than San Félix, and it's also advisable to stay there for convenience, the surroundings and security. The following listings are all in Puerto Ordaz.

La Casa del Lobo (Map p292; ☎ 961-6286; lobo_travel@yahoo.de; Calle Zambia No 2, Villa Africana, Manzana 39; s/d $7/10) This is the private house of a German, Wolf, who rents out four rooms with fan and bathroom and prepares great meals on request. He also provides a free pickup service from the Puerto Ordaz bus terminal, or take a taxi ($2.50). It's a friendly, inexpensive and safe place to stay. Excellent value.

Posada Turística Salto Ángel (Map p294; ☎ 922-6516; Vía Caracas, Campo A-2; d/tr $22/25; P ✖) A new kid on the block, Salto Ángel was built with an eye for every detail and is a comfy, clean spot. It's on a main road, but all of its eight rooms are on the quiet back end of the building. It has its own restaurant and bar.

Posada Turística Kaori (Map p294; ☎ 923-4038; kaoriposada@cantv.net; Calle Argentina, Campo B; d/tr $20/22; P ✖) This new, neat 14-room posada, within walking distance of the center, offers reasonable standards, tranquility and hot water.

Residencias Tore (Map p294; ☎ 923-0679; cnr Calle San Cristóbal & Carrera Los Andes, Campo A-2; d $22-25; P ✖) Puerto Ordaz's first posada is set in a quiet residential suburb, yet is still a manageable walking distance from the center. It now has an extension diagonally across the street. The old part has 30 simple rooms with hot water. The 20 rooms in the new part are a

bit larger and better, and accordingly pricier. The posada has a good restaurant providing hearty food, including 10 different breakfasts ($2 to $3) and set lunches ($3).

Residencia Ambato 19 (Map p294; ☎ 923-2072; Calle Ambato No 19; d $22; P ✖) This small family-run posada has no name on the door, just a number. It has seven tranquil and spotless rooms, all with a double bed and bathroom. It's often full, so call and check for vacancies.

Hotel Embajador (Map p294; ☎ 922-5511; hembajador@hotmail.com; cnr Av Principal de Castillito & Calle Urbana; s/d $25/30, ste $32-40; ✖) The seven-story, modern Embajador doesn't offer great luxuries, but is very central and well kept, and doesn't cost a fortune.

Hotel Dos Ríos (Map p294; ☎ 920-1600; h2rios@telcel.net.ve; Calle México; s/d/ste $30/40/55; P ✖ ▣) This quiet, well-located hotel is a bit faded, but some rooms have been refurbished and are reasonable value – be sure to ask for *habitación remodelada* (renovated room). A bonus is the hotel's pool, even if it's pretty small.

Hotel Mara Inn (Map p292; ☎ 953-0111; Calle Neverí; d $85-100, ste $100-150; P ✖ ▣) Right opposite the airport, the smart, modern Mara Inn is the most recent addition to the city's lodgings, and a very good one. It has impeccable rooms with safety box, fridge and Internet connection, and there's a classy restaurant downstairs.

Hotel Intercontinental Guayana (Map p292; ☎ 713-1000; guayana@interconti.com; Av Guayana; d $180-205; P ✖ ▣ ▣) Built in 1971 on the bank of the Caroní, this seven-story, slightly ageing block is still the city's best hotel, and one of the few that has a swimming pool. Book a room facing the river on one of the top floors, and you'll have a lovely view of the Caroní and La Llovizna falls. The rooms (205 in all) are clearly overpriced, but the rates can apparently be negotiated – be sure to try.

Eating

Boulevar de la Comida Guayanesa (Map p294; Calle Guasipati; meals $2-4; ☾ lunch) This is a line of 12 or so rustic food kiosks serving typical local fare on the street sidewalk. The food is cooked in front of you in a market-like atmosphere.

Fuente de Soda La Fuente (Map p294; ☎ 923-5038; Edificio La Meseta, Calle Guasipati; set lunch $2-4;

☺ 7am-9pm) La Fuente offers all you need for an unsophisticated meal at any time of the day, but it's at lunchtime that it gets packed with patrons who arrive en masse for one of the four appetizing set lunches.

Pastapoli (Map p294; Calle Urbana; pasta $2.50-3.50; ☺ 11:30am-3pm Mon-Sat) This tiny locale is an excellent place for a tasty pasta lunch at bargain prices.

Pasta Fresca Caroní (Map p294; ☎ 922-1587; Calle Moitaco; pasta $2.50-4; ☺ 11:30am-3pm) Another recommended place for quality homemade pasta, Caroní has tables to eat in or you can take-away.

Trattoria Da'Giulio (Map p294; ☎ 923-5698; Av Las Américas; mains $3-6; ☺ 11:30am-2:30pm & 7-9:30pm) This simple restaurant will come in handy if you feel like having an unpretentious, tasty Italian lunch or dinner.

Tasca Restaurant Jai-Alai (Map p294; ☎ 717-3072; Edificio Amazonas, Av Las Américas; mains $5-9; ☺ 11am-3pm & 6-11pm Mon-Sat) Jai-Alai brings a touch of Spain to town, with its well-prepared meat, fish and seafood in tasca-style surroundings. The specialties include *paella valenciana* ($14 for two) and *parrilla mar y tierra* (seafood grill for two $15).

El Bigote del Abuelo (Map p294; ☎ 922-8131; Av Las Américas; mains $5-9; ☺ 11:30am-midnight) The 'Grandfather's Mustache' is a large, relaxing timber-decked restaurant that offers popular Venezuelan grilled and barbequed fare, such as *parrilla* (mixed grill), *chuleta* (chop, rib steak), chicken and seafood, plus loads of beer to wash it down.

Ristorante La Romanina (Map p294; ☎ 922-4821; Carrera Ciudad Piar; mains $6-10; ☺ noon-3pm & 7-10pm) La Romanina is a well-appointed, respectable Italian restaurant, one of the best in town. Whatever you order – pasta, carpaccio or fish – you can expect a satisfying meal.

Pastelería ChiQuito's (Map p294; ☎ 923-4076; Carrera Tumeremo; snacks $0.50-2; ✕) A great place for a breakfast, ChiQuito's has beautifully fresh croissants, *pastelitos* (pastries) and *cachitos* (filled croissants), and delicious espresso. Eat inside or on the breezy terrace.

RicArepa (Map p294; ☎ 923-1483; Carrera Upata; arepas $1-2; ☺ 24hr) This most popular, central *arepera* offers 20 varieties round the clock.

Drinking & Dancing

El Ají (Map p294; ☎ 922-8651; Edificio Mefri, Calle Guasipati) This informal nightspot, popular with all ages, is open nightly, but it's at its best on Friday and Saturday night when salsa bands have gigs and play till late. The snaking bar serves streams of beer and a plethora of cocktails, and patrons rush to dance.

Cowboy Saloon (Map p292; ☎ 962-8527; Ciudad Comercial Alta Vista, Av Guayana) Aptly named, this cool bar-cum-disco brings the 'Wild West' to mind. The bar, swamped with saddles and the like, serves Tex-Mex fare and drinks till late. Behind it is a two-level disco room, beautifully decked with wood. Discos are Wednesday to Saturday, attracting mostly younger folks to a ragbag of music ranging from rock to merengue.

Strike Sport Bar & Grill (Map p292; ☎ 962-2121; Ciudad Comercial Alta Vista, Av Guayana) Strike is a cozy two-level spot revolving around rock music. It hosts rock bands Thursday to Saturday and taped rock on other nights. It also has food, including good salads, and obviously plenty of beer, rum and whisky.

Getting There & Around

AIR

The **Aeropuerto Puerto Ordaz** (Map p292; ☎ 951-2482; Av Guayana) is at the western end of Puerto Ordaz on the road to Ciudad Bolívar. Buses marked 'Sidor Directo' from Alta Vista will leave you at the terminal's entrance. Note that the airport appears in all schedules as 'Puerto Ordaz,' not 'Ciudad Guayana.'

Puerto Ordaz is the busiest air hub in eastern Venezuela and is serviced by most major domestic airlines, including **Aeropostal** (☎ 0800-284-6637), **Aserca** (☎ 962-9229), **Avior** (☎ 953-0064) and **Rutaca** (☎ 951-6904). There are direct flights to Caracas ($53 to $86), Porlamar ($56 to $83), Barcelona ($51 to $73) and Valencia ($82 to $107), and connections to other destinations.

BUS

Ciudad Guayana has two bus terminals. The **Terminal de Pasajeros San Félix** (Map p292; ☎ 974-2778; Av José Gumilla), about 1km south of San Félix's center, is the city's main terminal. Its environs can be unsafe, particularly after dark, so don't walk there; take a bus or taxi. Plenty of urban buses pass by the bus terminal on their way between Puerto Ordaz and San Félix, but they become infrequent after 8pm and stop running around 9pm. If you arrive later, you'll need a taxi to move around.

GUAYANA

GUAYANA

The **Terminal de Pasajeros Puerto Ordaz** (Map p292; Av Guayana) is 1km east of the airport. It's smaller, cleaner, quieter and safer, but handles far fewer buses than the San Félix station. It's essentially a pick-up/drop-off spot rather than the final bus destination or departure point, and not all buses pass through here.

From the San Félix terminal, buses to Caracas ($13 to $18, 10½ hours, 706km) depart either in the morning or, mostly, in the evening, and most of them stop en route at the Puerto Ordaz terminal. There are also direct buses to Maracay ($13 to $18, 11 hours, 742km) and Valencia ($14 to $19, 12 hours, 791km). They don't pass through Caracas, but take a shorter route via Los Llanos. They are convenient if you wish to go straight to Venezuela's northwest or the Andes, avoiding spending time and money on connections in Caracas.

Eight buses daily come through from Ciudad Bolívar on their way to Santa Elena de Uairén ($10 to $17, nine to 11 hours, 601km); all call at San Félix, but only a few stop in Puerto Ordaz. Buses to Ciudad Bolívar depart from both terminals every half-hour or so ($1.50, 1½ hours, 115km).

Expresos La Guayanesa has two buses a day from San Félix to Tucupita ($4, 3½ hours, 137km), or go by por puesto, which depart regularly ($6, 2½ hours). Expresos Maturín has buses from San Félix to Maturín every hour or two ($5, 3½ hours, 176km); some of these buses go further north to Carúpano ($9 to $12, seven hours, 350km). All these trips involve a ferry ride across the Orinoco from San Félix to Los Barrancos.

CASTILLOS DE GUAYANA

Downstream from Ciudad Guayana, two old forts sit on the hilly right (south) bank of the Orinoco, overlooking the river. They were built to protect Santo Tomás, the first Spanish settlement founded on the riverbank in 1595. The older fort, **Castillo de San Francisco** (admission $0.20; 9am-noon & 1-5pm Tue-Sun), dates from the 1670s and was named after the monastery of San Francisco de Asís that had previously stood on the site. As pirate raids continued unabated, a second fort, the **Castillo de San Diego de Alcalá** (admission $0.20; 9am-noon & 1-5pm Tue-Sun), went up in 1747 on a nearby higher

hill. However, it couldn't provide adequate protection for the town either.

Santo Tomás was eventually moved up-river and re-founded in 1764 as Santo Tomás de la Guayana de Angostura (present-day Ciudad Bolívar), and the forts were abandoned. At the end of the 19th century, the forts were remodeled and used to control river traffic, which they did until 1943. In the 1970s, the forts were restored to their original condition and opened as a tourist attraction. They were extensively refurbished again in 2003 and they look impressive. The higher fort commands long views over the Orinoco.

Getting There & Away

The forts are accessible by road from Ciudad Guayana's San Félix ($1.50, 1¼ hours, 41km). Buses depart a few times a day from the place known as 'El Mirador,' in an eastern suburb of San Félix, which can be reached by city buses. Alternatively, take a tour – some travel agencies in Puerto Ordaz organize half-day tours to the forts.

REPRESA DE GURI

South of Ciudad Guayana is the world's second-largest hydroelectric project (after Itaipú on the border of Brazil and Paraguay). It was built between 1963 and 1986 on the lower course of the Río Caroní, about 100km upstream from the Orinoco. With an electric potential of 10 million kilowatts, the complex satisfies over half of the country's electricity demand.

Officially named the Represa Raúl Leoni, but commonly referred to as the Represa de Guri, the mammoth dam is 1304m long and 162m high at its highest point. Eight million cubic meters of concrete were used to build it. **Embalse de Guri**, the 4250-sq-km reservoir created by the dam, is Venezuela's largest body of water after Lago de Maracaibo. The dam and some of the installations can be visited on a tour.

The state company that operates the dam, **EDELCA** (☎ 0286-960-8448, 960-8452), runs free daily tours at 9am, 10:30am, 2pm and 3:30pm. From the visitors center (called Asuntos Públicos), you are taken by bus for a one-hour trip around the complex. Although you don't see much of the installations, you get a feeling for how enormous the project is.

The tour includes a stop at a lookout, from where you get a good general view of the dam and of the Torre Solar, a 50m-high kinetic sculpture by Alejandro Otero. You are then shown one of the units of the powerhouse, embellished with a geometrical piece of art by another first-rank Venezuelan artist, Carlos Cruz Díez. Next you go to the Plaza del Sol y la Luna, noted for a huge sundial showing months, hours and minutes. Finally, you are taken up to the dam's crest for panoramic views.

Getting There & Away
The Represa de Guri is about 85km by road from Puerto Ordaz and you can get there pretty easily. From Ciudad Guayana's Puerto Ordaz bus terminal, take the morning Milenio bus to Pueblo Guri ($1, 1½ hours, 82km). Pueblo Guri is a village that was built close to the dam for the victims of the 1999 natural disaster in the Vargas state. Violent mudslides devastated a 100km stretch of the Caribbean coast, claiming up to 50,000 lives. A taxi from the village will take you to the visitor's center ($1, 4km). To return, go by taxi to Pueblo Guri (the staff in the visitors center will call a taxi for you) and change for a bus. Note that the last bus to Puerto Ordaz departs from Pueblo Guri at 3pm. You can do the whole trip by taxi (about $30 round-trip from Puerto Ordaz).

EL CALLAO
☎ 0288 / pop 12,000
El Callao is an old town on the Río Yuruarí, in what is Venezuela's richest gold region. The town is a product of the gold rush that hit Guayana in 1849 and made Venezuela the world's largest gold producer (see the boxed text, below). The town erupted dramatically during that period.

Today El Callao is a quiet town, and the gold-shopping mecca of the region. It boasts a huge number of gold jewelers – as many as 25 on Plaza Bolívar alone – and many more down nearby side streets. The jewelry is not renowned for its artistic quality, but it's the cheapest gold in the country.

Even if you are not on a gold-shopping spree, it's worth visiting some of the many small workshops where the jewelry is produced using traditional, rudimentary manual techniques. Just walk around the central streets and look for 'Taller de Oro' signs.

There are plenty of gold mines around the town, of which the Mina Colombia is the largest. Operated by the Minerven state company, it's the deepest gold mine in Venezuela, with galleries spread over seven levels, from 130m to 479m below the surface. It produces about three tons of gold per year. The mine is 3km south of El Callao, serviced by por puestos and taxis, and it's occasionally open to tourists for free

GUAYANA

THE SEARCH FOR EL DORADO

As soon as the first conquistadores arrived in Venezuela, the search for gold took off – the quest for the fabled golden city of El Dorado. Guayana was one of the regions where the Spaniards thought El Dorado might be hidden. In 1531, in the first serious attempt to explore the interior, Diego de Ordaz sailed up the Río Orinoco as far as Raudales de Atures, near what is now Puerto Ayacucho, yet he found nothing. Many other attempts followed, including the 1595 expedition led by Sir Walter Raleigh, but El Dorado didn't show up. In fact, 300 years of the colonial period turned up virtually no gold at all.

The Spaniards did, however, have the right presentiment – in 1849 prospectors found exceptionally rich lodes on the Río Yuruarí near the present-day town of El Callao in Guayana, and the gold rush took off. Fortune seekers from all corners of Venezuela, as well as Trinidad, British Guiana (present-day Guyana) and beyond, flooded in to join what became one of the greatest gold rushes in modern history. By the 1880s, the region was producing 15 tonnes of gold per year and Venezuela had become the world's biggest gold producer. El Dorado did finally materialize.

Larger gold deposits were later found in South Africa and elsewhere, and Venezuela is no longer the world's leader, yet it remains an important producer. Guayana's gold-rich basin spreads from El Callao southward up to the edge of the Gran Sabana, and is dotted with hundreds of gold mines. The total gold reserves of Guayana are estimated at about 10,000 metric tons, roughly 10% of the world's known reserves.

GUAYANA

tours, organized on request a few days in advance. Contact the mine's **Departamento de Relaciones Públicas** (☎ 762-0216) for details.

In addition to Mina Colombia, there are a dozen large private mines and perhaps a hundred smaller ones within a 20km radius of El Callao. They are not tourist sights, but some may be visited by arrangement – ask at the jewelry shops and hotels in town.

The town's other distinctive feature is its Trinidad-influenced carnival, accompanied by calypso, steel bands and floats – a tangible legacy of the influx of people from the Antilles during the gold rush.

Sleeping & Eating

Hotel Italia (☎ 762-0770; Calle Ricaurte; r $10; ☒) Two blocks northwest of Plaza Bolívar, the Italia has 24 rooms with bathroom and was in the process of building new rooms at the time of research. You pay the same for a single, double or triple, and the hotel restaurant provides inexpensive meals.

Hotel New Millenium (☎ 762-0448; Plaza Bolívar; d $16-19, tr $22; P ☒) Occupying the largest building on the plaza, this new hotel has the perfect location, spacious rooms and good views over the plaza. The adjacent restaurant is OK and a good place to watch the lazy world go by.

Hotel El Arte Dorado (☎ 762-0535; Calle Roscio; d $13-16, tr/q $19/22; P ☒) About 300m south of Plaza Bolívar, the 'Golden Art' has reasonable rooms that are neat and airy, and it has its own restaurant.

Getting There & Away

El Callao sits 1km off the Ciudad Guayana–Santa Elena road, but many of the long-distance buses enter the town and stop near the bridge. Buses to Ciudad Guayana's San Félix ($5, three hours, 177km) pass through every hour or two, and there are also por puestos ($7, 2½ hours) departing from the corner of Calle Heres and Calle Bolívar, one block north of the plaza. A few buses a day pass through on their way to Santa Elena ($8 to $12, six to eight hours, 424km).

ANGEL FALLS & AROUND

The world's highest waterfall, Angel Falls (Salto Ángel) has a total height of 979m (recorded by a National Geographic Society

---

AN ANGEL FALLS TO EARTH

Angel Falls is not named, as one might expect, after a divine creature, but after an American bush pilot, Jimmie Angel, who landed on the boggy top of Auyantepui in 1937 in his four-seater airplane in search of gold. The plane stuck fast in the marshy surface and Angel couldn't take off again. He, along with his wife and two companions, trekked through rough, virgin terrain to the edge of the plateau, then descended a steep cliff, returning to civilization after an 11-day odyssey. The plane was later removed from the top of the tepui by the air force, restored and placed in front of the airport terminal in Ciudad Bolívar, where it now resides.

---

expedition in 1949) and an uninterrupted drop of 807m, 16 times the height of Niagara Falls. Angel Falls spills off one of the largest tepuis, the heart-shaped Auyantepui ('Mountain of the God of Evil' in the local Pemón language), and drops into the Cañón del Diablo (Devil's Canyon). The waterfall has become Venezuela's number one promotional landmark, and you will find photos of it in just about every tourist brochure.

Orientation

Angel Falls is in a distant wilderness without any road access. The village of Canaima, about 50km northwest, is the major gateway to the falls. Canaima doesn't have any overland link to the rest of the country either, but it does have an airport. The small Indian settlement of Kavac, at the southeastern foot of Auyantepui, is another access point for the falls, but it's far less popular than Canaima and is used infrequently by organized tours. It's also isolated, but it has its own airstrip.

A visit to Angel Falls is normally undertaken in two stages, with Canaima as the stepping-stone. Most tourists fly into Canaima, where they take a light plane or boat to the falls. No walking trails go all the way from Canaima (or Kavac) to the falls.

There are other attractions in the Canaima area, mostly waterfalls, of which the most popular is Salto El Sapo. Around Kavac the most frequently visited sight is the Cueva de Kavac (see Tours p304).

Angel Falls, Auyantepui, Canaima and the surrounding area lie within the boundaries of the 30,000-sq-km Parque Nacional Canaima, Venezuela's second-largest national park, and the country's only park appearing on the Unesco World Natural Heritage list. It stretches eastward and southward almost to the international borders with Brazil and Guyana and encompasses most of the Gran Sabana. All visitors coming to Canaima pay a $6 national park entrance fee, which is collected upon arrival at the airport.

Planning
WHEN TO GO
The waterfall's volume much depends on the season, and the contrast can be quite dramatic. In the dry months (normally January to May), it can be pretty faint – just a thin ribbon of water fading into mist halfway down its drop. In the rainy season, and particularly in the wettest months (August and September), it's often voluminous and spectacular, but frequently covered by cloud.

Recent climatic anomalies make planning more uncertain. In late 1990 and early 2000 the rainy season continued well into February, and even in the dry season, rains occurred more frequently than before. In a drastic twist in early 2003, the region was affected by the biggest drought in living memory, with most of the region's waterfalls almost dry and the local rivers at a record low.

GUAYANA

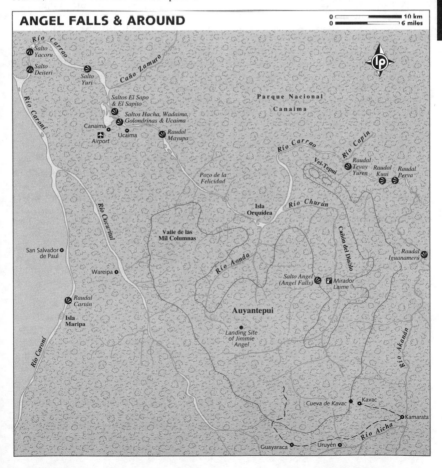

ANGEL FALLS & AROUND

For camera buffs, morning hours are the best for taking photos of Angel Falls, as it faces east and is in direct sunlight from sunrise until around noon.

WHAT KIND OF TRIP

The cheapest way to see Angels Falls is by taking a budget day trip from Ciudad Bolívar (p288), which includes a flight over the falls. The companies that organize tours via La Paragua may offer this package for as little as $120. Keep in mind, though, that you may end up not seeing the waterfall, especially in the rainy season, when it's frequently shrouded in clouds. Basically, it's luck-of-the-draw.

A more attractive option is a three-day package from Ciudad Bolívar, which includes a boat trip to the waterfall instead of a flight over it. Not only do you have a much better chance of actually seeing the falls, but the trip is more relaxed and easy-going. With some tour companies, you can negotiate an extra day in Canaima at no extra cost. Put aside a minimum of $140 for this package.

Some travelers may prefer to fly to Canaima on their own and arrange the flight over Angel Falls or the boat trip to the falls (or both) from there with local operators (see Tours, p302). This will be more expensive than a package from Ciudad Bolívar and will involve shopping around in Canaima, yet it gives you more flexibility, especially if you plan on staying longer in Canaima.

WHAT TO BRING

Bring waterproof gear, a swimsuit and plenty of film. Efficient insect repellent is essential – insects abound on the savanna, though less so in the jungle. A long-sleeved shirt will further protect you from insects and occasional chills at night. A hat or other head protection from sun and rain is advisable, and a flashlight. If you plan on boat excursions, make sure to have a plastic sheet or bag to protect your gear. A tent or hammock (preferably with a mosquito net) will save you from having to spend money at Canaima's hotels, while bringing your own food will save you money on restaurants.

CANAIMA

☎ 0286 / pop 1200

Canaima is a mixture of indigenous village and tourist center that serves as a base for Angel Falls. It lies on a peaceful, wide stretch of Río Carrao known as Laguna de Canaima, just below the point where the river turns into a line of seven magnificent falls.

The red wine–colored lagoon is bordered by a pink beach, and the falls, too, have conspicuously colored water, vaguely reminiscent of beer or brandy. The coloring of these (as well as of other rivers and falls in the region) is caused by tannin, a compound found in local trees and plants, especially in the Bonnetia tree.

In the center of the village is Campamento Canaima, a tourist camp spectacularly set right on the bank of the romantic lagoon. The airport is just a few minutes' walk to the west, while the indigenous community of some 150 Pemón families lives south of the tourist camp. There's an interesting thatched Pemón church at the southern end of the village.

Like most visitors, you'll probably spend some time in Campamento Canaima, enjoying the beach and views of the falls. The lagoon looks wonderfully calm, but the waterfalls cause treacherous undercurrents. Be careful and don't swim close to the waterfalls.

Information

Canaima has no specific tourist office (try tour operators for information instead) and no banks. The **Tienda Canaima** (☎ 962-0443, 0414-884-0940), a souvenir-cum-grocery shop near the airport, changes US dollars and traveler's checks. The rate is lower than in the cities, so it's best to come with bolívares. Most of Canaima's tour operators will accept payment in US dollars, but not credit cards, or will charge 10% more if you pay with plastic.

Tours

You can get to Angel Falls by boat or plane. Flights are in the light (usually five-seater) planes of various small airlines coming mostly from Ciudad Bolívar. The pilots fly two or three times back and forth over the face of the falls, circle the top of the tepui and then return. The roundtrip flight from Canaima takes about 40 minutes and costs $40 to $50. These trips can be arranged directly with the pilots at the airport or with local tour operators.

Boat tours are arguably even more fascinating than flights – they allow you to see the waterfall from a different perspective and, more importantly, enjoy it at a leisurely pace. The boat trip itself is a great fun and the scenery is spectacular, particularly in the Cañón del Diablo.

Motorized canoes depart from Ucaima, above the Canaima waterfalls, and go up the Carrao and Churún Rivers to Isla Ratoncito, at the foot of Angel Falls. From there, an hour's walk will take you uphill to Mirador Laime, the outcrop right in front of the falls.

Boats operate when the water level is sufficiently high, usually nine to 10 months a year, with some breaks between January and April. Tours are normally two- or three-day packages, with the nights spent in *campamentos* (in hammocks).

The all-inclusive boat package costs $100 to $180 per person, and normally includes a trip to Salto El Sapo, the most popular waterfall in the Canaima area. It's a 10-minute boat trip from Canaima plus a short walk. Salto El Sapo is beautiful and unusual in that you can walk under it. Be prepared to get drenched by the waterfall in the rainy season – take a swimsuit.

All Canaima-based tour companies run boat trips and can arrange flights. Following are the main operators:

Bernal Tours (☎ 0414-988-8140, 0414-854-8234; www.bernaltours.com) Small family-run company based on an island in Laguna de Canaima, where participants stay and eat before and after the tour. Bernal Tours has its *campamento* on Isla Ratoncito, opposite Angel Falls.

Canaima Tours (☎ 0286-962-5560 in Ciudad Guayana; canaimatours@hotmail.com) Based at its upmarket Wakü Lodge, this is by far the most expensive operator and its tours should be bought in advance in Ciudad Guayana.

Excursiones Kavac (☎ 0414-884-0511, 0414-880-3555) Agency managed by the indigenous Pemón community. Marginally cheaper than Bernal Tours, it too has its *campamento* in front of Angel Falls.

Tiuna Tours (☎ 962-4255, 0414-884-0502; tiunatours@hotmail.com) The biggest and cheapest local player, with a large *campamento* in Canaima and another one up the Río Carrao at the Aonda.

Save for Canaima Tours, all the other companies wait for incoming flights at the airport and service independent travelers who arrive at Canaima. Prices can be negotiated to some extent. Tiuna and Bernal have out-

lets at Ciudad Bolívar's airport. See Ciudad Bolívar (p288) for tours organized from that city, which are likely to work out to be cheaper and more convenient than coming to Canaima and buying a tour.

When choosing between the tour companies, an important factor to consider (apart from price) is the location of their camps. Bernal and Kavac are more attractive because their camps face Angel Falls and you'll be able to see the waterfall for most of the day (including in the spectacular sunrise light), whereas Tiuna visits the falls from its Aonda camp for just a few hours.

Sleeping & Eating

There are a dozen *campamentos* and posadas in Canaima, most of which also serve meals. Most accommodations are relatively inexpensive; expect to pay $4 to $7 for a hammock and $7 to $15 for a bed. Prices are volatile and largely depend on demand.

If you have your own tent, you can camp free in Canaima, but get a permit from the Inparques officer at the airport. The usual place to camp is on the beach next to the Guardia Nacional post, just behind Campamento Canaima. You may be able to arrange with guards to leave your stuff at the post while you are away.

A few shops in Canaima sell basic supplies such as bread, pasta, canned fish and biscuits, but prices are high. If you plan on self-catering, it's best to bring some essential supplies with you, though bear in mind the 10kg free luggage allowance limit on flights.

Campamento Canaima (☎ 961-3071; r per person $40, r per person incl all meals $75; breakfast $10, lunch $15, dinner $15) This is Canaima's oldest and best-known lodging and dining facility. The camp consists of 35 palm-thatched cabañas, featuring 109 rooms with fans and bathrooms, plus a restaurant, bar and *fuente de soda* (snack bar). The cabañas, which are scattered along the lagoon bank, are built in traditional style, and the elevated *churuata*-style restaurant offers an excellent view over the lagoon and falls. Accommodations are available as part of an expensive tour package or are offered separately. The buffet-style restaurant is open to all, but it's expensive.

Posada Wey Tüpü (☎ 0414-893-3170, 0414-884-0524; r per person $7; breakfast $3.50, lunch $3.50, dinner $7)

Opposite the school in the south part of the village, Wey Tüpü is one of the cheapest options and is quite good value. It has 21 simple, neat rooms (doubles, triples, quads) with fans and bathrooms, and provides some of the cheapest meals for guests. It also offers inexpensive boat tours.

Campamento Churún Vená (☎ 0414-884-0511, 0414-880-3555; hammocks/r per person $5/13; breakfast $5, lunch $8, dinner $8) Opposite the soccer pitch, this is the camp for the clients of Excursiones Kavac, but it often has vacancies available to all. It has four new rooms and a large palm-thatched room with hammocks. You can inquire with Vená's agent at the airport upon arrival.

Posada Kaikusé (☎ 0414-331-9010, 0414-918-1832; r per person $10; breakfast/lunch $5/9) This small place at the northern end of Canaima offers some of the cheapest beds. Rooms have fans and bathrooms, but otherwise are pretty basic.

Posada Kusarí (☎ 962-0443, 0414-884-0940; r per person $16) Near Kaikusé, this posada is better than Kaikusé and is well maintained. It has 14 rooms with fans and private facilities – inquire at the Tienda Canaima for vacancies and current rates.

Campamento Tiuna (☎ 962-4255, 0414-884-0502; hammocks/r per person $5/10; breakfast $4, lunch $6, dinner $6) The *campamento* of Tiuna Tours is in the northern part of the village. It offers vacant beds and hammocks to independent tourists and can also provide meals. Inquire at the airport when you arrive.

Wakü Lodge (☎ 962-5560; lunch/dinner $20/20) Close to Campamento Tiuna, this is Canaima's best and most expensive lodging and dining option, and home of Canaima Tours. The lodge offers 15 fine rooms with fans and bathrooms and a *churuata*-style upmarket restaurant. The *campamento* and tour agency are operated from Ciudad Guayana, where you can get information about prices and make a reservation.

Restaurant Imawary (set menú $9, pasta $6) Facing the soccer pitch, this is Canaima's only regular restaurant, locally known as Los Simons after the name of the owners. It also has a bakery.

Getting There & Away

Avior flies between Caracas and Canaima ($115 to $135) a couple of days a week. Several regional carriers fly between Canaima and Ciudad Bolívar on a semi-regular or charter basis ($50 to $60). Various small airlines, including LTA, Sasca and Rutaca, go to and from Porlamar ($120 to $140); check LTA first – it's usually the cheapest carrier. Rutaca has highly overpriced daily flights between Canaima and Santa Elena de Uairén ($145). Flights to Kavac can be chartered in Canaima.

KAMARATA

Kamarata is an old Pemón village on the Río Akanán, at the southeastern foot of Auyantepui. Some decades ago it was discovered as an alternative access point for Angel Falls, and since then it has been attracting adventurous travelers. There are a few simple places to stay and eat in town, and an airstrip serviced irregularly by air taxis and charter flights on light planes.

In order to attract tourists, the locals built the village of Kavac, which has since taken over most of Kamarata's tourist traffic – that is, the little there is. Kavac is a hot two-hour walk from Kamarata, or a short drive on a dirt road.

KAVAC

The touristy offspring of Kamarata, Kavac consists of 20-odd 'new' *churuatas* built in the traditional style, resembling a manicured Pemón settlement. Quiet and almost devoid of people, it sits on the savanna just southeast of Auyantepui.

The majority of tourists coming to Kavac are package groups put together by tour companies, mostly from Ciudad Bolívar. Independent travelers are rare guests here and risk being overcharged for tours, accommodations and food by the local operators, as has happened in the past.

The area's major attraction is the Cueva de Kavac which, despite its name, is not a cave but a deep gorge with a waterfall plunging into it. There's a natural pool at the foot of the waterfall, which you reach by swimming upstream in the canyon; be sure to bring your swimsuit with you. It's a pretty straightforward half-hour walk from Kavac to the caves, and you actually don't need a guide to get there.

Tours

Kavac plays host to three small tour/hotel operators that organize tours in the region – Asociación Civil Kamarata Kavac (the best), Makunaima Tours and Excursiones Pemón.

Boat trips to Angel Falls can be organized in the rainy season. The boats depart from Kamarata down the Akanán and Carrao Rivers, then up the Churún to Isla Ratoncito. Following a walk to the Mirador Laime, the boats then sail down the Churún and Carrao Rivers to Canaima, where the tours conclude. This is normally a four-day tour that costs $200 to $300 per person, with a minimum of about six persons. It may be a good idea to try to buy this tour in Ciudad Bolívar, to avoid wasting time and money in Kamarata searching for guides, preparing the boat etc.

Kavac and Kamarata are starting points for a fascinating trip to the top of Auyantepui. Guides for this long and adventurous hike can be contracted in either of the villages. The trail leads from Kavac via Uruyén to Guayaraca, from where it approaches the foot of the tepui before snaking uphill, following roughly the same route Jimmie Angel used for his descent in 1937 (see the boxed text, below). In three days (from Kavac), you'll reach a place called El Libertador, named after Bolívar, whose bust is placed here. You need another week or so to get to the point from where Angel Falls plunges. Count on roughly $25 a day per guide for the group, plus another $20 per porter.

The tour to Cueva de Kavac is a 2½ hour roundtrip from Kavac ($25 with lunch).

Sleeping

Any of the three tour operators will put you up for the night in a bed ($12 to $16) or a hammock ($7 to $10).

Getting There & Away

Kavac has an airstrip where light planes land several times a week from Ciudad Bolívar ($70 to $80). Flights to/from Canaima are mostly on a charter basis.

GRAN SABANA

Vast, wild, beautiful, empty and silent, the Gran Sabana is one of the country's most enchanting and unusual regions. This rolling, grassy highland in Venezuela's far southeastern corner is well worth a detour.

The most striking natural features are tepuis. More than 100 of these plateaus dot the vast region from the Colombian border in the west to Guyana and Brazil in the east, but most of them are here in the Gran Sabana. One of the tepuis, Roraima, can be climbed, and this trip is an extraordinary adventure. Other sights include a number of amazing waterfalls, some of them near the main road and easily accessible.

In geographical terms, the Gran Sabana is the highland lying in the basin of the upper Río Caroní at an elevation of over 800m. Its area is some 35,000 sq km, and much of it lies within the boundaries of

GUAYANA

THE MYSTERIOUS WORLD OF THE TEPUIS

Tepuis are flat-topped, cliff-edged sandstone mountains typical of southern Venezuela. Tepui (also spelled 'tepuy') is a Pemón Indian word for 'mountain,' and it has been adopted internationally as the term to identify this specific type of table mountain. Curiously, the term 'tepui' is used only in the Pemón linguistic area – in the Gran Sabana and its environs. Elsewhere, the table mountains are called either *cerros* or *montes*.

Geologically, these massive tablelands are the remnants of a thick layer of Precambrian sediment laid down some two billion years ago when South America, Africa and Australia were joined together as part of the supercontinent Gondwana. Warping of the continental plates created fissures and fractures in the sandstone plain, which gradually eroded, leaving behind only the most resistant rock 'islands' – present-day tepuis.

Effectively isolated for millions of years from each other and from the eroded lower level, the tops of tepuis allowed the independent evolution of fauna and flora. Developing in such a specific environment, many species have preserved features of their remote ancestors, and no longer exist away from the table tops except as fossilized remains.

Botanical research has found roughly 2000 plant species on top of the tepuis, half of which are endemic – that is, they grow nowhere else. This is almost the highest percentage of endemic flora found anywhere in the world.

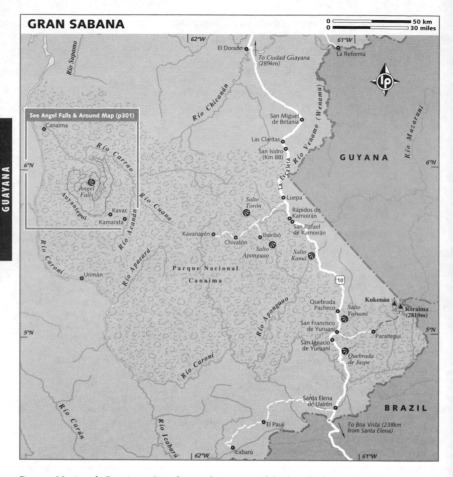

GRAN SABANA

Parque Nacional Canaima. Strictly speaking, the Gran Sabana doesn't include either the Valle de Kamarata or the sabanas of Urimán and Canaima.

The only town in the region is Santa Elena de Uairén, close to the Brazilian frontier. The remainder of the sparsely populated region is inhabited mostly by the 15,000 indigenous Pemón people, who live in some 270 scattered villages and hamlets.

Getting Around

Not long ago, the Gran Sabana was virtually inaccessible by land. It wasn't until 1973 that a road between El Dorado and Santa Elena was completed, and the last stretch of this road was finally paved in 1992. Today it's

one of the best highways in the country and one of the most spectacular. The road is signposted with kilometer marks from the El Dorado fork (Km 0) southward to Santa Elena (Km 316) – a great help in orientation.

Although this El Dorado–Santa Elena de Uairén highway provides access to this fascinating land, public transportation on this road is infrequent (eight buses a day in each direction, half of which run at night), making independent sightseeing inconvenient and time-consuming. Traveling away from the highway (eg to Kavanayén or Salto Aponguao) is still more difficult, as there are no buses on these side roads and traffic is sporadic. An easy solution is a tour from Ciudad Bolívar or Santa Elena de Uairén.

Whichever way you choose to explore the region, bring plenty of good insect repellent. The Gran Sabana is infested by small gnats known as *jejenes,* commonly (and justifiably) called *la plaga* (the plague). They are ubiquitous and voracious in the morning and late afternoon, and their bites itch for days.

Traveling the Gran Sabana

Traveling southward from El Dorado, at Km 85 you'll reach **Las Claritas**, a particularly dirty and busy ramshackle town, and 3km further south is **San Isidro** (often simply called 'Km 88'), another unsavory collection of tin-and-rubbish shacks. Both settlements have developed as gold-mining supply centers for what is today one of Venezuela's major gold-rush areas. These localities rekindle memories of the old American gold outposts you see in the movies, with prospectors much in evidence and noisy bars crammed with tipsy miners. Neither town seems to be the safest spot on earth, but for those who wish to hang around for a while anyway, both towns offer a choice of accommodations.

Proceeding south, at Km 95 the road begins to wind up the so-called **La Escalera** (Stairway). This portion of road, snaking through lush rain forest and ascending about 800m over 40km, is reputed to be one of the best bird-watching roads on the continent. One can see more than 15 species of parrots and six species of toucans on an average morning.

At Km 98 you pass a huge sandstone boulder, **Piedra de la Virgen**, and 5km further on is the entrance to Parque Nacional Canaima. A board signals the start of the park; you don't need a permit to enter. At Km 119 is a pretty 35m-high waterfall called **Salto El Danto**. It's not visible from the road, but is very close to it.

The road continues to wind uphill to Km 135, where the rain forest suddenly ends and you enter a vast, rolling grassland. This is the beginning of the Gran Sabana, which stretches south for nearly 200km. You are now at an altitude of about 1200m, which is evidenced by more moderate temperatures, particularly during cloudy days, and by chilly nights.

At Km 141 is the Inparques office, and 2km further on you'll pass by a military outpost at Luepa. At Km 147 a side road branches west for 70km to the village of **Kavanayén** (p308). Midway down this road, a dust trail departs south to the Indian hamlet of Iboribó, from where you will be able to walk to the marvelous **Salto Aponguao** (below).

The main road continues south to **Rápidos de Kamoirán** (Km 172), where there's a hotel, restaurant and gas station, and some small rapids behind the complex. At Km 195 is **Salto Kawí**, two small but lovely cascades spilling onto red jasper rock, and at Km 202 you'll find the spectacular, frequently visited **Salto Kamá** (p308).

The **Quebrada Pacheco** (p309), noted for yet another waterfall, is at Km 237, and **Balneario Soruapé**, 1km off the road at Km 244, is a popular place to bathe in natural pools. Just 3km further south you'll find the amazing **Salto Yuruaní** (p309) before reaching the village of **San Francisco de Yuruaní** (p311) at Km 250. Here a side road runs east to the Indian village of **Paraitepui** (p311), from where a fascinating hike will take you to the top of spectacular **Roraima** (p309).

The main road proceeds south to the impressive **Quebrada de Jaspe** (p311), at Km 273, one of the most popular falls in the region. About 5km down the highway, a rough jeep trail branches off to the east and runs for 3km to two picturesque waterfalls, **Salto Agua Fría** and **Salto Puerta del Cielo**.

At Km 316, you will finally reach **Santa Elena de Uairén** (p311), the region's only town to speak of. The highway heads south to the Brazilian border (Km 331) and continues to Boa Vista, 223km beyond the border.

There's an unpaved road heading west from Santa Elena to the mining settlement of **Icabarú**, 115km away. Tours around this part of Gran Sabana are available from Santa Elena, and usually go as far as the friendly village of **El Pauji**, 73km from Santa Elena. Tour attractions include **Salto Catedral**, **Pozo Esmeralda**, **Salto El Pauji** and **El Abismo**.

SALTO APONGUAO

One of the most impressive and photogenic waterfalls in the Gran Sabana, Salto Aponguao is about 105m high, and in the wet season it can be a wall of water nearly 80m wide. Even in the dry season it's spectacular. The waterfall is also known by its Indian name of Chinak-Merú (*merú* means 'waterfall' in the Pemón language).

GUAYANA

Just getting to the waterfall is an adventure – it's off the highway, 32km along an unpaved road toward Kavanayén, plus another 11km south to the Indian hamlet of Iboribó (there's no public transportation on these roads). Villagers in Iboribó offer rustic lodging in hammocks under a roof and serve simple meals, and there are plans to provide a few rooms with beds.

Locals will take you in a *curiara* (dugout canoe) to the opposite side of the Río Aponguao and provide a mandatory guide for a trip to the waterfall – a 40-minute walk along a well defined path. The fee for the boat ride and the guide is $3 per person roundtrip. Locals also offer a boat service all the way from Iboribó to the falls, which takes 25 minutes each way and costs $4 per person roundtrip, with a minimum of five passengers.

There's a well-marked path leading downhill to the foot of the falls, where you can bathe in natural pools and take excellent pictures; sunlight strikes the falls from mid-morning until very early afternoon.

KAVANAYÉN

Set on the top of a small plateau, Kavanayén is a small Indian village in a spectacular location in the middle of the Gran Sabana. The village is about 70km west of the highway, and accessible by dirt road. It's surrounded by tepuis, and has views of at least half a dozen of these table mountains, including the unique cone-shaped Wei Tepui (Mountain of the Sun).

Kavanayén developed around the Capuchin mission established here half a century ago. The missionaries erected a massive stone building for themselves and apparently assumed that the Indians wanted to live in a similar dwelling. Almost all the houses in the village are of heavy stone construction, a striking contrast to the thatched adobe *churuatas* you'll see elsewhere in the region.

A rough jeep trail leads from Kavanayén to the **Karuai-Merú**, a fine waterfall at the base of Ptari Tepui, 20km away. The road is bad and the trip may take up to 1½ hours, but the scenery is fabulous. You can walk, but it's a 10-hour roundtrip.

An adventurous trail goes from Karuai to Kamarata, but it takes at least a week to complete. Some of Santa Elena's tour companies, including Backpacker Tours and New Frontiers Adventure Tours, can organize trips on this route (see p313).

Sleeping & Eating
Hotel Kavanayén (d/tr $10/12) Located at the entrance to the village, this hotel provides simple but acceptable rooms.

La Misión (dm $5) Also offers accommodations in the town's heart, which offers basic dormitory-type accommodations.

Campamento Mantopai (d $16, breakfast $4, lunch $6, dinner $6), Provides meals and accommodations 8km north of Kavanayén, but has just two rooms.

Restaurant de la Señora Guadalupe (breakfast $3, lunch $3, dinner $5) Serves unsophisticated home-cooked meals.

Getting There & Away
The road leading to Kavanayén is almost traffic-free, so it may take a long time to hitchhike. A quicker option is a tour, but not all tours go as far as Kavanayén. The last stretch of the road to Kavanayén is in poor shape, especially in the wet season, and the road may sometimes be passable only by jeep.

SALTO KAMÁ

Salto Kamá, or Kamá-Merú, is a lovely 50m-high waterfall, 200m west of Km 202. Do not miss walking down to its base – paths go there along both sides of the waterfall, providing views of the falls from different angles. The locals can take you on a boat trip ($2) around the waterfall's pool and behind its water curtain; be prepared to get completely saturated. Sunlight strikes the falls from late morning to late afternoon.

Sleeping & Eating
Campamento Kama Wuena (r without bathroom $2.50, with bathroom $4; breakfast $2.50, lunch $5, dinner $5) Located near the waterfall. You can also pitch your tent for a small fee.

Campamento Kuranao (r without bathroom $3.50; breakfast $3, lunch $5, dinner $5). More basic than Kama Wuena and you can pitch your tent in for a small fee.

Campamento Rápidos de Kamoirán (☎ 0289-808-1505, 0414-870-0568; d/tr/q with bathroom $13/15/17; mains $3-5) Located at Km 172 on the highway, is a convenient point for motorists; in addition to lodging and dining facilities it has a shop (selling food, film, toiletries etc), public phones and a petrol station.

Getting There & Away
If you're traveling on your own, just stay on the road and flag down anything heading in the same direction. Keep an eye out for parked cars belonging to tourists visiting the falls; they may give you a ride when they leave.

QUEBRADA PACHECO
Also known as Arapán-Merú, this is a handsome multi-step cascade just 100m east of the road at Km 237. It's much nicer up close than you'd imagine from the road. The best light for photos is in the afternoon. Basic meals and accommodations in hammocks may be available during holiday periods.

SALTO YURUANÍ
This wonderful waterfall is about 6m high and 60m wide, with amazing beer-colored water. It's at Km 247, where you cross a bridge over the Río Yuruaní. From the bridge you'll see the waterfall, about 1km to the east, with the Yuruaní tepui in the background. The way to the falls is along both the southern and northern banks of the river. You can walk behind the curtain of water, but only during low-water periods, and you shouldn't do it without a guide. There's a place for camping next to the falls, but bring a lot of insect repellent as this waterfall is notorious for *jejenes*. The best sunlight strikes the falls in the late afternoon.

RORAIMA
One of Gran Sabana's greatest adventure destinations, the massive table mountain of Roraima provides some of the most memorable experiences of a trip to Venezuela. The hike up the steep walls is fascinating, and the top of the plateau is nothing short of a dream.

Roraima was the first of the tepuis on which a climb was recorded (in 1884) and it has since been much explored by botanists. It's the easiest table mountain to ascend and doesn't require any particular skills or technical climbing. It can be done by anyone who is reasonably fit and healthy, and is popular with travelers, but it's not an easy or short walk. It will take a minimum of five days to do the roundtrip, and you need camping equipment and food. Be prepared for a strenuous trek and some discomfort, including plenty of rain, cold and *jejenes*.

Orientation
Roraima lies approximately 40km east of the El Dorado–Santa Elena highway, just east of San Francisco de Yuruaní (p311), which is the usual starting point for the trip.

THE MOTHER OF ALL WATERS

Sitting on the three-way border between Venezuela, Guyana and Brazil, the 34-sq-km Roraima is the highest of all the tepuis – its plateau is at about 2700m and the tallest peak at 2810m. The indigenous Pemón people call it the 'Mother of all Waters,' presumably because Roraima is the source of rivers that feed all three of the surrounding great river basins – the Orinoco, the Essequibo and the Amazon.

Like most other tepuis in the region, Roraima has a rocky barren surface, swept by rain and wind, and few living organisms have adapted to these inhospitable conditions. Those that have include curious endemic species such as a little, black frog (*Oreophrynella*) that crawls instead of jumps, and the *heliamphora* (*Sarraceniaceae*), a carnivorous plant that traps unwary insects in beautiful, bucket-shaped, red flowers filled with rainwater.

The German explorer Robert Schomburgk was the first European to reach the base of Roraima, in 1838, yet he considered the summit inaccessible. Various expeditions then failed to climb the plateau, until British botanists Everald Im Thum and Harry Perkins made it to the top in 1884 in a two-month-long expedition and discovered its unique plant and animal life.

The news fired the imagination of Sir Arthur Conan Doyle, the creator of Sherlock Holmes. Inspired by the fabulous stories of the explorers, he wrote his famous adventure tale, *The Lost World*, in which dinosaurs were still living on a remote plateau in the Amazon basin – giving Roraima an aura of mystery and romance.

You can organize a guide in San Francisco, or walk or go by jeep to the Indian village of Paraitepui (p311), where you can also hire a (compulsory) guide. From Paraitepui you continue by path for two days to the top of Roraima. Give yourself at least two days on the top to be able to visit some of the major attractions and to enjoy the beauty and atmosphere of this unique place.

Planning
WHEN TO GO
The dry season in the region is from December to April, but the top of the tepui receives rain off the Atlantic year-round. The weather up there can change in a matter of minutes, with bright sunshine or heavy rain possible at any time.

WHAT KIND OF TRIP
You have basically two options: bring and carry all your camping gear and food and only hire a local guide, or purchase a tour and not worry about anything. There's obviously a big difference in price between the former and the latter, but take some time to calculate all the costs precisely.

Given that few travelers come to Venezuela with their own high-mountain camping equipment, you'll probably need to rent all of it locally, which will substantially add to your do-it-yourself costs. You must also buy all your food (and rent pots and pans to cook it). Finally, if you don't want to walk from San Francisco to Paraitepui and back, you'll need to rent a jeep, which will again add to the expense of your tour. In summary, the difference in cost between going solo and taking a tour may not be so drastic, while the advantages of a tour can be quite significant.

If you consider a tour option, shop around the tour operators in Santa Elena (p313); they are probably the best and cheapest you will find. If you want to go on your own, you will probably still need to speak with the same tour operators, as they rent out camping gear, organize jeep transportation to Paraitepui and may provide information and advice.

WHAT TO BRING
A good tent, preferably with a flysheet (an outer canvas layer), is a must. It gets bitterly cold at night on the top of the tepui,

so bring a good sleeping bag and warm clothes too. You also need reliable rain gear, sturdy shoes, a cooking stove and the usual hiking equipment. Bring enough food to share with your guide and to last one or two days more than planned – you may not be able to resist the temptation of staying longer on the top, or you may be stuck at Río Kukenán, unable to cross. A rope may be useful for crossing the river.

There are no *jejenes* atop Roraima, but you'll have plenty of these nasty biting gnats on the way, so take an effective insect repellent. Don't forget a good supply of film. A macro lens is a great help in photographing the unique, tiny plants. Make sure to bring along plastic bags to take all your garbage back down to civilization, and don't remove anything that belongs to the mountain – no plants, rocks, crystals. Searches are sometimes conducted on returning travelers, and those caught with crystals are subject to heavy fines. Furthermore, locals believe that these crystals bring bad luck.

Climbing Roraima
Once you have arranged your guide in San Francsico de Yuruaní (p311) or Paraitepui (p311), you can set off for Roraima. The trip to the top normally takes two days (total net walking time is about 12 hours up and 10 hours down). There are several good places to camp (with water) on the way. The most popular campsites are on the Río Tek (four hours from Paraitepui), on the Río Kukenán (30 minutes further on) and at the foot of Roraima at the so-called *campamento base* (base camp), three hours uphill from the Río Kukenán. The steep, tough four-hour ascent from the base camp to the top is the most spectacular (yet demanding) part of the hike.

The volume of Río Kukenán depends on the highly changeable and unpredictable rainfall on the Kukenán and Roraima tepuis, and the river level can change substantially in an hour or less. After rains, the river can be impassable, and you may need to wait for several hours, or even a day, until the level drops. As a rough rule, the water level is lower in the evening than in the morning. Don't camp right on the shore, unless you don't mind taking an unexpected bath.

Once you reach the top of the tepui, you will walk for 15 minutes to a place called

El Hotel, one of the few sites good for camping. It's actually just a patch of sand large enough for a few tents and is partly protected by an overhanging rock. Half a dozen other 'hotels' are in the area.

The scenery all around is a dreamscape, evocative of a science-fiction movie: impressive blackened rocks of every imaginable shape, gorges, creeks, pink beaches and gardens filled with unique flowering plants. Frequent and constantly changing mist and fog add to the mysterious air.

It's here that the guide finally becomes handy, as it's very easy to get lost on the vast plateau. Your guide will take you to some of the attractions, including **El Foso**, an intriguing round pool in a deep rocky hole. It's a three hour walk north from El Hotel, and on the way you'll pass by the amazingly lush **Valle Arabopo**. Beyond the pool are **Valle de los Cristales** and **Laberinto**. Another fascinating area is the southwestern part of Roraima, where attractions include **La Ventana** (Window), **El Abismo** (Abyss) and **Jacuzzis** (little ponds filled with quartz crystals). Plan on staying at least two days on the top.

San Francisco de Yuruaní

This small village, 66km north of Santa Elena de Uairén by the highway, is the starting point for a trip up Roraima. There's nothing much to do here except possibly arrange guides ($25 a day per group of up to six people). Porters, should you need one, charge $20 per day and can carry up to about 15kg. Both guides and porters can also be hired (for much the same price) in the village of Paraitepui, your next stop on the way to Roraima. San Francisco has a few basic accommodations along the main road near the bus stop, including **Roraima Tours** (☎ 0289-808-1037; r per person $4), **Posada El Caney de Yuruaní** (☎ 0414-886-6707; q $13; meals $3) and **Hospedaje Minina** (☎ 0289-808-2514; q $13). Food stalls at the Indian market and a few basic eateries will keep you going.

Paraitepui

Paraitepui is a nondescript Pemón village of about 250 people whose identity has been largely shattered by tourism. It's 26km east of San Francisco; to get there, you can either hire a jeep in San Francisco, which carries up to six people ($50, regardless of the number of passengers) or walk. The road to Paraitepui branches off the highway 1km south of San Francisco. It's a hot, steady seven-hour walk, mostly uphill, to Paraitepui.

The road is not difficult to follow, except for one point (about a five-hour walk from San Francisco) where it divides. The road going straight ahead leads to the hamlet of Chirimatá, while the Paraitepui road proper (which you should follow) branches off sharply to the right. Don't worry too much if you miss this turnoff, as there's a path from Chirimatá to Paraitepui. You may be lucky enough to hitch a jeep ride on the road, but traffic is sporadic and drivers are likely to charge you for the lift.

Upon arrival at Paraitepui, you will be greeted by the Inparques rangers, who will arrange a guide for you. Although you don't really need a guide to follow the track up to the tepui, you won't be allowed to continue without one. The village has no hotels or restaurants, but you can camp near the Inparques post. A few shops in the village sell basic food (canned fish, biscuits, packet soups) at inflated prices.

Getting There & Away

Eight buses a day run in each direction along the Ciudad Guayana–Santa Elena highway, stopping at San Francisco de Yuruaní. Buy all food at either starting point; don't count on shopping in San Francisco, let alone in Paraitepui.

QUEBRADA DE JASPE

Between San Francisco and Santa Elena, at Km 273, is another of the many Gran Sabana waterfalls. This one is small and faint, but what is truly amazing is the intense orange-red color of the pure jasper rock over which the creek flows. The Quebrada is 300m to the east of the highway, hidden in a stretch of woodland.

SANTA ELENA DE UAIRÉN

☎ 0289 / pop 16,000

This easygoing town is a good base for exploring the fascinating Gran Sabana with its waterfalls and tepuis, and for Roraima, the most popular of the tepuis. It's a pleasant border town with an agreeable climate and a Brazilian ambience thanks to the significant number of residents from across the border.

GUAYANA

SANTA ELENA DE UAIRÉN

0 ____ 200 m
0 ____ 0.1 miles

To Backpacker Tours (200m);
Villa Fairmont (400m)

To Bus Terminal (1.5km);
Ciudad Guayana (601km);
Ciudad Bolívar (716km)

Av Mariscal Sucre

Calle Bolívar
Calle Roscio
Calle Lucas Fernández Peña
Av Perimetral
Calle Urdaneta
Calle Zea
Plaza Bolívar
Calle Icabarú
Av Perimetral

Capilla de San Francisco

To Hotel Gran Sabana
& Raúl Helicopter's (3km);
Airport (7km);
Boa Vista (Brazil) (238km)

INFORMATION	
Banco Industrial de Venezuela	1 A2
Brazilian Consulate	2 C1
CANTV	3 B3
detodo.com	4 B3
Globalstar	5 B2
Ipostel	6 A2
Iruk Café	7 A2
Lavandería Lucrecia	8 C1
Lavandería Tonny	9 B2
Moneychangers	10 A2

SIGHTS & ACTIVITIES	(p313)
Kamadac	11 A2
Mystic Tours	12 B2
New Frontiers Adventure Tours	13 B2
Ruta Salvaje Tours	14 C1

SLEEPING	(pp313–14)
Hotel Augusta	15 A2
Hotel Lucrecia	16 C2
Hotel Michelle	17 C2
La Casa de Gladys	18 B2
Posada Michelle	(see 17)

EATING	(p314)
Alfredo's Restaurant	19 C2
Restaurant Michelle	(see 17)
Restaurant Nova Opção Sucursal I	20 A2
Restaurant Nova Opção	21 A2
Restaurant Oriental	22 A2

Founded in 1924, Santa Elena began to grow when diamonds were discovered in the 1930s in the Icabarú region, 115km to the west. However, as the village was isolated from the center of the country by a lack of roads, it remained small and insignificant. The second development push came with the opening of the highway from El Dorado in 1992, which is the only road link between Venezuela and Brazil, and you're sure to pass through if you travel overland between these two countries.

Information

IMMIGRATION
Brazilian Consulate (☎ 995-1256; Av Mariscal Sucre; ◷ 8am-noon Mon-Fri) The consulate is opposite the petrol station. If you want to play it safe, get your visa beforehand – the nearest Brazilian consulate before Santa Elena is in Ciudad Guayana. A yellow-fever vaccination certificate is likely to be required before issuing a visa (see Health p347).

INTERNET ACCESS
detodo.com (Calle Lucas Fernández Peña)
Globalstar (Calle Urdaneta)
Iruk Café (Calle Bolívar)

LAUNDRY
Lavandería Lucrecia (Av Perimetral)
Lavandería Tonny (Calle Urdaneta)

MONEY
US dollars can easily be exchanged with the moneychangers who hang around the corner of Calle Bolívar and Calle Urdaneta, popularly known as Cuatro Esquinas. They are there every day except Sunday afternoon and usually give quite good rates. There are also a couple of *casas de cambio* on the same corner, and they may cash traveler's checks, albeit at a poor rate. If you're heading south for Brazil, get rid of all your bolívares in Santa Elena and buy Brazilian currency from the moneychangers.
Banco Industrial de Venezuela (Calle Bolívar) Gives cash advances on Visa, but not on MasterCard.

POST
Ipostel (Calle Urdaneta btwn Calles Bolívar & Roscio)

TELEPHONE
CANTV (Calle Zea btwn Calles Roscio & Lucas Fernández Peña)

GUAYANA

TOURIST INFORMATION

The town's tour agencies (below) are good sources of information about the region.

Tours

Santa Elena has about a dozen tour agencies. Their staple is a one-, two- or three-day jeep tour around the Gran Sabana, with visits to the most interesting sights, mostly waterfalls. Budget on roughly $25 per person per day in a group of four or more. This price includes transportation and a guide, but no accommodations or food. However, tours normally stop in budget places to stay and eat. If you prefer an all-inclusive Gran Sabana tour, it will cost $40 to $60 per person per day.

Another local specialty is the Roraima tour, which is normally offered as an all inclusive six-day package for $140 to $250. The operators who organize this tour usually also rent out camping equipment and can provide transportation to Paraitepui, the starting point for the Roraima trek, for $60 to $80 per jeep each way for up to six people.

Some operators offer tours to El Paují area, noted for its natural attractions and gold and diamond mines. These are one- or two-day trips, with prices and conditions similar to those of the Gran Sabana tours.

Following is a list of recommended local tour companies:

Backpacker Tours (☎ 995-1524, 0414-886-7227; www.backpacker-tours.com; Urbanización Acurima, Sector Los Pinos) Just north of town, this small, responsible German-run company, led by knowledgeable Eric Buschbell, provides personalized service and well-organized tours.

Kamadac (☎ 995-1408, 0414-886-1196; www.aben teuer-venezuela.de; Calle Urdaneta) This German-owned agency, run by Andreas Hauer, offers staples (Gran Sabana, Roraima), as well as some more adventurous tours (Auyantepui, Akopán Tepui).

Mystic Tours (☎ 416-0558, 0414-886-1055; www .mystictours.com.ve; Calle Urdaneta) Run by Roberto Marrero, author of various maps and books on the region, this agency has good tours to the top of Roraima and some of the lowest prices. The Gran Sabana tours are guided personally by Roberto. It's one of the few operators that organizes El Paují tours.

New Frontiers Adventure Tours (☎ 995-1584, 0414-927-7140; www.newfrontiersadventures.com; Calle Urdaneta) Run by a team of experienced guides, this agency specializes in trekking tours, including trips to the top of Roraima, and provides competent guidance and good equipment.

Ruta Salvaje Tours (☎ 995-1134, 0414-889-4164; www.geocities.com/rutagransabana; Av Mariscal Sucre) Reliable company led by Iván Artal, offering the usual range of tours, including the Gran Sabana and Roraima. Also offers rafting trips and bicycle rental.

If money is not a problem, **Raúl Helicopter's** (☎ 995-1711, 0414-886-1191; www.raulhelicopteros.com; Hotel Gran Sabana, Vía Brasil) comes in handy, providing air taxi services in light planes and helicopters. It can take you anywhere – for example, to the top of Roraima (around $1400 roundtrip for four persons).

Festivals & Events

Santa Elena's Carnaval, held during February and March, has a distinctly Brazilian feel, with samba rhythms and a parade of *carrozas* (floats). In mid-August the town celebrates the feast of its patron saint.

Sleeping

Posada Michelle (☎ 995-1415; hotelmichelle@cantv .net; Calle Urdaneta; s/d/tr $4/7/10) This new place offers eight clean rooms with fans, bathrooms and plenty of water – important in Santa Elena due to its erratic water supply. The rooms are great value, and there was a backyard with a terrace being built at the time of research. Cheap laundry service is available for guests of the posada.

Hotel Michelle (☎ 995-1415; hotelmichelle@cantv .net; Calle Urdaneta; s/d/tr $6/11/15) Next door to Posada Michelle and administered by the same manager, the hotel has 10 still larger rooms and is equally spotless. Cheap laundry service is available for the guests of the hotel.

La Casa de Gladys (☎ 995-1171; Calle Urdaneta; s/d/tr/q $6/7/10/13) La Casa has long been a popular travelers' lodge and it is still so despite increasing competition. It is fairly basic, but all rooms have private facilities and guests can use the kitchen and fridge.

Hotel Augusta (☎ 995-1654; Calle Bolívar; d/tr/q $7/10/11) This pleasant 18-room hotel has fair-sized rooms with bathroom and fan. It's on a lively street but gets little noise. Rooms on the upper floor are prettier.

Hotel Lucrecia (☎ 995-1105; hotellucrecia@cantv .net; Av Perimetral; s/d/tr $13/15/20; P 🐶 🛱) Lucrecia is a friendly, family-run old-fashioned house with a lovely patio in bloom year-round. The rooms, arranged around the patio, have hot water. The hotel has a

GUAYANA

large water tank and a fair-sized pool, and breakfast and dinner is served on request.

Villa Fairmont (☎ 995-1022; Calle Kavanayén; s/d/tr/q incl breakfast $22/28/35/42; P ✷) In the northern suburb of Akurima, this is a comfy country-feel spot with large rooms, and a large *churuata* that accommodates a restaurant.

Hotel Gran Sabana (☎ 995-1810; www.hotelgran sabana.com; Vía Brasil; d/tr/ste $40/48/56; P ✷ ☂) On the road to Brazil, 3km from the town's center, Gran Sabana is Santa Elena's top lodge, providing 54 good-sized rooms with fridge and hot water, plus a large swimming pool.

Eating

Restaurant Nova Opção (☎ 995-1013; Plaza Bolívar; meals $2-4) This Brazilian self-service budget eatery, open roughly from lunchtime till evening, sells food (chicken, beef, potatoes, rice etc) by weight, so you can choose what you want and how much you want.

Restaurant Nova Opção Sucursal I (☎ 995-1702; cnr Calles Urdaneta & Roscio; meals $2-4) Nova Opção's new outlet offers fresh, hearty food, but it has a normal restaurant menu and table service. It also opens for breakfast.

Restaurant Michelle (☎ 995-1415; Calle Urdaneta; mains $2-4) Run by the manager of the two Michelle lodgings, this restaurant offers fairly authentic and tasty Chinese food, cooked personally by the manager.

Restaurant Oriental (Pasaje Morales, Calle Roscio; mains $2-4) This is another Chinese affair, particularly recommended for its vegetarian dishes.

Alfredo's Restaurant (☎ 995-1628; Av Perimertal; pasta & pizza $4-5, mains $5-9; ✷) This enjoyable restaurant has an unusually long menu, reasonable steaks, and fine pizzas from its wood-burning oven. You can either sit inside or at the front tables alfresco-style.

Getting There & Away
AIR
The airport is 7km southwest of town, off the road to the border with Brazil. There's no public transport; a taxi will cost around $5. Tour operators are often waiting for incoming flights and will usually give you a free lift to town, hoping you might be interested in their offer. Rutaca has daily flights on five-seater Cessnas to Ciudad Bolívar ($145), via Canaima ($145).

BUS
Santa Elena has a new bus terminal, on the Ciudad Guayana highway about 2km east of the town's center. There are no urban buses – you need to go by taxi ($1.50).

Eight buses depart daily to Ciudad Bolívar ($11 to $19, 10 to 12 hours, 716km), and they all pass through Ciudad Guayana ($10 to $17, nine to 11 hours, 601km).

To/From Brazil
Both Venezuelan and Brazilian passport formalities are now done at the border itself, locally known as La Línea, 15km south of Santa Elena. The bus stops at the border for passport formalities. Be sure to have your passport stamped upon leaving or entering Venezuela. Two buses a day run to Boa Vista, Brazil ($8, three to four hours, 238km). The road is now paved all the way.

AMAZONAS

Venezuela's southernmost state is Amazonas, a predominantly thick rain forest crisscrossed by rivers and sparsely populated by a mosaic of indigenous communities. The current indigenous population, estimated at 40,000 (half of what it was in 1925), comprises three main groups – the Piaroa, Yanomami and Guajibo – and a number of smaller communities, among them the Yekuana (Maquiritare), Curripaco and Piapoco.

Amazonas covers an area of 180,000 sq km, or one-fifth of the national territory, yet it's home to less than 1% of the country's population. Despite its name, most of the region lies in the Orinoco basin, while the Amazon basin occupies only the southwestern portion of the state. The two basins are linked by the unusual 320km-long Brazo Casiquiare, a natural channel that sends a portion of the water from the Orinoco to Río Negro and down to the Amazon. Amazonas boasts four large national parks that cover 30% of the state area.

In contrast to the central Amazon basin in Brazil, Venezuelan Amazonas is quite diverse topographically, its most noticeable feature being the tepuis. Though not as numerous or as classical as those in the Gran Sabana, they do give the green carpet

of rain forest a distinctive and spectacular appearance.

At the southernmost part of the Amazonas, along the border with Brazil, is the Serranía de la Neblina, a scarcely explored and virtually unknown mountain range. The highest peak reaches 3014m, making it the tallest mountain range on the continent east of the Andean chain, and the canyon running through its middle is one of the world's deepest. La Neblina has some of the richest endemic plant life in the world.

The climate is not uniform throughout the region. At the northern edge, there's a distinctive dry season from December to April; April is the hottest month. Heading south, the dry season becomes shorter and not so dry, and eventually disappears. Accordingly, the southern part of Amazonas is wet year-round. The best time to explore the region is from October to December, when the river level is high but rains are already easing.

Getting Around

As there are no roads in most of the region, transportation is by river or air. There's no regular passenger service on the rivers, which makes independent travel difficult, if not impossible, but tour operators in Puerto Ayacucho can take you just about everywhere – at a price, of course.

PUERTO AYACUCHO

☎ 0248 / pop 80,000

The capital of the Amazonas, Puerto Ayacucho is the gateway to the Venezuelan Amazon and the region's only significant urban center. It's a lively, bustling town set on a colorful stretch of the Orinoco, just down from spectacular rapids, the Raudales Atures. Puerto Ayacucho is a hot place, with frequent heavy downpours, but it's amazingly shaded by luxuriant mango trees – a pleasant sight for the eye and a relief (somewhat) from both the heat and rain.

The town has become a regional tourist center, home to a dozen tour companies that can take you up the Orinoco and its tributaries, and deep into the jungle. It is also a transit point on the adventurous back routes to Colombia and Brazil. The town itself has a few interesting sights, including an enchanting Indian craft market and the ethnographic museum.

Puerto Ayacucho was founded as a river port in 1924, together with another port, Samariapo, 63km upriver (south). The towns were linked by road to bypass a nonnavigable stretch of the Orinoco cut by a series of rapids; this enabled timber to be shipped from the upper Amazonas down to the country's center. For a long time the two ports were obscure and isolated villages as the only road connection to the rest of the country was just a rough track. Only in the late 1980s, when this track was improved and surfaced, did Puerto Ayacucho start to grow dramatically. Ironically, the port, which was responsible for the town's birth and initial growth, has lost its importance as most cargo is now carried by road.

Information

IMMIGRATION

DIEX (Av Aguerrevere; ☼ 8am–noon & 1-5pm Mon-Fri) This is where you have to get your passport stamped when leaving or entering Venezuela. Note that the opening hours listed above are strictly a guideline.

INTERNET ACCESS

Biblionet (Biblioteca Pública, Av Río Negro) Half-hour free access.
Cibercafé Compuserv (Calle Evelio Roa)
El Navegante (Centro Comercial Maniglia, Av Orinoco)
Infomanía Network (Centro Comercial Las Maravillas, cnr Avs Aguerrevere & Río Negro)
Windows PC (Centro Comercial Rapagna, Av Orinoco)

LAUNDRY

Lavandería Aquario (Av Aguerrevere)

MONEY

Banco de Venezuela (Av Orinoco)
Banco Provincial (Calle La Guardia)
Banesco (Av Orinoco)

TELEPHONE

CANTV (cnr Av Río Negro & Calle Atabapo)

TOURIST INFORMATION

Dirección de Turismo (☎ 521-0033; Plaza Bolívar; ☼ 8am–noon & 2-5:30pm Mon-Fri) The tourist office is in the building of the Gobernación (government offices).

Sights

The small but interesting **Museo Etnológico de Amazonas** (Av Río Negro; admission $0.50; ☼ 8:30am-11:30am & 2:30-6pm Tue-Fri, 9am-noon & 3:30-7pm Sat, 9am-1pm Sun) gives an insight into the culture

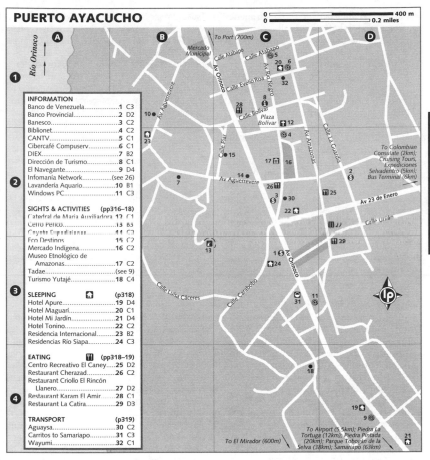

of regional indigenous groups, including the Piaroa, Guajibo, Yekuana and Yanomami. Note the Yekuana's ritual weapons laboriously carved in wood, the Yanomami's body adornments made of colorful feathers and the Piaroa's ceremonial masks used in their traditional dances.

The **Mercado Indígena** (Av Río Negro), held every morning (but busiest from Thursday to Saturday), on the square opposite the museum, has indigenous crafts for sale. Look for the handmade hammocks and human figures carved in wood. A few paces away is the **Catedral de María Auxiliadora** (Av Río Negro), worth entering to see its charming colorful interior.

The **Cerro Perico**, just southwest of the town's center, provides good views over Río Orinoco and the town. Another hill, Cerro El Zamuro, commonly known as **El Mirador**, 1.5km south of the center, overlooks the Raudales Atures, the spectacular rapids that block river navigation. The rapids are most impressive in the wet season, when the water is high.

Tours

Tour operators have some standard tours, but most can arrange a tour according to your interests and time. Be sure to shop around and negotiate the tour price, and carry your passport and tourist card on all trips. If you buy a tour, try to negotiate bonus side trips to Piedra Pintada, La Tortuga and/or Parque Tobogán. If there's a serious discrepancy between what an agency promises and what it actually provides, complain to the tourist office and insist on receiving part of your money back.

Among the popular shorter tours are a three-day trip up the Río Cuao and a three-day trip up the Sipapo and Autana Rivers to the foot of Cerro Autana. Expect to pay from $30 to $60 per person per day all-inclusive.

The Ruta Humboldt, following the route of the great explorer, is a longer and more adventurous trip. It goes along the Orinoco, Brazo Casiquiare and Guainía Rivers up to Maroa. The boat is then transported overland to Yavita, and returns down the Atabapo and Orinoco Rivers to Puerto Ayacucho. This trip takes 10 to 15 days and will cost around $70 to $100 per person per day. Tour operators don't usually do the whole loop, but only its most attractive fragments, including Brazo Casiquiare, skipping over the less interesting parts by plane.

The far southeastern part of Amazonas beyond La Esmeralda, basically all the Parima-Tapirapeco National Park, where the Yanomami live, is a restricted area; you need special permits that are virtually impossible to get – some agents get around the ban by visiting Yanomami villages on the Río Siapa off Brazo Casiquiare.

Recommended tour operators:

Coyote Expediciones (☎ 521-4583; coyotexpedition@cantv.net; Av Aguerrevere) A popular company with travelers, its main offerings are the three-day Autana and Cuao tours ($100 per person), but it also runs longer trips.

Cruising Tours (☎ 0416-785-5033, 0416-448-5391; cruisingtours@hotmail.com; Valle Verde Triángulo) One-man agency run by a friendly German, Axel Kelemen, who has lived in the region for over 20 years. He personally guides diverse tours and expeditions in the region and beyond at reasonable prices (from $30 a day), and offers accommodation in his home for tour participants. The office is 5km east of the centre.

Eco Destinos (☎ 521-3964, 0416-448-6394; henryamazonas@hotmail.com; Calle Piar) Roughly similar tour offer and prices to Coyote; the two often work together.

Expediciones Selvadentro (☎ 0414-486-8231, 0414-486-6835; www.selvadentro.com; Vía Alto Carinagua) Long, adventurous trips to distant destinations (around $100 per person per day) aboard a 17m-long comfortable catamaran with toilet and kitchen, personally guided by the experienced manager Lucho Navarro. The office is 5km east of the centre.

Tadae (☎ 521-4882, 0414-486-5923; Centro Comercial Maniglia, Av Orinoco) Apart from the staple Autana and Cuao tours, Tadeo offers rafting on Raudales Atures ($30) and rainforest walks guided by local indigenous people ($20).

Turismo Yutajé (☎ 521-0664, 521-3348; turismoamazonas@cantv.net; Barrio Monte Bello) One of the longest-established companies, with good experience and low tour prices (from $30 per day); also organizes fishing trips. Free accommodations for tour participants the night before and after the tour.

Sleeping

Residencia Internacional (☎ 521-0242; Av Aguerrevere; d with fan $10-12, d with air-con $13-16, tr with air-con $19; ✷) Simple, pleasant and friendly, this is the most popular choice with backpackers. It has 24 rooms (all with bathrooms) arranged around a long patio, and a rooftop terrace.

Hotel Maguarí (☎ 521-3189; Calle Evelio Roa; d with fan $9-11, d with air-con $12; ✷) Maguarí is one of the cheapest acceptable options and is very central. The rooms are basic but have private facilities.

Hotel Tonino (☎ 521-1464; Av 23 de Enero; d $10-12, tr $16; ✷) Tonino is a tiny spot with just five clean, ample rooms. The hotel is on a busy road, but rooms are well away from the city bustle.

Residencias Río Siapa (☎ 521-0138; Calle Carabobo; d/tr $12/15; P ✷) Another reasonably priced, central place, Río Siapa is friendly, pleasant and tranquil. Its 18 rooms overlook a central courtyard where you can sit and relax. There's no sign at the entrance, so keep your eyes peeled when walking down the street.

Hotel Mi Jardín (☎ 521-4647; Av Orinoco; d $14-18, tr/q $22/28; P ✷) South of the center, Mi Jardín has its own restaurant and 18 good, clean rooms arranged around a central patio-garden, which is probably where its name came from.

Hotel Apure (☎ 521-4443; Av Orinoco; d $15-18, tr/q $22/30; P ✷) Close to Mi Jardín, the Apure offers much the same rates and standards, including good-sized rooms, comfy beds and attentive service.

Eating

Centro Recreativo El Caney (Av Amazonas; meals $2-3) This rustic, open-air spot serves up copious hearty breakfasts and lunches at rock-bottom prices.

Restaurant Karam El Amir (Av Orinoco; sandwiches $2, mains $4) This is a great stop for a yummy falafel or *shawarma* (Arab sandwich with pieces of beef/chicken served in pitta bread), or some more elaborate Middle Eastern specialties.

Restaurant Cherazad (☎ 521-5679; cnr Avs Aguerrevere & Río Negro; mains $5-7) One of the best dining establishments in town, Cherazad provides a reasonable choice of pasta, steaks and fish, plus some Middle Eastern dishes – try the *plato mixto,* which has samples of various specialties.

One of the favorite inexpensive places to eat among locals is **Mercadito** (Little Market; Av Orinoco), which boasts half a dozen rudimentary eateries, including **Restaurant Criollo El Rincón Llanero** (Av Amazonas; mains $3-4) and **Restaurant La Catira** (Av Amazonas; mains $3-4). Both are very simple, with the menu posted on the wall and prices written in white chalk, but the food is savory and the portions generous. Try the fried fish, which comes straight from the river.

Getting There & Away
AIR
The airport, 6km southeast of town (accessible by taxi; $3), handles daily flights to Caracas ($68 to $93). Two small local carriers, **Aguaysa** (☎ 521-0026; Av Río Negro) and **Wayumi** (☎ 521-0635; Calle Evelio Roa), operate flights within Amazonas. There are daily flights (except Sunday) to San Fernando de Atabapo ($50) and San Juan de Manapiare ($50), three weekly flights to San Carlos de Río Negro ($80) and Maroa ($80), and one flight a week to La Esmeralda ($80).

BUS
The bus terminal is 6km east of the center, on the outskirts of town. City buses go there from Av 23 de Enero, or take a taxi ($2). Buses to Ciudad Bolívar ($10 to $13, 10 to 12 hours, 728km) depart regularly throughout the day. There are about six morning departures daily to San Fernando de Apure ($10, seven hours, 299km), from where you can get buses to Caracas, Maracay, Valencia, Barinas and San Cristóbal. Carritos to Samariapo ($2, 1¼ hours, 63km) depart from Av Orinoco, one block south of the Banco de Venezuela.

TO/FROM COLOMBIA
The nearest Colombian town, Puerto Carreño, at the confluence of the Meta and Orinoco Rivers, is accessible via Puerto Páez, a Venezuelan village 93km north of Puerto Ayacucho. You can get there by the San Fernando bus ($2, two hours); the trip includes a ferry crossing of the Orinoco from El Burro to Puerto Páez. You then take a boat from the village's wharf across the Río Meta to Puerto Carreño ($1); the boat runs regularly during the day. Remember to get an exit stamp in your passport at DIEX in Puerto Ayacucho before setting off.

Puerto Carreño is a long, one-street town with an airport, a half-dozen budget hotels and a number of places to eat. Go to the DAS office (Colombian immigration), one block west of the main plaza, for an entry stamp in your passport. A number of shops will change bolívares to pesos.

There are three flights per week from here to Bogotá ($95). Buses go only in the dry season, roughly from mid-December to mid-March, but they are not recommended because of the strong presence of guerrillas in the region.

TO/FROM BRAZIL
Take a flight from Puerto Ayacucho south to San Carlos de Río Negro, from where irregular boats will take you to San Simón de Cocuy, on the border. From here take a bus to São Gabriel da Cachoeira (Brazil) and continue by boat down the Río Negro to Manaus (three boats per week). Most of Puerto Ayacucho's tour companies can tailor a tour that concludes in San Carlos de Río Negro, or even escort you to São Gabriel.

AROUND PUERTO AYACUCHO
The **Piedra La Tortuga**, 12km south of Puerto Ayacucho, is a gigantic boulder reminiscent of a giant turtle, and you can walk up to the top for great views. There's an Inparques office close to the boulder where you should register before climbing, but be there before 2pm. The piedra is beside the Samariapo road; any Samariapo-bound carrito will let you off at the entrance to the Inparques office.

The **Piedra Pintada** is an enormous boulder covered with pre-Columbian petroglyphs carved high above the ground in a virtually inaccessible place. They include a 40m-long serpent and a 10m-long centipede. The best time to see the petroglyphs is in the afternoon, when they are in direct sunlight. To get there from Puerto Ayacucho, take the Ruta 17 bus from Av Orinoco to the village of Comunidad Pintao, 17km south of the city on the Samariapo road, and then take a side road left (east) for 3km. Visit the Inparques office (open till 4pm) in the village to register before walking to the petroglyphs (10 minutes).

Parque Tobogán de la Selva is a popular weekend picnic area developed around a large, steeply inclined smooth rock with water running over it – a sort of natural slide. The park has picnic tables, half a dozen restaurants, a natural swimming pool, toilets and a car park. You can camp in your tent ($2) or hang your hammock (free). The park

is 32km south of Puerto Ayacucho along the Samariapo road, then 6km off to the east. There's no public transportation all the way to the park, but the Ruta 17 bus (the same one you take to Piedra Pintada) will drop you at the road fork just 2km away from the park before it continues to the village of Comunidad Coromoto.

The best known of the Amazonas tepuis is **Cerro Autana**, about 80km south of Puerto Ayacucho. It is the sacred mountain of the Piaroa Indians, who consider it the birthplace of the universe. The tepui looks like a gigantic tree trunk, growing 700m above the surrounding plains (1208m above sea level). A unique cave about 200m below its top cuts right through the tepui.

Directory

CONTENTS

ACCOMMODATIONS

There are heaps of hotels throughout the country for every budget, and it's usually easy to find a room, except perhaps on major feast days and the three short peak tourist seasons – Christmas, Carnaval and Easter – when Venezuelans go mad about traveling. Camping grounds are virtually nonexistent, but you can camp rough in the countryside. Camping on the beach is popular, but be cautious and don't leave your tent unattended. Venezuela has no youth hostels.

An interesting kind of accommodation is the posada, a small, family-run guesthouse. These have mushroomed over past decades in the cities and, particularly, in the smaller localities and the countryside. They often have more character then hotels and offer more personalized attention. Most posadas are budget places but there are also some mid-range and a few top-end posadas.

Another kind of countryside lodging are the *campamentos* (literally 'camps'), which have sprung up even in the most remote areas. Not to be confused with campsites, *campamentos* can be anything from a rustic shelter with a few hammocks to a posh country lodge with a swimming pool and its own airstrip. More commonly, though, it will be a collection of cabañas plus a restaurant. *Campamentos* provide accommodation, food and usually tours, sometimes selling these services as all-inclusive packages.

Places to stay can legally charge a 16% VAT on top of the room price, though few

---

PRACTICALITIES

- Venezuela uses the metric system for weights and measures.

- Electrical current is 110V, 60 cycles AC throughout the country. Plugs are the US-type with two flat prongs.

- The two leading Caracas newspapers *El Universal* and *El Nacional* have country-wide distribution; both have reasonable coverage of national and international affairs, sports, economics and culture. The *Daily Journal* is the main English-language newspaper published in Venezuela, but it's hard to get outside Caracas.

- Videos sold in Venezuela use the NTSC image registration system, the same as in North America and Japan but incompatible with PAL which is used in most of Europe and Australia.

- Many hotels have cable TV, bringing some US stations to your hotel room.

budget hotels or posadas actually do it. The prices listed in this book have included this tax already. Most top-end hotels will accept payment by credit card, but this is rarely offered in budget places so make sure you have cash at hand. Hotels in the popular holiday destinations (eg Isla de Margarita) increase their rates in holiday periods. On the other hand, in the slow season it's possible to bargain, both in the budget and five-star hotels, but always try to do it in a friendly and easygoing manner.

Budget

In this book, budget category covers places where a double room costs about $20 or less. Budget places to stay have a variety of names, such as *hotel, residencia, hospedaje,* posada and *pensión.* The last two are meant to be small, family-run guesthouses, but don't jump to conclusions by just looking at the sign out the front, check inside.

Budget hotels tend to be grouped together in certain areas, usually around the market, bus terminal and in the backstreets of the city center. Most of the cheapies have a private bathroom, which includes a toilet and shower. Note that cheap hotel plumbing can't cope with toilet paper, so throw it in the wastebasket that is normally provided. Venezuelans love TV, so most budget hotels provide TVs in the rooms.

As most of the country lies in the lowland tropics, rooms have either a fan or air-con, but there's no hot water. Air-con may not always be advantageous. The equipment often dates from oil-rich years and, after decades of use, it may be in a desperate state of disrepair and very noisy. There's usually only the on/off switch, and it's not always clear which is better. Sometimes they're *very* efficient and turn the room into a freezer; other times they don't cool at all. Always have a look at the room and check the fan or air-con before you book in and pay.

Few budget hotels have single or twin rooms, but many do have *matrimoniales* (rooms with a double bed intended for couples). This type of room usually costs the same for one person as for two, so traveling as a couple significantly reduces the cost of accommodations. Single travelers are at a disadvantage. In this guide, price ranges given for doubles will include prices for *matrimoniales.*

Many cheap hotels double as 'love hotels' (that rent rooms by the hour), and it may be impossible to avoid staying in one from time to time.

Mid-Range

In this guide, mid-range covers the places where double rooms and/or *matrimoniales* cost between $20 and $50.

Many of the mid-range hotels nestle conveniently in city centers – you'll often find a few of them in the environs of the local Plaza Bolívar. Some of them can be booked online and paid for by credit card, but most still follow traditional style – reserve by phone and pay in cash.

Although often lacking in character, mid range hotels usually provide better rooms and more facilities than budget establishments, and virtually every room will have a TV, often cable TV. They will almost always have private bathrooms and air-con, and the air-con will usually be quieter than those in the cheapies. That said, it's a good idea to inspect the room in these hotels before you commit yourself.

Top End

Any hotel with double rooms costing $50 or more is considered top end. By and large, top-end hotels are outside downtown areas, in greener and wealthier residential suburbs, sometimes quite a way from the center. After all, if you have money enough to stay in such places, you'll also have some change for a taxi to get around.

Standards of these hotels vary, but you can expect silent, central air-con, hot water, a reception desk open around the clock and proper facilities to safeguard guests' valuables. An increasing number of these hotels have Internet connections in rooms or in a business center, and you can usually book these hotels by email. However, keep in mind that they are likely to charge you the full price online, while walk-in rates off the street can be much lower.

Prices vary greatly and don't always reflect quality. You can normally grab quite a good double with facilities for somewhere between $50 and $100, except in Caracas and Isla de Margarita, where prices are generally higher. Sometimes top-end hotels have much lower weekend rates. Only Caracas and Isla de Margarita, and to a lesser extent Puerto La Cruz and Maracaibo, have a choice of five-star hotels.

ACTIVITIES

Venezuela has much to offer those who love the great outdoors. Mérida, in particular, is known as Venezuela's adventure sports capital.

Fishing

Los Roques (p101) is renowned as one of the world's finest areas for game fishing, particularly for bonefish. You can also go piranha fishing in the *hatos* (large cattle ranches typical of Los Llanos; p224) and trout fishing in the mountain lakes around Mérida (p196).

Hiking & Trekking

Many of Venezuela's 40-odd national parks provide a choice of walks ranging from easy, well-signposted trails to wild jungle paths. Parque Nacional El Ávila (p93), near Caracas, offers some of the best easy walking trails, while Mérida's surrounds (p193) offer fabulous opportunities for high-mountain trekking. Other hiking possibilities include Parque Nacional Guatopo (p107), Parque Nacional Henri Pittier (p118), Parque Nacional San Esteban (p136), Sierra de San Luis (p150), La Teta de Niquitao (p204), Parque Nacional Península de Paria (p271), and one of the most adventurous and fascinating treks, to the top of Roraima (p309).

Mountain Biking

The region around Mérida (p195) is excellent for mountain biking, and the tour operators in the city organize biking trips and rent out bikes.

Paragliding

Mérida (p195) is the best place to go paragliding. Double gliders are available, so even greenhorns can try this breathtaking experience.

Rafting & Canyoning

Rafting trips are run on some Andean rivers (arranged in Mérida; p196), in the Parque Nacional Mochima (arranged in Mochima; p254), and over Río Orinoco rapids (arranged in Puerto Ayacucho; p317). The Mérida region is also the home of canyoning (climbing, rappelling and hiking down a river canyon), the newest adventure craze.

Snorkeling & Scuba Diving

Venezuela has excellent snorkeling and scuba diving around the offshore archipelagos such as Los Roques (p100). There's also some good snorkeling and diving around the islands closer to the mainland, including in Parque Nacional Mochima (p251) and Parque Nacional Morrocoy (p152). In all these places, local operators offer courses and diving trips, and rent equipment.

Spelunking

Spelunkers can explore some of Venezuela's several hundred caves. The most famous and among the most spectacular is the Cueva del Guácharo (p275). There are about 20 other lesser-known caves in the same area.

Wildlife & Bird-Watching

Los Llanos is one of the best regions to see wild animals, including caimans, capybaras (aquatic rodents), anacondas, anteaters and birds. Wildlife safaris are organized from the *hatos* (p224) and from Mérida (p186). If you are particularly interested in bird-watching, consider Parque Nacional Henri Pittier (p118) and Parque Nacional Yacambú (p165). There are also some good bird-watching spots around Mérida (p196) and along La Escalera (p307) on the Ciudad Guayana–Santa Elena road.

Windsurfing & Kitesurfing

Venezuela has some windsurfing areas of international reputation, including Adícora (p148) and El Yaque (p243). There is also fine windsurfing at Los Roques (p101).

BUSINESS HOURS

The working day is theoretically eight hours, from 8am to noon and 2pm to 6pm, Monday to Friday, but in practice, many businesses work shorter hours. Almost all offices, including tourist offices, are closed on Saturday and Sunday.

Usual shopping hours are 9am to 6pm or 7pm weekdays, and a half-day on Saturday. Many shops close for lunch but some work the *horario corrido*, without a lunchtime break. Restaurants normally open from around noon to 9pm or 11pm, but many are closed on Sunday.

Most museums are open on Sunday but closed on Monday.

For opening hours of banks, post offices, telephone centers and Internet cafés, see the respective sections in this chapter.

CHILDREN

Like most Latin Americans, Venezuelans adore children. Very few foreigners travel with children in Venezuela, but any visiting parents will easily find plenty of local companions for their kids.

Children enjoy numerous privileges on local transportation and in accommodations and entertainment. Age limits for discounts or freebies vary from place to place, but are rarely rigidly enforced. Officially children can ride free on buses and the Caracas metro if they don't occupy a separate seat.

In most major Venezuelan cities there are usually quite a few shops devoted to kids' clothing, shoes and toys, and you can buy disposable diapers (nappies) and baby food in most supermarkets and pharmacies. For more information, see Lonely Planet's *Travel with Children*.

CLIMATE CHARTS

See When to Go (p9) for general information about climate. Venezuela is close to the equator, so average temperatures vary little throughout the year. They do, however, change with altitude, dropping about 6°C with every 1000m increase. Since over 90% of Venezuela lies below 1000m, you'll experience temperatures between 22°C and 30°C in most places. The Andean and coastal mountain ranges have more moderate temperatures.

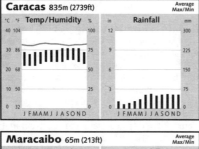

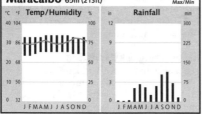

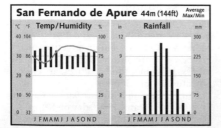

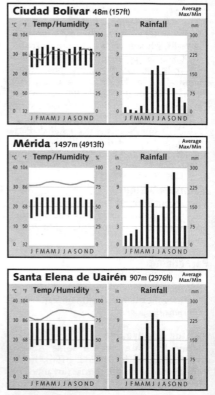

COURSES

Venezuela has Spanish language schools in most big cities. You can also find an independent teacher and arrange individual classes. Possibly the best place to learn Spanish is Mérida (p186), which has plenty of language-teaching facilities and is one of the cheapest places to study. You can also study Spanish in Caracas (p74) and in Pampatar on Isla de Margarita (p240).

CUSTOMS

Customs regulations don't differ much from those in other South American countries. You are allowed to bring in personal belongings and presents you intend to give to Venezuelan residents, as well as cameras (still, video and movie), camping equipment, sports accessories, a personal computer and the like.

According to Venezuelan law, possession, trafficking and consumption of drugs are all serious offenses subject to heavy penalties. You would have to be crazy to try smuggling drugs across the border.

DANGERS & ANNOYANCES

Venezuela is reasonably safe to travel in, though it's not a perfectly secure country. The country is getting poorer and, consequently, theft, robbery and common crime are on the increase. Theft is the most common travelers' danger, and the problem is more serious in the larger cities and urban centers than in the countryside. Caracas is the most dangerous place in the country, and you should take care while strolling around the streets, particularly at night.

The most common methods of theft are snatching your daypack, camera or watch, pickpocketing, or taking advantage of a moment's inattention to pick up your gear and run away. Thieves often work in pairs or groups; one or more will distract you, while an accomplice does the deed. Theft from hotel rooms, cars and unattended tents are also potential dangers.

If you can, leave your money and valuables somewhere safe before walking the streets. In practice, it's good to carry a decoy bundle of small notes, the equivalent of $5 to $10, ready to hand over in case of an assault; if you don't have anything, robbers can become frustrated and unpredictable.

Armed hold-ups in the cities can occur even in upmarket suburbs. If you are accosted by robbers, it is best to give them what they are after, but try to play it cool and don't rush to hand them all your

---

TEN BASIC PRECAUTIONS AGAINST THEFT & ROBBERY

- Keep your money and documents as secure as possible, preferably in a money belt next to your skin.
- Distribute your valuables about your person and luggage to avoid the risk of losing everything in one fell swoop.
- Don't venture into poor suburbs, desolate streets or suspicious-looking surroundings, especially after dark.
- Wear casual and inexpensive dress, preferably in plain, sober tones rather than in bright colors.
- Don't wear expensive jewelry or wristwatches, and keep your camera out of sight as much as possible.
- Behave confidently on the street; don't look lost or stand with a blank expression in the middle of the street.
- Before arriving in a new place, make sure you have a map or at least a rough idea about orientation.
- Use taxis if this seems the appropriate way to avoid walking through risky or unknown areas.
- Look around to see whether you're being observed or followed, especially while leaving a bank, *casa de cambio* (money-exchange office) or an ATM.
- Have good travel insurance just in case something goes wrong.

DIRECTORY

valuables at once – they may well be satisfied with just your decoy bundle. Don't try to escape or struggle, and don't count on any help from passers-by. There have been reports of armed robbery on remote hiking trails and deserted beaches, but they seem to be isolated cases. Some travelers warned us about the risks of using ATMs – see the boxed text (p330).

When traveling around the country, there are plenty of *alcabalas* (checkpoints), though not all are actually operating. They check the identity documents of passengers, and occasionally the luggage as well. In the cities, police checks are uncommon, but they do occur, so always have your passport with you. If you don't, you may end up at the police station.

If your passport, valuables or other belongings are stolen, go to the nearest PTJ (Policía Técnica Judicial) office to make a *denuncia* (report). The officer on duty will write a statement according to what you tell them. It should include the description of the events and the list of stolen articles. Pay attention to the wording you use, make sure you include every stolen item and document, and carefully check the statement before signing it to ensure it contains exactly what you've said. They will give you a copy of the statement, which serves as a temporary identity document, and you will need to present it to your insurer in order to make a claim. Don't expect your things to be found, as the police are unlikely to do anything about it. Stolen cars and motorcycles should also be reported at the PTJ.

Two Colombian guerrilla groups, the FARC and the ELN, have shown an increasing presence in Venezuela's remote border areas of Zulia, Táchira, Apure and Amazonas states. Travel in these areas may involve a risk of violence, skirmishes or even kidnapping.

DISABLED TRAVELERS

Venezuela offers very little to people with disabilities. Wheelchair ramps are available only at a few upmarket hotels and restaurants, and public transportation will be a challenge for any person with mobility limitations. Hardly any office, museum or bank provides special facilities for disabled persons, and wheelchair-accessible toilets are virtually nonexistent.

DISCOUNT CARDS

Students and senior citizens can get small discounts on airfares with some domestic carriers and on ferry tickets to Isla de Margarita, but that's about it. There are no discounts on intercity bus fares, urban transportation or cinema tickets, and most museums have free admission anyway.

EMBASSIES & CONSULATES
Venezuelan Embassies & Consulates

Venezuelan embassies abroad include the following:

Brazil (☎ 06-1223-9375; Quadra 803, Ses Av Das Naçoes, Brasilia DF)

Canada (☎ 613-235-5151, 235-0551; www.mision venezuela.org; 32 Range Rd, Ottawa, Ontario K1N 4J8)

Colombia (☎ 1-640-1213; embajada@embaven.org.co; Carrera 11 No 87-51, Bogotá)

France (☎ 01-45-53-29-98, 01-47-55-00-11; www .embavenez-paris.com; 11 rue Copernic, Paris 75116)

Germany (☎ 030-832-24-00; www.botschaft-venezuela .de; Schillstrasse 9-10, 10785 Berlin)

Italy (☎ 068-07-97-97, 068-07-94-64; embaveit@iol.it; Via Nicolo Tartaglia 11, 00197 Rome)

Japan (☎ 0334-091-501; embavene@interlink.or.jp; 38 Kowa Building, 12-24 Nishi Azabu, 4 Chrome, Minato Ku, Tokyo 106)

Netherlands (☎ 0703-65-12-56, 0703-63-38-05; embavene@xs4all.nl; Nassaulaan 2, 2514 JS The Hague)

Spain (☎ 01-598-12-00; embvenez@teleline.es; Edificio Eurocentro, Calle Capitan Haya No 1, 28020 Madrid)

Trinidad & Tobago (☎ 627-9821; embaveneztt@ carib-link.net; Venezuelan Centre, 16 Victoria Av, Port of Spain)

UK (☎ 020-7581-2776, 7584-4206; www.venezlon .demon.co.uk; 1 Cromwell Rd, London SW7 2HW)

USA (☎ 202-342-2214; www.embavenez-us.org; 1099 30th St NW, Washington DC 20007)

YOUR OWN EMBASSY

It's important to realize what your own embassy – the embassy of the country of which you are a citizen – can and can't do to help if you get into trouble. Generally speaking, it won't be much help if the trouble you're in is remotely your own fault. Remember that you are bound by the laws of the country you are in. Your embassy will not be sympathetic if you end up in jail after committing a crime locally, even if such actions are legal in your own country.

In genuine emergencies you might get some assistance, but only if other channels have been exhausted. For example, if you need to get home urgently, a free ticket home is exceedingly unlikely – the embassy would expect you to have insurance. If all your money and documents are stolen, it should assist you with getting a new passport, but a loan for onward travel is out of the question.

Embassies & Consulates in Venezuela

The following embassies are located in Caracas. Consulates are at the same address as the embassies unless otherwise noted. If you can't find your home embassy, check a Caracas phone directory.

Brazil (Map p70; ☎ 261-5505; www.embajadabrasil .org.ve; Centro Gerencial Mohedano, cnr Calle Los Chaguaramos & Av Mohedano, La Castellana, Caracas); Consulate in Ciudad Guayana (**Map p294;** ☎ 923-5243; Edificio Amazonas, Av Las Américas, Puerto Ordaz); Consulate in Santa Elena de Uairén (**Map p312;** ☎ 995-1256; Av Gran Mariscal)

Canada (Map p70; ☎ 264-0833, 266-7176; crcas@ dfait-maeci.gc.ca; cnr Avs Francisco de Miranda & Sur Altamira, Altamira, Caracas)

Colombia (Map p80; ☎ 261-5584; Torre Credival, cnr 2a Av de Campo Alegre & Av Francisco de Miranda, Campo Alegre, Caracas); Consulate in Caracas (**Map p98;** ☎ 951-3631, 951-1697; Edificio Consulado de Colombia, Calle Guaicaipuro, El Rosal, Caracas); Consulate in Maracaibo (☎ 792-1483; Av 3Y No 70-16); Consulate in Puerto Ayacucho (☎ 521-0789; Calle Yapacana off Av Rómulo Gallegos)

France (Map p80; ☎ 909-6500; www.francia.org.ve; Edificio Embajada de Francia, cnr Calle Madrid & Av La Trinidad, Las Mercedes, Caracas)

Germany Consulate (Map p70; ☎ 261-0181; diplogermacara@cantv.net; Torre La Castellana, Av Principal de la Castellana, La Castellana, Caracas)

Guyana (☎ 977-1158; embaguy@caracas-office .org.ve; Quinta Roraima, Av El Paseo, Prados del Este, Caracas)

Israel (Map pp56-7; ☎ 239-4921; Centro Empresarial Miranda, cnr Av Francisco de Miranda & Av Principal de Los Ruices, Los Ruices, Caracas)

Italy (Map p80; ☎ 952-7311; ambcara@italamb .org.ve; Edificio Atrium, Calle Sorocaima; El Rosal, Caracas)

Japan Consulate (Map p70; ☎ 261-8333; csjapon@ genesisbci.net; Edificio Bancaracas, Plaza La Castellana, La Castellana, Caracas)

Netherlands Consulate (Map p70; ☎ 263-3076, 263-3622; www.embholanda.org.ve; Edificio San Juan, cnr 2a Transversal & Av San Juan Bosco, Altamira, Caracas)

Spain (Map pp56-7; ☎ 263-2855; espanve@cantv.net; Quinta Marmolejo, Av Mohedano btwn 1a & 2a Transversal, La Castellana, Caracas)

Suriname (Map p70; ☎ 261-2724; embsur1@cantv.net; Quinta Los Milagros, 4a Av btwn 7a & 8a Transversal, Altamira, Caracas)

Trinidad & Tobago (Map p70; ☎ 261-3748; embassytt@cantv.net; Quinta Serrana, 4a Av btwn 7a & 8a Transversal, Altamira, Caracas)

UK (Map p70; ☎ 263-8411; www.britain.org.ve; Torre La Castellana, Av Principal de la Castellana, La Castellana, Caracas)

USA (Map p80; ☎ 975-6411, 975-7811; www .embajadausa.org.ve; cnr Calle F & Calle Suapure, Colinas del Valle Arriba, Caracas)

FESTIVALS & EVENTS

Given the strong Catholic character of Venezuela, many feasts and celebrations follow the Church calendar – Christmas, Carnaval, Easter and Corpus Christi are celebrated all over the country. The religious calendar is dotted with saints' days, and every village and town has its own patron saint and will hold a celebratory feast on that day. Cultural events such as festivals of theater, film or classical music are almost exclusively confined to Caracas. Venezuela's main religious and cultural events are listed below. See the respective sections for more information.

JANUARY

Feria de San Sebastián Main event of San Cristóbal, taking place in the second half of January (p207).

Fiesta Patronales de la Divina Pastora Barquisimeto's major feast, held in mid-January (p159).

Paradura del Niño Celebrated for the whole month in Mérida state (p187).

FEBRUARY/MARCH

Carnaval Celebrated throughout the country on the Monday and Tuesday prior to Ash Wednesday; particularly elaborate in Mérida, El Callao and Carúpano.

MARCH/APRIL

Festival Internacional de Teatro Cultural festival held in Caracas on even years.

Semana Santa Easter week (the week leading up to Easter Sunday) sees solemn celebrations in the churches all around the country and processions on Maundy Thursday and Good Friday.

MAY/JUNE

Festival de Los Diablos Danzantes Colorful Dancing Devils invade San Francisco de Yare, Chuao and some other villages in the northern-central region on Corpus Christi (60 days after Easter, in May or June; see p106).

SEPTEMBER

Fiesta de la Virgen de Coromoto Major pilgrimage gathering in Guanare on September 8, to honor the anniversary of the Virgin's appearance.

Fiesta de la Virgen del Valle Another focus of religious fervor, on September 8 at Valle del Espíritu Santo on Isla de Margarita (p240).

NOVEMBER

Feria de la Chinita Maracaibo's major annual bash, held for a week and culminating with the coronation of Zulia's patron saint on November 18 (p172).

FOOD

See the Food & Drink chapter (p47) to read up on what you can eat, where and when. In this guide, we have only divided eating sections into budget, mid-range and top end in major cities such as Caracas. Expect main dishes to cost under $5 in a budget eatery, $5 to $10 in a mid-range eatery, and over $10 in a top-end restaurant.

GAY & LESBIAN TRAVELERS

Homosexuality isn't illegal in Venezuela, but the overwhelmingly Catholic society tends to both deny and suppress it. The gay and lesbian movement is at present still very underdeveloped. Caracas has the largest gay and lesbian community and the most open gay life, and is the best place to make contacts and get to know what's going on (p87). Get as much information there as you can, because elsewhere in Venezuela it can be difficult to contact the gay community.

Caracas' contacts include the **Movimiento Ambiente de Venezuela** (☎ 0212-321-9470) and the gay 'what's on' guide **En Ambiente** (☎ 0414-219-1837; enambiente@latinmail.com). Also check local gay websites www.republicagay.com and www.rumbacaracas.com (both are in Spanish).

HOLIDAYS

Official public holidays include:
New Year's Day January 1
Carnaval Monday and Tuesday prior to Ash Wednesday, February/March
Easter Maundy Thursday and Good Friday, March/April
Declaration of Independence April 19
Labor Day May 1
Battle of Carabobo June 24
Independence Day July 5
Bolívar's Birthday July 24
Discovery of America October 12
Christmas Day December 25

INSURANCE

A travel insurance policy to cover theft, loss and medical problems is a good idea. Some policies specifically exclude 'dangerous activities,' which can include scuba diving, motorcycling, even trekking. You may prefer a policy which pays doctors or hospitals directly rather than you having to pay on the spot and claim later. If you have to claim later make sure you keep all documentation. Check that the policy covers ambulances or an emergency flight home. For more information on insurance, see the Health chapter (p342).

INTERNET ACCESS

Virtually all cities and most towns have cybercafés; Caracas alone has over 100. A selection of them is listed in the Internet Access sections under each town in this book, but new ones are popping up every day, so you're likely to find many more (and perhaps better, faster and cheaper) places by the time you travel. Also note that CANTV and Telcel, the two major local telephone operators (see the Telephone section under each town), also provide Internet facilities.

An hour of surfing the Web or emailing normally costs between $0.50 and $1, except for Caracas, where it may cost up to $2. Mérida has some of the cheapest Internet facilities. Many cybercafés in major cities now have broadband (*banda ancha*), so connection is fast. Opening hours of cyber-cafés vary, but many are open 9am to 9pm or longer. In the larger cities, you'll usually find a place open till 11pm or longer, and there may be some open round the clock. Most cybercafés provide a range of related facilities, such as printing, scanning and faxing, and some offer cheap international phone calls via the Internet.

Many travelers use free Web-based email accounts (such as Yahoo! or Hotmail), so they can access their email in any cybercafé anywhere. You can also open a free ekit Web-based email account online at www .lonelyplanet.ekit.com. To access a specific account of your own, you'll need to know your incoming (POP or IMAP) mail server name, your account name and your pass word. Get these from your Internet service provider (ISP). Using your own laptop for access may not be easy or cheap, as only a handful of upmarket hotels have Internet connections in rooms. For more information on traveling with a portable computer, see www.teleadapt.com. See Internet Resources (p12) for some useful Venezuelan sites.

LEGAL MATTERS

Venezuelan police have a mixed reputation. Cases of police corruption, abuse of power and use of undue force have been known, so it's probably best to stay a safe distance from them if you don't need them. This, of course, doesn't mean that they will stay away from you. If you happen to get involved with the police, keep calm and be polite, but not overly friendly. Don't get angry or hostile – it only works against you.

Keep well away from drugs; penalties for trafficking, possessing and using illegal drugs are stiff in Venezuela, and perpetrators usually end up with long jail terms. Don't carry even the smallest quantity – the police can be very thorough in searching travelers, and if they find any, you're in deep trouble. Needless to say, smuggling dope across borders is a crazy idea. Venezuelan prisons are not the most pleasant places you've ever seen. Also be aware that your embassy is of limited help if you get into trouble with the law – foreigners here, as elsewhere, are subject to the laws of the host country.

While your embassy or consulate is the best stop in any emergency, bear in mind

that there are some things it cannot do for you. These include getting local laws or regulations waived because you're a foreigner, investigating a crime, providing legal advice or representation in civil or criminal cases, getting you out of jail, and lending you money. An embassy or consulate can, however, issue emergency passports, contact relatives and friends, advise on how to transfer funds, provide lists of reliable local doctors, lawyers and interpreters, and visit you if you've been arrested or jailed. Also see the boxed text (p327).

MAPS

The best general map of Venezuela (scale 1:1,750,000) is published by International Travel Maps (Canada). Within Venezuela, folded road maps of the country are produced by several local publishers. For large-scale regional maps, contact IGVSB (Instituto Geográfico de Venezuela Simón Bolívar), the Caracas-based state map publisher; see p56 for details.

MONEY

The unit of Venezuelan currency is bolívar, abbreviated to Bs. There are 50-, 100- and 500-bolívar coins, and paper notes of 1000, 2000, 5000, 10,000, 20,000 and 50,000 bolívares. Confusingly, there are two different kind of notes of 1000, 2000, 5000 and 10,000 bolívares in circulation, and both are legal. Watch carefully the notes you pay and receive because some notes of various denominations have similar colors and are easily confused.

By far the most popular foreign currency is the US dollar, so stick strictly to the greenback. For this reason, all the prices quoted in this guide are in US dollar unless specified.

For exchange rates, see the Quick Reference page on the inside front cover of this guide. For information on costs in Venezuela, see p9.

ATMs & Banks

ATMs *(cajeros automáticos)* are the easiest way of getting cash, but there are some risks; see the boxed text p330. ATMs can be found at most major banks, including Banco de Venezuela, Banco Mercantil, Banco Provincial and Banesco (these are listed in the individual regional sections). ATMs are normally open 24 hours.

DIRECTORY

ATM WARNING

Withdrawing money from an ATM in Venezuela is easy, fast and convenient, but it has some small if potentially serious risks. To start with, the machine can swallow your card, as some travelers have reported. If it happens during the bank's business hours, someone from the bank is likely to help you retrieve your card. It will be less fun, however, when the bank is closed: no money, no card and no help.

Or maybe you'll get your card back, but no money. One traveler reported that he tried once but the money didn't come out. Believing that there might have been some temporary problem with the machine, he repeated the operation, with the same negative result. A couple of months later at home, he wasn't particularly happy with his bank statement, which recorded two withdrawals.

Even if the machine gives back your card and the money, there is not always a happy ending. Some ATMs are targeted by robbers who watch discreetly and then kill two birds with one shot – they get your cash and your credit card, and may even extract the PIN from the victim. So far, travelers have reported incidents of this occurring only in Caracas, but the problem may spread.

The chance that something like this will happen to you is slim, but if you want to minimize the risk, get your cash advance inside the bank from a cashier, even if this does take half an hour or more.

Most ATMs are linked to Cirrus and Plus and should accept international Visa and MasterCard, though some don't. If this is the case go inside the bank and get a cash advance from the cashier. The usual opening hours of banks are 8:30am to 3:30pm Monday to Friday countrywide. Venezuelan banks are almost always crowded, inefficient and painfully slow. Remember that your bank at home will usually charge a fee for each foreign ATM and cashier transaction.

Black Market

A black market is likely to operate as long as the exchange controls are in place (see the boxed text p331). Visitors with cash

US dollars will get a better rate on the black market than officially. Don't bring any currency other than greenbacks. The black-market exchange rates vary widely from day to day and place to place, but at the time of research it was possible to get up to 60% more than changing on official rate. Of course the black market is illegal, so travelers should be aware of the potential dangers. Check before traveling if the current exchange controls still apply.

Cash

The usual official place to change cash is at a *casa de cambio* (an authorized money-exchange office). They exist in most major cities and buy foreign currency (but don't sell it) at the official exchange rate. There are a number of them in Caracas, Puerto La Cruz and Porlamar, but there may be just one or two in other large cities. Italcambio is the biggest and best known company, with branches all over the country.

By far the most popular foreign currency is the US dollar. Other internationally known currencies, such as the euro or pound sterling, can be exchanged in a *casa de cambio*, but not all will accept them and the rates are usually poor.

Banks which previously changed foreign currencies at good rates are now very reluctant to do so, but they may do it again once the exchange controls are lifted. US dollars are normally accepted by tour operators as payment for tours.

Credit Cards

Visa and MasterCard are the most useful credit cards in Venezuela. Both are widely accepted as a means of payment for goods and services (though many tour operators may refuse payment by credit card or charge 10% more for the service). They are also useful for taking cash advances from banks or ATMs (see earlier). Make sure you know the number to call if you lose your credit card, and be quick to cancel it if it's lost or stolen.

Traveler's Checks

American Express is the most recognized traveler's check brand. Corp Banca was the best bank for changing Amex checks, but it stopped cashing them after exchange restrictions were introduced. The bank is likely to reintroduce exchange transactions

MONEY EXCHANGE WARNING

The Venezuelan economy is in serious trouble. The inflation rate in 2003 was an alarming 27% while the GDP in that year contracted 7%. The country has been South America's worst economic performer in recent years. Early in 2003 the Chávez government introduced restrictions on importing and exporting currency, and fixed the exchange rate of the bolívar against the US dollar (US$1 = 1600 Bs), well above the bolívar's free-market value. Banks stopped changing foreign currency, both cash and traveler's checks. The move didn't cure the financial problems but sparked a widespread black market. Early in 2004, the government was forced to devalue the currency by nearly 20% (US$1 = 1920 Bs), yet the black-market dollar responded immediately, jumping to a new record high.

Exchange controls have been introduced several times in the past in Venezuela, but have never worked. The government was always forced to abolish them, and then face the inevitable hyper-inflation. It's impossible to predict how long they will stay this time, but they were still in place as this book was going to press. Foreign visitors should be aware of the following repercussions:

■ There's a flourishing black market where cash dollars buy much more than in the bank (see Black Market p330).

■ Banks that previously changed foreign currency no longer do so (eg Corp Banca); see Traveler's Checks p330.

■ Some ATMs don't give cash advances on foreign credit cards (see ATMs & Banks 329).

■ Prices of goods and services are extremely volatile. Consequently, the prices listed in this book are particularly vulnerable to change and should be regarded as guidelines only (see Costs & Money p9).

■ Before you travel, check an exchange rate site such as www.oanda.com to see if the exchange controls still apply.

in the future, but for now you need a *casa de cambio* to cash your checks. Same *casas de cambio* will change traveler's checks (try Italcambio), but will charge a commission of about 3% or more. Some tour operators will accept traveler's checks as payment.

NATIONAL PARKS

You don't have to go to the Instituto Nacional de Parques Nacionales (Inparques) for permits to the parks, as they are no longer necessary, but **Inparques** (Map p70; ☎ 285-4859; www.inparques.gov.ve; Av Rómulo Gallegos; ✆ 8am-noon & 1.30-4pm Mon-Fri) does have a main office just east of the Parque del Este metro station in Caracas. The office doesn't provide maps or brochures about the parks, but it has a specialized library.

POST

The postal service is run by Ipostel, which has post offices throughout the country. The usual opening hours are 8am to 5pm Monday to Friday, with regional variations. Some offices in the main cities may open longer hours and on Saturday. Airmailing a letter up to 20g costs $0.50 to anywhere in the Americas, $0.60 to Europe or Africa and $0.70 to the rest of the world. Sending a package of up to 500g will cost $6/8/10, respectively. The service is unreliable and slow. Airmail to Europe can take up to a month to arrive, if it arrives at all.

Ipostel also handles poste restante (general delivery mail). This service is also slow and not very reliable. Letters sent to Venezuela from abroad take a long time to be delivered and sometimes simply never make it. If you decide to use poste restante, stick to the main offices in major cities.

SHOPPING

Venezuela offers varied, good-quality craftwork. It's particularly renowned for its fine basketry, pottery and woodcarving, which differs significantly from region to region. Other attractive crafts include handwoven hammocks of the Guajiros, papier-mâché devil masks from San Francisco de Yare, and woolen ponchos from the Andes.

Try to buy crafts in their region of origin, ideally from the artisans themselves: not only are the crafts more authentic, but they are also cheaper, and the money goes directly to the artisan. If you can't get to the remote Indian communities, shop in the markets in nearby towns. However, don't ignore handicraft shops in the large cities, particularly in Caracas (p89), where you can find the best collections and best-quality crafts from around the country.

If you are interested in local music (*joropo, gaita,* salsa), the Caracas CD shops have the best selection. The price of locally produced CDs ranges from about $8 to $15.

Venezuela is noted for gold and diamonds, but don't expect to find great bargains everywhere. Possibly the cheapest place to buy gold jewelry is El Callao (p299), but you'll find better quality in Ciudad Bolívar (p291) and Caracas (p89).

SOLO TRAVELERS

Traveling solo certainly has its pros and cons. The undeniable advantage is being able to do what you want when you want and the way you want, but many travelers prefer to sacrifice the *libertad* and share the experiences of the trip with someone else.

While traveling on your own, you need to be more alert to what's going on around you and more cautious about where you go. You also face more potential risks, whether you're walking the city streets or trekking remote mountains. Solo females may face an additional problem of being the target of unwanted attention; see Women Travelers (p334).

Traveling solo is likely to be more expensive, principally due to the higher accommodation costs. Few hotels have single rooms, so you will need to pay for a *matrimonial* or double.

TELEPHONE

Venezuela's telephone system is operated by CANTV and is largely automated for both domestic and international connections. All phone numbers in the country are seven digits and area codes are three digits. A three-minute local call within a city costs about $0.10. The cost of long-distance calls is around $0.25 per minute, and it doesn't depend on the distance, so

calling the neighboring city costs the same as calling anywhere within the country.

Area Codes

Area codes are listed under the headings of the relevant destinations throughout this guide.

The country code for Venezuela is ☎ 58. To call Venezuela from abroad, dial the international access code of the country you're calling from, Venezuela's code (☎ 58), the area code (drop the initial 0) and the local phone number.

If making an international call from Venezuela, dial the international access code (00), the country code, the area code (without the initial 0), then the local number.

Mobile Phones

Telcel (numbers begin with ☎ 0414) is the major operator of mobile telephone services, followed by **Mobilnet** (☎ 0416) and **Digitel** (☎ 0412). Venezuela has one of the highest cellular-phone-per-capita ratios in Latin America. Cellular phones have become both a status symbol and a more reliable alternative to overloaded fixed lines and the often inoperable public phones. Note that calling cellular numbers is expensive and eats quickly into your phonecard.

Phonecards

Public telephones exist in the cities and larger towns, though some are out of order. All public phones operate only on phone-cards, not coins. If you plan on using public phones at all, it's worth buying a card (Tarjeta CANTV), which costs $3. You can also use services of another telecommunications operator, Telcel, which has its own public phones operating on its own phonecards (Tarjeta Telcel), but far fewer phones than CANTV.

You can save using the Multiphone or Entel pre-paid phonecards, available from newsagents and some other businesses, but they can only be used from private phones. Also, some cybercafés provide cheap Internet phone calls. Finally, you can call reverse-charge (collect) to most countries.

Phone Centers

Long-distance and international calls can be made from public phones or from the communication offices of CANTV and

Telcel – called Centro de Comunicaciones CANTV and Centro de Conexiones Telcel respectively. In large cities, these centers are everywhere, from downtown to the suburbs, and most of them also offer fast Internet connections. Telephone centers are normally open from about 7am to 9pm daily, with some regional variations, and are listed in the Information sections of each town.

Sample per-minute phone rates of CANTV/Telcel are $0.15/0.10 to the USA, $0.45/0.35 to the UK and $0.80/0.75 to Australia.

TIME

All of Venezuela lies within the same time zone, four hours behind Greenwich Mean Time. There's no daylight saving time. When it's noon in Venezuela, it's 11am in New York, 8am in San Francisco, 4pm in London and 2am next day in Sydney (add one hour to these times during daylight saving).

TOILETS

There are virtually no self-contained public toilets in Venezuela. If you are unexpectedly in need, use a toilet in a restaurant. Museums and large shopping malls usually have toilets, as do bus and airport terminals. Toilets are usually the sit-down style, but they often lack seats, so they effectively become the squat variety.

You will rarely find toilet paper in toilets, so carry your own at all times. Some toilets charge fees (normally not exceeding $0.20), for which you receive a piece of toilet paper. If it doesn't seem like enough, do not hesitate to ask for more.

Except for toilets in upmarket establishments, the plumbing might not be of a standard you are accustomed to. The tubes are narrow and water pressure is weak, so toilets can't cope with toilet paper. A wastebasket is normally provided.

The most common word for toilet is *baño*. Men's toilets will usually bear a label reading *señores* or *caballeros,* while women's toilets will be marked *señoras* or *damas.*

TOURIST INFORMATION

Inatur (Instituto Autónomo de Turismo de Aragua; www .inatur.gov.ve) is the Caracas-based government agency that promotes tourism and provides tourist information; see p60 for contact details. Outside the capital, tourist information is handled by regional tourist bodies which have offices in their respective state capitals and in some other cities. Some are better than others, but on the whole they lack city maps and brochures, and the staff members rarely speak English.

TOURS

Tours are a common way to visit some of Venezuela's attractions, because vast areas of the country are virtually inaccessible by public transport (eg the Orinoco Delta or Amazon Basin) or because a solitary visit to scattered sights in a large territory (eg the Gran Sabana) may be inconvenient, time-consuming and expensive.

Tours booked from abroad are expensive; you are likely to save a lot of money by arranging a tour in Venezuela. It's cheapest to arrange a tour from the regional center closest to the area you are going to visit. For hikes in the Andes, the place to look for a guide is Mérida; for excursions around the Gran Sabana and to the top of Roraima, the cheapest organized trips are from Santa Elena de Uairén; for the Amazon Basin, book a tour in Puerto Ayacucho; and for tours to Angel Falls, Ciudad Bolívar is the place to shop around. Information about local tour operators is included in the relevant destination sections.

VISAS

Nationals of the US, Canada, Australia, New Zealand, Japan, the UK and most of Western and Scandinavian Europe don't need a visa to enter Venezuela; a free Tourist Card (Tarjeta de Ingreso, officially denominated DEX-2) is all that is required. The card is normally valid for 90 days (unless immigration officers note on the card a shorter period) and can be extended. Airlines flying into Venezuela provide these cards to passengers while on the plane. Overland visitors bearing passports of the countries listed above can obtain the card from the immigration official at the border crossing (it's best to check this beforehand at the nearest consulate).

On entering Venezuela, your passport and tourist card will be stamped (make sure this happens) by Dirección de Identificación y Extranjería (DIEX or DEX) bor

DIRECTORY

officials. Keep the yellow copy of the tourist card while traveling in Venezuela (you may be asked for it during passport controls), and return it to immigration officials when leaving the country – although not all are interested in collecting the cards.

Visa and tourist card extensions are handled by the office of DIEX in Caracas (p58).

WOMEN TRAVELERS

Like most of Latin America, Venezuela is very much a man's country. Women travelers will attract more curiosity, attention and advances from local men than they would from men in North America or Western Europe. Local males will quickly pick you out in a crowd and are not shy to show their admiration through whistles, endearments and flirtatious comments. These advances are usually lighthearted, though they can seem rude to the outsider at first.

The best way to deal with unwanted attention is simply to ignore it. Dressing modestly will make you less conspicuous to the local peacocks. Don't follow local fashions in dressing, as most Venezuelan women dress up to the nines and are always beautifully turned out with lots of makeup, high heels and skintight clothes – regardless of whether they are on the beach, the bus or in the local launderette.

Harassment aside, women travelers are also more vulnerable to assault and bag-snatchers than men. Always stay conscious of your surroundings and aware of situations that could be dangerous. Shabby *barrios* (shantytowns), solitary streets and beaches, and all places considered 'male territory,' such as bars, sports events, mines and construction sites, should be considered risky. Never hitchhike alone.

WORK

Travelers looking for a paid job in Venezuela may be disappointed. The economic situation is a mess, unemployment is around 20% and over three-quarters of the population live in poverty. Qualified English teachers may have the best chance of getting a job, but it's not easy. Try English-teaching institutions such as the **British Council** (www.britishcouncil.com), private language schools or linguistic departments at universities. Note that you need a work visa to work legally in Venezuela, and getting one is a journey through hell.

Transportation

GETTING THERE & AWAY

ENTERING THE COUNTRY

Entering Venezuela by air, sea or land is pretty straightforward. Most visitors from Western countries don't need a visa, just a *tarjeta de ingreso* (tourist card), officially known as DEX-2, which is free and will be provided upon entry to the country. You need to fill the card in and present it, along with your valid passport, to the immigration officials, who will then stamp both the passport and the card and give you a yellow carbon copy of the card. For information on visas, see p333.

Upon departure, you need to return the tourist card to the immigration officials, though not all are interested in collecting them. Make sure they put an exit stamp in your passport; without one you may have problems entering Venezuela next time around. All travelers, at both airports and road crossings, are charged a $13 *impuesto de salida* (departure tax).

AIR

Set at the northern edge of South America, Venezuela has the cheapest air links with both Europe and North America and is therefore the most convenient northern gateway to the continent.

Airports & Airlines

Most international visitors arrive at Caracas' airport in Maiquetía, the **Aeropuerto Internacional 'Simón Bolívar'** (www.aeropuerto-maiquetia.com.ve in Spanish), 26km from Caracas. Venezuela has several other airports servicing international flights, but these change frequently and unexpectedly. Isla de Margarita's airport (p231) is used by charter flights bringing international package tourists, but few independent travelers fly in here.

Following is a list of national and international airlines flying to and from Venezuela (addresses and phone numbers listed are in Caracas):

Aerocaribe Coro (☎ 252-1837)

Aero Continente (☎ 263-4114; www.aerocontinente.com)

Aerolíneas Argentinas (Map p80; ☎ 951-3005; www.aerolineas.com.ar; Calle Guaicaipuro, Torre Hener 1-A, El Rosal)

Aeropostal (Map p70; ☎ 0800-337-8466, 266-1059; www.aeropostal.com; 1st fl, Torre ING Bank, La Castellana) The country's largest airline, with the widest international coverage, serving Bogotá, Guayaquil, Havana, Lima, Miami, Madrid, Port of Spain, Quito and Santo Domingo.

Air Europa (☎ 951-1910; www.air-europa.com)

Air France (Map p70; ☎ 283-5855, 0800-100-3459; www.airfrance.com; 2nd fl, Torre Este, Parque Cristal, Av Francisco de Miranda, Los Palos Grandes)

Alitalia (Map p70; ☎ 208-4120, 208-4111; www.alitalia.it; 5th fl, Edificio Atlantic, Av Andrés Bello, Los Palos Grandes)

American Airlines (Map p70; ☎ 209-8111; www.aa.com; 7th fl, Torre ING Bank, Centro Letonia)

THINGS CHANGE

The information in this chapter is particularly vulnerable to change. Check directly with the airline or a travel agent to make sure you understand how a fare (and ticket you may buy) works and be aware of the security requirements for international travel. Shop carefully. The details given in this chapter should be regarded as pointers and are not a substitute for your own careful, up-to-date research.

DEPARTURE TAX

Venezuela's international *tasa aeroportuaria* (airport tax) is $30. On top of it, an additional *impuesto de salida* (departure tax) of $13 must be paid by all visitors. The taxes are payable in either US dollars or bolívares, but not by credit card. Check the Caracas airport website (www.aeropuerto -maiquetia.com.ve in Spanish) for possible increases.

Aserca (Map p80; ☎ 0800-648-8356, 905-5333; www.asercaairlines.com; Ground fl, Edificio Taeca, Calle Guaicaipuro, El Rosal)
Avianca (Alianza Summa) (Map p80; ☎ 953-7254; www.summa.aero; Ground fl, Edificio Roraima, Av Francisco de Miranda, El Bosque)
Avior (www.avior.com.ve) Sabana Grande (Map p68; ☎ 238-4622; Lincoln Suites, Av Solano López); Las Mercedes (Map p80; Tamanaco InterContinental Caracas, Av Principal de las Mercedes)
British Airways (Map p80; ☎ 266-0122; www .british-airways.com; 3rd fl, Centro San Ignacio, Torre Copérnico, La Castellana)
BWIA (Map p80; ☎ 953-6424; www.bwee.com; 8th fl, Edificio EXA, No 803-4, Avs Libertador & Alameda, El Rosal)
Continental Airlines (☎ 0800-359-2600, 953-3107; www.continental.com) El Rosal (Map p80; Centro Lido, Nivel Miranda, No M-22, Av Francisco de Miranda) Las Mercedes (Map p80; Tamanaco InterContinental Caracas, Av Principal de las Mercedes)
Cubana de Aviación (Map p70; ☎ 286-8639; www.cubana.cu; 4th fl, Edificio Atlantic, No 5, Av Andrés Bello & 1a Transversal, Los Palos Grandes)
Delta Airlines (☎ 0800-100-3453; www.delta.com)
Dutch Caribbean Airlines (www.flydca.net)
Iberia (Map p70; ☎ 267-8666; www.iberia .com; 4th fl, Centro Altamira, Av San Juan Bosco, Altamira)
KLM (Map p70; ☎ 285-3333; www.klm.com/ve _sp; Torre KLM, Av Rómulo Gallegos)
LanChile (Map p70; ☎ 284-1211; www.lanchile.com; Av Francisco de Miranda, Edificio Parque Cristal, No Lcc1-1, Los Palos Grandes)
Lufthansa (Map p70; ☎ 210-2111; www.lufthansa .com; 1st fl, Torre Centro Coinasa, Av San Felipe No 16, La Castellana)
Santa Bárbara (Map pp56-7; ☎ 204-4000; www .santabarbaraairlines.com; Edificio Tokay, Calle 3B, Industrial La Urbina) Young, but already well-established airline with international flights to Lima, Madrid, Quito and Tenerife.

TAP Air Portugal (Map p80; ☎ 951-0511; www .tap-airportugal.pt; Edificio Canaima, Av Francisco de Miranda, El Rosal)

Tickets

Venezuela is not a good place to buy international air tickets – avoid arriving on a one-way ticket as you may be disappointed: airfares to Europe and Australia are high, and there are virtually no discounted tickets available. Only flights to Florida are reasonably cheap, simply because it's close and the route is serviced by local airlines that may offer discount fares. It's always better to have the whole route covered by a ticket bought at home. Students and teachers will find the best deals at IVI Idiomas Vivos (see Travel Agencies, p61).

Just about every travel agency in Caracas will sell you tickets for flights with most airlines and, consequently, will know which is the cheapest carrier on a particular route. When it comes to more complex intercontinental connections, however, not all agencies are experts, so shop around.

It may be cheapest to fly to Miami and take one of the relatively cheap transatlantic flights to Europe (eg with United Airlines). Some Caracas travel agencies will sell combined tickets for the whole route.

Many travelers now buy tickets online. While this is safe, Web prices vary enormously. Try the following international online sites, but don't stop here because there are plenty of other sites which may offer deals that are just as good, if not better.

Expedia (www.expedia.com)
Flight Centre International (www.flightcentre.com)
Flights.com (www.eltexpress.com)
STA (www.sta.com)
Travelocity (www.travelocity.com)

Check the weekend travel sections of major newspapers for more companies, and see the suggestions listed under the following destinations.

Australia & New Zealand

The shortest route between Australia and South America goes over the South Pole. You can fly with either LanChile to Santiago or Aerolíneas Argentinas to Buenos Aires. Both carriers fly from Sydney through Auckland and have connections to Caracas. Expect to pay between A$2200 and A$2800 for the Sydney–Caracas roundtrip flight, depending on the length of stay and the season. The Auckland–Caracas fare will be only marginally lower.

Another possible route goes via Los Angeles and Miami, and will cost much the same as those via Chile or Argentina, though you'll probably need to change twice, in both LA and Miami. You can also fly to Venezuela through Europe – it's the longest route, but not as absurd as it may sound. You can stop in London, Amsterdam or Paris, and the total fare may be comparable to or even lower than traveling via Los Angeles. Finally, you can buy a RTW (Round-the-World) ticket that includes South America, or at least Miami, from where you can make a side trip to Venezuela.

The following are well-known agents for cheap fares:

Flight Centre Australia (☎ 133-133; www.flightcentre .com.au); New Zealand (☎ 0800-243-544; www.flight centre.co.nz)

STA Travel Australia (☎ 1300-733-035; www.statravel .com.au); New Zealand (☎ 0508-782-872; www.statravel .co.nz)

Travel.com (www.travel.com.au)

Canada

There are no direct flights to Venezuela – you need to go via a US city, usually Miami. Expect a roundtrip fare from Toronto or Montreal to Caracas to cost C$1100 to C$1500. **Travel CUTS** (☎ 800-667-2887; www.travel cuts.com) is Canada's national student travel agency. For online booking try www.expedia .ca and www.travelocity.ca.

Caribbean
NETHERLANDS ANTILLES

Dutch Caribbean Airlines (DCA) flies between Caracas and Aruba, Curaçao and Bonaire. It also has flights between Maracaibo and Aruba and Curaçao, and between Las Piedras (Punto Fijo) and Curaçao. Aeropostal serves Aruba and Curaçao from Caracas. Aserca and Avior fly between Caracas and Aruba. Aerocaribe Coro has flights between Coro and Curaçao and between Las Piedras and Aruba. Expect to pay roughly $120 to $140 one-way, and $100 to $150 roundtrip for any of the routes. Discount fares are available on seven- and 14-day roundtrip flights.

TRINIDAD
Aeropostal and BWIA fly daily between Port of Spain and Caracas ($150 one-way, $205 for a 21-day roundtrip). Aeropostal and Rutaca fly between Porlamar and Port of Spain ($110 one-way, $155 for a 21-day roundtrip).

South America
BRAZIL
Flying between Brazil and Venezuela is expensive. The flight from São Paulo or Rio de Janeiro to Caracas will cost around $840 one-way and $890 for a 60-day roundtrip. There are no direct flights between Manaus and Caracas, nor between Boa Vista and Santa Elena de Uairén.

COLOMBIA
Avianca and Aeropostal fly between Bogotá and Caracas ($229 one-way, $251 for a 30-day roundtrip, $281 for a 60-day roundtrip).

GUYANA
There are no direct flights between Venezuela and Guyana. You need to fly via Port of Spain (Trinidad) with BWIA ($257 one-way, $347 for a 30-day roundtrip).

UK

Caracas is the cheapest South American destination from the UK, with prices for discounted flights from London to Caracas starting at around UK£250 one-way and UK£400 roundtrip. Bargain hunters should have little trouble finding even lower prices. Discount air travel is big in London. Advertisements for many travel agencies appear in weekend newspapers, and in *Time Out, Evening Standard* and the free magazine, *TNT*. Recommended ticket agencies:

Flight Centre (☎ 0870-890-8099; www.flightcentre.co.uk)
Journey Latin America (☎ 020-8747-3108; www .journeylatinamerica.co.uk)
STA Travel (☎ 0870-160-0599; www.statravel.co.uk)
Trailfinders (☎ 020-7937-1234; www.trailfinders.co.uk)
Travel Bag (☎ 0870-890-1456; www.travelbag.co.uk)

For online bookings try www.dialaflight.com or www.lastminute.com.

USA
The major US gateway for Venezuela is Miami, from where several carriers, including American Airlines, LanChile and Aeropostal,

fly to Caracas. APEX roundtrip tickets normally costs $400 to $600, but Aeropostal may offer cut-down airfares. Other US cities serving direct flights to Caracas include Atlanta (Delta Airlines), Houston and New York (both Continental Airlines).

Two of the most reputable discount travel agencies in the USA are **STA Travel** (☎ 800-777 0112; www.sta-travel.com) and **Council Travel** (☎ 800-226 8624; www.counciltravel.com). Contact these head offices for the branch nearest you.

The following websites are recommended for online bookings:

- www.cheaptickets.com
- www.exitotravel.com
- www.expedia.com
- www.itn.net
- www.lowestfare.com
- www.orbitz.com
- www.sta.com

LAND
Border Crossings
Venezuela has road connections with Brazil and Colombia only. There is no road link with Guyana; you must go via Brazil.

BRAZIL
Only one road connects Brazil and Venezuela; it leads from Manaus through Boa Vista (Brazil) to Santa Elena de Uairén (Venezuela) and continues to Ciudad Guayana – see Santa Elena de Uairén (p314).

You can also enter Venezuela from Manaus via the Río Negro at San Simón de Cocuy. This is an adventurous river/road route seldom used by travelers – see To/From Brazil (p319).

COLOMBIA
You can enter Venezuela from Colombia at four border crossings. In the northwest is a fairly popular coastal route between Maicao and Maracaibo (see To/From Columbia, p176). Further south is the most popular border crossing, between Cúcuta and San Antonio del Táchira (see To/From Colombia, p211). There is a crossing from Arauca to El Amparo de Apure, but it is inconvenient and dangerous (because of Colombian guerrilla activity) and is rarely used.

Finally, there's an uncommon but interesting outback route from Puerto Carreño in Colombia to Puerto Páez in Venezuela (see To/From Colombia, p319).

Remember to wind your watch forward one hour when crossing from Colombia to Venezuela.

SEA
Weekly passenger boats operate between Güiria in Venezuela and Port of Spain on Trinidad (p271), but there are no longer ferries between Venezuela and Netherlands Antilles.

GETTING AROUND

AIR
Venezuela has a number of airlines and a reasonable network of air routes. Caracas (or, more precisely, Maiquetía, where Caracas' airport is located) is the country's major aviation hub and handles flights to most airports around the country. Cities most frequently serviced from Caracas include Porlamar, Maracaibo and Puerto Ordaz (Ciudad Guayana). The most popular destinations with travelers are Mérida, Ciudad Bolívar, Canaima and Porlamar. See the map (p339) for major domestic air routes.

Flying in Venezuela is still relatively cheap when compared to neighboring Colombia or Brazil, but it's no longer the bargain it used to be. Fares vary between carriers (sometimes substantially), so if the route you're flying is serviced by several airlines, check all fares before buying your ticket. Approximate fares are given in the relevant sections in the book; see the table (p90) for fares on the main routes out of Caracas. The fares listed in this book include the domestic airport tax ($5), which you normally pay when purchasing your ticket.

Some airlines offer discount fares for students and/or senior citizens, but these change frequently and may apply only to Venezuelans; check with the airlines or agencies. Reconfirm your flight at least 72 hours before departure and arm yourself with patience, as not all flights depart on time.

Airlines in Venezuela
Venezuela has half a dozen major commercial airlines servicing main domestic routes, and a dozen minor provincial carriers that cover regional and remote routes on a regular or charter basis. The big cities are served mostly by large modern jets, while light

planes fly to obscure destinations. The airline safety record is appreciably good – you can check www.airsafe.com/index.html for statistical data.

The airline situation changes frequently. Avensa, which a few years ago controlled half of the domestic air market, is now virtually dead. Meanwhile Aeropostal, which was grounded in the mid-1990s, was miraculously resuscitated to become Venezuela's major carrier. The other carriers are relatively young – most no older than five years.

Venezuelan airlines include the following (the listed addresses and phone numbers are for Caracas):

Aereotuy/LTA (Map p68; ☎ 761-6231, 761-6247; www.tuy.com/aereotuy.htm; 5th fl, Edificio Gran Sabana,

Av Abraham Lincoln at Blvd Sabana Grande, Sabana Grande) This tourist carrier has small propeller aircrafts to major tourist destinations such as Los Roques, Porlamar and Canaima. Most flights are sold as packages, but on some routes (eg Los Roques) you can buy an air ticket only.

Aeropostal (Map p70; ☎ 0800-337-8466, 266-1059; www.aeropostal.com; 1st fl, Torre ING Bank, La Castellana) The country's largest airline, with flights to most major domestic destinations, including Barcelona, Barquisimeto, Maracaibo, Maturín, Porlamar, Puerto Ordaz (Ciudad Guayana), San Antonio del Táchira and Valencia.

Aserca (Map p80; ☎ 0800-648-8356, 905-5333; www.asercaairlines.com; Ground fl, Edificio Taeca, Calle Guaicaipuro, El Rosal) Airline operating jet flights between several major airports, including Caracas, Barcelona, Maracaibo, Porlamar and San Antonio del Táchira. Aserca also has international flights to Aruba and Santo Domingo.

ensa (domestic ☎ 355-1609, international ☎ 355-1889; www.avensa.com.ve; Maiquetía airport)
Avior (www.avior.com.ve) Las Mercedes (Map p80; Tamanaco InterContinental Caracas, Av Principal de las Mercedes); Sabana Grande (Map p68; ☎ 238-4622; Lincoln Suites, Av Solano López) Young, progressive carrier flying on fairly new propeller crafts to many airports around the country, including Caracas, Barcelona, Barinas, Barquisimeto, Canaima, Ciudad Bolívar, Coro, Cumaná, Maturín, Mérida, Porlamar and Valera.
LAI (☎ 355-2333, 355-2322; Maiquetía airport)
Laser (☎ 0800-527-3700, 355-2584; www.laser.com.ve; Maiquetía airport) Carrier focusing on a few main cities, including Caracas, Maracaibo and Porlamar.
Rutaca (☎ 576-0304) Small but expanding airline with planes ranging from old Cessnas to new jets, serving Caracas, Canaima, Ciudad Bolívar, Porlamar, San Antonio del Táchira and Santa Elena de Uairén.
Santa Bárbara (Map pp56-7; ☎ 204-4000; www.santabarbaraairlines.com; Edificio Tokay, Calle 3B, Industrial La Urbina) A young but already well-established airline serving Caracas, Cumaná, Las Piedras, Maracaibo, Mérida, Puerto Ayacucho and San Antonio del Táchira.

BICYCLE

Cycling around a country is a cheap, healthy, and above all, fun way of traveling. Unfortunately, Venezuela is not the best place for cyclists. There are almost no bike tracks, bike rentals or any other facilities. Drivers don't show much courtesy to cyclists either. Cycling is not a popular means of transportation among locals, and foreign travelers with their own bikes are a rarity. Mérida is currently one of the few places where mountain biking tours are organized and bikes can be hired (see Tours, p186).

BOAT

Venezuela has many islands off its Caribbean coast, but only Isla de Margarita is serviced by regular boats and ferries; see Caracas (p91), Puerto La Cruz (p250), Cumaná (p259) and Isla de Margarita (p233).

The Río Orinoco is the country's major inland waterway. It's navigable from its mouth up to Puerto Ayacucho, but there's no regular passenger service on any part of it.

BUS & POR PUESTO

As there is no passenger train service in Venezuela, most traveling is done by bus. Buses are generally fast, and they run regularly day and night between major population centers. Bus transportation is reasonably cheap in Venezuela; you probably won't go wrong if you allow $1.50 to $2 per hour (or roughly 60km) on a bus.

Venezuela's dozens of bus companies own buses ranging from archaic pieces of junk to the most recent models. All major companies offer *servicio ejecutivo* in comfortable air-conditioned buses, which now cover virtually all the major long-distance routes and are the dominant means of intercity transportation. Still better is the so-called *bus-cama*, the most recent achievement of bus technology, where seats can be reclined almost into beds. These buses are the most comfy means of transport – they have air-conditioning, television and often a toilet. Note that the air-con is often very efficient, so have plenty of warm clothing at hand to avoid freezing.

If various companies operate the same route, fares are much the same though some may offer discounts. Figures given in the regional sections of this book are approximate minimum-to-maximum fares you are likely to pay on a given route.

All intercity buses depart from and arrive at the *terminal de pasajeros* (bus terminal). Every city has such a terminal, usually outside the city center, but always linked to it by local transport. Caracas is the most important transport hub, handling buses to just about every corner of the country. In general, there's no need to buy tickets in advance for major routes, except around Christmas, Carnaval and Easter.

Many short-distance regional routes are served by por puesto (literally 'by the seat'), a cross between a bus and a taxi. Por puestos are usually large US-made cars (less often minibuses) of the '60s and '70s vintages that ply fixed routes and depart when all seats are filled. They cost about 40% to 80% more than buses, but they're faster and usually more comfortable. On some routes, they are the dominant or even the exclusive means of transport. Depending on the region and kind of vehicle, por puestos may also be called *carros* or *carritos*.

CAR & MOTORCYCLE

Traveling by car is a comfortable and attractive way of getting around Venezuela. The country is reasonably safe, and the network of roads is extensive and usually in acceptable shape. Gas stations are numerous and fuel is just about the cheapest in the world – $0.03 to $0.06 per liter, depending on the octane level. You can fill up your tank for a dollar!

This rosy picture is slightly obscured by Venezuelan traffic and local driving manners. Traffic in Venezuela, especially in Caracas, is wild, chaotic, noisy, polluting and anarchic.

Bringing a car to Venezuela (or to South America in general) is expensive, time-consuming and involves plenty of paperwork, and few people do it. It's much more convenient and cheaper to rent a car locally.

Hire

A number of international and local car rental companies, including Hertz, Avis and Budget, operate in Venezuela. They have offices at major airports and in city centers, often in top end hotels. See individual destinations for details. As a rough guide, a small car will cost $40 to $60 per day, with discount rates applying for a full week or longer. A 4WD vehicle is considerably more expensive and difficult to obtain.

Rental agencies require a credit card and driver's license (your home-country license is valid in Venezuela). You need to be at least 21 years of age to rent a car, although renting some cars (particularly 4WDs and luxury models) may require you to be at least 23 or 25 years. Some companies also have a maximum age of about 65 years.

Read the rental contract carefully before signing (most contracts are in Spanish only). Pay close attention to any theft clause, as it will probably load any loss onto the renter. Look at the car carefully, and insist on listing any defects (including scratches) on the rental form. Check the spare tire, and take note of whether there is a jack.

This said, it's a good idea to contact the international rental companies at home before your trip and check what they can offer in Venezuela. It's likely to be more convenient and cheaper to book at home rather than in Venezuela, and you can be pretty sure that the car will be waiting for you upon arrival.

Road Rules

Watching Venezuela's crazy traffic, reminiscent of Formula One racing, you'd never suspect that there are speed limits, but they do legally exist. Unless traffic signs say otherwise, the maximum speed limit in urban areas is 40km/h, and outside built-up areas it's 80km/h. Officially, traffic coming from the right has priority, unless indicated otherwise by signs. In practice, however, it seems that right-of-way depends on the size of vehicle rather than the regulations.

Cars must be equipped with seat belts for front seats (which always have to be used), and they must have a spare tire, wheel block, jack and a special reflector triangle, which in case of accident or breakdown has to be placed 50m behind the car. Motorcyclists have to wear a crash helmet, and motorcycles cannot be ridden at night. However, once again, all this is theoretical.

HITCHING

Hitchhiking is never entirely safe in any country and is not recommended. Travelers who decide to hitchhike should understand that they are taking a small, but potentially serious risk. People who do choose to hitchhike will be safer if they travel in pairs and let someone know where they are planning to go. Women traveling on their own should not hitchhike at all.

Safety apart, Venezuela is not good for hitchhiking. Although many people have cars, they are reluctant to stop to pick up strangers. As bus transportation is fast, efficient and relatively cheap, it's probably not worth wasting time hitchhiking.

LOCAL TRANSPORT
Bus & Metro

All cities and many major towns have their own urban transportation systems, which in most places are small buses or minibuses. Depending on the region, these are called busetas, *carros*, carritos, *micros* or *camionetas*, and fares are usually no more than $0.20. In many larger cities you can also find urban por puestos, swinging faster than buses through the chaotic traffic. Caracas is the only city in Venezuela with a subway system.

Taxi

Taxis are inexpensive and worth considering, particularly for transport between the bus terminal and city center when you are carrying luggage. Taxis don't have meters, so always fix the fare with the driver before boarding the cab. It's a good idea to find out the correct fare from a terminal official or a hotel reception desk beforehand.

TRANSPORTATION

Health Dr David Goldberg

CONTENTS

Prevention is the key to staying healthy while abroad. Travelers who receive the recommended vaccines and follow common-sense precautions usually come away with nothing more than a little diarrhea.

BEFORE YOU GO

Most vaccines don't produce immunity until at least two weeks after they're given, so visit a physician four to eight weeks before departure. Ask your doctor for an International Certificate of Vaccination (otherwise known as the yellow booklet), which will list all the vaccinations you've received. This is mandatory for countries that require proof of yellow fever vaccination upon entry, but it's a good idea to carry it wherever you travel.

INSURANCE

If your health insurance does not cover you for medical expenses abroad, consider supplemental insurance. Check the Subwwway section of the **Lonely Planet website** (www.lonelyplanet.com/subwwway) for more information. Find out in advance if your insurance plan will make payments directly to providers or reimburse you later for overseas health expenditures.

MEDICAL CHECKLIST

- acetaminophen/paracetamol (Tylenol) or aspirin
- adhesive or paper tape
- antibacterial ointment (eg Bactroban) for cuts and abrasions
- antibiotics
- antidiarrheal drugs (eg loperamide)
- antihistamines (for hay fever and allergic reactions)
- anti-inflammatory drugs (eg ibuprofen)
- bandages, gauze, gauze rolls
- DEET-containing insect repellent for the skin
- iodine tablets (for water purification)
- oral rehydration salts
- permethrin-containing insect spray for clothing, tents and bed nets
- pocket knife
- scissors, safety pins, tweezers
- steroid cream or cortisone (for poison ivy and other allergic rashes)
- sunblock
- syringes and sterile needles
- thermometer

INTERNET RESOURCES

There is a wealth of travel health advice on the Internet. For further information, the **Lonely Planet website** (www.lonelyplanet.com /subwwway) is a good place to start. A superb book called *International Travel and Health*, revised annually and available online at no cost, is published by the **World Health Organization** (www.who.int/ith/). Another website of general interest is **MD Travel Health** (www.mdtravelhealth.com), which provides complete travel health recommendations for every country, updated daily, also at no cost.

It's usually a good idea to consult your government's travel health website before departure, if one is available.

Australia (www.dfat.gov.au/travel/)
Canada (www.hc-sc.gc.ca/pphb-dgspsp/tmp-pmv/pub _e.html)
United Kingdom (www.doh.gov.uk/traveladvice /index.htm)
United States (www.cdc.gov/travel/)

FURTHER READING

For further information, see *Healthy Travel Central & South America*, published by Lonely Planet. If you're traveling with children, Lonely Planet's *Travel with Children* may also be useful. The *ABC of Healthy Travel*, by E. Walker et al, and *Medicine for the Outdoors*, by Paul S Auerbach, are other valuable resources.

IN TRANSIT

DEEP VEIN THROMBOSIS (DVT)

Blood clots may form in the legs during plane flights, chiefly because of prolonged immobility. The longer the flight, the greater the risk. Though most blood clots are reabsorbed uneventfully, some may break off and travel through the blood vessels to the lungs, where they could cause life-threatening complications.

The chief symptom of DVTs is swelling or pain of the foot, ankle or calf, usually but not always on just one side. When a blood clot travels to the lungs, it may cause chest pain and difficulty breathing. Travelers with any of these symptoms should immediately seek medical attention.

To prevent the development of DVT on long flights you should walk about the cabin, perform isometric compressions of

RECOMMENDED VACCINATIONS

There are no required vaccines for Venezuela, but a number are recommended. Note that some of these are not approved for use by children or pregnant women – check with your physician.

Vaccine	Recommended for	Dosage	Side effects
chickenpox	travelers who've never had chickenpox	2 doses 1 month apart	fever; mild case of chickenpox
hepatitis A	all travelers	1 dose before trip; booster 6-12 months later	soreness at injection site; headaches; body aches
hepatitis B	long-term travelers in close contact with the local population	3 doses over 6 months	soreness at injection site; low-grade fever
measles	travelers who have never had measles or completed a vaccination course	1 dose	fever; rash; joint pain; allergic reactions
rabies	travelers who may have contact with animals and may not have access to medical care	3 doses over 3-4 weeks	soreness at injection site; headaches; body aches
tetanus-diphtheria	all travelers who haven't had booster within 10 years	1 dose lasts 10 years	soreness at injection site
typhoid	all travelers	4 capsules orally, 1 taken every other day	abdominal pain; nausea; rash
yellow fever	travelers to all areas, but especially rural areas of the following states: Apure, Amazonas, Barinas, Bolívar, Sucre, Táchira, Delta Amacuro, Angel Falls	1 dose lasts 10 years	headaches; body aches; severe reactions are rare

Bring medications in their original containers, clearly labeled. A signed, dated letter from your physician describing all medical conditions and medications, including generic names, is also a good idea. If carrying syringes or needles, be sure to have a physician's letter documenting their medical necessity.

HEALTH

the leg muscles (ie contract the leg muscles while sitting), drink plenty of fluids, and avoid alcohol and tobacco.

JET LAG & MOTION SICKNESS

Jet lag is common when crossing more than five time zones, and can result in insomnia, fatigue, malaise or nausea. To avoid jet lag try drinking plenty of fluids (non-alcoholic) and eating light meals. Upon arrival, get exposure to natural sunlight and readjust your schedule (for meals, sleep etc) as soon as possible.

Antihistamines such as dimenhydrinate (Dramamine) and meclizine (Antivert or Bonine) are usually the first choice for treating motion sickness. Their main side effect is drowsiness. A herbal alternative is ginger, which works like a charm for some people.

IN VENEZUELA

AVAILABILITY & COST OF HEALTH CARE

Good medical care is available in Caracas, but may be difficult to find in rural areas. Public hospitals are free, but the quality of medical care is better in private facilities. For an online list of physicians, dentists, and other health care providers, most of whom speak English, go to the **US embassy web-site** (http://embajadausa.org.ve/wwwh005.html). Many doctors and hospitals expect payment in cash, regardless of whether you have travel health insurance.

For an ambulance in Venezuela, call ☎ 171. If you develop a life-threatening medical problem, you'll probably want to be evacuated to a country with state-of-the-art medical care. Since this may cost tens of thousands of dollars, be sure you have insurance to cover this before you depart. You can find a list of medical evacuation and travel insurance companies on the **US state department website** (www.travel.state.gov/medical.html).

Venezuelan *farmacias* (pharmacies) are identifiable by a red light in the store window. The quality and availability of medication is comparable to that in most other countries. The pharmacies keep a rotating schedule of 24-hour availability, so that different pharmacies are open on different nights. To find a late-night pharmacy,

you can either look in the local newspaper under 'turnos,' call ☎ 800-88766 (that is, 800-TURNO), check the list posted on most pharmacy doors or search for a pharmacy with its red light still on.

INFECTIOUS DISEASES
Brucellosis

This is an infection of domestic and wild animals that may be transmitted to humans through direct animal contact or by consumption of unpasteurized dairy products from infected animals. In Venezuela, most human cases are related to infected cattle. Symptoms may include fever, malaise, depression, loss of appetite, headache, muscle ache and back pain. Complications may include arthritis, hepatitis, meningitis and endocarditis (heart-valve infection).

Cholera

Cholera is an intestinal infection acquired through ingestion of contaminated food or water. The main symptom is profuse, watery diarrhea, which may be so severe that it causes life-threatening dehydration. The key treatment is drinking an oral rehydration solution. Antibiotics are also given, usually tetracycline or doxycycline, though quinolone antibiotics such as ciprofloxacin and levofloxacin are also effective.

Cholera sometimes occurs in Venezuela, but it's rare among travelers. Cholera vaccine is no longer required, and is in fact no longer available in some countries, including the United States, because the old vaccine was relatively ineffective and caused side effects. There are new vaccines that are safer and more effective, but they're not available in many countries and are only recommended for those at particularly high risk.

Dengue Fever (Breakbone Fever)

Dengue fever is a viral infection found throughout South America. In Venezuela, large numbers of cases are reported each year, especially from the states of Barinas, Amazonas, Aragua, Mérida, Táchira and Lara, and the Caracas district. Dengue is transmitted by aedes mosquitoes, which bite preferentially during the daytime and are usually found close to human habitations, often indoors. They breed primarily in artificial water containers, such as jars, barrels, cans, cisterns, metal drums, plastic containers and discarded tires. As a result, dengue is especially common in densely populated, urban environments.

Dengue usually causes flu-like symptoms, including fever, muscle ache, joint pain, headache, nausea and vomiting, often followed by a rash. The body aches may be quite uncomfortable, but most cases resolve uneventfully in a few days. Severe cases usually occur in children under the age of 15 who are experiencing their second dengue infection.

There is no treatment as yet for dengue fever, except to take analgesics such as acetaminophen/paracetamol (Tylenol) and drink plenty of fluids. Severe cases may require hospitalization for intravenous fluids and supportive care. There is no vaccine. The cornerstone of prevention is protecting against insect bites, as described on p348.

Hepatitis A

Hepatitis A is the second most common travel-related infection (after travelers' diarrhea). It's a viral infection of the liver that is usually acquired by ingestion of contaminated water, food or ice, though it may also be acquired by direct contact with infected persons. The illness occurs throughout the world, but the incidence is higher in developing nations. Symptoms may include fever, malaise, jaundice, nausea, vomiting and abdominal pain. Most cases resolve without complications, though hepatitis A occasionally causes severe liver damage. There is no treatment.

The vaccine for hepatitis A is extremely safe and highly effective. If you get a booster six to 12 months later, it lasts for at least 10 years. You really should get it before you go to Venezuela or any other developing nation. Because the safety of hepatitis A vaccine has not been established for pregnant women or children under the age of two, they should instead be given a gamma-globulin injection.

Hepatitis B

Like hepatitis A, hepatitis B is a liver infection that occurs worldwide, but is more common in developing nations. Unlike hepatitis A, the disease is usually acquired by sexual contact or by exposure to infected blood, generally through blood transfusions or contaminated needles. The vaccine is recommended only for long-term travelers (on the road more than six months) who expect to live in rural areas or have close physical contact with the local population. Additionally, the vaccine is recommended for anyone who anticipates sexual contact with the local inhabitants or a possible need for medical, dental or other treatments while abroad, especially if a need for transfusions or injections is expected.

Hepatitis B vaccine is safe and highly effective. A total of three injections however, are necessary to establish full immunity. Several countries added hepatitis B vaccine to the list of routine childhood immunizations in the 1980s, so many young adults are already protected.

HIV/AIDS

This has been reported in all South American countries. Be sure to use condoms for all sexual encounters.

Leishmaniasis

This disease occurs in the mountains and jungles of all South American countries except Chile, Uruguay and the Falkland Islands. In Venezuela it is widespread in rural areas, especially the west-central part of the country. The infection is transmitted by sand flies, which are about one-third the size of mosquitoes. Leishmaniasis may be particularly severe in those with HIV. There is no vaccine. To protect yourself from sand flies, follow the same precautions as for mosquitoes (p348), except that netting must be finer mesh (at least 18 holes to the linear inch).

Malaria

Malaria occurs in every South American country except Chile, Uruguay and the Falkland Islands. It's transmitted by mosquito bites, usually between dusk and dawn. The main symptom is high spiking fevers, which may be accompanied by chills, sweats, headache, body aches, weakness, vomiting or diarrhea. Severe cases may involve the central nervous system and lead to seizures, confusion, coma and death.

Taking malaria pills is strongly recommended for those visiting Angel Falls and for rural areas in the states of Apure, Amazonas, Barinas, Bolívar, Delta Amacuro, Sucre, Táchira and Zulia. In general, the risk of malaria is greatest between February and August, especially after the onset of the rainy season in late May.

There is a choice of three malaria pills, all of which work equally well. Mefloquine (Lariam) is taken once weekly in a dosage of 250mg, starting one to two weeks before arriving in Venezuela and continuing until four weeks after departure. A certain percentage of people (the number is controversial) develop neuropsychiatric side effects, which may range from mild to severe. Atovaquone/proguanil (Malarone) is a newly approved combination pill; it's taken once daily with food, starting two days before arrival and continuing until seven days after departure. Side effects are typically mild. Doxycycline is a third alternative, but may cause an exaggerated sunburn reaction.

In general, Malarone seems to cause fewer side effects than Lariam and is becoming more popular. The chief disadvantage is that it has to be taken daily. For longer trips, it's probably worth trying Lariam; for shorter trips, Malarone will be the drug of choice for most people.

Protecting yourself against mosquito bites (see the recommendations p348), is just as important as taking malaria pills since none of the pills are 100% effective.

Since you may not have access to medical care while traveling, you should bring along additional pills for emergency self-treatment; take these if you can't reach a doctor and you develop symptoms that suggest malaria, such as high spiking fevers. One self-treatment option is to take four tablets of Malarone once daily for three days. However, Malarone should not be used for treatment if you're already taking it for prevention. An alternative is to take 650mg quinine three times daily and 100mg doxycycline twice daily for one week. If you start self-medication, see a doctor at the earliest possible opportunity.

If you develop a fever after returning home, see a physician, as malaria symptoms may not occur for months.

Measles

A large measles outbreak recently occurred in Venezuela, related to the inadequate vaccination of many children. All travelers should be sure they have had either two measles vaccinations or a blood test proving they're immune. Although measles immunization usually doesn't begin until the age of 12 months, children between six and 11 months should probably receive an initial dose of measles vaccine before traveling to Venezuela.

Rabies

Rabies is a viral infection of the brain and spinal cord that is almost always fatal. The rabies virus is carried in the saliva of infected animals and is typically transmitted through an animal bite, though contamination of any break in the skin with infected saliva may result in rabies. Rabies occurs in all South American countries. In Venezuela, most cases are related to dog bites.

Rabies vaccine is safe, but a full series requires three injections and is quite expensive. Those at high risk for rabies, such as animal handlers and spelunkers (cave explorers), should certainly get the vaccine. In addition, those at lower risk for animal bites should consider asking for the vaccine if they might be traveling to remote areas and might not have access to appropriate medical care if needed. The treatment for a possibly rabid bite consists of rabies vaccine with rabies immune globulin. It's effective, but must be given promptly. Most travelers don't need rabies vaccine.

All animal bites and scratches must be promptly and thoroughly cleansed with large amounts of soap and water, and local health authorities contacted to determine whether or not further treatment is necessary.

Schistosomiasis

This parasitic infection is acquired by exposure to contaminated fresh water, and is reported from isolated spots in the north-central part of the country, including the areas around Caracas (but not Caracas) and the states of Aragua, Carabobo, Guárico and Miranda. When traveling in these areas, you should avoid swimming, wading, bathing or washing in bodies of fresh water, including lakes, ponds, streams and rivers. Salt water and chlorinated pools carry no risk of schistosomiasis.

Tick-borne Relapsing Fever

This fever, which may be transmitted by either ticks or lice, is caused by bacteria that is closely related to those that cause Lyme disease and syphilis. The illness is characterized by periods of fever, chills, headache, body aches, muscle aches and coughs, alternating with periods when the fever subsides and the person feels relatively well. To minimize the risk of relapsing fever, follow tick precautions as outlined on p348 and practice good personal hygiene at all times.

Typhoid Fever

Typhoid is caused by ingestion of food or water contaminated by a species of salmonella known as *Salmonella typhi*. Fever occurs in virtually all cases. Other symptoms may include headache, malaise, muscle aches, dizziness, loss of appetite, nausea and abdominal pain. Either diarrhea or constipation may occur. Possible complications include intestinal perforation, intestinal bleeding, confusion, delirium or (rarely) coma.

Unless you expect to take all your meals in major hotels and restaurants, typhoid vaccine is a good idea. It's usually given orally, but is also available as an injection. Neither vaccine is approved for use in children under the age of two.

The drug of choice for typhoid fever is usually a quinolone antibiotic such as ciprofloxacin (Cipro) or levofloxacin (Levaquin), which many travelers carry for treatment of traveler's diarrhea. However, if you self-treat for typhoid fever, you may also need to self-treat for malaria, since the symptoms of the two diseases may be indistinguishable.

Venezuelan Equine Encephalitis

This viral infection, transmitted by mosquitoes, reached epidemic levels in 1995 after unusually heavy rainfalls, especially in the northwestern states of Zulia, Lara, Falcón, Yaracuy, Carabobo and Trujillo. The greatest incidence was reported among the Warao population. Cases still occur, but in smaller numbers, chiefly in the west between the Península de la Guajira and the Río Catatumbo. This illness comes on suddenly and symptoms are malaise, fevers, rigors , severe headache, photophobia and myalgias. Possible complications can include convulsions, coma, and paralysis.

Yellow Fever

Yellow fever is a life-threatening viral infection transmitted by mosquitoes in forested areas. The illness begins with flu-like symptoms, which may include fever, chills, headache, muscle aches, backache, loss of appetite, nausea and vomiting. These symptoms usually subside in a few days, but one person in six enters a second, toxic phase characterized by recurrent fever, vomiting, listlessness, jaundice, kidney failure and hemorrhage, leading to death in up to half of the cases. There is no treatment except for supportive care.

Given recent yellow fever outbreaks in Venezuela, the yellow fever vaccine is strongly recommended for all travelers (except pregnant women), especially anyone traveling beyond Caracas and the northern coast.

Yellow fever vaccine is given only in approved yellow fever vaccination centers, which provide validated International Certificates of Vaccination (yellow booklets). The vaccine should be given at least 10 days before any potential exposure to yellow fever, and remains effective for approximately 10 years. Reactions to the vaccine are generally mild and may include headache, muscle ache, low-grade fevers or discomfort at the injection site. Severe, life-threatening reactions have been described, but are extremely rare. In general, the risk of becoming ill from the vaccine is far less than the risk of becoming ill from yellow fever, and you're strongly encouraged to get the vaccine.

Taking measures to protect yourself from mosquito bites (p348) is an essential part of preventing yellow fever.

TRAVELER'S DIARRHEA

To prevent diarrhea, avoid tap water unless it has been boiled, filtered or chemically disinfected (iodine tablets); only eat fresh fruit or vegetables if cooked or peeled; be wary of dairy products that might contain unpasteurized milk; and be highly selective when eating food from street vendors.

If you develop diarrhea, be sure to drink plenty of fluids, preferably an oral rehydration solution containing lots of salt and sugar. A few loose stools don't require treatment but, if you start having more than four or five stools a day, you should start taking an antibiotic (usually a quinolone drug) and an antidiarrheal agent (such as loperamide). If diarrhea is bloody or persists for more than 72 hours or is accompanied by fever, shaking chills or severe abdominal pain, you should seek medical attention.

ENVIRONMENTAL HAZARDS
Altitude Sickness

Altitude sickness may develop in those who ascend rapidly to altitudes greater than 2500m. Being physically fit offers no protection. Those who have experienced altitude sickness in the past are prone to future episodes. The risk increases with faster ascents, higher altitudes and greater exertion. Symptoms may include headaches, nausea, vomiting, dizziness, malaise, insomnia and loss of appetite. Severe cases may be complicated by fluid in the lungs (high-altitude pulmonary edema) or swelling of the brain (high-altitude cerebral edema).

The best treatment for altitude sickness is descent. If you are exhibiting symptoms, do not ascend. If symptoms are severe or persistent, descent immediately.

One option for the prevention of altitude sickness is to take acetazolamide (Diamox). The recommended dosage ranges from 125mg (twice daily) to 250mg (three times daily). It should be taken 24 hours before ascent and continued for 48 hours after arrival at altitude. Possible side effects include increased urinary volume, numbness, tingling, nausea, drowsiness, myopia and temporary impotence. Acetazolamide should not be given to pregnant women or anyone with a history of sulfa allergy. For those who cannot tolerate acetazolamide, the next best option is 4mg of dexamethasone taken four times daily. Unlike acetazolamide, dexamethasone must be tapered gradually upon arrival at altitude, since there is a risk that altitude sickness will occur as the dosage is reduced. Dexamethasone is a steroid, so it should not be given to diabetics or anyone for whom steroids are contraindicated. A natural alternative is gingko, which some people find quite helpful.

When traveling to high altitudes, it's also important to avoid overexertion, eat light meals and abstain from alcohol.

If your symptoms are more than mild or don't resolve promptly, see a doctor. Altitude sickness should be taken seriously; it can be life threatening when severe.

Insect Bites
MOSQUITOES

To prevent mosquito bites, wear long sleeves, long pants, hats and shoes (rather than sandals). Bring along a good insect repellent, preferably one containing DEET, which should be applied to exposed skin and clothing, but not to eyes, mouth, cuts, wounds or irritated skin. Products containing lower concentrations of DEET are as effective, but for shorter periods of time. In general, adults and children over 12 years of age should use preparations containing 25% to 35% DEET, which usually lasts about six hours. Children between two and 12 years of age should use preparations containing no more than 10% DEET, applied sparingly, which will usually last about three hours. Neurological toxicity has been reported from using DEET, especially in children, but appears to be extremely uncommon and generally related to overuse. DEET-containing compounds should not be used on children under the age of two.

Insect repellents containing certain botanical products, including oil of eucalyptus and soybean oil, are effective but last only 1½ to two hours. DEET-containing repellents are preferable for areas where there is a high risk of malaria or yellow fever. Citronella-based products are not effective.

For additional protection, you can apply permethrin to clothing, shoes, tents and bed nets. Permethrin treatments are safe and remain effective for at least two weeks, even when items are laundered. Permethrin should not be applied directly to skin.

Don't sleep with the window open unless there is a screen. If sleeping outdoors or in accommodations that allow entry of mosquitoes, use a bed net, preferably treated with permethrin, with edges tucked in under the mattress. The mesh size should be less than 1.5mm. If the sleeping area is not otherwise protected, use a mosquito coil, which will fill the room with insecticide through the night. Repellent-impregnated wristbands are not effective.

TICKS

To protect yourself from tick bites, follow the same precautions as for mosquitoes, except that boots are preferable to shoes, with pants tucked in. Be sure to perform a thorough tick check at the end of each day.

You'll generally need the assistance of a friend or mirror for a full examination. Ticks should be removed with tweezers, grasping them firmly by the head. Insect repellents based on botanical products (described under Mosquitoes p348) have not been adequately studied for insects other than mosquitoes and cannot be recommended to prevent tick bites.

Snake Bites

Snakes and leeches are a hazard in some areas of South America. In the event of a venomous snake bite, place the victim at rest, keep the bitten area immobilized, and move the victim immediately to the nearest medical facility. Avoid tourniquets, which are no longer recommended.

Sun

To protect yourself from excessive sun exposure, you should stay out of the midday sun, wear sunglasses and a wide-brimmed sun hat, and apply sunblock with SPF 15 or higher, with both UVA and UVB protection. Sunblock should be generously applied to all exposed parts of the body approximately 30 minutes before sun exposure, and should be reapplied after swimming or vigorous activity. Travelers should also drink plenty of fluids and avoid strenuous exercise when the temperature is high.

Water

Tap water in Venezuela is not safe to drink – buying bottled water is your best bet. If you have the means, vigorous boiling for one minute is the most effective means of water purification. At altitudes greater than 2000m, boil for three minutes. Another option is to disinfect water with iodine pills; add 2% tincture of iodine to 1L of water (five drops to clear water, 10 drops to cloudy water) and let stand for 30 minutes. If the water is cold, longer times may be required.

TRAVELING WITH CHILDREN

Children under nine months should not be taken to areas where yellow fever occurs,

---

TRADITIONAL MEDICINE

The following are some traditional remedies for common travel-related conditions.

Problem	Treatment
altitude sickness	gingko
jet lag	melatonin
motion sickness	ginger
mosquito bite prevention	oil of eucalyptus or soybean

---

since the vaccine is not safe for this age group. Although measles immunisation doesn't begin until the age of 12 months, children between the ages six and 11 months should probably receive an initial dose of measles vaccine before traveling to Venezuela.

When traveling with young children, be particularly careful about what you allow them to eat and drink, because diarrhea can be especially dangerous in this age group and because the vaccines for hepatitis A and typhoid fever are not approved for use in children under the age of two.

The two main malaria medications, Lariam and Malarone, may be given to children, but insect repellents must be applied in lower concentrations.

WOMEN'S HEALTH

There are English-speaking obstetricians in Venezuela, listed on the **US embassy website** (http://embajadausa.org.ve/wwwh005.html). However, medical facilities will probably not compare favorably to those in your home country. It's safer to avoid travel to Venezuela late in pregnancy, so that you don't have to deliver here. Yellow fever vaccine should not be given during pregnancy because the vaccine contains a live virus that may infect the fetus.

Also it isn't advisable for pregnant women to spend time at altitudes where the air is thin. If you need to take malaria pills, mefloquine (Lariam) is the safest during pregnancy.

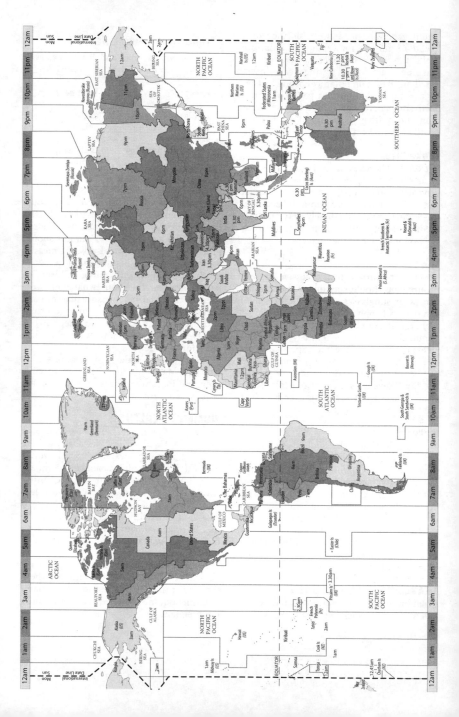

Language

CONTENTS

Spanish is Venezuela's official language, and except for some remote Indian groups, all of the population speaks it. There are over 25 Indian languages spoken in the country as well.

English-speakers can be found in large urban centers, but it's certainly not a commonly understood or spoken language, even though it's taught as a mandatory second language in the public school system.

Spanish is quite an easy language to learn and a language course taken before departure can considerably enhance your stay in Venezuela. Language courses are also available once you're there; Mérida (p186), and Caracas (p74) have the most options, but Pamapatar (p240) on Isla de Margarita has some facilities too. Even if classes are impractical, you should make the effort to learn a few basic phrases and pleasantries. Don't hesitate to practice your new skills – in general, Latin Americans meet attempts to communicate in their language, however halting, with enthusiasm and appreciation.

Lonely Planet's *Latin American Spanish Phrasebook* is a worthwhile addition to your backpack. Another useful resource is the *University of Chicago Spanish-English, English-Spanish Dictionary* – its small size, light weight and thorough entries make it ideal for travel. It also makes a great gift for any new friends upon your departure.

SPANISH IN VENEZUELA

Throughout Latin America, the Spanish language is referred to as *castellano* more often than *español*. Probably the most notable difference between the sound of Latin American Spanish and the principal language of Spain is that the letters **c** and **z** are never lisped; attempts to do so could well provoke amusement or even scorn.

Venezuelan Spanish is not the clearest or easiest to understand. Venezuelans (except those from the Andes) speak more rapidly than most other South Americans and tend to drop some endings, especially plurals.

The use of the forms *tú* (informal 'you') and *usted* (polite 'you') is very flexible in Venezuela. Both are used, but with regional variations. Either is OK, though it's best to answer using the same form in which you are addressed. Always use the *usted* form when talking to the police and the Guardia Nacional.

Greetings in Venezuela are more elaborate than in Spain. The short Spanish *hola* has given way to a number of expressions, which are exchanged at the beginning of a conversation. Listen to how the locals greet you and learn some of their local idiom.

Although Venezuelans don't seem to be devoutly religious, the expressions *si Dios quiere* (God willing) and *gracias a Dios* (thanks to God) are frequently heard in conversation.

PRONUNCIATION

Spanish spelling is phonetically consistent, meaning that there's a clear and consistent relationship between what you see in writing and how it's pronounced.

Vowels

a	as in 'father'
e	as in 'met'
i	as in 'marine'
o	as in 'or' (without the 'r' sound)
u	as in 'rule;' the 'u' is not pronounced after **q** and in the letter combinations **gue** and **gui**, unless it's marked with a diaeresis (eg *argüir*), in which case it's pronounced as English 'w'

y at the end of a word or when it stands alone, it's pronounced as the Spanish **i** (eg *ley*); between vowels within a word it's as the 'y' in 'yonder'

Consonants

As a rule, Spanish consonants resemble their English counterparts. The exceptions are listed below. Note that while the consonants **ch**, **ll** and **ñ** are generally considered distinct letters, **ch** and **ll** are now often listed alphabetically under **c** and **l** respectively. The letter **ñ** is still treated as a separate letter and comes after **n** in dictionaries.

b	similar to English 'b,' but softer; referred to as 'b larga'
c	as in 'celery' before **e** and **i**; otherwise as English 'k'
ch	as in 'church'
d	as in 'dog,' but between vowels and after **l** or **n**, the sound is closer to the 'th' in 'this'
g	as the 'ch' in the Scottish *loch* before **e** and **i** ('kh' in our guides to pronunciation); elsewhere, as in 'go'
h	invariably silent. If your name begins with this letter, listen carefully if you're waiting for public officials to call you.
j	as the 'ch' in the Scottish *loch* (written as 'kh' in our guides to pronunciation)
ll	as the 'y' in 'yellow'
ñ	as the 'ni' in 'onion'
r	a short **r** except at the beginning of a word, and after **l**, **n** or **s**, when it's often rolled
rr	very strongly rolled
v	similar to English 'b,' but softer; referred to as 'b corta'
x	as in 'taxi' except for a very few words, when it's pronounced as **j**
z	as the 's' in 'sun'

Semiconsonant

The Spanish **y** is a semiconsonant; it's pronounced as the Spanish **i** when it stands alone or appears at the end of a word. Normally, **y** is pronounced like the 'y' in 'yesterday'; however, in some regions it may be pronounced as the 's' in 'pleasure' or even the 'j' in 'jacket.' Hence, *yo me llamo* can sound like 'joe meh jahm-oh.'

Word Stress

In general, words ending in vowels or the letters **n** or **s** have stress on the next-to-last syllable, while those with other endings have stress on the last syllable.

Written accents denote stress, and override the rules above, eg *sótano* (basement), *América* and *porción* (portion).

GENDER & PLURALS

In Spanish, nouns are either masculine or feminine, and there are rules to help determine gender – with exceptions, of course! Feminine nouns generally end with -a or with the groups -ción, -sión or -dad. Other endings typically signify a masculine noun. Endings for adjectives also change to agree with the gender of the noun they modify (masculine/feminine -o/-a). Where both masculine and feminine forms are included in this language guide, they are separated by a slash, with the masculine form first, eg *perdido/a*.

If a noun or adjective ends in a vowel, the plural is formed by adding **s** to the end. If it ends in a consonant, the plural is formed by adding **es** to the end.

ACCOMMODATIONS

I'm looking for ...	*Estoy buscando ...*	e·stoy boos·kan·do ...
Where is ...?	*¿Dónde hay ...?*	don·de ai ...
a hotel	*un hotel*	oon o·tel
a guesthouse	*una pensión/ casa de huéspedes*	oo·na pen·syon/ ka·sa de we·spe·des
a camping ground	*un terreno de cámping*	oon te·re·no de kam·peen
a youth hostel	*un albergue juvenil*	oon al·ber·ge khoo·ve·neel
I'd like a ... room.	*Quisiera una habitación ...*	kee·sye·ra oo·na a·bee·ta·syon ...
single	*sencilla*	sen·see·la
double	*doble*	do·ble
twin	*con dos camas*	kon dos ka·mas
How much is it per ...?	*¿Cuánto cuesta por ...?*	kwan·to kwes·ta por ...
night	*noche*	no·che
person	*persona*	per·so·na
week	*semana*	se·ma·na

Does it include breakfast?

¿Incluye el desayuno?   een·kloo·ye el de·sa·yoo·no

May I see the room?
¿Puedo ver la — pwe-do ver la
habitación? — a-bee-ta-*syon*
I don't like it.
No me gusta. — no me *goos*-ta
It's fine. I'll take it.
OK. La alquilo. — o-*kay* la al-*kee*-lo
I'm leaving now.
Me voy ahora. — me *voy* a-o-ra

private/shared	*baño privado/*	*ba*-nyo pree-*va*-do/
bathroom	*compartido*	kom-par-*tee*-do
full board	*pensión completa*	pen-*syo*-ne kom-*ple*-ta
too expensive	*demasiado caro*	de-ma-*sya*-do *ka*-ro
cheaper	*más barato/*	mas ba-*ra*-to/
	económico	e-ko-*no*-mee-ko
discount	*descuento*	des-*kwen*-to

MAKING A RESERVATION

(for phone or written requests)

To ...	*A ...*
From ...	*De ...*
Date	*Fecha*
I'd like to book ...	*Quisiera reservar ...* (see 'Accommodations' on p352 for bed and room options)
in the name of ...	*en nombre de ...*
for the nights of ...	*para las noches del ...*
credit card ...	*tarjeta de crédito ...*
number	*número*
expiry date	*fecha de vencimiento*
Please confirm ...	*Puede confirmar ...*
availability	*la disponibilidad*
price	*el precio*

CONVERSATION & ESSENTIALS

In their public behavior, South Americans are very conscious of civilities, sometimes to the point of ceremoniousness. Never approach a stranger for information without extending a greeting and use only the polite form of address, especially with the police and public officials. Young people may be less likely to expect this, but it's best to stick to the polite form unless you're quite sure you won't offend by using the informal mode. The polite form is used in all cases in this guide; where options are given, the form is indicated by the abbreviations 'pol' and 'inf.'

Hello. — *Hola.* — o-la
Good morning. — *Buenos días.* — bwe-nos dee-as
Good afternoon. — *Buenas tardes.* — bwe-nas tar-des
Good evening/ — *Buenas noches.* — bwe-nas no-ches
night.
Goodbye. — *Adiós.* — a-dyos
Bye/See you soon. — *Hasta luego.* — as-ta lwe-go
Yes. — *Sí.* — see
No. — *No.* — no
Please. — *Por favor.* — por fa-*vor*
Thank you. — *Gracias.* — *gra*-syas
Many thanks. — *Muchas gracias.* — *moo*-chas *gra*-syas
You're welcome. — *De nada.* — de *na*-da
Pardon me. — *Perdón.* — per-*don*
Excuse me. — *Permiso.* — per-*mee*-so
(used when asking permission)
Forgive me. — *Disculpe.* — dees-*kool*-pe
(used when apologizing)

How are things?
¿Qué tal? — ke tal
What's your name?
¿Cómo se llama? — *ko*-mo se *ya*-ma (pol)
¿Cómo te llamas? — *ko*-mo te *ya*-mas (inf)
My name is ...
Me llamo ... — me *ya*-mo ...
It's a pleasure to meet you.
Mucho gusto. — *moo*-cho *goos*-to
The pleasure is mine.
El gusto es mío. — el *goos*-to es *mee*-o
Where are you from?
¿De dónde es/eres? — de *don*-de es/e-res (pol/inf)
I'm from ...
Soy de ... — soy de ...
Where are you staying?
¿Dónde está alojado? — *don*-de es-ta a-lo-*kha*-do (pol)
¿Dónde estás alojado? — *don*-de es-tas a-lo-*kha*-do (inf)
May I take a photo?
¿Puedo sacar una foto? — pwe-do sa-*kar* oo-na *fo*-to

DIRECTIONS

How do I get to ...?
¿Cómo puedo llegar a ...? — *ko*-mo pwe-do lye-*gar* a ...
Is it far?
¿Está lejos? — es-ta le-khos
Go straight ahead.
Siga/Vaya derecho. — see-ga/va-ya de-*re*-cho
Turn left.
Voltée a la izquierda. — vol-*te*-e a la ees-*kyer*-da
Turn right.
Voltée a la derecha. — vol-*te*-e a la de-*re*-cha
I'm lost.
Estoy perdido/a. — es-toy per-*dee*-do/a
Can you show me (on the map)?
¿Me lo podría indicar — me lo po-*dree*-a een-dee-*kar*
(en el mapa)? — (en el *ma*-pa)

SIGNS

Entrada	Entrance
Salida	Exit
Información	Information
Abierto	Open
Cerrado	Closed
Prohibido	Prohibited
Comisaria	Police Station
Servicios/Baños	Toilets
Hombres/Varones	Men
Señoras/Damas	Women

north	*norte*	*nor*·te
south	*sur*	soor
east	*este/oriente*	es·te/o·*ryen*·te
west	*oeste/occidente*	o·es·te/ok·see·*den*·te
here	*aquí*	a·*kee*
there	*allí*	a·*yee*
avenue	*avenida*	a·ve·*nee*·da
block	*cuadra*	*kwa*·dra
street	*calle/paseo*	*ka*·lye/pa·*se*·o

HEALTH

I'm sick.
  Estoy enfermo/a.   es·*toy* en·*fer*·mo/a

I need a doctor.
  Necesito un médico.   ne·se·*see*·to oon *me*·dee·ko

Where's the hospital?
  ¿Dónde está el hospital?   don·de es·*ta* el os·pee·*tal*

I'm pregnant.
  Estoy embarazada.   es·*toy* em·ba·ra·*sa*·da

I've been vaccinated.
  Estoy vacunado/a.   es·*toy* va·koo·*na*·do/a

I'm allergic	*Soy alérgico/a*	soy a·*ler*·khee·ko/a
to ...	*a ...*	a ...
antibiotics	*los antibióticos*	los an·tee·*byo*·tee·kos
penicillin	*la penicilina*	la pe·nee·see·*lee*·na
nuts	*las fruta secas*	las *froo*·tas *se*·kas

I'm ...	*Soy ...*	soy ...
asthmatic	*asmático/a*	as·*ma*·tee·ko/a
diabetic	*diabético/a*	dya·*be*·tee·ko/a
epileptic	*epiléptico/a*	e·pee·*lep*·tee·ko/a

I have ...	*Tengo ...*	*ten*·go ...
altitude sickness	*soroche*	so·*ro*·che
diarrhea	*diarrea*	dya·*re*·a
nausea	*náusea*	*now*·se·a
a headache	*un dolor de cabeza*	oon do·*lor* de ka·*be*·sa
a cough	*tos*	tos

EMERGENCIES

Help!	*¡Socorro!*	so·*ko*·ro
Fire!	*¡Incendio!*	een·*sen*·dyo
I've been robbed.	*Me robaron.*	me ro·*ba*·ron
Go away!	*¡Déjeme!*	*de*·khe·me
Get lost!	*¡Váyase!*	*va*·ya·se

Call ...!	*¡Llame a ...!*	*ya*·me a
an ambulance	*una ambulancia*	oo·na am·boo·*lan*·sya
a doctor	*un médico*	oon *me*·dee·ko
the police	*la policía*	la po·lee·*see*·a

It's an emergency.
  Es una emergencia.   es oo·na e·mer·*khen*·sya

Could you help me, please?
  ¿Me puede ayudar, por favor?   me *pwe*·de a·yoo·*dar* por fa·*vor*

I'm lost.
  Estoy perdido/a.   es·*toy* per·*dee*·do/a

Where are the toilets?
  ¿Dónde están los baños?   don·de es·*tan* los *ba*·nyos

LANGUAGE DIFFICULTIES

Do you speak (English)?
  ¿Habla/Hablas (inglés)?   a·bla/a·blas (een·*gles*) (pol/inf)

Does anyone here speak English?
  ¿Hay alguien que hable inglés?   ai al·*gyen* ke a·ble een·*gles*

I (don't) understand.
  Yo (no) entiendo.   yo (no) en·*tyen*·do

How do you say ...?
  ¿Cómo se dice ...?   *ko*·mo se *dee*·se ...

What does ...mean?
  ¿Qué quiere decir ...?   ke *kye*·re de·*seer* ...

Could you please ...?	*¿Puede ..., por favor?*	*pwe*·de ... por fa·*vor*
repeat that	*repetirlo*	re·pe·*teer*·lo
speak more slowly	*hablar más despacio*	a·*blar* mas des·*pa*·syo
write it down	*escribirlo*	es·kree·*beer*·lo

NUMBERS

1	*uno*	*oo*·no
2	*dos*	dos
3	*tres*	tres
4	*cuatro*	*kwa*·tro
5	*cinco*	*seen*·ko
6	*seis*	says
7	*siete*	*sye*·te
8	*ocho*	*o*·cho

9	nueve	nwe·ve
10	diez	dyes
11	once	on·se
12	doce	do·se
13	trece	tre·se
14	catorce	ka·tor·se
15	quince	keen·se
16	dieciséis	dye·see·says
17	diecisiete	dye·see·sye·te
18	dieciocho	dye·see·o·cho
19	diecinueve	dye·see·nwe·ve
20	veinte	vayn·te
21	veintiuno	vayn·tee·oo·no
30	treinta	trayn·ta
31	treinta y uno	trayn·ta ee oo·no
40	cuarenta	kwa·ren·ta
50	cincuenta	seen·kwen·ta
60	sesenta	se·sen·ta
70	setenta	se·ten·ta
80	ochenta	o·chen·ta
90	noventa	no·ven·ta
100	cien	syen
101	ciento uno	syen·to oo·no
200	doscientos	do·syen·tos
1000	mil	meel
5000	cinco mil	seen·ko meel
10,000	diez mil	dyes meel
50,000	cincuenta mil	seen·kwen·ta meel
100,000	cien mil	syen meel
1,000,000	un millón	oon mee·yon

credit cards	tarjetas de crédito	tar·khe·tas de kre·dee·to
traveler's checks	cheques de viajero	che·kes de vya·khe·ro
less	menos	me·nos
more	más	mas
large	grande	gran·de
small	pequeño/a	pe·ke·nyo/a
I'm looking for (a/the) ...	Estoy buscando ...	es·toy boos·kan·do
ATM	un cajero automático	oon ka·khe·ro ow·to·ma·tee·ko
bank	el banco	el ban·ko
bookstore	una librería	oo·na lee·bre·ree·a
embassy	la embajada	la em·ba·kha·da
exchange house	una casa de cambio	oo·na ka·sa de kam·byo
general store	la tienda	la tyen·da
laundry	la lavandería	la la·van·de·ree·a
market	el mercado	el mer·ka·do
pharmacy/ chemist	la farmacia/ la botica	la far·ma·sya/ la bo·tee·ka
post office	el correo	el ko·re·o
public telephone	un teléfono público	oon te·le·fo·no poob·lee·ko
supermarket	el supermercado	el soo·per·mer·ka·do
tourist office	la oficina de turismo	la o·fee·see·na de too·rees·mo

SHOPPING & SERVICES

I'd like to buy ...
Quisiera comprar ...   kee·sye·ra kom·prar
I'm just looking.
Sólo estoy mirando.   so·lo es·toy mee·ran·do
May I look at it?
¿Puedo mirar(lo/la)?   pwe·do mee·rar·(lo/la)
How much is it?
¿Cuánto cuesta?   kwan·to kwes·ta
That's too expensive for me.
Es demasiado caro   es de·ma·sya·do ka·ro
para mí.   pa·ra mee
Could you lower the price?
¿Podría bajar un poco   po·dree·a ba·khar oon po·ko
el precio?   el pre·syo
I don't like it.
No me gusta.   no me goos·ta
I'll take it.
Lo llevo.   lo ye·vo

| **Do you accept ...?** | ¿Aceptan ...? | a·sep·tan |
| **American dollars** | dólares americanos | do·la·res a·me·ree·ka·nos |

What time does it open/close?
¿A qué hora abre/cierra?   a ke o·ra a·bre/sye·ra
I want to change some money/traveler's checks.
Quiero cambiar dinero/   kye·ro kam·byar dee·ne·ro/
cheques de viajero.   che·kes de vya·khe·ro
What is the exchange rate?
¿Cuál es el tipo de   kwal es el tee·po de
cambio?   kam·byo
I want to call ...
Quiero llamar a ...   kye·ro lya·mar a ...

airmail	correo aéreo	ko·re·o a·e·re·o
black market	mercado (negro/ paralelo)	mer·ka·do ne·gro/ pa·ra·le·lo
collect call	llamada a cobro revertido	ya·ma·da a ko·bro re·ver·tee·do
email	correo electrónico	ko·re·yo e·le·tro·nee·ko
letter	carta	kar·ta
local call	llamada local	ya·ma·da lo·kal
long-distance call	llamada de larga distancia	ya·ma·da de lar·ga dis·tan·sa
parcel	paquete	pa·ke·te

person to	persona a	per·so·na a
person	persona	per·so·na
postcard	postal	pos·tal
registered mail	certificado	ser·tee·fee·ka·do
stamps	estampillas	es·tam·pee·lyas

TIME & DATES

The time is expressed by saying *la* or *las* followed by the hour number and how far it is past or until the hour. Thus, eight o'clock is *las ocho*, while 8:30 is *las ocho y treinta* (eight and thirty) or *las ocho y media* (eight and a half). However, 7:45 is *las ocho menos quince* (eight minus fifteen) or *las ocho menos cuarto* (eight minus a quarter).

Times are modified by morning (*de la mañana*) or afternoon (*de la tarde*) instead of am or pm. Use of the 24-hour clock, or military time, is also common, especially with transportation schedules.

What time is it?	¿Qué hora es?	ke o·ra es
It's one o'clock.	Es la una.	es la oo·na
It's two/three ... (etc) o'clock.	Son las dos/tres ...	son las dos/tres ...
At three o'clock.	A las tres.	a las tres
midnight	medianoche	me·dya·no·che
noon	mediodía	me·dyo·dee·a
half past two	dos y media	dos ee me·dya

now	ahora	a·o·ra
today	hoy	oy
tonight	esta noche	es·ta no·che
tomorrow	mañana	ma·nya·na
yesterday	ayer	a·yer

Monday	lunes	loo·nes
Tuesday	martes	mar·tes
Wednesday	miércoles	myer·ko·les
Thursday	jueves	khwe·ves
Friday	viernes	vyer·nes
Saturday	sábado	sa·ba·do
Sunday	domingo	do·meen·go

January	enero	e·ne·ro
February	febrero	fe·bre·ro
March	marzo	mar·so
April	abril	a·breel
May	mayo	ma·yo
June	junio	khoo·nyo
July	julio	khoo·lyo
August	agosto	a·gos·to
September	septiembre	sep·tyem·bre
October	octubre	ok·too·bre
November	noviembre	no·vyem·bre
December	diciembre	dee·syem·bre

GEOGRAPHICAL EXPRESSIONS

The expressions below are among the most common you'll encounter in Spanish-language maps and guides.

avenida	avenue
bahía	bay
calle	street
camino	road
campo/finca/fundo/ hacienda	farm
carretera/camino/ruta	highway
cascada/salto	waterfall
cerro	hill
cerro	mount
cordillera	mountain range
estancia/granja/rancho	ranch
estero	marsh, estuary
lago	lake
montaña	mountain
parque nacional	national park
paso	pass
puente	bridge
río	river
seno	sound
valle	valley

TRANSPORTATION
Public Transportation

airport	el aeropuerto	el a·e·ro·pwer·to
bus stop	la parada de autobuses	la pa·ra·da de ow·to·boo·ses
bus terminal	la terminal de pasajeros	la tair·mee·nal de pa·sa·khe·ros
luggage check room	guardería/ equipaje	gwar·de·ree·a/ e·kee·pa·khe
ticket office	la boletería	la bo·le·te·ree·a
train station	la estación de ferrocarril	la es·ta·syon de fe·ro·ka·reel

What time does ... leave/arrive?	¿A qué hora ... sale/llega?	a ke o·ra ... sa·le/ye·ga
the boat	el bongo/ la lancha/ el bote	el bon·go/ la lan·cha/ el bo·te
the bus	el autobus	el ow·to·boos
the plane	el avión	el a·vyon
the ship	el barco/buque	el bar·ko/boo·ke
the small bus	el por puesto/ la buseta/ el carrito	el por·pwes·to/ la boo·se·ta/ el ka·ree·to
the train	el tren	el tren

I'd like a ticket to ...
Quiero un boleto a ...   kye-ro oon bo-*le*-to a ...
What's the fare to ...?
¿Cuánto cuesta hasta ...?   kwan-to *kwes*-ta a-sta ...

1st class	*primera clase*	pree-me-ra *kla*-se
2nd class	*segunda clase*	se-*goon*-da *kla*-se
single/one-way	*ida*	ee-da
return/roundtrip	*ida y vuelta*	ee-da ee *vwel*-ta
taxi	*taxi*	tak-see

Private Transportation

pickup (truck)	*camioneta*	ka-myo-*ne*-ta
truck	*camión*	*ka*-myon
hitchhike	*hacer dedo/*	a-ser de-do/
	pedir una cola	pe-*deer* oon *ko*-la

I'd like to	*Quisiera*	kee-*sye*-ra
hire a/an ...	*alquilar ...*	al-kee-*lar* ...
4WD	*un todo terreno*	oon *to*-do te-*re*-no
car	*un auto/carro*	oon ow-to/*ka*-ro
motorcycle	*una moto*	*oo*-na mo-to
bicycle	*una bicicleta*	*oo*-na bee-see-*kle*-ta

Is this the road to (...)?
¿Se va a (...) por   se va a (...) por
esta carretera?   es-ta ka-re-*te*-ra
Where's a petrol station?
¿Dónde hay una   don-de ai oo-na
gasolinera/un grifo?   ga-so-lee-*ne*-ra/oon *gree*-fo
Please fill it up.
Lleno, por favor.   ye-no por fa-*vor*
I'd like (20) liters.
Quiero (veinte) litros.   kye-ro (*vayn*-te) *lee*-tros

diesel	*diesel*	dee-sel
leaded (regular)	*gasolina con*	ga-so-*lee*-na kon
	plomo	*plo*-mo
petrol (gas)	*gasolina*	ga-so-*lee*-na
unleaded	*gasolina sin*	ga-so-*lee*-na seen
	plomo	*plo*-mo

(How long) Can I park here?
¿(Por cuánto tiempo)   (por *kwan*-to *tyem*-po)
Puedo aparcar aquí?   pwe-do a-par-*kar* a-*kee*
Where do I pay?
¿Dónde se paga?   don-de se *pa*-ga
I need a mechanic.
Necesito un   ne-se-*see*-to oon
mecánico.   me-*ka*-nee-ko
The car has broken down (in ...).
El carro se ha averiado   el *ka*-ro se a a-ve-*rya*-do
(en ...).   (en ...)

ROAD SIGNS
Keep in mind that traffic signs will invariably be in Spanish and may not be accompanied by internationally recognized symbols. Pay especially close attention to *Peligro* (Danger), *Ceda el Paso* (Yield/Give Way; especially prevalent on one-lane bridges), and *Hundimiento* (Dip; this is often a euphemistic term for 'axle-breaking sinkhole'). Disregarding these warnings could result in disaster.

Acceso	Entrance
Alto	Stop
Aparcamiento	Parking
Ceda el Paso	Yield/Give way
Curva Peligrosa	Dangerous Curve
Derrumbes en la Vía	Landslides/Rockfalls
Despacio	Slow
Desvío	Detour
Dirección Única	One-way
Hundimiento	Dip
Mantenga Su Derecha	Keep to the Right
No Adelantar/No Rebase	No Passing
No Estacionar	No Parking
No Hay Paso	No Entrance
Peaje	Toll
Peligro	Danger
Prohibido Aparcar/	No Parking
No Estacionar	
Prohibido el Paso	No Entry
Pare/Stop	Stop
Salida de Autopista	Freeway Exit
Trabajos en la Vía	Roadwork
Tránsito Entrando	Entering Traffic

The motorbike won't start.
No arranca la moto.   no a-*ran*-ka la *mo*-to
I have a flat tyre.
Tengo un pinchazo.   ten-go oon peen-*cha*-so
I've run out of petrol.
Me quedé sin gasolina.   me ke-*de* seen ga-so-*lee*-na
I've had an accident.
Tuve un accidente.   *too*-ve oon ak-see-*den*-te

TRAVEL WITH CHILDREN
Do you mind if I breast-feed here?
¿Le molesta que dé   le mo-*les*-ta ke de
de pecho aquí?   de *pe*-cho a-*kee*
Are children allowed?
¿Se admiten niños?   se ad-*mee*-ten *nee*-nyos

I need ...
Necesito ...   ne-se-*see*-to ...

Do you have ...?
¿Hay ...?   ai ...

a car baby seat
un asiento de seguridad   oon a·*syen*·to de se·goo·ree·*da*
   para bebés   pa·ra be·*bes*

a child-minding service
un servicio de cuidado   oon ser·*vee*·syo de kwee·*da*·do
   de niños   de *nee*·nyos

a children's menu
una carta infantil   oona *kar*·ta een·fan·*teel*

a creche
una guardería   oo·na gwar·de·*ree*·a

(disposable) diapers/nappies
pañoles (de usar y tirar)   pa·*nyo*·les (de oo·*sar* ee tee·*rar*)

an (English-speaking) babysitter
una niñera   oo·na nee·*nye*·ra
   (de habla inglesa)   (de *a*·bla een·*gle*·sa)

formula (milk)
leche en polvo   *le*·che en *pol*·vo

a highchair
una trona   oo·na *tro*·na

a potty
una pelela   oo·na pe·*le*·la

a pusher/stroller
un cochecito   oon ko·che·*see*·to

Also available from Lonely Planet:
Latin American Spanish Phrasebook

Glossary

See the Food & Drink chapter (p49) for useful words and phrases dealing with food and dining. See the Language chapter (p351) for general-use words and phrases.

abasto – small rural store selling anything from bread and batteries to sunblock and beer

acure – hare-sized rodent, species of agouti

AD – Acción Democrática, or Democratic Action Party; populist party created in 1941 by Rómulo Betancourt as one of the two major traditional parties

adobe – sun-dried brick made of mud and straw, used in traditional rural constructions

alcabala – road checkpost operated by the Guardia Nacional

alcaldía – mayor's office

andino/a – inhabitant of the Andes

araguaney – trumpet tree *(Tabebuia chrysantha),* a large tree with yellow flowers; Venezuela's national tree

atarraya – kind of traditional circular fishing net used on the coast and rivers

ateneo – cultural center

autopista – freeway

azulejos – ornamental handmade tiles brought to South America from Spain and Portugal in colonial times

baba – spectacled caiman, the smallest of the family of local crocodiles

baloncesto – basketball

bandola – four-string, pear-shaped guitar-type instrument used by some *joropo* bands instead of the harp

barrio – shantytown built of *ranchos* around the big city centers; they are particularly numerous and extensive in Caracas

béisbol – baseball

bodega – warehouse; also used to mean 'grocery,' especially in small localities and rural areas

bolo – informal term for the *bolívar* (Venezuela's currency); see also *real*

bonche – party (informal)

bongo – large dugout canoe; traditionally hand-hewn, today usually equipped with outboard motor

buhonero – street vendor

bus-cama – new-generation, long-distance bus with seats almost reclining into a bed. The most comfy means of intercity transportation.

buseta – small bus, frequently used in city transportation

cabalgata – horseback ride

cabaña – cabin, found mostly on the coast and in the mountains

cachicamo – armadillo

caimán – caiman, or American crocodile; similar to alligators, but with a more heavily armored belly

cajero automático – automated teller machine (ATM)

calle – street

callejón – alley or narrow, short street

caminata – trek, hike

campamento – countryside lodging facility, usually in cabins, with its own food services and often a tour program

campesino/a – rural dweller, usually of modest economic means; peasant

caney – palm-thatched open-sided large hut

canoa – a dugout canoe

canotaje – rafting

CANTV – the national telecommunications company

caño – natural water channel

capybara – a tailless largely aquatic South American rodent; also called *chigüire*

carabobeño/a – inhabitant of Carabobo state, particularly Valencia

Caracazo – violent Caracas riots of February 27–29, 1989, in which more than 300 people died

caraqueño/a – person born and/or residing in Caracas

cardón – columnar type of cactus typical of the Península de Paraguaná

carrito – term used for *por puesto*

casa – house; used for anything from a rustic hut to a rambling colonial mansion

casa de cambio – money-exchange office

cascabel – rattlesnake

caserío – hamlet

casona – large, rambling old mansion; stately home

catire – person of light complexion

caudillo – South American dictator, normally a military man who assumes power by force and is noted for autocratic rule. Caudillos governed Venezuela from 1830 to 1958.

CC – common abbreviation for Centro Comercial, or shopping mall

cédula – identity document of Venezuelan citizens and residents

ceiba – common tree of the tropics that can reach a huge size

chalana – flatbed river ferry for people and vehicles

chaguaramo – popular term for royal palm

chamo/a – boy/girl, young person, friend, pal, mate (informal)

cheque viajero – traveler's check

chévere – good, fine (informal)

chigüire – capybara, the world's largest rodent

chinchorro – hammock woven of cotton threads or palm fiber like a fishing net; typical of many Indian groups, including the Warao and Guajiro

churuata – traditional palm-thatched large circular Indian hut

ciénaga – shallow lake or lagoon

cinemateca – arthouse cinema that focuses on screening films of a high artistic quality

coleo – form of rodeo practiced in Los Llanos, also known as *toros coleados*. The aim is to overthrow a bull by grabbing its tail from a galloping horse.

colibrí – hummingbird

comida criolla – typical Venezuelan cuisine

cónchale – informal tag word, used on its own or added to the beginning of a sentence to emphasize emotional involvement

conuco – small cultivated plot, usually obtained by slashing-and-burning

Copei – Partido Social Cristiano, or Social Christian Party; founded by Rafael Caldera in 1946 in opposition to the leftist AD party. Until the 1993 election, Copei and AD almost monopolized the popular vote.

corrida – bullfight

costeño/a – inhabitant of the coastal regions

criollo/a – Creole, a person of European (especially Spanish) ancestry but born in the Americas

cuadra – city block

cuatro – a small four-stringed guitar, used in *joropo* and *gaita* music

cuñado – literally 'brother-in-law'; pal, friend, mate (informal)

curiara – small dugout canoe

Curripaco – Indian community living in Amazonas state

danta – tapir; large hoofed mammal of tropical and subtropical forests

denuncia – official report/statement to the police

DIEX or DEX – Dirección Nacional de Identificación y Extranjería, the Venezuelan immigration authority

embalse – reservoir formed by a dam built for hydroelectric or water-supply purposes

embarcadero – landing dock

esquina – street corner

estacionamiento (vigilado) – (guarded) car park

estera – a sort of mat made from a papyrus-like reed

farmacia – pharmacy

flamenco – flamingo

flor de mayo – species of orchid that is Venezuela's national flower

fortín – small fort

frailejón – espeletia; a species of plant typical of the *páramo*

franela – literally 'flannel'; commonly refers to a T-shirt

fuerte – fort

fundo – country estate

fútbol – soccer

furruco – musical instrument consisting of a drum and a wooden pole piercing the drumhead; used in some kinds of popular music including the *gaita*. The sound is produced via striking the drumhead by moving the pole up and down.

gaita – popular music played in Zulia state

gallera – cockfight ring

garimpeiro – illegal gold miner

garza – heron

gavilán – sparrow hawk

gringo/a – any white foreigner; sometimes, not always, derogatory

guacamaya – macaw

guácharo – oilbird, a species of nocturnal bird living in caves

Guajibo – Indian group living in parts of Los Llanos and Amazonas along the frontier with Colombia

Guajiro – Venezuela's most numerous Indian group, living in Zulia state (Venezuela) and Península de la Guajira (Colombia)

guardaequipaje – left-luggage office; checkroom

guardaparque – national-park ranger

Guardia Nacional – military police responsible for security

guarupa – jacaranda; a tall tropical tree with lavender-blue blossoms

hacienda – country estate

hato – large cattle ranch, typical of Los Llanos

hospedaje – cheap hotel

iglesia – church

impuesto – tax

invierno – literally 'winter'; refers to the rainy season

Ipostel – company operating a network of post offices

isla – island

IVA – *impuesto de valor agregado,* a value-added sales tax (VAT)

jején – species of small biting gnat that infests the Gran Sabana and, to a lesser extent, some other regions

joropo – typical music of Los Llanos, today widespread throughout the country; considered Venezuelan national rhythm

lapa – species of agouti, a rabbit-sized rodent whose brown skin is dotted with white spots

lavandería – launderette

libre – taxi

liqui liqui – men's traditional costume, typical of most of the Caribbean; a white or beige suit comprising trousers and a shirt with a collar, usually accompanied by white hat and shoes
llanero/a – inhabitant of Los Llanos
(Los) Llanos – literally 'plains'; Venezuela's vast central region
loro – parrot

malecón – waterfront boulevard
manatí – manatee; a cetaceous herbivore living in calm rivers. Manatees can reach up to 5m in length.
manga de coleo – place where *coleos* are held
manta – long, loose, usually colorful dress worn by Guajiro Indian women
mapanare – venomous snake common in Venezuela
Maquiritare – see *Yekuana*
maracas – gourd rattles; an indispensable accompanying instrument of *joropo*
maracucho/a – person from Maracaibo; often extended to mean anyone from the Zulia state
margariteño/a – person from the Isla de Margarita
matrimonial – hotel room with a double bed intended for couples
médanos – sand dunes near Coro
menú del día – set lunch or dinner
merengue – musical rhythm originating from the Dominican Republic, today widespread throughout the Caribbean
merú – Pemón Indian word for 'waterfall'
mestizo/a – person of mixed European-Indian blood
micro – in some regions, a term for a minibus or van used as local transportation
mirador – lookout, viewpoint
mochilero – backpacker
monedero – originally a term referring to a public telephone operated by coins, but now extended to any public phone
moriche – palm common in Los Llanos and the Delta del Orinoco, used by indigenous people for construction, food, household items, handicrafts etc
morocho/a – person of dark complexion; usually a mix of black and white ancestry
morrocoy – tortoise typical of some regions, including Los Llanos and Guayana
mosquitero – mosquito net
mucuposadas – traditional rural lodges
muelle – pier, wharf
mulatto – a person of mixed European-African ancestry
MVR – Movimiento Quinta República; populist leftist party formed by Hugo Chávez

Navidad – Christmas
nevado – snowcapped peak

orquídea – orchid
oso hormiguero – anteater

palafito – house built on stilts over the water; a typical Warao dwelling in the Delta del Orinoco. Also found in Zulia state, especially in Laguna de Sinamaica
palos – literally 'sticks'; drinks (informal)
pana – pal, mate (informal)
paño – small towel, the one you'll get in cheap hotels
parada – bus stop
páramo – open highland above about 3300m; typical of Venezuela, Colombia and Ecuador
parapente – paragliding
pardo/a – mulatto; person of mixed European and African descent
parrilla – mixed grill
paují – a black bird that inhabits cloud forest in the north and west of Venezuela
Pemón – Indian group inhabiting the Gran Sabana and neighboring areas
peñero – open fishing boat made from wood
pereza – sloth
Piapoco – Indian community living in Amazonas state
Piaroa – Indian community living in Amazonas state
piscina – swimming pool
playa – beach
plaza de toros – bullfight ring
por puesto – cross between a bus and taxi that plies fixed routes and departs when full, a popular means of transportation
posada – small, family-run guesthouse
primo – literally 'cousin'; pal, brother (informal)
propina – tip
puri-puri – small biting flies, similar to *jejenes*

quebrada – a steep ravine which may or may not have a creek or river at the bottom of it
quinta – house with a garden. Quintas originally took up a fifth of a city block – hence the name.

ranchería – Indian hamlet
rancho or **ranchito** – ramshackle dwelling built of waste materials
raudales – rapids
real – informal term for the bolívar (Venezuela's currency)
redoma – traffic circle, roundabout
refugio – rustic shelter in a remote area, mostly in the mountains
residencia – cheap hotel or, more often, apartment building
río – river
roqueño/a – inhabitants of the Archipiélago Los Roques
rumba – party
rústico – jeep

salinas – seaside salt pans or shallow lagoons used for extraction of salt

salsa – type of Caribbean dance music of Cuban origin

Semana Santa – Holy Week, the week before Easter Sunday

shabono – large circular house typical of the Yanomami

SIDA – AIDS

sifrino/a – yuppie (informal)

sima – sinkhole; depression in the ground, usually circular and deep, with vertical walls

soroche – altitude sickness

tambora – large wooden drum

tarjeta de crédito – credit card

tarjetero – public telephone operated by phone cards

tasca – Spanish bar-restaurant

teleférico – cable car

telenovela – TV soap opera

tepui – also spelled *tepuy*; a flat-topped sandstone mountain with vertical flanks. The term is derived from the Pemón Indian word for 'mountain.'

terminal de pasajeros – bus terminal

tienda – small store that sells food, toiletries, batteries etc

tigre – jaguar

tonina – freshwater dolphin

toros coleados – see *coleo*

trapiche – traditional sugarcane mill

turpial – small black, red and yellow bird; Venezuela's national bird

urbanización – suburb

vallenato – typical Colombian music, now widespread throughout Venezuela

vaquero – cowboy of Los Llanos

vená – the Pemón Indian word for 'high waterfall'

verano – literally 'summer'; used in the sense of 'dry season'

viajero – traveler

Warao – Indian group living in the Delta del Orinoco

yagrumo – tree with large palmate silver-colored leaves

Yanomami – indigenous group living in the Venezuelan and Brazilian Amazon

Yekuana – also referred to as *Maquiritare*; an Indian group inhabiting parts of Amazonas and Bolívar states

zambo/a – person of mixed Indian-African ancestry

Behind the Scenes

THIS BOOK

This 4th edition of *Venezuela* was written by Krzysztof Dydyński and Charlotte Beech. Charlotte wrote the Culture, Food & Drink, Caracas, Central North and Northeast chapters. Krzysztof, the coordinating author, wrote the rest of the book. The Environment chapter was written by Tobias Mendelovici, and the Health chapter was written by Dr David Goldberg MD. The last three editions have been researched and written by Krzysztof Dydyński.

THANKS from the Authors

Krzysztof Dydyński Many friends, colleagues and travelers have kindly contributed to this book and deserve the highest praise. I would like to thank all those people for their advice, information, hospitality and much else. Warmest thanks to Walter Bernal, Eric Buschbell, Gert Altmann, Nico de Greiff, Raquel and Tom Evenou, Jesús García, Axel Kelemen, Slawek Kociecki, Eric Migliore, Peter Rothfuss, Roger Ruffenach, Claude Saint-Pierre and the Inatur tourist office in Caracas. My special thanks goes to Angela Melendro.

Charlotte Beech Many people generously spared time to help me during my research. An especially warm vote of thanks goes to Marjored Pérez and Felix González in Caracas. Also to Carla Salanova and her family, who welcomed me into their home, fed me *arepas* and plentiful *guarapita* and worried about me as I disappeared off to research. I must also extend my gratitude to Emilio Rodríguez, Arnaldo Morales, the Thomas Merle Association,

Elsy Goerke, Jimmy Capriles, Margarita's Cámara de Turismo, Gabriela Bender, Emma Banks, Alex Amelines, Lorena, Bibi and Gabriela Torres. And, as ever, a huge thank you to all the travelers I met on the road and to the Lonely Planet readers who wrote in with their hints and tips.

CREDITS

Venezuela 4 was commissioned and developed in Lonely Planet's Oakland office by Wendy Smith. The manuscript was assessed by Alex Hershey, with help from Sam Benson, Erin Corrigan and Suki Gear. Cartography for this title was developed by Alison Lyall. The book was coordinated by Katrina Webb (editorial), and Anneka Imkamp and Owen Eszeki (cartography). Imogen Bannister, Pete Cruttenden, Kate Evans, Katie Lynch, Kate McLeod, Melanie Dankel and Jennifer Garrett assisted with editing and proofing. Jimi Ellis, Herman So, Jack Gavran and Anthony Phelan assisted with cartography. The layout team consisted of Vicki Beale and Nick Stebbing. Nic Lehman designed the cover and cover artwork was prepared by Maria Vallianos. Quentin Frayne prepared the Language chapter, and Katrina Webb prepared the index. Overseeing the production were Eoin Dunlevy (Project Manager), Bruce Evans (Managing Editor) and Alison Lyall (Managing Cartographer), with assistance from Anthony Phelan and Laurie Mikkelsen. Series Publishing Manager Virginia Maxwell oversaw the redevelopment of the country guides series with help from Maria Donohoe, who was also the Regional Publishing Manager and steered the development of this title. The series was designed by James Hardy, with

---

THE LONELY PLANET STORY

The story begins with a classic travel adventure: Tony and Maureen Wheeler's 1972 journey across Europe and Asia to Australia. There was no useful information about the overland trail then, so Tony and Maureen published the first Lonely Planet guidebook to meet a growing need.

From a kitchen table, Lonely Planet has grown to become the largest independent travel publisher in the world, with offices in Melbourne (Australia), Oakland (USA), London (UK) and Paris (France).

Today Lonely Planet guidebooks cover the globe. There is an ever-growing list of books and information in a variety of media. Some things haven't changed. The main aim is still to make it possible for adventurous travelers to get out there – to explore and better understand the world.

At Lonely Planet we believe travelers can make a positive contribution to the countries they visit – if they respect their host communities and spend their money wisely.

mapping development by Paul Piaia. The series development team included Shahara Ahmed, Susie Ashworth, Gerilyn Attebery, Jenny Blake, Anna Bolger, Verity Campbell, Erin Corrigan, Nadine Fogale, Dave McClymont, Leonie Mugavin, Lynne Preston, Rachel Peart and Howard Rally.

THANKS from Lonely Planet

Many thanks to the hundreds of travelers who used the last edition and wrote to us with helpful hints, useful advice and interesting anecdotes:

A Lynn Achee, Holly Ackerman, Sherry Ackerman, Robert Ajlumi, Wolf Albermann, Beth & Skip Albertson, Carmen Alfonso, Brett Allen, Bodil Almberg, Tanya Ammann, Marzio Andrea Pistilli, Harold Armitage, Dan Arrowood, Andrea Aster, Guy Atherton, Nicolas Atwood, Alain Aucordier, Christie Ayral **B** Ted Bachrach, Susie Bailey, Francoise Balconi, Brad Ballard, RA Balmanoukian, Sebastien Baron, Hugo Baudert, C J Bayman, Carsten Behme, Federico Belline, Martin Benedicto, Tony Bennee, Kim Bennett, Robert J Bennett, Marty Berke, A Bernard, Hermann Bersch, Katrin Beurger, Petra Biderman, Fabio Biserna, R Bisset, Erica Blatchford, Sam Blowes, Brian W Boag, Roland Bogers, Sue Bokowski, Craig Booker, William Bookhammer, Lotte Boot, Stephane Borella, Fabienne Borzeix, Martijn van den Bosch, Marco Bottacini, Roy & Audrey Bradford, Christopher Branahan, Nicholas Branch, Kerstin Brandes, Carl Bray, Richard J Bray, Benno Breitenmoser, M J Bristow, Mag Bruno Korinek, Nina Bryggemann, Ziemowit Buchalski, Rhonda Bueche, Wim Buesink, Neil & Sandra Burditt, CD Burgess, Nicki Burston, Martina Bussmann, Veronica Byrne **C** Lorena Caleffi, Jon Camfield, Elisabetta Cammarota, Alistair Campbell, Fabio Cannavale, Georg Capart, Pernille Carlson, Georg Caspary, Sabas Castillo, Rowan Castle, Andzea Cesillo, Stephen Chan, Simon Channon, Morag Chase, Kelly Chisholm, Thomas Christen, Dale R Christiansen, Eva Christiansen, C Christopher Gaunt, Liam Clancy, Lucy Claridge, Deborah Clarke, Claudia Cleff, Barry Clements, Paolo Cocchiglia, Nick Cocks, Juan Claudio Coello Pantojo, Tracey Collins, Rachel Cook, David & Diana Copp, Aaron Corcoran, Erika Cordes, Josselin Cormier, James Cornish, Sandra Cottam, Bruce Cowley, John Crandon, Andy Crawford, Matthew Creeden, Martin Crone, Jim Crooks, Juan Cruz Escardo, Benoit Cuvelier **D** Wojciech Dabrowski, Kerstin Daemen, Natasha Dahanayake, Christopher & Victoria Darke, Lucy de Alio, Lindsay DeHart, Justa Denning, Richard Derichs, Pieter Dings, Vicki Dischler, Jens Dube, Andrea Duerr **E** Vanessa Eden Evans, David Edwards, Ron Edwardson, Michael Eiche, Anna Elfors, Sarah Ellis, Hans & Marjan van der Eng, P Enea, Omar Enriquez, Manon Ensing, Mariella Erkens, Cristina Esther Pulido, Chris P Evans, Sabine Exner **F** Igor Fabjan, Donatella Fachin, Brian Fagan, Caryll Fagan, Carlos Fagi, Kristen Faith, Mike Farrell, Marek Feldman, Patrik Ferkl, Tracy Ferrell, Christian Finkbeiner, Jaromir Folders, Alex Fontanini, Matt Fordham, Rolf Forster, Nicholas Foster, Richard Fowkes, Jill Frazer **G** Markus Gajer, Daryl Galloway, S Garrett, Jeannie Gellatly, David Gerez, Michael Gerth, Thomas Gibbins, Sherry Gibson, William Gibson, Gregory Gilbert, Werner Ginzky, David Godfrey, Peter Goeltenboth, Tulio Gomez, Diane B Goodpasture, Shannon Gorman, John Gravley, Stephanie Greene, Lance Greenwood, Harald Gries, Danny Grobben, Michael Grundke, Katja Grunow, Daniel Guerrero C, Tim Gunn, Antje Günther **H** Johannes Hajek, Ellen Hakstege, Eileen Hallstrom, Ayscha Hamdani, Lysia Hand, Jessica Hanlaoui, Paula Hanna, Joan Hannum, Marjolein Hanson, Donna & Dan Hardy, John C Harley, William Harris, Richard Harrold, Colin Harvey, Ineke van Hassel, Jenny Hassenbach, Annick Hauser, Steve Hauser, J Hayes, Roland Helmi, Jacob Henriksen, D Herbint, Janet Higgs, Silvia Hincapie, Heidi Hirsh, Anita Hoback, Beth Hocking, Tamara Hofman, Carla Holden, John Holman, Rick Hoogenboom, Susanne Hrinkov, Winona Hubbard, Denis Hughes, Serge Huguet, Diana Humple, David L Huntzinger, Hugo Hus, Eva Huthoefer, Jan Hutta **I** Andrew Inchley, Peter Ingerfeld, Stephanie Inglesfield, Judy Isikow, Pablo Iveli **J** Bill Johnson, Greg Jones, Peter Jones, D Josephson, Sabine Joyce, Admir Jukanovic **K** Leonard Kahansky, David Kaiser, D Kakimoto, Georg Karl, Nils Karmann, Kryss Katsiavriades, Grainne Kavanagh, Mike Kaye, Chris Kelley, R & R Key, M Kilpatrick, Andy King, Katie Kipper, Rachel Kirsch, Marc Kish, Claas Koenig, Robert Koepcke, Jaap Koeree, Michael Koest, Fuat Koro, Nadja Kos, Margaret Kostaszuk, Ken Kramer **L** P Lack, Coby Laird, Stan Lampard, Derek Larney, Lewis Laura, Ino Laurensse, Jenny Lawrence, Justin Lawson, Robert Layne, Gregg Le Blanc, Danilo Leal, Jonathan Legg, Brian Lema, Kevin Lentz, Dominque Leon, Guy Leonard, Frank Lepannetier, Wim Leuppens, Asaf Levy, Nadine Lewin, Laura Lewis, Rachel Lewis, Verhofstadt Lieven, John P Linstroth, Cor Lionel, Stephen Lloyd, Lutz Logemann, Lutz & Beate Logemann, Sara Logie, Mark Loney, Rachel Look, David Low, Kate Low, Dieter Lubitz, Mariam

Lunrein, Massimo Luppi, Hermann Luyken **M** Hugh MacDonald, Ruth Magden, Silvia Makovnikova, Edith Mann, Arlette Marcer, Chris Marks, Sebastian Marks, Sandra Marquez, Allegra Marshall, Alyssa Martin, Philip B Martin, Arfilio Martinez, Miguel Martinez-Lafuente, Bob Masters, Beth Masterson, Laurence Mathelin, Akira Maya, Ronan McCabe, Rick McCaffrey, Anderson McCammot, S McCullagh, Kathleen McGurk, Kenneth McIntosh, Bill McKnight, Randy Mead, Julia Meinke, Alison Melbourne, Manfred Melchinger, Tony Mendoza, Johan van der Merwe, Christian Messerschmidt, Elizabeth MG Court, Deborah Miller, Gabriele Mills, Simon Moore, Gregorio Morales, Samantha & Russell Mort, Jacob E Moss, Asia Motyl, David Muffon, Mohan Mukhoty, Kevin Murphy **N** Juan Nagel, John T Nasci, Tino Naumann, Peter Necas, Robert Neill, Angie & Yannick Neron, Christph Neunzig, Victoria Neves Pedro, Grant Nielsen, Charles Noirot, Gitte Norgaard, Loma Norgrove, F Nunerol **O** Michal Obrebski, Mike O'Connor, N Okwudili, Conny Olde Olthof, Ottar Olsen, Anders Olsson, Adrie Omtzigt, Śian Óram, Tommy Órme, Simon Urr, Keith Uttö **P** Robert H Packard, Natalie Paganelli, Markus Pallör, Beryl Park, Adela Parzanese, Rhonda Payget, Kim Pearson, Sacha Pearson, Phil Pellmann, G Percontino, Gustavo Perez, Denise Perreault, Marshall Peterson, Cheryl Petreman, Eric Phan-Kim, M Philippe Queriaux, Cameron Phillips, Paseal Pin, Helen & Anthony Pink, Boris Polania, Michael Post, Inga Poy, Barbara Preiswerk, Carl Pressley, Philip Preston, Alex Price, Martyn Pronk, Franca Pugnaghi, Ray Purdy **R** Kevin Ransom, Claudia Rantes, Kris Borring Prasada Rao, Lisa Rasmussen, Sandra Reauu, Sarah Reid, Teus Renes, Marco Antonio Reyes, Kristen Reynolds, David Rheault, Thomas Ribisel, Mary Richards, Alexander Robinson, Don Rogers, Valerio Romano, Robin Romberg, Peter Roose, Bet Ross, Daniel Ross, Steffen Rossel, Tom Roth, Nareg Roubinian, Delvenia Rounds, Ollie Royer, Jan Ruis, Thomas Runker, Diarmuid Russell, Stephen Ryan Chan **S** Emily Sachs, Raul Saguillo, Rania Salameh, Francisco Sanabria, Victor Sanavia, Jeanette Sautner, Scott Savoie, Sue Savoy, René Schaap, Paul Schaffrath, Andreas Scharew, Ron Scharis, H Schicks, Gabriele Schindl, Ulrike Schipf, Marc Schipperheyn, Marc Schlichtner, Helen Schoenmaker, Robert Schweiger, Uta Schwoerke, Matt Scott, Steve Seamark, Davide Selva, Yiftah Shalev, Mark Sharp, Eran Shayshon, Ron Shell, Andrew Sherwin, Martin Shippen, Gayle Short, Andy Shorwin, Jochen Siepmann, Christian Silkenath, Monica Silva, Tom Simpson, Tony Sirotkin, Luke Skinner, Wanda Skinner, Siri Skroppa, Caroline Smith, Peter Smith, TJ Snow, Fabio Sorrentino, E G Stack III, Stephanie Stasse, Danielle Stemmer van Duren, David Stephnes, Morten Stige, Thomas Stodulka, Emma Stone, David Strachan, Luis Streckman, Sarah Stubblefield, Francesca Symmons **T** Danko Taborosi, Carlos J Tarazona, Beth Taylor, M Taylor, Carolina Tenias, Isabel B Terry, Jonas Teubner, Elke Thape, Stig Thomsen, Stéphane Tiberghien, Steve Tietsworth, M Tilman, Anne Tobin, Carole Tomaszewicz, C Topas, GB Toppelwell, Albert Toune, Alistair Towers, Chiara Trapani, Samuel Trickey **U** Roland Ulrich **V** Richard Vader, Nathan Valentine, L Valles, Theo van Aerts, Peter van Boxstael, Natalie van de Beek, Eric van de Keuken, Ruud van Leeuwen, Patrick van Riswick, Gijs van Tilburg, Michel van Velde, Maaike van Westen, Ronny van Zijl, Brian Vats-Fournier, Pascal Vervacke, Thomas Villette, Marcella Vinciguerra, Antonio Vizamora, Mario Vogt, Paul Volk, Jurg Vosbeck, Michal Vossberg, Helene Vroegh **W** Mike Wagner, Jonathan Waldie, Peter Walker, Peter Ward, Hans Warmerdam, Paul Webb, Jonathan Weber, Jorn Weigle, Douglas H Weller, Ina Wenig, Michael Wheelahon, Richard Wherry, Warwick White, Eric Whittington, Matthias Wiesner, Jim Wills, R A Wilmore, Ian Wilson, Steve Wilson, Tristram Winfield, Robert Wingfield, Thomas & Judith Winter, Bert Winthorst, Alan H Witz, Anja Wohlgemuth, Meike Wolf, Christopher Woods, Jonathan Woolrich, Alexander Wuerfel, Dirk Wutherich, Jackie Wynn **Y** Andrew Yale Esq **Z** Vamosi Zoltan

ACKNOWLEDGMENTS

Many thanks to the following for the use of their content:

Globe on back cover © Mountain High Maps 1993 Digital Wisdom, Inc.

Index

000 Map pages
000 Location of colour photographs

INDEX

MAP LEGEND
ROUTES

Tollway	One-Way Street
Freeway	Unsealed Road
Primary Road	Street Mall/Steps
Secondary Road	Tunnel
Tertiary Road	Walking Tour
Lane	Walking Tour Detour
Under Construction	Walking Trail
Track	Walking Path

TRANSPORT

Ferry	Rail (Underground)
Metro	Tram
Bus Route	Cable Car, Funicular
Rail	

HYDROGRAPHY

River, Creek	Canal
Intermittent River	Water
Swamp	Lake (Dry)
Mangrove	Lake (Salt)
Reef	Mudflats

BOUNDARIES

International	Regional, Suburb
State, Provincial	Cliff
Disputed	

AREA FEATURES

Airport	Land
Area of Interest	Mall
Beach, Desert	Park
Building	Reserve
Campus	Rocks
Cemetery	Sports
Forest	Urban

Text Abbreviations: Parque Nacional (PN)

POPULATION

○ **CAPITAL (NATIONAL)**	◉ CAPITAL (STATE)
● **Large City**	○ Medium City
○ Small City	○ Town, Village

SYMBOLS

Information
- Bank, ATM
- Embassy/Consulate
- Hospital, Medical
- Information
- Internet Facilities
- Petrol Station
- Police Station
- Post Office, GPO
- Telephone

Sights/Activities
- Beach
- Castle, Fortress
- Cathedral
- Monument
- Museum, Gallery
- Ruin
- Zoo, Bird Sanctuary

Sleeping
- Sleeping
- Camping

Eating
- Eating

Drinking
- Drinking

Entertainment
- Entertainment

Shopping
- Shopping

Other
- Picnic Area

Transport
- Airport, Airfield
- Bus Station
- General Transport
- Taxi Rank

Geographic
- Lighthouse
- Lookout
- Mountain, Volcano
- National Park
- Pass, Canyon
- River Flow
- Shelter, Hut
- Waterfall

LONELY PLANET OFFICES

Australia
Head Office
Locked Bag 1, Footscray, Victoria 3011
☎ 03 8379 8000, fax 03 8379 8111
talk2us@lonelyplanet.com.au

USA
150 Linden St, Oakland, CA 94607
☎ 510 893 8555, toll free 800 275 8555
fax 510 893 8572, info@lonelyplanet.com

UK
72–82 Rosebery Ave,
Clerkenwell, London EC1R 4RW
☎ 020 7841 9000, fax 020 7841 9001
go@lonelyplanet.co.uk

France
1 rue du Dahomey, 75011 Paris
☎ 01 55 25 33 00, fax 01 55 25 33 01
bip@lonelyplanet.fr, www.lonelyplanet.fr

Published by Lonely Planet Publications Pty Ltd
ABN 36 005 607 983

© Lonely Planet 2004

© photographers as indicated 2004

Cover photographs by Lonely Planet Images: Laguna de Canaima waterfalls, Krzysztof Dydyński (front); Ceramic masks of the dancing devils *(diablos danzantes)*, Krzysztof Dydyński (back). Many of the images in this guide are available for licensing from Lonely Planet Images: www.lonelyplanetimages.com.

Printed through The Bookmaker International Ltd
Printed in China